ADVANCED

MS-DOS®

PROGRAMMING

RAY DUNCAN

ADVANCED

MSDOS®

PROGRAMMING

Microsoft PRESS ®

The

Microsoft®

guide for

Assembly

Language

and C

programmers

PUBLISHED BY

Microsoft Press
A Division of Microsoft Corporation
16011 NE 36th Way, Box 97017, Redmond, Washington 98073-9717

Library of Congress Cataloging in Publication Data

Duncan, Ray, 1952-
Advanced MS-DOS programming.
Rev. ed. of: Advanced MS-DOS. ©1986.
Includes index.
1. MS-DOS (Computer operating system)   2. Assembler language
(Computer program language)   3. C (Computer program language)
I. Duncan, Ray, 1952-   Advanced MS-DOS.   II. Title.
QA76.76.063D858   1988   005.4'46   88-1251
ISBN 1-55615-157-8
Printed and bound in the United States of America.

1 2 3 4 5 6 7 8 9   FGFG   3 2 1 0 9 8

Distributed to the book trade in the United States
by Harper & Row.

Distributed to the book trade in Canada by General
Publishing Company, Ltd.

Penguin Books Ltd., Harmondworth, Middlesex, England
Penguin Books Australia Ltd., Ringwood, Victoria, Australia
Penguin Books N.Z. Ltd., 182-190 Wairu Road, Auckland 10, New Zealand

British Cataloging in Publication Data available

IBM®, PC/AT®, and PS/2® are registered trademarks of International Business Machines Corporation. CodeView®, Microsoft®, MS-DOS®, and XENIX® are registered trademarks and InPort™ is a trademark of Microsoft Corporation.

Technical Editor: Mike Halvorson   **Production Editor:** Mary Ann Jones

For Carolyn

Contents

Road Map to Figures and Tables

Acknowledgments

My renewed thanks to the outstanding editors and production staff at Microsoft Press, who make beautiful books happen, and to the talented Microsoft developers, who create great programs to write books about. Special thanks to Mike Halvorson, Jeff Hinsch, Mary Ann Jones, Claudette Moore, Dori Shattuck, and Mark Zbikowski; if this book has anything unique to offer, these people deserve most of the credit.

Introduction

Advanced MS-DOS Programming is written for the experienced C or assembly-language programmer. It provides all the information you need to write robust, high-performance applications under the MS-DOS operating system. Because I believe that working, well-documented programs are unbeatable learning tools, I have included detailed programming examples throughout—including complete utility programs that you can adapt to your own needs.

This book is both a tutorial and a reference and is divided into four sections, so that you can find information more easily. Section I discusses MS-DOS capabilities and services by functional group in the context of common programming issues, such as user input, control of the display, memory management, and file handling. Special classes of programs, such as interrupt handlers, device drivers, and filters, have their own chapters.

Section II provides a complete reference guide to MS-DOS function calls, organized so that you can see the calling sequence, results, and version dependencies of each function at a glance. I have also included notes, where relevant, about quirks and special uses of functions as well as cross-references to related functions. An assembly-language example is included for each entry in Section II.

Sections III and IV are references to IBM ROM BIOS, Microsoft Mouse driver, and Lotus/Intel/Microsoft Expanded Memory Specification functions. The entries in these two sections have the same form as in Section II, except that individual programming examples have been omitted.

The programs in this book were written with the marvelous Brief editor from Solution Systems and assembled or compiled with Microsoft Macro Assembler version 5.1 and Microsoft C Compiler version 5.1. They have been tested under MS-DOS versions 2.1, 3.1, 3.3, and 4.0 on an 8088-based IBM PC, an 80286-based IBM PC/AT, and an 80386-based IBM PS/2 Model 80. As far as I am aware, they do not contain any software or hardware dependencies that will prevent them from running properly on any IBM PC–compatible machine running MS-DOS version 2.0 or later.

Changes from the First Edition

Readers who are familiar with the first edition will find many changes in the second edition, but the general structure of the book remains the same. Most of the material comparing MS-DOS to CP/M and UNIX/XENIX has been removed; although these comparisons were helpful a few years ago, MS-DOS has become its own universe and deserves to be considered on its own terms.

The previously monolithic chapter on character devices has been broken into three more manageable chapters focusing on the keyboard and mouse, the display, and the serial port and printer. Hardware-dependent video techniques have been de-emphasized; although this topic is more important than ever, it has grown so complex that it requires a book of its own. A new chapter discusses compatibility and portability of MS-DOS applications and also contains a brief introduction to Microsoft OS/2, the new multitasking, protected-mode operating system.

A road map to vital figures and tables has been added, following the Table of Contents, to help you quickly locate the layouts of the program segment prefix, file control block, and the like.

The reference sections at the back of the book have been extensively updated and enlarged and are now complete through MS-DOS version 4.0, the IBM PS/2 Model 80 ROM BIOS and the VGA video adapter, the Microsoft Mouse driver version 6.0, and the Lotus/Intel/Microsoft Expanded Memory Specification version 4.0.

In the two years since *Advanced MS-DOS Programming* was first published, hundreds of readers have been kind enough to send me their comments, and I have tried to incorporate many of their suggestions in this new edition. As before, please feel free to contact me via MCI Mail (user name LMI), CompuServe (user ID 72406,1577), or BIX (user name rduncan).

Ray Duncan
Los Angeles, California
September 1988

SPECIAL OFFER

Companion Disk to
ADVANCED MS-DOS PROGRAMMING,
2nd edition

Microsoft Press has created a Companion Disk to ADVANCED MS-DOS PROGRAMMING, 2nd edition, available in either 5.25-inch or 3.5-inch format. This disk contains all of the source files and executable files from the book and is an essential resource for anyone who wants to forgo the drudgery of typing code (and the time required to find and correct those inevitable typing errors).

The Companion Disk to ADVANCED MS-DOS PROGRAMMING is available only from Microsoft Press. To order, use the special reply card bound in the back of the book. If the card has already been used, send $19.95, plus sales tax if applicable (CA residents 5% plus local option tax, CT 7.5%, FL 6%, MA 5%, MN 6%, MO 4.225%, NY 4% plus local option tax, WA State 7.8%) and $2.50 per disk for domestic postage and handling, $6.00 per disk for foreign orders to: Microsoft Press, Attn: Companion Disk Offer, 21919 20th Ave S.E., Box 3011, Bothell, WA 98041-3011. Please specify 5.25-inch or 3.5-inch format. Payment must be in U.S. funds. You may pay by check or money order (payable to Microsoft Press) or by American Express, VISA, or MasterCard; please include both your credit card number and the expiration date. All orders are shipped 2nd day air upon receipt of order to Microsoft.

If you have questions or comments about this disk, please contact Ray Duncan via MCI Mail (user name LMI), CompuServe (user ID 72406,1577), or BIX (user name rduncan).

If this disk proves defective, please send the defective disk along with your packing slip to: Microsoft Press, Consumer Sales, 16011 NE 36th Way, Box 97017, Redmond, WA 98073-9717.

SECTION I

Chapter 1

Genealogy of MS-DOS

In only seven years, MS-DOS has evolved from a simple program loader into a sophisticated, stable operating system for personal computers that are based on the Intel 8086 family of microprocessors (Figure 1-1). MS-DOS supports networking, graphical user interfaces, and storage devices of every description; it serves as the platform for thousands of application programs; and it has over 10 million licensed users—dwarfing the combined user bases of all of its competitors.

The progenitor of MS-DOS was an operating system called 86-DOS, which was written by Tim Paterson for Seattle Computer Products in mid-1980. At that time, Digital Research's CP/M-80 was the operating system most commonly used on microcomputers based on the Intel 8080 and Zilog Z-80 microprocessors, and a wide range of application software (word processors, database managers, and so forth) was available for use with CP/M-80.

To ease the process of porting 8-bit CP/M-80 applications into the new 16-bit environment, 86-DOS was originally designed to mimic CP/M-80 in both available functions and style of operation. Consequently, the structures of 86-DOS's file control blocks, program segment prefixes, and executable files were nearly identical to those of CP/M-80. Existing CP/M-80 programs could be converted mechanically (by processing their source-code files through a special translator program) and, after conversion, would run under 86-DOS either immediately or with very little hand editing.

Because 86-DOS was marketed as a proprietary operating system for Seattle Computer Products' line of S-100 bus, 8086-based microcomputers, it made very little impact on the microcomputer world in general. Other vendors of 8086-based microcomputers were understandably reluctant to adopt a competitor's operating system and continued to wait impatiently for the release of Digital Research's CP/M-86.

In October 1980, IBM approached the major microcomputer-software houses in search of an operating system for the new line of personal computers it was designing. Microsoft had no operating system of its own to offer (other than a stand-alone version of Microsoft BASIC) but paid a fee to Seattle Computer Products for the right to sell Paterson's 86-DOS. (At that time, Seattle Computer Products received a license to use and sell Microsoft's languages and all 8086 versions of Microsoft's operating system.) In July 1981, Microsoft purchased all rights to 86-DOS, made substantial alterations to it, and renamed it MS-DOS. When the first IBM PC was released in the fall of 1981, IBM offered MS-DOS (referred to as PC-DOS 1.0) as its primary operating system.

IBM also selected Digital Research's CP/M-86 and Softech's P-system as alternative operating systems for the PC. However, they were both very slow to appear at IBM PC dealers and suffered the additional disadvantages of higher prices and lack of available programming languages. IBM threw its considerable weight behind PC-DOS by releasing all the IBM-logo PC application software and development tools to run under it. Consequently, most third-party software developers targeted their products for PC-DOS from the start, and CP/M-86 and P-system never became significant factors in the IBM PC–compatible market.

In spite of some superficial similarities to its ancestor CP/M-80, MS-DOS version 1.0 contained a number of improvements over CP/M-80, including the following:

- An improved disk-directory structure that included information about a file's attributes (such as whether it was a system or a hidden file), its exact size in bytes, and the date that the file was created or last modified

- A superior disk-space allocation and management method, allowing extremely fast sequential or random record access and program loading

- An expanded set of operating-system services, including hardware-independent function calls to set or read the date and time, a filename parser, multiple-block record I/O, and variable record sizes

- An AUTOEXEC.BAT batch file to perform a user-defined series of commands when the system was started or reset

IBM was the only major computer manufacturer (sometimes referred to as OEM, for *original equipment manufacturer*) to ship MS-DOS version 1.0 (as PC-DOS 1.0) with its products. MS-DOS version 1.25 (equivalent to IBM PC-DOS 1.1) was released in June 1982 to fix a number of bugs and also to support double-sided disks and improved hardware independence in the DOS kernel. This version was shipped by several vendors besides IBM, including Texas Instruments, COMPAQ, and Columbia, who all entered the personal computer market early. Due to rapid decreases in the prices of RAM and fixed disks, MS-DOS version 1 is no longer in common use.

MS-DOS version 2.0 (equivalent to PC-DOS 2.0) was first released in March 1983. It was, in retrospect, a new operating system (though great care was taken to maintain compatibility with MS-DOS version 1). It contained many significant innovations and enhanced features, including those listed on the following page.

- Support for both larger-capacity floppy disks and hard disks
- Many UNIX/XENIX-like features, including a hierarchical file structure, file handles, I/O redirection, pipes, and filters
- Background printing (print spooling)
- Volume labels, plus additional file attributes
- Installable device drivers
- A user-customizable system-configuration file that controlled the loading of additional device drivers, the number of system disk buffers, and so forth
- Maintenance of environment blocks that could be used to pass information between programs
- An optional ANSI display driver that allowed programs to position the cursor and control display characteristics in a hardware-independent manner
- Support for the dynamic allocation, modification, and release of memory by application programs
- Support for customized user command interpreters (shells)
- System tables to assist application software in modifying its currency, time, and date formats (known as *international support*)

MS-DOS version 2.11 was subsequently released to improve international support (table-driven currency symbols, date formats, decimal-point symbols, currency separators, and so forth), to add support for 16-bit Kanji characters throughout, and to fix a few minor bugs. Version 2.11 rapidly became the base version shipped for 8086/8088-based personal computers by every major OEM, including Hewlett-Packard, Wang, Digital Equipment Corporation, Texas Instruments, COMPAQ, and Tandy.

MS-DOS version 2.25, released in October 1985, was distributed in the Far East but was never shipped by OEMs in the United States and Europe. In this version, the international support for Japanese and Korean character sets was extended even further, additional bugs were repaired, and many of the system utilities were made compatible with MS-DOS version 3.0.

MS-DOS version 3.0 was introduced by IBM in August 1984 with the release of the 80286-based PC/AT machines. It represented another major rewrite of the entire operating system and included the important new features listed on the following page.

- Direct control of the print spooler by application software

- Further expansion of international support for currency formats

- Extended error reporting, including a code that suggests a recovery strategy to the application program

- Support for file and record locking and sharing

- Support for larger fixed disks

MS-DOS version 3.1, which was released in November 1984, added support for the sharing of files and printers across a network. Beginning with version 3.1, a new operating-system module called the *redirector* intercepts an application program's requests for I/O and filters out the requests that are directed to network devices, passing these requests to another machine for processing.

Since version 3.1, the changes to MS-DOS have been evolutionary rather than revolutionary. Version 3.2, which appeared in 1986, generalized the definition of device drivers so that new media types (such as 3.5-inch floppy disks) could be supported more easily. Version 3.3 was released in 1987, concurrently with the new IBM line of PS/2 personal computers, and drastically expanded MS-DOS's multilanguage support for keyboard mappings, printer character sets, and display fonts. Version 4.0, delivered in 1988, was enhanced with a visual shell as well as support for very large file systems.

While MS-DOS has been evolving, Microsoft has also put intense efforts into the areas of user interfaces and multitasking operating systems. Microsoft Windows, first shipped in 1985, provides a multitasking, graphical user "desktop" for MS-DOS systems. Windows has won widespread support among developers of complex graphics applications such as desktop publishing and computer-aided design because it allows their programs to take full advantage of whatever output devices are available without introducing any hardware dependence.

Microsoft Operating System/2 (MS OS/2), released in 1987, represents a new standard for application developers: a protected-mode, multitasking, virtual-memory system specifically designed for applications requiring high-performance graphics, networking, and interprocess communications. Although MS OS/2 is a new product and is not a derivative of MS-DOS, its user interface and file system are compatible with MS-DOS and Microsoft Windows, and it offers the ability to run one real-mode (MS-DOS) application alongside MS OS/2 protected-mode applications. This compatibility allows users to move between the MS-DOS and OS/2 environments with a minimum of difficulty.

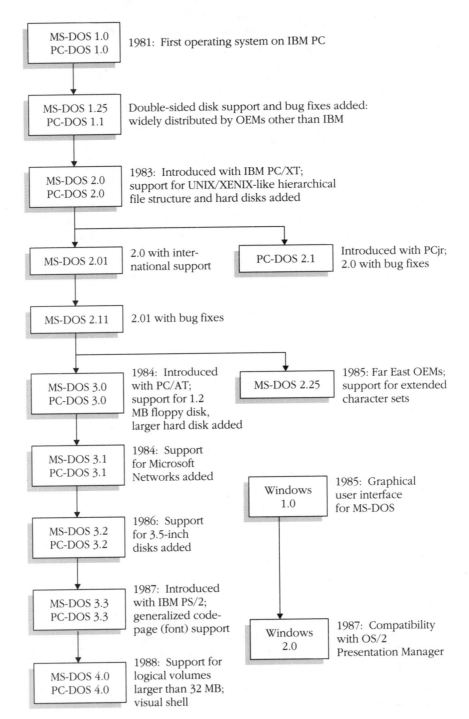

Figure 1-1. *The evolution of MS-DOS.*

What does the future hold for MS-DOS? Only the long-range planning teams at Microsoft and IBM know for sure. But it seems safe to assume that MS-DOS, with its relatively small memory requirements, adaptability to diverse hardware configurations, and enormous base of users, will remain important to programmers and software publishers for years to come.

Chapter 2

MS-DOS in Operation

It is unlikely that you will ever be called upon to configure the MS-DOS software for a new model of computer. Still, an acquaintance with the general structure of MS-DOS can often be very helpful in understanding the behavior of the system as a whole. In this chapter, we will discuss how MS-DOS is organized and how it is loaded into memory when the computer is turned on.

The Structure of MS-DOS

MS-DOS is partitioned into several layers that serve to isolate the kernel logic of the operating system, and the user's perception of the system, from the hardware it is running on. These layers are

- The BIOS (Basic Input/Output System)
- The DOS kernel
- The command processor (shell)

We'll discuss the functions of each of these layers separately.

The BIOS Module

The BIOS is specific to the individual computer system and is provided by the manufacturer of the system. It contains the default resident hardware-dependent drivers for the following devices:

- Console display and keyboard (CON)
- Line printer (PRN)
- Auxiliary device (AUX)
- Date and time (CLOCK$)
- Boot disk device (block device)

The MS-DOS kernel communicates with these device drivers through I/O request packets; the drivers then translate these requests into the proper commands for the various hardware controllers. In many MS-DOS systems, including the IBM PC, the most primitive parts of the hardware drivers are located in read-only memory (ROM) so that they can be used by stand-alone applications, diagnostics, and the system startup program.

The terms *resident* and *installable* are used to distinguish between the drivers built into the BIOS and the drivers installed during system initialization by DEVICE commands in the CONFIG.SYS file. (Installable drivers will be discussed in more detail later in this chapter and in Chapter 14.)

The BIOS is read into random-access memory (RAM) during system initialization as part of a file named IO.SYS. (In PC-DOS, the file is called IBMBIO.COM.) This file is marked with the special attributes *hidden* and *system*.

The DOS Kernel

The DOS kernel implements MS-DOS as it is seen by application programs. The kernel is a proprietary program supplied by Microsoft Corporation and provides a collection of hardware-independent services called *system functions*. These functions include the following:

- File and record management
- Memory management
- Character-device input/output
- Spawning of other programs
- Access to the real-time clock

Programs can access system functions by loading registers with function-specific parameters and then transferring to the operating system by means of a *software interrupt*.

The DOS kernel is read into memory during system initialization from the MSDOS.SYS file on the boot disk. (The file is called IBMDOS.COM in PC-DOS.) This file is marked with the attributes *hidden* and *system*.

The Command Processor

The command processor, or shell, is the user's interface to the operating system. It is responsible for parsing and carrying out user commands, including the loading and execution of other programs from a disk or other mass-storage device.

The default shell that is provided with MS-DOS is found in a file called COMMAND.COM. Although COMMAND.COM prompts and responses constitute the ordinary user's complete perception of MS-DOS, it is important to realize that COMMAND.COM is not the operating system, but simply a special class of program running under the control of MS-DOS.

COMMAND.COM can be replaced with a shell of the programmer's own design by simply adding a SHELL directive to the system-configuration file (CONFIG.SYS) on the system startup disk. The product COMMAND-PLUS from ESP Systems is an example of such an alternative shell.

More about COMMAND.COM

The default MS-DOS shell, COMMAND.COM, is divided into three parts:

- A resident portion
- An initialization section
- A transient module

The resident portion is loaded in lower memory, above the DOS kernel and its buffers and tables. It contains the routines to process Ctrl-C and Ctrl-Break, critical errors, and the termination (final exit) of other transient programs. This part of COMMAND.COM issues error messages and is responsible for the familiar prompt

```
Abort, Retry, Ignore?
```

The resident portion also contains the code required to reload the transient portion of COMMAND.COM when necessary.

The initialization section of COMMAND.COM is loaded above the resident portion when the system is started. It processes the AUTOEXEC.BAT batch file (the user's list of commands to execute at system startup), if one is present, and is then discarded.

The transient portion of COMMAND.COM is loaded at the high end of memory, and its memory can also be used for other purposes by application programs. The transient module issues the user prompt, reads the commands from the keyboard or batch file, and causes them to be executed. When an application program terminates, the resident portion of COMMAND.COM does a checksum of the transient module to determine whether it has been destroyed and fetches a fresh copy from the disk if necessary.

The user commands that are accepted by COMMAND.COM fall into three categories:

- Internal commands
- External commands
- Batch files

Internal commands, sometimes called *intrinsic* commands, are those carried out by code embedded in COMMAND.COM itself. Commands in this category include COPY, REN(AME), DIR(ECTORY), and DEL(ETE). The routines for the internal commands are included in the transient part of COMMAND.COM.

External commands, sometimes called *extrinsic* commands or *transient programs,* are the names of programs stored in disk files. Before these programs can be executed, they must be loaded from the disk into the *transient program area* (TPA) of memory. (See "How MS-DOS Is Loaded" in this chapter.) Familiar examples of external commands are CHKDSK, BACKUP, and RESTORE. As soon as an external command has completed its work, it is discarded from memory; hence, it must be reloaded from disk each time it is invoked.

Batch files are text files that contain lists of other intrinsic, extrinsic, or batch commands. These files are processed by a special interpreter that is built into the transient portion of COMMAND.COM. The interpreter reads the batch file one line at a time and carries out each of the specified operations in order.

In order to interpret a user's command, COMMAND.COM first looks to see if the user typed the name of a built-in (intrinsic) command that it can carry out directly. If not, it searches for an external command (executable program file) or batch file by the same name. The search is carried out first in the current directory of the current disk drive and then in each of the directories specified in the most recent PATH command. In each directory inspected, COMMAND.COM first tries to find a file with the extension .COM, then .EXE, and finally .BAT. If the search fails for all three file types in all of the possible locations, COMMAND.COM displays the familiar message

Bad command or file name

If a .COM file or a .EXE file is found, COMMAND.COM uses the MS-DOS EXEC function to load and execute it. The EXEC function builds a special data structure called a *program segment prefix* (PSP) above the resident portion of COMMAND.COM in the transient program area. The PSP contains various linkages and pointers needed by the application program. Next, the EXEC function loads the program itself, just above the PSP, and performs any relocation that may be necessary. Finally, it sets up the registers appropriately and transfers control to the entry point for the program. (Both the PSP and the EXEC function will be discussed in more detail in Chapters 3 and 12.) When the transient program has finished its job, it calls a special MS-DOS termination function that releases the transient program's memory and returns control to the program that caused the transient program to be loaded (COMMAND.COM, in this case).

A transient program has nearly complete control of the system's resources while it is executing. The only other tasks that are accomplished are those performed by interrupt handlers (such as the keyboard input driver and the real-time clock) and operations that the transient program requests from the operating system. MS-DOS does not support sharing of the central processor among several tasks executing concurrently, nor can it wrest control away from a program when it crashes or executes for too long. Such capabilities are the province of MS OS/2, which is a protected-mode system with preemptive multitasking (time-slicing).

How MS-DOS Is Loaded

When the system is started or reset, program execution begins at address 0FFFF0H. This is a feature of the 8086/8088 family of microprocessors and has nothing to do with MS-DOS. Systems based on these processors are designed so that address 0FFFF0H lies within an area of ROM and contains a jump machine instruction to transfer control to system test code and the ROM bootstrap routine (Figure 2-1).

The ROM bootstrap routine reads the disk bootstrap routine from the first sector of the system startup disk (the *boot sector*) into memory at some arbitrary address and then transfers control to it (Figure 2-2). (The boot sector also contains a table of information about the disk format.)

The disk bootstrap routine checks to see if the disk contains a copy of MS-DOS. It does this by reading the first sector of the root directory and determining whether the first two files are IO.SYS and MSDOS.SYS (or IBMBIO.COM and IBMDOS.COM), in that order. If these files are not present, the user is prompted to change disks and strike any key to try again.

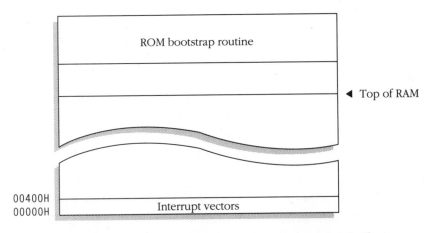

Figure 2-1. *A typical 8086/8088-based computer system immediately after system startup or reset. Execution begins at location 0FFFF0H, which contains a jump instruction that directs program control to the ROM bootstrap routine.*

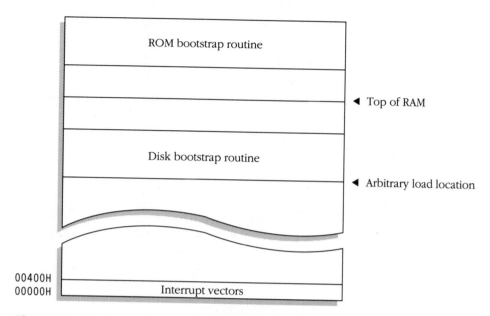

Figure 2-2. *The ROM bootstrap routine loads the disk bootstrap routine into memory from the first sector of the system startup disk and then transfers control to it.*

If the two system files are found, the disk bootstrap reads them into memory and transfers control to the initial entry point of IO.SYS (Figure 2-3). (In some implementations, the disk bootstrap reads only IO.SYS into memory, and IO.SYS in turn loads the MSDOS.SYS file.)

The IO.SYS file that is loaded from the disk actually consists of two separate modules. The first is the BIOS, which contains the linked set of resident device drivers for the console, auxiliary port, printer, block, and clock devices, plus some hardware-specific initialization code that is run only at system startup. The second module, SYSINIT, is supplied by Microsoft and linked into the IO.SYS file, along with the BIOS, by the computer manufacturer.

SYSINIT is called by the manufacturer's BIOS initialization code. It determines the amount of contiguous memory present in the system and then relocates itself to high memory. Then it moves the DOS kernel, MSDOS.SYS, from its original load location to its final memory location, overlaying the original SYSINIT code and any other expendable initialization code that was contained in the IO.SYS file (Figure 2-4).

Next, SYSINIT calls the initialization code in MSDOS.SYS. The DOS kernel initializes its internal tables and work areas, sets up the interrupt vectors 20H through 2FH, and traces through the linked list of resident device drivers, calling the initialization function for each. (See Chapter 14.)

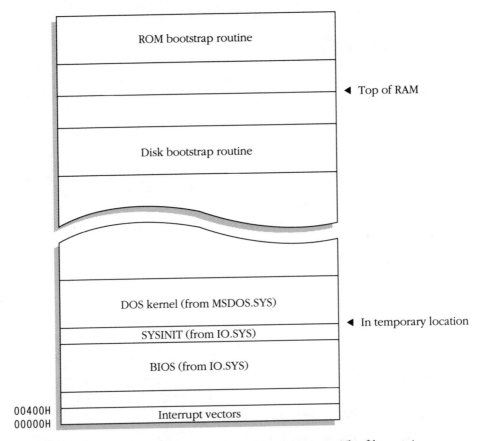

ROM bootstrap routine

◄ Top of RAM

Disk bootstrap routine

DOS kernel (from MSDOS.SYS)

◄ In temporary location

SYSINIT (from IO.SYS)

BIOS (from IO.SYS)

00400H
00000H Interrupt vectors

Figure 2-3. *The disk bootstrap reads the file IO.SYS into memory. This file contains the MS-DOS BIOS (resident device drivers) and the SYSINIT module. Either the disk bootstrap or the BIOS (depending upon the manufacturer's implementation) then reads the DOS kernel into memory from the MSDOS.SYS file.*

These driver functions determine the equipment status, perform any necessary hardware initialization, and set up the vectors for any external hardware interrupts the drivers will service.

As part of the initialization sequence, the DOS kernel examines the disk-parameter blocks returned by the resident block-device drivers, determines the largest sector size that will be used in the system, builds some drive-parameter blocks, and allocates a disk sector buffer. Control then returns to SYSINIT.

When the DOS kernel has been initialized and all resident device drivers are available, SYSINIT can call on the normal MS-DOS file services to open the CONFIG.SYS file. This optional file can contain a variety of commands that enable the user to customize the MS-DOS environment. For

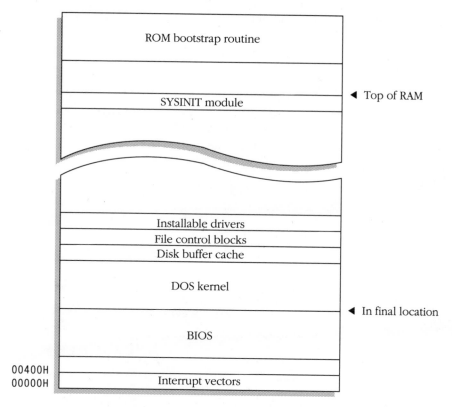

Figure 2-4. *SYSINIT moves itself to high memory and relocates the DOS kernel, MSDOS.SYS, downward to its final address. The MS-DOS disk buffer cache and file control block areas are allocated, and then the installable device drivers specified in the CONFIG.SYS file are loaded and linked into the system.*

instance, the user can specify additional hardware device drivers, the number of disk buffers, the maximum number of files that can be open at one time, and the filename of the command processor (shell).

If it is found, the entire CONFIG.SYS file is loaded into memory for processing. All lowercase characters are converted to uppercase, and the file is interpreted one line at a time to process the commands. Memory is allocated for the disk buffer cache and the internal file control blocks used by the handle file and record system functions. (See Chapter 8.) Any device drivers indicated in the CONFIG.SYS file are sequentially loaded into memory, initialized by calls to their *init* modules, and linked into the device-driver list. The *init* function of each driver tells SYSINIT how much memory to reserve for that driver.

After all installable device drivers have been loaded, SYSINIT closes all file handles and reopens the console (CON), printer (PRN), and auxiliary

(AUX) devices as the standard input, standard output, standard error, standard list, and standard auxiliary devices. This allows a user-installed character-device driver to override the BIOS's resident drivers for the standard devices.

Finally, SYSINIT calls the MS-DOS EXEC function to load the command interpreter, or shell. (The default shell is COMMAND.COM, but another shell can be substituted by means of the CONFIG.SYS file.) Once the shell is loaded, it displays a prompt and waits for the user to enter a command. MS-DOS is now ready for business, and the SYSINIT module is discarded (Figure 2-5).

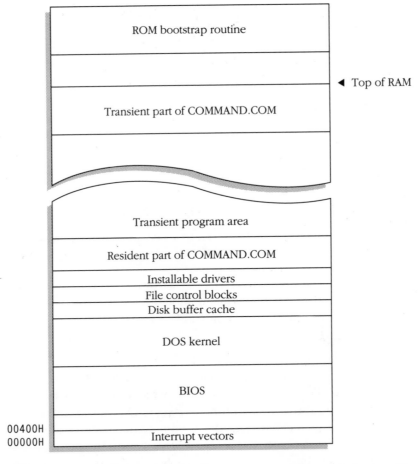

Figure 2-5. *The final result of the MS-DOS startup process for a typical system. The resident portion of COMMAND.COM lies in low memory, above the DOS kernel. The transient portion containing the batch-file interpreter and intrinsic commands is placed in high memory, where it can be overlaid by extrinsic commands and application programs running in the transient program area.*

Chapter 3

Structure of MS-DOS Application Programs

Programs that run under MS-DOS come in two basic flavors: .COM programs, which have a maximum size of approximately 64 KB, and .EXE programs, which can be as large as available memory. In Intel 8086 parlance, .COM programs fit the tiny model, in which all segment registers contain the same value; that is, the code and data are mixed together. In contrast, .EXE programs fit the small, medium, or large model, in which the segment registers contain different values; that is, the code, data, and stack reside in separate segments. .EXE programs can have multiple code and data segments, which are respectively addressed by long calls and by manipulation of the data segment (DS) register.

A .COM-type program resides on the disk as an absolute memory image, in a file with the extension .COM. The file does not have a header or any other internal identifying information. A .EXE program, on the other hand, resides on the disk in a special type of file with a unique header, a relocation map, a checksum, and other information that is (or can be) used by MS-DOS.

Both .COM and .EXE programs are brought into memory for execution by the same mechanism: the EXEC function, which constitutes the MS-DOS loader. EXEC can be called with the filename of a program to be loaded by COMMAND.COM (the normal MS-DOS command interpreter), by other shells or user interfaces, or by another program that was previously loaded by EXEC. If there is sufficient free memory in the transient program area, EXEC allocates a block of memory to hold the new program, builds the program segment prefix (PSP) at its base, and then reads the program into memory immediately above the PSP. Finally, EXEC sets up the segment registers and the stack and transfers control to the program.

When it is invoked, EXEC can be given the addresses of additional information, such as a command tail, file control blocks, and an environment block; if supplied, this information will be passed on to the new program. (The exact procedure for using the EXEC function in your own programs is discussed, with examples, in Chapter 12.)

.COM and .EXE programs are often referred to as *transient programs*. A transient program "owns" the memory block it has been allocated and has nearly total control of the system's resources while it is executing. When the program terminates, either because it is aborted by the operating system or because it has completed its work and systematically performed a final exit back to MS-DOS, the memory block is then freed (hence the term *transient*) and can be used by the next program in line to be loaded.

The Program Segment Prefix

A thorough understanding of the program segment prefix is vital to successful programming under MS-DOS. It is a reserved area, 256 bytes long, that is set up by MS-DOS at the base of the memory block allocated to a transient program. The PSP contains some linkages to MS-DOS that can be used by the transient program, some information MS-DOS saves for its own purposes, and some information MS-DOS passes to the transient program—to be used or not, as the program requires (Figure 3-1).

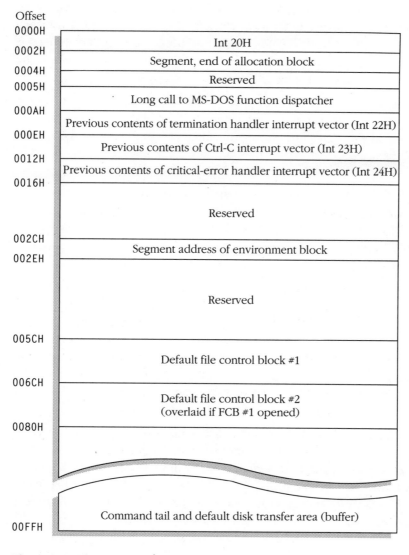

Figure 3-1. *The structure of the program segment prefix.*

In the first versions of MS-DOS, the PSP was designed to be compatible with a control area that was built beneath transient programs under Digital Research's venerable CP/M operating system, so that programs could be ported to MS-DOS without extensive logical changes. Although MS-DOS has evolved considerably since those early days, the structure of the PSP is still recognizably similar to its CP/M equivalent. For example, offset 0000H in the PSP contains a linkage to the MS-DOS process-termination handler, which cleans up after the program has finished its job and performs a final exit. Similarly, offset 0005H in the PSP contains a linkage to the MS-DOS function dispatcher, which performs disk operations, console input/output, and other such services at the request of the transient program. Thus, calls to *PSP:0000* and *PSP:0005* have the same effect as *CALL 0000* and *CALL 0005* under CP/M. (These linkages are not the "approved" means of obtaining these services, however.)

The word at offset 0002H in the PSP contains the segment address of the top of the transient program's allocated memory block. The program can use this value to determine whether it should request more memory to do its job or whether it has extra memory that it can release for use by other processes.

Offsets 000AH through 0015H in the PSP contain the previous contents of the interrupt vectors for the termination, Ctrl-C, and critical-error handlers. If the transient program alters these vectors for its own purposes, MS-DOS restores the original values saved in the PSP when the program terminates.

The word at PSP offset 002CH holds the segment address of the environment block, which contains a series of ASCIIZ strings (sequences of ASCII characters terminated by a null, or zero, byte). The environment block is inherited from the program that called the EXEC function to load the currently executing program. It contains such information as the current search path used by COMMAND.COM to find executable programs, the location on the disk of COMMAND.COM itself, and the format of the user prompt used by COMMAND.COM.

The *command tail*—the remainder of the command line that invoked the transient program, after the program's name—is copied into the PSP starting at offset 0081H. The length of the command tail, not including the return character at its end, is placed in the byte at offset 0080H. Redirection or piping parameters and their associated filenames do not appear in the portion of the command line (the command tail) that is passed to the transient program, because redirection is transparent to applications.

To provide compatibility with CP/M, MS-DOS parses the first two parameters in the command tail into two default *file control blocks* (FCBs) at PSP:005CH and PSP:006CH, under the assumption that they may be filenames. However, if the parameters are filenames that include a path specification, only the drive code will be valid in these default FCBs, because FCB-type file- and record-access functions do not support hierarchical file structures. Although the default FCBs were an aid in earlier years, when compatibility with CP/M was more of a concern, they are essentially useless in modern MS-DOS application programs that must provide full path support. (File control blocks are discussed in detail in Chapter 8 and hierarchical file structures are discussed in Chapter 9.)

The 128-byte area from 0080H through 00FFH in the PSP also serves as the default *disk transfer area* (DTA), which is set by MS-DOS before passing control to the transient program. If the program does not explicitly change the DTA, any file read or write operations requested with the FCB group of function calls automatically use this area as a data buffer. This is rarely useful and is another facet of MS-DOS's handling of the PSP that is present only for compatibility with CP/M.

❑ **WARNING** *Programs must not alter any part of the PSP below offset 005CH.*

Introduction to .COM Programs

Programs of the .COM persuasion are stored in disk files that hold an absolute image of the machine instructions to be executed. Because the files contain no relocation information, they are more compact, and are loaded for execution slightly faster, than equivalent .EXE files. Note that MS-DOS does not attempt to ascertain whether a .COM file actually contains executable code (there is no signature or checksum, as in the case of a .EXE file); it simply brings any file with the .COM extension into memory and jumps to it.

Because .COM programs are loaded immediately above the program segment prefix and do not have a header that can specify another entry point, they must always have an origin of 0100H, which is the length of the PSP. Location 0100H must contain an executable instruction. The maximum length of a .COM program is 65,536 bytes, minus the length of the PSP (256 bytes) and a mandatory word of stack (2 bytes).

When control is transferred to the .COM program from MS-DOS, all of the segment registers point to the PSP (Figure 3-2). The stack pointer (SP)

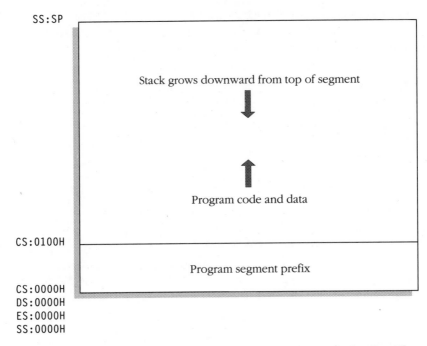

SS:SP

Stack grows downward from top of segment

Program code and data

CS:0100H

Program segment prefix

CS:0000H
DS:0000H
ES:0000H
SS:0000H

Figure 3-2. *A memory image of a typical .COM-type program after loading. The contents of the .COM file are brought into memory just above the program segment prefix. Program, code, and data are mixed together in the same segment, and all segment registers contain the same value.*

register contains 0FFFEH if memory allows; otherwise, it is set as high as possible in memory minus 2 bytes. (MS-DOS pushes a zero word on the stack before entry.)

Although the size of an executable .COM file can't exceed 64 KB, the current versions of MS-DOS allocate all of the transient program area to .COM programs when they are loaded. Because many such programs date from the early days of MS-DOS and are not necessarily "well-behaved" in their approach to memory management, the operating system simply makes the worst-case assumption and gives .COM programs everything that is available. If a .COM program wants to use the EXEC function to invoke another process, it must first shrink down its memory allocation to the minimum memory it needs in order to continue, taking care to protect its stack. (This is discussed in more detail in Chapter 12.)

When a .COM program finishes executing, it can return control to MS-DOS by several means. The preferred method is Int 21H Function 4CH, which allows the program to pass a return code back to the program, shell, or batch file that invoked it. However, if the program is running under MS-DOS version 1, it must exit by means of Int 20H, Int 21H Function 0, or a NEAR RETURN. (Because a word of zero was pushed onto the stack at entry, a NEAR RETURN causes a transfer to PSP:0000, which contains an Int 20H instruction.)

A .COM-type application can be linked together from many separate object modules. All of the modules must use the same code-segment name and class name, and the module with the entry point at offset 0100H within the segment must be linked first. In addition, all of the procedures within a .COM program should have the NEAR attribute, because all executable code resides in one segment.

When linking a .COM program, the linker will display the message

```
Warning: no stack segment
```

This message can be ignored. The linker output is a .EXE file, which must be converted into a .COM file with the MS-DOS EXE2BIN utility before execution. You can then delete the .EXE file. (An example of this process is provided in Chapter 4.)

An Example .COM Program

The *HELLO.COM* program listed in Figure 3-3 demonstrates the structure of a simple assembly-language program that is destined to become a .COM file. (You may find it helpful to compare this listing with the *HELLO.EXE* program later in this chapter.) Because this program is so short and simple, a relatively high proportion of the source code is actually assembler directives that do not result in any executable code.

The NAME statement simply provides a module name for use during the linkage process. This aids understanding of the map that the linker produces. In MASM versions 5.0 and later, the module name is always the same as the filename, and the NAME statement is ignored.

The PAGE command, when used with two operands, as in line 2, defines the length and width of the page. These default respectively to 66 lines and 80 characters. If you use the PAGE command without any operands, a formfeed is sent to the printer and a heading is printed. In larger programs, use the PAGE command liberally to place each of your subroutines on separate pages for easy reading.

The TITLE command, in line 3, specifies the text string (limited to 60 characters) that is to be printed at the upper left corner of each page. The TITLE command is optional and cannot be used more than once in each assembly-language source file.

```
 1:          name    hello
 2:          page    55,132
 3:          title   HELLO.COM--print hello on terminal
 4:
 5: ;
 6: ; HELLO.COM:    demonstrates various components
 7: ;               of a functional .COM-type assembly-
 8: ;               language program, and an MS-DOS
 9: ;               function call.
10: ;
11: ; Ray Duncan, May 1988
12: ;
13:
14: stdin   equ     0               ; standard input handle
15: stdout  equ     1               ; standard output handle
16: stderr  equ     2               ; standard error handle
17:
18: cr      equ     0dh             ; ASCII carriage return
19: lf      equ     0ah             ; ASCII linefeed
20:
21:
22: _TEXT   segment word public 'CODE'
23:
24:         org     100h            ; .COM files always have
25:                                 ; an origin of 100h
26:
27:         assume  cs:_TEXT,ds:_TEXT,es:_TEXT,ss:_TEXT
28:
29: print   proc    near            ; entry point from MS-DOS
30:
31:         mov     ah,40h          ; function 40h = write
32:         mov     bx,stdout       ; handle for standard output
33:         mov     cx,msg_len      ; length of message
34:         mov     dx,offset msg   ; address of message
35:         int     21h             ; transfer to MS-DOS
36:
37:         mov     ax,4c00h        ; exit, return code = 0
38:         int     21h             ; transfer to MS-DOS
39:
40: print   endp
41:
42:
43: msg     db      cr,lf           ; message to display
44:         db      'Hello World!',cr,lf
45:
46: msg_len equ     $-msg           ; length of message
47:
```

Figure 3-3. *The* HELLO.COM *program listing.* *(continued)*

Figure 3-3. *continued*

```
48:
49: _TEXT    ends
50:
51:          end     print            ; defines entry point
```

Dropping down past a few comments and EQU statements, we come to a declaration of a code segment that begins in line 22 with a SEGMENT command and ends in line 49 with an ENDS command. The label in the leftmost field of line 22 gives the code segment the name _TEXT. The operand fields at the right end of the line give the segment the attributes WORD, PUBLIC, and 'CODE'. (You might find it helpful to read the Microsoft Macro Assembler manual for detailed explanations of each possible segment attribute.)

Because this program is going to be converted into a .COM file, all of its executable code and data areas must lie within one code segment. The program must also have its origin at offset 0100H (immediately above the program segment prefix), which is taken care of by the ORG statement in line 24.

Following the ORG instruction, we encounter an ASSUME statement on line 27. The concept of ASSUME often baffles new assembly-language programmers. In a way, ASSUME doesn't "do" anything; it simply tells the assembler which segment registers you are going to use to point to the various segments of your program, so that the assembler can provide segment overrides when they are necessary. It's important to notice that the ASSUME statement doesn't take care of loading the segment registers with the proper values; it merely notifies the assembler of *your* intent to do that within the program. (Remember that, in the case of a .COM program, MS-DOS initializes all the segment registers before entry to point to the PSP.)

Within the code segment, we come to another type of block declaration that begins with the PROC command on line 29 and closes with ENDP on line 40. These two instructions declare the beginning and end of a *procedure*, a block of executable code that performs a single distinct function. The label in the leftmost field of the PROC statement (in this case, *print*) gives the procedure a name. The operand field gives it an attribute. If the procedure carries the NEAR attribute, only other code in the same segment can call it, whereas if it carries the FAR attribute, code located anywhere in the CPU's memory-addressing space can call it. In .COM programs, all procedures carry the NEAR attribute.

For the purposes of this example program, I have kept the *print* procedure ridiculously simple. It calls MS-DOS Int 21H Function 40H to send the message *Hello World!* to the video screen, and calls Int 21H Function 4CH to terminate the program.

The END statement in line 51 tells the assembler that it has reached the end of the source file and also specifies the entry point for the program. If the entry point is not a label located at offset 0100H, the .EXE file resulting from the assembly and linkage of this source program cannot be converted into a .COM file.

Introduction to .EXE Programs

We have just discussed a program that was written in such a way that it could be assembled into a .COM file. Such a program is simple in structure, so a programmer who needs to put together this kind of quick utility can concentrate on the program logic and do a minimum amount of worrying about control of the assembler. However, .COM-type programs have some definite disadvantages, and so most serious assembly-language efforts for MS-DOS are written to be converted into .EXE files.

Although .COM programs are effectively restricted to a total size of 64 KB for machine code, data, and stack combined, .EXE programs can be practically unlimited in size (up to the limit of the computer's available memory). .EXE programs also place the code, data, and stack in separate parts of the file. Although the normal MS-DOS program loader does not take advantage of this feature of .EXE files, the ability to load different parts of large programs into several separate memory fragments, as well as the opportunity to designate a "pure" code portion of your program that can be shared by several tasks, is very significant in multitasking environments such as Microsoft Windows.

The MS-DOS loader always brings a .EXE program into memory immediately above the program segment prefix, although the order of the code, data, and stack segments may vary (Figure 3-4). The .EXE file has a *header*, or block of control information, with a characteristic format (Figures 3-5 and 3-6). The size of this header varies according to the number of program instructions that need to be relocated at load time, but it is always a multiple of 512 bytes.

Before MS-DOS transfers control to the program, the initial values of the code segment (CS) register and instruction pointer (IP) register are calculated from the entry-point information in the .EXE file header and the program's load address. This information derives from an END statement

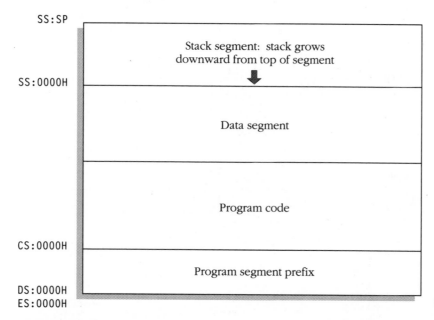

```
SS:SP ─────┐
           │ ┌──────────────────────────────────────┐
           │ │       Stack segment: stack grows      │
           │ │       downward from top of segment    │
SS:0000H ──┤ │                   ⬇                   │
           │ ├──────────────────────────────────────┤
           │ │                                       │
           │ │             Data segment              │
           │ │                                       │
           │ ├──────────────────────────────────────┤
           │ │                                       │
           │ │             Program code              │
           │ │                                       │
CS:0000H ──┤ ├──────────────────────────────────────┤
           │ │         Program segment prefix        │
DS:0000H ──┤ └──────────────────────────────────────┘
ES:0000H ──┘
```

Figure 3-4. *A memory image of a typical .EXE-type program immediately after loading. The contents of the .EXE file are relocated and brought into memory above the program segment prefix. Code, data, and stack reside in separate segments and need not be in the order shown here. The entry point can be anywhere in the code segment and is specified by the END statement in the main module of the program. When the program receives control, the DS (data segment) and ES (extra segment) registers point to the program segment prefix; the program usually saves this value and then resets the DS and ES registers to point to its data area.*

in the source code for one of the program's modules. The data segment (DS) and extra segment (ES) registers are made to point to the PSP so that the program can access the environment-block pointer, command tail, and other useful information contained there.

The initial contents of the stack segment (SS) and stack pointer (SP) registers come from the header. This information derives from the declaration of a segment with the attribute STACK somewhere in the program's source code. The memory space allocated for the stack may be initialized or uninitialized, depending on the stack-segment definition; many programmers like to initialize the stack memory with a recognizable data pattern so that they can inspect memory dumps and determine how much stack space is actually used by the program.

When a .EXE program finishes processing, it should return control to MS-DOS through Int 21H Function 4CH. Other methods are available, but they offer no advantages and are considerably less convenient (because they usually require the CS register to point to the PSP).

Byte offset

0000H	First part of .EXE file signature (4DH)
0001H	Second part of .EXE file signature (5AH)
0002H	Length of file MOD 512
0004H	Size of file in 512-byte pages, including header
0006H	Number of relocation-table items
0008H	Size of header in paragraphs (16-byte units)
000AH	Minimum number of paragraphs needed above program
000CH	Maximum number of paragraphs desired above program
000EH	Segment displacement of stack module
0010H	Contents of SP register at entry
0012H	Word checksum
0014H	Contents of IP register at entry
0016H	Segment displacement of code module
0018H	Offset of first relocation item in file
001AH	Overlay number (0 for resident part of program)
001BH	Variable reserved space
	Relocation table
	Variable reserved space
	Program and data segments
	Stack segment

Figure 3-5. *The format of a .EXE load module.*

The input to the linker for a .EXE-type program can be many separate object modules. Each module can use a unique code-segment name, and the procedures can carry either the NEAR or the FAR attribute, depending on naming conventions and the size of the executable code. The programmer must take care that the modules linked together contain only one segment with the STACK attribute and only one entry point defined with an END assembler directive. The output from the linker is a file with a .EXE extension. This file can be executed immediately.

```
C>DUMP HELLO.EXE
        0  1  2  3  4  5  6  7  8  9  A  B  C  D  E  F
0000   4D 5A 28 00 02 00 01 00 20 00 09 00 FF FF 03 00    MZ(..... .......
0010   80 00 20 05 00 00 00 00 1E 00 00 00 01 00 01 00    .. ............
0020   00 00 00 00 00 00 00 00 00 00 00 00 00 00 00 00    ...............
0030   00 00 00 00 00 00 00 00 00 00 00 00 00 00 00 00    ...............
0040   00 00 00 00 00 00 00 00 00 00 00 00 00 00 00 00    ...............
0050   00 00 00 00 00 00 00 00 00 00 00 00 00 00 00 00    ...............
        .
        .
        .
0200   B8 01 00 8E D8 B4 40 BB 01 00 B9 10 00 90 BA 08    ......@.........
0210   00 CD 21 B8 00 4C CD 21 0D 0A 48 65 6C 6C 6F 20    ..!..L.!..Hello
0220   57 6F 72 6C 64 21 0D 0A                            World!..
```

Figure 3-6. *A hex dump of the* HELLO.EXE *program, demonstrating the contents of a simple .EXE load module. Note the following interesting values: the .EXE signature in bytes 0000H and 0001H, the number of relocation-table items in bytes 0006H and 0007H, the minimum extra memory allocation (MIN_ALLOC) in bytes 000AH and 000BH, the maximum extra memory allocation (MAX_ALLOC) in bytes 000CH and 000DH, and the initial IP (instruction pointer) register value in bytes 0014H and 0015H. See also Figure 3-5.*

An Example .EXE Program

The *HELLO.EXE* program in Figure 3-7 demonstrates the fundamental structure of an assembly-language program that is destined to become a .EXE file. At minimum, it should have a module name, a code segment, a stack segment, and a primary procedure that receives control of the computer from MS-DOS after the program is loaded. The *HELLO.EXE* program also contains a data segment to provide a more complete example.

The NAME, TITLE, and PAGE directives were covered in the *HELLO.COM* example program and are used in the same manner here, so we'll move to the first new item of interest. After a few comments and EQU statements, we come to a declaration of a code segment that begins on line 21 with a SEGMENT command and ends on line 41 with an ENDS command. As in the *HELLO.COM* example program, the label in the leftmost field of the line gives the code segment the name _TEXT. The operand fields at the right end of the line give the attributes WORD, PUBLIC, and 'CODE'.

Following the code-segment instruction, we find an ASSUME statement on line 23. Notice that, unlike the equivalent statement in the *HELLO.COM* program, the ASSUME statement in this program specifies several different segment names. Again, remember that this statement has no direct effect on the contents of the segment registers but affects only the operation of the assembler itself.

```
 1:          name    hello
 2:          page    55,132
 3:          title   HELLO.EXE--print Hello on terminal
 4:  ;
 5:  ; HELLO.EXE:    demonstrates various components
 6:  ;               of a functional .EXE-type assembly-
 7:  ;               language program, use of segments,
 8:  ;               and an MS-DOS function call.
 9:  ;
10:  ; Ray Duncan, May 1988
11:  ;
12:
13: stdin    equ     0               ; standard input handle
14: stdout   equ     1               ; standard output handle
15: stderr   equ     2               ; standard error handle
16:
17: cr       equ     0dh             ; ASCII carriage return
18: lf       equ     0ah             ; ASCII linefeed
19:
20:
21: _TEXT    segment word public 'CODE'
22:
23:          assume  cs:_TEXT,ds:_DATA,ss:STACK
24:
25: print    proc    far             ; entry point from MS-DOS
26:
27:          mov     ax,_DATA        ; make our data segment
28:          mov     ds,ax           ; addressable...
29:
30:          mov     ah,40h          ; function 40h = write
31:          mov     bx,stdout       ; standard output handle
32:          mov     cx,msg_len      ; length of message
33:          mov     dx,offset msg   ; address of message
34:          int     21h             ; transfer to MS-DOS
35:
36:          mov     ax,4c00h        ; exit, return code = 0
37:          int     21h             ; transfer to MS-DOS
38:
39: print    endp
40:
41: _TEXT    ends
42:
43:
44: _DATA    segment word public 'DATA'
45:
46: msg      db      cr,lf           ; message to display
47:          db      'Hello World!',cr,lf
48:
```

Figure 3-7. *The HELLO.EXE program listing.*   *(continued)*

Figure 3–7. *continued*

```
49:    msg_len equ     $-msg            ; length of message
50:
51:    _DATA   ends
52:
53:
54:    STACK   segment para stack 'STACK'
55:
56:            db      128 dup (?)
57:
58:    STACK   ends
59:
60:            end     print            ; defines entry point
```

Within the code segment, the main *print* procedure is declared by the PROC command on line 25 and closed with ENDP on line 39. Because the procedure resides in a .EXE file, we have given it the FAR attribute as an example, but the attribute is really irrelevant because the program is so small and the procedure is not called by anything else in the same program.

The *print* procedure first initializes the DS register, as indicated in the earlier ASSUME statement, loading it with a value that causes it to point to the base of the data area. (MS-DOS automatically sets up the CS and SS registers.) Next, the procedure uses MS-DOS Int 21H Function 40H to display the message *Hello World!* on the screen, just as in the *HELLO.COM* program. Finally, the procedure exits back to MS-DOS with an Int 21H Function 4CH on lines 36 and 37, passing a return code of zero (which by convention means a success).

Lines 44 through 51 declare a data segment named _DATA, which contains the variables and constants the program will use. If the various modules of a program contain multiple data segments with the same name, the linker will collect them and place them in the same physical memory segment.

Lines 54 through 58 establish a stack segment; PUSH and POP instructions will access this area of scratch memory. Before MS-DOS transfers control to a .EXE program, it sets up the SS and SP registers according to the declared size and location of the stack segment. Be sure to allow enough room for the maximum stack depth that can occur at runtime, plus a safe number of extra words for registers pushed onto the stack during an MS-DOS service call. If the stack overflows, it may damage your other code and data segments and cause your program to behave strangely or even to crash altogether!

The END statement on line 60 winds up our brief *HELLO.EXE* program, telling the assembler that it has reached the end of the source file and providing the label of the program's point of entry from MS-DOS.

The differences between .COM and .EXE programs are summarized in Figure 3-8.

	.COM program	*.EXE program*
Maximum size	65,536 bytes minus 256 bytes for PSP and 2 bytes for stack	No limit
Entry point	PSP:0100H	Defined by END statement
AL at entry	00H if default FCB #1 has valid drive, 0FFH if invalid drive	Same
AH at entry	00H if default FCB #2 has valid drive, 0FFH if invalid drive	Same
CS at entry	PSP	Segment containing module with entry point
IP at entry	0100H	Offset of entry point within its segment
DS at entry	PSP	PSP
ES at entry	PSP	PSP
SS at entry	PSP	Segment with STACK attribute
SP at entry	0FFFEH or top word in available memory, whichever is lower	Size of segment defined with STACK attribute
Stack at entry	Zero word	Initialized or uninitialized
Stack size	65,536 bytes minus 256 bytes for PSP and size of executable code and data	Defined in segment with STACK attribute
Subroutine calls	Usually NEAR	NEAR or FAR
Exit method	Int 21H Function 4CH preferred, NEAR RET if MS-DOS version 1	Int 21H Function 4CH preferred
Size of file	Exact size of program	Size of program plus header (multiple of 512 bytes)

Figure 3-8. *Summary of the differences between .COM and .EXE programs, including their entry conditions.*

More About Assembly-Language Programs

Now that we've looked at working examples of .COM and .EXE assembly-language programs, let's backtrack and discuss their elements a little more formally. The following discussion is based on the Microsoft Macro Assembler, hereafter referred to as *MASM*. If you are familiar with MASM and are an experienced assembly-language programmer, you may want to skip this section.

MASM programs can be thought of as having three structural levels:

- The module level
- The segment level
- The procedure level

Modules are simply chunks of source code that can be independently maintained and assembled. *Segments* are physical groupings of like items (machine code or data) within a program and a corresponding segregation of dissimilar items. *Procedures* are functional subdivisions of an executable program—routines that carry out a particular task.

Program Modules

Under MS-DOS, the module-level structure consists of files containing the source code for individual routines. Each source file is translated by the assembler into a relocatable object module. An object module can reside alone in an individual file or with many other object modules in an object-module library of frequently used or related routines. The Microsoft Object Linker (LINK) combines object-module files, often with additional object modules extracted from libraries, into an executable program file.

Using modules and object-module libraries reduces the size of your application source files (and vastly increases your productivity), because these files need not contain the source code for routines they have in common with other programs. This technique also allows you to maintain the routines more easily, because you need to alter only one copy of their source code stored in one place, instead of many copies stored in different applications. When you improve (or fix) one of these routines, you can simply reassemble it, put its object module back into the library, relink all of the programs that use the routine, and *voilà*: instant upgrade.

Program Segments

The term *segments* refers to two discrete programming concepts: physical segments and logical segments.

Physical segments are 64 KB blocks of memory. The Intel 8086/8088 and 80286 microprocessors have four segment registers, which are essentially used as pointers to these blocks. (The 80386 has six segment registers, which are a superset of those found on the 8086/8088 and 80286.) Each segment register can point to the bottom of a different 64 KB area of memory. Thus, a program can address any location in memory by appropriate manipulation of the segment registers, but the maximum amount of memory that it can address simultaneously is 256 KB.

As we discussed earlier in the chapter, .COM programs assume that all four segment registers always point to the same place—the bottom of the program. Thus, they are limited to a maximum size of 64 KB. .EXE programs, on the other hand, can address many different physical segments and can reset the segment registers to point to each segment as it is needed. Consequently, the only practical limit on the size of a .EXE program is the amount of available memory. The example programs throughout the remainder of this book focus on .EXE programs.

Logical segments are the program components. A minimum of three logical segments must be declared in any .EXE program: a code segment, a data segment, and a stack segment. Programs with more than 64 KB of code or data have more than one code or data segment. The routines or data that are used most frequently are put into the primary code and data segments for speed, and routines or data that are used less frequently are put into secondary code and data segments.

Segments are declared with the SEGMENT and ENDS directives in the following form:

```
name    SEGMENT attributes
   .
   .
   .
name    ENDS
```

The attributes of a segment include its *align* type (BYTE, WORD, or PARA), *combine* type (PUBLIC, PRIVATE, COMMON, or STACK), and *class* type. The segment attributes are used by the linker when it is combining logical segments to create the physical segments of an executable program. Most of the time, you can get by just fine using a small selection of attributes in a rather stereotypical way. However, if you want to use the full range of attributes, you might want to read the detailed explanation in the MASM manual.

Programs are classified into one *memory model* or another based on the number of their code and data segments. The most commonly used memory model for assembly-language programs is the small model, which has one code and one data segment, but you can also use the medium, compact, and large models (Figure 3-9). (Two additional models exist with which we will not be concerning ourselves further: the tiny model, which consists of intermixed code and data in a single segment— for example, a .COM file under MS-DOS; and the huge model, which is supported by the Microsoft C Optimizing Compiler and which allows use of data structures larger than 64 KB.)

Model	Code segments	Data segments
Small	One	One
Medium	Multiple	One
Compact	One	Multiple
Large	Multiple	Multiple

Figure 3-9. *Memory models commonly used in assembly-language and C programs.*

For each memory model, Microsoft has established certain segment and class names that are used by all its high-level-language compilers (Figure 3-10). Because segment names are arbitrary, you may as well adopt the Microsoft conventions. Their use will make it easier for you to integrate your assembly-language routines into programs written in languages such as C, or to use routines from high-level-language libraries in your assembly-language programs.

Another important Microsoft high-level-language convention is to use the GROUP directive to name the near data segment (the segment the program expects to address with offsets from the DS register) and the stack segment as members of DGROUP (the automatic data group), a special name recognized by the linker and also by the program loaders in Microsoft Windows and Microsoft OS/2. The GROUP directive causes logical segments with different names to be combined into a single physical segment so that they can be addressed using the same segment base address. In C programs, DGROUP also contains the local heap, which is used by the C runtime library for dynamic allocation of small amounts of memory.

Memory model	Segment name	Align type	Combine type	Class type	Group
Small	_TEXT	WORD	PUBLIC	CODE	
	_DATA	WORD	PUBLIC	DATA	DGROUP
	STACK	PARA	STACK	STACK	DGROUP
Medium	*module*_TEXT	WORD	PUBLIC	CODE	
	.				
	.				
	_DATA	WORD	PUBLIC	DATA	DGROUP
	STACK	PARA	STACK	STACK	DGROUP
Compact	_TEXT	WORD	PUBLIC	CODE	
	data	PARA	PRIVATE	FAR_DATA	
	.				
	.				
	_DATA	WORD	PUBLIC	DATA	DGROUP
	STACK	PARA	STACK	STACK	DGROUP
Large	*module*_TEXT	WORD	PUBLIC	CODE	
	.				
	.				
	data	PARA	PRIVATE	FAR_DATA	
	.				
	.				
	_DATA	WORD	PUBLIC	DATA	DGROUP
	STACK	PARA	STACK	STACK	DGROUP

Figure 3-10. *Segments, groups, and classes for the standard memory models as used with assembly-language programs. The Microsoft C Optimizing Compiler and other high-level-language compilers use a superset of these segments and classes.*

For pure assembly-language programs that will run under MS-DOS, you can ignore DGROUP. However, if you plan to integrate assembly-language routines and programs written in high-level languages, you'll want to follow the Microsoft DGROUP convention. For example, if you are planning to link routines from a C library into an assembly-language program, you should include the line

```
DGROUP group _DATA,STACK
```

near the beginning of the program.

The final Microsoft convention of interest in creating .EXE programs is segment order. The high-level compilers assume that code segments always come first, followed by far data segments, followed by the near data segment, with the stack and heap last. This order won't concern you much until you begin integrating assembly-language code with routines from high-level-language libraries, but it is easiest to learn to use the convention right from the start.

Program Procedures

The procedure level of program structure is partly real and partly conceptual. Procedures are basically just a fancy guise for subroutines.

Procedures within a program are declared with the PROC and ENDP directives in the following form:

```
name    PROC attribute
    .
    .
    .
        RET
name    ENDP
```

The attribute carried by a PROC declaration, which is either NEAR or FAR, tells the assembler what type of call you expect to use to enter the procedure—that is, whether the procedure will be called from other routines in the same segment or from routines in other segments. When the assembler encounters a RET instruction within the procedure, it uses the attribute information to generate the correct opcode for either a near (intra-segment) or far (inter-segment) return.

Each program should have a main procedure that receives control from MS-DOS. You specify the entry point for the program by including the name of the main procedure in the END statement in one of the program's source files. The main procedure's attribute (NEAR or FAR) is really not too important, because the program returns control to MS-DOS with a function call rather than a RET instruction. However, by convention, most programmers assign the main procedure the FAR attribute anyway.

You should break the remainder of the program into procedures in an orderly way, with each procedure performing a well-defined single function, returning its results to its caller, and avoiding actions that have global effects within the program. Ideally procedures invoke each other only by CALL instructions, have only one entry point and one exit point, and always exit by means of a RET instruction, never by jumping to some other location within the program.

For ease of understanding and maintenance, a procedure should not exceed one page (about 60 lines); if it is longer than a page, it is probably too complex and you should delegate some of its function to one or more subsidiary procedures. You should preface the source code for each procedure with a detailed comment that states the procedure's calling sequence, results returned, registers affected, and any data items accessed or modified. The effort invested in making your procedures compact, clean, flexible, and well-documented will be repaid many times over when you reuse the procedures in other programs.

Chapter 4

MS-DOS Programming Tools

Preparing a new program to run under MS-DOS is an iterative process with four basic steps:

- Use of a text editor to create or modify an ASCII source-code file

- Use of an assembler or high-level-language compiler (such as the Microsoft Macro Assembler or the Microsoft C Optimizing Compiler) to translate the source file into relocatable object code

- Use of a linker to transform the relocatable object code into an executable MS-DOS load module

- Use of a debugger to methodically test and debug the program

Additional utilities the MS-DOS software developer may find necessary or helpful include the following:

- LIB, which creates and maintains object-module libraries

- CREF, which generates a cross-reference listing

- EXE2BIN, which converts .EXE files to .COM files

- MAKE, which compares dates of files and carries out operations based on the result of the comparison

This chapter gives an operational overview of the Microsoft programming tools for MS-DOS, including the assembler, the C compiler, the linker, and the librarian. In general, the information provided here also applies to the IBM programming tools for MS-DOS, which are really the Microsoft products with minor variations and different version numbers. Even if your preferred programming language is not C or assembly language, you will need at least a passing familiarity with these tools because all of the examples in the IBM and Microsoft DOS reference manuals are written in one of these languages.

The survey in this chapter, together with the example programs and reference section elsewhere in the book, should provide the experienced programmer with sufficient information to immediately begin writing useful programs. Readers who do not have a background in C, assembly language, or the Intel 80x86 microprocessor architecture should refer to the tutorial and reference works listed at the end of this chapter.

File Types

The MS-DOS programming tools can create and process many different file types. The following extensions are used by convention for these files:

Extension	File type
.ASM	Assembly-language source file
.C	C source file
.COM	MS-DOS executable load module that does not require relocation at runtime
.CRF	Cross-reference information file produced by the assembler for processing by CREF.EXE
.DEF	Module-definition file describing a program's segment behavior (MS OS/2 and Microsoft Windows programs only; not relevant to normal MS-DOS applications)
.EXE	MS-DOS executable load module that requires relocation at runtime
.H	C header file containing C source code for constants, macros, and functions; merged into another C program with the *#include* directive
.INC	Include file for assembly-language programs, typically containing macros and/or equates for systemwide values such as error codes
.LIB	Object-module library file made up of one or more .OBJ files; indexed and manipulated by LIB.EXE
.LST	Program listing, produced by the assembler, that includes memory locations, machine code, the original program text, and error messages
.MAP	Listing of symbols and their locations within a load module; produced by the linker
.OBJ	Relocatable-object-code file produced by an assembler or compiler
.REF	Cross-reference listing produced by CREF.EXE from the information in a .CRF file

The Microsoft Macro Assembler

The Microsoft Macro Assembler (MASM) is distributed as the file MASM.EXE. When beginning a program translation, MASM needs the following information:

- The name of the file containing the source program

- The filename for the object program to be created

- The destination of the program listing

- The filename for the information that is later processed by the cross-reference utility (CREF.EXE)

You can invoke MASM in two ways. If you enter the name of the assembler alone, it prompts you for the names of each of the various input and output files. The assembler supplies reasonable defaults for all the responses except the source filename, as shown in the following example:

```
C>MASM  <Enter>

Microsoft (R) Macro Assembler Version 5.10
Copyright (C) Microsoft Corp 1981, 1988. All rights reserved.

Source filename [.ASM]: HELLO  <Enter>
Object filename [HELLO.OBJ]:  <Enter>
Source listing  [NUL.LST]:  <Enter>
Cross-reference [NUL.CRF]:  <Enter>

  49006 Bytes symbol space free

      0 Warning Errors
      0 Severe Errors

C>
```

You can use a logical device name (such as PRN or COM1) at any of the MASM prompts to send that output of the assembler to a character device rather than a file. Note that the default for the listing and cross-reference files is the NUL device—that is, no file is created. If you end any response with a semicolon, MASM assumes that the remaining responses are all to be the default.

A more efficient way to use MASM is to supply all parameters in the command line, as follows:

MASM [*options*] *source*,[*object*],[*listing*],[*crossref*]

For example, the following command lines are equivalent to the preceding interactive session:

```
C>MASM HELLO,,NUL,NUL  <Enter>
```

or

```
C>MASM HELLO;  <Enter>
```

These commands use the file *HELLO.ASM* as the source, generate the object-code file *HELLO.OBJ*, and send the listing and cross-reference files to the bit bucket.

MASM accepts several optional switches in the command line, to control code generation and output files. Figure 4-1 lists the switches accepted by MASM version 5.1. As shown in the following example, you can put frequently used options in a MASM environment variable, where they will be found automatically by the assembler:

```
C>SET MASM=/T /Zi  <Enter>
```

The switches in the environment variable will be overridden by any that you enter in the command line.

In other versions of the Microsoft Macro Assembler, additional or fewer switches may be available. For exact instructions, see the manual for the version of MASM that you are using.

Switch	Meaning
/A	Arrange segments in alphabetic order.
/B*n*	Set size of source-file buffer (in KB).
/C	Force creation of a cross-reference (.CRF) file.
/D	Produce listing on both passes (to find phase errors).
/D*symbol*	Define *symbol* as a null text string (*symbol* can be referenced by conditional assembly directives in file).
/E	Assemble for 80x87 numeric coprocessor emulator using IEEE real-number format.
/I*path*	Set search path for include files.
/L	Force creation of a program-listing file.
/LA	Force listing of all generated code.
/ML	Preserve case sensitivity in all names (uppercase names distinct from their lowercase equivalents).
/MX	Preserve lowercase in external names only (names defined with PUBLIC or EXTRN directives).
/MU	Convert all lowercase names to uppercase.
/N	Suppress generation of tables of macros, structures, records, segments, groups, and symbols at the end of the listing.
/P	Check for impure code in 80286/80386 protected mode.
/S	Arrange segments in order of occurrence (default).
/T	"Terse" mode; suppress all messages unless errors are encountered during the assembly.
/V	"Verbose" mode; report number of lines and symbols at end of assembly.
/W*n*	Set error display (warning) level; *n*=0–2.
/X	Force listing of false conditionals.
/Z	Display source lines containing errors on the screen.
/Zd	Include line-number information in .OBJ file.
/Zi	Include line-number and symbol information in .OBJ file.

Figure 4-1. *Microsoft Macro Assembler version 5.1 switches.*

MASM allows you to override the default extensions on any file—a feature that can be rather dangerous. For example, if in the preceding example you had responded to the *Object filename* prompt with *HELLO.ASM*, the assembler would have accepted the entry without comment and destroyed your source file. This is not too likely to happen in the interactive command mode, but you must be very careful with file extensions when MASM is used in a batch file.

The Microsoft C Optimizing Compiler

The Microsoft C Optimizing Compiler consists of three executable files—C1.EXE, C2.EXE, and C3.EXE—that implement the C preprocessor, language translator, code generator, and code optimizer. An additional control program, CL.EXE, executes the three compiler files in order, passing each the necessary information about filenames and compilation options.

Before using the C compiler and the linker, you need to set up four environment variables:

Variable	*Action*
PATH=*path*	Specifies the location of the three executable C compiler files (C1, C2, and C3) if they are not in the current directory; used by CL.EXE.
INCLUDE=*path*	Specifies the location of *#include* files (default extension .H) that are not found in the current directory.
LIB=*path*	Specifies the location(s) for object-code libraries that are not found in the current directory.
TMP=*path*	Specifies the location for temporary working files created by the C compiler and linker.

CL.EXE does not support an interactive mode or response files. You always invoke it with a command line of the following form:

CL [*options*] *file* [*file* ...]

You may list any number of files—if a file has a .C extension, it will be compiled into a relocatable-object-module (.OBJ) file. Ordinarily, if the compiler encounters no errors, it automatically passes all resulting .OBJ files and any additional .OBJ files specified in the command line to the linker, along with the names of the appropriate runtime libraries.

The C compiler has many optional switches controlling its memory models, output files, code generation, and code optimization. These are summarized in Figure 4-2. The C compiler's arcane switch syntax is derived largely from UNIX/XENIX, so don't expect it to make any sense.

Switch	Meaning
/A*x*	Select memory model:
	C = compact model
	H = huge model
	L = large model
	M = medium model
	S = small model (default)
/c	Compile only; do not invoke linker.
/C	Do not strip comments.
/D<*name*>[=*text*]	Define macro.
/E	Send preprocessor output to standard output.
/EP	Send preprocessor output to standard output without line numbers.
/F<*n*>	Set stack size (in hexadecimal bytes).
/Fa [*filename*]	Generate assembly listing.
/Fc [*filename*]	Generate mixed source/object listing.
/Fe [*filename*]	Force executable filename.
/Fl [*filename*]	Generate object listing.
/Fm [*filename*]	Generate map file.
/Fo [*filename*]	Force object-module filename.
/FP*x*	Select floating-point control:
	a = calls with alternate math library
	c = calls with emulator library
	c87 = calls with 8087 library
	i = in-line with emulator (default)
	i87 = in-line with 8087
/Fs [*filename*]	Generate source listing.
/G*x*	Select code generation:
	0 = 8086 instructions (default)
	1 = 186 instructions
	2 = 286 instructions
	c = Pascal style function calls
	s = no stack checking
	t[n] = data size threshold
/H<*n*>	Specify external name length.
/I<*path*>	Specify additional *#include* path.
/J	Specify default *char* type as *unsigned*.
/link [*options*]	Pass switches and library names to linker.
/O*x*	Select optimization:
	a = ignore aliasing
	d = disable optimizations
	i = enable intrinsic functions
	l = enable loop optimizations
	n = disable "unsafe" optimizations
	p = enable precision optimizations
	r = disable in-line return
	s = optimize for space

Figure 4-2. *Microsoft C Optimizing Compiler version 5.1 switches.*   *(continued)*

Figure 4-2. *continued*

Switch	Meaning
/O*x*	t = optimize for speed (default)
(continued)	w = ignore aliasing except across function calls
	x = enable maximum optimization (equivalent to /Oailt /Gs)
/P	Send preprocessor output to file.
/S*x*	Select source-listing control:
	l<columns> = set line width
	p<lines> = set page length
	s<string> = set subtitle string
	t<string> = set title string
/Tc<*file*>	Compile file without .C extension.
/u	Remove all predefined macros.
/U<*name*>	Remove specified predefined macro.
/V<*string*>	Set version string.
/W<*n*>	Set warning level (0–3).
/X	Ignore "standard places" for include files.
/Z*x*	Select miscellaneous compilation control:
	a = disable extensions
	c = make Pascal functions case-insensitive
	d = include line-number information
	e = enable extensions (default)
	g = generate declarations
	i = include symbolic debugging information
	l = remove default library info
	p<*n*> = pack structures on *n*-byte boundary
	s = check syntax only

The Microsoft Object Linker

The object module produced by MASM from a source file is in a form that contains relocation information and may also contain unresolved references to external locations or subroutines. It is written in a common format that is also produced by the various high-level compilers (such as FORTRAN and C) that run under MS-DOS. The computer cannot execute object modules without further processing.

The Microsoft Object Linker (LINK), distributed as the file LINK.EXE, accepts one or more of these object modules, resolves external references, includes any necessary routines from designated libraries, performs any necessary offset relocations, and writes a file that can be loaded and executed by MS-DOS. The output of LINK is always in .EXE load-module format. (See Chapter 3.)

As with MASM, you can give LINK its parameters interactively or by entering all the required information in a single command line. If you enter the name of the linker alone, the following type of dialog ensues:

```
C>LINK  <Enter>

Microsoft (R) Overlay Linker  Version 3.61
Copyright (C) Microsoft Corp 1983-1987. All rights reserved.

Object Modules [.OBJ]: HELLO  <Enter>
Run File [HELLO.EXE]:  <Enter>
List File [NUL.MAP]: HELLO  <Enter>
Libraries [.LIB]:  <Enter>

C>
```

If you are using LINK version 4.0 or later, the linker also asks for the name of a module-definition (.DEF) file. Simply press the Enter key in response to such a prompt. Module-definition files are used when building Microsoft Windows or MS OS/2 "new .EXE" executable files but are not relevant in normal MS-DOS applications.

The input file for this example was *HELLO.OBJ*; the output files were *HELLO.EXE* (the executable program) and *HELLO.MAP* (the load map produced by the linker after all references and addresses were resolved). Figure 4-3 shows the load map.

```
 Start   Stop   Length Name                    Class
 00000H  00017H 00018H _TEXT                   CODE
 00018H  00027H 00010H _DATA                   DATA
 00030H  000AFH 00080H STACK                   STACK
 000B0H  000BBH 0000CH $$TYPES                 DEBTYP
 000C0H  000D6H 00017H $$SYMBOLS               DEBSYM


  Address          Publics by Name


  Address          Publics by Value

Program entry point at 0000:0000
```

Figure 4-3. *Map produced by the Microsoft Object Linker (LINK) during the generation of the* HELLO.EXE *program from Chapter 3. The program contains one CODE, one DATA, and one STACK segment. The first instruction to be executed lies in the first byte of the CODE segment. The $$TYPES and $$SYMBOLS segments contain information for the CodeView debugger and are not part of the program; these segments are ignored by the normal MS-DOS loader.*

You can obtain the same result more quickly by entering all parameters in the command line, in the following form:

LINK *options objectfile*, [*exefile*], [*mapfile*], [*libraries*]

Thus, the command-line equivalent to the preceding interactive session is

```
C>LINK HELLO,HELLO,HELLO,,   <Enter>
```

or

```
C>LINK HELLO,,HELLO;  <Enter>
```

If you enter a semicolon as the last character in the command line, LINK assumes the default values for all further parameters.

A third method of commanding LINK is with a *response file*. A response file contains lines of text that correspond to the responses you would give the linker interactively. You specify the name of the response file in the command line with a leading @ character, as follows:

LINK *@filename*

You can also enter the name of a response file at any prompt. If the response file is not complete, LINK will prompt you for the missing information.

When entering linker commands, you can specify multiple object files with the + operator or with spaces, as in the following example:

```
C>LINK HELLO+VMODE+DOSINT,MYPROG,,GRAPHICS;   <Enter>
```

This command would link the files *HELLO.OBJ*, *VMODE.OBJ*, and *DOSINT.OBJ*, searching the library file *GRAPHICS.LIB* to resolve any references to symbols not defined in the specified object files, and would produce a file named *MYPROG.EXE*. LINK uses the current drive and directory when they are not explicitly included in a filename; it will not automatically use the same drive and directory you specified for a previous file in the same command line.

By using the + operator or space characters in the *libraries* field, you can specify up to 32 library files to be searched. Each high-level-language compiler provides default libraries that are searched automatically during the linkage process if the linker can find them (unless they are explicitly excluded with the /NOD switch). LINK looks for libraries first in the current directory of the default disk drive, then along any paths that were provided in the command line, and finally along the path(s) specified by the LIB variable if it is present in the environment.

LINK accepts several optional switches as part of the command line or at the end of any interactive prompt. Figure 4-4 lists these switches. The number of switches available and their actions vary among different versions of LINK. See your Microsoft Object Linker instruction manual for detailed information about your particular version.

Switch	Full form	Meaning
/A:n	/ALIGNMENT:n	Set segment sector alignment factor. N must be a power of 2 (default = 512). Not related to logical-segment alignment (BYTE, WORD, PARA, PAGE, and so forth). Relevant to segmented executable files (Microsoft Windows and MS OS/2) only.
/B	/BATCH	Suppress linker prompt if a library cannot be found in the current directory or in the locations specified by the LIB environment variable.
/CO	/CODEVIEW	Include symbolic debugging information in the .EXE file for use by CodeView.
/CP	/CPARMAXALLOC	Set the field in the .EXE file header controlling the amount of memory allocated to the program in addition to the memory required for the program's code, stack, and initialized data.
/DO	/DOSSEG	Use standard Microsoft segment naming and ordering conventions.
/DS	/DSALLOCATE	Load data at high end of the data segment. Relevant to real-mode programs only.
/E	/EXEPACK	Pack executable file by removing sequences of repeated bytes and optimizing relocation table.
/F	/FARCALLTRANSLATION	Optimize far calls to labels within the same physical segment for speed by replacing them with near calls and NOPs.
/HE	/HELP	Display information about available options.
/HI	/HIGH	Load program as high in memory as possible.
/I	/INFORMATION	Display information about progress of linking, including pass numbers and the names of object files being linked.

(continued)

Figure 4-4. *Switches accepted by the Microsoft Object Linker (LINK) version 5.0. Earlier versions use a subset of these switches. Note that any abbreviation for a switch is acceptable as long as it is sufficient to specify the switch uniquely.*

Figure 4-4. *continued*

Switch	Full form	Meaning
/INC	/INCREMENTAL	Force production of .SYM and .ILK files for subsequent use by ILINK (incremental linker). May not be used with /EXEPACK. Relevant to segmented executable files (Microsoft Windows and MS OS/2) only.
/LI	/LINENUMBERS	Write address of the first instruction that corresponds to each source-code line to the map file. Has no effect if the compiler does not include line-number information in the object module. Force creation of a map file.
/M[:n]	/MAP[:n]	Force creation of a .MAP file listing all public symbols, sorted by name and by location. The optional value n is the maximum number of symbols that can be sorted (default = 2048); when n is supplied, the alphabetically sorted list is omitted.
/NOD	/NODEFAULTLIBRARYSEARCH	Skip search of any default compiler libraries specified in the .OBJ file.
/NOE	/NOEXTENDEDDICTSEARCH	Ignore extended library dictionary (if it is present). The extended dictionary ordinarily provides the linker with information about inter-module dependencies, to speed up linking.
/NOF	/NOFARCALLTRANSLATION	Disable optimization of far calls to labels within the same segment.
/NOG	/NOGROUPASSOCIATION	Ignore group associations when assigning addresses to data and code items.
/NOI	/NOIGNORECASE	Do not ignore case in names during linking.
/NON	/NONULLSDOSSEG	Arrange segments as for /DOSSEG but do not insert 16 null bytes at start of _TEXT segment.
/NOP	/NOPACKCODE	Do not pack contiguous logical code segments into a single physical segment.
/O:n	/OVERLAYINTERRUPT:n	Use interrupt number n with the overlay manager supplied with some Microsoft high-level languages.
/PAC[:n]	/PACKCODE[:n]	Pack contiguous logical code segments into a single physical code segment. The optional value n is the maximum size for each packed physical code segment (default = 65,536 bytes). Segments in different groups are not packed.
/PADC:n	/PADCODE:n	Add n filler bytes to end of each code module so that a larger module can be inserted later with ILINK. Relevant to segmented executable files (Windows and MS OS/2) only.

(continued)

Figure 4-4. *continued*

Switch	Full form	Meaning
/PADD:*n*	/PADDATA:*n*	Add *n* filler bytes to end of each data module so that a larger module can be inserted later with ILINK. Relevant to segmented executable files (Microsoft Windows and MS OS/2) only.
/PAU	/PAUSE	Pause during linking, allowing a change of disks before .EXE file is written.
/SE:*n*	/SEGMENTS:*n*	Set maximum number of segments in linked program (default = 128).
/ST:*n*	/STACK:*n*	Set stack size of program in bytes; ignore stack segment size declarations within object modules and definition file.
/W	/WARNFIXUP	Display warning messages for offsets relative to a segment base that is not the same as the group base. Relevant to segmented executable files (Microsoft Windows and MS OS/2) only.

The EXE2BIN Utility

The EXE2BIN utility (EXE2BIN.EXE) transforms a .EXE file created by LINK into an executable .COM file, if the program meets the following prerequisites:

- It cannot contain more than one declared segment and cannot define a stack.

- It must be less than 64 KB in length.

- It must have an origin at 0100H.

- The first location in the file must be specified as the entry point in the source code's END directive.

Although .COM files are somewhat more compact than .EXE files, you should avoid using them. Programs that use separate segments for code, data, and stack are much easier to port to protected-mode environments such as MS OS/2; in addition, .COM files do not support the symbolic debugging information used by CodeView.

Another use for the EXE2BIN utility is to convert an installable device driver—after it is assembled and linked into a .EXE file—into a memory-image .BIN or .SYS file with an origin of zero. This conversion is required in MS-DOS version 2, which cannot load device drivers as .EXE files. The process of writing an installable device driver is discussed in more detail in Chapter 14.

Unlike most of the other programming utilities, EXE2BIN does not have an interactive mode. It always takes its source and destination filenames, separated by spaces, from the MS-DOS command line, as follows:

EXE2BIN *sourcefile* [*destinationfile*]

If you do not supply the source-file extension, it defaults to .EXE; the destination-file extension defaults to .BIN. If you do not specify a name for the destination file, EXE2BIN gives it the same name as the source file, with a .BIN extension.

For example, to convert the file *HELLO.EXE* into *HELLO.COM*, you would use the following command line:

```
C>EXE2BIN HELLO.EXE HELLO.COM  <Enter>
```

The EXE2BIN program also has other capabilities, such as pure binary conversion with segment fixup for creating program images to be placed in ROM; but because these features are rarely used during MS-DOS application development, they will not be discussed here.

The CREF Utility

The CREF cross-reference utility CREF.EXE processes a .CRF file produced by MASM, creating an ASCII text file with the default extension .REF. The file contains a cross-reference listing of all symbols declared in the program and the line numbers in which they are referenced. (See Figure 4-5.) Such a listing is very useful when debugging large assembly-language programs with many interdependent procedures and variables.

CREF may be supplied with its parameters interactively or in a single command line. If you enter the utility name alone, CREF prompts you for the input and output filenames, as shown in the following example:

```
C>CREF  <Enter>

Microsoft (R) Cross-Reference Utility  Version 5.10
Copyright (C) Microsoft Corp 1981-1985, 1987. All rights reserved.

Cross-reference [.CRF]: HELLO  <Enter>
Listing [HELLO.REF]:

15 Symbols

C>
```

```
Microsoft Cross-Reference  Version 5.10      Thu May 26 11:09:34 1988
HELLO.EXE --- print Hello on terminal

  Symbol Cross-Reference    (# definition, + modification)Cref-1

@CPU . . . . . . . . . . . . .  1#
@VERSION . . . . . . . . . . .  1#


CODE . . . . . . . . . . . . .  21
CR . . . . . . . . . . . . . . 17#    46     47


DATA . . . . . . . . . . . . .  44


LF . . . . . . . . . . . . . . 18#    46     47


MSG. . . . . . . . . . . . . .  33    46#
MSG_LEN. . . . . . . . . . . .  32    49#


PRINT. . . . . . . . . . . . . 25#    39     60


STACK. . . . . . . . . . . . .  23    54#    54     58
STDERR . . . . . . . . . . . . 15#
STDIN. . . . . . . . . . . . . 13#
STDOUT . . . . . . . . . . . . 14#    31


_DATA. . . . . . . . . . . . .  23    27    44#    51
_TEXT. . . . . . . . . . . . . 21#    23     41


15 Symbols
```

Figure 4-5. *Cross-reference listing* HELLO.REF *produced by the CREF utility from the file* HELLO.CRF, *for the* HELLO.EXE *program example from Chapter 3. The symbols declared in the program are listed on the left in alphabetic order. To the right of each symbol is a list of all the lines where that symbol is referenced. The number with a # sign after it denotes the line where the symbol is declared. Numbers followed by a + sign indicate that the symbol is modified at the specified line. The line numbers given in the cross-reference listing correspond to the line numbers generated by the assembler in the program-listing (.LST) file, not to any physical line count in the original source file.*

The parameters may also be entered in the command line in the following form:

CREF *CRF_file, listing_file*

For example, the command-line equivalent to the preceding interactive session is:

```
C>CREF HELLO,HELLO  <Enter>
```

If CREF cannot find the specified .CRF file, it displays an error message. Otherwise, it leaves the cross-reference listing in the specified file on the disk. You can send the file to the printer with the COPY command, in the following form:

COPY *listing_file* PRN:

You can also send the cross-reference listing directly to a character device as it is generated by responding to the *Listing* prompt with the name of the device.

The Microsoft Library Manager

Although the object modules that are produced by MASM or by high-level-language compilers can be linked directly into executable load modules, they can also be collected into special files called *object-module libraries*. The modules in a library are indexed by name and by the public symbols they contain, so that they can be extracted by the linker to satisfy external references in a program.

The Microsoft Library Manager (LIB) is distributed as the file LIB.EXE. LIB creates and maintains program libraries, adding, updating, and deleting object files as necessary. LIB can also check a library file for internal consistency or print a table of its contents (Figure 4-6).

LIB follows the command conventions of most other Microsoft programming tools. You must supply it with the name of a library file to work on, one or more operations to perform, the name of a listing file or device, and (optionally) the name of the output library. If you do not specify a name for the output library, LIB gives it the same name as the input library and changes the extension of the input library to .BAK.

The LIB operations are simply the names of object files, with a prefix character that specifies the action to be taken:

Prefix	Meaning
–	Delete an object module from the library.
*	Extract a module and place it in a separate .OBJ file.
+	Add an object module or the entire contents of another library to the library.

You can combine command prefixes. For example, –+ replaces a module, and *– extracts a module into a new file and then deletes it from the library.

```
_abort...........abort              _abs.............abs
_access..........access             _asctime.........asctime
_atof............atof               _atoi............atoi
_atol............atol               _bdos............bdos
_brk.............brk                _brkctl..........brkctl
_bsearch.........bsearch            _calloc..........calloc
_cgets...........cgets              _chdir...........dir
_chmod...........chmod              _chsize..........chsize
      .                                   .
      .                                   .
      .                                   .

_exit              Offset: 00000010H  Code and data size: 44H
  __exit


_filbuf            Offset: 00000160H  Code and data size: BBH
  __filbuf


_file              Offset: 00000300H  Code and data size: CAH
  __iob                  __iob2                 __lastiob
      .
      .
      .
```

Figure 4-6. *Extract from the table-of-contents listing produced by the Microsoft Library Manager (LIB) for the Microsoft C library SLIBC.LIB. The first part of the listing is an alphabetic list of all public names declared in all of the modules in the library. Each name is associated with the object module to which it belongs. The second part of the listing is an alphabetic list of the object-module names in the library, each followed by its offset within the library file and the actual size of the module in bytes. The entry for each module is followed by a summary of the public names that are declared within it.*

When you invoke LIB with its name alone, it requests the other information it needs interactively, as shown in the following example:

```
C>LIB  <Enter>

Microsoft (R) Library Manager  Version 3.08
Copyright (C) Microsoft Corp 1983-1987. All rights reserved.

Library name:  SLIBC  <Enter>
Operations: +VIDEO  <Enter>
List file:  SLIBC.LST  <Enter>
Output library:  SLIBC2  <Enter>

C>
```

In this example, LIB added the object module *VIDEO.OBJ* to the library *SLIBC.LIB*, wrote a library table of contents into the file *SLIBC.LST*, and named the resulting new library *SLIBC2.LIB*.

The Library Manager can also be run with a command line of the following form:

LIB *library* [*commands*],[*list*],[*newlibrary*]

For example, the following command line is equivalent to the preceding interactive session:

```
C>LIB SLIBC +VIDEO,SLIBC.LST,SLIBC2;  <Enter>
```

As with the other Microsoft utilities, a semicolon at the end of the command line causes LIB to use the default responses for any parameters that are omitted.

Like LINK, LIB can also accept its commands from a response file. The contents of the file are lines of text that correspond exactly to the responses you would give LIB interactively. You specify the name of the response file in the command line with a leading @ character, as follows:

LIB @*filename*

LIB has only three switches: /I (/IGNORECASE), /N (/NOIGNORECASE), and /PAGESIZE:*number*. The /IGNORECASE switch is the default. The /NOIGNORECASE switch causes LIB to regard as distinct any symbols that differ only in the case of their component letters. You should place the /PAGESIZE switch, which defines the size of a unit of allocation space for a given library, immediately after the library filename. The library page size is in bytes and must be a power of 2 between 16 and 32,768 (16, 32, 64, and so forth); the default is 16 bytes. Because the index to a library is always a fixed number of pages, setting a larger page size allows you to store more object modules in that library; on the other hand, it will result in more wasted space within the file.

The MAKE Utility

The MAKE utility (MAKE.EXE) compares dates of files and carries out commands based on the result of that comparison. Because of this single, rather basic capability, MAKE can be used to maintain complex programs built from many modules. The dates of source, object, and executable files are simply compared in a logical sequence; the assembler, compiler, linker, and other programming tools are invoked as appropriate.

The MAKE utility processes a plain ASCII text file called, as you might expect, a *make file*. You start the utility with a command-line entry in the following form:

MAKE *makefile* [*options*]

By convention, a make file has the same name as the executable file that is being maintained, but without an extension. The available MAKE switches are listed in Figure 4-7.

A simple make file contains one or more *dependency statements* separated by blank lines. Each dependency statement can be followed by a list of MS-DOS commands, in the following form:

targetfile : *sourcefile* ...

  command

  command

  .

  .

  .

If the date and time of any source file are later than those of the target file, the accompanying list of commands is carried out. You may use comment lines, which begin with a # character, freely in a make file. MAKE can also process inference rules and macro definitions. For further details on these advanced capabilities, see the Microsoft or IBM documentation.

Switch	Meaning
/D	Display last modification date of each file as it is processed.
/I	Ignore exit (return) codes returned by commands and programs executed as a result of dependency statements.
/N	Display commands that would be executed as a result of dependency statements but do not execute those commands.
/S	Do not display commands as they are executed.
/X <*filename*>	Direct error messages from MAKE, or any program that MAKE runs, to the specified file. If *filename* is a hyphen (-), direct error messages to the standard output.

Figure 4-7. *Switches for the MAKE utility.*

A Complete Example

Let's put together everything we've learned about using the MS-DOS programming tools so far. Figure 4-8 shows a sketch of the overall process of building an executable program.

Assume that we have the source code for the *HELLO.EXE* program from Chapter 3 in the file *HELLO.ASM*. To assemble the source program into the relocatable object module *HELLO.OBJ* with symbolic debugging information included, also producing a program listing in the file *HELLO.LST* and a cross-reference data file *HELLO.CRF*, we would enter

```
C>MASM /C /L /Zi /T HELLO;  <Enter>
```

To convert the cross-reference raw-data file *HELLO.CRF* into a cross-reference listing in the file *HELLO.REF*, we would enter

```
C>CREF HELLO,HELLO  <Enter>
```

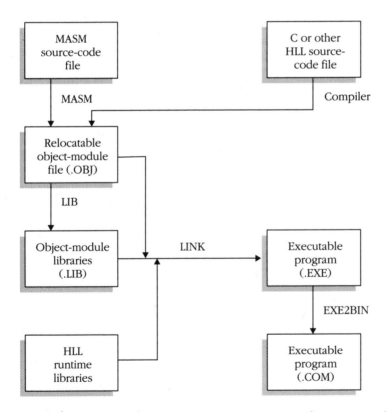

Figure 4-8. *Creation of an MS-DOS application program, from source code to executable file.*

To convert the relocatable object file *HELLO.OBJ* into the executable file *HELLO.EXE*, creating a load map in the file *HELLO.MAP* and appending symbolic debugging information to the executable file, we would enter

```
C>LINK /MAP /CODEVIEW HELLO;  <Enter>
```

We could also automate the entire process just described by creating a make file named *HELLO* (with no extension) and including the following instructions:

```
hello.obj : hello.asm
 masm /C /L /Zi /T hello;
 cref hello,hello

hello.exe : hello.obj
 link /MAP /CODEVIEW hello;
```

Then, when we have made some change to *HELLO.ASM* and want to rebuild the executable *HELLO.EXE* file, we need only enter

```
C>MAKE HELLO  <Enter>
```

Programming Resources and References

The literature on IBM PC–compatible personal computers, the Intel 80x86 microprocessor family, and assembly-language and C programming is vast. The list below contains a selection of those books that I have found to be useful and reliable. The list should not be construed as an endorsement by Microsoft Corporation.

MASM Tutorials

Assembly Language Primer for the IBM PC and XT, by Robert Lafore. New American Library, New York, NY, 1984. ISBN 0-452-25711-5.

8086/8088/80286 Assembly Language, by Leo Scanlon. Brady Books, Simon and Schuster, New York, NY, 1988. ISBN 0-13-246919-7.

C Tutorials

Microsoft C Programming for the IBM, by Robert Lafore. Howard K. Sams & Co., Indianapolis, IN, 1987. ISBN 0-672-22515-8.

Proficient C, by Augie Hansen. Microsoft Press, Redmond, WA, 1987. ISBN 1-55615-007-5.

Intel 80x86 Microprocessor References

iAPX 88 Book. Intel Corporation, Literature Department SV3-3, 3065 Bowers Ave., Santa Clara, CA 95051. Order no. 210200.

iAPX 286 Programmer's Reference Manual. Intel Corporation, Literature Department SV3-3, 3065 Bowers Ave., Santa Clara, CA 95051. Order no. 210498.

iAPX 386 Programmer's Reference Manual. Intel Corporation, Literature Department SV3-3, 3065 Bowers Ave., Santa Clara, CA 95051. Order no. 230985.

PC, PC/AT, and PS/2 Architecture

The IBM Personal Computer from the Inside Out (Revised Edition), by Murray Sargent and Richard L. Shoemaker. Addison-Wesley Publishing Company, Reading, MA, 1986. ISBN 0-201-06918-0.

Programmer's Guide to PC & PS/2 Video Systems, by Richard Wilton. Microsoft Press, Redmond, WA, 1987. ISBN 1-55615-103-9.

Personal Computer Technical Reference. IBM Corporation, IBM Technical Directory, P. O. Box 2009, Racine, WI 53404. Part no. 6322507.

Personal Computer AT Technical Reference. IBM Corporation, IBM Technical Directory, P. O. Box 2009, Racine, WI 53404. Part no. 6280070.

Options and Adapters Technical Reference. IBM Corporation, IBM Technical Directory, P. O. Box 2009, Racine, WI 53404. Part no. 6322509.

Personal System/2 Model 30 Technical Reference. IBM Corporation, IBM Technical Directory, P. O. Box 2009, Racine, WI 53404. Part no. 68X2201.

Personal System/2 Model 50/60 Technical Reference. IBM Corporation, IBM Technical Directory, P. O. Box 2009, Racine, WI 53404. Part no. 68X2224.

Personal System/2 Model 80 Technical Reference. IBM Corporation, IBM Technical Directory, P. O. Box 2009, Racine, WI 53404. Part no. 68X2256.

Chapter 5

Keyboard and Mouse Input

The fundamental means of user input under MS-DOS is the keyboard. This follows naturally from the MS-DOS command-line interface, whose lineage can be traced directly to minicomputer operating systems with Teletype consoles. During the first few years of MS-DOS's existence, when 8088/8086-based machines were the norm, nearly every popular application program used key-driven menus and text-mode displays.

However, as high-resolution graphics adapters (and 80286/80386-based machines with enough power to drive them) have become less expensive, programs that support windows and a graphical user interface have steadily grown more popular. Such programs typically rely on a pointing device such as a mouse, stylus, joystick, or light pen to let the user navigate in a "point-and-shoot" manner, reducing keyboard entry to a minimum. As a result, support for pointing devices has become an important consideration for all software developers.

Keyboard Input Methods

Applications running under MS-DOS on IBM PC–compatible machines can use several methods to obtain keyboard input:

- MS-DOS handle-oriented functions

- MS-DOS traditional character functions

- IBM ROM BIOS keyboard-driver functions

These methods offer different degrees of flexibility, portability, and hardware independence.

The handle, or stream-oriented, functions are philosophically derived from UNIX/XENIX and were first introduced in MS-DOS version 2.0. A program uses these functions by supplying a *handle,* or token, for the desired device, plus the address and length of a buffer.

When a program begins executing, MS-DOS supplies it with predefined handles for certain commonly used character devices, including the keyboard:

Handle	Device name	Opened to
0	Standard input (*stdin*)	CON
1	Standard output (*stdout*)	CON
2	Standard error (*stderr*)	CON
3	Standard auxiliary (*stdaux*)	AUX
4	Standard printer (*stdprn*)	PRN

These handles can be used for read and write operations without further preliminaries. A program can also obtain a handle for a character device by explicitly opening the device for input or output using its logical name (as though it were a file). The handle functions support *I/O redirection,* allowing a program to take its input from another device or file instead of the keyboard, for example. Redirection is discussed in detail in Chapter 15.

The traditional character-input functions are a superset of the character I/O functions that were present in CP/M. Originally included in MS-DOS simply to facilitate the porting of existing applications from CP/M, they are still widely used. In MS-DOS versions 2.0 and later, most of the traditional functions also support I/O redirection (although not as well as the handle functions do).

Use of the IBM ROM BIOS keyboard functions presupposes that the program is running on an IBM PC–compatible machine. The ROM BIOS keyboard driver operates at a much more primitive level than the MS-DOS functions and allows a program to circumvent I/O redirection or MS-DOS's special handling of certain control characters. Programs that use the ROM BIOS keyboard driver are inherently less portable than those that use the MS-DOS functions and may interfere with the proper operation of other programs; many of the popular terminate-and-stay-resident (TSR) utilities fall into this category.

Keyboard Input with Handles

The principal MS-DOS function for keyboard input using handles is Int 21H Function 3FH (Read File or Device). The parameters for this function are a handle, the segment and offset of a buffer, and the length of the buffer. (For a more detailed explanation of this function, see Section II of this book, "MS-DOS Functions Reference.")

As an example, let's use the predefined standard input handle (0) and Int 21H Function 3FH to read a line from the keyboard:

```
buffer  db   80 dup (?)      ; keyboard input buffer
        .
        .
        .
        mov   ah,3fh          ; function 3fh = read file or device
        mov   bx,0            ; handle for standard input
        mov   cx,80           ; maximum bytes to read
        mov   dx,seg buffer   ; DS:DX = buffer address
        mov   ds,dx
        mov   dx,offset buffer
```

(continued)

(continued)

```
        int   21h              ; transfer to MS-DOS
        jc    error            ; jump if error detected
        .
        .
        .
```

When control returns from Int 21H Function 3FH, the carry flag is clear if the function was successful, and AX contains the number of characters read. If there was an error, the carry flag is set and AX contains an error code; however, this should never occur when reading the keyboard.

The standard input is redirectable, so the code just shown is not a foolproof way of obtaining input from the keyboard. Depending upon whether a redirection parameter was included in the command line by the user, program input might be coming from the keyboard, a file, another character device, or even the bit bucket (NUL device). To bypass redirection and be absolutely certain where your input is coming from, you can ignore the predefined standard input handle and open the console as though it were a file, using the handle obtained from that open operation to perform your keyboard input, as in the following example:

```
buffer  db    80 dup (?)    ; keyboard input buffer
fname   db    'CON',0       ; keyboard device name
handle  dw    0             ; keyboard device handle
        .
        .
        .
        mov   ah,3dh        ; function 3dh = open
        mov   al,0          ; mode = read
        mov   dx,seg fname  ; DS:DX = device name
        mov   ds,dx
        mov   dx,offset fname
        int   21h           ; transfer to MS-DOS
        jc    error         ; jump if open failed
        mov   handle,ax     ; save handle for CON
        .
        .
        .
        mov   ah,3fh        ; function 3fh = read file or device
        mov   bx,handle     ; BX = handle for CON
        mov   cx,80         ; maximum bytes to read
        mov   dx,offset buffer ; DS:DX = buffer address
```

(continued)

(continued)

```
int     21h          ; transfer to MS-DOS
jc      error        ; jump if error detected
  .
  .
  .
```

When a programmer uses Int 21H Function 3FH to read from the keyboard, the exact result depends on whether MS-DOS regards the handle to be in ASCII mode or binary mode (sometimes known as *cooked mode* and *raw mode*). ASCII mode is the default, although binary mode can be selected with Int 21H Function 44H (IOCTL) when necessary.

In ASCII mode, MS-DOS initially places characters obtained from the keyboard in a 128-byte internal buffer, and the user can edit the input with the Backspace key and the special function keys. MS-DOS automatically echoes the characters to the standard output, expanding tab characters to spaces (although they are left as the ASCII code 09H in the buffer). The Ctrl-C, Ctrl-S, and Ctrl-P key combinations receive special handling, and the Enter key is translated to a carriage return–linefeed pair. When the user presses Enter or Ctrl-Z, MS-DOS copies the requested number of characters (or the actual number of characters entered, if less than the number requested) out of the internal buffer into the calling program's buffer.

In binary mode, MS-DOS never echoes input characters. It passes the Ctrl-C, Ctrl-S, Ctrl-P, and Ctrl-Z key combinations and the Enter key through to the application unchanged, and Int 21H Function 3FH does not return control to the application until the exact number of characters requested has been received.

Ctrl-C checking is discussed in more detail at the end of this chapter. For now, simply note that the application programmer can substitute a custom handler for the default MS-DOS Ctrl-C handler and thereby avoid having the application program lose control of the machine when the user enters a Ctrl-C or Ctrl-Break.

Keyboard Input with Traditional Calls

The MS-DOS traditional keyboard functions offer a variety of character and line-oriented services with or without echo and Ctrl-C detection. These functions are summarized on the following page.

Int 21H Function	Action	Ctrl-C checking
01H	Keyboard input with echo	Yes
06H	Direct console I/O	No
07H	Keyboard input without echo	No
08H	Keyboard input without echo	Yes
0AH	Buffered keyboard input	Yes
0BH	Input-status check	Yes
0CH	Input-buffer reset and input	Varies

In MS-DOS versions 2.0 and later, redirection of the standard input affects all these functions. In other words, they act as though they were special cases of an Int 21H Function 3FH call using the predefined standard input handle (0).

The character-input functions (01H, 06H, 07H, and 08H) all return a character in the AL register. For example, the following sequence waits until a key is pressed and then returns it in AL:

```
        mov     ah,1        ; function 01h — read keyboard
        int     21h         ; transfer to MS-DOS
```

The character-input functions differ in whether the input is echoed to the screen and whether they are sensitive to Ctrl-C interrupts. Although MS-DOS provides no pure keyboard-status function that is immune to Ctrl-C, a program can read keyboard status (somewhat circuitously) without interference by using Int 21H Function 06H. Extended keys, such as the IBM PC keyboard's special function keys, require two calls to a character-input function.

As an alternative to single-character input, a program can use buffered-line input (Int 21H Function 0AH) to obtain an entire line from the keyboard in one operation. MS-DOS builds up buffered lines in an internal buffer and does not pass them to the calling program until the user presses the Enter key. While the line is being entered, all the usual editing keys are active and are handled by the MS-DOS keyboard driver. You use Int 21H Function 0AH as follows:

```
buff    db      81          ; maximum length of input
        db      0           ; actual length (from MS-DOS)
        db      81 dup (0)  ; receives keyboard input
```

(continued)

(continued)

```
        .
        .
        .
    mov     ah,0ah      ; function 0ah = read buffered line
    mov     dx,seg buff ; DS:DX = buffer address
    mov     ds,dx
    mov     dx,offset buff
    int     21h         ; transfer to MS-DOS
        .
        .
        .
```

Int 21H Function 0AH differs from Int 21H Function 3FH in several important ways. First, the maximum length is passed in the first byte of the
buffer, rather than in the CX register. Second, the actual length is returned
in the second byte of the structure, rather than in the AX register. Finally,
when the user has entered one less than the specified maximum number
of characters, MS-DOS ignores all subsequent characters and sounds a
warning beep until the Enter key is pressed.

For detailed information about each of the traditional keyboard-input
functions, see Section II of this book, "MS-DOS Functions Reference."

Keyboard Input with ROM BIOS Functions

Programmers writing applications for IBM PC compatibles can bypass the
MS-DOS keyboard functions and choose from two hardware-dependent
techniques for keyboard input.

The first method is to call the ROM BIOS keyboard driver using Int 16H.
For example, the following sequence reads a single character from the
keyboard input buffer and returns it in the AL register:

```
    mov     ah,0        ; function 0=read keyboard
    int     16h         ; transfer to ROM BIOS
```

Int 16H Function 00H also returns the keyboard scan code in the AH
register, allowing the program to detect key codes that are not ordinarily
returned by MS-DOS. Other Int 16H services return the keyboard status
(that is, whether a character is waiting) or the keyboard shift state (from
the ROM BIOS data area 0000:0417H). For a more detailed explanation of
ROM BIOS keyboard functions, see Section III of this book, "IBM ROM
BIOS and Mouse Functions Reference."

You should consider carefully before building ROM BIOS dependence into an application. Although this technique allows you to bypass any I/O redirection that may be in effect, ways exist to do this without introducing dependence on the ROM BIOS. And there are real disadvantages to calling the ROM BIOS keyboard driver:

- It always bypasses I/O redirection, which sometimes may not be desirable.

- It is dependent on IBM PC compatibility and does not work correctly, unchanged, on some older machines such as the Hewlett-Packard TouchScreen or the Wang Professional Computer.

- It may introduce complicated interactions with TSR utilities.

The other and more hardware-dependent method of keyboard input on an IBM PC is to write a new handler for ROM BIOS Int 09H and service the keyboard controller's interrupts directly. This involves translation of scan codes to ASCII characters and maintenance of the type-ahead buffer. In ordinary PC applications, there is no reason to take over keyboard I/O at this level; therefore, I will not discuss this method further here. If you are curious about the techniques that would be required, the best reference is the listing for the ROM BIOS Int 09H handler in the IBM PC or PC/AT technical reference manual.

Ctrl-C and Ctrl-Break Handlers

In the discussion of keyboard input with the MS-DOS handle and traditional functions, I made some passing references to the fact that Ctrl-C entries can interfere with the expected behavior of those functions. Let's look at this subject in more detail now.

During most character I/O operations, MS-DOS checks for a Ctrl-C (ASCII code 03H) waiting at the keyboard and executes an Int 23H if one is detected. If the system break flag is on, MS-DOS also checks for a Ctrl-C entry during certain other operations (such as file reads and writes). Ordinarily, the Int 23H vector points to a routine that simply terminates the currently active process and returns control to the parent process— usually the MS-DOS command interpreter.

In other words, if your program is executing and you enter a Ctrl-C, accidentally or intentionally, MS-DOS simply aborts the program. Any files the program has opened using file control blocks will not be closed properly, any interrupt vectors it has altered may not be restored correctly, and if it is performing any direct I/O operations (for example, if it contains an interrupt driver for the serial port), all kinds of unexpected events may occur.

Although you can use a number of partially effective methods to defeat Ctrl-C checking, such as performing keyboard input with Int 21H Functions 06H and 07H, placing all character devices into binary mode, or turning off the system break flag with Int 21H Function 33H, none of these is completely foolproof. The simplest and most elegant way to defeat Ctrl-C checking is simply to substitute your own Int 23H handler, which can take some action appropriate to your program. When the program terminates, MS-DOS automatically restores the previous contents of the Int 23H vector from information saved in the program segment prefix. The following example shows how to install your own Ctrl-C handler (which in this case does nothing at all):

```
          push    ds              ; save data segment
                                  ; set int 23h vector...
          mov     ax,2523h        ; function 25h = set interrupt
                                  ; int 23h = vector for
                                  ; Ctrl-C handler
          mov     dx,seg handler  ; DS:DX = handler address
          mov     ds,dx
          mov     dx,offset handler
          int     21h             ; transfer to MS-DOS

          pop     ds              ; restore data segment
          .
          .
          .
handler:                          ; a Ctrl-C handler
          iret                    ; that does nothing
```

The first part of the code (which alters the contents of the Int 23H vector) would be executed in the initialization part of the application. The handler receives control whenever MS-DOS detects a Ctrl-C at the keyboard. (Because this handler consists only of an interrupt return, the Ctrl-C will remain in the keyboard input stream and will be passed to the application when it requests a character from the keyboard, appearing on the screen as ^C.)

When an Int 23H handler is called, MS-DOS is in a stable state. Thus, the handler can call any MS-DOS function. It can also reset the segment registers and the stack pointer and transfer control to some other point in the application without ever returning control to MS-DOS with an IRET.

On IBM PC compatibles, an additional interrupt handler must be taken into consideration. Whenever the ROM BIOS keyboard driver detects the key combination Ctrl-Break, it calls a handler whose address is stored in the vector for Int 1BH. The default ROM BIOS Int 1BH handler does nothing. MS-DOS alters the Int 1BH vector to point to its own handler, which sets a flag and returns; the net effect is to remap the Ctrl-Break into a Ctrl-C that is forced ahead of any other characters waiting in the keyboard buffer.

Taking over the Int 1BH vector in an application is somewhat tricky but extremely useful. Because the keyboard is interrupt driven, a press of Ctrl-Break lets the application regain control under almost any circumstance—often, even if the program has crashed or is in an endless loop.

You cannot, in general, use the same handler for Int 1BH that you use for Int 23H. The Int 1BH handler is more limited in what it can do, because it has been called as a result of a hardware interrupt and MS-DOS may have been executing a critical section of code at the time the interrupt was serviced. Thus, all registers except CS:IP are in an unknown state; they may have to be saved and then modified before your interrupt handler can execute. Similarly, the depth of the stack in use when the Int 1BH handler is called is unknown, and if the handler is to perform stack-intensive operations, it may have to save the stack segment and the stack pointer and switch to a new stack that is known to have sufficient depth.

In normal application programs, you should probably avoid retaining control in an Int 1BH handler, rather than performing an IRET. Because of subtle differences among non-IBM ROM BIOSes, it is difficult to predict the state of the keyboard controller and the 8259 Programmable Interrupt Controller (PIC) when the Int 1BH handler begins executing. Also, MS-DOS itself may not be in a stable state at the point of interrupt, a situation that can manifest itself in unexpected critical errors during subsequent I/O operations. Finally, MS-DOS versions 3.2 and later allocate a stack from an internal pool for use by the Int 09H handler. If the Int 1BH handler never returns, the Int 09H handler never returns either, and repeated entries of Ctrl-Break will eventually exhaust the stack pool, halting the system.

Because Int 1BH is a ROM BIOS interrupt and not an MS-DOS interrupt, MS-DOS does not restore the previous contents of the Int 1BH vector when a program exits. If your program modifies this vector, it must save the original value and restore it before terminating. Otherwise, the vector will be left pointing to some random area in the next program that runs, and the next time the user presses Ctrl-Break a system crash is the best you can hope for.

Ctrl-C and Ctrl-Break Handlers and High-Level Languages

Capturing the Ctrl-C and Ctrl-Break interrupts is straightforward when you are programming in assembly language. The process is only slightly more difficult with high-level languages, as long as you have enough information about the language's calling conventions that you can link in a small assembly-language routine as part of the program.

The *BREAK.ASM* listing in Figure 5-1 contains source code for a Ctrl-Break handler that can be linked with small-model Microsoft C programs running on an IBM PC compatible. The short C program in Figure 5-2 demonstrates use of the handler. (This code should be readily portable to other C compilers.)

```
        page    55,132
        title   Ctrl-C & Ctrl-Break Handlers
        name    break


;
; Ctrl-C and Ctrl-Break handler for Microsoft C
; programs running on IBM PC compatibles
;
; by Ray Duncan
;
; Assemble with:  C>MASM /Mx BREAK;
;
; This module allows C programs to retain control
; when the user enters a Ctrl-Break or Ctrl-C.
; It uses Microsoft C parameter-passing conventions
; and assumes the C small memory model.
;
; The procedure _capture is called to install
; a new handler for the Ctrl-C and Ctrl-Break
; interrupts (1bh and 23h).  _capture is passed
; the address of a static variable, which will be
; set to true by the handler whenever a Ctrl-C
; or Ctrl-Break is detected.  The C syntax is:
;
;               static int flag;
;               capture(&flag);
;
; The procedure _release is called by the C program
; to restore the original Ctrl-Break and Ctrl-C
; handler. The C syntax is:
```

(continued)

Figure 5-1. BREAK.ASM: *A Ctrl-C and Ctrl-Break interrupt handler that can be linked with Microsoft C programs.*

Figure 5-1. *continued*

```
;
;                    release();
;
; The procedure ctrlbrk is the actual interrupt
; handler.  It receives control when a software
; int 1bh is executed by the ROM BIOS or int 23h
; is executed by MS-DOS.  It simply sets the C
; program's variable to true (1) and returns.
;

args     equ     4                    ; stack offset of arguments,
                                      ; C small memory model

cr       equ     0dh                  ; ASCII carriage return
lf       equ     0ah                  ; ASCII linefeed


_TEXT    segment word public 'CODE'

         assume cs:_TEXT



         public  _capture
_capture proc    near                 ; take over Ctrl-Break
                                      ; and Ctrl-C interrupt vectors

         push    bp                   ; set up stack frame
         mov     bp,sp

         push    ds                   ; save registers
         push    di
         push    si

                                      ; save address of
                                      ; calling program's "flag"
         mov     ax,word ptr [bp+args]
         mov     word ptr cs:flag,ax
         mov     word ptr cs:flag+2,ds

                                      ; save address of original
         mov     ax,3523h             ; int 23h handler
         int     21h
         mov     word ptr cs:int23,bx
         mov     word ptr cs:int23+2,es
         mov     ax,351bh             ; save address of original
         int     21h                  ; int 1bh handler
         mov     word ptr cs:int1b,bx
         mov     word ptr cs:int1b+2,es
```

(continued)

Figure 5-1. *continued*

```
        push    cs              ; set DS:DX = address
        pop     ds              ; of new handler
        mov     dx,offset _TEXT:ctrlbrk

        mov     ax,02523h       ; set int 23h vector
        int     21h

        mov     ax,0251bh       ; set int 1bh vector
        int     21h

        pop     si              ; restore registers
        pop     di
        pop     ds

        pop     bp              ; discard stack frame
        ret                     ; and return to caller

_capture endp


        public  _release
_release proc   near            ; restore original Ctrl-C
                                ; and Ctrl-Break handlers

        push    bp              ; save registers
        push    ds
        push    di
        push    si

        lds     dx,cs:int1b     ; get address of previous
                                ; int 1bh handler

        mov     ax,251bh        ; set int 1bh vector
        int     21h

        lds     dx,cs:int23     ; get address of previous
                                ; int 23h handler

        mov     ax,2523h        ; set int 23h vector
        int     21h

        pop     si              ; restore registers
        pop     di              ; and return to caller
        pop     ds
        pop     bp
        ret
```

(continued)

Figure 5-1. *continued*

```
_release endp

ctrlbrk proc    far                 ; Ctrl-C and Ctrl-Break
                                    ; interrupt handler

        push    bx                  ; save registers
        push    ds

        lds     bx,cs:flag          ; get address of C program's
                                    ; "flag variable"

                                    ; and set the flag "true"
        mov     word ptr ds:[bx],1

        pop     ds                  ; restore registers
        pop     bx

        iret                        ; return from handler

ctrlbrk endp

flag    dd      0                   ; far pointer to caller's
                                    ; Ctrl-Break or Ctrl-C flag

int23   dd      0                   ; address of original
                                    ; Ctrl-C handler

int1b   dd      0                   ; address of original
                                    ; Ctrl-Break handler

_TEXT   ends

        end
```

```
/*
    TRYBREAK.C

    Demo of BREAK.ASM Ctrl-Break and Ctrl-C
    interrupt handler, by Ray Duncan

    To create the executable file TRYBREAK.EXE, enter:
```

(continued)

Figure 5-2. TRYBREAK.C: *A simple Microsoft C program that demonstrates use of the interrupt handler* BREAK.ASM *from Figure 5-1.*

Figure 5-2. *continued*

```
    MASM /Mx BREAK;
    CL TRYBREAK.C BREAK.OBJ
*/

#include <stdio.h>

main(int argc, char *argv[])
{
    int hit = 0;                    /* flag for key press      */
    int c = 0;                      /* character from keyboard */
    static int flag = 0;            /* true if Ctrl-Break
                                       or Ctrl-C detected      */

    puts("\n*** TRYBREAK.C running ***\n");
    puts("Press Ctrl-C or Ctrl-Break to test handler,");
    puts("Press the Esc key to exit TRYBREAK.\n");

    capture(&flag);                 /* install new Ctrl-C and
                                       Ctrl-Break handler and
                                       pass address of flag    */

    puts("TRYBREAK has captured interrupt vectors.\n");

    while(1)
    {
        hit = kbhit();              /* check for key press     */
                                    /* (MS-DOS sees Ctrl-C
                                        when keyboard polled)  */

        if(flag != 0)               /* if flag is true, an     */
        {                           /* interrupt has occurred  */
            puts("\nControl-Break detected.\n");
            flag = 0;               /* reset interrupt flag    */
        }
        if(hit != 0)                /* if any key waiting      */
        {
            c = getch();            /* read key, exit if Esc   */
            if( (c & 0x7f) == 0x1b) break;
            putch(c);               /* otherwise display it    */
        }
    }
    release();                      /* restore original Ctrl-C
                                       and Ctrl-Break handlers */

    puts("\n\nTRYBREAK has released interrupt vectors.");
}
```

In the example handler, the procedure named *capture* is called with the address of an integer variable within the C program. It saves the address of the variable, points the Int 1BH and Int 23H vectors to its own interrupt handler, and then returns.

When MS-DOS detects a Ctrl-C or Ctrl-Break, the interrupt handler sets the integer variable within the C program to true (1) and returns. The C program can then poll this variable at its leisure. Of course, to detect more than one Ctrl-C, the program must reset the variable to zero again.

The procedure named *release* simply restores the Int 1BH and Int 23H vectors to their original values, thereby disabling the interrupt handler. Although it is not strictly necessary for *release* to do anything about Int 23H, this action does give the C program the option of restoring the default handler for Int 23H without terminating.

Pointing Devices

Device drivers for pointing devices are supplied by the hardware manufacturer and are loaded with a DEVICE statement in the CONFIG.SYS file. Although the hardware characteristics of the available pointing devices differ greatly, nearly all of their drivers present the same software interface to application programs: the Int 33H protocol used by the Microsoft Mouse driver. Version 6 of the Microsoft Mouse driver (which was current as this was written) offers the following functions:

Function	Meaning
00H	Reset mouse and get status.
01H	Show mouse pointer.
02H	Hide mouse pointer.
03H	Get button status and pointer position.
04H	Set pointer position.
05H	Get button-press information.
06H	Get button-release information.
07H	Set horizontal limits for pointer.
08H	Set vertical limits for pointer.
09H	Set graphics pointer type.
0AH	Set text pointer type.
0BH	Read mouse-motion counters.
0CH	Install interrupt handler for mouse events.
0DH	Turn on light pen emulation.
0EH	Turn off light pen emulation.
0FH	Set mickeys to pixel ratio.
10H	Set pointer exclusion area.

(continued)

Function	Meaning
13H	Set double-speed threshold.
14H	Swap mouse-event interrupt routines.
15H	Get buffer size for mouse-driver state.
16H	Save mouse-driver state.
17H	Restore mouse-driver state.
18H	Install alternate handler for mouse events.
19H	Get address of alternate handler.
1AH	Set mouse sensitivity.
1BH	Get mouse sensitivity.
1CH	Set mouse interrupt rate.
1DH	Select display page for pointer.
1EH	Get display page for pointer.
1FH	Disable mouse driver.
20H	Enable mouse driver.
21H	Reset mouse driver.
22H	Set language for mouse-driver messages.
23H	Get language number.
24H	Get driver version, mouse type, and IRQ number.

Although this list of mouse functions may appear intimidating, the average application will only need a few of them.

A program first calls Int 33H Function 00H to initialize the mouse driver for the current display mode and to check its status. At this point, the mouse is "alive" and the application can obtain its state and position; however, the pointer does not become visible until the process calls Int 33H Function 01H.

The program can then call Int 33H Functions 03H, 05H, and 06H to monitor the mouse position and the status of the mouse buttons. Alternatively, the program can register an interrupt handler for mouse events, using Int 33H Function 0CH. This latter technique eliminates the need to poll the mouse driver; the driver will notify the program by calling the interrupt handler whenever the mouse is moved or a button is pressed or released.

When the application is finished with the mouse, it can call Int 33H Function 02H to hide the mouse pointer. If the program has registered an interrupt handler for mouse events, it should disable further calls to the handler by resetting the mouse driver again with Int 33H Function 00H.

For a complete description of the mouse-driver functions, see Section III of this book, "IBM ROM BIOS and Mouse Functions Reference." Figure 5-3 shows a small demonstration program that polls the mouse continually, to display its position and status.

```
/*
    Simple Demo of Int 33H Mouse Driver
    (C) 1988 Ray Duncan

    Compile with: CL MOUDEMO.C
*/

#include <stdio.h>
#include <dos.h>

union REGS regs;

void cls(void);                     /* function prototypes      */
void gotoxy(int, int);

main(int argc, char *argv[])
{
    int x,y,buttons;                /* some scratch variables   */
                                    /* for the mouse state      */

    regs.x.ax = 0;                  /* reset mouse driver       */
    int86(0x33, &regs, &regs);      /* and check status         */

    if(regs.x.ax == 0)              /* exit if no mouse         */
    {   printf("\nMouse not available\n");
        exit(1);
    }

    cls();                          /* clear the screen         */
    gotoxy(45,0);                   /* and show help info       */
    puts("Press Both Mouse Buttons To Exit");

    regs.x.ax = 1;                  /* display mouse cursor     */
    int86(0x33, &regs, &regs);

    do {
        regs.x.ax = 3;              /* get mouse position       */
        int86(0x33, &regs, &regs);  /* and button status        */
        buttons = regs.x.bx & 3;
        x = regs.x.cx;
        y = regs.x.dx;
```

(continued)

Figure 5-3. MOUDEMO.C: *A simple Microsoft C program that polls the mouse and continually displays the coordinates of the mouse pointer in the upper left corner of the screen. The program uses the ROM BIOS video driver, which is discussed in Chapter 6, to clear the screen and position the text cursor.*

Figure 5-3. *continued*

```
        gotoxy(0,0);                    /* display mouse position  */
        printf("X = %3d  Y = %3d", x, y);

    } while(buttons != 3);              /* exit if both buttons down */

    regs.x.ax = 2;                      /* hide mouse cursor         */
    int86(0x33, &regs, &regs);

    cls();                              /* display message and exit */
    gotoxy(0,0);
    puts("Have a Mice Day!");
}

/*
    Clear the screen
*/
void cls(void)
{
    regs.x.ax = 0x0600;                 /* ROM BIOS video driver     */
    regs.h.bh = 7;                      /* int 10h function 06h      */
    regs.x.cx = 0;                      /* initializes a window      */
    regs.h.dh = 24;
    regs.h.dl = 79;
    int86(0x10, &regs, &regs);
}


/*
    Position cursor to (x,y)
*/
void gotoxy(int x, int y)
{
    regs.h.dl = x;                      /* ROM BIOS video driver     */
    regs.h.dh = y;                      /* int 10h function 02h      */
    regs.h.bh = 0;                      /* positions the cursor      */
    regs.h.ah = 2;
    int86(0x10, &regs, &regs);
}
```

Chapter 6

Video Display

The visual presentation of an application program is one of its most important elements. Users frequently base their conclusions about a program's performance and "polish" on the speed and attractiveness of its displays. Therefore, a feel for the computer system's display facilities and capabilities at all levels, from MS-DOS down to the bare hardware, is important to you as a programmer.

Video Display Adapters

The video display adapters found in IBM PC–compatible computers have a hybrid interface to the central processor. The overall display characteristics, such as vertical and horizontal resolution, background color, and palette, are controlled by values written to I/O ports whose addresses are hardwired on the adapter, whereas the appearance of each individual character or graphics pixel on the display is controlled by a specific location within an area of memory called the *regen buffer* or *refresh buffer*. Both the CPU and the video controller access this memory; the software updates the display by simply writing character codes or bit patterns directly into the regen buffer. (This is called *memory-mapped I/O*.)

The following adapters are in common use as this book is being written:

■ Monochrome/Printer Display Adapter (MDA). Introduced with the original IBM PC in 1981, this adapter supports 80-by-25 text display on a green (monochrome) screen and has no graphics capabilities at all.

■ Color/Graphics Adapter (CGA). Also introduced by IBM in 1981, this adapter supports 40-by-25 and 80-by-25 text modes and 320-by-200, 4-color or 640-by-200, 2-color graphics (all-points-addressable, or APA) modes on composite or digital RGB monitors.

■ Enhanced Graphics Adapter (EGA). Introduced by IBM in 1985 and upwardly compatible from the CGA, this adapter adds support for 640-by-350, 16-color graphics modes on digital RGB monitors. It also supports an MDA-compatible text mode.

■ Multi-Color Graphics Array (MCGA). Introduced by IBM in 1987 with the Personal System/2 (PS/2) models 25 and 30, this adapter is partially compatible with the CGA and EGA and supports 640-by-480, 2-color or 320-by-200, 256-color graphics on analog RGB monitors.

■ Video Graphics Array (VGA). Introduced by IBM in 1987 with the PS/2 models 50, 60, and 80, this adapter is upwardly compatible from the EGA and supports 640-by-480, 16-color or 320-by-200, 256-color graphics on analog RGB monitors. It also supports an MDA-compatible text mode.

- Hercules Graphics Card, Graphics CardPlus, and InColor Cards. These are upwardly compatible from the MDA for text display but offer graphics capabilities that are incompatible with all of the IBM adapters.

The locations of the regen buffers for the various IBM PC–compatible adapters are shown in Figure 6-1.

FE000H	ROM BIOS
F4000H	System ROM, Stand-alone BASIC, etc.
C0000H	Reserved for BIOS extensions (hard-disk controller, etc.)
BC000H	Reserved
B8000H	16 KB regen buffer for CGA, EGA, MCGA, and VGA in text modes and 200-line graphics modes
B1000H	Reserved
B0000H	4 KB Monochrome Adapter regen buffer
A0000H	Regen buffer area for EGA, MCGA, and VGA in 350-line or 480-line graphics modes
	Transient part of COMMAND.COM
varies	Transient program area
00400H	MS-DOS and its buffers, tables, and device drivers
00000H	Interrupt vectors

Figure 6-1. *Memory diagram of an IBM PC–compatible personal computer, showing the locations of the regen buffers for various adapters.*

Support Considerations

MS-DOS offers several functions to transfer text to the display. Version 1 supported only Teletype-like output capabilities; version 2 added an optional ANSI console driver to allow the programmer to clear the screen, position the cursor, and select colors and attributes with standard escape sequences embedded in the output. Programs that use only the MS-DOS functions will operate properly on any computer system that runs MS-DOS, regardless of the level of IBM hardware compatibility.

On IBM PC–compatible machines, the ROM BIOS contains a video driver that programs can invoke directly, bypassing MS-DOS. The ROM BIOS functions allow a program to write text or individual pixels to the screen or to select display modes, video pages, palette, and foreground and background colors. These functions are relatively efficient (compared with the MS-DOS functions, at least), although the graphics support is primitive.

Unfortunately, the display functions of both MS-DOS and the ROM BIOS were designed around the model of a cursor-addressable terminal and therefore do not fully exploit the capabilities of the memory-mapped, high-bandwidth display adapters used on IBM PC–compatible machines. As a result, nearly every popular interactive application with full-screen displays or graphics capability ignores both MS-DOS and the ROM BIOS and writes directly to the video controller's registers and regen buffer.

Programs that control the hardware directly are sometimes called "ill-behaved," because they are performing operations that are normally reserved for operating-system device drivers. These programs are a severe management problem in multitasking real-mode environments such as DesqView and Microsoft Windows, and they are the main reason why such environments are not used more widely. It could be argued, however, that the blame for such problematic behavior lies not with the application programs but with the failure of MS-DOS and the ROM BIOS—even six years after the first appearance of the IBM PC—to provide display functions of adequate range and power.

MS-DOS Display Functions

Under MS-DOS versions 2.0 and later, the preferred method for sending text to the display is to use handle-based Int 21H Function 40H (Write File or Device). When an application program receives control, MS-DOS has already assigned it handles for the standard output (1) and standard error (2) devices, and these handles can be used immediately. For example, the sequence at the top of the following page writes the message *hello* to the display using the standard output handle.

```
msg      db      'hello'        ; message to display
msg_len  equ     $-msg          ; length of message
         .
         .
         .
         mov     ah,40h         ; function 40h = write file or device
         mov     bx,1           ; BX = standard output handle
         mov     cx,msg_len     ; CX = message length
         mov     dx,seg msg     ; DS:DX = address of message
         mov     ds,dx
         mov     dx,offset msg
         int     21h            ; transfer to MS-DOS
         jc      error          ; jump if error detected
         .
         .
         .
```

If there is no error, the function returns the carry flag cleared and the number of characters actually transferred in register AX. Unless a Ctrl-Z is embedded in the text or the standard output is redirected to a disk file and the disk is full, this number should equal the number of characters requested.

As in the case of keyboard input, the user's ability to specify command-line redirection parameters that are invisible to the application means that if you use the predefined standard output handle, you can't always be sure where your output is going. However, to ensure that your output actually goes to the display, you can use the predefined standard error handle, which is always opened to the CON (logical console) device and is not redirectable.

As an alternative to the standard output and standard error handles, you can bypass any output redirection and open a separate channel to CON, using the handle obtained from that open operation for character output. For example, the following code opens the console display for output and then writes the string *hello* to it:

```
fname    db      'CON',0        ; name of CON device
handle   dw      0              ; handle for CON device
msg      db      'hello'        ; message to display
msg_len  equ     $-msg          ; length of message
         .
         .
         .
```

(continued)

(continued)

```
        mov     ax,3d02h        ; AH = function 3dh = open
                                ; AL = mode = read/write
        mov     dx,seg fname    ; DS:DX = device name
        mov     ds,dx
        mov     dx,offset fname
        int     21h             ; transfer to MS-DOS
        jc      error           ; jump if open failed
        mov     handle,ax       ; save handle for CON
        .
        .
        .
        mov     ah,40h          ; function 40h = write
        mov     cx,msg_len      ; CX = message length
        mov     dx,seg msg      ; DS:DX = address of message
        mov     ds,dx
        mov     dx,offset msg
        mov     bx,handle       ; BX = CON device handle
        int     21h             ; transfer to MS-DOS
        jc      error           ; jump if error detected
        .
        .
        .
```

As with the keyboard input functions, MS-DOS also supports traditional display functions that are upwardly compatible from the corresponding CP/M output calls:

- Int 21H Function 02H sends the character in the DL register to the standard output device. It is sensitive to Ctrl-C interrupts, and it handles carriage returns, linefeeds, bell codes, and backspaces appropriately.

- Int 21H Function 06H transfers the character in the DL register to the standard output device, but it is not sensitive to Ctrl-C interrupts. You must take care when using this function, because it can also be used for input and for status requests.

- Int 21H Function 09H sends a string to the standard output device. The string is terminated by the $ character.

With MS-DOS version 2 or later, these three traditional functions are converted internally to handle-based writes to the standard output and thus are susceptible to output redirection.

The sequence at the top of the following page sounds a warning beep by sending an ASCII bell code (07H) to the display driver using the traditional character-output call Int 21H Function 02H.

```
                 .
                 .
                 .
        mov      dl,7          ; 07h = ASCII bell code
        mov      ah,2          ; function 02h = display character
        int      21h           ; transfer to MS-DOS
                 .
                 .
                 .
```

The following sequence uses the traditional string-output call Int 21H
Function 09H to display a string:

```
msg     db       'hello$'
                 .
                 .
                 .
        mov      dx,seg msg  ; DS:DX = message address
        mov      ds,dx
        mov      dx,offset msg
        mov      ah,9          ; function 09h = write string
        int      21h           ; transfer to MS-DOS
                 .
                 .
                 .
```

Note that MS-DOS detects the $ character as a terminator and does not
display it on the screen.

Screen Control with MS-DOS Functions

With version 2.0 or later, if MS-DOS loads the optional device driver
ANSI.SYS in response to a DEVICE directive in the CONFIG.SYS file, programs can clear the screen, control the cursor position, and select foreground and background colors by embedding escape sequences in the
text output. Escape sequences are so called because they begin with an
escape character (1BH), which alerts the driver to intercept and interpret
the subsequent characters in the sequence. When the ANSI driver is not
loaded, MS-DOS simply passes the escape sequence to the display like any
other text, usually resulting in a chaotic screen.

The escape sequences that can be used with the ANSI driver for screen
control are a subset of those defined in the ANSI 3.64–1979 Standard.
These standard sequences are summarized in Figure 6-2. Note that case is

significant for the last character in an escape sequence and that numbers must always be represented as ASCII digit strings, not as their binary values. (A separate set of escape sequences supported by ANSI.SYS, but not compatible with the ANSI standard, may be used for reprogramming and remapping the keyboard.)

Escape sequence	*Meaning*
Esc[2J	Clear screen; place cursor in upper left corner (home position).
Esc[K	Clear from cursor to end of line.
Esc[*row*;*col*H	Position cursor. (*Row* is the *y* coordinate in the range 1–25 and *col* is the *x* coordinate in the range 1–80 for 80-by-25 text display modes.) Escape sequences terminated with the letter *f* instead of *H* have the same effect.
Esc[*n*A	Move cursor up *n* rows.
Esc[*n*B	Move cursor down *n* rows.
Esc[*n*C	Move cursor right *n* columns.
Esc[*n*D	Move cursor left *n* columns.
Esc[s	Save current cursor position.
Esc[u	Restore cursor to saved position.
Esc[6n	Return current cursor position on the standard input handle in the format *Esc*[*row*;*col*R.
Esc[*n*m	Select character attributes:
	0 = no special attributes
	1 = high intensity
	2 = low intensity
	3 = italic
	4 = underline
	5 = blink
	6 = rapid blink
	7 = reverse video
	8 = concealed text (no display)
	30 = foreground black
	31 = foreground red
	32 = foreground green
	33 = foreground yellow
	34 = foreground blue
	35 = foreground magenta

(continued)

Figure 6-2. *The ANSI escape sequences supported by the MS-DOS ANSI.SYS driver. Programs running under MS-DOS 2.0 or later may use these functions, if ANSI.SYS is loaded, to control the appearance of the display in a hardware-independent manner. The symbol* Esc *indicates an ASCII escape code — a character with the value 1BH. Note that cursor positions in ANSI escape sequences are one-based, unlike the cursor coordinates used by the IBM ROM BIOS, which are zero-based. Numbers embedded in an escape sequence must always be represented as a string of ASCII digits, not as their binary values.*

Figure 6-2. *continued*

Escape sequence	Meaning
	36 = foreground cyan
	37 = foreground white
	40 = background black
	41 = background red
	42 = background green
	43 = background yellow
	44 = background blue
	45 = background magenta
	46 = background cyan
	47 = background white
Esc[=*n*h	Select display mode:
	0 = 40-by-25, 16-color text (color burst off)
	1 = 40-by-25, 16-color text
	2 = 80-by-25, 16-color text (color burst off)
	3 = 80-by-25, 16-color text
	4 = 320-by-200, 4-color graphics
	5 = 320-by-200, 4-color graphics (color burst off)
	6 = 620-by-200, 2-color graphics
	14 = 640-by-200, 16-color graphics (EGA and VGA, MS-DOS 4.0)
	15 = 640-by-350, 2-color graphics (EGA and VGA, MS-DOS 4.0)
	16 = 640-by-350, 16-color graphics (EGA and VGA, MS-DOS 4.0)
	17 = 640-by-480, 2-color graphics (MCGA and VGA, MS-DOS 4.0)
	18 = 640-by-480, 16-color graphics (VGA, MS-DOS 4.0)
	19 = 320-by-200, 256-color graphics (MCGA and VGA, MS-DOS 4.0)
	Escape sequences terminated with *l* instead of *h* have the same effect.
Esc[= 7h	Enable line wrap.
Esc[= 7l	Disable line wrap.

Binary Output Mode

Under MS-DOS version 2 or later, you can substantially increase display speeds for well-behaved application programs without sacrificing hardware independence by selecting binary (raw) mode for the standard output. In binary mode, MS-DOS does not check between each character it transfers to the output device for a Ctrl-C waiting at the keyboard, nor does it filter the output string for certain characters such as Ctrl-Z.

Bit 5 in the device information word associated with a device handle controls binary mode. Programs access the device information word by using Subfunctions 00H and 01H of the MS-DOS IOCTL function (I/O Control, Int 21H Function 44H). For example, the sequence on the following page places the standard output handle into binary mode.

```
                         ; get device information...
        mov    bx,1      ; standard output handle
        mov    ax,4400h  ; function 44h subfunction 00h
        int    21h       ; transfer to MS-DOS

        mov    dh,0      ; set upper byte of DX = 0
        or     dl,20h    ; set binary mode bit in DL

                         ; write device information...
                         ; (BX still has handle)
        mov    ax,4401h  ; function 44h subfunction 01h
        int    21h       ; transfer to MS-DOS
```

Note that if a program changes the mode of any of the standard handles, it should restore those handles to ASCII (cooked) mode before it exits. Otherwise, subsequent application programs may behave in unexpected ways. For more detailed information on the IOCTL function, see Section II of this book, "MS-DOS Functions Reference."

The ROM BIOS Display Functions

You can somewhat improve the display performance of programs that are intended for use only on IBM PC–compatible machines by using the ROM BIOS video driver instead of the MS-DOS output functions. Accessed by means of Int 10H, the ROM BIOS driver supports the following functions for all of the currently available IBM display adapters:

Function	*Action*
Display mode control	
00H	Set display mode.
0FH	Get display mode.
Cursor control	
01H	Set cursor size.
02H	Set cursor position.
03H	Get cursor position and size.
Writing to the display	
09H	Write character and attribute at cursor.
0AH	Write character-only at cursor.
0EH	Write character in teletype mode.

(continued)

Function	*Action*
Reading from the display	
08H	Read character and attribute at cursor.
Graphics support	
0CH	Write pixel.
0DH	Read pixel.
Scroll or clear display	
06H	Scroll up or initialize window.
07H	Scroll down or initialize window.
Miscellaneous	
04H	Read light pen.
05H	Select display page.
0BH	Select palette/set border color.

Additional ROM BIOS functions are available on the EGA, MCGA, VGA, and PCjr to support the enhanced features of these adapters, such as programmable palettes and character sets (fonts). Some of the functions are valid only in certain display modes.

Each display mode is characterized by the number of colors it can display, its vertical resolution, its horizontal resolution, and whether it supports text or graphics memory mapping. The ROM BIOS identifies it with a unique number. Section III of this book, "IBM ROM BIOS and Mouse Functions Reference," documents all of the ROM BIOS Int 10H functions and display modes.

As you can see from the preceding list, the ROM BIOS offers several desirable capabilities that are not available from MS-DOS, including initialization or scrolling of selected screen windows, modification of the cursor shape, and reading back the character being displayed at an arbitrary screen location. These functions can be used to isolate your program from the hardware on any IBM PC–compatible adapter. However, the ROM BIOS functions do not suffice for the needs of a high-performance, interactive, full-screen program such as a word processor. They do not support the rapid display of character strings at an arbitrary screen position, and they do not implement graphics operations at the level normally required by applications (for example, bit-block transfers and rapid drawing of lines, circles, and filled polygons). And, of course, they are of no use whatsoever in non-IBM display modes such as the monochrome graphics mode of the Hercules Graphics Card.

Let's look at a simple example of a call to the ROM BIOS video driver. The following sequence writes the string *hello* to the screen:

```
msg      db       'hello'
msg_len  equ      $-msg
         .
         .
         .
         mov      si,seg msg   ; DS:SI = message address
         mov      ds,si
         mov      si,offset msg
         mov      cx,msg_len   ; CX = message length
         cld
next:    lodsb                 ; get AL = next character
         push     si           ; save message pointer
         mov      ah,0eh       ; int 10h function 0eh = write
                               ; character in teletype mode
         mov      bh,0         ; assume video page 0
         mov      bl,color     ; (use in graphics modes only)
         int      10h          ; transfer to ROM BIOS
         pop      si           ; restore message pointer
         loop     next         ; loop until message done
         .
         .
         .
```

(Note that the SI and DI registers are not necessarily preserved across a call to a ROM BIOS video function.)

Memory-mapped Display Techniques

Display performance is best when an application program takes over complete control of the video adapter and the refresh buffer. Because the display is memory-mapped, the speed at which characters can be put on the screen is limited only by the CPU's ability to copy bytes from one location in memory to another. The trade-off for this performance is that such programs are highly sensitive to hardware compatibility and do not always function properly on "clones" or even on new models of IBM video adapters.

Text Mode

Direct programming of the IBM PC–compatible video adapters in their text display modes (sometimes also called alphanumeric display modes) is straightforward. The character set is the same for all, and the cursor home position—(x,y) = (0,0)—is defined to be the upper left corner of the screen (Figure 6-3). The MDA uses 4 KB of memory starting at segment B000H as a regen buffer, and the various adapters with both text and graphics capabilities (CGA, EGA, MCGA, and VGA) use 16 KB of memory starting at segment B800H. (See Figure 6-1.) In the latter case, the 16 KB is divided into "pages" that can be independently updated and displayed.

Figure 6-3. *Cursor addressing for 80-by-25 text display modes (IBM ROM BIOS modes 2, 3, and 7).*

Each character-display position is allotted 2 bytes in the regen buffer. The first byte (even address) contains the ASCII code of the character, which is translated by a special hardware character generator into a dot-matrix pattern for the screen. The second byte (odd address) is the attribute byte. Several bit fields in this byte control such features as blinking, intensity (highlighting), and reverse video, depending on the adapter type and display mode (Figures 6-4 and 6-5). Figure 6-6 shows a hex and ASCII dump of part of the video map for the MDA.

7	6	5	4	3	2	1	0
B	Background			I	Foreground		

B = Blink
I = Intensity

Display	Background	Foreground
No display (black)	000	000
No display (white) *	111	111
Underline	000	001
Normal video	000	111
Reverse video	111	000

*VGA only

Figure 6-4. *Attribute byte for 80-by-25 monochrome text display mode on the MDA, Hercules cards, EGA, and VGA (IBM ROM BIOS mode 7).*

7	6	5	4	3	2	1	0
B	Background			I	Foreground		

B = Blink or background intensity (default = blink)
I = Foreground intensity or character select (default = intensity)

Value	Color
0	Black
1	Blue
2	Green
3	Cyan
4	Red
5	Magenta
6	Brown
7	White
8	Gray
9	Light blue
10	Light green
11	Light cyan
12	Light red
13	Light magenta
14	Yellow
15	Intense white

Figure 6-5. *Attribute byte for the 40-by-25 and 80-by-25 text display modes on the CGA, EGA, MCGA, and VGA (IBM ROM BIOS modes 0–3). The table of color values assumes default palette programming and that the B or I bit controls intensity.*

```
B000:0000 3e 07 73 07 65 07 6c 07 65 07 63 07 74 07 20 07
B000:0010 74 07 65 07 6d 07 70 07 20 07 20 07 20 07 20 07
B000:0020 20 07 20 07 20 07 20 07 20 07 20 07 20 07 20 07
B000:0030 20 07 20 07 20 07 20 07 20 07 20 07 20 07 20 07
B000:0040 20 07 20 07 20 07 20 07 20 07 20 07 20 07 20 07
B000:0050 20 07 20 07 20 07 20 07 20 07 20 07 20 07 20 07
B000:0060 20 07 20 07 20 07 20 07 20 07 20 07 20 07 20 07
B000:0070 20 07 20 07 20 07 20 07 20 07 20 07 20 07 20 07
B000:0080 20 07 20 07 20 07 20 07 20 07 20 07 20 07 20 07
B000:0090 20 07 20 07 20 07 20 07 20 07 20 07 20 07 20 07
```

Figure 6-6. *Example dump of the first 160 bytes of the MDA's regen buffer. These bytes correspond to the first visible line on the screen. Note that ASCII character codes are stored in even bytes and their respective character attributes in odd bytes; all the characters in this example line have the attribute normal video.*

You can calculate the memory offset of any character on the display as the line number (y coordinate) times 80 characters per line times 2 bytes per character, plus the column number (x coordinate) times 2 bytes per character, plus (for the text/graphics adapters) the page number times the size of the page (4 KB per page in 80-by-25 modes; 2 KB per page in 40-by-25 modes). In short, the formula for the offset of the character-attribute pair for a given screen position (x,y) in 80-by-25 text modes is

$$offset = ((y * 50H + x) * 2) + (page * 1000H)$$

In 40-by-25 text modes, the formula is

$$offset = ((y * 50H + x) * 2) + (page * 0800H)$$

Of course, the segment register being used to address the video buffer must be set appropriately, depending on the type of display adapter.

As a simple example, assume that the character to be displayed is in the AL register, the desired attribute byte for the character is in the AH register, the x coordinate (column) is in the BX register, and the y coordinate (row) is in the CX register. The following code stores the character and attribute byte into the MDA's video refresh buffer at the proper location:

```
        push    ax          ; save char and attribute
        mov     ax,160
        mul     cx          ; DX:AX = Y * 160
        shl     bx,1        ; multiply X by 2
        add     bx,ax       ; BX = (Y*160) + (X*2)
        mov     ax,0b000h   ; ES = segment of monochrome
        mov     es,ax       ; adapter refresh buffer
        pop     ax          ; restore char and attribute
        mov     es:[bx],ax  ; write them to video buffer
```

More frequently, we wish to move entire strings into the refresh buffer, starting at a given coordinate. In the next example, assume that the DS:SI registers point to the source string, the ES:DI registers point to the starting position in the video buffer (calculated as shown in the previous example), the AH register contains the attribute byte to be assigned to every character in the string, and the CX register contains the length of the string. The following code moves the entire string into the refresh buffer:

```
xfer:   lodsb               ; fetch next character
        stosw               ; store char + attribute
        loop    xfer        ; until all chars moved
```

Of course, the video drivers written for actual application programs must take into account many additional factors, such as checking for special control codes (linefeeds, carriage returns, tabs), line wrap, and scrolling.

Programs that write characters directly to the CGA regen buffer in text modes must deal with an additional complicating factor—they must examine the video controller's status port and access the refresh buffer only during the horizontal retrace or vertical retrace intervals. (A *retrace interval* is the period when the electron beam that illuminates the screen phosphors is being repositioned to the start of a new scan line.) Otherwise, the contention for memory between the CPU and the video controller is manifest as unsightly "snow" on the display. (If you are writing programs for any of the other IBM PC–compatible video adapters, such as the MDA, EGA, MCGA, or VGA, you can ignore the retrace intervals; snow is not a problem with these video controllers.)

A program can detect the occurrence of a retrace interval by monitoring certain bits in the video controller's status register. For example, assume that the offset for the desired character position has been calculated as in the preceding example and placed in the BX register, the segment for the CGA's refresh buffer is in the ES register, and an ASCII character code to be displayed is in the CL register. The following code waits for the beginning of a new horizontal retrace interval and then writes the character into the buffer:

```
        mov     dx,03dah    ; DX = video controller's
                            ; status port address
        cli                 ; disable interrupts

                            ; if retrace is already
                            ; in progress, wait for
                            ; it to end...
wait1:  in      al,dx       ; read status port
        and     al,1        ; check if retrace bit on
        jnz     wait1       ; yes, wait

                            ; wait for new retrace
                            ; interval to start...
wait2:  in      al,dx       ; read status port
        and     al,1        ; retrace bit on yet?
        jz      wait2       ; jump if not yet on

        mov     es:[bx],cl  ; write character to
                            ; the regen buffer
        sti                 ; enable interrupts again
```

The first wait loop "synchronizes" the code to the beginning of a horizontal retrace interval. If only the second wait loop were used (that is, if a character were written when a retrace interval was already in progress), the write would occasionally begin so close to the end of a horizontal retrace "window" that it would partially miss the retrace, resulting in scattered snow at the left edge of the display. Notice that the code also disables interrupts during accesses to the video buffer, so that service of a hardware interrupt won't disrupt the synchronization process.

Because of the retrace-interval constraints just outlined, the rate at which you can update the CGA in text modes is severely limited when the updating is done one character at a time. You can obtain better results by calculating all the relevant addresses and setting up the appropriate registers, disabling the video controller by writing to register 3D8H, moving the entire string to the buffer with a *REP MOVSW* operation, and then reenabling the video controller. If the string is of reasonable length, the user won't even notice a flicker in the display. Of course, this procedure introduces additional hardware dependence into your code because it requires much greater knowledge of the 6845 controller. Luckily, snow is not a problem in CGA graphics modes.

Graphics Mode

Graphics-mode memory-mapped programming for IBM PC–compatible adapters is considerably more complicated than text-mode programming. Each bit or group of bits in the regen buffer corresponds to an addressable point, or *pixel,* on the screen. The mapping of bits to pixels differs for each of the available graphics modes, with their differences in resolution and number of supported colors. The newer adapters (EGA, MCGA, and VGA) also use the concept of *bit planes,* where bits of a pixel are segregated into multiple banks of memory mapped at the same address; you must manipulate these bit planes by a combination of memory-mapped I/O and port addressing.

IBM-video-systems graphics programming is a subject large enough for a book of its own, but we can use the 640-by-200, 2-color graphics display mode of the CGA (which is also supported by all subsequent IBM text/graphics adapters) to illustrate a few of the techniques involved. This mode is simple to deal with because each pixel is represented by a single bit. The pixels are assigned (x,y) coordinates in the range $(0,0)$ through $(639,199)$, where x is the horizontal displacement, y is the vertical displacement, and the home position $(0,0)$ is the upper left corner of the display. (See Figure 6-7.)

(0,0)   (639,0)

(0,199)   (639,199)

Figure 6-7. *Point addressing for 640-by-200, 2-color graphics modes on the CGA, EGA, MCGA, and VGA (IBM ROM BIOS mode 6).*

Each successive group of 80 bytes (640 bits) represents one horizontal scan line. Within each byte, the bits map one-for-one onto pixels, with the most significant bit corresponding to the leftmost displayed pixel of a set of eight pixels and the least significant bit corresponding to the rightmost displayed pixel of the set. The memory map is set up so that all the even y coordinates are scanned as a set and all the odd y coordinates are scanned as a set; this mapping is referred to as the memory *interlace*.

To find the regen buffer offset for a particular (x,y) coordinate, you would use the following formula:

offset = $((y$ AND $1) * 2000$H$) + (y/2 * 50$H$) + (x/8)$

The assembly-language implementation of this formula is as follows:

```
                        ; assume AX = Y, BX = X
        shr     bx,1    ; divide X by 8
        shr     bx,1
        shr     bx,1
        push    ax      ; save copy of Y
        shr     ax,1    ; find (Y/2) * 50h
        mov     cx,50h  ; with product in DX:AX
        mul     cx
        add     bx,ax   ; add product to X/8
        pop     ax      ; add (Y AND 1) * 2000h
        and     ax,1
        jz      label1
        add     bx,2000h
label1:                 ; now BX = offset into
                        ; video buffer
```

After calculating the correct byte address, you can use the following formula to calculate the bit position for a given pixel coordinate:

bit = $7 - (x$ MOD $8)$

where bit 7 is the most significant bit and bit 0 is the least significant bit. It is easiest to build an 8-byte table, or array of bit masks, and use the operation *X AND 7* to extract the appropriate entry from the table:

(X AND 7)	Bit mask	(X AND 7)	Bit mask
0	80H	4	08H
1	40H	5	04H
2	20H	6	02H
3	10H	7	01H

The assembly-language implementation of this second calculation is as follows:

```
table   db      80h             ; X AND 7 = offset 0
        db      40h             ; X AND 7 = offset 1
        db      20h             ; X AND 7 = offset 2
        db      10h             ; X AND 7 = offset 3
        db      08h             ; X AND 7 = offset 4
        db      04h             ; X AND 7 = offset 5
        db      02h             ; X AND 7 = offset 6
        db      01h             ; X AND 7 = offset 7
        .
        .
        .
                                ; assume BX = X coordinate
        and     bx,7            ; isolate 0-7 offset
        mov     al,[bx+table]
                                ; now AL = mask from table
        .
        .
        .
```

The program can then use the mask, together with the byte offset previously calculated, to set or clear the appropriate bit in the video controller's regen buffer.

Chapter 7

Printer and Serial Port

MS-DOS supports printers, plotters, modems, and other hard-copy output or communication devices with device drivers for *parallel ports* and *serial ports*. Parallel ports are so named because they transfer a byte—8 bits—in parallel to the destination device over eight separate physical paths (plus additional status and handshaking signals). The serial port, on the other hand, communicates with the CPU with bytes but sends data to or receives data from its destination device serially—a bit at a time—over a single physical connection.

Parallel ports are typically used for high-speed output devices, such as line printers, over relatively short distances (less than 50 feet). They are rarely used for devices that require two-way communication with the computer. Serial ports are used for lower-speed devices, such as modems and terminals, that require two-way communication (although some printers also have serial interfaces). A serial port can drive its device reliably over much greater distances (up to 1000 feet) over as few as three wires—transmit, receive, and ground.

The most commonly used type of serial interface follows a standard called RS-232. This standard specifies a 25-wire interface with certain electrical characteristics, the use of various handshaking signals, and a standard DB-25 connector. Other serial-interface standards exist—for example, the RS-422, which is capable of considerably higher speeds than the RS-232—but these are rarely used in personal computers (except for the Apple Macintosh) at this time.

MS-DOS has built-in device drivers for three parallel adapters, and for two serial adapters on the PC or PC/AT and three serial adapters on the PS/2. The logical names for these devices are LPT1, LPT2, LPT3, COM1, COM2, and COM3. The standard printer (PRN) and standard auxiliary (AUX) devices are normally aliased to LPT1 and COM1, but you can redirect PRN to one of the serial ports with the MS-DOS MODE command.

As with keyboard and video display I/O, you can manage printer and serial-port I/O at several levels that offer different degrees of flexibility and hardware independence:

- MS-DOS handle-oriented functions

- MS-DOS traditional character functions

- IBM ROM BIOS driver functions

In the case of the serial port, direct control of the hardware by application programs is also common. I will discuss each of these I/O methods briefly, with examples, in the following pages.

Printer Output

The preferred method of printer output is to use the handle write function (Int 21H Function 40H) with the predefined standard printer handle (4). For example, you could write the string *hello* to the printer as follows:

```
msg      db       'hello'     ; message for printer
msg_len equ      $-msg        ; length of message
         .
         .
         .

         mov      ah,40h       ; function 40h = write file or device
         mov      bx,4         ; BX = standard printer handle
         mov      cx,msg_len   ; CX = length of string
         mov      dx,seg msg   ; DS:DX = string address
         mov      ds,dx
         mov      dx,offset msg
         int      21h          ; transfer to MS-DOS
         jc       error        ; jump if error
         .
         .
         .
```

If there is no error, the function returns the carry flag cleared and the number of characters actually transferred to the list device in register AX. Under normal circumstances, this number should always be the same as the length requested and the carry flag indicating an error should never be set. However, the output will terminate early if your data contains an end-of-file mark (Ctrl-Z).

You can write independently to several list devices (for example, LPT1, LPT2) by issuing a specific open request (Int 21H Function 3DH) for each device and using the handles returned to access the printers individually with Int 21H Function 40H. You have already seen this general approach in Chapters 5 and 6.

An alternative method of printer output is to use the traditional Int 21H Function 05H, which transfers the character in the DL register to the printer. (This function is sensitive to Ctrl-C interrupts.) For example, the assembly-language code sequence at the top of the following page would write the the string *hello* to the line printer.

```
msg      db      'hello'      ; message for printer
msg_len  equ     $-msg        ; length of message
         .
         .
         .
         mov     bx,seg msg   ; DS:BX = string address
         mov     ds,bx
         mov     bx,offset msg
         mov     cx,msg_len   ; CX = string length

next:    mov     dl,[bx]      ; get next character
         mov     ah,5         ; function 05h = printer output
         int     21h          ; transfer to MS-DOS
         inc     bx           ; bump string pointer
         loop    next         ; loop until string done
         .
         .
         .
```

Programs that run on IBM PC–compatible machines can obtain improved printer throughput by bypassing MS-DOS and calling the ROM BIOS printer driver directly by means of Int 17H. Section III of this book, "IBM ROM BIOS and Mouse Functions Reference," documents the Int 17H functions in detail. Use of the ROM BIOS functions also allows your program to test whether the printer is off line or out of paper, a capability that MS-DOS does not offer.

For example, the following sequence of instructions calls the ROM BIOS printer driver to send the string *hello* to the line printer:

```
msg      db      'hello'      ; message for printer
msg_len  equ     $-msg        ; length of message
         .
         .
         .
         mov     bx,seg msg   ; DS:BX = string address
         mov     ds,bx
         mov     bx,offset msg
         mov     cx,msg_len   ; CX = string length
         mov     dx,0         ; DX = printer number

next:    mov     al,[bx]      ; AL = character to print
         mov     ah,0         ; function 00h = printer output
         int     17h          ; transfer to ROM BIOS
         inc     bx           ; bump string pointer
```

(continued)

(continued)

```
loop    next        ; loop until string done
  .
  .
  .
```

Note that the printer numbers used by the ROM BIOS are zero-based, whereas the printer numbers in MS-DOS logical-device names are one-based. For example, ROM BIOS printer 0 corresponds to LPT1.

Finally, the most hardware-dependent technique of printer output is to access the printer controller directly. Considering the functionality already provided in MS-DOS and the IBM ROM BIOS, as well as the speeds of the devices involved, I cannot see any justification for using direct hardware control in this case. The disadvantage of introducing such extreme hardware dependence for such a low-speed device would far outweigh any small performance gains that might be obtained.

The Serial Port

MS-DOS support for serial ports (often referred to as the *auxiliary device* in MS-DOS manuals) is weak compared with its keyboard, video-display, and printer support. This is one area where the application programmer is justified in making programs hardware dependent to extract adequate performance.

Programs that restrict themselves to MS-DOS functions to ensure portability can use the handle read and write functions (Int 21H Functions 3FH and 40H), with the predefined standard auxiliary handle (3) to access the serial port. For example, the following code writes the string *hello* to the serial port that is currently defined as the AUX device:

```
msg     db      'hello'      ; message for serial port
msg_len equ     $-msg        ; length of message
          .
          .
          .
        mov     ah,40h       ; function 40h = write file or device
        mov     bx,3         ; BX = standard aux handle
        mov     cx,msg_len   ; CX = string length
        mov     dx,seg msg   ; DS:DX = string address
        mov     ds,dx
```

(continued)

(continued)

```
        mov     dx,offset msg
        int     21h         ; transfer to MS-DOS
        jc      error       ; jump if error
        .
        .
        .
```

The standard auxiliary handle gives access to only the first serial port (COM1). If you want to read or write COM2 and COM3 using the handle calls, you must issue an open request (Int 21H Function 3DH) for the desired serial port and use the handle returned by that function with Int 21H Functions 3FH and 40H.

Some versions of MS-DOS have a bug in character-device handling that manifests itself as follows: If you issue a read request with Int 21H Function 3FH for the exact number of characters that are waiting in the driver's buffer, the length returned in the AX register is the number of characters transferred minus one. You can circumvent this problem by always requesting more characters than you expect to receive or by placing the device handle into binary mode using Int 21H Function 44H.

MS-DOS also supports two traditional functions for serial-port I/O. Int 21H Function 03H inputs a character from COM1 and returns it in the AL register; Int 21H Function 04H transmits the character in the DL register to COM1. Like the other traditional calls, these two are direct descendants of the CP/M auxiliary-device functions.

For example, the following code sends the string *hello* to COM1 using the traditional Int 21H Function 04H:

```
msg     db      'hello'     ; message for serial port
msg_len equ     $-msg       ; length of message
        .
        .
        .
        mov     bx,seg msg  ; DS:BX = string address
        mov     ds,bx
        mov     bx,offset msg
        mov     cx,msg_len  ; CX = length of string
```

(continued)

```
next:   mov     dl,[bx]        ; get next character
        mov     ah,4           ; function 04h = aux output
        int     21h            ; transfer to MS-DOS
        inc     bx             ; bump pointer to string
        loop    next           ; loop until string done
        .
        .
        .
```

MS-DOS translates the traditional auxiliary-device functions into calls on the same device driver used by the handle calls. Therefore, it is generally preferable to use the handle functions in the first place, because they allow very long strings to be read or written in one operation, they give access to serial ports other than COM1, and they are symmetrical with the handle video-display, keyboard, printer, and file I/O methods described elsewhere in this book.

Although the handle or traditional serial-port functions allow you to write programs that are portable to any machine running MS-DOS, they have a number of disadvantages:

- The built-in MS-DOS serial-port driver is slow and is not interrupt driven.

- MS-DOS serial-port I/O is not buffered.

- Determining the status of the auxiliary device requires a separate call to the IOCTL function (Int 21H Function 44H)—if you request input and no characters are ready, your program will simply hang.

- MS-DOS offers no standardized function to configure the serial port from within a program.

For programs that are going to run on the IBM PC or compatibles, a more flexible technique for serial-port I/O is to call the IBM ROM BIOS serial-port driver by means of Int 14H. You can use this driver to initialize the serial port to a desired configuration and baud rate, examine the status of the controller, and read or write characters. Section III of this book, "IBM ROM BIOS and Mouse Functions Reference," documents the functions available from the ROM BIOS serial-port driver.

For example, the following sequence sends the character *X* to the first serial port (COM1):

```
        .
        .
        .
mov     ah,1        ; function 01h = send character
mov     al,'X'      ; AL = character to transmit
mov     dx,0        ; DX = serial-port number
int     14h         ; transfer to ROM BIOS
and     ah,80h      ; did transmit fail?
jnz     error       ; jump if transmit error
        .
        .
        .
```

As with the ROM BIOS printer driver, the serial-port numbers used by the ROM BIOS are zero-based, whereas the serial-port numbers in MS-DOS logical-device names are one-based. In this example, serial port 0 corresponds to COM1.

Unfortunately, like the MS-DOS auxiliary-device driver, the ROM BIOS serial-port driver is not interrupt driven. Although it will support higher transfer speeds than the MS-DOS functions, at rates greater than 2400 baud it may still lose characters. Consequently, most programmers writing high-performance applications that use a serial port (such as telecommunications programs) take complete control of the serial-port controller and provide their own interrupt driver. The built-in functions provided by MS-DOS, and by the ROM BIOS in the case of the IBM PC, are simply not adequate.

Writing such programs requires a good understanding of the hardware. In the case of the IBM PC, the chips to study are the INS8250 Asynchronous Communications Controller and the Intel 8259A Programmable Interrupt Controller. The IBM technical reference documentation for these chips is a bit disorganized, but most of the necessary information is there if you look for it.

The *TALK* Program

The simple terminal-emulator program *TALK.ASM* (Figure 7-1) is an example of a useful program that performs screen, keyboard, and serial-port I/O. This program recapitulates all of the topics discussed in Chapters 5 through 7. *TALK* uses the IBM PC's ROM BIOS video driver to put characters on the screen, to clear the display, and to position the cursor; it uses the MS-DOS character-input calls to read the keyboard; and it contains its own interrupt driver for the serial-port controller.

```
        name    talk
        page    55,132
        .lfcond                 ; List false conditionals too
        title   TALK--Simple terminal emulator


;
; TALK.ASM--Simple IBM PC terminal emulator
;
; Copyright (c) 1988 Ray Duncan
;
; To assemble and link this program into TALK.EXE:
;
;       C>MASM TALK;
;       C>LINK TALK;
;


stdin   equ     0               ; standard input handle
stdout  equ     1               ; standard output handle
stderr  equ     2               ; standard error handle


cr      equ     0dh             ; ASCII carriage return
lf      equ     0ah             ; ASCII linefeed
bsp     equ     08h             ; ASCII backspace
escape  equ     1bh             ; ASCII escape code


dattr   equ     07h             ; display attribute to use
                                ; while in emulation mode


bufsiz  equ     4096            ; size of serial-port buffer


echo    equ     0               ; 0 = full-duplex, -1 = half-duplex
```

(continued)

Figure 7-1. TALK.ASM: *A simple terminal-emulator program for IBM PC–compatible computers. This program demonstrates use of the MS-DOS and ROM BIOS video and keyboard functions and direct control of the serial-communications adapter.*

Figure 7-1. *continued*

```
true     equ     -1
false    equ     0


com1     equ     true          ; use COM1 if nonzero
com2     equ     not com1      ; use COM2 if nonzero


pic_mask equ     21h           ; 8259 interrupt mask port
pic_eoi  equ     20h           ; 8259 EOI port


         if      com1
com_data equ     03f8h         ; port assignments for COM1
com_ier  equ     03f9h
com_mcr  equ     03fch
com_sts  equ     03fdh
com_int  equ     0ch           ; COM1 interrupt number
int_mask equ     10h           ; IRQ4 mask for 8259
         endif


         if      com2
com_data equ     02f8h         ; port assignments for COM2
com_ier  equ     02f9h
com_mcr  equ     02fch
com_sts  equ     02fdh
com_int  equ     0bh           ; COM2 interrupt number
int_mask equ     08h           ; IRQ3 mask for 8259
         endif


_TEXT    segment word public 'CODE'

         assume  cs:_TEXT,ds:_DATA,es:_DATA,ss:STACK

talk     proc    far           ; entry point from MS-DOS

         mov     ax,_DATA      ; make data segment addressable
         mov     ds,ax
         mov     es,ax
                               ; initialize display for
                               ; terminal emulator mode...

         mov     ah,15         ; get display width and
         int     10h           ; current display mode
         dec     ah            ; save display width for use
         mov     columns,ah    ; by the screen-clear routine

         cmp     al,7          ; enforce text display mode
         je      talk2         ; mode 7 ok, proceed
```

(continued)

Figure 7-1. *continued*

```
        cmp     al,3
        jbe     talk2           ; modes 0-3 ok, proceed

        mov     dx,offset msg1
        mov     cx,msg1_len
        jmp     talk6           ; print error message and exit

talk2:  mov     bh,dattr        ; clear screen and home cursor
        call    cls

        call    asc_enb         ; capture serial-port interrupt
                                ; vector and enable interrupts

        mov     dx,offset msg2  ; display message
        mov     cx,msg2_len     ; 'terminal emulator running'
        mov     bx,stdout       ; BX = standard output handle
        mov     ah,40h          ; function 40h = write file or device
        int     21h             ; transfer to MS-DOS

talk3:  call    pc_stat         ; keyboard character waiting?
        jz      talk4           ; nothing waiting, jump

        call    pc_in           ; read keyboard character

        cmp     al,0            ; is it a function key?
        jne     talk32          ; not function key, jump

        call    pc_in           ; function key, discard 2nd
                                ; character of sequence
        jmp     talk5           ; then terminate program

talk32:                         ; keyboard character received
        if      echo
        push    ax              ; if half-duplex, echo
        call    pc_out          ; character to PC display
        pop     ax
        endif

        call    com_out         ; write char to serial port

talk4:  call    com_stat        ; serial-port character waiting?
        jz      talk3           ; nothing waiting, jump

        call    com_in          ; read serial-port character

        cmp     al,20h          ; is it control code?
        jae     talk45          ; jump if not
```

(continued)

Figure 7-1. *continued*

```
        call    ctrl_code       ; control code, process it

        jmp     talk3           ; check keyboard again

talk45:                         ; noncontrol char received,
        call    pc_out          ; write it to PC display

        jmp     talk4           ; see if any more waiting

talk5:                          ; function key detected,
                                ; prepare to terminate...

        mov     bh,07h          ; clear screen and home cursor
        call    cls

        mov     dx,offset msg3  ; display farewell message
        mov     cx,msg3_len

talk6:  push    dx              ; save message address
        push    cx              ; and message length

        call    asc_dsb         ; disable serial-port interrupts
                                ; and release interrupt vector

        pop     cx              ; restore message length
        pop     dx              ; and address

        mov     bx,stdout       ; handle for standard output
        mov     ah,40h          ; function 40h = write device
        int     21h             ; transfer to MS-DOS

        mov     ax,4c00h        ; terminate program with
        int     21h             ; return code = 0

talk    endp

com_stat proc   near            ; check asynch status; returns
                                ; Z = false if character ready
                                ; Z = true if nothing waiting
        push    ax
        mov     ax,asc_in       ; compare ring buffer pointers
        cmp     ax,asc_out
        pop     ax
        ret                     ; return to caller
```

(continued)

Figure 7-1. *continued*

```
com_stat endp

com_in  proc    near            ; get character from serial-
                                ; port buffer; returns
                                ; new character in AL

        push    bx              ; save register BX

com_in1:                        ; if no char waiting, wait
        mov     bx,asc_out      ; until one is received
        cmp     bx,asc_in
        je      com_in1         ; jump, nothing waiting

        mov     al,[bx+asc_buf] ; character is ready,
                                ; extract it from buffer

        inc     bx              ; update buffer pointer
        cmp     bx,bufsiz
        jne     com_in2
        xor     bx,bx           ; reset pointer if wrapped
com_in2:
        mov     asc_out,bx      ; store updated pointer
        pop     bx              ; restore register BX
        ret                     ; and return to caller

com_in  endp

com_out proc    near            ; write character in AL
                                ; to serial port

        push    dx              ; save register DX
        push    ax              ; save character to send
        mov     dx,com_sts      ; DX = status port address

com_out1:                       ; check if transmit buffer
        in      al,dx           ; is empty (TBE bit = set)
        and     al,20h
        jz      com_out1        ; no, must wait

        pop     ax              ; get character to send
        mov     dx,com_data     ; DX = data port address
        out     dx,al           ; transmit the character
        pop     dx              ; restore register DX
        ret                     ; and return to caller

com_out endp
```

(continued)

Figure 7-1. *continued*

```
pc_stat proc    near            ; read keyboard status; returns
                                ; Z = false if character ready
                                ; Z = true if nothing waiting
                                ; register DX destroyed

        mov     al,in_flag      ; if character already
        or      al,al           ; waiting, return status
        jnz     pc_stat1

        mov     ah,6            ; otherwise call MS-DOS to
        mov     dl,0ffh         ; determine keyboard status
        int     21h

        jz      pc_stat1        ; jump if no key ready

        mov     in_char,al      ; got key, save it for
        mov     in_flag,0ffh    ; "pc_in" routine

pc_stat1:                       ; return to caller with
        ret                     ; Z flag set appropriately

pc_stat endp

pc_in   proc    near            ; read keyboard character,
                                ; return it in AL
                                ; DX may be destroyed

        mov     al,in_flag      ; key already waiting?
        or      al,al
        jnz     pc_in1          ; yes, return it to caller

        call    pc_stat         ; try to read a character
        jmp     pc_in

pc_in1: mov     in_flag,0       ; clear char-waiting flag
        mov     al,in_char      ; and return AL = character
        ret

pc_in   endp

pc_out  proc    near            ; write character in AL
                                ; to the PC's display

        mov     ah,0eh          ; ROM BIOS function 0eh =
                                ; "teletype output"
```

(continued)

Figure 7-1. *continued*

```
        push    bx              ; save register BX
        xor     bx,bx           ; assume page 0
        int     10h             ; transfer to ROM BIOS
        pop     bx              ; restore register BX
        ret                     ; and return to caller

pc_out  endp


cls     proc    near            ; clear display using
                                ; char attribute in BH
                                ; registers AX, CX,
                                ; and DX destroyed

        mov     dl,columns      ; set DL,DH = X,Y of
        mov     dh,24           ; lower right corner
        mov     cx,0            ; set CL,CH = X,Y of
                                ; upper left corner
        mov     ax,600h         ; ROM BIOS function 06h =
                                ; "scroll or initialize
                                ; window"
        int     10h             ; transfer to ROM BIOS
        call    home            ; set cursor at (0,0)
        ret                     ; and return to caller

cls     endp


clreol  proc    near            ; clear from cursor to end
                                ; of line using attribute
                                ; in BH, registers AX, CX,
                                ; and DX destroyed

        call    getxy           ; get current cursor position
        mov     cx,dx           ; current position = "upper
                                ; left corner" of window;
        mov     dl,columns      ; "lower right corner" X is
                                ; max columns, Y is same
                                ; as upper left corner
        mov     ax,600h         ; ROM BIOS function 06h =
                                ; "scroll or initialize
                                ; window"
        int     10h             ; transfer to ROM BIOS
        ret                     ; return to caller

clreol  endp
```

(continued)

Figure 7-1. *continued*

```
home     proc     near               ; put cursor at home position

         mov      dx,0               ; set (X,Y) = (0,0)
         call     gotoxy             ; position the cursor
         ret                         ; return to caller

home     endp

gotoxy   proc     near               ; position the cursor
                                     ; call with DL = X, DH = Y

         push     bx                 ; save registers
         push     ax

         mov      bh,0               ; assume page 0
         mov      ah,2               ; ROM BIOS function 02h =
                                     ; set cursor position
         int      10h                ; transfer to ROM BIOS

         pop      ax                 ; restore registers
         pop      bx
         ret                         ; and return to caller

gotoxy   endp


getxy    proc     near               ; get cursor position,
                                     ; returns DL = X, DH = Y

         push     ax                 ; save registers
         push     bx
         push     cx

         mov      ah,3               ; ROM BIOS function 03h =
                                     ; get cursor position
         mov      bh,0               ; assume page 0
         int      10h                ; transfer to ROM BIOS

         pop      cx                 ; restore registers
         pop      bx
         pop      ax
         ret                         ; and return to caller

getxy    endp
```

(continued)

Figure 7-1. *continued*

```
ctrl_code proc   near              ; process control code
                                   ; call with AL = char

         cmp     al,cr             ; if carriage return
         je      ctrl8             ; just send it

         cmp     al,lf             ; if linefeed
         je      ctrl8             ; just send it

         cmp     al,bsp            ; if backspace
         je      ctrl8             ; just send it

         cmp     al,26             ; is it cls control code?
         jne     ctrl7             ; no, jump

         mov     bh,dattr          ; cls control code, clear
         call    cls               ; screen and home cursor

         jmp     ctrl9

ctrl7:
         cmp     al,escape         ; is it Escape character?
         jne     ctrl9             ; no, throw it away

         call    esc_seq           ; yes, emulate CRT terminal
         jmp     ctrl9

ctrl8:   call    pc_out            ; send CR, LF, or backspace
                                   ; to the display

ctrl9:   ret                       ; return to caller

ctrl_code endp


esc_seq proc     near              ; decode Televideo 950 escape
                                   ; sequence for screen control

         call    com_in            ; get next character
         cmp     al,84             ; is it clear to end of line?
         jne     esc_seq1          ; no, jump

         mov     bh,dattr          ; yes, clear to end of line
         call    clreol
         jmp     esc_seq2          ; then exit
```

(continued)

Figure 7-1. *continued*

```
esc_seq1:
        cmp     al,61           ; is it cursor positioning?
        jne     esc_seq2        ; no jump

        call    com_in          ; yes, get Y parameter
        sub     al,33           ; and remove offset
        mov     dh,al

        call    com_in          ; get X parameter
        sub     al,33           ; and remove offset
        mov     dl,al
        call    gotoxy          ; position the cursor

esc_seq2:                       ; return to caller
        ret

esc_seq endp


asc_enb proc    near            ; capture serial-port interrupt
                                ; vector and enable interrupt

                                ; save address of previous
                                ; interrupt handler...
        mov     ax,3500h+com_int ; function 35h = get vector
        int     21h             ; transfer to MS-DOS
        mov     word ptr oldvec+2,es
        mov     word ptr oldvec,bx

                                ; now install our handler...
        push    ds              ; save our data segment
        mov     ax,cs           ; set DS:DX = address
        mov     ds,ax           ; of our interrupt handler
        mov     dx,offset asc_int
        mov     ax,2500h+com_int ; function 25h = set vector
        int     21h             ; transfer to MS-DOS
        pop     ds              ; restore data segment

        mov     dx,com_mcr      ; set modem-control register
        mov     al,0bh          ; DTR and OUT2 bits
        out     dx,al

        mov     dx,com_ier      ; set interrupt-enable
        mov     al,1            ; register on serial-
        out     dx,al           ; port controller
```

(continued)

Figure 7-1. *continued*

```
        in      al,pic_mask     ; read current 8259 mask
        and     al,not int_mask ; set mask for COM port
        out     pic_mask,al     ; write new 8259 mask

        ret                     ; back to caller

asc_enb endp


asc_dsb proc    near            ; disable interrupt and
                                ; release interrupt vector

        in      al,pic_mask     ; read current 8259 mask
        or      al,int_mask     ; reset mask for COM port
        out     pic_mask,al     ; write new 8259 mask

        push    ds              ; save our data segment
        lds     dx,oldvec       ; load address of
                                ; previous interrupt handler
        mov     ax,2500h+com_int ; function 25h = set vector
        int     21h             ; transfer to MS-DOS
        pop     ds              ; restore data segment

        ret                     ; back to caller

asc_dsb endp


asc_int proc    far             ; interrupt service routine
                                ; for serial port

        sti                     ; turn interrupts back on

        push    ax              ; save registers
        push    bx
        push    dx
        push    ds

        mov     ax,_DATA        ; make our data segment
        mov     ds,ax           ; addressable

        cli                     ; clear interrupts for
                                ; pointer manipulation

        mov     dx,com_data     ; DX = data port address
        in      al,dx           ; read this character
```

(continued)

Figure 7-1. *continued*

```
        mov     bx,asc_in           ; get buffer pointer
        mov     [asc_buf+bx],al     ; store this character
        inc     bx                  ; bump pointer
        cmp     bx,bufsiz           ; time for wrap?
        jne     asc_int1            ; no, jump
        xor     bx,bx               ; yes, reset pointer

asc_int1:                           ; store updated pointer
        mov     asc_in,bx

        sti                         ; turn interrupts back on

        mov     al,20h              ; send EOI to 8259
        out     pic_eoi,al

        pop     ds                  ; restore all registers
        pop     dx
        pop     bx
        pop     ax

        iret                        ; return from interrupt

asc_int endp

_TEXT   ends


_DATA   segment word public 'DATA'

in_char db      0                   ; PC keyboard input char
in_flag db      0                   ; <>0 if char waiting

columns db      0                   ; highest numbered column in
                                    ; current display mode (39 or 79)

msg1    db      cr,lf
        db      'Display must be text mode.'
        db      cr,lf
msg1_len equ $-msg1

msg2    db      'Terminal emulator running...'
        db      cr,lf
msg2_len equ $-msg2

msg3    db      'Exit from terminal emulator.'
        db      cr,lf
msg3_len equ $-msg3
```

(continued)

Figure 7-1. *continued*

```
oldvec   dd      0                    ; original contents of serial-
                                      ; port interrupt vector

asc_in   dw      0                    ; input pointer to ring buffer
asc_out  dw      0                    ; output pointer to ring buffer

asc_buf  db      bufsiz dup (?)  ; communications buffer

_DATA    ends


STACK    segment para stack 'STACK'

         db      128 dup (?)

STACK    ends

         end     talk              ;  defines entry point
```

The *TALK* program illustrates the methods that an application should use to take over and service interrupts from the serial port without running afoul of MS-DOS conventions.

The program begins with some equates and conditional assembly statements that configure the program for half- or full-duplex and for the desired serial port (COM1 or COM2). At entry from MS-DOS, the main routine of the program—the procedure named *talk*—checks the status of the serial port, initializes the display, and calls the *asc_enb* routine to take over the serial-port interrupt vector and enable interrupts. The *talk* procedure then enters a loop that reads the keyboard and sends the characters out the serial port and then reads the serial port and puts the characters on the display—in other words, it causes the PC to emulate a simple CRT terminal.

The *TALK* program intercepts and handles control codes (carriage return, linefeed, and so forth) appropriately. It detects escape sequences and handles them as a subset of the Televideo 950 terminal capabilities. (You can easily modify the program to emulate any other cursor-addressable terminal.) When one of the PC's special function keys is pressed, the program disables serial-port interrupts, releases the serial-port interrupt vector, and exits back to MS-DOS.

There are several *TALK* program procedures that are worth your attention because they can easily be incorporated into other programs. These are listed in the table on the following page.

Procedure	Action
asc_enb	Takes over the serial-port interrupt vector and enables interrupts by writing to the modem-control register of the INS8250 and the interrupt-mask register of the 8259A.
asc_dsb	Restores the original state of the serial-port interrupt vector and disables interrupts by writing to the interrupt-mask register of the 8259A.
asc_int	Services serial-port interrupts, placing received characters into a ring buffer.
com_stat	Tests whether characters from the serial port are waiting in the ring buffer.
com_in	Removes characters from the interrupt handler's ring buffer and increments the buffer pointers appropriately.
com_out	Sends one character to the serial port.
cls	Calls the ROM BIOS video driver to clear the screen.
clreol	Calls the ROM BIOS video driver to clear from the current cursor position to the end of the line.
home	Places the cursor in the upper left corner of the screen.
gotoxy	Positions the cursor at the desired position on the display.
getxy	Obtains the current cursor position.
pc_out	Sends one character to the PC's display.
pc_stat	Gets status for the PC's keyboard.
pc_in	Returns a character from the PC's keyboard.

Chapter 8

File Management

The dual heritage of MS-DOS—CP/M and UNIX/XENIX—is perhaps most clearly demonstrated in its file-management services. In general, MS-DOS provides at least two distinct operating-system calls for each major file or record operation. This chapter breaks this overlapping battery of functions into two groups and explains the usage, advantages, and disadvantages of each.

I will refer to the set of file and record functions that are compatible with CP/M as *FCB functions*. These functions rely on a data structure called a *file control block* (hence, FCB) to maintain certain bookkeeping information about open files. This structure resides in the application program's memory space. The FCB functions allow the programmer to create, open, close, and delete files and to read or write records of any size at any record position within such files. These functions do not support the hierarchical (treelike) file structure that was first introduced in MS-DOS version 2.0, so they can be used only to access files in the current subdirectory for a given disk drive.

I will refer to the set of file and record functions that provide compatibility with UNIX/XENIX as the *handle functions*. These functions allow the programmer to open or create files by passing MS-DOS a null-terminated string that describes the file's location in the hierarchical file structure (the drive and path), the file's name, and its extension. If the open or create operation is successful, MS-DOS returns a 16-bit token, or *handle*, that is saved by the application program and used to specify the file in subsequent operations.

When you use the handle functions, the operating system maintains the data structures that contain bookkeeping information about the file inside its own memory space, and these structures are not accessible to the application program. The handle functions fully support the hierarchical file structure, allowing the programmer to create, open, close, and delete files in any subdirectory on any disk drive and to read or write records of any size at any byte offset within such files.

Although we are discussing the FCB functions first in this chapter for historical reasons, new MS-DOS applications should always be written using the more powerful handle functions. Use of the FCB functions in new programs should be avoided, unless compatibility with MS-DOS version 1.0 is needed.

Using the FCB Functions

Understanding the structure of the file control block is the key to success with the FCB family of file and record functions. An FCB is a 37-byte data structure allocated within the application program's memory space; it is divided into many fields (Figure 8-1). Typically, the program initializes an FCB with a drive code, a filename, and an extension (conveniently accomplished with the parse-filename service, Int 21H Function 29H) and then passes the address of the FCB to MS-DOS to open or create the file. If the file is successfully opened or created, MS-DOS fills in certain fields of the FCB with information from the file's entry in the disk directory. This information includes the file's exact size in bytes and the date and time the file was created or last updated. MS-DOS also places certain other information within a reserved area of the FCB; however, this area is used by the operating system for its own purposes and varies among different versions of MS-DOS. Application programs should never modify the reserved area.

For compatibility with CP/M, MS-DOS automatically sets the record-size field of the FCB to 128 bytes. If the program does not want to use this default record size, it must place the desired size (in bytes) into the record-size field *after* the open or create operation. Subsequently, when the program needs to read or write records from the file, it must pass the address of the FCB to MS-DOS; MS-DOS, in turn, keeps the FCB updated with information about the current position of the file pointer and the size of the

Byte offset

00H	
Drive identification	Note 1
01H	
Filename (8 characters)	Note 2
09H	
Extension (3 characters)	Note 2
0CH	
Current-block number	Note 9
0EH	
Record size	Note 10
10H	
File size (4 bytes)	Notes 3, 6
14H	
Date created/updated	Note 7
16H	
Time created/updated	Note 8
18H	
Reserved	
20H	
Current-record number	Note 9
21H	
Relative-record number (4 bytes)	Note 5

Figure 8-1. *Normal file control block. Total length is 37 bytes (25H bytes). See notes on pages 133–34.*

file. Data is always read to or written from the current disk transfer area (DTA), whose address is set with Int 21H Function 1AH. If the application program wants to perform random record access, it must set the record number into the FCB *before* issuing each function call; when sequential record access is being used, MS-DOS maintains the FCB and no special intervention is needed from the application.

In general, MS-DOS functions that use FCBs accept the full address of the FCB in the DS:DX register and pass back a return code in the AL register (Figure 8-2). For file-management calls (open, close, create, and delete), this return code is zero if the function was successful and 0FFH (255) if the function failed. For the FCB-type record read and write functions, the success code returned in the AL register is again zero, but there are several failure codes. Under MS-DOS version 3.0 or later, more detailed error reporting can be obtained by calling Int 21H Function 59H (Get Extended Error Information) after a failed FCB function call.

When a program is loaded under MS-DOS, the operating system sets up two FCBs in the program segment prefix, at offsets 005CH and 006CH. These are often referred to as the *default FCBs*, and they are included to provide upward compatibility from CP/M. MS-DOS parses the first two parameters in the command line that invokes the program (excluding any redirection directives) into the default FCBs, under the assumption that they may be file specifications. The application must determine whether they really *are* filenames or not. In addition, because the default FCBs overlap and are not in a particularly convenient location (especially for .EXE programs), they usually must be copied elsewhere in order to be used safely. (See Chapter 3.)

```
                                    ; filename was previously
                                    ; parsed into "my_fcb"
            mov     dx,seg my_fcb   ; DS:DX = address of
            mov     ds,dx           ; file control block
            mov     dx,offset my_fcb
            mov     ah,0fh          ; function 0fh = open
            int     21h
            or      al,al           ; was open successful?
            jnz     error           ; no, jump to error routine
            .
            .
            .
my_fcb      db      37 dup (0)      ; file control block
```

Figure 8-2. *A typical FCB file operation. This sequence of code attempts to open the file whose name was previously parsed into the FCB named* my_fcb.

Note that the structures of FCBs under CP/M and MS-DOS are not identical. However, the differences lie chiefly in the reserved areas of the FCBs (which should not be manipulated by application programs in any case), so well-behaved CP/M applications should be relatively easy to port into MS-DOS. It seems, however, that few such applications exist. Many of the tricks that were played by clever CP/M programmers to increase performance or circumvent the limitations of that operating system can cause severe problems under MS-DOS, particularly in networking environments. At any rate, much better performance can be achieved by thoroughly rewriting the CP/M applications to take advantage of the superior capabilities of MS-DOS.

You can use a special FCB variant called an *extended file control block* to create or access files with special attributes (such as hidden or read-only files), volume labels, and subdirectories. An extended FCB has a 7-byte header followed by the 37-byte structure of a normal FCB (Figure 8-3). The first byte contains 0FFH, which could never be a legal drive code and thus indicates to MS-DOS that an extended FCB is being used. The next 5 bytes are reserved and are unused in current versions of MS-DOS. The

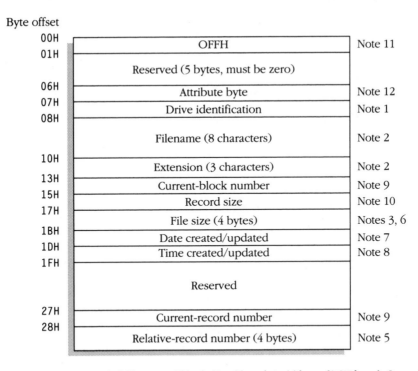

Figure 8-3. *Extended file control block. Total length is 44 bytes (2CH bytes). See notes on pages 133–34.*

seventh byte contains the attribute of the special file type that is being accessed. (Attribute bytes are discussed in more detail in Chapter 9.) Any MS-DOS function that uses a normal FCB can also use an extended FCB.

The FCB file- and record-management functions may be gathered into the following broad classifications:

Function	Action
Common FCB file operations	
0FH	Open file.
10H	Close file.
16H	Create file.
Common FCB record operations	
14H	Perform sequential read.
15H	Perform sequential write.
21H	Perform random read.
22H	Perform random write.
27H	Perform random block read.
28H	Perform random block write.
Other vital FCB operations	
1AH	Set disk transfer address.
29H	Parse filename.
Less commonly used FCB file operations	
13H	Delete file.
17H	Rename file.
Less commonly used FCB record operations	
23H	Obtain file size.
24H	Set relative-record number.

Several of these functions have special properties. For example, Int 21H Functions 27H (Random Block Read) and 28H (Random Block Write) allow reading and writing of multiple records of any size and also update the random-record field automatically (unlike Int 21H Functions 21H and 22H). Int 21H Function 28H can truncate a file to any desired size, and Int 21H Function 17H used with an extended FCB can alter a volume label or rename a subdirectory.

Section II of this book, "MS-DOS Functions Reference," gives detailed specifications for each of the FCB file and record functions, along with assembly-language examples. It is also instructive to compare the preceding groups with the corresponding groups of handle-type functions listed on pages 140–41.

Notes for Figures 8-1 and 8-3

1. The drive identification is a binary number: 00=default drive, 01=drive A:, 02=drive B:, and so on. If the application program supplies the drive code as zero (default drive), MS-DOS fills in the code for the actual current disk drive after a successful open or create call.

2. File and extension names must be left justified and padded with blanks.

3. The file size, date, time, and reserved fields should not be modified by applications.

4. All word fields are stored with the least significant byte at the lower address.

5. The relative-record field is treated as 4 bytes if the record size is less than 64 bytes; otherwise, only the first 3 bytes of this field are used.

6. The file-size field is in the same format as in the directory, with the less significant word at the lower address.

7. The date field is mapped as in the directory. Viewed as a 16-bit word (as it would appear in a register), the field is broken down as follows:

F E D C B A 9 8	7 6 5	4 3 2 1 0
Year	Month	Day

Bits	Contents
00H–04H	Day (1–31)
05H–08H	Month (1–12)
09H–0FH	Year, relative to 1980

8. The time field is mapped as in the directory. Viewed as a 16-bit word (as it would appear in a register), the field is broken down as follows:

F E D C B	A 9 8 7 6 5	4 3 2 1 0
Hours	Minutes	2-second increments

Bits	Contents
00H–04H	2-second increments (0–29)
05H–0AH	Minutes (0–59)
0BH–0FH	Hours (0–23)

(continued)

9. The current-block and current-record numbers are used together on sequential reads and writes. This simulates the behavior of CP/M.

10. The Int 21H open (0FH) and create (16H) functions set the record-size field to 128 bytes, to provide compatibility with CP/M. If you use another record size, you must fill it in *after* the open or create operation.

11. An 0FFH (255) in the first byte of the structure signifies that it is an extended file control block. You can use extended FCBs with any of the functions that accept an ordinary FCB. (See also note 12.)

12. The attribute byte in an extended FCB allows access to files with the special characteristics hidden, system, or read-only. You can also use extended FCBs to read volume labels and the contents of special subdirectory files.

FCB File-Access Skeleton

The following is a typical program sequence to access a file using the FCB, or traditional, functions (Figure 8-4):

1. Zero out the prospective FCB.

2. Obtain the filename from the user, from the default FCBs, or from the command tail in the PSP.

3. If the filename was not obtained from one of the default FCBs, parse the filename into the new FCB using Int 21H Function 29H.

4. Open the file (Int 21H Function 0FH) or, if writing new data only, create the file or truncate any existing file of the same name to zero length (Int 21H Function 16H).

5. Set the record-size field in the FCB, unless you are using the default record size. Recall that it is important to do this *after* a successful open or create operation. (See Figure 8-5.)

6. Set the relative-record field in the FCB if you are performing random record I/O.

7. Set the disk transfer area address using Int 21H Function 1AH, unless the buffer address has not been changed since the last call to this function. If the application never performs a set DTA, the DTA address defaults to offset 0080H in the PSP.

8. Request the needed read- or write-record operation (Int 21H Function 14H–Sequential Read, 15H–Sequential Write, 21H–Random Read, 22H–Random Write, 27H–Random Block Read, 28H–Random Block Write).

(continued)

```
recsize      equ    1024                    ; file record size
             .
             .
             .
             mov    ah,29h                  ; parse input filename
             mov    al,1                    ; skip leading blanks
             mov    si,offset fname1        ; address of filename
             mov    di,offset fcb1          ; address of FCB
             int    21h
             or     al,al                   ; jump if name
             jnz    name_err                ; was bad
             .
             .
             .
             mov    ah,29h                  ; parse output filename
             mov    al,1                    ; skip leading blanks
             mov    si,offset fname2        ; address of filename
             mov    di,offset fcb2          ; address of FCB
             int    21h
             or     al,al                   ; jump if name
             jnz    name_err                ; was bad
             .
             .
             .
             mov    ah,0fh                  ; open input file
             mov    dx,offset fcb1
             int    21h
             or     al,al                   ; open successful?
             jnz    no_file                 ; no, jump
             .
             .
             .
             mov    ah,16h                  ; create and open
             mov    dx,offset fcb2          ; output file
             int    21h
             or     al,al                   ; create successful?
             jnz    disk_full               ; no, jump
             .
             .
             .                              ; set record sizes
             mov    word ptr fcb1+0eh,recsize
             mov    word ptr fcb2+0eh,recsize
             .
             .
             .
```

(continued)

Figure 8-4. *Skeleton of an assembly-language program that performs file and record I/O using the FCB family of functions.*

Figure 8-4. *continued*

```
             mov    ah,1ah               ; set disk transfer
             mov    dx,offset buffer     ; address for reads
             int    21h                  ; and writes
             .
next:        .                           ; process next record
             .
             mov    ah,14h               ; sequential read from
             mov    dx,offset fcb1       ; input file
             int    21h
             cmp    al,01                ; check for end of file
             je     file_end             ; jump if end of file
             cmp    al,03
             je     file_end             ; jump if end of file
             or     al,al                ; other read fault?
             jnz    bad_read             ; jump if bad read
             .
             .
             mov    ah,15h               ; sequential write to
             mov    dx,offset fcb2       ; output file
             int    21h
             or     al,al                ; write successful?
             jnz    bad_write            ; jump if write failed
             .
             .
             .
             jmp    next                 ; process next record
             .
file_end:    .                           ; reached end of input
             .
             mov    ah,10h               ; close input file
             mov    dx,offset fcb1
             int    21h
             .
             .
             .
             mov    ah,10h               ; close output file
             mov    dx,offset fcb2
             int    21h
             .
             .
             .
             mov    ax,4c00h             ; exit with return
             int    21h                  ; code of zero
             .
             .
             .
```

(continued)

Figure 8-4. *continued*

```
fname1      db      'OLDFILE.DAT',0      ; name of input file
fname2      db      'NEWFILE.DAT',0      ; name of output file
fcb1        db      37 dup (0)           ; FCB for input file
fcb2        db      37 dup (0)           ; FCB for output file
buffer      db      recsize dup (?)      ; buffer for file I/O
```

Byte offset	FCB before open	FCB contents	FCB after open
00H	00	Drive	03
01H	4D		4D
02H	59		59
03H	46		46
04H	49	Filename	49
05H	4C		4C
06H	45		45
07H	20		20
08H	20		20
09H	44		44
0AH	41	Extension	41
0BH	54		54
0CH	00	Current block	00
0DH	00		00
0EH	00	Record size	80
0FH	00		00
10H	00		80
11H	00	File size	3D
12H	00		00
13H	00		00
14H	00	File date	43
15H	00		0B
16H	00	File time	A1
17H	00		52
18H	00		03
19H	00		02
1AH	00		42
1BH	00	Reserved	73
1CH	00		00
1DH	00		01
1EH	00		35
1FH	00		0F
20H	00	Current record	00
21H	00		00
22H	00	Relative-record number	00
23H	00		00
24H	00		00

Figure 8-5. *A typical file control block before and after a successful open call (Int 21H Function 0FH).*

9. If the program is not finished processing the file, go to step 6; otherwise, close the file (Int 21H Function 10H). If the file was used for reading only, you can skip the close operation under early versions of MS-DOS. However, this shortcut can cause problems under MS-DOS versions 3.0 and later, especially when the files are being accessed across a network.

Points to Remember

Here is a summary of the pros and cons of using the FCB-related file and record functions in your programs.

Advantages:

- Under MS-DOS versions 1 and 2, the number of files that can be open concurrently when using FCBs is unlimited. (This is not true under MS-DOS versions 3.0 and later, especially if networking software is running.)

- File-access methods using FCBs are familiar to programmers with a CP/M background, and well-behaved CP/M applications require little change in logical flow to run under MS-DOS.

- MS-DOS supplies the size, time, and date for a file to its FCB after the file is opened. The calling program can inspect this information.

Disadvantages:

- FCBs take up room in the application program's memory space.

- FCBs offer no support for the hierarchical file structure (no access to files outside the current directory).

- FCBs provide no support for file locking/sharing or record locking in networking environments.

- In addition to the read or write call itself, file reads or writes using FCBs require manipulation of the FCB to set record size and record number, plus a previous call to a separate MS-DOS function to set the DTA address.

- Random record I/O using FCBs for a file containing variable-length records is very clumsy and inconvenient.

- You must use extended FCBs, which are incompatible with CP/M anyway, to access or create files with special attributes such as hidden, read-only, or system.

- The FCB file functions have poor error reporting. This situation has been improved somewhat in MS-DOS version 3 because a program can call the added Int 21H Function 59H (Get Extended Error Information) after a failed FCB function to obtain additional information.

- Microsoft discourages use of FCBs. FCBs will make your program more difficult to port to MS OS/2 later because MS OS/2 does not support FCBs in protected mode at all.

Using the Handle Functions

The handle file- and record-management functions access files in a fashion similar to that used under the UNIX/XENIX operating system. Files are designated by an ASCIIZ string (an ASCII character string terminated by a null, or zero, byte) that can contain a drive designator, path, filename, and extension. For example, the file specification

```
C:\SYSTEM\COMMAND.COM
```

would appear in memory as the following sequence of bytes:

```
43 3A 5C 53 59 53 54 45 4D 5C 43 4F 4D 4D 41 4E 44 2E 43 4F 4D 00
```

When a program wishes to open or create a file, it passes the address of the ASCIIZ string specifying the file to MS-DOS in the DS:DX registers (Figure 8-6). If the operation is successful, MS-DOS returns a 16-bit handle to the program in the AX register. The program must save this handle for further reference.

```
          mov    ah,3dh              ; function 3dh = open
          mov    al,2                ; mode 2 = read/write
          mov    dx,seg filename     ; address of ASCIIZ
          mov    ds,dx               ; file specification
          mov    dx,offset filename
          int    21h                 ; request open from DOS
          jc     error               ; jump if open failed
          mov    handle,ax           ; save file handle
          .
          .
          .
filename  db     'C:\MYDIR\MYFILE.DAT',0 ; filename
handle    dw     0                   ; file handle
```

Figure 8-6. *A typical handle file operation. This sequence of code attempts to open the file designated in the ASCIIZ string whose address is passed to MS-DOS in the DS:DX registers.*

When the program requests subsequent operations on the file, it usually places the handle in the BX register before the call to MS-DOS. All the handle functions return with the CPU's carry flag cleared if the operation was successful, or set if the operation failed; in the latter case, the AX register contains a code describing the failure.

MS-DOS restricts the number of handles that can be active at any one time—that is, the number of files and devices that can be open concurrently when using the handle family of functions—in two different ways:

- The maximum number of concurrently open files in the system, for all active processes combined, is specified by the entry

  FILES=*nn*

  in the CONFIG.SYS file. This entry determines the number of entries to be allocated in the *system file table*; under MS-DOS version 3, the default value is 8 and the maximum is 255. After MS-DOS is booted and running, you cannot expand this table to increase the total number of files that can be open. You must use an editor to modify the CON-FIG.SYS file and then restart the system.

- The maximum number of concurrently open files for a single process is 20, assuming that sufficient entries are also available in the system file table. When a program is loaded, MS-DOS preassigns 5 of its potential 20 handles to the standard devices. Each time the process issues an open or create call, MS-DOS assigns a handle from the process's private allocation of 20, until all the handles are used up or the system file table is full. In MS-DOS versions 3.3 and later, you can expand the per-process limit of 20 handles with a call to Int 21H Function 67H (Set Handle Count).

The handle file- and record-management calls may be gathered into the following broad classifications for study:

Function	Action
Common handle file operations	
3CH	Create file (requires ASCIIZ string).
3DH	Open file (requires ASCIIZ string).
3EH	Close file.
Common handle record operations	
42H	Set file pointer (also used to find file size).
3FH	Read file.
40H	Write file.

(continued)

Function	Action
Less commonly used handle operations	
41H	Delete file.
43H	Get or modify file attributes.
44H	IOCTL (I/O Control).
45H	Duplicate handle.
46H	Redirect handle.
56H	Rename file.
57H	Get or set file date and time.
5AH	Create temporary file (versions 3.0 and later).
5BH	Create file (fails if file already exists; versions 3.0 and later).
5CH	Lock or unlock file region (versions 3.0 and later).
67H	Set handle count (versions 3.3 and later).
68H	Commit file (versions 3.3 and later).
6CH	Extended open file (version 4).

Compare the groups of handle-type functions in the preceding table with the groups of FCB functions outlined earlier, noting the degree of functional overlap. Section II of this book, "MS-DOS Functions Reference," gives detailed specifications for each of the handle functions, along with assembly-language examples.

Handle File-Access Skeleton

The following is a typical program sequence to access a file using the handle family of functions (Figure 8-7):

1. Get the filename from the user by means of the buffered input service (Int 21H Function 0AH) or from the command tail supplied by MS-DOS in the PSP.

2. Put a zero at the end of the file specification in order to create an ASCIIZ string.

3. Open the file using Int 21H Function 3DH and mode 2 (read/write access), or create the file using Int 21H Function 3CH. (Be sure to set the CX register to zero, so that you don't accidentally make a file with special attributes.) Save the handle that is returned.

4. Set the file pointer using Int 21H Function 42H. You may set the file-pointer position relative to one of three different locations: the start of the file, the current pointer position, or the end of the file. If you are performing sequential record I/O, you can usually skip this step because MS-DOS will maintain the file pointer for you automatically.

5. Read from the file (Int 21H Function 3FH) or write to the file (Int 21H Function 40H). Both of these functions require that the BX register contain the file's handle, the CX register contain the length of the record, and the DS:DX registers point to the data being transferred. Both return the actual number of bytes transferred in the AX register.

   In a read operation, if the number of bytes read is less than the number requested, the end of the file has been reached. In a write operation, if the number of bytes written is less than the number requested, the disk containing the file is full. *Neither of these conditions is returned as an error code;* that is, the carry flag is *not* set.

6. If the program is not finished processing the file, go to step 4; otherwise, close the file (Int 21H Function 3EH). Any normal exit from the program will also close all active handles.

```
recsize      equ     1024                    ; file record size
             .
             .
             .
             mov     ah,3dh                  ; open input file
             mov     al,0                    ; mode = read only
             mov     dx,offset fname1        ; name of input file
             int     21h
             jc      no_file                 ; jump if no file
             mov     handle1,ax              ; save token for file
             .
             .
             .
             mov     ah,3ch                  ; create output file
             mov     cx,0                    ; attribute = normal
             mov     dx,offset fname2        ; name of output file
             int     21h
             jc      disk_full               ; jump if create fails
             mov     handle2,ax              ; save token for file
             .
next:        .                               ; process next record
             .
```

(continued)

Figure 8-7. *Skeleton of an assembly-language program that performs sequential processing on an input file and writes the results to an output file using the handle file and record functions. This code assumes that the DS and ES registers have already been set to point to the segment containing the buffers and filenames.*

Figure 8-7. *continued*

```
        mov   ah,3fh              ; sequential read from
        mov   bx,handle1          ; input file
        mov   cx,recsize
        mov   dx,offset buffer
        int   21h
        jc    bad_read            ; jump if read error
        or    ax,ax               ; check bytes transferred
        jz    file_end            ; jump if end of file
        .
        .
        .
        mov   ah,40h              ; sequential write to
        mov   bx,handle2          ; output file
        mov   cx,recsize
        mov   dx,offset buffer
        int   21h
        jc    bad_write           ; jump if write error
        cmp   ax,recsize          ; whole record written?
        jne   disk_full           ; jump if disk is full
        .
        .
        .
        jmp   next                ; process next record
        .
file_end:     .                   ; reached end of input
        .
        mov   ah,3eh              ; close input file
        mov   bx,handle1
        int   21h
        .
        .
        .
        mov   ah,3eh              ; close output file
        mov   bx,handle2
        int   21h
        .
        .
        .
        mov   ax,4c00h            ; exit with return
        int   21h                 ; code of zero
        .
        .
        .
fname1  db    'OLDFILE.DAT',0     ; name of input file
fname2  db    'NEWFILE.DAT',0     ; name of output file
handle1 dw    0                   ; token for input file
handle2 dw    0                   ; token for output file
buffer  db    recsize dup (?)     ; buffer for file I/O
```

Points to Remember

Here is a summary of the pros and cons of using the handle file and record operations in your program. Compare this list with the one given earlier in the chapter for the FCB family of functions.

Advantages:

- The handle calls provide direct support for I/O redirection and pipes with the standard input and output devices in a manner functionally similar to that used by UNIX/XENIX.

- The handle functions provide direct support for directories (the hierarchical file structure) and special file attributes.

- The handle calls support file sharing/locking and record locking in networking environments.

- Using the handle functions, the programmer can open channels to character devices and treat them as files.

- The handle calls make the use of random record access extremely easy. The current file pointer can be moved to any byte offset relative to the start of the file, the end of the file, or the current pointer position. Records of any length, up to an entire segment (65,535 bytes), can be read to any memory address in one operation.

- The handle functions have relatively good error reporting in MS-DOS version 2, and error reporting has been enhanced even further in MS-DOS versions 3.0 and later.

- Microsoft strongly encourages use of the handle family of functions in order to provide upward compatibility with MS OS/2.

Disadvantages:

- There is a limit per program of 20 concurrently open files and devices using handles in MS-DOS versions 2.0 through 3.2.

- Minor gaps still exist in the implementation of the handle functions. For example, you must still use extended FCBs to change volume labels and to access the contents of the special files that implement directories.

MS-DOS Error Codes

When one of the handle file functions fails with the carry flag set, or when a program calls Int 21H Function 59H (Get Extended Error Information) following a failed FCB function or other system service, one of the following error codes may be returned:

Value	Meaning
MS-DOS version 2 error codes	
01H	Function number invalid
02H	File not found
03H	Path not found
04H	Too many open files
05H	Access denied
06H	Handle invalid
07H	Memory control blocks destroyed
08H	Insufficient memory
09H	Memory block address invalid
0AH (10)	Environment invalid
0BH (11)	Format invalid
0CH (12)	Access code invalid
0DH (13)	Data invalid
0EH (14)	Unknown unit
0FH (15)	Disk drive invalid
10H (16)	Attempted to remove current directory
11H (17)	Not same device
12H (18)	No more files
Mappings to critical-error codes	
13H (19)	Write-protected disk
14H (20)	Unknown unit
15H (21)	Drive not ready
16H (22)	Unknown command
17H (23)	Data error (CRC)
18H (24)	Bad request-structure length
19H (25)	Seek error
1AH (26)	Unknown media type
1BH (27)	Sector not found
1CH (28)	Printer out of paper
1DH (29)	Write fault
1EH (30)	Read fault
1FH (31)	General failure
MS-DOS version 3 and later extended error codes	
20H (32)	Sharing violation
21H (33)	File-lock violation
22H (34)	Disk change invalid

(continued)

Value	Meaning
MS-DOS version 3 and later extended error codes, continued	
23H (35)	FCB unavailable
24H (36)	Sharing buffer exceeded
25H–31H (37–49)	Reserved
32H (50)	Unsupported network request
33H (51)	Remote machine not listening
34H (52)	Duplicate name on network
35H (53)	Network name not found
36H (54)	Network busy
37H (55)	Device no longer exists on network
38H (56)	NetBIOS command limit exceeded
39H (57)	Error in network adapter hardware
3AH (58)	Incorrect response from network
3BH (59)	Unexpected network error
3CH (60)	Remote adapter incompatible
3DH (61)	Print queue full
3EH (62)	Not enough room for print file
3FH (63)	Print file was deleted
40H (64)	Network name deleted
41H (65)	Network access denied
42H (66)	Incorrect network device type
43H (67)	Network name not found
44H (68)	Network name limit exceeded
45H (69)	NetBIOS session limit exceeded
46H (70)	Temporary pause
47H (71)	Network request not accepted
48H (72)	Print or disk redirection paused
49H–4FH (73–79)	Reserved
50H (80)	File already exists
51H (81)	Reserved
52H (82)	Cannot make directory
53H (83)	Fail on Int 24H (critical error)
54H (84)	Too many redirections
55H (85)	Duplicate redirection
56H (86)	Invalid password
57H (87)	Invalid parameter
58H (88)	Net write fault

Under MS-DOS versions 3.0 and later, you can also use Int 21H Function 59H to obtain other information about the error, such as the error locus and the recommended recovery action.

Critical-Error Handlers

In Chapter 5, we discussed how an application program can take over the Ctrl-C handler vector (Int 23H) and replace the MS-DOS default handler, to avoid losing control of the computer when the user enters a Ctrl-C or Ctrl-Break at the keyboard. Similarly, MS-DOS provides a critical-error-handler vector (Int 24H) that defines the routine to be called when unrecoverable hardware faults occur. The default MS-DOS critical-error handler is the routine that displays a message describing the error type and the cue

```
Abort, Retry, Ignore?
```

This message appears after such actions as the following:

- Attempting to open a file on a disk drive that doesn't contain a floppy disk or whose door isn't closed

- Trying to read a disk sector that contains a CRC error

- Trying to print when the printer is off line

The unpleasant thing about MS-DOS's default critical-error handler is, of course, that if the user enters an *A* for *Abort*, the application that is currently executing is terminated abruptly and never has a chance to clean up and make a graceful exit. Intermediate files may be left on the disk, files that have been extended using FCBs are not properly closed so that the directory is updated, interrupt vectors may be left pointing into the transient program area, and so forth.

To write a truly bombproof MS-DOS application, you must take over the critical-error-handler vector and point it to your own routine, so that your program intercepts all catastrophic hardware errors and handles them appropriately. You can use MS-DOS Int 21H Function 25H to alter the Int 24H vector in a well-behaved manner. When your application exits, MS-DOS will automatically restore the previous contents of the Int 24H vector from information saved in the program segment prefix.

MS-DOS calls the critical-error handler for two general classes of errors—disk-related and non-disk-related—and passes different information to the handler in the registers for each of these classes.

For disk-related errors, MS-DOS sets the registers as shown on the following page. (Bits 3–5 of the AH register are relevant only in MS-DOS versions 3.1 and later.)

Register	Bit(s)	Significance
AH	7	0, to signify disk error
	6	Reserved
	5	0 = ignore response not allowed
		1 = ignore response allowed
	4	0 = retry response not allowed
		1 = retry response allowed
	3	0 = fail response not allowed
		1 = fail response allowed
	1–2	Area where disk error occurred
		00 = MS-DOS area
		01 = file allocation table
		10 = root directory
		11 = files area
	0	0 = read operation
		1 = write operation
AL	0–7	Drive code (0 = A, 1 = B, and so forth)
DI	0–7	Driver error code
	8–15	Not used
BP:SI		Segment:offset of device-driver header

For non-disk-related errors, the interrupt was generated either as the result of a character-device error or because a corrupted memory image of the file allocation table was detected. In this case, MS-DOS sets the registers as follows:

Register	Bit(s)	Significance
AH	7	1, to signify a non-disk error
DI	0–7	Driver error code
	8–15	Not used
BP:SI		Segment:offset of device-driver header

To determine whether the critical error was caused by a character device, use the address in the BP:SI registers to examine the device attribute word at offset 0004H in the presumed device-driver header. If bit 15 is set, then the error was indeed caused by a character device, and the program can inspect the name field of the driver's header to determine the device.

At entry to a critical-error handler, MS-DOS has already disabled interrupts and set up the stack as shown in Figure 8-8. A critical-error handler cannot use any MS-DOS services except Int 21H Functions 01H through 0CH (Traditional Character I/O), Int 21H Function 30H (Get MS-DOS Version), and Int 21H Function 59H (Get Extended Error Information). These functions use a special stack so that the context of the original function (which generated the critical error) will not be lost.

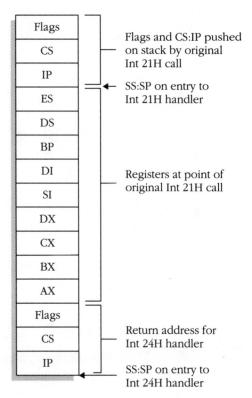

Figure 8-8. *The stack at entry to a critical-error handler.*

The critical-error handler should return to MS-DOS by executing an IRET, passing one of the following action codes in the AL register:

Code	Meaning
0	Ignore the error (MS-DOS acts as though the original function call had succeeded).
1	Retry the operation.
2	Terminate the process that encountered the error.
3	Fail the function (an error code is returned to the requesting process). Versions 3.1 and later only.

The critical-error handler should preserve all other registers and must not modify the device-driver header pointed to by BP:SI. A skeleton example of a critical-error handler is shown in Figure 8-9.

```
                                ; prompt message used by
                                ; critical-error handler
prompt  db      cr,lf,'Critical Error Occurred: '
        db      'Abort, Retry, Ignore, Fail? $'

keys    db      'aArRiIfF'      ; possible user response keys
keys_len equ $-keys             ; (both cases of each allowed)

codes   db      2,2,1,1,0,0,3,3 ; codes returned to MS-DOS kernel
                                ; for corresponding response keys


;
; This code is executed during program's initialization
; to install the new critical-error handler.
;
        .
        .
        .

        push    ds              ; save our data segment

        mov     dx,seg int24    ; DS:DX = handler address
        mov     ds,dx
        mov     dx,offset int24
        mov     ax,2524h        ; function 25h = set vector
        int     21h             ; transfer to MS-DOS

        pop     ds              ; restore data segment
        .
        .
        .

;
; This is the replacement critical-error handler. It
; prompts the user for Abort, Retry, Ignore, or Fail, and
; returns the appropriate code to the MS-DOS kernel.
;

int24   proc    far             ; entered from MS-DOS kernel

        push    bx              ; save registers
        push    cx
        push    dx
        push    si
        push    di
        push    bp
        push    ds
        push    es
```

Figure 8-9. *A skeleton example of a replacement critical-error handler.*   *(continued)*

Figure 8-9. *continued*

```
int24a: mov      ax,seg prompt    ; display prompt for user
        mov      ds,ax            ; using function 9 (print string
        mov      es,ax            ; terminated by $ character)
        mov      dx,offset prompt
        mov      ah,9
        int      21h

        mov      ah,1             ; get user's response
        int      21h             ; function 1 = read one character

        mov      di,offset keys  ; look up code for response key
        mov      cx,keys_len
        cld
        repne scasb
        jnz      int24a          ; prompt again if bad response

                                 ; set AL = action code for MS-DOS
                                 ; according to key that was entered:
                                 ; 0 = ignore, 1 = retry, 2 = abort,
                                 ; 3 = fail
        mov      al,[di+keys_len-1]

        pop      es              ; restore registers
        pop      ds
        pop      bp
        pop      di
        pop      si
        pop      dx
        pop      cx
        pop      bx
        iret                     ; exit critical-error handler

int24   endp
```

Example Programs: *DUMP.ASM* and *DUMP.C*

The programs *DUMP.ASM* (Figure 8-10) and *DUMP.C* (Figure 8-11) are parallel examples of the use of the handle file and record functions. The assembly-language version, in particular, illustrates features of a well-behaved MS-DOS utility:

- The program checks the version of MS-DOS to ensure that all the functions it is going to use are really available.

- The program parses the drive, path, and filename from the command tail in the program segment prefix.

- The program uses buffered I/O for speed.

- The program sends error messages to the standard error device.

- The program sends normal program output to the standard output device, so that the dump output appears by default on the system console but can be redirected to other character devices (such as the line printer) or to a file.

The same features are incorporated into the C version of the program, but some of them are taken care of behind the scenes by the C runtime library.

```
        name    dump
        page    55,132
        title   DUMP--display file contents

;
;   DUMP--Display contents of file in hex and ASCII
;
;   Build:    C>MASM DUMP;
;             C>LINK DUMP;
;
;   Usage:    C>DUMP unit:\path\filename.exe [ >device ]
;
;   Copyright (C) 1988 Ray Duncan
;

cr        equ     0dh                ; ASCII carriage return
lf        equ     0ah                ; ASCII line feed
tab       equ     09h                ; ASCII tab code
blank     equ     20h                ; ASCII space code

cmd       equ     80h                ; buffer for command tail

blksize   equ     16                 ; input file record size

stdin     equ     0                  ; standard input handle
stdout    equ     1                  ; standard output handle
stderr    equ     2                  ; standard error handle
```

Figure 8-10. *The assembly-language version:* DUMP.ASM.   *(continued)*

Figure 8-10. *continued*

```
_TEXT    segment word public 'CODE'

         assume  cs:_TEXT,ds:_DATA,es:_DATA,ss:STACK

dump     proc    far             ; entry point from MS-DOS

         push    ds              ; save DS:0000 for final
         xor     ax,ax           ; return to MS-DOS, in case
         push    ax              ; function 4ch can't be used

         mov     ax,_DATA        ; make our data segment
         mov     ds,ax           ; addressable via DS register

                                 ; check MS-DOS version
         mov     ax,3000h        ; function 30h = get version
         int     21h             ; transfer to MS-DOS
         cmp     al,2            ; major version 2 or later?
         jae     dump1           ; yes, proceed

                                 ; if MS-DOS 1.x, display
                                 ; error message and exit
         mov     dx,offset msg3  ; DS:DX = message address
         mov     ah,9            ; function 9 = print string
         int     21h             ; transfer to MS-DOS
         ret                     ; then exit the old way

dump1:                           ; check if filename present
         mov     bx,offset cmd   ; ES:BX = command tail
         call    argc            ; count command arguments
         cmp     ax,2            ; are there 2 arguments?
         je      dump2           ; yes, proceed

                                 ; missing filename, display
                                 ; error message and exit
         mov     dx,offset msg2  ; DS:DX = message address
         mov     cx,msg2_len     ; CX = message length
         jmp     dump9           ; go display it

dump2:                           ; get address of filename
         mov     ax,1            ; AX = argument number
                                 ; ES:BX still = command tail
         call    argv            ; returns ES:BX = address,
                                 ; and AX = length

         mov     di,offset fname ; copy filename to buffer
         mov     cx,ax           ; CX = length
```

(continued)

Figure 8-10. *continued*

```
dump3:   mov     al,es:[bx]      ; copy one byte
         mov     [di],al
         inc     bx              ; bump string pointers
         inc     di
         loop    dump3           ; loop until string done
         mov     byte ptr [di],0 ; add terminal null byte

         mov     ax,ds           ; make our data segment
         mov     es,ax           ; addressable by ES too
                                 ; now open the file
         mov     ax,3d00h        ; function 3dh = open file
                                 ; mode 0 = read only
         mov     dx,offset fname ; DS:DX = filename
         int     21h             ; transfer to MS-DOS
         jnc     dump4           ; jump, open successful

                                 ; open failed, display
                                 ; error message and exit
         mov     dx,offset msg1  ; DS:DX = message address
         mov     cx,msg1_len     ; CX = message length
         jmp     dump9           ; go display it

dump4:   mov     fhandle,ax      ; save file handle

dump5:                           ; read block of file data
         mov     bx,fhandle      ; BX = file handle
         mov     cx,blksize      ; CX = record length
         mov     dx,offset fbuff ; DS:DX = buffer
         mov     ah,3fh          ; function 3fh = read
         int     21h             ; transfer to MS-DOS

         mov     flen,ax         ; save actual length
         cmp     ax,0            ; end of file reached?
         jne     dump6           ; no, proceed

         cmp     word ptr fptr,0 ; was this the first read?
         jne     dump8           ; no, exit normally

                                 ; display empty file
                                 ; message and exit
         mov     dx,offset msg4  ; DS:DX = message address
         mov     cx,msg4_len     ; CX = length
         jmp     dump9           ; go display it
```

(continued)

Figure 8-10. *continued*

```
dump6:                              ; display heading at
                                    ; each 128-byte boundary
        test    fptr,07fh           ; time for a heading?
        jnz     dump7               ; no, proceed

                                    ; display a heading
        mov     dx,offset hdg       ; DS:DX = heading address
        mov     cx,hdg_len          ; CX = heading length
        mov     bx,stdout           ; BX = standard output
        mov     ah,40h              ; function 40h = write
        int     21h                 ; transfer to MS-DOS

dump7:  call    conv                ; convert binary record
                                    ; to formatted ASCII

                                    ; display formatted output
        mov     dx,offset fout      ; DX:DX = output address
        mov     cx,fout_len         ; CX = output length
        mov     bx,stdout           ; BX = standard output
        mov     ah,40h              ; function 40h = write
        int     21h                 ; transfer to MS-DOS
        jmp     dump5               ; go get another record

dump8:                              ; close input file
        mov     bx,fhandle          ; BX = file handle
        mov     ah,3eh              ; function 3eh = close
        int     21h                 ; transfer to MS-DOS

        mov     ax,4c00h            ; function 4ch = terminate,
                                    ; return code = 0
        int     21h                 ; transfer to MS-DOS

dump9:                              ; display message on
                                    ; standard error device
                                    ; DS:DX = message address
                                    ; CX = message length
        mov     bx,stderr           ; standard error handle
        mov     ah,40h              ; function 40h = write
        int     21h                 ; transfer to MS-DOS

        mov     ax,4c01h            ; function 4ch = terminate,
                                    ; return code = 1
        int     21h                 ; transfer to MS-DOS

dump    endp
```

(continued)

Figure 8-10. *continued*

```
conv      proc     near                ; convert block of data
                                       ; from input file

          mov      di,offset fout      ; clear output format
          mov      cx,fout_len-2       ; area to blanks
          mov      al,blank
          rep stosb

          mov      di,offset fout      ; convert file offset
          mov      ax,fptr             ; to ASCII for output
          call     w2a

          mov      bx,0                ; init buffer pointer

conv1:    mov      al,[fbuff+bx]       ; fetch byte from buffer
          mov      di,offset foutb     ; point to output area

                                       ; format ASCII part...
                                       ; store '.' as default
          mov      byte ptr [di+bx],'.'

          cmp      al,blank            ; in range 20h-7eh?
          jb       conv2               ; jump, not alphanumeric

          cmp      al,7eh              ; in range 20h-7eh?
          ja       conv2               ; jump, not alphanumeric

          mov      [di+bx],al          ; store ASCII character

conv2:                                 ; format hex part...
          mov      di,offset fouta     ; point to output area
          add      di,bx               ; base addr + (offset*3)
          add      di,bx
          add      di,bx
          call     b2a                 ; convert byte to hex

          inc      bx                  ; advance through record
          cmp      bx,flen             ; entire record converted?
          jne      conv1               ; no, get another byte

                                       ; update file pointer
          add      word ptr fptr,blksize

          ret

conv      endp
```

(continued)

Figure 8-10. *continued*

```
w2a     proc    near            ; convert word to hex ASCII
                                ; call with AX = value
                                ;           DI = addr for string
                                ; returns AX, DI, CX destroyed

        push    ax              ; save copy of value
        mov     al,ah
        call    b2a             ; convert upper byte

        pop     ax              ; get back copy
        call    b2a             ; convert lower byte
        ret

w2a     endp

b2a     proc    near            ; convert byte to hex ASCII
                                ; call with AL = binary value
                                ;           DI = addr for string
                                ; returns  AX, DI, CX modified

        sub     ah,ah           ; clear upper byte
        mov     cl,16
        div     cl              ; divide byte by 16
        call    ascii           ; quotient becomes the first
        stosb                   ; ASCII character
        mov     al,ah
        call    ascii           ; remainder becomes the
        stosb                   ; second ASCII character
        ret

b2a     endp

ascii   proc    near            ; convert value 0-0fh in AL
                                ; into "hex ASCII" character

        add     al,'0'          ; offset to range 0-9
        cmp     al,'9'          ; is it > 9?
        jle     ascii2          ; no, jump
        add     al,'A'-'9'-1    ; offset to range A-F,

ascii2: ret                     ; return AL = ASCII char

ascii   endp

argc    proc    near            ; count command-line arguments
                                ; call with ES:BX = command line
                                ; returns  AX = argument count
```

(continued)

Figure 8-10. *continued*

```
        push    bx              ; save original BX and CX
        push    cx              ; for later
        mov     ax,1            ; force count >= 1

argc1:  mov     cx,-1           ; set flag = outside argument

argc2:  inc     bx              ; point to next character
        cmp     byte ptr es:[bx],cr
        je      argc3           ; exit if carriage return
        cmp     byte ptr es:[bx],blank
        je      argc1           ; outside argument if ASCII blank
        cmp     byte ptr es:[bx],tab
        je      argc1           ; outside argument if ASCII tab

                                ; otherwise not blank or tab,
        jcxz    argc2           ; jump if already inside argument

        inc     ax              ; else found argument, count it
        not     cx              ; set flag = inside argument
        jmp     argc2           ; and look at next character

argc3:  pop     cx              ; restore original BX and CX
        pop     bx
        ret                     ; return AX = argument count

argc    endp


argv    proc    near            ; get address & length of
                                ; command line argument
                                ; call with ES:BX = command line
                                ;           AX   = argument #
                                ; returns   ES:BX = address
                                ;           AX   = length

        push    cx              ; save original CX and DI
        push    di

        or      ax,ax           ; is it argument 0?
        jz      argv8           ; yes, jump to get program name

        xor     ah,ah           ; initialize argument counter

argv1:  mov     cx,-1           ; set flag = outside argument
```

(continued)

Figure 8-10. *continued*

```
argv2:  inc     bx                   ; point to next character
        cmp     byte ptr es:[bx],cr
        je      argv7                ; exit if carriage return
        cmp     byte ptr es:[bx],blank
        je      argv1                ; outside argument if ASCII blank
        cmp     byte ptr es:[bx],tab
        je      argv1                ; outside argument if ASCII tab

                                     ; if not blank or tab...
        jcxz    argv2                ; jump if already inside argument

        inc     ah                   ; else count arguments found
        cmp     ah,al                ; is this the one we're looking for?
        je      argv4                ; yes, go find its length
        not     cx                   ; no, set flag = inside argument
        jmp     argv2                ; and look at next character

argv4:                               ; found desired argument, now
                                     ; determine its length...
        mov     ax,bx                ; save param starting address

argv5:  inc     bx                   ; point to next character
        cmp     byte ptr es:[bx],cr
        je      argv6                ; found end if carriage return
        cmp     byte ptr es:[bx],blank
        je      argv6                ; found end if ASCII blank
        cmp     byte ptr es:[bx],tab
        jne     argv5                ; found end if ASCII tab

argv6:  xchg    bx,ax                ; set ES:BX = argument address
        sub     ax,bx                ; and AX = argument length
        jmp     argvx                ; return to caller

argv7:  xor     ax,ax                ; set AX = 0, argument not found
        jmp     argvx                ; return to caller

argv8:                               ; special handling for argv = 0
        mov     ax,3000h             ; check if DOS 3.0 or later
        int     21h                  ; (force AL = 0 in case DOS 1)
        cmp     al,3
        jb      argv7                ; DOS 1 or 2, return null param
        mov     es,es:[2ch]          ; get environment segment from PSP
        xor     di,di                ; find the program name by
        xor     al,al                ; first skipping over all the
        mov     cx,-1                ; environment variables...
        cld
```

(continued)

Figure 8-10. *continued*

```
argv9:  repne scasb             ; scan for double null (can't use
        scasb                   ; SCASW since might be odd addr)
        jne    argv9            ; loop if it was a single null
        add    di,2             ; skip count word in environment
        mov    bx,di            ; save program name address
        mov    cx,-1            ; now find its length...
        repne scasb             ; scan for another null byte
        not    cx               ; convert CX to length
        dec    cx
        mov    ax,cx            ; return length in AX

argvx:                          ; common exit point
        pop    di               ; restore original CX and DI
        pop    cx
        ret                     ; return to caller


argv    endp


_TEXT   ends


_DATA   segment word public 'DATA'


fname   db     64 dup (0)       ; buffer for input filespec

fhandle dw     0                ; token from PCDOS for input file

flen    dw     0                ; actual length read

fptr    dw     0                ; relative address in file

fbuff   db     blksize dup (?) ; data from input file

fout    db     'nnnn'           ; formatted output area
        db     blank,blank
fouta   db     16 dup ('nn',blank)
        db     blank
foutb   db     16 dup (blank),cr,lf
fout_len equ   $-fout

hdg     db     cr,lf            ; heading for each 128 bytes
        db     7 dup (blank)    ; of formatted output
        db     '0  1  2  3  4  5  6  7  '
        db     '8  9  A  B  C  D  E  F',cr,lf
hdg_len equ    $-hdg
```

(continued)

Figure 8-10. *continued*

```
msg1    db      cr,lf
        db      'dump: file not found'
        db      cr,lf
msg1_len equ    $-msg1

msg2    db      cr,lf
        db      'dump: missing file name'
        db      cr,lf
msg2_len equ    $-msg2

msg3    db      cr,lf
        db      'dump: wrong MS-DOS version'
        db      cr,lf,'$'

msg4    db      cr,lf
        db      'dump: empty file'
        db      cr,lf
msg4_len equ    $-msg4

_DATA   ends

STACK   segment para stack 'STACK'

        db      64 dup (?)

STACK   ends

        end     dump
```

```
/*
    DUMP.C      Displays the binary contents of a file in
                hex and ASCII on the standard output device.

    Compile:    C>CL DUMP.C

    Usage:      C>DUMP unit:path\filename.ext

    Copyright (C) 1988 Ray Duncan
*/

#include <stdio.h>
#include <io.h>
#include <fcntl.h>
```

Figure 8-11. *The C version:* DUMP.C. *(continued)*

Figure 8-11. *continued*

```
#define REC_SIZE 16                    /* input file record size    */

main(int argc, char *argv[])
{
    int fd;                            /* input file handle         */
      int status = 0;                  /* status from file read     */
    long fileptr = 0L;                 /* current file byte offset  */
    char filebuf[REC_SIZE];            /* data from file            */

    if(argc != 2)                      /* abort if missing filename */
    {   fprintf(stderr,"\ndump: wrong number of parameters\n");
        exit(1);
    }

                                       /* open file in binary mode,
                                          abort if open fails       */
    if((fd = open(argv[1],O_RDONLY | O_BINARY) ) == -1)
    {   fprintf(stderr, "\ndump: can't find file %s \n", argv[1]);
        exit(1);
    }

                                       /* read and dump records
                                          until end of file         */
    while((status = read(fd,filebuf,REC_SIZE) ) != 0)
    {   dump_rec(filebuf, fileptr, status);
        fileptr += REC_SIZE;
    }

    close(fd);                         /* close input file          */
    exit(0);                           /* return success code       */
}

/*
   Display record (16 bytes) in hex and ASCII on standard output
*/

dump_rec(char *filebuf, long fileptr, int length)
{
    int i;                             /* index to current record   */

    if(fileptr % 128 == 0)             /* display heading if needed */
        printf("\n\n      0 1 2 3 4 5 6 7 8 9 A B C D E F");

    printf("\n%041X ",fileptr);        /* display file offset       */

                                       /* display hex equivalent of
                                          each byte from file        */
```

(continued)

Figure 8-11. *continued*

```
for(i = 0; i < length; i++)
    printf(" %02X", (unsigned char) filebuf[i]);

if(length != 16)                    /* spaces if partial record */
    for (i=0; i<(16-length); i++) printf("   ");

                            /* display ASCII equivalent of
                                  each byte from file      */
printf("  ");
for(i = 0; i < length; i++)
{   if(filebuf[i] < 32 || filebuf[i] > 126) putchar('.');
    else putchar(filebuf[i]);
}
}
```

The assembly-language version of the *DUMP* program contains a number of subroutines that you may find useful in your own programming efforts. These include the following:

Subroutine	Action
argc	Returns the number of command-line arguments.
argv	Returns the address and length of a particular command-line argument.
w2a	Converts a binary word (16 bits) into hex ASCII for output.
b2a	Converts a binary byte (8 bits) into hex ASCII for output.
ascii	Converts 4 bits into a single hex ASCII character.

It is interesting to compare these two equivalent programs. The C program contains only 77 lines, whereas the assembly-language program has 436 lines. Clearly, the C source code is less complex and easier to maintain. On the other hand, if size and efficiency are important, the *DUMP.EXE* file generated by the C compiler is 8563 bytes, whereas the assembly-language *DUMP.EXE* file is only 1294 bytes and runs twice as fast as the C program.

Chapter 9

Volumes and Directories

Each file in an MS-DOS system is uniquely identified by its name and its location. The location, in turn, has two components: the logical drive that contains the file and the directory on that drive where the filename can be found.

Logical drives are specified by a single letter followed by a colon (for example, A:). The number of logical drives in a system is not necessarily the same as the number of physical drives; for example, it is common for large fixed-disk drives to be divided into two or more logical drives. The key aspect of a logical drive is that it contains a self-sufficient *file system;* that is, it contains one or more directories, zero or more complete files, and all the information needed to locate the files and directories and to determine which disk space is free and which is already in use.

Directories are simply lists or catalogs. Each entry in a directory consists of the name, size, starting location, attributes, and last modification date and time of a file or another directory that the disk contains. The detailed information about the location of every block of data assigned to a file or directory is in a separate control area on the disk called the file allocation table (FAT). (See Chapter 10 for a detailed discussion of the internal format of directories and the FAT.)

Every disk potentially has two distinct kinds of directories: the *root directory* and all other directories. The root directory is always present and has a maximum number of entries, determined when the disk is formatted; this number cannot be changed. The subdirectories of the root directory, which may or may not be present on a given disk, can be nested to any level and can grow to any size (Figure 9-1). This is the *hierarchical*, or tree, directory structure referred to in earlier chapters. Every directory has a name, except for the root directory, which is designated by a single backslash (\) character.

MS-DOS keeps track of a "current drive" for the system and uses this drive when a file specification does not include an explicit drive code. Similarly, MS-DOS maintains a "current directory" for each logical drive. You can select any particular directory on a drive by naming in order—either from the root directory or relative to the current directory—the directories that lead to its location in the tree structure. Such a list of directories, separated by backslash delimiters, is called a *path*. When a complete path from the root directory is prefixed by a logical drive code and followed by a filename and extension, the resulting string is a *fully qualified filename* and unambiguously specifies a file.

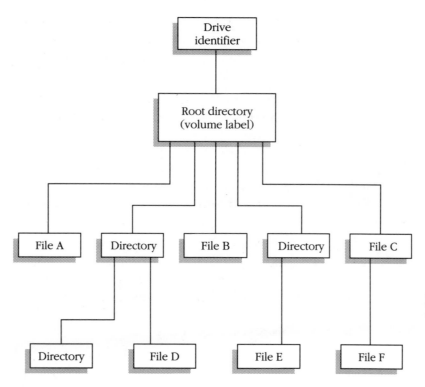

Figure 9-1. *An MS-DOS file-system structure.*

Drive and Directory Control

You can examine, select, create, and delete disk directories interactively with the DIR, CHDIR (CD), MKDIR (MD), and RMDIR (RD) commands. You can select a new current drive by entering the letter of the desired drive, followed by a colon. MS-DOS provides the following Int 21H functions to give application programs similar control over drives and directories:

Function	Action
0EH	Select current drive.
19H	Get current drive.
39H	Create directory.
3AH	Remove directory.
3BH	Select current directory.
47H	Get current directory.

The two functions that deal with disk drives accept or return a binary drive code—0 represents drive A, 1 represents drive B, and so on. This differs from most other MS-DOS functions, which use 0 to indicate the current drive, 1 for drive A, and so on.

The first three directory functions in the preceding list require an ASCIIZ string that describes the path to the desired directory. As with the handle-based file open and create functions, the address of the ASCIIZ string is passed in the DS:DX registers. On return, the carry flag is clear if the function succeeds or set if the function failed, with an error code in the AX register. The directory functions can fail for a variety of reasons, but the most common cause of an error is that some element of the indicated path does not exist.

The last function in the preceding list, Int 21H Function 47H, allows you to obtain an ASCIIZ path for the current directory on the specified or default drive. MS-DOS supplies the path string without the drive identifier or a leading backslash. Int 21H Function 47H is most commonly used with Int 21H Function 19H to build fully qualified filenames. Such filenames are desirable because they remain valid if the user changes the current drive or directory.

Section II of this book, "MS-DOS Functions Reference," gives detailed information on the drive and directory control functions.

Searching Directories

When you request an open operation on a file, you are implicitly performing a search of a directory. MS-DOS examines each entry of the directory to find a match for the filename you have given as an argument; if the file is found, MS-DOS copies certain information from the directory into a data structure that it can use to control subsequent read or write operations to the file. Thus, if you wish to test for the existence of a specific file, you need only perform an open operation and observe whether it is successful. (If it is, you should, of course, perform a subsequent close operation to avoid needless expenditure of handles.)

Sometimes you may need to perform more elaborate searches of a disk directory. Perhaps you wish to find all the files with a certain extension, a file with a particular attribute, or the names of the subdirectories of a certain directory. Although the locations of a disk's directories and the specifics of the entries that are found in them are of necessity hardware dependent (for example, interpretation of the field describing the starting location of a file depends upon the physical disk format), MS-DOS does provide functions that will allow examination of a disk directory in a hardware-independent fashion.

In order to search a disk directory successfully, you must understand two types of MS-DOS search services. The first type is the "search for first" function, which accepts a file specification—possibly including wildcard characters—and looks for the first matching file in the directory of interest. If it finds a match, the function fills a buffer owned by the requesting program with information about the file; if it does not find a match, it returns an error flag.

A program can call the second type of search service, called "search for next," only after a successful "search for first." If the file specification that was originally passed to "search for first" included wildcard characters and at least one matching file was present, the program can call "search for next" as many times as necessary to find all additional matching files. Like "search for first," "search for next" returns information about the matched files in a buffer designated by the requesting program. When it can find no more matching files, "search for next" returns an error flag.

As with nearly every other operation, MS-DOS provides two parallel sets of directory-searching services:

Action	FCB function	Handle function
Search for first	11H	4EH
Search for next	12H	4FH

The FCB directory functions allow searches to match a filename and extension, both possibly containing wildcard characters, within the current directory for the specified or current drive. The handle directory functions, on the other hand, allow a program to perform searches within any directory on any drive, regardless of the current directory.

Searches that use normal FCBs find only normal files. Searches that use extended FCBs, or the handle-type functions, can be qualified with file attributes. The attribute bits relevant to searches are as follows:

Bit	Significance
0	Read-only file
1	Hidden file
2	System file
3	Volume label
4	Directory
5	Archive needed (set when file modified)

The remaining bits of a search function's attribute parameter should be zero. When any of the preceding attribute bits are set, the search function returns all normal files plus any files with the specified attributes, except in the case of the volume-label attribute bit, which receives special treatment as described later in this chapter. Note that by setting bit 4 you can include directories in a search, exactly as though they were files.

Both the FCB and handle directory-searching functions require that the disk transfer area address be set (with Int 21H Function 1AH), *before* the call to "search for first," to point to a working buffer for use by MS-DOS. The DTA address should not be changed between calls to "search for first" and "search for next." When it finds a matching file, MS-DOS places the information about the file in the buffer and then inspects the buffer on the next "search for next" call, to determine where to resume the search. The format of the data returned in the buffer is different for the FCB and handle functions, so read the detailed descriptions in Section II of this book, "MS-DOS Functions Reference," before attempting to interpret the buffer contents.

Figures 9-2 and 9-3 provide equivalent examples of searches for all files in a given directory that have the .ASM extension, one example using the FCB directory functions (Int 21H Functions 11H and 12H) and the other using the handle functions (Int 21H Functions 4EH and 4FH). (Both programs use the handle write function with the standard output handle to display the matched filenames, to avoid introducing tangential differences in the listings.)

```
start:                              ; set DTA address for buffer
                                    ; used by search functions
        mov     dx,seg buff         ; DS:DX = buffer address
        mov     ds,dx
        mov     dx,offset buff
        mov     ah,1ah              ; function 1ah = search for first
        int     21h                 ; transfer to MS-DOS
```

(continued)

Figure 9-2. *Example of an FCB-type directory search using Int 21H Functions 11H and 12H. This routine displays the names of all files in the current directory that have the .ASM extension.*

Figure 9-2. *(continued)*

```
                                ; search for first match...
        mov     dx,offset fcb   ; DS:DX = FCB address
        mov     ah,11h          ; function 11h = search for first
        int     21h             ; transfer to MS-DOS
        or      al,al           ; any matches at all?
        jnz     exit            ; no, quit

disp:                           ; go to a new line...
        mov     dx,offset crlf  ; DS:DX = CR-LF string
        mov     cx,2            ; CX = string length
        mov     bx,1            ; BX = standard output handle
        mov     ah,40h          ; function 40h = write
        int     21h             ; transfer to MS-DOS

                                ; display matching file
        mov     dx,offset buff+1 ; DS:DX = filename
        mov     cx,11           ; CX = length
        mov     bx,1            ; BX = standard output handle
        mov     ah,40h          ; function 40h = write
        int     21h             ; transfer to MS-DOS

                                ; search for next match...
        mov     dx,offset fcb   ; DS:DX = FCB address
        mov     ah,12h          ; function 12h = search for next
        int     21h             ; transfer to MS-DOS
        or      al,al           ; any more matches?
        jz      disp            ; yes, go show filename

exit:                           ; final exit point
        mov     ax,4c00h        ; function 4ch = terminate,
                                ; return code = 0
        int     21h             ; transfer to MS-DOS

        .
        .
        .


crlf    db      0dh,0ah         ; ASCII carriage return-
                                ; linefeed string

fcb     db      0               ; drive = current
        db      8 dup ('?')     ; filename = wildcard
        db      'ASM'           ; extension = ASM
        db      25 dup (0)      ; remainder of FCB = zero

buff    db      64 dup (0)      ; receives search results
```

```
start:                              ; set DTA address for buffer
                                    ; used by search functions
        mov     dx,seg buff         ; DS:DX = buffer address
        mov     ds,dx
        mov     dx,offset buff
        mov     ah,1ah              ; function 1ah = search for first
        int     21h                 ; transfer to MS-DOS


                                    ; search for first match...
        mov     dx,offset fname     ; DS:DX = wildcard filename
        mov     cx,0                ; CX = normal file attribute
        mov     ah,4eh              ; function 4eh = search for first
        int     21h                 ; transfer to MS-DOS
        jc      exit                ; quit if no matches at all

disp:                               ; go to a new line...
        mov     dx,offset crlf      ; DS:DX = CR-LF string
        mov     cx,2                ; CX = string length
        mov     bx,1                ; BX = standard output handle
        mov     ah,40h              ; function 40h = write
        int     21h                 ; transfer to MS-DOS
                                    ; find length of filename...
        mov     cx,0                ; CX will be char count
                                    ; DS:SI = start of name
        mov     si,offset buff+30

disp1:  lodsb                       ; get next character
        or      al,al               ; is it null character?
        jz      disp2               ; yes, found end of string
        inc     cx                  ; else count characters
        jmp     disp1               ; and get another

disp2:                              ; display matching file...
                                    ; CX already contains length
                                    ; DS:DX = filename
        mov     dx,offset buff+30
        mov     bx,1                ; BX = standard output handle
        mov     ah,40h              ; function 40h = write
        int     21h                 ; transfer to MS-DOS
```

(continued)

Figure 9-3. *Example of a handle-type directory search using Int 21H Functions 4EH and 4FH. This routine also displays the names of all files in the current directory that have a .ASM extension.*

Figure 9-3. *(continued)*

```
                                     ; find next matching file...
          mov     ah,4fh           ; function 4fh = search for next
          int     21h              ; transfer to MS-DOS
          jnc     disp             ; jump if another match found

exit:                              ; final exit point
          mov     ax,4c00h         ; function 4ch = terminate,
                                   ; return code = 0
          int     21h              ; transfer to MS-DOS

                .
                .
                .

crlf      db      0dh,0ah          ; ASCII carriage return-
                                   ; linefeed string

fname     db      '*.ASM',0        ; ASCIIZ filename to
                                   ; be matched

buff      db      64 dup (0)       ; receives search results
```

Moving Files

The rename file function that was added in MS-DOS version 2.0, Int 21H Function 56H, has the little-advertised capability to move a file from one directory to another. The function has two ASCIIZ parameters: the "old" and "new" names for the file. If the old and new paths differ, MS-DOS moves the file; if the filename or extension components differ, MS-DOS renames the file. MS-DOS can carry out both of these actions in the same function call.

Of course, the old and new directories must be on the same drive, because the file's actual data is not moved at all; only the information that *describes* the file is removed from one directory and placed in another directory. Function 56H fails if the two ASCIIZ strings include different logical-drive codes, if the file is read-only, or if a file with the same name and location as the "new" filename already exists.

The FCB-based rename file service, Int 21H Function 17H, works only on the current directory and cannot be used to move files.

Volume Labels

Support for volume labels was first added to MS-DOS in version 2.0. A volume label is an optional name of from 1 to 11 characters that the user assigns to a disk during a FORMAT operation. You can display a volume label with the DIR, TREE, CHKDSK, or VOL command. Beginning with MS-DOS version 3.0, you can use the LABEL command to add, display, or alter the label after formatting. In MS-DOS version 4, the FORMAT program also assigns a semi-random 32-bit binary ID to each disk it formats; you can display this value, but you cannot change it.

The distinction between volumes and drives is important. A volume label is associated with a specific storage medium. A drive identifier (such as A) is associated with a physical device that a storage medium can be mounted on. In the case of fixed-disk drives, the medium associated with a drive identifier does not change (hence the name). In the case of floppy disks or other removable media, the disk accessed with a given drive identifier might have any volume label or none at all.

Hence, volume labels do not take the place of the logical-drive identifier and cannot be used as part of a pathname to identify a file. In fact, in MS-DOS version 2, the system does not use volume labels internally at all. In MS-DOS versions 3.0 and later, a disk driver can use volume labels to detect whether the user has replaced a disk while a file is open; this use is optional, however, and is not implemented in all systems.

MS-DOS volume labels are implemented as a special type of entry in a disk's root directory. The entry contains a time-and-date stamp and has an attribute value of 8 (i.e., bit 3 set). Except for the attribute, a volume label is identical to the directory entry for a file that was created but never had any data written into it, and you can manipulate volume labels with Int 21H functions much as you manipulate files. However, a volume label receives special handling at several levels:

- When you create a volume label after a disk is formatted, MS-DOS always places it in the root directory, regardless of the current directory.

- A disk can contain only one volume label; attempts to create additional volume labels (even with different names) will fail.

- MS-DOS always carries out searches for volume labels in the root directory, regardless of the current directory, and does not also return all normal files.

In MS-DOS version 2, support for volume labels is not completely integrated into the handle file functions, and you must use extended FCBs instead to manipulate volume labels. For example, the code in Figure 9-4 searches for the volume label in the root directory of the current drive. You can also change volume labels with extended FCBs and the rename file function (Int 21H Function 17H), but you should not attempt to remove an existing volume label with Int 21H Function 13H under MS-DOS version 2, because this operation can damage the disk's FAT in an unpredictable manner.

In MS-DOS versions 3.0 and later, you can create a volume label in the expected manner, using Int 21H Function 3CH and an attribute of 8, and you can use the handle-type "search for first" function (4EH) to obtain an existing volume label for a logical drive (Figure 9-5). However, you still must use extended FCBs to change a volume label.

```
buff      db      64 dup (?)    ; receives search results

xfcb      db      0ffh          ; flag signifying extended FCB
          db      5 dup (0)     ; reserved
          db      8             ; volume attribute byte
          db      0             ; drive code (0 = current)
          db      11 dup ('?')  ; wildcard filename and extension
          db      25 dup (0)    ; remainder of FCB (not used)
          .
          .
          .
                                ; set DTA address for buffer
                                ; used by search functions
          mov     dx,seg buff   ; DS:DX = buffer address
          mov     ds,dx
          mov     dx,offset buff
          mov     ah,1ah        ; function 1ah = set DTA
          int     21h           ; transfer to MS-DOS

                                ; now search for label...
                                ; DS:DX = extended FCB
          mov     dx,offset xfcb
          mov     ah,11h        ; function 11h = search for first
          int     21h           ; transfer to MS-DOS
          cmp     al,0ffh       ; search successful?
          je      no_label      ; jump if no volume label
          .
          .
          .
```

Figure 9-4. *A volume-label search under MS-DOS version 2, using an extended file control block. If the search is successful, the volume label is returned in* buff, *formatted in the filename and extension fields of an extended FCB.*

```
buff      db      64 dup (?)      ; receives search results

wildcd    db      '*.*',0         ; wildcard ASCIIZ filename
          .
          .
          .
                                  ; set DTA address for buffer
                                  ; used by search functions
          mov     dx,seg buff     ; DS:DX = buffer address
          mov     ds,dx
          mov     dx,offset buff
          mov     ah,1ah          ; function 1ah = set DTA
          int     21h             ; transfer to MS-DOS

                                  ; now search for label...
                                  ; DS:DX = ASCIIZ string
          mov     dx,offset wildcd
          mov     cx,8            ; CX = volume attribute
          mov     ah,4eh          ; function 4eh = search for first
          int     21h             ; transfer to MS-DOS
          jc      no_label        ; jump if no volume label
          .
          .
          .
```

Figure 9-5. *A volume-label search under MS-DOS version 3, using the handle-type file functions. If the search is successful (carry flag returned clear), the volume name is placed at location* buff+1EH *in the form of an ASCIIZ string.*

Chapter 10

Disk Internals

MS-DOS disks are organized according to a rather rigid scheme that is easily understood and therefore easily manipulated. Although you will probably never need to access the special control areas of a disk directly, an understanding of their internal structure leads to a better understanding of the behavior and performance of MS-DOS as a whole.

From the application programmer's viewpoint, MS-DOS presents disk devices as logical volumes that are associated with a drive code (A, B, C, and so on) and that have a volume name (optional), a root directory, and from zero to many additional directories and files. MS-DOS shields the programmer from the physical characteristics of the medium by providing a battery of disk services through Int 21H. Using these services, the programmer can create, open, read, write, close, and delete files in a uniform way, regardless of the disk drive's size, speed, number of read/write heads, number of tracks, and so forth.

Requests from an application program for file operations actually go through two levels of translation before resulting in the physical transfer of data between the disk device and random-access memory:

1. Beneath the surface, MS-DOS views each logical volume, whether it is an entire physical unit such as a floppy disk or only a part of a fixed disk, as a continuous sequence of logical sectors, starting at sector 0. (A logical disk volume can also be implemented on other types of storage. For example, RAM disks map a disk structure onto an area of random-access memory.) MS-DOS translates an application program's Int 21H file-management requests into requests for transfers of logical sectors, using the information found in the volume's directories and allocation tables. (For those rare situations where it is appropriate, programs can also access logical sectors directly with Int 25H and Int 26H.)

2. MS-DOS then passes the requests for logical sectors to the disk device's driver, which maps them onto actual physical addresses (head, track, and sector). Disk drivers are extremely hardware dependent and are always written in assembly language for maximum speed. In most versions of MS-DOS, a driver for IBM-compatible floppy- and fixed-disk drives is built into the MS-DOS BIOS module (IO.SYS) and is always loaded during system initialization; you can install additional drivers for non-IBM-compatible disk devices by including the appropriate DEVICE directives in the CONFIG.SYS file.

Each MS-DOS logical volume is divided into several fixed-size control areas and a files area (Figure 10-1). The size of each control area depends on several factors—the size of the volume and the version of FORMAT used to initialize the volume, for example—but all of the information

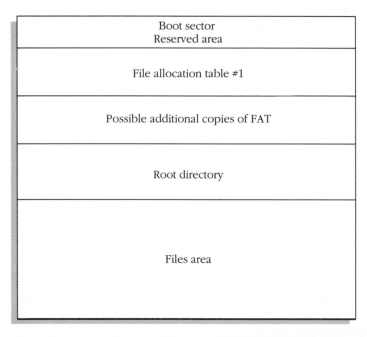

+--+
| Boot sector |
| Reserved area |
+--+
| File allocation table #1 |
+--+
| Possible additional copies of FAT |
+--+
| Root directory |
+--+
| |
| |
| Files area |
| |
| |
+--+

Figure 10-1. *Map of a typical MS-DOS logical volume. The boot sector (logical sector 0) contains the OEM identification, BIOS parameter block (BPB), and disk bootstrap. The remaining sectors are divided among an optional reserved area, one or more copies of the file allocation table, the root directory, and the files area.*

needed to interpret the structure of a particular logical volume can be found *on the volume itself* in the boot sector.

The Boot Sector

Logical sector 0, known as the *boot sector*, contains all of the critical information regarding the disk medium's characteristics (Figure 10-2). The first byte in the sector is always an 80x86 jump instruction—either a normal intrasegment JMP (opcode 0E9H) followed by a 16-bit displacement or a "short" JMP (opcode 0EBH) followed by an 8-bit displacement and then by an NOP (opcode 90H). If neither of these two JMP opcodes is present, the disk has not been formatted or was not formatted for use with MS-DOS. (Of course, the presence of the JMP opcode does not in itself ensure that the disk has an MS-DOS format.)

Following the initial JMP instruction is an 8-byte field that is reserved by Microsoft for OEM identification. The disk-formatting program, which is specialized for each brand of computer, disk controller, and medium, fills in this area with the name of the computer manufacturer and the manufacturer's internal MS-DOS version number.

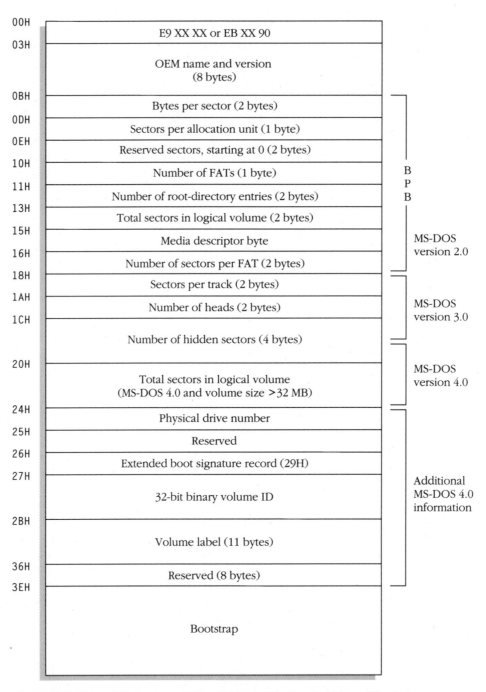

Figure 10-2. *Map of the boot sector of an MS-DOS disk. Note the JMP at offset 0, the OEM identification field, the MS-DOS version 2 compatible BIOS parameter block (bytes 0BH–17H), the three additional WORD fields for MS-DOS version 3, the double-word number-of-sectors field and 32-bit binary volume ID for MS-DOS version 4.0, and the bootstrap code.*

The third major component of the boot sector is the BIOS parameter block (BPB) in bytes 0BH through 17H. (Additional fields are present in MS-DOS versions 3.0 and later.) This data structure describes the physical disk characteristics and allows the device driver to calculate the proper physical disk address for a given logical-sector number; it also contains information that is used by MS-DOS and various system utilities to calculate the address and size of each of the disk control areas (file allocation tables and root directory).

The final element of the boot sector is the disk bootstrap routine. The disk bootstrap is usually read into memory by the ROM bootstrap, which is executed automatically when the computer is turned on. The ROM bootstrap is usually just smart enough to home the head of the disk drive (move it to track 0), read the first physical sector into RAM at a predetermined location, and jump to it. The disk bootstrap is more sophisticated. It calculates the physical disk address of the beginning of the files area, reads the files containing the operating system into memory, and transfers control to the BIOS module at location 0070:0000H. (See Chapter 2.)

Figures 10-3 and 10-4 show a partial hex dump and disassembly of a PC-DOS 3.3 floppy-disk boot sector.

```
        0  1  2  3  4  5  6  7  8  9  A  B  C  D  E  F
0000  EB 34 90 49 42 4D 20 20 33 2E 33 00 02 02 01 00   .4.IBM  3.3.....
0010  02 70 00 D0 02 FD 02 00 09 00 02 00 00 00 00 00   .p..............
0020  00 00 00 00 00 00 00 00 00 00 00 00 00 00 00 12   ...............
0030  00 00 00 00 01 00 FA 33 C0 8E D0 BC 00 7C 16 07   .......3.....|..
          .
          .
          .
01C0  0D 0A 44 69 73 6B 20 42 6F 6F 74 20 66 61 69 6C   ..Disk Boot fail
01D0  75 72 65 0D 0A 00 49 42 4D 42 49 4F 20 20 43 4F   ure...IBMBIO  CO
01E0  4D 49 42 4D 44 4F 53 20 20 43 4F 4D 00 00 00 00   MIBMDOS  COM....
01F0  00 00 00 00 00 00 00 00 00 00 00 00 00 00 55 AA   ..............U.
```

Figure 10-3. *Partial hex dump of the boot sector (track 0, head 0, sector 1) of a PC-DOS version 3.3 floppy disk. This sector contains the OEM identification, a copy of the BIOS parameter block describing the medium, and the bootstrap routine that reads the BIOS into memory and transfers control to it. See also Figures 10-2 and 10-4.*

```
        jmp     $+54            ; jump to bootstrap
        nop

        db      'IBM  3.3'      ; OEM identification

                                ; BIOS parameter block
        dw      512             ; bytes per sector
        db      2               ; sectors per cluster
        dw      1               ; reserved sectors
        db      2               ; number of FATs
        dw      112             ; root directory entries
        dw      720             ; total sectors
        db      0fdh            ; media descriptor byte
        dw      2               ; sectors per FAT

        dw      9               ; sectors per track
        dw      2               ; number of heads
        dd      0               ; hidden sectors
        .
        .
        .
```

Figure 10-4. *Partial disassembly of the boot sector shown in Figure 10-3.*

The Reserved Area

The boot sector is actually part of a *reserved area* that can span from one to several sectors. The reserved-sectors word in the BPB, at offset 0EH in the boot sector, describes the size of this area. Remember that the number in the BPB field includes the boot sector itself, so if the value is 1 (as it is on IBM PC floppy disks), the length of the reserved area is actually 0 sectors.

The File Allocation Table

When a file is created or extended, MS-DOS assigns it groups of disk sectors from the files area in powers of 2. These are known as *allocation units* or *clusters*. The number of sectors per cluster for a given medium is defined in the BPB and can be found at offset 0DH in the disk's boot sector. Below are some example cluster sizes:

Disk type	Power of 2	Sectors/cluster
5.25" 180 KB floppy disk	0	1
5.25" 360 KB floppy disk	1	2
PC/AT fixed disk	2	4
PC/XT fixed disk	3	8

The *file allocation table* (FAT) is divided into fields that correspond directly to the assignable clusters on the disk. These fields are 12 bits in MS-DOS versions 1 and 2 and may be either 12 bits or 16 bits in versions 3.0 and later, depending on the size of the medium (12 bits if the disk contains fewer than 4087 clusters, 16 bits otherwise).

The first two fields in the FAT are always reserved. On IBM-compatible media, the first 8 bits of the first reserved FAT entry contain a copy of the media descriptor byte, which is also found in the BPB in the boot sector. The second, third, and (if applicable) fourth bytes, which constitute the remainder of the first two reserved FAT fields, always contain 0FFH. The currently defined IBM-format media descriptor bytes are as follows:

Descriptor	Medium	MS-DOS version where first supported
0F0H	3.5" floppy disk, 2-sided, 18-sector	3.3
0F8H	Fixed disk	2.0
0F9H	5.25" floppy disk, 2-sided, 15-sector	3.0
	3.5" floppy disk, 2-sided, 9-sector	3.2
0FCH	5.25" floppy disk, 1-sided, 9-sector	2.0
0FDH	5.25" floppy disk, 2-sided, 9-sector	2.0
	8" floppy disk, 1-sided, single-density	
0FEH	5.25" floppy disk, 1-sided, 8-sector	1.0
	8" floppy disk, 1-sided, single-density	
	8" floppy disk, 2-sided, double-density	
0FFH	5.25" floppy disk, 2-sided, 8-sector	1.1

The remainder of the FAT entries describe the use of their corresponding disk clusters. The contents of the FAT fields are interpreted as follows:

Value	Meaning
(0)000H	Cluster available
(F)FF0–(F)FF6H	Reserved cluster
(F)FF7H	Bad cluster, if not part of chain
(F)FF8–(F)FFFH	Last cluster of file
(X)XXX	Next cluster in file

Each file's entry in a directory contains the number of the first cluster assigned to that file, which is used as an entry point into the FAT. From the entry point on, each FAT slot contains the cluster number of the next cluster in the file, until a last-cluster mark is encountered.

At the computer manufacturer's option, MS-DOS can maintain two or more identical copies of the FAT on each volume. MS-DOS updates all copies simultaneously whenever files are extended or the directory is modified. If access to a sector in a FAT fails due to a read error, MS-DOS tries the other copies until a successful disk read is obtained or all copies are exhausted. Thus, if one copy of the FAT becomes unreadable due to wear or a software accident, the other copies may still make it possible to salvage the files on the disk. As part of its procedure for checking the integrity of a disk, the CHKDSK program compares the multiple copies (usually two) of the FAT to make sure they are all readable and consistent.

The Root Directory

Following the file allocation tables is an area known in MS-DOS versions 2.0 and later as the *root directory*. (Under MS-DOS version 1, it was the only directory on the disk.) The root directory contains 32-byte entries that describe files, other directories, and the optional volume label (Figure 10-5). An entry beginning with the byte value E5H is available for reuse; it represents a file or directory that has been erased. An entry beginning with a null (zero) byte is the logical end-of-directory; that entry and all subsequent entries have never been used.

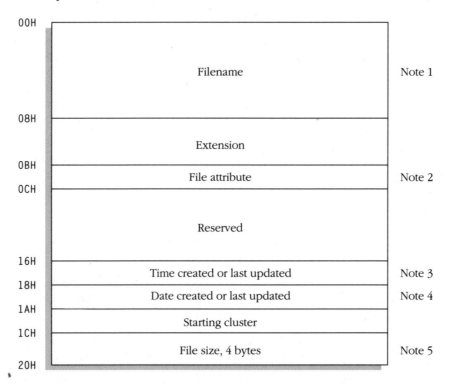

Figure 10-5. *Format of a single entry in a disk directory. Total length is 32 bytes (20H bytes).*

Notes for Figure 10-5

1. The first byte of the filename field of a directory entry may contain the following special information:

Value	Meaning
00H	Directory entry has never been used; end of occupied portion of directory.
05H	First character of filename is actually E5H.
2EH	Entry is an alias for the current or parent directory. If the next byte is also 2EH, the cluster field contains the cluster number of the parent directory (zero if the parent directory is the root directory).
E5H	File has been erased.

2. The attribute byte of the directory entry is mapped as follows:

Bit	Meaning
0	Read-only; attempts to open file for write or to delete file will fail.
1	Hidden file; excluded from normal searches.
2	System file; excluded from normal searches.
3	Volume label; can exist only in root directory.
4	Directory; excluded from normal searches.
5	Archive bit; set whenever file is modified.
6	Reserved.
7	Reserved.

3. The time field is encoded as follows:

Bits	Contents
00H–04H	Binary number of 2-second increments (0–29, corresponding to 0–58 seconds)
05H–0AH	Binary number of minutes (0–59)
0BH–0FH	Binary number of hours (0–23)

4. The date field is encoded as follows:

Bits	Contents
00H–04H	Day of month (1–31)
05H–08H	Month (1–12)
09H–0FH	Year (relative to 1980)

5. The file-size field is interpreted as a 4-byte integer, with the low-order 2 bytes of the number stored first.

The root directory has a number of special properties. Its size and position are fixed and are determined by the FORMAT program when a disk is initialized. This information can be obtained from the boot sector's BPB. If the disk is bootable, the first two entries in the root directory always describe the files containing the MS-DOS BIOS and the MS-DOS kernel. The disk bootstrap routine uses these entries to bring the operating system into memory and start it up.

Figure 10-6 shows a partial hex dump of the first sector of the root directory on a bootable PC-DOS 3.3 floppy disk.

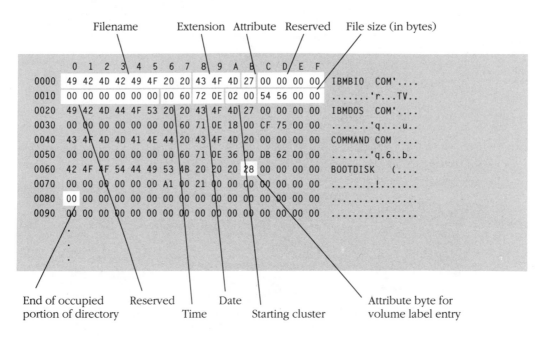

Figure 10-6. *Partial hex dump of the first sector of the root directory for a PC-DOS 3.3 disk containing the three system files and a volume label.*

The Files Area

The remainder of the volume after the root directory is known as the *files area*. MS-DOS views the sectors in this area as a pool of clusters, each containing one or more logical sectors, depending on the disk format. Each cluster has a corresponding entry in the FAT that describes its current use: available, reserved, assigned to a file, or unusable (because of defects in the medium). Because the first two fields of the FAT are reserved, the first cluster in the files area is assigned the number 2.

When a file is extended under versions 1 and 2, MS-DOS searches the FAT from the beginning until it finds a free cluster (designated by a zero FAT field); it then changes that FAT field to a last-cluster mark and updates the previous last cluster of the file's chain to point to the new last cluster. Under versions 3.0 and later, however, MS-DOS searches the FAT from the most recently allocated cluster; this reduces file fragmentation and improves overall access times.

Directories other than the root directory are simply a special type of file. Their storage is allocated from the files area, and their contents are 32-byte entries—in the same format as those used in the root directory—that describe files or other directories. Directory entries that describe other directories contain an attribute byte with bit 4 set, zero in the file-length field, and the date and time that the directory was created (Figure 10-7). The first cluster field points, of course, to the first cluster in the files area that belongs to the directory. (The directory's other clusters can be found only by tracing through the FAT.)

All directories except the root directory contain two special directory entries with the names . and ... MS-DOS puts these entries in place when it creates a directory, and they cannot be deleted. The . entry is an alias for the current directory; its cluster field points to the cluster in which it is

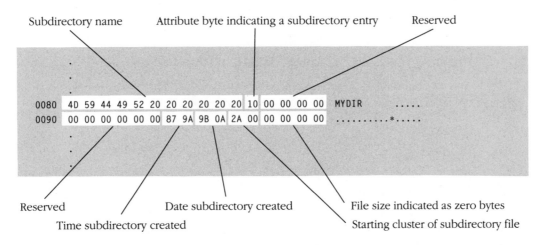

Figure 10-7. *Extract from the root directory of an MS-DOS disk, showing the entry for a subdirectory named* MYDIR. *Bit 4 in the attribute byte is set, the cluster field points to the first cluster of the subdirectory file, the date and time stamps are valid, but the file length is zero.*

found. The **..** entry is an alias for the directory's parent (the directory immediately above it in the tree structure); its cluster field points to the first cluster of the parent directory. If the parent is the root directory, the cluster field of the **..** entry contains zero (Figure 10-8).

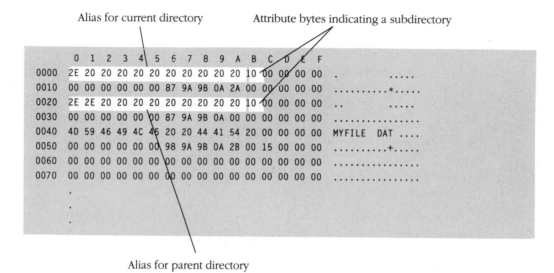

Alias for current directory   Attribute bytes indicating a subdirectory

Alias for parent directory

Figure 10-8. *Hex dump of the first block of the directory* MYDIR. *Note the* **.** *and* **..** *entries. This directory contains exactly one file,* MYFILE.DAT.

Interpreting the File Allocation Table

Now that we understand how the disk is structured, let's see how we can use this knowledge to find a FAT position from a cluster number.

If the FAT has 12-bit entries, use the following procedure:

1. Use the directory entry to find the starting cluster of the file in question.

2. Multiply the cluster number by 1.5.

3. Use the integral part of the product as the offset into the FAT and move the word at that offset into a register. Remember that a FAT position can span a physical disk-sector boundary.

4. If the product is a whole number, AND the register with 0FFFH.

5. Otherwise, "logical shift" the register right 4 bits.

6. If the result is a value from 0FF8H through 0FFFH, the file has no more clusters. Otherwise, the result is the number of the next cluster in the file.

On disks with at least 4087 clusters formatted under MS-DOS version 3.0 or later, the FAT entries use 16 bits, and the extraction of a cluster number from the table is much simpler:

1. Use the directory entry to find the starting cluster of the file in question.

2. Multiply the cluster number by 2.

3. Use the product as the offset into the FAT and move the word at that offset into a register.

4. If the result is a value from 0FFF8H through 0FFFFH, the file has no more clusters. Otherwise, the result is the number of the next cluster in the file.

To convert cluster numbers to logical sectors, subtract 2, multiply the result by the number of sectors per cluster, and add the logical-sector number of the beginning of the data area (this can be calculated from the information in the BPB).

As an example, let's work out the disk location of the file IBMBIO.COM, which is the first entry in the directory shown in Figure 10-6. First, we need some information from the BPB, which is in the boot sector of the medium. (See Figures 10-3 and 10-4.) The BPB tells us that there are

- 512 bytes per sector

- 2 sectors per cluster

- 2 sectors per FAT

- 2 FATs

- 112 entries in the root directory

From the BPB information, we can calculate the starting logical-sector number of each of the disk's control areas and the files area by constructing a table, as follows:

Area	Length (sectors)	Sector numbers
Boot sector	1	00H
2 FATs * 2 sectors/FAT	4	01H–04H
112 directory entries *32 bytes/entry / 512 bytes/sector	7	05H–0BH
Total sectors occupied by bootstrap, FATs, and root directory	12	

Therefore, the first sector of the files area is 12 (0CH).

The word at offset 01AH in the directory entry for IBMBIO.COM gives us the starting cluster number for that file: cluster 2. To find the logical-sector number of the first block in the file, we can follow the procedure given earlier:

1. Cluster number − 2 = 2 − 2 = 0.

2. Multiply by sectors per cluster = 0 ∗ 2 = 0.

3. Add logical-sector number of start of the files area = 0 + 0CH = 0CH.

So the calculated sector number of the beginning of the file IBMBIO.COM is 0CH, which is exactly what we expect knowing that the FORMAT program always places the system files in contiguous sectors at the beginning of the data area.

Now let's trace IBMBIO.COM's chain through the file allocation table (Figures 10-9 and 10-10). This will be a little tedious, but a detailed understanding of the process is crucial. In an actual program, we would first read the boot sector using Int 25H, then calculate the address of the FAT from the contents of the BPB, and finally read the FAT into memory, again using Int 25H.

From IBMBIO.COM's directory entry, we already know that the first cluster in the file is cluster 2. To examine that cluster's entry in the FAT, we multiply the cluster number by 1.5, which gives 0003H as the FAT offset, and fetch the word at that offset (which contains 4003H). Because the product of the cluster and 1.5 is a whole number, we AND the word from the FAT with 0FFFH, yielding the number 3, which is the number of the second cluster assigned to the file.

```
        0  1  2  3  4  5  6  7  8  9  A  B  C  D  E  F
0000   FD FF FF 03 40 00 05 60 00 07 80 00 09 A0 00 0B   ....@..'........
0010   C0 00 0D E0 00 0F 00 01 11 20 01 13 40 01 15 60   ......... ..@..'
0020   01 17 F0 FF 19 A0 01 1B C0 01 1D E0 01 1F 00 02   ................
0030   21 20 02 23 40 02 25 60 02 27 80 02 29 A0 02 2B   ! .#@.%'.'..)..+
   .
   .
   .
```

Figure 10-9. *Hex dump of the first block of the file allocation table (track 0, head 0, sector 2) for the PC-DOS 3.3 disk whose root directory is shown in Figure 10-6. Notice that the first byte of the FAT contains the media descriptor byte for a 5.25-inch, 2-sided, 9-sector floppy disk.*

```
getfat    proc      near        ; extracts the FAT field
                                 ; for a given cluster
                                 ; call    AX = cluster #
                                 ;         DS:BX = addr of FAT
                                 ; returns AX = FAT field
                                 ; other registers unchanged

          push      bx          ; save affected registers
          push      cx
          mov       cx,ax
          shl       ax,1        ; cluster * 2
          add       ax,cx       ; cluster * 3
          test      ax,1
          pushf                 ; save remainder in Z flag
          shr       ax,1        ; cluster * 1.5
          add       bx,ax
          mov       ax,[bx]
          popf                  ; was cluster * 1.5 whole number?
          jnz       getfat1     ; no, jump
          and       ax,0fffh    ; yes, isolate bottom 12 bits
          jmp       getfat2
getfat1:  mov       cx,4        ; shift word right 4 bits
          shr       ax,cx
getfat2:  pop       cx          ; restore registers and exit
          pop       bx
          ret
getfat    endp
```

Figure 10-10. *Assembly-language procedure to access the file allocation table
(assumes 12-bit FAT fields). Given a cluster number, the procedure returns the contents of that cluster's FAT entry in the AX register. This simple example ignores the fact
that FAT entries can span sector boundaries.*

To examine cluster 3's entry in the FAT, we multiply 3 by 1.5, which gives
4.5, and fetch the word at offset 0004H (which contains 0040H). Because
the product of 3 and 1.5 is not a whole number, we shift the word right
4 bits, yielding the number 4, which is the number of the third cluster
assigned to IBMBIO.COM.

In this manner, we can follow the chain through the FAT until we come to
a cluster (number 23, in this case) whose FAT entry contains the value
0FFFH, which is an end-of-file marker in FATs with 12-bit entries.

We have now established that the file IBMBIO.COM contains clusters 2
through 23 (02H–17H), from which we can calculate that logical sectors
0CH through 38H are assigned to the file. Of course, the last cluster may

be only partially filled with actual data; the portion of the last cluster used is the remainder of the file's size in bytes (found in the directory entry) divided by the bytes per cluster.

Fixed-Disk Partitions

Fixed disks have another layer of organization beyond the logical volume structure already discussed: *partitions*. The FDISK utility divides a fixed disk into one or more partitions consisting of an integral number of cylinders. Each partition can contain an independent file system and, for that matter, its own copy of an operating system.

The first physical sector on a fixed disk (track 0, head 0, sector 1) contains the *master boot record*, which is laid out as follows:

Bytes	Contents
000–1BDH	Reserved
1BE–1CDH	Partition #1 descriptor
1CE–1DDH	Partition #2 descriptor
1DE–1EDH	Partition #3 descriptor
1EE–1FDH	Partition #4 descriptor
1FE–1FFH	Signature word (AA55H)

The partition descriptors in the master boot record define the size, location, and type of each partition, as follows:

Byte(s)	Contents
00H	Active flag (0 = not bootable, 80H = bootable)
01H	Starting head
02H–03H	Starting cylinder/sector
04H	Partition type
	00H not used
	01H FAT file system, 12-bit FAT entries
	04H FAT file system, 16-bit FAT entries
	05H extended partition
	06H "huge partition" (MS-DOS versions 4.0 and later)
05H	Ending head
06H–07H	Ending cylinder/sector
08H–0BH	Starting sector for partition, relative to beginning of disk
0CH–0FH	Partition length in sectors

The active flag, which indicates that the partition is bootable, can be set on only one partition at a time.

MS-DOS treats partition types 1, 4, and 6 as normal logical volumes and assigns them their own drive identifiers during the system boot process. Partition type 5 can contain multiple logical volumes and has a special extended boot record that describes each volume. The FORMAT utility initializes MS-DOS fixed-disk partitions, creating the file system within the partition (boot record, file allocation table, root directory, and files area) and optionally placing a bootable copy of the operating system in the file system.

Figure 10-11 contains a partial hex dump of a master block from a fixed disk formatted under PC-DOS version 3.3. This dump illustrates the partition descriptors for a normal partition with a 16-bit FAT and an extended partition.

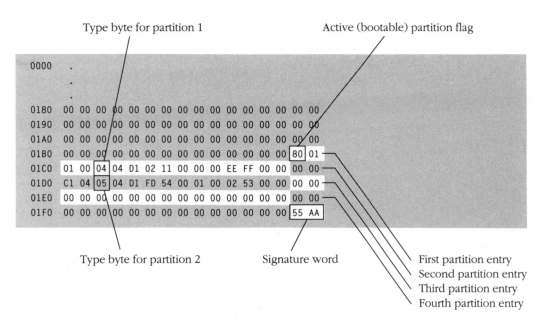

Figure 10-11. *A partial hex dump of a master block from a fixed disk formatted under PC-DOS version 3.3. This disk contains two partitions. The first partition has a 16-bit FAT and is marked "active" to indicate that it contains a bootable copy of PC-DOS. The second partition is an "extended" partition. The third and fourth partition entries are not used in this example.*

Chapter 11

Memory Management

Current versions of MS-DOS can manage as much as 1 megabyte of contiguous random-access memory. On IBM PCs and compatibles, the memory occupied by MS-DOS and other programs starts at address 0000H and may reach as high as address 09FFFFH; this 640 KB area of RAM is sometimes referred to as *conventional memory*. Memory above this address is reserved for ROM hardware drivers, video refresh buffers, and the like. Computers that are not IBM compatible may use other memory layouts.

The RAM area under the control of MS-DOS is divided into two major sections:

- The operating-system area

- The transient-program area

The operating-system area starts at address 0000H—that is, it occupies the lowest portion of RAM. It holds the interrupt vector table, the operating system proper and its tables and buffers, any additional installable drivers specified in the CONFIG.SYS file, and the resident part of the COMMAND.COM command interpreter. The amount of memory occupied by the operating-system area varies with the version of MS-DOS used, the number of disk buffers, the size of installed device drivers, and so forth.

The transient-program area (TPA), sometimes called the *memory arena,* is the remainder of memory above the operating-system area. The memory arena is dynamically allocated in blocks called *arena entries*. Each arena entry has a special control structure called an *arena header*, and all of the arena headers are chained together. Three MS-DOS Int 21H functions allow programs to allocate, resize, and release blocks of memory from the TPA:

Function	Action
48H	Allocate memory block.
49H	Release memory block.
4AH	Resize memory block.

MS-DOS itself uses these functions when loading a program from disk at the request of COMMAND.COM or another program. The EXEC function, which is the MS-DOS program loader, calls Int 21H Function 48H to allocate a memory block for the loaded program's environment and another for the program itself and its program segment prefix. It then reads the program from the disk into the assigned memory area. When the program terminates, MS-DOS calls Int 21H Function 49H to release all memory owned by the program.

Transient programs can also employ the MS-DOS memory-management functions to dynamically manage the memory available in the TPA. Proper use of these functions is one of the most important criteria of whether a program is well behaved under MS-DOS. Well-behaved programs are most likely to be portable to future versions of the operating system and least likely to cause interference with other processes under multitasking user interfaces such as Microsoft Windows.

Using the Memory-Allocation Functions

The memory-allocation functions have two common uses:

- To shrink a program's initial memory allocation so that there is enough room to load and execute another program under its control.

- To dynamically allocate additional memory required by the program and to release the same memory when it is no longer needed.

Shrinking the Initial Memory Allocation

Although many MS-DOS application programs simply assume they own all memory, this assumption is a relic of MS-DOS version 1 (and CP/M), which could support only one active process at a time. Well-behaved MS-DOS programs take pains to modify only memory that they actually own and to release any memory that they don't need.

Unfortunately, under current versions of MS-DOS, the amount of memory that a program will own is not easily predicted in advance. It turns out that the amount of memory allocated to a program when it is first loaded depends upon two factors:

- The type of file the program is loaded from

- The amount of memory available in the TPA

MS-DOS always allocates all of the largest available memory block in the TPA to programs loaded from .COM (memory-image) files. Because .COM programs contain no file header that can pass segment and memory-use information to MS-DOS, MS-DOS simply assumes the worst case and gives such a program everything. MS-DOS will load the program as long as there is an available memory block as large as the size of the file plus 256 bytes for the PSP and 2 bytes for the stack. The .COM program, when it receives control, must determine whether enough memory is available to carry out its functions.

MS-DOS uses more complicated rules to allocate memory to programs loaded from .EXE files. First, of course, a memory block large enough to hold the declared code, data, and stack segments must be available in the TPA. In addition, the linker sets two fields in a .EXE file's header to inform MS-DOS about the program's memory requirements. The first field, MIN_ALLOC, defines the minimum number of paragraphs required by the program, in addition to those for the code, data, and stack segments. The second, MAX_ALLOC, defines the maximum number of paragraphs of additional memory the program would use if they were available.

When loading a .EXE file, MS-DOS first attempts to allocate the number of paragraphs in MAX_ALLOC plus the number of paragraphs required by the program itself. If that much memory is not available, MS-DOS assigns all of the largest available block to the program, provided that this is at least the amount specified by MIN_ALLOC plus the size of the program image. If that condition is not satisfied, the program cannot be executed.

After a .COM or .EXE program is loaded and running, it can use Int 21H Function 4AH (Resize Memory Block) to release all the memory it does not immediately need. This is conveniently done right after the program receives control from MS-DOS, by calling the resize function with the segment of the program's PSP in the ES register and the number of paragraphs that the program requires to run in the BX register (Figure 11-1).

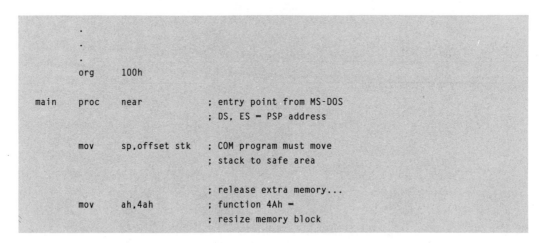

```
            .
            .
            .
            org     100h

main        proc    near            ; entry point from MS-DOS
                                    ; DS, ES = PSP address

            mov     sp,offset stk   ; COM program must move
                                    ; stack to safe area

                                    ; release extra memory...
            mov     ah,4ah          ; function 4Ah =
                                    ; resize memory block
```

(continued)

Figure 11-1. *An example of a .COM program releasing excess memory after it receives control from MS-DOS. Int 21H Function 4AH is called with ES pointing to the program's PSP and BX containing the number of paragraphs that the program needs to execute. In this case, the new size for the program's memory block is calculated as the program image size plus the size of the PSP (256 bytes), rounded up to the next paragraph. .EXE programs use similar code.*

Figure 11-1. *continued*

```
                                ; BX = paragraphs to keep
        mov     bx,(offset stk - offset main + 10FH) / 16
        int     21h             ; transfer to MS-DOS
        jc      error           ; jump if resize failed
    (   .
        .
        .
        .
main    endp


        .
        .
        .


        dw      64 dup (?)      ; new stack area
stk     equ     $               ; new base of stack

        end     main            ; defines entry point
```

Dynamic Allocation of Additional Memory

When a well-behaved program needs additional memory space—for an I/O buffer or an array of intermediate results, for example—it can call Int 21H Function 48H (Allocate Memory Block) with the desired number of paragraphs. If a sufficiently large block of unallocated memory is available, MS-DOS returns the segment address of the base of the assigned area and clears the carry flag (0), indicating that the function was successful.

If no unallocated block of sufficient size is available, MS-DOS sets the carry flag (1), returns an error code in the AX register, and returns the size (in paragraphs) of the largest block available in the BX register (Figure 11-2). In this case, no memory has yet been allocated. The program can use the value returned in the BX register to determine whether it can continue in a "degraded" fashion, with less memory. If it can, it must call Int 21H Function 48H again to allocate the smaller memory block.

When the MS-DOS memory manager is searching the chain of arena headers to satisfy a memory-allocation request, it can use one of the following strategies:

- First fit: Use the arena entry at the lowest address that is large enough to satisfy the request.

- Best fit: Use the smallest arena entry that will satisfy the request, regardless of its location.

- Last fit: Use the arena entry at the highest address that is large enough to satisfy the request.

```
                      .
                      .
                      .
              mov     ah,48h              ; function 48h = allocate mem block
              mov     bx,0800h            ; 800h paragraphs = 32 KB
              int     21h                 ; transfer to MS-DOS
              jc      error               ; jump if allocation failed
              mov     buff_seg,ax         ; save segment of allocated block
                      .
                      .
                      .
              mov     es,buff_seg         ; ES:DI = address of block
              xor     di,di
              mov     cx,08000h           ; store 32,768 bytes
              mov     al,0ffh             ; fill buffer with -1s
              cld
              rep     stosb               ; now perform fast fill
                      .
                      .
                      .
              mov     cx,08000h           ; length to write, bytes
              mov     bx,handle           ; handle for prev opened file
              push    ds                  ; save our data segment
              mov     ds,buff_seg         ; let DS:DX = buffer address
              mov     dx,0
              mov     ah,40h              ; function 40h = write
              int     21h                 ; transfer to MS-DOS
              pop     ds                  ; restore our data segment
              jc      error               ; jump if write failed
                      .
                      .
                      .
              mov     es,buff_seg         ; ES = seg of prev allocated block
              mov     ah,49h              ; function 49h = release mem block
              int     21h                 ; transfer to MS-DOS
              jc      error               ; jump if release failed
                      .
error:                .
                      .
handle        dw      0                   ; file handle
buff_seg      dw      0                   ; segment of allocated block
                      .
                      .
```

Figure 11-2. *Example of dynamic memory allocation. The program requests a 32 KB memory block from MS-DOS, fills it with −1s, writes it to disk, and then releases it.*

If the arena entry selected is larger than the size requested, MS-DOS divides it into two parts: one block of the size requested, which is assigned to the program that called Int 21H Function 48H, and an unowned block containing the remaining memory.

The default MS-DOS allocation strategy is first fit. However, under MS-DOS versions 3.0 and later, an application program can change the strategy with Int 21H Function 58H.

When a program is through with an allocated memory block, it should use Int 21H Function 49H to release the block. If it does not, MS-DOS will automatically release all memory allocations for the program when it terminates.

Arena Headers

Microsoft has not officially documented the internal structure of *arena headers* for the outside world at present. This is probably to deter programmers from trying to manipulate their memory allocations directly instead of through the MS-DOS functions provided for that purpose.

Arena headers have identical structures in MS-DOS versions 2 and 3. They are 16 bytes (one paragraph) and are located immediately before the memory area that they control (Figure 11-3). An arena header contains the following information:

- A byte signifying whether the header is a member or the last entry in the entire chain of such headers

- A word indicating whether the area it controls is available or whether it already belongs to a program (if the latter, the word points to the program's PSP)

- A word indicating the size (in paragraphs) of the controlled memory area (arena entry)

MS-DOS inspects the chain of arena headers whenever the program requests a memory-block allocation, modification, or release function, or when a program is EXEC'd or terminated. If any of the blocks appear to be corrupted or if the chain is broken, MS-DOS displays the dreaded message

```
Memory allocation error
```

and halts the system.

In the example illustrated in Figure 11-3, *COMMAND.COM* originally loaded *PROGRAM1.COM* into the TPA and, because it was a .COM file, *COMMAND.COM* allocated it all of the TPA, controlled by arena header #1. *PROGRAM1.COM* then used Int 21H Function 4AH (Resize Memory Block) to shrink its memory allocation to the amount it actually needed to run and loaded and executed *PROGRAM2.EXE* with the EXEC function (Int 21H Function 4BH). The EXEC function obtained a suitable amount of memory, controlled by arena header #2, and loaded *PROGRAM2.EXE* into it. *PROGRAM2.EXE*, in turn, needed some additional memory to store some intermediate results, so it called Int 21H Function 48H (Allocate Memory Block) to obtain the area controlled by arena header #3. The highest arena header (#4) controls all of the remaining TPA that has not been allocated to any program.

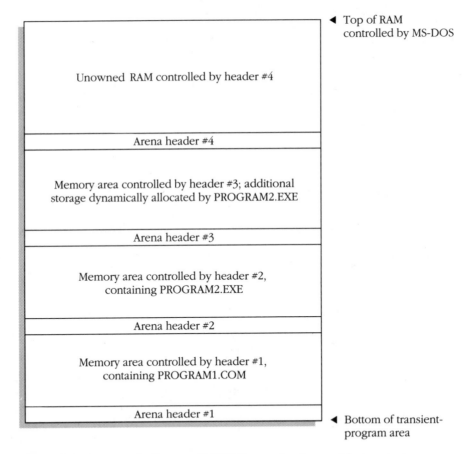

Figure 11-3. *An example diagram of MS-DOS arena headers and the transient-program area. The environment blocks and their associated headers have been omitted from this figure to increase its clarity.*

Lotus/Intel/Microsoft Expanded Memory

When the IBM Personal Computer and MS-DOS were first released, the 640 KB limit that IBM placed on the amount of RAM that could be directly managed by MS-DOS seemed almost unimaginably huge. But as MS-DOS has grown in both size and capabilities and the popular applications have become more powerful, that 640 KB has begun to seem a bit crowded. Although personal computers based on the 80286 and 80386 have the potential to manage up to 16 megabytes of RAM under operating systems such as MS OS/2 and XENIX, this is little comfort to the millions of users of 8086/8088-based computers and MS-DOS.

At the spring COMDEX in 1985, Lotus Development Corporation and Intel Corporation jointly announced the Expanded Memory Specification 3.0 (EMS), which was designed to head off rapid obsolescence of the older PCs because of limited memory. Shortly afterward, Microsoft announced that it would support the EMS and would enhance Microsoft Windows to use the memory made available by EMS hardware and software. EMS versions 3.2 and 4.0, released in fall 1985 and summer 1987, expanded support for multitasking operating systems.

The LIM EMS (as it is usually known) has been an enormous success. EMS memory boards are available from scores of manufacturers, and "EMS-aware" software—especially spreadsheets, disk caches, and terminate-and-stay-resident utilities—has become the rule rather than the exception.

What Is Expanded Memory?

The Lotus/Intel/Microsoft Expanded Memory Specification is a functional definition of a bank-switched memory-expansion subsystem. It consists of hardware expansion modules and a resident driver program specific to those modules. In EMS versions 3.0 and 3.2, the expanded memory is made available to application software as 16 KB pages mapped into a contiguous 64 KB area called the *page frame*, somewhere above the main memory area used by MS-DOS/PC-DOS (0–640 KB). The exact location of the page frame is user configurable, so it need not conflict with other hardware options. In EMS version 4.0, the pages may be mapped anywhere in memory and can have sizes other than 16 KB.

The EMS provides a uniform means for applications to access as much as 8 megabytes of memory (32 megabytes in EMS 4.0). The supporting software, which is called the Expanded Memory Manager (EMM), provides a hardware-independent interface between application software and the expanded memory board(s). The EMM is supplied in the form of an installable device driver that you link into the MS-DOS/PC-DOS system by adding a line to the CONFIG.SYS file on the system boot disk.

Internally, the Expanded Memory Manager consists of two major portions, which may be referred to as the *driver* and the *manager*. The driver portion mimics some of the actions of a genuine installable device driver, in that it includes initialization and output status functions and a valid device header. The second, and major, portion of the EMM is the true interface between application software and the expanded-memory hardware. Several classes of services are provided:

- Verification of functionality of hardware and software modules

- Allocation of expanded-memory pages

- Mapping of logical pages into the physical page frame

- Deallocation of expanded-memory pages

- Support for multitasking operating systems

Application programs communicate with the EMM directly, by means of software Int 67H. MS-DOS versions 3.3 and earlier take no part in (and in fact are completely oblivious to) any expanded-memory manipulations that may occur. MS-DOS version 4.0 and Microsoft Windows, on the other hand, are "EMS-aware" and can use the EMS memory when it is available.

Expanded memory should not be confused with *extended memory*. Extended memory is the term used by IBM to refer to the memory at physical addresses above 1 megabyte that can be accessed by an 80286 or 80386 CPU in protected mode. Current versions of MS-DOS run the 80286 and 80386 in real mode (8086-emulation mode), and *extended* memory is therefore not directly accessible.

Checking for Expanded Memory

An application program can use either of two methods to test for the existence of the Expanded Memory Manager:

- Issue an open request (Int 21H Function 3DH) using the guaranteed device name of the EMM driver: *EMMXXXX0*. If the open function succeeds, either the driver is present or a file with the same name coincidentally exists on the default disk drive. To rule out the latter, the application can use IOCTL (Int 21H Function 44H) subfunctions 00H and 07H to ensure that EMM is present. In either case, the application should then use Int 21H Function 3EH to close the handle that was obtained from the open function, so that the handle can be reused for another file or device.

- Use the address that is found in the Int 67H vector to inspect the device header of the presumed EMM. Interrupt handlers and device drivers *must* use this method. If the EMM is present, the name field at offset 0AH of the device header contains the string *EMMXXXX0*. This approach is nearly foolproof and avoids the relatively high overhead of an MS-DOS open function. However, it is somewhat less well behaved because it involves inspection of memory that does not belong to the application.

These two methods of testing for the existence of the Expanded Memory Manager are illustrated in Figures 11-4 and 11-5.

```
            .
            .
            .
                             ; attempt to "open" EMM...
    mov  dx,seg emm_name     ; DS:DX = address of name
    mov  ds,dx               ; of Expanded Memory Manager
    mov  dx,offset emm_name
    mov  ax,3d00h            ; function 3dh, mode = 00h
                             ; = open, read only
    int  21h                 ; transfer to MS-DOS
    jc   error               ; jump if open failed

                             ; open succeeded, be sure
                             ; it was not a file...
    mov  bx,ax               ; BX = handle from open
    mov  ax,4400h            ; function 44h subfunction 00h
                             ; = IOCTL get device information
    int  21h                 ; transfer to MS-DOS
    jc   error               ; jump if IOCTL call failed
    and  dx,80h              ; bit 7 = 1 if character device
    jz   error               ; jump if it was a file

                             ; EMM is present, be sure
                             ; it is available...
                             ; (BX still contains handle)
    mov  ax,4407h            ; function 44h subfunction 07h
                             ; = IOCTL get output status
    int  21h                 ; transfer to MS-DOS
    jc   error               ; jump if IOCTL call failed
    or   al,al               ; test device status
    jz   error               ; if AL = 0 EMM is not avail
```

(continued)

Figure 11-4. *Testing for the Expanded Memory Manager by means of the MS-DOS open and IOCTL functions.*

Figure 11-4. *continued*

```
                        ; now close handle ...
                        ; (BX still contains handle)
        mov   ah,3eh    ; function 3eh = close
        int   21h       ; transfer to MS-DOS
        jc    error     ; jump if close failed
        .
        .
        .
emm_name  db  'EMMXXXX0',0  ; guaranteed device name for
                            ; Expanded Memory Manager
```

```
emm_int  equ  67h       ; Expanded Memory Manager
                        ; software interrupt
        .
        .
        .
                        ; first fetch contents of
                        ; EMM interrupt vector...
        mov   al,emm_int  ; AL = EMM int number
        mov   ah,35h       ; function 35h = get vector
        int   21h          ; transfer to MS-DOS
                        ; now ES:BX = handler address

                        ; assume ES:0000 points
                        ; to base of the EMM...
        mov   di,10     ; ES:DI = address of name
                        ; field in device header
                        ; DS:SI = EMM driver name
        mov   si,seg emm_name
        mov   ds,si
        mov   si,offset emm_name
        mov   cx,8      ; length of name field
        cld
        repz cmpsb      ; compare names...
        jnz   error     ; jump if driver absent
        .
        .
        .


emm_name  db  'EMMXXXX0'  ; guaranteed device name for
                          ; Expanded Memory Manager
```

Figure 11-5. *Testing for the Expanded Memory Manager by inspection of the name field in the driver's device header.*

Using Expanded Memory

After establishing that the memory-manager software is present, the application program communicates with it directly by means of the "user interrupt" 67H, bypassing MS-DOS/PC-DOS. The calling sequence for the EMM is as follows:

```
        mov   ah,function          ; AH determines service type
        .                          ; load other registers with
        .                          ; values specific to the
        .                          ; requested service
        int   67h
```

In general, AH contains the EMM function number, AL holds the subfunction number (if any), BX holds a number of pages (if applicable), and DX contains an EMM handle. Registers DS:SI and ES:DI are used to pass the addresses of arrays or buffers. Section IV of this book, "Lotus/Intel/Microsoft EMS Functions Reference," details each of the expanded memory functions.

Upon return from an EMM function, the AH register contains zero if the function was successful; otherwise, it contains an error code with the most significant bit set (Figures 11-6 and 11-7). Other values are typically returned in the AL and BX registers or in a user-specified buffer.

Error code	Meaning
00H	Function successful.
80H	Internal error in Expanded Memory Manager software (could be caused by corrupted memory image of driver).
81H	Malfunction in expanded-memory hardware.
82H	Memory manager busy.
83H	Invalid handle.
84H	Function requested by application not defined.
85H	No more handles available.
86H	Error in save or restore of mapping context.
87H	Allocation request specified more logical pages than physically available in system; no pages allocated.
88H	Allocation request specified more logical pages than currently available in system (request does not exceed physical pages that exist, but some are already allocated to other handles); no pages allocated.

(continued)

Figure 11-6. *Expanded Memory Manager error codes common to EMS versions 3.0, 3.2, and 4.0. After a call to EMM, the AH register contains zero if the function was successful or an error code in the range 80H through 8FH if the function failed.*

Figure 11-6. *continued*

Error code	Meaning
89H	Zero pages; cannot be allocated.
8AH	Logical page requested to be mapped located outside range of logical pages assigned to handle.
8BH	Illegal physical page number in mapping request (not in range 0–3).
8CH	Page-mapping hardware-state save area full.
8DH	Save of mapping context failed; save area already contains context associated with requested handle.
8EH	Restore of mapping context failed; save area does not contain context for requested handle.
8FH	Subfunction parameter not defined.

Error code	Meaning
90H	Attribute type not defined.
91H	Feature not supported.
92H	Source and destination memory regions have same handle and overlap; requested move was performed, but part of source region was overwritten.
93H	Specified length for source or destination memory region is longer than actual allocated length.
94H	Conventional-memory region and expanded-memory region overlap.
95H	Specified offset is outside logical page.
96H	Region length exceeds 1 MB.
97H	Source and destination memory regions have same handle and overlap; exchange cannot be performed.
98H	Memory source and destination types undefined.
99H	This error code currently unused.
9AH	Alternate map or DMA register sets supported, but the alternate register set specified is not supported.
9BH	Alternate map or DMA register sets supported, but all alternate register sets currently allocated.
9CH	Alternate map or DMA register sets not supported, and specified alternate register set not zero.
9DH	Alternate map or DMA register sets supported, but alternate register set specified is either not defined or not allocated.

(continued)

Figure 11-7. *Expanded Memory Manager error codes unique to EMS version 4.0. Most of these errors are related to the EMS functions for use by operating systems and would not normally be encountered by application programs.*

Figure 11-7. *continued*

Error code	Meaning
9EH	Dedicated DMA channels not supported.
9FH	Dedicated DMA channels supported, but specified DMA channel not supported.
A0H	No handle found for specified name.
A1H	Handle with this name already exists.
A2H	Memory address wrap; sum of the source or destination region base address and length exceeds 1 MB.
A3H	Invalid pointer passed to function, or contents of source array corrupted.
A4H	Access to function denied by operating system.

An application program that uses expanded memory should regard that memory as a system resource, like a file or a device, and employ only the documented EMM services to allocate, access, and release expanded-memory pages. Such a program can use the following general strategy:

1. Establish the presence of the Expanded Memory Manager by one of the two methods demonstrated in Figures 11-4 and 11-5.

2. After the driver is known to be present, check its operational status with EMS Function 40H.

3. Check the version number of EMM with EMS Function 46H, to ensure that all services the application will request are available.

4. Obtain the segment of the page frame used by EMM with EMS Function 41H.

5. Allocate the desired number of expanded-memory pages with EMS Function 43H. If the allocation is successful, EMM returns a handle that the application can use to refer to the expanded-memory pages that it owns. This step is exactly analogous to opening a file and using the handle obtained from the open function for read/write operations on the file.

6. If the requested number of pages are not available, the application can query EMM for the actual number of pages available (EMS Function 42H) and determine whether it can continue.

7. After the application has successfully allocated the needed number of expanded-memory pages, it uses EMS Function 44H to map logical pages in and out of the physical page frame in order to store and retrieve data in expanded memory.

8. When the program finishes using its expanded-memory pages, it must release them by calling EMS Function 45H. Otherwise, the pages will be lost to use by other programs until the system is restarted.

Figure 11-8 shows a skeleton program that illustrates this general approach.

An interrupt handler or device driver that uses EMS follows the same general procedure outlined in steps 1 through 8, with a few minor variations. It may need to acquire an EMS handle and allocate pages before the operating system is fully functional; in particular, you cannot assume that the MS-DOS Open File or Device, IOCTL, and Get Interrupt Vector functions are available. Thus, such a handler or driver must use a modified version of the "get interrupt vector" technique (Figure 11-5) to test for the existence of EMM, fetching the contents of the Int 67H vector directly.

A device driver or interrupt handler typically owns its expanded-memory pages permanently (until the system is restarted) and never deallocates them. Such a program must also take care to save and restore EMM's page-mapping context (EMS Functions 47H and 48H) whenever it accesses expanded memory, so that use of EMS by a foreground program will not be disturbed.

The EMM relies on the good behavior of application software to avoid the corruption of expanded memory. If several applications that use expanded memory are running under a multitasking manager such as Microsoft Windows and one or more of them does not abide strictly by EMM conventions, the data of some or all of the applications may be destroyed.

```
        .
        .
        .
        mov  ah,40h       ; test EMM status
        int  67h
        or   ah,ah
        jnz  error        ; jump if bad status from EMM

        mov  ah,46h       ; check EMM version
        int  67h
        or   ah,ah
        jnz  error        ; jump if couldn't get version

        cmp  al,030h      ; make sure at least ver 3.0
        jb   error        ; jump if wrong EMM version
```

(continued)

Figure 11-8. *A program illustrating the general strategy for using expanded memory.*

Figure 11-8. *continued*

```
    mov  ah,41h           ; get page frame segment
    int  67h
    or   ah,ah
    jnz  error            ; jump if failed to get frame
    mov  page_frame,bx    ; save segment of page frame

    mov  ah,42h           ; get number of available pages
    int  67h
    or   ah,ah
    jnz  error            ; jump if get pages error
    mov  total_pages,dx   ; save total EMM pages
    mov  avail_pages,bx   ; save available EMM pages
    or   bx,bx
    jz   error            ; abort if no pages available

    mov  ah,43h           ; try to allocate EMM pages
    mov  bx,needed_pages
    int  67h              ; if allocation is successful
    or   ah,ah
    jnz  error            ; jump if allocation failed

    mov  emm_handle,dx    ; save handle for allocated pages

    .
    .                     ; now we are ready for other
    .                     ; processing using EMM pages
    .
                          ; map in EMS memory page...
    mov  bx,log_page      ; BX <- EMS logical page number
    mov  al,phys_page     ; AL <- EMS physical page (0-3)
    mov  dx,emm_handle    ; EMM handle for our pages
    mov  ah,44h           ; function 44h — map EMS page
    int  67h
    or   ah,ah
    jnz  error            ; jump if mapping error

    .
    .
    .                     ; program ready to terminate,
                          ; give up allocated EMM pages...
    mov  dx,emm_handle    ; handle for our pages
    mov  ah,45h           ; EMS function 45h — release pages
    int  67h
    or   ah,ah
    jnz  error            ; jump if release failed
    .
    .
    .
```

Extended Memory

Extended memory is RAM storage at addresses above 1 megabyte (100000H) that can be accessed by an 80286 or 80386 processor running in protected mode. IBM PC/AT– and PS/2–compatible machines can (theoretically) have as much as 15 MB of extended memory installed, in addition to the usual 1 MB of conventional memory.

Protected-mode operating systems such as Microsoft XENIX or MS OS/2 can use extended memory for execution of programs. MS-DOS, on the other hand, runs in real mode on an 80286 or 80386, and programs running under its control cannot ordinarily execute from extended memory or even address that memory for storage of data. However, the ROM BIOS contains two routines that allow real-mode programs restricted access to extended memory:

ROM BIOS function	Action
Int 15H Function 87H	Move extended-memory block.
Int 15H Function 88H	Get extended-memory size.

These routines can be used by electronic disks (RAMdisks) and by other programs that want to use extended memory for fast storage and retrieval of information that would otherwise have to be written to a slower physical disk drive. Section III of this book, "IBM ROM BIOS and Mouse Functions Reference," documents both of these functions.

You should use these ROM BIOS routines with caution. Data stored in extended memory is, of course, volatile; it is lost if the machine is turned off. The transfer of data to or from extended memory involves a switch from real mode to protected mode and back, which is a relatively slow process on 80286-based machines; in some cases it is only marginally faster than actually reading the data from a fixed disk. In addition, programs that use the ROM BIOS extended-memory functions are not compatible with the MS-DOS compatibility mode of MS OS/2.

Finally, a major deficit in these ROM BIOS functions is that they do not make any attempt to arbitrate between two or more programs or drivers that are using extended memory for temporary storage. For example, if an application program and an installed RAMdisk driver attempt to put data in the same area of extended memory, no error will be returned to either program, but the data of one or both may be destroyed.

Figure 11-9 shows an example of the code necessary to transfer data to and from extended memory.

```
bmdt      db       30h dup (0)       ; block move descriptor table

buff1     db       80h dup ('?')     ; source buffer
buff2     db       80h dup (0)       ; destination buffer

             .
             .
             .


                                     ; copy 'buff1' to extended-
                                     ; memory address 100000h
          mov      dx,10h            ; DX:AX = destination
          mov      ax,0              ; extended-memory address
          mov      bx,seg buff1      ; DS:BX = source conventional-
          mov      ds,bx             ; memory address
          mov      bx,offset buff1
          mov      cx,80h            ; CX = bytes to move
          mov      si,seg bmdt       ; ES:SI = block move
          mov      es,si             ; descriptor table
          mov      si,offset bmdt
          call     putblk            ; request transfer


                                     ; fill buff2 from extended-
                                     ; memory address 100000h
          mov      dx,10h            ; DX:AX = source extended-
          mov      ax,0              ; memory address
          mov      bx,seg buff2      ; DS:BX = destination
          mov      ds,bx             ; conventional-memory address
          mov      bx,offset buff2
          mov      cx,80h            ; CX = bytes to move
          mov      si,seg bmdt       ; ES:SI = block move
          mov      es,si             ; descriptor table
          mov      si,offset bmdt
          call     getblk            ; request transfer

             .
             .
             .
```

(continued)

Figure 11-9. *Moving blocks of data between conventional memory and extended memory, using the ROM BIOS extended-memory functions. For additional information on the format of the block move descriptor table, see the entry for Int 15H Function 87H in Section III of this book, "IBM ROM BIOS and Mouse Functions Reference." Note that you must specify the extended-memory address as a 32-bit linear address rather than as a segment and offset.*

Figure 11-9. *continued*

```
getblk  proc    near                    ; transfer block from extended
                                        ; memory to real memory
                                        ; call with
                                        ; DX:AX - source linear 32-bit
                                        ;          extended-memory address
                                        ; DS:BX - segment and offset
                                        ;          destination address
                                        ; CX    - length in bytes
                                        ; ES:SI - block move descriptor
                                        ;          table
                                        ; returns
                                        ; AH    - 0 if transfer OK

        mov     es:[si+10h],cx  ; store length into descriptors
        mov     es:[si+18h],cx


                                ; store access rights bytes
        mov     byte ptr es:[si+15h],93h
        mov     byte ptr es:[si+1dh],93h


        mov     es:[si+12h],ax  ; source extended-memory address
        mov     es:[si+14h],dl


                                ; convert destination segment
                                ; and offset to linear address
        mov     ax,ds           ; segment * 16
        mov     dx,16
        mul     dx
        add     ax,bx           ; + offset -> linear address
        adc     dx,0


        mov     es:[si+1ah],ax  ; store destination address
        mov     es:[si+1ch],dl


        shr     cx,1            ; convert length to words
        mov     ah,87h          ; int 15h function 87h - block move
        int     15h             ; transfer to ROM BIOS


        ret                     ; back to caller

getblk  endp
```

(continued)

Figure 11-9. *continued*

```
putblk  proc    near            ; transfer block from real
                                 ; memory to extended memory
                                 ; call with
                                 ; DX:AX - dest linear 32-bit
                                 ;         extended-memory address
                                 ; DS:BX - segment and offset
                                 ;         source address
                                 ; CX    - length in bytes
                                 ; ES:SI - block move descriptor
                                 ;         table
                                 ; returns
                                 ; AH    - 0 if transfer OK

        mov     es:[si+10h],cx  ; store length into descriptors
        mov     es:[si+18h],cx


                                 ; store access rights bytes
        mov     byte ptr es:[si+15h],93h
        mov     byte ptr es:[si+1dh],93h


        mov     es:[si+1ah],ax  ; store destination extended-
        mov     es:[si+1ch],dl  ; memory address


                                 ; convert source segment and
                                 ; offset to linear address
        mov     ax,ds           ; segment * 16
        mov     dx,16
        mul     dx
        add     ax,bx           ; + offset -> linear address
        adc     dx,0
        mov     es:[si+12h],ax  ; store source address
        mov     es:[si+14h],dl


        shr     cx,1            ; convert length to words
        mov     ah,87h          ; int 15h function 87h - block move
        int     15h             ; transfer to ROM BIOS


        ret                     ; back to caller

putblk  endp
```

Chapter 12

The EXEC Function

The MS-DOS EXEC function (Int 21H Function 4BH) allows a program (called the *parent*) to load any other program (called the *child*) from a storage device, execute it, and then regain control when the child program is finished.

A parent program can pass information to the child in a command line, in default file control blocks, and by means of a set of strings called the environment block (discussed later in this chapter). All files or devices that the parent opened using the handle file-management functions are duplicated in the newly created child task; that is, the child inherits all the active handles of the parent task. Any file operations on those handles by the child, such as seeks or file I/O, also affect the file pointers associated with the parent's handles.

MS-DOS suspends execution of the parent program until the child program terminates. When the child program finishes its work, it can pass an exit code back to the parent, indicating whether it encountered any errors. It can also, in turn, load other programs, and so on through many levels of control, until the system runs out of memory.

The MS-DOS command interpreter, COMMAND.COM, uses the EXEC function to run its external commands and other application programs. Many popular commercial programs, such as database managers and word processors, use EXEC to run other programs (spelling checkers, for example) or to load a second copy of COMMAND.COM, thereby allowing the user to list directories or copy and rename files without closing all the application files and stopping the main work in progress. EXEC can also be used to load program overlay segments, although this use is uncommon.

Making Memory Available

In order for a parent program to use the EXEC function to load a child program, sufficient unallocated memory must be available in the transient program area.

When the parent itself was loaded, MS-DOS allocated it a variable amount of memory, depending upon its original file type—.COM or .EXE—and any other information that was available to the loader. (See Chapter 11 for further details.) Because the operating system has no foolproof way of predicting how much memory any given program will require, it generally allocates far more memory to a program than is really necessary.

Therefore, a prospective parent program's first action should be to use Int 21H Function 4AH (Resize Memory Block) to release any excess memory allocation of its own to MS-DOS. In this case, the program should call Int 21H Function 4AH with the ES register pointing to the program segment prefix of the program releasing memory and the BX register containing the number of paragraphs of memory to retain for that program. (See Figure 11-1 for an example.)

❑ **WARNING** *A .COM program must move its stack to a safe area if it is reducing its memory allocation to less than 64 KB.*

Requesting the EXEC Function

To load and execute a child program, the parent must execute an Int 21H with the registers set up as follows:

AH = 4BH

AL = 00H (subfunction to load child program)

DS:DX = segment:offset of pathname for child program

ES:BX = segment:offset of parameter block

The parameter block, in turn, contains addresses of other information needed by the EXEC function.

The Program Name

The name of the program to be run, which the calling program provides to the EXEC function, must be an unambiguous file specification (no wild-card characters) and must include an explicit .COM or .EXE extension. If the path and disk drive are not supplied in the program name, MS-DOS uses the current directory and default disk drive. (The sequential search for .COM, .EXE, and .BAT files in all the locations listed in the PATH variable is not a function of EXEC, but rather of the internal logic of COMMAND.COM.)

You cannot EXEC a batch file directly; instead, you must EXEC a copy of COMMAND.COM and pass the name of the batch file in the command tail, along with the /C switch.

The Parameter Block

The parameter block contains the addresses of four data objects:

- The environment block
- The command tail
- Two default file control blocks

The space reserved in the parameter block for the address of the environment block is only 2 bytes and holds a segment address. The remaining three addresses are all double-word addresses; that is, they are 4 bytes, with the offset in the first 2 bytes and the segment address in the last 2 bytes.

The Environment Block

Each program that the EXEC function loads inherits a data structure called an *environment block* from its parent. The pointer to the segment of the block is at offset 002CH in the PSP. The environment block holds certain information used by the system's command interpreter (usually COMMAND.COM) and may also hold information to be used by transient programs. It has no effect on the operation of the operating system proper.

If the environment-block pointer in the EXEC parameter block contains zero, the child program acquires a copy of the parent program's environment block. Alternatively, the parent program can provide a segment pointer to a different or expanded environment. The maximum size of the environment block is 32 KB, so very large chunks of information can be passed between programs by this mechanism.

The environment block for any given program is static, implying that if more than one generation of child programs is resident in RAM, each one will have a distinct and separate copy of the environment block. Furthermore, the environment block for a program that terminates and stays resident is not updated by subsequent PATH and SET commands.

You will find more details about the environment block later in this chapter.

The Command Tail

MS-DOS copies the command tail into the child program's PSP at offset 0080H, as described in Chapter 3. The information takes the form of a count byte, followed by a string of ASCII characters, terminated by a carriage return; the carriage return is not included in the count.

The command tail can include filenames, switches, or other parameters. From the child program's point of view, the command tail should provide the same information that would be present if the program had been run by a direct user command at the MS-DOS prompt. EXEC ignores any I/O-redirection parameters placed in the command tail; the parent program must provide for redirection of the standard devices *before* the EXEC call is made.

The Default File Control Blocks

MS-DOS copies the two default file control blocks pointed to by the EXEC parameter block into the child program's PSP at offsets 005CH and 006CH. To emulate the function of COMMAND.COM from the child program's point of view, the parent program should use Int 21H Function 29H (the system parse-filename service) to parse the first two parameters of the command tail into the default file control blocks before invoking the EXEC function.

File control blocks are not much use under MS-DOS versions 2 and 3, because they do not support the hierarchical file structure, but some application programs do inspect them as a quick way to get at the first two switches or other parameters in the command tail. Chapter 8 discusses file control blocks in more detail.

Returning from the EXEC Function

In MS-DOS version 2, the EXEC function destroys the contents of all registers except the code segment (CS) and instruction pointer (IP). Therefore, *before* making the EXEC call, the parent program must push the contents of any other registers that are important onto the stack and then save the stack segment (SS) and stack pointer (SP) registers in variables. Upon return from a successful EXEC call (that is, the child program has finished executing), the parent program should reload SS and SP from the variables where they were saved and then pop the other saved registers off the stack. In MS-DOS versions 3.0 and later, the stack and other registers are preserved across the EXEC call in the usual fashion.

Finally, the parent can use Int 21H Function 4DH to obtain the termination type and return code of the child program.

The EXEC function will fail under the following conditions:

- Not enough unallocated memory is available to load and execute the requested program file.

- The requested program can't be found on the disk.

■ The transient portion of COMMAND.COM in highest RAM (which contains the actual loader) has been destroyed and not enough free memory is available to reload it (PC-DOS version 2 only).

Figure 12-1 summarizes the calling convention for function 4BH. Figure 12-2 shows a skeleton of a typical EXEC call. This particular example uses the EXEC function to load and run the MS-DOS utility CHKDSK.COM. The *SHELL.ASM* program listing later in this chapter (Figure 12-5) presents a more complete example that includes the use of Int 21H Function 4AH to free unneeded memory.

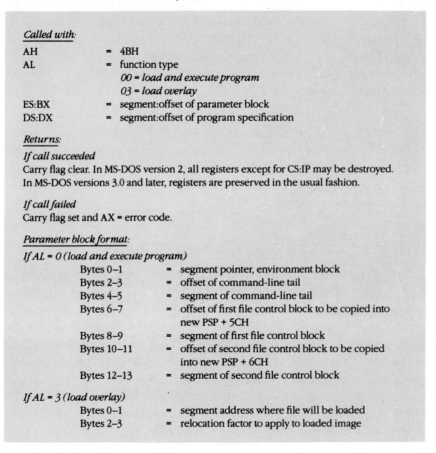

Called with:

AH	=	4BH
AL	=	function type
		00 = load and execute program
		03 = load overlay
ES:BX	=	segment:offset of parameter block
DS:DX	=	segment:offset of program specification

Returns:

If call succeeded
Carry flag clear. In MS-DOS version 2, all registers except for CS:IP may be destroyed. In MS-DOS versions 3.0 and later, registers are preserved in the usual fashion.

If call failed
Carry flag set and AX = error code.

Parameter block format:

If AL = 0 (load and execute program)

Bytes 0–1	=	segment pointer, environment block
Bytes 2–3	=	offset of command-line tail
Bytes 4–5	=	segment of command-line tail
Bytes 6–7	=	offset of first file control block to be copied into new PSP + 5CH
Bytes 8–9	=	segment of first file control block
Bytes 10–11	=	offset of second file control block to be copied into new PSP + 6CH
Bytes 12–13	=	segment of second file control block

If AL = 3 (load overlay)

Bytes 0–1	=	segment address where file will be loaded
Bytes 2–3	=	relocation factor to apply to loaded image

Figure 12-1. *Calling convention for the EXEC function (Int 21H Function 4BH).*

```
cr        egu      Odh              ; ASCII carriage return
          .
          .
          .
          mov      stkseg,ss        ; save stack pointer
          mov      stkptr,sp

          mov      dx,offset pname  ; DS:DX - program name
          mov      bx,offset pars   ; ES:BX - param block
          mov      ax,4b00h         ; function 4bh, subfunction 00h
          int      21h              ; transfer to MS-DOS

          mov      ax,_DATA         ; make our data segment
          mov      ds,ax            ; addressable again
          mov      es,ax

          cli                       ; (for bug in some 8088s)
          mov      ss,stkseg        ; restore stack pointer
          mov      sp,stkptr
          sti                       ; (for bug in some 8088s)

          jc       error            ; jump if EXEC failed
          .
          .
          .


stkseg    dw       0               ; original SS contents
stkptr    dw       0               ; original SP contents

pname     db       '\CHKDSK.COM',0 ; pathname of child program

pars      dw       envir           ; environment segment
          dd       cmdline         ; command line for child
          dd       fcb1            ; file control block #1
          dd       fcb2            ; file control block #2

cmdline   db       4,' *.*',cr     ; command line for child

fcb1      db       0               ; file control block #1
          db       11 dup ('?')
          db       25 dup (0)
```

(continued)

Figure 12-2. *A brief example of the use of the MS-DOS EXEC call, with all necessary variables and command blocks. Note the protection of the registers for MS-DOS version 2 and the masking of interrupts during loading of SS:SP to circumvent a bug in some early 8088 CPUs.*

Figure 12-2. *continued*

```
fcb2    db      0                   ; file control block #2
        db      11 dup (' ')
        db      25 dup (0)


envir   segment para 'ENVIR'   ; environment segment

        db      'PATH=',0          ; empty search path
                                   ; location of COMMAND.COM
        db      'COMSPEC=A:\COMMAND.COM',0
        db      0                  ; end of environment

envir   ends
```

More About the Environment Block

The environment block is always paragraph aligned (starts at an address that is a multiple of 16 bytes) and contains a series of ASCIIZ strings. Each of the strings takes the following form:

NAME=PARAMETER

An additional zero byte (Figure 12-3) indicates the end of the entire set of strings. Under MS-DOS version 3, the block of environment strings and the extra zero byte are followed by a word count and the complete drive, path, filename, and extension used by EXEC to load the program.

```
        0  1  2  3  4  5  6  7  8  9  A  B  C  D  E  F  0123456789ABCDEF
0000   43 4F 4D 53 50 45 43 3D 43 3A 5C 43 4F 4D 4D 41  COMSPEC=C:\COMMA
0010   4E 44 2E 43 4F 4D 00 50 52 4F 4D 50 54 3D 24 70  ND.COM.PROMPT=$p
0020   24 5F 24 64 20 20 20 24 74 24 68 24 68 24 68 24  $_$d   $t$h$h$h$
0030   68 24 68 24 68 20 24 71 24 71 24 67 00 50 41 54  h$h$h $q$q$g.PAT
0040   48 3D 43 3A 5C 53 59 53 54 45 4D 3B 43 3A 5C 41  H=C:\SYSTEM;C:\A
0050   53 4D 3B 43 3A 5C 57 53 3B 43 3A 5C 45 54 48 45  SM;C:\WS;C:\ETHE
0060   52 4E 45 54 3B 43 3A 5C 46 4F 52 54 48 5C 50 43  RNET;C:\FORTH\PC
0070   33 31 3B 00 00 01 00 43 3A 5C 46 4F 52 54 48 5C  31;....C:\FORTH\
0080   50 43 33 31 5C 46 4F 52 54 48 2E 43 4F 4D 00 20  PC31\FORTH.COM.
```

Figure 12-3. *Dump of a typical environment block under MS-DOS version 3. This particular example contains the default COMSPEC parameter and two relatively complex PATH and PROMPT control strings that were set up by entries in the user's AUTOEXEC file. Note the path and file specification of the executing program following the double zeros at offset 0073H that denote the end of the environment block.*

Under normal conditions, the environment block inherited by a program will contain at least three strings:

COMSPEC=variable
PATH=variable
PROMPT=variable

MS-DOS places these three strings into the environment block at system initialization, during the interpretation of SHELL, PATH, and PROMPT directives in the CONFIG.SYS and AUTOEXEC.BAT files. The strings tell the MS-DOS command interpreter, COMMAND.COM, the location of its executable file (to enable it to reload the transient portion), where to search for executable external commands or program files, and the format of the user prompt.

You can add other strings to the environment block, either interactively or in batch files, with the SET command. Transient programs can use these strings for informational purposes. For example, the Microsoft C Compiler looks in the environment block for INCLUDE, LIB, and TMP strings to tell it where to find its *#include* files and library files and where to build its temporary working files.

Example Programs: *SHELL.C* and *SHELL.ASM*

As a practical example of use of the MS-DOS EXEC function, I have included a small command interpreter called *SHELL,* with equivalent Microsoft C (Figure 12-4) and Microsoft Macro Assembler (Figure 12-5) source code. The source code for the assembly-language version is considerably more complex than the code for the C version, but the names and functionality of the various procedures are quite parallel.

```
/*
    SHELL.C       Simple extendable command interpreter
                  for MS-DOS versions 2.0 and later

    Copyright 1988 Ray Duncan

    Compile:   C>CL SHELL.C

    Usage:     C>SHELL
*/
```

(continued)

Figure 12-4. SHELL.C: *A table-driven command interpreter written in Microsoft C.*

Figure 12-4. *continued*

```
#include <stdio.h>
#include <process.h>
#include <stdlib.h>
#include <signal.h>

                                    /* macro to return number of
                                       elements in a structure  */
#define dim(x) (sizeof(x) / sizeof(x[0]))

unsigned intrinsic(char *);         /* function prototypes       */
void extrinsic(char *);
void get_cmd(char *);
void get_comspec(char *);
void break_handler(void);
void cls_cmd(void);
void dos_cmd(void);
void exit_cmd(void);

struct cmd_table {                  /* intrinsic commands table */
                char *cmd_name;
                int  (*cmd_fxn)();
                }  commands[] =

                { "CLS",   cls_cmd,
                  "DOS",   dos_cmd,
                  "EXIT",  exit_cmd, };

static char com_spec[64];           /* COMMAND.COM filespec      */

main(int argc, char *argv[])
{
    char inp_buf[80];               /* keyboard input buffer     */

    get_comspec(com_spec);          /* get COMMAND.COM filespec  */

                                    /* register new handler
                                       for Ctrl-C interrupts     */
    if(signal(SIGINT, break_handler) == (int(*)()) -1)
    {
        fputs("Can't capture Control-C Interrupt", stderr);
        exit(1);
    }

    while(1)                        /* main interpreter loop     */
```

(continued)

Figure 12-4. *continued*

```
    {
        get_cmd(inp_buf);              /* get a command            */
        if (! intrinsic(inp_buf) )  /* if it's intrinsic,
                                        run its subroutine        */
            extrinsic(inp_buf);        /* else pass to COMMAND.COM */
    }
}


/*
    Try to match user's command with intrinsic command
    table. If a match is found, run the associated routine
    and return true; else return false.
*/

unsigned intrinsic(char *input_string)
{
    int i, j;                          /* some scratch variables   */

                                       /* scan off leading blanks  */
    while(*input_string == '\x20') input_string++ ;

                                       /* search command table     */
    for(i=0; i < dim(commands); i++)
    {
        j = strcmp(commands[i].cmd_name, input_string);

        if(j == 0)                     /* if match, run routine    */
        {
            (*commands[i].cmd_fxn)();
            return(1);                 /* and return true          */
        }
    }
    return(0);                         /* no match, return false   */
}


/*
    Process an extrinsic command by passing it
    to an EXEC'd copy of COMMAND.COM.
*/

void extrinsic(char *input_string)
{
    int status;
```

Figure 12-4. *continued*

```
    status = system(input_string);       /* call EXEC function  */

    if(status)                           /* if failed, display
                                            error message        */
        fputs("\nEXEC of COMMAND.COM failed\n", stderr);
}


/*
    Issue prompt, get user's command from standard input,
    fold it to uppercase.
*/

void get_cmd(char *buffer)
{
    printf("\nsh: ");                    /* display prompt       */
    gets(buffer);                        /* get keyboard entry   */
    strupr(buffer);                      /* fold to uppercase    */
}


/*
    Get the full path and file specification for COMMAND.COM
    from the COMSPEC variable in the environment.
*/

void get_comspec(char *buffer)
{
    strcpy(buffer, getenv("COMSPEC"));

    if(buffer[0] == NULL)
    {
        fputs("\nNo COMSPEC in environment\n", stderr);
        exit(1);
    }
}


/*
    This Ctrl-C handler keeps SHELL from losing control.
    It just reissues the prompt and returns.
*/
```

(continued)

Figure 12-4. *continued*

```
void break_handler(void)
{
    signal(SIGINT, break_handler);      /* reset handler       */
    printf("\nsh: ");                   /* display prompt      */
}



/*
    These are the subroutines for the intrinsic commands.
*/

void cls_cmd(void)                      /* CLS command         */
{
    printf("\033[2J");                  /* ANSI escape sequence */
}                                       /* to clear screen     */

void dos_cmd(void)                      /* DOS command         */
{
    int status;
                                        /* run COMMAND.COM     */
    status = spawnlp(P_WAIT, com_spec, com_spec, NULL);

    if (status)
        fputs("\nEXEC of COMMAND.COM failed\n",stderr);
}

void exit_cmd(void)                     /* EXIT command        */
{
    exit(0);                            /* terminate SHELL     */
}
```

```
        name    shell
        page    55,132
        title   SHELL.ASM--simple MS-DOS shell
;
; SHELL.ASM     Simple extendable command interpreter
;               for MS-DOS versions 2.0 and later
;
; Copyright 1988 by Ray Duncan
```

(continued)

Figure 12-5. SHELL.ASM: *A simple table-driven command interpreter written in Microsoft Macro Assembler.*

Figure 12-5. *continued*

```
;
; Build:          C>MASM SHELL;
;                 C>LINK SHELL;
;
; Usage:          C>SHELL;
;

stdin    equ    0                       ; standard input handle
stdout   equ    1                       ; standard output handle
stderr   equ    2                       ; standard error handle


cr       equ    0dh                     ; ASCII carriage return
lf       equ    0ah                     ; ASCII linefeed
blank    equ    20h                     ; ASCII blank code
escape   equ    01bh                    ; ASCII escape code


_TEXT    segment word public 'CODE'

         assume  cs:_TEXT,ds:_DATA,ss:STACK

shell    proc    far                    ; at entry DS = ES = PSP

         mov    ax,_DATA                ; make our data segment
         mov    ds,ax                   ; addressable

         mov    ax,es:[002ch]           ; get environment segment
         mov    env_seg,ax              ; from PSP and save it

                                        ; release unneeded memory...
                                        ; ES already = PSP segment
         mov    bx,100h                 ; BX = paragraphs needed
         mov    ah,4ah                  ; function 4ah = resize block
         int    21h                     ; transfer to MS-DOS
         jnc    shell1                  ; jump if resize OK

         mov    dx,offset msg1          ; resize failed, display
         mov    cx,msg1_length          ; error message and exit
         jmp    shell4

shell1:  call   get_comspec             ; get COMMAND.COM filespec
         jnc    shell2                  ; jump if it was found

         mov    dx,offset msg3          ; COMSPEC not found in
         mov    cx,msg3_length          ; environment, display error
         jmp    shell4                  ; message and exit
```

(continued)

Figure 12-5. *continued*

```
shell2:  mov     dx,offset shell3        ; set Ctrl-C vector (int 23h)
         mov     ax,cs                   ; for this program's handler
         mov     ds,ax                   ; DS:DX - handler address
         mov     ax,2523h                ; function 25h - set vector
         int     21h                     ; transfer to MS-DOS

         mov     ax,_DATA                ; make our data segment
         mov     ds,ax                   ; addressable again
         mov     es,ax

shell3:                                  ; main interpreter loop

         call    get_cmd                 ; get a command from user

         call    intrinsic               ; check if intrinsic function
         jnc     shell3                  ; yes, it was processed

         call    extrinsic               ; no, pass it to COMMAND.COM
         jmp     shell3                  ; then get another command

shell4:                                  ; come here if error detected
                                         ; DS:DX - message address
                                         ; CX - message length
         mov     bx,stderr               ; BX - standard error handle
         mov     ah,40h                  ; function 40h - write
         int     21h                     ; transfer to MS-DOS

         mov     ax,4c01h                ; function 4ch - terminate with
                                         ; return code - 1
         int     21h                     ; transfer to MS-DOS

shell    endp



intrinsic proc  near                     ; decode user entry against
                                         ; the table "COMMANDS"
                                         ; if match, run the routine,
                                         ; and return carry - false
                                         ; if no match, carry - true
                                         ; return carry - true

         mov     si,offset commands      ; DS:SI - command table

intr1:   cmp     byte ptr [si],0         ; end of table?
         je      intr7                   ; jump, end of table found
```

(continued)

Figure 12-5. *continued*

```
          mov     di,offset inp_buf      ; no, let DI = addr of user input

intr2:    cmp     byte ptr [di],blank    ; scan off any leading blanks
          jne     intr3

          inc     di                     ; found blank, go past it
          jmp     intr2

intr3:    mov     al,[si]                ; next character from table

          or      al,al                  ; end of string?
          jz      intr4                  ; jump, entire string matched

          cmp     al,[di]                ; compare to input character
          jnz     intr6                  ; jump, found mismatch

          inc     si                     ; advance string pointers
          inc     di
          jmp     intr3

intr4:    cmp     byte ptr [di],cr       ; be sure user's entry
          je      intr5                  ; is the same length...
          cmp     byte ptr [di],blank    ; next character in entry
          jne     intr6                  ; must be blank or return

intr5:    call    word ptr [si+1]        ; run the command routine

          clc                            ; return carry flag = false
          ret                            ; as success flag

intr6:    lodsb                          ; look for end of this
          or      al,al                  ; command string (null byte)
          jnz     intr6                  ; not end yet, loop

          add     si,2                   ; skip over routine address
          jmp     intr1                  ; try to match next command

intr7:    stc                            ; command not matched, exit
          ret                            ; with carry = true

intrinsic endp
```

(continued)

Figure 12-5. *continued*

```
extrinsic proc   near                        ; process extrinsic command
                                             ; by passing it to
                                             ; COMMAND.COM with a
                                             ; " /C " command tail

        mov     al,cr                        ; find length of command
        mov     cx,cmd_tail_length           ; by scanning for carriage
        mov     di,offset cmd_tail+1         ; return
        cld
        repnz scasb

        mov     ax,di                        ; calculate command-tail
        sub     ax,offset cmd_tail+2         ; length without carriage
        mov     cmd_tail,al                  ; return, and store it

                                             ; set command-tail address
        mov     word ptr par_cmd,offset cmd_tail
        call    exec                         ; and run COMMAND.COM
        ret

extrinsic endp


get_cmd proc     near                        ; prompt user, get command

                                             ; display the shell prompt
        mov     dx,offset prompt             ; DS:DX = message address
        mov     cx,prompt_length             ; CX = message length
        mov     bx,stdout                    ; BX = standard output handle
        mov     ah,40h                       ; function 40h = write
        int     21h                          ; transfer to MS-DOS

                                             ; get entry from user
        mov     dx,offset inp_buf            ; DS:DX = input buffer
        mov     cx,inp_buf_length            ; CX = max length to read
        mov     bx,stdin                     ; BX = standard input handle
        mov     ah,3fh                       ; function 3fh = read
        int     21h                          ; transfer to MS-DOS

        mov     si,offset inp_buf            ; fold lowercase characters
        mov     cx,inp_buf_length            ; in entry to uppercase
```

(continued)

Figure 12-5. *continued*

```
gcmd1:  cmp     byte ptr [si],'a'       ; check if 'a-z'
        jb      gcmd2                   ; jump, not in range
        cmp     byte ptr [si],'z'       ; check if 'a-z'
        ja      gcmd2                   ; jump, not in range
        sub     byte ptr [si],'a'-'A'   ; convert to uppercase

gcmd2:  inc     si                      ; advance through entry
        loop    gcmd1
        ret                             ; back to caller

get_cmd endp



get_comspec proc near                   ; get location of COMMAND.COM
                                        ; from environment "COMSPEC="
                                        ; returns carry = false
                                        ; if COMSPEC found
                                        ; returns carry = true
                                        ; if no COMSPEC

        mov     si,offset com_var       ; DS:SI = string to match...
        call    get_env                 ; search environment block
        jc      gcsp2                   ; jump if COMSPEC not found

                                        ; ES:DI points past "="
        mov     si,offset com_spec      ; DS:SI = local buffer

gcsp1:  mov     al,es:[di]              ; copy COMSPEC variable
        mov     [si],al                 ; to local buffer
        inc     si
        inc     di
        or      al,al                   ; null char? (turns off carry)
        jnz     gcsp1                   ; no, get next character

gcsp2:  ret                             ; back to caller

get_comspec endp



get_env proc    near                    ; search environment
                                        ; call DS:SI = "NAME="
                                        ; uses contents of "ENV_SEG"
                                        ; returns carry = false and ES:DI
                                        ; pointing to parameter if found,
                                        ; returns carry = true if no match
```

(continued)

Figure 12-5. *continued*

```
        mov     es,env_seg          ; get environment segment
        xor     di,di               ; initialize env offset

genv1:  mov     bx,si               ; initialize pointer to name
        cmp     byte ptr es:[di],0  ; end of environment?
        jne     genv2               ; jump, end not found

        stc                         ; no match, return carry set
        ret

genv2:  mov     al,[bx]             ; get character from name
        or      al,al               ; end of name? (turns off carry)
        jz      genv3               ; yes, name matched

        cmp     al,es:[di]          ; compare to environment
        jne     genv4               ; jump if match failed

        inc     bx                  ; advance environment
        inc     di                  ; and name pointers
        jmp     genv2

genv3:                              ; match found, carry = clear,
        ret                         ; ES:DI = variable

genv4:  xor     al,al               ; scan forward in environment
        mov     cx,-1               ; for zero byte
        cld
        repnz   scasb
        jmp     genv1               ; go compare next string

get_env endp


exec    proc    near                ; call MS-DOS EXEC function
                                    ; to run COMMAND.COM

        mov     stkseg,ss           ; save stack pointer
        mov     stkptr,sp

                                    ; now run COMMAND.COM
        mov     dx,offset com_spec  ; DS:DX = filename
        mov     bx,offset par_blk   ; ES:BX = parameter block
        mov     ax,4b00h            ; function 4bh = EXEC
                                    ; subfunction 0 =
                                    ; load and execute
```

(continued)

Figure 12-5. *continued*

```
        int     21h                     ; transfer to MS-DOS

        mov     ax,_DATA                ; make data segment
        mov     ds,ax                   ; addressable again
        mov     es,ax

        cli                             ; (for bug in some 8088s)
        mov     ss,stkseg               ; restore stack pointer
        mov     sp,stkptr
        sti                             ; (for bug in some 8088s)

        jnc     exec1                   ; jump if no errors

                                        ; display error message
        mov     dx,offset msg2          ; DS:DX = message address
        mov     cx,msg2_length          ; CX = message length
        mov     bx,stderr               ; BX = standard error handle
        mov     ah,40h                  ; function 40h = write
        int     21h                     ; transfer to MS-DOS

exec1:  ret                             ; back to caller

exec    endp




cls_cmd proc    near                    ; intrinsic CLS command

        mov     dx,offset cls_str       ; send the ANSI escape
        mov     cx,cls_str_length       ; sequence to clear
        mov     bx,stdout               ; the screen
        mov     ah,40h
        int     21h
        ret

cls_cmd endp


dos_cmd proc    near                    ; intrinsic DOS command

                                        ; set null command tail
        mov     word ptr par_cmd,offset nultail
        call    exec                    ; and run COMMAND.COM
        ret

dos_cmd endp
```

(continued)

Figure 12-5. *continued*

```
exit_cmd proc   near                    ; intrinsic EXIT command

        mov     ax,4c00h                ; call MS-DOS terminate
        int     21h                     ; function with
                                        ; return code of zero
exit_cmd endp

_TEXT   ends


STACK   segment para stack 'STACK'      ; declare stack segment

        dw      64 dup (?)

STACK   ends

_DATA   segment word public 'DATA'

commands equ $                          ; "intrinsic" commands table
                                        ; each entry is ASCIIZ string
                                        ; followed by the offset
                                        ; of the procedure to be
                                        ; executed for that command

        db      'CLS',0
        dw      cls_cmd

        db      'DOS',0
        dw      dos_cmd

        db      'EXIT',0
        dw      exit_cmd

        db      0                       ; end of table

com_var db      'COMSPEC=',0            ; environment variable

                                        ; COMMAND.COM filespec
com_spec db     80 dup (0)              ; from environment COMSPEC=

nultail db      0,cr                    ; null command tail for
                                        ; invoking COMMAND.COM
                                        ; as another shell

cmd_tail db     0,' /C '                ; command tail for invoking
                                        ; COMMAND.COM as a transient
```

(continued)

Figure 12-5. *continued*

```
inp_buf db      80 dup (0)              ; command line from standard input

inp_buf_length equ $-inp_buf
cmd_tail_length equ $-cmd_tail-1

prompt  db      cr,lf,'sh: '            ; SHELL's user prompt
prompt_length equ $-prompt

env_seg dw      0                       ; segment of environment block

msg1    db      cr,lf
        db      'Unable to release memory.'
        db      cr,lf
msg1_length equ $-msg1

msg2    db      cr,lf
        db      'EXEC of COMMAND.COM failed.'
        db      cr,lf
msg2_length equ $-msg2

msg3    db      cr,lf
        db      'No COMSPEC variable in environment.'
        db      cr,lf
msg3_length equ $-msg3

cls_str db      escape,'[2J'            ; ANSI escape sequence
cls_str_length equ $-cls_str           ; to clear the screen

                                        ; EXEC parameter block
par_blk dw      0                       ; environment segment
par_cmd dd      cmd_tail                ; command line
        dd      fcb1                    ; file control block #1
        dd      fcb2                    ; file control block #2

fcb1    db      0                       ; file control block #1
        db      11 dup (' ')
        db      25 dup (0)

fcb2    db      0                       ; file control block #2
        db      11 dup (' ')
        db      25 dup (0)

stkseg  dw      0                       ; original SS contents
stkptr  dw      0                       ; original SP contents

_DATA   ends

        end     shell
```

The *SHELL* program is table driven and can easily be extended to provide a powerful customized user interface for almost any application. When *SHELL* takes control of the system, it displays the prompt

sh:

and waits for input from the user. After the user types a line terminated by a carriage return, *SHELL* tries to match the first token in the line against its table of internal (intrinsic) commands. If it finds a match, it calls the appropriate subroutine. If it does not find a match, it calls the MS-DOS EXEC function and passes the user's input to COMMAND.COM with the /C switch, essentially using COMMAND.COM as a transient command processor under its own control.

As supplied in these listings, *SHELL* "knows" exactly three internal commands:

Command	*Action*
CLS	Uses the ANSI standard control sequence to clear the display screen and home the cursor.
DOS	Runs a copy of COMMAND.COM.
EXIT	Exits SHELL, returning control of the system to the next lower command interpreter.

You can quickly add new intrinsic commands to either the C version or the assembly-language version of *SHELL*. Simply code a procedure with the appropriate action and insert the name of that procedure, along with the text string that defines the command, into the table *COMMANDS*. In addition, you can easily prevent *SHELL* from passing certain "dangerous" commands (such as MKDIR or ERASE) to COMMAND.COM simply by putting the names of the commands to be screened out into the intrinsic command table with the address of a subroutine that prints an error message.

To summarize, the basic flow of both versions of the SHELL program is as follows:

1. The program calls MS-DOS Int 21H Function 4AH (Resize Memory Block) to shrink its memory allocation, so that the maximum possible space will be available for COMMAND.COM if it is run as an overlay. (This is explicit in the assembly-language version only. To keep the example code simple, the number of paragraphs to be reserved is coded as a generous literal value, rather than being figured out at runtime from the size and location of the various program segments.)

2. The program searches the environment for the COMSPEC variable, which defines the location of an executable copy of COMMAND.COM. If it can't find the COMSPEC variable, it prints an error message and exits.

3. The program puts the address of its own handler in the Ctrl-C vector (Int 23H) so that it won't lose control if the user enters a Ctrl-C or a Ctrl-Break.

4. The program issues a prompt to the standard output device.

5. The program reads a buffered line from the standard input device to get the user's command.

6. The program matches the first blank-delimited token in the line against its table of intrinsic commands. If it finds a match, it executes the associated procedure.

7. If the program does not find a match in the table of intrinsic commands, it synthesizes a command-line tail by appending the user's input to the /C switch and then EXECs a copy of COMMAND.COM, passing the address of the synthesized command tail in the EXEC parameter block.

8. The program repeats steps 4 through 7 until the user enters the command EXIT, which is one of the intrinsic commands, and which causes *SHELL* to terminate execution.

In its present form, *SHELL* allows COMMAND.COM to inherit a full copy of the current environment. However, in some applications it may be helpful, or safer, to pass a modified copy of the environment block so that the secondary copy of COMMAND.COM will not have access to certain information.

Using EXEC to Load Overlays

Loading overlays with the EXEC function is much less complex than using EXEC to run another program. The overlay can be constructed as either a memory image (.COM) or relocatable (.EXE) file and need not be the same type as the program that loads it. The main program, called the root segment, must carry out the following steps to load and execute an overlay:

1. Make a memory block available to receive the overlay. The program that calls EXEC must own the memory block for the overlay.

2. Set up the overlay parameter block to be passed to the EXEC function. This block contains the segment address of the block that will receive the overlay, plus a segment relocation value to be applied to the contents of the overlay file (if it is a .EXE file). These are normally the same value.

3. Call the MS-DOS EXEC function to load the overlay by issuing an Int 21H with the registers set up as follows:

AH = 4BH

AL = 03H (EXEC subfunction to load overlay)

DS:DX = segment:offset of overlay file pathname

ES:BX = segment:offset of overlay parameter block

Upon return from the EXEC function, the carry flag is clear if the overlay was found and loaded. The carry flag is set if the file could not be found or if some other error occurred.

4. Execute the code within the overlay by transferring to it with a far call. The overlay should be designed so that either the entry point or a pointer to the entry point is at the beginning of the module after it is loaded. This technique allows you to maintain the root and overlay modules separately, because the root module does not contain any "magical" knowledge of addresses within the overlay segment.

To prevent users from inadvertently running an overlay directly from the command line, you should assign overlay files an extension other than .COM or .EXE. It is most convenient to relate overlays to their root segment by assigning them the same filename but a different extension, such as .OVL or .OV1, .OV2, and so on.

Figure 12-6 shows the use of EXEC to load and execute an overlay.

```
        .
        .
        .
                        ; allocate memory for overlay
        mov     bx,1000h        ; get 64 KB (4096 paragraphs)
        mov     ah,48h          ; function 48h = allocate block
```

(continued)

Figure 12-6. *A code skeleton for loading and executing an overlay with the EXEC function. The overlay file may be in either .COM or .EXE format.*

Figure 12-6. *continued*

```
        int     21h                 ; transfer to MS-DOS
        jc      error               ; jump if allocation failed

        mov     pars,ax             ; set load address for overlay
        mov     pars+2,ax           ; set relocation segment for overlay

                                    ; set segment of entry point
        mov     word ptr entry+2,ax

        mov     stkseg,ss           ; save root's stack pointer
        mov     stkptr,sp

        mov     ax,ds               ; set ES = DS
        mov     es,ax

        mov     dx,offset oname ; DS:DX = overlay pathname
        mov     bx,offset pars  ; ES:BX = parameter block
        mov     ax,4b03h            ; function 4bh, subfunction 03h
        int     21h                 ; transfer to MS-DOS

        mov     ax,_DATA            ; make our data segment
        mov     ds,ax               ; addressable again
        mov     es,ax

        cli                         ; (for bug in some early 8088s)
        mov     ss,stkseg           ; restore stack pointer
        mov     sp,stkptr
        sti                         ; (for bug in some early 8088s)

        jc      error               ; jump if EXEC failed

                                    ; otherwise EXEC succeeded...
        push    ds                  ; save our data segment
        call    dword ptr entry ; now call the overlay
        pop     ds                  ; restore our data segment
        .
        .
        .

oname   db      'OVERLAY.OVL',0 ; pathname of overlay file

pars    dw      0                   ; load address (segment) for file
        dw      0                   ; relocation (segment) for file

entry   dd      0                   ; entry point for overlay

stkseg  dw      0                   ; save SS register
stkptr  dw      0                   ; save SP register
```

Chapter 13

Interrupt Handlers

Interrupts are signals that cause the computer's central processing unit to suspend what it is doing and transfer to a program called an interrupt handler. Special hardware mechanisms that are designed for maximum speed force the transfer. The interrupt handler determines the cause of the interrupt, takes the appropriate action, and then returns control to the original process that was suspended.

Interrupts are typically caused by events external to the central processor that require immediate attention, such as the following:

- Completion of an I/O operation
- Detection of a hardware failure
- "Catastrophes" (power failures, for example)

In order to service interrupts more efficiently, most modern processors support multiple *interrupt types,* or levels. Each type usually has a reserved location in memory, called an *interrupt vector,* that specifies where the interrupt-handler program for that interrupt type is located. This design speeds processing of an interrupt because the computer can transfer control directly to the appropriate routine; it does not need a central routine that wastes precious machine cycles determining the cause of the interrupt. The concept of interrupt types also allows interrupts to be prioritized, so that if several interrupts occur simultaneously, the most important one can be processed first.

CPUs that support interrupts must also have the capability to block interrupts while they are executing critical sections of code. Sometimes the CPU can block interrupt levels selectively, but more frequently the effect is global. While an interrupt is being serviced, the CPU masks all other interrupts of the same or lower priority until the active handler has completed its execution; similarly, it can preempt the execution of a handler if a different interrupt with higher priority requires service. Some CPUs can even draw a distinction between selectively masking interrupts (they are recognized, but their processing is deferred) and simply disabling them (the interrupt is thrown away).

The creation of interrupt handlers has traditionally been considered one of the most arcane of programming tasks, suitable only for the elite cadre of system hackers. In reality, writing an interrupt handler is, in itself, straightforward. Although the exact procedure must, of course, be customized for the characteristics of the particular CPU and operating system, the guidelines on the following page are applicable to almost any computer system.

A program preparing to handle interrupts must do the following:

1. Disable interrupts, if they were previously enabled, to prevent them from occurring while interrupt vectors are being modified.

2. Initialize the vector for the interrupt of interest to point to the program's interrupt handler.

3. Ensure that, if interrupts were previously disabled, all other vectors point to some valid handler routine.

4. Enable interrupts again.

The interrupt handler itself must follow a simple but rigid sequence of steps:

1. Save the system context (registers, flags, and anything else that the handler will modify and that wasn't saved automatically by the CPU).

2. Block any interrupts that might cause interference if they were allowed to occur during this handler's processing. (This is often done automatically by the computer hardware.)

3. Enable any interrupts that should still be allowed to occur during this handler's processing.

4. Determine the cause of the interrupt.

5. Take the appropriate action for the interrupt: receive and store data from the serial port, set a flag to indicate the completion of a disk-sector transfer, and so forth.

6. Restore the system context.

7. Reenable any interrupt levels that were blocked during this handler's execution.

8. Resume execution of the interrupted process.

As in writing any other program, the key to success in writing an interrupt handler is to program defensively and cover all the bases. The main reason interrupt handlers have acquired such a mystical reputation is that they are so difficult to debug when they contain obscure errors. Because interrupts can occur asynchronously—that is, because they can be caused by external events without regard to the state of the currently executing process—bugs in interrupt handlers can cause the system as a whole to behave quite unpredictably.

Interrupts and the Intel 80x86 Family

The Intel 80x86 family of microprocessors supports 256 levels of prioritized interrupts, which can be triggered by three types of events:

- Internal hardware interrupts
- External hardware interrupts
- Software interrupts

Internal Hardware Interrupts

Internal hardware interrupts, sometimes called *faults,* are generated by certain events encountered during program execution, such as an attempt to divide by zero. The assignment of such events to certain interrupt numbers is wired into the processor and is not modifiable (Figure 13-1).

Interrupt level	Vector address	Interrupt trigger	8086/88	80286	80386
00H	00H–03H	Divide-by-zero	x	x	x
01H	04H–07H	Single step	x	x	x
02H	08H–0BH	Nonmaskable interrupt (NMI)	x	x	x
03H	0CH–0FH	Breakpoint	x	x	x
04H	10H–13H	Overflow	x	x	x
05H	14H–17H	BOUND exceeded		x	x
06H	18H–1BH	Invalid opcode		x	x
07H	1CH–1FH	Processor extension not available		x	x
08H	20H–23H	Double fault		x	x
09H	24H–27H	Segment overrun		x	x
0AH	28H–2BH	Invalid task-state segment		x	x
0BH	2CH–2FH	Segment not present		x	x
0CH	30H–33H	Stack segment overrun		x	x
0DH	34H–37H	General protection fault		x	x
0EH	38H–3BH	Page fault			x
0FH	3CH–3FH	Reserved			
10H	40H–43H	Numeric coprocessor error		x	x
11H–1FH	44H–7FH	Reserved			

Figure 13-1. *Internal interrupts (faults) on the Intel 8086/88, 80286, and 80386 microprocessors.*

External Hardware Interrupts

External hardware interrupts are triggered by peripheral device controllers or by coprocessors such as the 8087/80287. These can be tied to either the CPU's nonmaskable-interrupt (NMI) pin or its maskable-interrupt (INTR) pin. The NMI line is usually reserved for interrupts caused by such catastrophic events as a memory parity error or a power failure.

Instead of being wired directly to the CPU, the interrupts from external devices can be channeled through a device called the Intel 8259A Programmable Interrupt Controller (PIC). The CPU controls the PIC through a set of I/O ports, and the PIC, in turn, signals the CPU through the INTR pin. The PIC allows the interrupts from specific devices to be enabled and disabled, and their priorities to be adjusted, under program control.

A single PIC can handle only eight levels of interrupts. However, PICs can be cascaded together in a treelike structure to handle as many levels as desired. For example, 80286- and 80386-based machines with a PC/AT-compatible architecture use two PICs wired together to obtain 16 individually configurable levels of interrupts.

INTR interrupts can be globally enabled and disabled with the CPU's STI and CLI instructions. As you would expect, these instructions have no effect on interrupts received on the CPU's NMI pin.

The manufacturer of the computer system and/or the manufacturer of the peripheral device assigns external devices to specific 8259A PIC interrupt levels. These assignments are realized as physical electrical connections and cannot be modified by software.

Software Interrupts

Any program can trigger software interrupts synchronously simply by executing an INT instruction. MS-DOS uses Interrupts 20H through 3FH to communicate with its modules and with application programs. (For instance, the MS-DOS function dispatcher is reached by executing an Int 21H.) The IBM PC ROM BIOS and application software use other interrupts, with either higher or lower numbers, for various purposes (Figure 13-2). These assignments are simply conventions and are not wired into the hardware in any way.

Interrupt	Usage	Machine
00H	Divide-by-zero	PC, AT, PS/2
01H	Single step	PC, AT, PS/2
02H	NMI	PC, AT, PS/2
03H	Breakpoint	PC, AT, PS/2
04H	Overflow	PC, AT, PS/2
05H	ROM BIOS PrintScreen	PC, AT, PS/2
	BOUND exceeded	AT, PS/2
06H	Reserved	PC
	Invalid opcode	AT, PS/2
07H	Reserved	PC
	80287/80387 not present	AT, PS/2
08H	IRQ0 timer tick	PC, AT, PS/2
	Double fault	AT, PS/2
09H	IRQ1 keyboard	PC, AT, PS/2
	80287/80387 segment overrun	AT, PS/2
0AH	IRQ2 reserved	PC
	IRQ2 cascade from slave 8259A PIC	AT, PS/2
	Invalid task-state segment (TSS)	AT, PS/2
0BH	IRQ3 serial communications (COM2)	PC, AT, PS/2
	Segment not present	AT, PS/2
0CH	IRQ4 serial communications (COM1)	PC, AT, PS/2
	Stack segment overflow	AT, PS/2
0DH	IRQ5 fixed disk	PC
	IRQ5 parallel printer (LPT2)	AT
	Reserved	PS/2
	General protection fault	AT, PS/2
0EH	IRQ6 floppy disk	PC, AT, PS/2
	Page fault	AT, PS/2
0FH	IRQ7 parallel printer (LPT1)	PC, AT, PS/2
10H	ROM BIOS video driver	PC, AT, PS/2
	Numeric coprocessor fault	AT, PS/2
11H	ROM BIOS equipment check	PC, AT, PS/2
12H	ROM BIOS conventional-memory size	PC, AT, PS/2
13H	ROM BIOS disk driver	PC, AT, PS/2
14H	ROM BIOS communications driver	PC, AT, PS/2
15H	ROM BIOS cassette driver	PC
	ROM BIOS I/O system extensions	AT, PS/2
16H	ROM BIOS keyboard driver	PC, AT, PS/2
17H	ROM BIOS printer driver	PC, AT, PS/2
18H	ROM BASIC	PC, AT, PS/2
19H	ROM BIOS bootstrap	PC, AT, PS/2

(continued)

Figure 13-2. *Interrupts with special significance on the IBM PC, PC/AT, and PS/2 and compatible computers. Note that the IBM ROM BIOS uses several interrupts in the range 00H–1FH, even though they were reserved by Intel for CPU faults. IRQ numbers refer to Intel 8259A PIC priority levels.*

Figure 13-2. *continued*

Interrupt	Usage	Machine
1AH	ROM BIOS time of day	AT, PS/2
1BH	ROM BIOS Ctrl-Break	PC, AT, PS/2
1CH	ROM BIOS timer tick	PC, AT, PS/2
1DH	ROM BIOS video parameter table	PC, AT, PS/2
1EH	ROM BIOS floppy-disk parameters	PC, AT, PS/2
1FH	ROM BIOS font (characters 80H–FFH)	PC, AT, PS/2
20H	MS-DOS terminate process	
21H	MS-DOS function dispatcher	
22H	MS-DOS terminate address	
23H	MS-DOS Ctrl-C handler address	
24H	MS-DOS critical-error handler address	
25H	MS-DOS absolute disk read	
26H	MS-DOS absolute disk write	
27H	MS-DOS terminate and stay resident	
28H	MS-DOS idle interrupt	
29H	MS-DOS reserved	
2AH	MS-DOS network redirector	
2BH–2EH	MS-DOS reserved	
2FH	MS-DOS multiplex interrupt	
30H–3FH	MS-DOS reserved	
40H	ROM BIOS floppy-disk driver (if fixed disk installed)	PC, AT, PS/2
41H	ROM BIOS fixed-disk parameters	PC
	ROM BIOS fixed-disk parameters (drive 0)	AT, PS/2
42H	ROM BIOS default video driver (if EGA installed)	PC, AT, PS/2
43H	EGA, MCGA, VGA character table	PC, AT, PS/2
44H	ROM BIOS font (characters 00H–7FH)	PCjr
46H	ROM BIOS fixed-disk parameters (drive 1)	AT, PS/2
4AH	ROM BIOS alarm handler	AT, PS/2
5AH	Cluster adapter	PC, AT
5BH	Used by cluster program	PC, AT
60H–66H	User interrupts	PC, AT, PS/2
67H	LIM EMS driver	PC, AT, PS/2
68H–6FH	Unassigned	
70H	IRQ8 CMOS real-time clock	AT, PS/2
71H	IRQ9 software diverted to IRQ2	AT, PS/2
72H	IRQ10 reserved	AT, PS/2
73H	IRQ11 reserved	AT, PS/2
74H	IRQ12 reserved	AT
	IRQ12 mouse	PS/2
75H	IRQ13 numeric coprocessor	AT, PS/2
76H	IRQ14 fixed-disk controller	AT, PS/2
77H	IRQ15 reserved	AT, PS/2
78H–7FH	Unassigned	
80H–F0H	BASIC	PC, AT, PS/2
F1H–FFH	Not used	PC, AT, PS/2

The Interrupt-Vector Table

The bottom 1024 bytes of system memory are called the *interrupt-vector table*. Each 4-byte position in the table corresponds to an interrupt type (0 through 0FFH) and contains the segment and offset of the interrupt handler for that level. Interrupts 0 through 1FH (the lowest levels) are used for internal hardware interrupts; MS-DOS uses Interrupts 20H through 3FH; all the other interrupts are available for use by either external hardware devices or system drivers and application software.

When an 8259A PIC or other device interrupts the CPU by means of the INTR pin, it must also place the interrupt type as an 8-bit number (0 through 0FFH) on the system bus, where the CPU can find it. The CPU then multiplies this number by 4 to find the memory address of the interrupt vector to be used.

Servicing an Interrupt

When the CPU senses an interrupt, it pushes the program status word (which defines the various CPU flags), the code segment (CS) register, and the instruction pointer (IP) onto the machine stack and disables the interrupt system. It then uses the 8-bit number that was jammed onto the system bus by the interrupting device to fetch the address of the handler from the vector table and resumes execution at that address.

Usually the handler immediately reenables the interrupt system (to allow higher-priority interrupts to occur), saves any registers it is going to use, and then processes the interrupt as quickly as possible. Some external devices also require a special acknowledgment signal so that they will know the interrupt has been recognized.

If the interrupt was funneled through an 8259A PIC, the handler must send a special code called *end of interrupt* (EOI) to the PIC through its control port to tell it when interrupt processing is completed. (The EOI has no effect on the CPU itself.) Finally, the handler executes the special IRET (INTERRUPT RETURN) instruction that restores the original state of the CPU flags, the CS register, and the instruction pointer (Figure 13-3).

Whether an interrupt was triggered by an external device or forced by software execution of an INT instruction, there is no discernible difference in the system state at the time the interrupt handler receives control. This fact is convenient when you are writing and testing external interrupt handlers because you can debug them to a large extent simply by invoking them with software drivers.

```
pic_ctl          equ  20h                    ; control port for 8259A
                                             ; interrupt controller

                  .
                  .
                  .
                 sti                          ; turn interrupts back on,
                 push  ax                     ; save registers
                 push  bx
                 push  cx
                 push  dx
                 push  si
                 push  di
                 push  bp
                 push  ds
                 push  es

                 mov   ax,cs                  ; make local data addressable
                 mov   ds,ax
                  .                           ; do some stuff appropriate
                  .                           ; for this interrupt here
                  .
                 mov   al,20h                 ; send EOI to 8259A PIC
                 mov   dx,pic_ctl
                 out   dx,al

                 pop   es                     ; restore registers
                 pop   ds
                 pop   bp
                 pop   di
                 pop   si
                 pop   dx
                 pop   cx
                 pop   bx
                 pop   ax
                 iret                         ; resume previous processing
```

Figure 13-3. *Typical handler for hardware interrupts on the 80x86 family of micro-processors. In real life, the interrupt handler would need to save and restore only the registers that it actually modified. Also, if the handler made extensive use of the machine stack, it would need to save and restore the SS and SP registers of the interrupted process and use its own local stack.*

Interrupt Handlers and MS-DOS

The introduction of an interrupt handler into your program brings with it considerable hardware dependence. It goes without saying (but I am saying it again here anyway) that you should avoid such hardware dependence in MS-DOS applications whenever possible, to ensure that your programs will be portable to any machine running current versions of MS-DOS and that they will run properly under future versions of the operating system.

Valid reasons do exist, however, for writing your own interrupt handler for use under MS-DOS:

- To supersede the MS-DOS default handler for an internal hardware interrupt (such as divide-by-zero, BOUND exceeded, and so forth).

- To supersede the MS-DOS default handler for a defined system exception, such as the critical-error handler or Ctrl-C handler.

- To chain your own interrupt handler onto the default system handler for a hardware device, so that both the system's actions *and* your own will occur on an interrupt. (A typical example of this is the "clock-tick" interrupt.)

- To service interrupts not supported by the default MS-DOS device drivers (such as the serial communications port, which can be used at much higher speeds with interrupts than with polling).

- To provide a path of communication between a program that terminates and stays resident and other application software.

MS-DOS provides the following facilities to enable you to install well-behaved interrupt handlers in a manner that does not interfere with operating-system functions or other interrupt handlers:

Function	*Action*
Int 21H Function 25H	Set interrupt vector.
Int 21H Function 35H	Get interrupt vector.
Int 21H Function 31H	Terminate and stay resident.

These functions allow you to examine or modify the contents of the system interrupt-vector table and to reserve memory for the use of a handler without running afoul of other processes in the system or causing memory use conflicts. Section II of this book, "MS-DOS Functions Reference," describes each of these functions in detail, with programming examples.

Handlers for external hardware interrupts under MS-DOS must operate under some fairly severe restrictions:

- Because the current versions of MS-DOS are not reentrant, a hardware interrupt handler should never call the MS-DOS functions during the actual interrupt processing.

- The handler must reenable interrupts as soon as it gets control, to avoid crippling other devices or destroying the accuracy of the system clock.

- A program should access the 8259A PIC with great care. The program should not access the PIC unless that program is known to be the only process in the system concerned with that particular interrupt level. And it is vital that the handler issue an end-of-interrupt code to the 8259A PIC before performing the IRET; otherwise, the processing of further interrupts for that priority level or lower priority levels will be blocked.

Restrictions on handlers that replace the MS-DOS default handlers for internal hardware interrupts or system exceptions (such as Ctrl-C or critical errors) are not quite so stringent, but you must still program the handlers with extreme care to avoid destroying system tables or leaving the operating system in an unstable state.

The following are a few rules to keep in mind when you are writing an interrupt driver:

- Use Int 21H Function 25H (Set Interrupt Vector) to modify the interrupt vector; do not write directly to the interrupt-vector table.

- If your program is not the only process in the system that uses this interrupt level, chain back to the previous handler after performing your own processing on an interrupt.

- If your program is not going to stay resident, fetch and save the current contents of the interrupt vector before modifying it and then restore the original contents when your program exits.

- If your program is going to stay resident, use one of the terminate-and-stay-resident functions (preferably Int 21H Function 31H) to reserve the proper amount of memory for your handler.

- If you are going to process hardware interrupts, keep the time that interrupts are disabled and the total length of the service routine to an absolute minimum. Remember that even after interrupts are reenabled with an STI instruction, interrupts of the same or lower priority remain blocked if the interrupt was received through the 8259A PIC.

ZERODIV, an Example Interrupt Handler

The listing *ZERODIV.ASM* (Figure 13-4) illustrates some of the principles and guidelines on the previous pages. It is an interrupt handler for the divide-by-zero internal interrupt (type 0). *ZERODIV* is loaded as a .COM file (usually by a command in the system's AUTOEXEC file) but makes itself permanently resident in memory as long as the system is running.

The *ZERODIV* program has two major portions: the initialization portion and the interrupt handler.

The initialization procedure (called *init* in the program listing) is executed only once, when the *ZERODIV* program is executed from the MS-DOS level. The *init* procedure takes over the type 0 interrupt vector, prints a sign-on message, then performs a terminate-and-stay-resident exit to MS-DOS. This special exit reserves the memory occupied by the *ZERODIV* program, so that it is not overwritten by subsequent application programs.

The interrupt handler (called *zdiv* in the program listing) receives control when a divide-by-zero interrupt occurs. The handler preserves all registers and then prints a message to the user asking whether to continue or to abort the program. We can use the MS-DOS console I/O functions within this particular interrupt handler because we can safely presume that the application was in control when the interrupt occurred; thus, there should be no chance of accidentally making overlapping calls upon the operating system.

If the user enters a *C* to continue, the handler simply restores all the registers and performs an IRET (INTERRUPT RETURN) to return control to the application. (Of course, the results of the divide operation will be useless.) If the user enters *Q* to quit, the handler exits to MS-DOS. Int 21H Function 4CH is particularly convenient in this case because it allows the program to pass a return code and at the same time is the only termination function that does not rely on the contents of any of the segment registers.

For an example of an interrupt handler for external (communications port) interrupts, see the *TALK* terminal-emulator program in Chapter 7. You may also want to look again at the discussions of Ctrl-C and critical-error exception handlers in Chapters 5 and 8.

```
        name      zdivide
        page      55,132
        title     ZERODIV--Divide-by-zero handler


;
; ZERODIV.ASM--Terminate-and-stay-resident handler
;             for divide-by-zero interrupts
;
; Copyright 1988 Ray Duncan
;
; Build:          C>MASM ZERODIV;
;                 C>LINK ZERODIV;
;                 C>EXE2BIN ZERODIV.EXE ZERODIV.COM
;                 C>DEL ZERODIV.EXE
;
; Usage:          C>ZERODIV
;


cr      equ      0dh              ; ASCII carriage return
lf      equ      0ah              ; ASCII linefeed
beep    equ      07h              ; ASCII bell code
backsp  equ      08h              ; ASCII backspace code


_TEXT   segment word public 'CODE'

        org      100H

        assume   cs:_TEXT,ds:_TEXT,es:_TEXT,ss:_TEXT

init    proc     near             ; entry point at load time

                                  ; capture vector for
                                  ; interrupt zero...
        mov      dx,offset zdiv   ; DS:DX = handler address
        mov      ax,2500h         ; function 25h = set vector
                                  ; interrupt type = 0
        int      21h              ; transfer to MS-DOS

                                  ; print sign-on message
        mov      dx,offset msg1   ; DS:DX = message address
        mov      ah,9             ; function 09h = display string
        int      21h              ; transfer to MS-DOS

                                  ; DX = paragraphs to reserve
```

(continued)

Figure 13-4. *A simple example of an interrrupt handler for use within the MS-DOS environment.* ZERODIV *makes itself permanently resident in memory and handles the CPU's internal divide-by-zero interrupt.*

Figure 13-4. *continued*

```
        mov     dx,((offset pgm_len+15)/16)+10h
        mov     ax,3100h        ; function 31h - terminate and
                                ; stay resident
        int     21h             ; transfer to MS-DOS

init    endp


zdiv    proc    far             ; this is the divide-by-
                                ; zero interrupt handler

        sti                     ; enable interrupts

        push    ax              ; save registers
        push    bx
        push    cx
        push    dx
        push    si
        push    di
        push    bp
        push    ds
        push    es

        mov     ax,cs           ; make data addressable
        mov     ds,ax

                                ; display message
                                ; "Continue or Quit?"
        mov     dx,offset msg2  ; DS:DX - message address
        mov     ah,9            ; function 09h - display string
        int     21h             ; transfer to MS-DOS

zdiv1:  mov     ah,1            ; function 01h - read keyboard
        int     21h             ; transfer to MS-DOS

        or      al,20h          ; fold char to lowercase

        cmp     al,'c'          ; is it C or Q?
        je      zdiv3           ; jump, it's a C

        cmp     al,'q'
        je      zdiv2           ; jump, it's a Q

                                ; illegal entry, send beep
                                ; and erase the character
```

(continued)

Figure 13-4. *continued*

```
        mov     dx,offset msg3  ; DS:DX = message address
        mov     ah,9            ; function 09h = display string
        int     21h             ; transfer to MS-DOS

        jmp     zdiv1           ; try again

zdiv2:                          ; user chose "Quit"
        mov     ax,4cffh        ; terminate current program
        int     21h             ; with return code = 255

zdiv3:                          ; user chose "Continue"
                                ; send CR-LF pair
        mov     dx,offset msg4  ; DS:DX = message address
        mov     ah,9            ; function 09h = print string
        int     21h             ; transfer to MS-DOS

                                ; what CPU type is this?
        xor     ax,ax           ; to find out, we'll put
        push    ax              ; zero in the CPU flags
        popf                    ; and see what happens
        pushf
        pop     ax
        and     ax,0f000h       ; 8086/8088 forces
        cmp     ax,0f000h       ; bits 12-15 true
        je      zdiv5           ; jump if 8086/8088

                                ; otherwise we must adjust
                                ; return address to bypass
                                ; the divide instruction...
        mov     bp,sp           ; make stack addressable

        lds     bx,[bp+18]      ; get address of the
                                ; faulting instruction

        mov     bl,[bx+1]       ; get addressing byte
        and     bx,0c7h         ; isolate mod & r/m fields

        cmp     bl,6            ; mod 0, r/m 6 = direct
        jne     zdiv4           ; not direct, jump

        add     word ptr [bp+18],4
        jmp     zdiv5
```

(continued)

Figure 13-4. *continued*

```
zdiv4:  mov     cl,6            ; otherwise isolate mod
        shr     bx,cl           ; field and get instruction
        mov     bl,cs:[bx+itab] ; size from table
        add     [bp+18],bx

zdiv5:  pop     es              ; restore registers
        pop     ds
        pop     bp
        pop     di
        pop     si
        pop     dx
        pop     cx
        pop     bx
        pop     ax
        iret                    ; return from interrupt


zdiv    endp


msg1    db      cr,lf           ; load-time sign-on message
        db      'Divide by Zero Interrupt '
        db      'Handler installed.'
        db      cr,lf,'$'

msg2    db      cr,lf,lf        ; interrupt-time message
        db      'Divide by Zero detected: '
        db      cr,lf,'Continue or Quit (C/Q) ? '
        db      '$'

msg3    db      beep            ; used if bad entry
        db      backsp,' ',backsp,'$'

msg4    db      cr,lf,'$'       ; carriage return-linefeed

                                ; instruction size table
itab    db      2               ; mod = 0
        db      3               ; mod = 1
        db      4               ; mod = 2
        db      2               ; mod = 3

pgm_len equ     $-init          ; program length

_TEXT   ends

        end     init
```

Chapter 14

Installable Device Drivers

Device drivers are the modules of an operating system that control the hardware. They isolate the operating-system kernel from the specific characteristics and idiosyncrasies of the peripheral devices interfaced to the central processor. Thus, the driver's relationship to the kernel is analogous to the operating system's relationship to application programs.

The installable device drivers that were introduced in MS-DOS version 2 give the user great flexibility. They allow the user to customize and configure the computer for a wide range of peripheral devices, with a minimum of troublesome interactions and without having to "patch" the operating system. Even the most inexperienced user can install a new device into a system by plugging in a card, copying a driver file to the boot disk, and editing the system configuration file.

For those inclined to do their own programming, the MS-DOS installable device drivers are interfaced to the hardware-independent kernel through a simple and clearly defined scheme of function codes and data structures. Given adequate information about the hardware, any competent assembly-language programmer can expect to successfully interface even the most bizarre device to MS-DOS without altering the operating system in the slightest and without acquiring any special or proprietary knowledge about its innards.

In retrospect, installable device drivers have proven to be one of the key usability features of MS-DOS. I feel that they have been largely responsible for the rapid proliferation and competitive pricing of high-speed mass-storage devices for MS-DOS machines, and for the growing confidence of the average user toward "tampering with" (upgrading) his or her machine.

MS-DOS Device-Driver Types

Drivers written for MS-DOS fall into two distinct classes:

- Block-device drivers
- Character-device drivers

A driver's class determines what functions it must support, how it is viewed by MS-DOS, and how it makes the associated physical device appear to behave when an application program makes a request for I/O.

Character-Device Drivers

Character-device drivers control peripheral devices that perform input and output one character (or byte) at a time, such as a terminal or printer. A single character-device driver ordinarily supports a single hardware unit. Each character device has a one-to-eight-character logical name, and an application program can use this name to open the device for input or output, as though it were a file. The logical name is strictly a means of identification for MS-DOS and has no physical equivalent on the device.

MS-DOS's built-in character-device drivers for the console, serial port, and printer are unique in that an application program can access them in three different ways:

- It can open them by name (CON, AUX, PRN, etc.) for input and output, like any other character device.

- It can use the special-purpose MS-DOS function calls (Int 21H Functions 01–0CH).

- It can use the default handles (standard input, standard output, standard error, standard auxiliary, and standard printer), which do not need to be opened to be used.

The number of additional character-device drivers that can be installed is limited only by available memory and by the requirement that each driver have a unique logical name. If more than one driver uses the same logical name, the last driver to be loaded will supersede any others and will receive all I/O requests addressed to that logical name. This fact can occasionally be turned to advantage; for example, it allows the user to replace the system's default CON driver, which does not support cursor positioning or character attributes, with the more powerful ANSI.SYS driver.

ASCII *vs* Binary Mode

MS-DOS regards a handle associated with a character device to be in either ASCII (cooked) mode or binary (raw) mode. The mode affects MS-DOS's buffering of data for read and write requests. The driver itself is not aware of the mode, and the mode does not affect its operation. An application can select the mode of a handle with the IOCTL function (Int 21H Function 44H).

During ASCII-mode input, MS-DOS requests characters one at a time from the driver and places them into its own internal buffer, echoing each to the screen (if the input device is the keyboard) and checking each character for a Ctrl-C (03H). When the number of characters requested by the application program has been received, when a Ctrl-Z is detected, or when the Enter key is pressed (in the case of the keyboard), MS-DOS terminates the input and copies the data from its internal buffer into the requesting program's buffer. Similarly, during ASCII-mode output, MS-DOS passes the characters to the device driver one at a time and checks for a Ctrl-C pending at the keyboard between each character. When a Ctrl-C is detected, MS-DOS aborts the input or output operation and transfers to the routine whose address is stored in the Int 23H vector.

In binary mode, MS-DOS reads or writes the exact number of bytes requested by the application program, without regard to any control characters such as Enter or Ctrl-C. MS-DOS passes the entire request through to the driver in a single operation, instead of breaking it into single-character reads or writes, and transfers the characters directly to or from the requesting program's buffer.

Block-Device drivers

Block-device drivers usually control random-access mass-storage devices such as floppy-disk drives and fixed disks, although they can also be used to control non-random-access devices such as magnetic-tape drives. Block devices transfer data in chunks, rather than one byte at a time. The size of the blocks may be either fixed (disk drives) or variable (tape drives).

A block driver can support more than one hardware unit, map a single physical unit onto two or more logical units, or both. Block devices do not have file-like logical names, as character devices do. Instead, MS-DOS assigns drive designators to the block-device units or logical drives in an alphabetic sequence: A, B, and so forth. Each logical drive contains a file system: boot block, file allocation table, root directory, and so forth. (See Chapter 10.)

A block-device driver's position in the chain of all drivers determines the first letter assigned to that driver. The number of logical drive units that the driver supports determines the total number of letters assigned to it.

Block-device drivers always read or write exactly the number of sectors requested (barring hardware or addressing errors) and never filter or otherwise manipulate the contents of the blocks being transferred.

Structure of an MS-DOS Device Driver

A device driver consists of three major parts (Figure 14-1):

- A device header
- A strategy (*strat*) routine
- An interrupt (*intr*) routine

We'll discuss each of these in more detail as we work through this chapter.

Interrupt routine	Initialization
	Media check
	Build BPB
	IOCTL read and write
	Status
	Read
	Write, write/verify
	Output until busy
	Flush buffers
	Device open
	Device close
	Check whether removable
	Generic IOCTL
	Get/Set logical device
Strategy routine	
Device-driver header	

Figure 14-1. *General structure of an MS-DOS installable device driver.*

The Device Header

The device header (Figure 14-2) lies at the beginning of the driver. It contains a link to the next driver in the chain, a set of attribute flags for the device (Figure 14-3), offsets to the executable strategy and interrupt routines for the device, and the logical-device name (if it is a character device such as PRN or COM1) or the number of logical units (if it is a block device).

```
00H  ┌─────────────────────────────────────────────┐
02H  │          Link to next driver, offset         │
     ├─────────────────────────────────────────────┤
04H  │         Link to next driver, segment         │
     ├─────────────────────────────────────────────┤
06H  │             Device attribute word            │
     ├─────────────────────────────────────────────┤
08H  │          Strategy entry point, offset        │
     ├─────────────────────────────────────────────┤
0AH  │          Interrupt entry point, offset       │
     ├─────────────────────────────────────────────┤
     │                                             │
     │   Logical name (8 bytes) if character device │
     │   Number of units (1 byte) if block device,  │
     │      followed by 7 bytes of reserved space   │
     │                                             │
     └─────────────────────────────────────────────┘
```

Figure 14-2. *Device-driver header. The offsets to the* strat *and* intr *routines are off-sets from the same segment used to point to the device header.*

Bit	Significance
15	1 if character device, 0 if block device
14	1 if IOCTL read and write supported
13	*for block devices:* 1 if BIOS parameter block in boot sector should be used to determine media characteristics, 0 if media ID byte should be used *for character devices:* 1 if output until busy supported
12	Reserved (should be 0)
11	1 if open/close/removable media supported (MS-DOS 3.0 and later)
7–10	Reserved (should be 0)
6	1 if generic IOCTL and get/set logical drive supported (MS-DOS 3.2 and later)
5	Reserved (should be 0)
4	1 if CON driver and Int 29H fast-output function supported
3	1 if current CLOCK$ device
2	1 if current NUL device
1	*for block devices:* 1 if driver supports 32-bit sector addressing (MS-DOS 4.0) *for character devices:* 1 if standard output device (*stdout*)
0	1 if current standard input device (*stdin*)

Figure 14-3. *Device attribute word in device header. In block-device drivers, only bits 6, 11, and 13–15 (and bit 1 in MS-DOS version 4.0) have significance; the remainder should always be zero.*

The Strategy Routine

MS-DOS calls the strategy routine (*strat*) for the device when the driver is first loaded and installed, and again whenever an application program issues an I/O request for the device. MS-DOS passes the strategy routine a double-word pointer to a data structure called a *request header*. This structure contains information about the type of operation to be performed. In current versions of MS-DOS, the strategy routine never actually performs any I/O operation but simply saves the pointer to the request header. The *strat* routine must *not* make any Int 21H function calls.

The first 13 bytes of the request header are the same for all device-driver functions and are therefore referred to as the *static* portion of the header. The number and contents of the subsequent bytes vary according to the type of function being requested (Figure 14-4). Both MS-DOS and the driver read and write information in the request header.

The request header's most important component is a *command code*, or function number, passed in its third byte to select a driver subfunction such as read, write, or status. Other information passed to the driver in the header includes unit numbers, transfer addresses, and sector or byte counts.

```
;
; MS-DOS request header structure definition
;
Request         struc                   ; request header template structure

Rlength         db      ?               ; 0  length of request header
Unit            db      ?               ; 1  unit number for this request
Command         db      ?               ; 2  request header's command code
Status          dw      ?               ; 3  driver's return status word
Reserve         db      8 dup (?)       ; 5  reserved area
Media           db      ?               ; 13 media descriptor byte
Address         dd      ?               ; 14 memory address for transfer
Count           dw      ?               ; 18 byte/sector count value
Sector          dw      ?               ; 20 starting sector value

Request         ends                    ; end of request header template
```

Figure 14-4. *Format of request header. Only the first 13 bytes are common to all driver functions; the number and definition of the subsequent bytes vary, depending upon the function type. The structure shown here is the one used by the read and write subfunctions of the driver.*

The Interrupt Routine

The last and most complex part of a device driver is the interrupt routine (*intr*), which MS-DOS calls immediately after it calls the strategy routine. The interrupt routine implements the device driver proper; it performs (or calls other resident routines to perform) the actual input or output operations, based on the information passed in the request header. The *strat* routine may *not* make any Int 21H function calls, except for a restricted set during driver initialization.

When an I/O function is completed, the interrupt routine uses the status field in the request header to inform the DOS kernel about the outcome of the requested I/O operation. It can use other fields in the request header to pass back such useful information as counts of the actual sectors or bytes transferred.

The interrupt routine usually consists of the following elements:

- A collection of subroutines to implement the various function types that may be requested by MS-DOS (sometimes called the command-code routines)

- A centralized entry point that saves all affected registers, extracts the desired function code from the request header, and branches to the appropriate command-code routine (typically accomplished with a jump table)
- A centralized exit point that stores status and error codes into the request header (Figures 14-5 and 14-6) and restores the previous contents of the affected registers

The command-code routines that implement the various functions supported by an installable device driver are discussed in detail in the following pages.

Bit(s)	Significance
15	Error
12–14	Reserved
9	Busy
8	Done
0–7	Error code if bit 15 = 1

Figure 14-5. *Values for the return status word of the request header.*

Code	Meaning
0	Write-protect violation
1	Unknown unit
2	Drive not ready
3	Unknown command
4	Data error (CRC)
5	Bad request-structure length
6	Seek error
7	Unknown medium
8	Sector not found
9	Printer out of paper
0AH	Write fault
0BH	Read fault
0CH	General failure
0D–0EH	Reserved
0FH	Invalid disk change (MS-DOS versions 3.0 and later)

Figure 14-6. *Driver error codes returned in bits 0 through 7 of the return status word of the request header.*

Although its name suggests otherwise, the interrupt routine is never entered asynchronously (on an I/O completion interrupt, for example). Thus, the division of function between strategy and interrupt routines is completely artificial in the current versions of MS-DOS.

The Command-Code Routines

A total of 20 command codes are defined for MS-DOS device drivers. The command codes (which are not consecutive), the names of the associated driver-interrupt routines, and the MS-DOS versions in which they are first supported are as follows:

Command code	Function	Character driver	Block driver	MS-DOS version
0	Init (Initialization)	X	X	2.0
1	Media Check		X	2.0
2	Build BPB		X	2.0
3	IOCTL Read	X	X	2.0
4	Read	X	X	2.0
5	Nondestructive Read	X		2.0
6	Input Status	X		2.0
7	Flush Input Buffers	X		2.0
8	Write	X	X	2.0

(continued)

Command code	Function	Character driver	Block driver	MS-DOS version
9	Write with Verify		X	2.0
10	Output Status	X		2.0
11	Flush Output Buffers	X		2.0
12	IOCTL Write	X	X	2.0
13	Device Open	X	X	3.0
14	Device Close	X	X	3.0
15	Removable Media		X	3.0
16	Output Until Busy	X		3.0
19	Generic IOCTL	X	X	3.2
23	Get Logical Device		X	3.2
24	Set Logical Device		X	3.2

As you can see from the preceding table, a driver's interrupt section must support functions 0 through 12 under all versions of MS-DOS. Drivers tailored for MS-DOS 3.0 and 3.1 can optionally support an additional four functions, and MS-DOS drivers for versions 3.2 and later can support three more (for a total of 20). MS-DOS inspects the bits in the attribute word of the device-driver header to determine which of the optional functions a driver supports, if any.

Some of the functions are relevant only for character-device drivers and some only for block-device drivers; a few have meaning to both types. In any case, both driver types should have an executable routine present for each function, even if it does nothing except set the done flag in the status word of the request header.

In the command-code descriptions that follow, RH refers to the request header whose address was passed to the strategy routine in ES:BX, BYTE is an 8-bit parameter, WORD is a 16-bit parameter, and DWORD is a far pointer (a 16-bit offset followed by a 16-bit segment).

Function 00H (0): Driver Initialization

MS-DOS requests the driver's initialization function (*init*) only once, when the driver is first loaded. This function performs any necessary device hardware initialization, setup of interrupt vectors, and so forth. The initialization routine must return the address of the position where free memory begins after the driver code (the *break* address), so that MS-DOS knows where it can build certain control structures and then load the next installable driver. If this is a block-device driver, *init* must also return the number of units and the address of a BPB pointer array.

MS-DOS uses the number of units returned by a block driver in the request header to assign drive identifiers. For example, if the current maximum drive is D and the driver being initialized supports four units, MS-DOS will assign it the drive letters E, F, G, and H. Although the *device-driver* header also has a field for number of units, MS-DOS does not inspect it.

The BPB pointer array is an array of word offsets to BIOS parameter blocks (Figure 14-7). Each unit defined by the driver must have one entry in the array, although the entries can all point to the same BPB to conserve memory. During the operating-system boot sequence, MS-DOS scans all the BPBs defined by all the units in all the block-device drivers to determine the largest sector size that exists on any device in the system and uses this information to set its cache buffer size.

The operating-system services that the initialization code can invoke at load time are very limited—only Int 21H Functions 01H through 0CH and 30H. These are just adequate to check the MS-DOS version number and display a driver-identification or error message.

Many programmers position the initialization code at the end of the driver and return that address as the location of the first free memory, so that MS-DOS will reclaim the memory occupied by the initialization routine after the routine is finished with its work. If the initialization routine finds that the device is missing or defective and wants to abort the installation of the driver completely so that it does not occupy any memory, it should return

Byte(s)	Contents
00–01H	Bytes per sector
02H	Sectors per allocation unit (power of 2)
03H–04H	Number of reserved sectors (starting at sector 0)
05H	Number of file allocation tables
06H–07H	Maximum number of root-directory entries
08H–09H	Total number of sectors in medium
0AH	Media descriptor byte
0BH–0CH	Number of sectors occupied by a single FAT
0DH–0EH	Sectors per track (versions 3.0 and later)
0FH–10H	Number of heads (versions 3.0 and later)
11H–12H	Number of hidden sectors (versions 3.0 and later)
13H–14H	High-order word of number of hidden sectors (version 4.0)
15H–18H	If bytes 8–9 are zero, total number of sectors in medium (version 4.0)
19H–1EH	Reserved, should be zero (version 4.0)

Figure 14-7. *Structure of a BIOS parameter block (BPB). Every formatted disk contains a copy of its BPB in the boot sector. (See Chapter 10.)*

number of units as zero and set the free memory address to CS:0000H. (A character-device driver that wants to abort its installation should clear bit 15 of the attribute word in the driver header and then set the units field and free memory address as though it were a block-device driver.)

The initialization function is called with

RH + 2	BYTE	Command code = 0
RH + 18	DWORD	Pointer to character after equal sign on CONFIG.SYS line that loaded driver (this information is read-only)
RH + 22	BYTE	Drive number for first unit of this block driver (0 = A, 1 = B, and so forth) (MS-DOS version 3 only)

It returns:

RH + 3	WORD	Status
RH + 13	BYTE	Number of units (block devices only)
RH + 14	DWORD	Address of first free memory above driver (break address)
RH + 18	DWORD	BPB pointer array (block devices only)

Function 01H (1): Media Check

The media-check function applies only to block devices, and in character-device drivers it should do nothing except set the done flag. This function is called when a drive-access call other than a simple file read or write is pending. MS-DOS passes to the function the media descriptor byte for the disk that it assumes is in the drive (Figure 14-8). If feasible, the media-check routine returns a code indicating whether the disk has been changed since the last transfer. If the media-check routine can assert that the disk has not been changed, MS-DOS can bypass rereading the FAT before a directory access, which improves overall performance.

Code	Meaning
0F0H	3.5", 2-sided, 18-sector
0F8H	fixed disk
0F9H	3.5", 2-sided, 9-sector
0F9H	5.25", 2-sided, 15-sector
0FCH	5.25", 1-sided, 9-sector
0FDH	5.25", 2-sided, 9-sector
0FEH	5.25", 1-sided, 8-sector
0FFH	5.25", 2-sided, 8-sector

Figure 14-8. *Current valid MS-DOS codes for the media descriptor byte of the request header, assuming bit 13 in the attribute word of the driver header is zero.*

MS-DOS responds to the results of the media-check function in the following ways:

- If the disk has not been changed, MS-DOS proceeds with the disk access.

- If the disk has been changed, MS-DOS invalidates all buffers associated with this unit, including buffers containing data waiting to be written (this data is simply lost), performs a BUILD BPB call, and then reads the disk's FAT and directory.

- If the disk-change status is unknown, the action taken by MS-DOS depends upon the state of its internal buffers. If data that needs to be written out is present in the buffers, MS-DOS assumes no disk change has occurred and writes the data (taking the risk that, if the disk really was changed, the file structure on the new disk may be damaged). If the buffers are empty or have all been previously flushed to the disk, MS-DOS assumes that the disk was changed, and then proceeds as described above for the disk-changed return code.

If bit 11 of the device-header attribute word is set (that is, the driver supports the optional open/close/removable-media functions), the host system is MS-DOS version 3.0 or later, and the function returns the disk-changed code (–1), the function must also return the segment and offset of the ASCIIZ volume label for the previous disk in the drive. (If the driver does not have the volume label, it can return a pointer to the ASCIIZ string *NO NAME*.) If MS-DOS determines that the disk was changed with unwritten data still present in its buffers, it issues a critical-error 0FH (invalid disk change). Application programs can trap this critical error and prompt the user to replace the original disk.

The media-check function is called with

RH + 1	BYTE	Unit code
RH + 2	BYTE	Command code = 1
RH + 13	BYTE	Media descriptor byte

It returns

RH + 3	WORD	Status
RH + 14	BYTE	Media-change code: –1 if disk changed 0 if don't know whether disk changed 1 if disk not changed
RH + 15	DWORD	Pointer to previous volume label, if device attribute bit 11 = 1 and disk has been changed (MS-DOS versions 3.0 and later)

Function 02H (2): Build BIOS Parameter Block (BPB)

The build BPB function applies only to block devices, and in character-device drivers should do nothing except set the done flag. The kernel uses this function to get a pointer to the valid BPB (see Figure 14-7) for the current disk and calls it when the disk-changed code is returned by the media-check routine or the don't-know code is returned and there are no dirty buffers (buffers with changed data that have not yet been written to disk). Thus, a call to this function indicates that the disk has been legally changed.

The build BPB function receives a pointer to a one-sector buffer in the request header. If bit 13 in the driver header's attribute word is zero, the buffer contains the first sector of the FAT (which includes the media identification byte) and should not be altered by the driver. If bit 13 is set, the driver can use the buffer as scratch space.

The build BPB function is called with

RH + 1	BYTE	Unit code
RH + 2	BYTE	Command code = 2
RH + 13	BYTE	Media descriptor byte
RH + 14	DWORD	Buffer address

It returns

RH + 3	WORD	Status
RH + 18	DWORD	Pointer to new BPB

Under MS-DOS versions 3.0 and later, if bit 11 of the header's device attribute word is set, this routine should also read the volume label off the disk and save it.

Function 03H (3): I/O-Control Read

The IOCTL read function allows the device driver to pass information directly to the application program. This function is called only if bit 14 is set in the device attribute word. MS-DOS performs no error check on IOCTL I/O calls.

The IOCTL read function is called with

RH + 1	BYTE	Unit code (block devices)
RH + 2	BYTE	Command code = 3
RH + 13	BYTE	Media descriptor byte
RH + 14	DWORD	Transfer address
RH + 18	WORD	Byte/sector count
RH + 20	WORD	Starting sector number (block devices)

It returns

RH + 3	WORD	Status
RH + 18	WORD	Actual bytes or sectors transferred

Function 04H (4): Read

The read function transfers data from the device into the specified memory buffer. If an error is encountered during the read, the function must set the error status and, in addition, report the number of bytes or sectors successfully transferred; it is not sufficient to simply report an error.

The read function is called with

RH + 1	BYTE	Unit code (block devices)
RH + 2	BYTE	Command code = 4
RH + 13	BYTE	Media descriptor byte
RH + 14	DWORD	Transfer address
RH + 18	WORD	Byte/sector count
RH + 20	WORD	Starting sector number (block devices)

For block-device read operations in MS-DOS version 4, if the logical unit is larger than 32 MB and bit 1 of the driver's attribute word is set, the following request structure is used instead:

RH + 1	BYTE	Unit code
RH + 2	BYTE	Command code = 4
RH + 13	BYTE	Media descriptor byte
RH + 14	DWORD	Transfer address
RH + 18	WORD	Sector count
RH + 20	WORD	Contains −1 to signal use of 32-bit sector number
RH + 26	DWORD	32-bit starting sector number

The read function returns

RH + 3	WORD	Status
RH + 18	WORD	Actual bytes or sectors transferred
RH + 22	DWORD	Pointer to volume label if error 0FH is returned (MS-DOS versions 3.0 and later)

Under MS-DOS versions 3.0 and later, this routine can use the count of open files maintained by the open and close functions (0DH and 0EH) and the media descriptor byte to determine whether the disk has been illegally changed.

Function 05H (5): Nondestructive Read

The nondestructive read function applies only to character devices, and in block devices it should do nothing except set the done flag. It returns the next character that would be obtained with a read function (command code 4), without removing that character from the driver's internal buffer. MS-DOS uses this function to check the console driver for pending Control-C characters during other operations.

The nondestructive read function is called with

RH + 2	BYTE	Command code = 5

It returns

RH + 3	WORD	Status
		If busy bit = 0, at least one character is waiting
		If busy bit = 1, no characters are waiting
RH + 13	BYTE	Character (if busy bit = 0)

Function 06H (6): Input Status

The input-status function applies only to character devices, and in block-device drivers it should do nothing except set the done flag. This function returns the current input status for the device, allowing MS-DOS to test whether characters are waiting in a type-ahead buffer. If the character device does not have a type-ahead buffer, the input-status routine should always return the busy bit equal to zero, so that MS-DOS will not wait forever to call the read (04H) or nondestructive read (05H) function.

The input-status function is called with

RH + 2	BYTE	Command code = 6

It returns

RH + 3	WORD	Status:
		If busy bit = 1, read request goes to physical device.
		If busy bit = 0, characters already in device buffer and read request returns quickly.

Function 07H (7): Flush Input Buffers

The flush-input-buffers function applies only to character devices, and in block-device drivers it should do nothing except set the done flag. This function causes any data waiting in the input buffer to be discarded.

The flush-input-buffers function is called with

RH + 2   BYTE   Command code = 7

It returns

RH + 3   WORD   Status

Function 08H (8): Write

The write function transfers data from the specified memory buffer to the device. If an error is encountered during the write, the write function must set the error status and, in addition, report the number of bytes or sectors successfully transferred; it is not sufficient to simply report an error.

The write function is called with

RH + 1	BYTE	Unit code (block devices)
RH + 2	BYTE	Command code = 8
RH + 13	BYTE	Media descriptor byte
RH + 14	DWORD	Transfer address
RH + 18	WORD	Byte/sector count
RH + 20	WORD	Starting sector number (block devices)

For block-device write operations in MS-DOS version 4, if the logical unit is larger than 32 MB and bit 1 of the driver's attribute word is set, the following request structure is used instead:

RH + 1	BYTE	Unit code
RH + 2	BYTE	Command code = 8
RH + 13	BYTE	Media descriptor byte
RH + 14	DWORD	Transfer address
RH + 18	WORD	Sector count
RH + 20	WORD	Contains −1 to signal use of 32-bit sector number
RH + 26	DWORD	32-bit starting sector number

The write function returns

RH + 3	WORD	Status
RH + 18	WORD	Actual bytes or sectors transferred
RH + 22	DWORD	Pointer to volume label if error 0FH returned (MS-DOS versions 3.0 and later)

Under MS-DOS versions 3.0 and later, this routine can use the reference count of open files maintained by the open and close functions (0DH and 0EH) and the media descriptor byte to determine whether the disk has been illegally changed.

Function 09H (9): Write with Verify

The write-with-verify function transfers data from the specified memory buffer to the device. If feasible, it should perform a read-after-write verification of the data to confirm that the data was written correctly. Otherwise, Function 09H is exactly like Function 08H.

Function 0AH (10): Output Status

The output-status function applies only to character devices, and in block-device drivers it should do nothing except set the done flag. This function returns the current output status for the device.

The output-status function is called with

RH + 2   BYTE   Command code = 10 (0AH)

It returns

RH + 3   WORD   Status:
                      If busy bit = 1, write request waits for completion of current request.
                      If busy bit = 0, device idle and write request starts immediately.

Function 0BH (11): Flush Output Buffers

The flush-output-buffers function applies only to character devices, and in block-device drivers it should do nothing except set the done flag. This function empties the output buffer, if any, and discards any pending output requests.

The flush-output-buffers function is called with

RH + 2   BYTE   Command code = 11 (0BH)

It returns

RH + 3   WORD   Status

Function 0CH (12): I/O-Control Write

The IOCTL write function allows an application program to pass control information directly to the driver. This function is called only if bit 14 is set in the device attribute word. MS-DOS performs no error check on IOCTL I/O calls.

The IOCTL write function is called with

RH + 1	BYTE	Unit code (block devices)
RH + 2	BYTE	Command code = 12 (0CH)
RH + 13	BYTE	Media descriptor byte
RH + 14	DWORD	Transfer address
RH + 18	WORD	Byte/sector count
RH + 20	WORD	Starting sector number (block devices)

It returns

RH + 3	WORD	Status
RH + 18	WORD	Actual bytes or sectors transferred

Function 0DH (13): Device Open

The device-open function is supported only under MS-DOS versions 3.0 and later and is called only if bit 11 is set in the device attribute word of the device header.

On block devices, the device-open function can be used to manage local buffering and to increment a reference count of the number of open files on the device. This capability must be used with care, however, because programs that access files through FCBs frequently fail to close them, thus invalidating the open-files count. One way to protect against this possibility is to reset the open-files count to zero, without flushing the buffers, whenever the answer to a media-change call is *yes* and a subsequent build BPB call is made to the driver.

On character devices, the device-open function can be used to send a device-initialization string (which can be set into the driver by an application program by means of an IOCTL write function) or to deny simultaneous access to a character device by more than one process. Note that the predefined handles for the CON, AUX, and PRN devices are always open.

The device-open function is called with

RH + 1	BYTE	Unit code (block devices)
RH + 2	BYTE	Command code = 13 (0DH)

It returns

RH + 3	WORD	Status

Function 0EH (14): Device Close

The device-close function is supported only under MS-DOS versions 3.0 and later and is called only if bit 11 is set in the device attribute word of the device header.

On block devices, this function can be used to manage local buffering and to decrement a reference count of the number of open files on the device; when the count reaches zero, all files have been closed and the driver should flush buffers because the user may change disks.

On character devices, the device-close function can be used to send a device-dependent post-I/O string such as a formfeed. (This string can be set into the driver by an application program by means of an IOCTL write function.) Note that the predefined handles for the CON, PRN, and AUX devices are never closed.

The device-close function is called with

RH + 1	BYTE	Unit code (block devices)
RH + 2	BYTE	Command code = 14 (0EH)

It returns

RH + 3	WORD	Status

Function 0FH (15): Removable Media

The removable-media function is supported only under MS-DOS versions 3.0 and later and only on block devices; in character-device drivers it should do nothing except set the done flag. This function is called only if bit 11 is set in the device attribute word in the device header.

The removable-media function is called with

RH + 1	BYTE	Unit code
RH + 2	BYTE	Command code = 15 (0FH)

It returns

RH + 3	WORD	Status:
		If busy bit = 1, medium nonremovable
		If busy bit = 0, medium removable

Function 10H (16): Output Until Busy

The output-until-busy function is supported only under MS-DOS versions 3.0 and later, and only on character devices; in block-device drivers it should do nothing except set the done flag. This function transfers data from the specified memory buffer to a device, continuing to transfer bytes until the device is busy. It is called only if bit 13 of the device attribute word is set in the device header.

This function is an optimization included specifically for the use of print spoolers. It is not an error for this function to return a number of bytes transferred that is less than the number of bytes requested.

The output-until-busy function is called with

RH + 2	BYTE	Command code = 16 (10H)
RH + 14	DWORD	Transfer address
RH + 18	WORD	Byte count

It returns

RH + 3	WORD	Status
RH + 18	WORD	Actual bytes transferred

Function 13H (19) Generic IOCTL

The generic IOCTL function is supported only under MS-DOS versions 3.2 and later and is called only if bit 6 is set in the device attribute word of the device header. This function corresponds to the MS-DOS generic IOCTL service supplied to application programs by Int 21H Function 44H Subfunctions 0CH and 0DH.

The generic IOCTL function is passed a category (major) code, a function (minor) code, the contents of the SI and DI registers at the point of the IOCTL call, and the segment and offset of a data buffer. This buffer in turn contains other information whose format depends on the major and minor IOCTL codes passed in the request header. The driver must interpret the major and minor codes in the request header and the contents of the additional buffer to determine which operation it will carry out, then set the done flag in the request-header status word, and return any other applicable information in the request header or the data buffer.

Services that the generic IOCTL function may invoke, if the driver supports them, include configuration of the driver for nonstandard disk formats, reading and writing entire disk tracks of data, and formatting and verifying tracks. The generic IOCTL function has been designed to be open-ended, so that it can be used to easily extend the device-driver definition under future versions of MS-DOS.

The generic IOCTL function is called with

RH + 1	BYTE	Unit number (block devices)
RH + 2	BYTE	Command code = 19 (13H)
RH + 13	BYTE	Category (major) code
RH + 14	BYTE	Function (minor) code
RH + 15	WORD	SI register contents
RH + 17	WORD	DI register contents
RH + 19	DWORD	Address of generic IOCTL data packet

It returns

RH + 3	WORD	Status

Function 17H (23): Get Logical Device

The get-logical-device function is supported only under MS-DOS versions 3.2 and later and only on block devices; in character-device drivers it should do nothing except set the done bit in the status word. This function is called only if bit 6 is set in the device attribute word of the device header. It corresponds to the get-logical-device-map service supplied to application programs through Int 21H Function 44H Subfunction 0EH.

The get-logical-device function returns a code for the last drive letter used to reference the device; if only one drive letter is assigned to the device, the returned unit code should be zero. Thus, this function can be used to determine whether more than one drive letter is assigned to the same physical device.

The get-logical-device function is called with

RH + 1	BYTE	Unit code
RH + 2	BYTE	Command code = 23 (17H)

It returns

RH + 1	BYTE	Last unit referenced, or zero
RH + 3	WORD	Status

Function 18H (24): Set Logical Device

The set-logical-device function is supported only under MS-DOS versions 3.2 and later and only on block devices; in character-device drivers it should do nothing except set the done bit in the status word. This function is called only if bit 6 is set in the device attribute word of the device header. It corresponds to the set-logical-device-map service supplied to application programs by MS-DOS through Int 21H Function 44H Subfunction 0FH.

The set-logical-device function informs the driver of the next logical-drive identifier that will be used to reference the physical device. The unit code passed by the MS-DOS kernel in this case is zero-based relative to the number of logical drives supported by this particular driver. For example, if the driver supports two floppy-disk units (A and B), only one physical floppy-disk drive exists in the system, and the set-logical-device function is called with a unit number of 1, the driver is being informed that the next read or write request from the kernel will be directed to drive B.

The set-logical-device function is called with

RH + 1	BYTE	Unit code
RH + 2	BYTE	Command code = 24 (18H)

It returns

RH + 3	WORD	Status

The Processing of a Typical I/O Request

An application program requests an I/O operation from MS-DOS by loading registers with the appropriate values and executing an Int 21H. This results in the following sequence of actions:

1. MS-DOS inspects its internal tables and determines which device driver should receive the I/O request.

2. MS-DOS creates a request-header data packet in a reserved area of memory. (Disk I/O requests are transformed from file and record information into logical-sector requests by MS-DOS's interpretation of the disk directory and FAT.)

3. MS-DOS calls the device driver's *strat* entry point, passing the address of the request header in the ES:BX registers.

4. The device driver saves the address of the request header in a local variable and performs a FAR RETURN.

5. MS-DOS calls the device driver's *intr* entry point.

6. The interrupt routine saves all registers, retrieves the address of the request header that was saved by the strategy routine, extracts the function code, and branches to the appropriate command-code subroutine to perform the function.

7. If a data transfer on a block device was requested, the driver's read or write subroutine translates the logical-sector number into a head, track, and physical-sector address for the requested unit and then performs the I/O operation. Because a multiple-sector transfer can be requested in a single request header, a single request by MS-DOS to the driver can result in multiple read or write commands to the disk controller.

8. When the requested function is complete, the interrupt routine sets the status word and any other required information into the request header, restores all registers to their state at entry, and performs a FAR RETURN.

9. MS-DOS translates the driver's return status into the appropriate return code and carry-flag status for the MS-DOS Int 21H function that was requested and returns control to the application program.

Note that a single request by an application program can result in MS-DOS passing many request headers to the driver. For example, attempting to open a file in a subdirectory on a previously unaccessed disk drive might require the following actions:

- Reading the disk's boot sector to get the BPB

- Reading from one to many sectors of the root directory to find the entry for the subdirectory and obtain its starting-cluster number

- Reading from one to many sectors of both the FAT and the subdirectory itself to find the entry for the desired file

The CLOCK Driver: A Special Case

MS-DOS uses the CLOCK device for marking file control blocks and directory entries with the date and time, as well as for providing the date and time services to application programs. This device has a unique type of interaction with MS-DOS—a 6-byte sequence is read from or written to the driver that obtains or sets the current date and time. The sequence has the following format:

0 Days low byte	1 Days high byte	2 Minutes	3 Hours	4 Seconds/ 100	5 Seconds

The value passed for days is a 16-bit integer representing the number of days elapsed since January 1, 1980.

The clock driver can have any logical-device name because MS-DOS uses the CLOCK bit in the device attribute word of the driver's device header to identify the device, rather than its name. On IBM PC systems, the clock device has the logical-device name CLOCK$.

Writing and Installing a Device Driver

Now that we have discussed the structure and capabilities of installable device drivers for the MS-DOS environment, we can discuss the mechanical steps of assembling and linking them.

Assembly

Device drivers for MS-DOS always have an origin of zero but are otherwise assembled, linked, and converted into an executable module as though they were .COM files. (Although MS-DOS is also capable of loading installable drivers in the .EXE file format, this introduces unnecessary complexity into writing and debugging drivers and offers no significant advantages. In addition, it is not possible to use .EXE-format drivers with some IBM versions of MS-DOS because the .EXE loader is located in COMMAND.COM, which is not present when the installable device drivers are being loaded.) The driver should not have a declared stack segment and must, in general, follow the other restrictions outlined in Chapter 3 for memory-image (.COM) programs. A driver can be loaded anywhere, so beware that you do not make any assumptions in your code about the driver's location in physical memory. Figure 14-9 presents a skeleton example that you can follow as you read the next few pages.

```
        name    driver
        page    55,132
        title   DRIVER.ASM Device-Driver Skeleton


;
; DRIVER.ASM   MS-DOS device-driver skeleton
;
; The driver command-code routines are stubs only and have
; no effect but to return a nonerror "done" status.
;
; Copyright 1988 Ray Duncan
;

_TEXT   segment word public 'CODE'

        assume  cs:_TEXT,ds:_TEXT,es:NOTHING


        org     0

MaxCmd  equ     24              ; maximum allowed command code:
                                ; 12 for MS-DOS 2
                                ; 16 for MS-DOS 3.0-3.1
                                ; 24 for MS-DOS 3.2-3.3
```

(continued)

Figure 14-9. DRIVER.ASM: *A functional skeleton from which you can implement your own working device driver.*

Figure 14-9. *continued*

```
cr        equ       0dh              ; ASCII carriage return
lf        equ       0ah              ; ASCII linefeed
eom       equ       '$'              ; end-of-message signal


Header:                              ; device-driver header
          dd        -1               ; link to next device driver
          dw        0c840h           ; device attribute word
          dw        Strat            ; "strategy" routine entry point
          dw        Intr             ; "interrupt" routine entry point
          db        'SKELETON'       ; logical-device name


RHPtr     dd        ?                ; pointer to request header, passed
                                     ; by MS-DOS kernel to strategy routine


Dispatch:                            ; interrupt-routine command-code
                                     ; dispatch table:
          dw        Init             ; 0  = initialize driver
          dw        MediaChk         ; 1  = media check
          dw        BuildBPB         ; 2  = build BPB
          dw        IoctlRd          ; 3  = IOCTL read
          dw        Read             ; 4  = read
          dw        NdRead           ; 5  = nondestructive read
          dw        InpStat          ; 6  = input status
          dw        InpFlush         ; 7  = flush input buffers
          dw        Write            ; 8  = write
          dw        WriteVfy         ; 9  = write with verify
          dw        OutStat          ; 10 = output status
          dw        OutFlush         ; 11 = flush output buffers
          dw        IoctlWt          ; 12 = IOCTL write
          dw        DevOpen          ; 13 = device open       (MS-DOS 3.0+)
          dw        DevClose         ; 14 = device close      (MS-DOS 3.0+)
          dw        RemMedia         ; 15 = removable media   (MS-DOS 3.0+)
          dw        OutBusy          ; 16 = output until busy (MS-DOS 3.0+)
          dw        Error            ; 17 = not used
          dw        Error            ; 18 = not used
          dw        GenIOCTL         ; 19 = generic IOCTL     (MS-DOS 3.2+)
          dw        Error            ; 20 = not used
          dw        Error            ; 21 = not used
          dw        Error            ; 22 = not used
          dw        GetLogDev        ; 23 = get logical device (MS-DOS 3.2+)
          dw        SetLogDev        ; 24 = set logical device (MS-DOS 3.2+)
```

(continued)

Figure 14-9. *continued*

```
Strat   proc    far             ; device-driver strategy routine,
                                ; called by MS-DOS kernel with
                                ; ES:BX = address of request header

                                ; save pointer to request header
        mov     word ptr cs:[RHPtr],bx
        mov     word ptr cs:[RHPtr+2],es

        ret                     ; back to MS-DOS kernel

Strat   endp


Intr    proc    far             ; device-driver interrupt routine,
                                ; called by MS-DOS kernel immediately
                                ; after call to strategy routine

        push    ax              ; save general registers
        push    bx
        push    cx
        push    dx
        push    ds
        push    es
        push    di
        push    si
        push    bp

        push    cs              ; make local data addressable
        pop     ds              ; by setting DS = CS

        les     di,[RHPtr]      ; let ES:DI = request header

                                ; get BX = command code
        mov     bl,es:[di+2]
        xor     bh,bh
        cmp     bx,MaxCmd       ; make sure it's legal
        jle     Intr1           ; jump, function code is ok
        call    Error           ; set error bit, "unknown command" code
        jmp     Intr2

Intr1:  shl     bx,1            ; form index to dispatch table
                                ; and branch to command-code routine
        call    word ptr [bx+Dispatch]

        les     di,[RHPtr]      ; ES:DI = addr of request header
```

(continued)

Figure 14-9. *continued*

```
Intr2:  or      ax,0100h        ; merge 'done' bit into status and
        mov     es:[di+3],ax    ; store status into request header

        pop     bp              ; restore general registers
        pop     si
        pop     di
        pop     es
        pop     ds
        pop     dx
        pop     cx
        pop     bx
        pop     ax
        ret                     ; back to MS-DOS kernel


; Command-code routines are called by the interrupt routine
; via the dispatch table with ES:DI pointing to the request
; header.  Each routine should return AX = 0 if function was
; completed successfully or AX = (8000h + error code) if
; function failed.


MediaChk proc   near            ; function 1 - media check

        xor     ax,ax
        ret

MediaChk endp


BuildBPB proc   near            ; function 2 - build BPB

        xor     ax,ax
        ret

BuildBPB endp


IoctlRd proc    near            ; function 3 - IOCTL read

        xor     ax,ax
        ret

IoctlRd endp
```

(continued)

Figure 14-9. *continued*

```
Read      proc    near            ; function 4 - read (input)

          xor     ax,ax
          ret

Read      endp


NdRead    proc    near            ; function 5 - nondestructive read

          xor     ax,ax
          ret

NdRead    endp


InpStat   proc    near            ; function 6 - input status

          xor     ax,ax
          ret

InpStat   endp


InpFlush  proc    near            ; function 7 - flush input buffers

          xor     ax,ax
          ret

InpFlush  endp


Write     proc    near            ; function 8 - write (output)

          xor     ax,ax
          ret

Write     endp


WriteVfy  proc    near            ; function 9 - write with verify

          xor     ax,ax
          ret
```

(continued)

Figure 14-9. *continued*

```
WriteVfy endp


OutStat  proc    near              ; function 10 = output status

         xor     ax,ax
         ret

OutStat  endp


OutFlush proc    near              ; function 11 = flush output buffers

         xor     ax,ax
         ret

OutFlush endp


IoctlWt  proc    near              ; function 12 = IOCTL write

         xor     ax,ax
         ret

IoctlWt  endp


DevOpen  proc    near              ; function 13 = device open

         xor     ax,ax
         ret

DevOpen  endp


DevClose proc    near              ; function 14 = device close

         xor     ax,ax
         ret

DevClose endp
```

(continued)

Figure 14-9. *continued*

```
RemMedia proc    near              ; function 15 = removable media

         xor     ax,ax
         ret

RemMedia endp


OutBusy  proc    near              ; function 16 = output until busy

         xor     ax,ax
         ret

OutBusy  endp


GenIOCTL proc    near              ; function 19 = generic IOCTL

         xor     ax,ax
         ret

GenIOCTL endp


GetLogDev proc   near              ; function 23 = get logical device

         xor     ax,ax
         ret

GetLogDev endp


SetLogDev proc   near              ; function 24 = set logical device

         xor     ax,ax
         ret

SetLogDev endp


Error    proc    near              ; bad command code in request header

         mov     ax,8003h          ; error bit + "unknown command" code
         ret
```

(continued)

Figure 14-9. *continued*

```
Error   endp


Init    proc    near            ; function 0 - initialize driver

        push    es              ; save address of request header
        push    di

        mov     ax,cs           ; convert load address to ASCII
        mov     bx,offset Ident1
        call    hexasc

        mov     ah,9            ; display driver sign-on message
        mov     dx,offset Ident
        int     21h

        pop     di              ; restore request-header address
        pop     es

                                ; set address of free memory
                                ; above driver (break address)
        mov     word ptr es:[di+14],offset Init
        mov     word ptr es:[di+16],cs

        xor     ax,ax           ; return status
        ret

Init    endp


hexasc  proc    near            ; converts word to hex ASCII
                                ; call with AX = value,
                                ; DS:BX = address for string
                                ; returns AX, BX destroyed

        push    cx              ; save registers
        push    dx

        mov     dx,4            ; initialize character counter
```

(continued)

Figure 14-9. *continued*

```
hexasc1:
        mov     cx,4            ; isolate next four bits
        rol     ax,cl
        mov     cx,ax
        and     cx,0fh
        add     cx,'0'          ; convert to ASCII
        cmp     cx,'9'          ; is it 0-9?
        jbe     hexasc2         ; yes, jump
        add     cx,'A'-'9'-1    ; add fudge factor for A-F

hexasc2:                        ; store this character
        mov     [bx],cl
        inc     bx              ; bump string pointer

        dec     dx              ; count characters converted
        jnz     hexasc1         ; loop, not four yet

        pop     dx              ; restore registers
        pop     cx
        ret                     ; back to caller


hexasc  endp


Ident   db      cr,1f,1f
        db      'Advanced MS-DOS Example Device Driver'
        db      cr,1f
        db      'Device driver header at: '
Ident1  db      'XXXX:0000'
        db      cr,1f,1f,eom

Intr    endp

_TEXT   ends

        end
```

The driver's device header must be located at the beginning of the file (offset 0000H). Both words in the link field in the header should be set to −1. The attribute word must be set up correctly for the device type and other options. The offsets to the strategy and interrupt routines must be relative to the same segment base as the device header itself. If the driver is for a character device, the *name* field should be filled in properly with the device's logical name. The logical name can be any legal 8-character filename, padded with spaces and without a colon. Beware of accidentally duplicating the names of existing character devices, unless you are intentionally superseding a resident driver.

MS-DOS calls the strategy and interrupt routines for the device by means of an intersegment call (CALL FAR) when the driver is first loaded and installed and again whenever an application program issues an I/O request for the device. MS-DOS uses the ES:BX registers to pass the *strat* routine a double-word pointer to the request header; this address should be saved internally in the driver so that it is available for use during the subsequent call to the *intr* routine.

The command-code routines for function codes 0 through 12 (0CH) must be present in *every* installable device driver, regardless of device type. Functions 13 (0DH) and above are optional for drivers used with MS-DOS versions 3.0 and later and can be handled in one of the following ways:

- Don't implement them, and leave the associated bits in the device header cleared. The resulting driver will work in either version 2 or version 3 but does not take full advantage of the augmented functionality of version 3.

- Implement them, and test the MS-DOS version during the initialization sequence, setting bits 6 and 11 of the device header appropriately. Write all command-code routines so that they test this bit and adjust to accommodate the host version of MS-DOS. Such a driver requires more work and testing but will take full advantage of both the version 2 and the version 3 environments.

- Implement them, and assume that all the version 3 facilities are available. With this approach, the resulting driver may not work properly under version 2.

Remember that device drivers must preserve the integrity of MS-DOS. The driver must preserve all registers, including flags (especially the direction flag and interrupt enable bits), and if the driver makes heavy use of the stack, it should switch to an internal stack of adequate depth (the MS-DOS stack has room for only 40 to 50 bytes when a driver is called).

If you install a new CON driver, be sure to set the bits for standard input and standard output in the device attribute word in the device header.

You'll recall that one file can contain multiple drivers. In this case, the device-header link field of each driver should point to the segment offset of the next, all using the same segment base, and the link field for the last driver in the file should be set to -1,-1. The initialization routines for all the drivers in the file should return the same break address.

Linking

Use the standard MS-DOS linker to transform the .OBJ file that is output from the assembler into a relocatable .EXE module. Then, use the EXE2BIN utility (see Chapter 4) to convert the .EXE file into a memory-image program. The extension on the final driver file can be anything, but .BIN and .SYS are most commonly used in MS-DOS systems, and it is therefore wise to follow one of these conventions.

Installation

After the driver is assembled, linked, and converted to a .BIN or .SYS file, copy it to the root directory of a bootable disk. If it is a character-device driver, do not use the same name for the file as you used for the logical device listed in the driver's header, or you will not be able to delete, copy, or rename the file after the driver is loaded.

Use your favorite text editor to add the line

DEVICE=[*D:*][*PATH*]*FILENAME.EXT*

to the CONFIG.SYS file on the bootable disk. (In this line, *D:* is an optional drive designator and *FILENAME.EXT* is the name of the file containing your new device driver. You can include a path specification in the entry if you prefer not to put the driver file in your root directory.) Now restart your computer system to load the modified CONFIG.SYS file.

During the MS-DOS boot sequence, the SYSINIT module (which is part of IO.SYS) reads and processes the CONFIG.SYS file. It loads the driver into memory and inspects the device header. If the driver is a character-device driver, SYSINIT links it into the device chain ahead of the other character devices; if it is a block-device driver, SYSINIT places it *behind* all previously linked block devices and the resident block devices (Figures 14-10, 14-11, and 14-12). It accomplishes the linkage by updating the link field in the device header to point to the segment and offset of the next driver in the chain. The link field of the last driver in the chain contains –1,–1.

Next, SYSINIT calls the *strat* routine with a request header that contains a command code of zero, and then it calls the *intr* routine. The driver executes its initialization routine and returns the break address, telling MS-DOS how much memory to reserve for this driver. Now MS-DOS can proceed to the next entry in the CONFIG.SYS file.

You cannot supersede a built-in block-device driver—you can only add supplemental block devices. However, you can override the default system driver for a character device (such as CON) with an installed driver by giving it the same logical-device name in the device header. When processing a character I/O request, MS-DOS always scans the list of installed drivers before it scans the list of default devices and takes the first match.

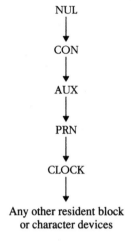

Figure 14-10. *MS-DOS device-driver chain before any installable device drivers have been loaded.*

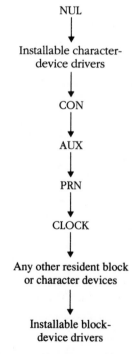

Figure 14-11. *MS-DOS device-driver chain after installable device drivers have been loaded.*

Address	Attribute	Strategy routine	Interrupt routine	Type	Units	Name
00E3:0111	8004	0FD5	0FE0	C		NUL
0070:0148	8013	008E	0099	C		CON
0070:01DD	8000	008E	009F	C		AUX
0070:028E	8000	008E	00AE	C		PRN
0070:0300	8008	008E	00C3	C		CLOCK
0070:03CC	0000	008E	00C9	B	02	
0070:01EF	8000	008E	009F	C		COM1
0070:02A0	8000	008E	00AE	C		LPT1
0070:06F0	8000	008E	00B4	C		LPT2
0070:0702	8000	008E	00BA	C		LPT3
0070:0714	8000	008E	00A5	C		COM2
End of device chain						

Figure 14-12. *Example listing of device chain under MS-DOS version 2.1, "plain vanilla" IBM PC with no fixed disks or user device drivers. (C=character device, B=block device)*

Debugging a Device Driver

The most important thing to remember when testing new device drivers is to maintain adequate backups and a viable fallback position. Don't modify the CONFIG.SYS file and install the new driver on your fixed disk before it is proven! Be prudent—create a bootable floppy disk and put the modified CONFIG.SYS file and the new driver on that for debugging. When everything is working properly, copy the finished product to its permanent storage medium.

The easiest way to test a new device driver is to write a simple assembly-language front-end routine that sets up a simulated request packet and then performs FAR CALLs to the *strat* and *intr* entry points, exactly as MS-DOS would. You can then link the driver and the front end together into a .COM or .EXE file that can be run under the control of CodeView or another debugger. This arrangement makes it easy to trace each of the command-code routines individually, to observe the results of the I/O, and to examine the status codes returned in the request header.

Tracing the installed driver when it is linked into the MS-DOS system in the normal manner is more difficult. Breakpoints must be chosen carefully, to yield the maximum possible information per debugging run. Because current versions of MS-DOS maintain only one request header internally, the request header that was being used by the driver you are tracing will be overwritten as soon as your debugger makes an output request to display information. You will find it helpful to add a routine to your initialization subroutine that displays the driver's load address on the console when you boot MS-DOS; you can then use this address to inspect the device-driver header and set breakpoints within the body of the driver.

Debugging a device driver can also be somewhat sticky when interrupt handling is involved, especially if the device uses the same interrupt-request priority level (IRQ level) as other peripherals in the system. Cautious, conservative programming is needed to avoid unexpected and unreproducible interactions with other device drivers and interrupt handlers. If possible, prove out the basic logic of the driver using polled I/O, rather than interrupt-driven I/O, and introduce interrupt handling only when you know the rest of the driver's logic to be solid.

Typical device-driver errors or problems that can cause system crashes or strange system behavior include the following:

- Failure to set the linkage address of the last driver in a file to −1

- Overflow of the MS-DOS stack by driver-initialization code, corrupting the memory image of MS-DOS (can lead to unpredictable behavior during boot; remedy is to use a local stack)

- Incorrect break-address reporting by the initialization routine (can lead to a system crash if the next driver loaded overwrites vital parts of the driver)

- Improper BPBs supplied by the build BPB routine, or incorrect BPB pointer array supplied by the initialization routine (can lead to many confusing problems, ranging from out-of-memory errors to system boot failure)

- Incorrect reporting of the number of bytes or sectors successfully transferred at the time an I/O error occurs (can manifest itself as a system crash after you enter *R* to the *Abort, Retry, Ignore?* prompt)

Although the interface between the DOS kernel and the device driver is fairly simple, it is also quite strict. The command-code routines must perform exactly as they are defined, or the system will behave erratically. Even a very subtle discrepancy in the action of a command-code routine can have unexpectedly large global effects.

Chapter 15

Filters

A filter is, essentially, a program that operates on a stream of characters. The source and destination of the character stream can be files, another program, or almost any character device. The transformation applied by the filter to the character stream can range from an operation as simple as character substitution to one as elaborate as generating splines from sets of coordinates.

The standard MS-DOS package includes three simple filters: SORT, which alphabetically sorts text on a line-by-line basis; FIND, which searches a text stream to match a specified string; and MORE, which displays text one screenful at a time.

System Support for Filters

The operation of a filter program relies on two MS-DOS features that first appeared in version 2.0: standard devices and redirectable I/O.

The standard devices are represented by five handles that are originally established by COMMAND.COM. Each process inherits these handles from its immediate parent. Thus, the standard device handles are already open when a process acquires control of the system, and it can use them with Interrupt 21H Functions 3FH and 40H for read and write operations without further preliminaries. The default assignments of the standard device handles are as follows:

Handle	Name	Default device
0	*stdin* (standard input)	CON
1	*stdout* (standard output)	CON
2	*stderr* (standard error)	CON
3	*stdaux* (standard auxiliary)	AUX
4	*stdprn* (standard printer)	PRN

The CON device is assigned by default to the system's keyboard and video display. AUX and PRN are respectively associated by default with COM1 (the first physical serial port) and LPT1 (the first parallel printer port). You can use the MODE command to redirect LPT1 to one of the serial ports; the MODE command will also redirect PRN.

When executing a program by entering its name at the COMMAND.COM prompt, you can redirect the standard input, the standard output, or both from their default device (CON) to another file, a character device, or a process. You do this by including one of the special characters <, >, >>, and ¦ in the command line, in the form shown on the following page.

Symbol	Effect
< *file*	Takes standard input from the specified *file* instead of the keyboard.
< *device*	Takes standard input from the named *device* instead of the keyboard.
> *file*	Sends standard output to the specified *file* instead of the display.
>> *file*	Appends standard output to the current contents of the specified *file* instead of sending it to the display.
> *device*	Sends standard output to the named *device* instead of the display.
p1 ¦ p2	Routes standard output of program *p1* to become the standard input of program *p2*. (Output of *p1* is said to be *piped* to *p2*.)

For example, the command

```
C>SORT <MYFILE.TXT >PRN <Enter>
```

causes the SORT filter to read its input from the file *MYFILE.TXT*, sort the lines alphabetically, and write the resulting text to the character device PRN (the logical name for the system's list device).

The redirection requested by the <, >, >>, and ¦ characters takes place at the level of COMMAND.COM and is invisible to the program it affects. Any other process can achieve a similar effect by redirecting the standard input and standard output with Int 21H Function 46H before calling the EXEC function (Int 21H Function 4BH) to run a child process.

Note that if a program circumvents MS-DOS to perform its input and output, either by calling ROM BIOS functions or by manipulating the keyboard or video controller directly, redirection commands placed in the program's command line do not have the expected effect.

How Filters Work

By convention, a filter program reads its text from the standard input device and writes the results of its operations to the standard output device. When it reaches the end of the input stream, the filter simply terminates. As a result, filters are both flexible and simple.

Filter programs are flexible because they do not know, and do not care about, the source of the data they process or the destination of their output. Thus, any character device that has a logical name within the system (CON, AUX, COM1, COM2, PRN, LPT1, LPT2, LPT3, and so on), any file on any block device (local or network) known to the system, or any other program can supply a filter's input or accept its output. If necessary, you can concatenate several functionally simple filters with pipes to perform very complex operations.

Although flexible, filters are also simple because they rely on their parent processes to supply standard input and standard output handles that have already been appropriately redirected. The parent must open or create any necessary files, check the validity of logical character-device names, and load and execute the preceding or following process in a pipe. The filter concerns itself only with the transformation it applies to the data.

Building a Filter

Creating a new filter for MS-DOS is a straightforward process. In its simplest form, a filter need only use the handle-oriented read (Interrupt 21H Function 3FH) and write (Interrupt 21H Function 40H) functions to get characters or lines from standard input and send them to standard output, performing any desired alterations on the text stream on a character-by-character or line-by-line basis.

Figures 15-1 and 15-2 contain prototype character-oriented filters in both assembly language and C. In these examples, the *translate* routine, which is called for each character transferred from the standard input to the standard output, does nothing at all. As a result, both filters function rather like a very slow COPY command. You can quickly turn these primitive filters into useful programs by substituting your own *translate* routine.

If you try out these programs, you'll notice that the C prototype filter runs much faster than its MASM equivalent. This is because the C runtime library is performing hidden blocking and deblocking of the input and output stream, whereas the MASM filter is doing exactly what it appears to be doing: making two calls to MS-DOS for each character processed. You can easily restore the MASM filter's expected speed advantage by adapting it to read and write lines instead of single characters.

```
        name    proto
        page    55,132
        title   PROTO.ASM--prototype filter
;
; PROTO.ASM:  prototype character-oriented filter
;
; Copyright 1988 Ray Duncan
;

stdin   equ     0               ; standard input handle
stdout  equ     1               ; standard output handle
stderr  equ     2               ; standard error handle


cr      equ     0dh             ; ASCII carriage return
lf      equ     0ah             ; ASCII linefeed


_TEXT   segment word public 'CODE'

        assume  cs:_TEXT,ds:_DATA,ss:STACK

main    proc    far             ; entry point from MS-DOS

        mov     ax,_DATA        ; set DS = our data segment
        mov     ds,ax

main1:                          ; read char from stdin...
        mov     dx,offset char  ; DS:DX = buffer address
        mov     cx,1            ; CX = length to read
        mov     bx,stdin        ; BX = standard input handle
        mov     ah,3fh          ; function 3fh = read
        int     21h             ; transfer to MS-DOS
        jc      main3           ; if error, terminate

        cmp     ax,1            ; any character read?
        jne     main2           ; if end of file, terminate

        call    translate       ; translate character

                                ; write char to stdout...
        mov     dx,offset char  ; DS:DX = buffer address
        mov     cx,1            ; CX = length to write
        mov     bx,stdout       ; BX = standard output handle
        mov     ah,40h          ; function 40h = write
        int     21h             ; transfer to MS-DOS
        jc      main3           ; if error, terminate
```

(continued)

Figure 15-1. PROTO.ASM, *the source code for a prototype character-oriented MASM filter.*

Figure 15-1. *continued*

```
            cmp     ax,1            ; was character written?
            jne     main3           ; if disk full, terminate

            jmp     main1           ; get another character

main2:                              ; end of file reached
            mov     ax,4c00h        ; function 4ch = terminate
                                    ; return code = 0
            int     21h             ; transfer to MS-DOS

main3:                              ; error or disk full
            mov     ax,4c01h        ; function 4ch = terminate
                                    ; return code = 1
            int     21h             ; transfer to MS-DOS

main        endp


;
; Perform any necessary translation on character
; from standard input stored in variable 'char'.
; This example simply leaves character unchanged.
;
translate proc  near

            ret                     ; does nothing

translate endp

_TEXT   ends


_DATA   segment word public 'DATA'

char    db      0                   ; storage for input character

_DATA   ends


STACK   segment para stack 'STACK'

        dw      64 dup (?)

STACK   ends

        end     main                ; defines program entry point
```

```
/*
    PROTO.C:  prototype character-oriented filter

    Copyright 1988 Ray Duncan
*/

#include <stdio.h>

main(int argc, char *argv[])
{
    char ch;

    while((ch=getchar()) != EOF)      /* read a character          */
    {
        ch = translate(ch);           /* translate it if necessary */

        putchar(ch);                  /* write the character       */
    }
    exit(0);                          /* terminate at end of file  */
}


/*
    Perform any necessary translation on character
    from input file. This example simply returns
    the same character.
*/

int translate(char ch)
{
    return (ch);
}
```

Figure 15-2. PROTO.C, *the source code for a prototype character-oriented C filter.*

The *CLEAN* Filter

As a more practical example of MS-DOS filters, let's look at a simple but very useful filter called *CLEAN*. Figures 15-3 and 15-4 show the assembly-language and C source code for this filter. *CLEAN* processes a text stream by stripping the high bit from all characters, expanding tabs to spaces, and throwing away all control codes except carriage returns, linefeeds, and formfeeds. Consequently, *CLEAN* can transform almost any kind of word-processed document file into a plain ASCII text file.

```
        name    clean
        page    55,132
        title   CLEAN--Text-file filter
;
; CLEAN.ASM      Filter to turn document files into
;                normal text files.
;
; Copyright 1988 Ray Duncan
;
; Build:         C>MASM CLEAN;
;                C>LINK CLEAN;
;
; Usage:         C>CLEAN  <infile  >outfile
;
; All text characters are passed through with high
; bit stripped off. Formfeeds, carriage returns,
; and linefeeds are passed through. Tabs are expanded
; to spaces. All other control codes are discarded.
;

tab     equ     09h             ; ASCII tab code
lf      equ     0ah             ; ASCII linefeed
ff      equ     0ch             ; ASCII formfeed
cr      equ     0dh             ; ASCII carriage return
blank   equ     020h            ; ASCII space code
eof     equ     01ah            ; Ctrl-Z end-of-file

tabsiz  equ     8               ; width of tab stop

bufsiz  equ     128             ; size of input and
                                ; output buffers

stdin   equ     0000            ; standard input handle
stdout  equ     0001            ; standard output handle
stderr  equ     0002            ; standard error handle


_TEXT   segment word public 'CODE'

        assume  cs:_TEXT,ds:_DATA,es:_DATA,ss:STACK

clean   proc    far             ; entry point from MS-DOS

        push    ds              ; save DS:0000 for final
        xor     ax,ax           ; return to MS-DOS, in case
        push    ax              ; function 4ch can't be used
```

(continued)

Figure 15-3. CLEAN.ASM, *the source code for the MASM version of the* CLEAN *filter.*

Figure 15-3. *continued*

```
        mov     ax,_DATA        ; make data segment addressable
        mov     ds,ax
        mov     es,ax

        mov     ah,30h          ; check version of MS-DOS
        int     21h
        cmp     al,2            ; MS-DOS 2.0 or later?
        jae     clean1          ; jump if version OK

                                ; MS-DOS 1, display error
                                ; message and exit...
        mov     dx,offset msg1  ; DS:DX = message address
        mov     ah,9            ; function 9 = display string
        int     21h             ; transfer to MS-DOS
        ret                     ; then exit the old way

clean1: call    init            ; initialize input buffer

clean2: call    getc            ; get character from input
        jc      clean9          ; exit if end of stream

        and     al,07fh         ; strip off high bit

        cmp     al,blank        ; is it a control char?
        jae     clean4          ; no, write it

        cmp     al,eof          ; is it end of file?
        je      clean8          ; yes, write EOF and exit

        cmp     al,tab          ; is it a tab?
        je      clean6          ; yes, expand it to spaces

        cmp     al,cr           ; is it a carriage return?
        je      clean3          ; yes, go process it

        cmp     al,lf           ; is it a linefeed?
        je      clean3          ; yes, go process it

        cmp     al,ff           ; is it a formfeed?
        jne     clean2          ; no, discard it

clean3: mov     column,0        ; if CR, LF, or FF,
        jmp     clean5          ; reset column to zero

clean4: inc     column          ; if non-control character,
                                ; increment column counter
```

(continued)

Figure 15-3. *continued*

```
clean5: call   putc            ; write char to stdout
        jnc    clean2          ; if disk not full,
                               ; get another character


                               ; write failed...
        mov    dx,offset msg2  ; DS:DX = error message
        mov    cx,msg2_len     ; CX = message length
        mov    bx,stderr       ; BX = standard error handle
        mov    ah,40h          ; function 40h = write
        int    21h             ; transfer to MS-DOS

        mov    ax,4c01h        ; function 4ch = terminate
                               ; return code = 1
        int    21h             ; transfer to MS-DOS

clean6: mov    ax,column       ; tab code detected
        cwd                    ; tabsiz - (column MOD tabsiz)
        mov    cx,tabsiz       ; is number of spaces needed
        idiv   cx              ; to move to next tab stop
        sub    cx,dx

        add    column,cx       ; also update column counter

clean7: push   cx              ; save spaces counter

        mov    al,blank        ; write an ASCII space
        call   putc

        pop    cx              ; restore spaces counter
        loop   clean7          ; loop until tab stop

        jmp    clean2          ; get another character

clean8: call   putc            ; write EOF mark

clean9: call   flush           ; write last output buffer
        mov    ax,4c00h        ; function 4ch = terminate
                               ; return code = 0
        int    21h             ; transfer to MS-DOS

clean   endp


getc    proc   near            ; get character from stdin
                               ; returns carry = 1 if
                               ; end of input, else
                               ; AL = char, carry = 0
```

(continued)

Figure 15-3. *continued*

```
          mov     bx,iptr          ; get input buffer pointer
          cmp     bx,ilen          ; end of buffer reached?
          jne     getc1            ; not yet, jump

                                   ; more data is needed...
          mov     bx,stdin         ; BX = standard input handle
          mov     cx,bufsiz        ; CX = length to read
          mov     dx,offset ibuff  ; DS:DX = buffer address
          mov     ah,3fh           ; function 3fh = read
          int     21h              ; transfer to MS-DOS
          jc      getc2            ; jump if read failed

          or      ax,ax            ; was anything read?
          jz      getc2            ; jump if end of input

          mov     ilen,ax          ; save length of data
          xor     bx,bx            ; reset buffer pointer

getc1:    mov     al,[ibuff+bx]    ; get character from buffer
          inc     bx               ; bump buffer pointer

          mov     iptr,bx          ; save updated pointer
          clc                      ; return character in AL
          ret                      ; and carry = 0 (clear)

getc2:    stc                      ; end of input stream
          ret                      ; return carry = 1 (set)

getc      endp


putc      proc    near             ; send character to stdout,
                                   ; returns carry = 1 if
                                   ; error, else carry = 0

          mov     bx,optr          ; store character into
          mov     [obuff+bx],al    ; output buffer

          inc     bx               ; bump buffer pointer
          cmp     bx,bufsiz        ; buffer full?
          jne     putc1            ; no, jump

          mov     bx,stdout        ; BX = standard output handle
          mov     cx,bufsiz        ; CX = length to write
          mov     dx,offset obuff  ; DS:DX = buffer address
```

(continued)

Figure 15-3. *continued*

```
           mov     ah,40h          ; function 40h = write
           int     21h             ; transfer to MS-DOS
           jc      putc2           ; jump if write failed

           cmp     ax,cx           ; was write complete?
           jne     putc2           ; jump if disk full

           xor     bx,bx           ; reset buffer pointer

putc1:     mov     optr,bx         ; save buffer pointer
           clc                     ; write successful,
           ret                     ; return carry = 0 (clear)

putc2:     stc                     ; write failed or disk full,
           ret                     ; return carry = 1 (set)

putc       endp


init       proc    near            ; initialize input buffer

           mov     bx,stdin        ; BX = standard input handle
           mov     cx,bufsiz       ; CX = length to read
           mov     dx,offset ibuff ; DS:DX = buffer address
           mov     ah,3fh          ; function 3fh = read
           int     21h             ; transfer to MS-DOS
           jc      init1           ; jump if read failed
           mov     ilen,ax         ; save actual bytes read
init1:     ret

init       endp


flush      proc    near            ; flush output buffer

           mov     cx,optr         ; CX = bytes to write
           jcxz    flush1          ; exit if buffer empty
           mov     dx,offset obuff ; DS:DX = buffer address
           mov     bx,stdout       ; BX = standard output handle
           mov     ah,40h          ; function 40h = write
           int     21h             ; transfer to MS-DOS
flush1:    ret

flush      endp

_TEXT      ends
```

(continued)

Figure 15-3. *continued*

```
_DATA    segment word public 'DATA'

ibuff    db       bufsiz dup (0)  ; input buffer
obuff    db       bufsiz dup (0)  ; output buffer

iptr     dw       0               ; ibuff pointer
ilen     dw       0               ; bytes in ibuff
optr     dw       0               ; obuff pointer

column   dw       0               ; current column counter

msg1     db       cr,lf
         db       'clean: need MS-DOS version 2 or greater.'
         db       cr,lf,'$'

msg2     db       cr,lf
         db       'clean: disk is full.'
         db       cr,lf
msg2_len equ      $-msg2

_DATA    ends


STACK    segment para stack 'STACK'

         dw       64 dup (?)

STACK    ends

         end      clean
```

```
/*
    CLEAN.C    Filter to turn document files into
               normal text files.

    Copyright 1988 Ray Duncan

    Compile:   C>CL CLEAN.C

    Usage:     C>CLEAN  <infile >outfile
```

(continued)

Figure 15-4. CLEAN.C, *the source code for the C version of the* CLEAN *filter.*

Figure 15-4. *continued*

```
    All text characters are passed through with high bit stripped
    off. Formfeeds, carriage returns, and linefeeds are passed
    through. Tabs are expanded to spaces. All other control codes
    are discarded.
*/

#include <stdio.h>

#define TAB_WIDTH   8              /* width of a tab stop      */
#define TAB        '\x09'          /* ASCII tab character      */
#define LF         '\x0A'          /* ASCII linefeed           */
#define FF         '\x0C'          /* ASCII formfeed           */
#define CR         '\x0D'          /* ASCII carriage return    */
#define BLANK      '\x20'          /* ASCII space code         */
#define EOFMK      '\x1A'          /* Ctrl-Z end of file       */


main(int argc, char *argv[])
{
    char c;                        /* character from stdin     */
    int col = 0;                   /* column counter           */

    while((c = getchar()) != EOF)  /* read input character     */
    {
        c &= 0x07F;                /* strip high bit           */

        switch(c)                  /* decode character         */
        {
            case LF:               /* if linefeed or           */
            case CR:               /* carriage return,         */
                col=0;             /* reset column count       */

            case FF:               /* if formfeed, carriage    */
                wchar(c);          /* return, or linefeed,     */
                break;             /* pass character through   */

            case TAB:              /* if tab, expand to spaces */
                do wchar(BLANK);
                while((++col % TAB_WIDTH) != 0);
                break;

            default:               /* discard other control    */
                if(c >= BLANK)     /* characters, pass text     */
```

(continued)

Figure 15-4. *continued*

```
                    {                        /* characters through    */
                  wchar(c);
                  col++;                      /* bump column counter   */
                }
              break;
        }
    }
    wchar(EOFMK);                          /* write end-of-file mark */
    exit(0);
}



/*
    Write a character to the standard output. If
    write fails, display error message and terminate.
*/

wchar(char c)
{
    if((putchar(c) == EOF) && (c != EOFMK))
    {
        fputs("clean: disk full",stderr);
        exit(1);
    }
}
```

When using the *CLEAN* filter, you must specify the source and destination files with redirection parameters in the command line; otherwise, *CLEAN* will simply read the keyboard and write to the display. For example, to filter the document file *MYFILE.DOC* and leave the result in the file *MYFILE.TXT*, you would enter the following command:

```
C>CLEAN <MYFILE.DOC >MYFILE.TXT  <Enter>
```

(Note that the original file, *MYFILE.DOC*, is unchanged.)

One valuable application of this filter is to rescue assembly-language source files. If you accidentally edit such a source file in document mode, the resulting file may cause the assembler to generate spurious or confusing error messages. *CLEAN* lets you turn the source file back into something the assembler can cope with, without losing the time you spent to edit it.

Another handy application for *CLEAN* is to list a word-processed document in raw form on the printer, using a command such as

```
C>CLEAN <MYFILE.DOC >PRN  <Enter>
```

Contrasting the C and assembly-language versions of this filter provides some interesting statistics. The C version contains 79 lines and compiles to a 5889-byte .EXE file, whereas the assembly-language version contains 265 lines and builds an 1107-byte .EXE file. The size and execution-speed advantages of implementing such tools in assembly language is obvious, even compared with such an excellent compiler as the Microsoft C Optimizing Compiler. However, you must balance performance considerations against the time and expense required for programming, particularly when a program will not be used very often.

Chapter 16

Compatibility and Portability

At the beginning of this book, we surveyed the history of MS-DOS and saw that new versions come along nearly every year, loosely coupled to the introduction of new models of personal computers. We then focused on each of the mainstream issues of MS-DOS applications programming: the user interface; mass storage; memory management; control of "child" processes; and special classes of programs, such as filters, interrupt handlers, and device drivers.

It's now time to close the circle and consider two global concerns of MS-DOS programming: compatibility and portability. For your programs to remain useful in a constantly evolving software and hardware environment, you must design them so that they perform reliably on any reasonable machine configuration and exploit available system resources; in addition, you should be able to upgrade them easily for new versions of MS-DOS, for new machines, and, for that matter, for completely new environments such as MS OS/2.

Degrees of Compatibility

If we look at how existing MS-DOS applications use the operating system and hardware, we find that we can assign them to one of four categories:

- MS-DOS–compatible applications

- ROM BIOS–compatible applications

- Hardware-compatible applications

- "Ill-behaved" applications

MS-DOS–compatible applications use only the documented MS-DOS function calls and do not call the ROM BIOS or access the hardware directly. They use ANSI escape sequences for screen control, and their input and output is redirectable. An MS-DOS–compatible application will run on any machine that supports MS-DOS, regardless of the machine configuration. Because of the relatively poor performance of MS-DOS's built-in display and serial port drivers, few popular programs other than compilers, assemblers, and linkers fall into this category.

ROM BIOS–compatible applications use the documented MS-DOS and ROM BIOS function calls but do not access the hardware directly. As recently as three years ago, this strategy might have significantly limited a program's potential market. Today, the availability of high-quality IBM-compatible ROM BIOSes from companies such as Phoenix has ensured the dominance of the IBM ROM BIOS standard; virtually no machines are being sold in which a program cannot rely as much on the ROM BIOS interface as it might on the MS-DOS interface. However, as we noted in Chapters 6 and 7, the ROM BIOS display and serial drivers are still not adequate to the needs of high-performance interactive applications, so the popular programs that fall into this category are few.

Hardware-compatible applications generally use MS-DOS functions for mass storage, memory management, and the like, and use a mix of MS-DOS and ROM BIOS function calls and direct hardware access for their user interfaces. The amount of hardware dependence in such programs varies widely. For example, some programs only write characters and attributes into the video controller's regen buffer and use the ROM BIOS to switch modes and position the cursor; others bypass the ROM BIOS video driver altogether and take complete control of the video adapter. As this book is written, the vast majority of the popular MS-DOS "productivity" applications (word processors, databases, telecommunications programs, and so on) can be placed somewhere in this category.

"Ill-behaved" applications are those that rely on undocumented MS-DOS function calls or data structures, interception of MS-DOS or ROM BIOS interrupts, or direct access to mass storage devices (bypassing the MS-DOS file system). These programs tend to be extremely sensitive to their environment and typically must be "adjusted" in order to work with each new MS-DOS version or PC model. Virtually all popular terminate-and-stay-resident (TSR) utilities, network programs, and disk repair/optimization packages are in this category.

Writing Well-Behaved MS-DOS Applications

Your choice of MS-DOS functions, ROM BIOS functions, or direct hardware access to solve a particular problem must always be balanced against performance needs; and, of course, the user is the final judge of a program's usefulness and reliability. Nevertheless, you can follow some basic guidelines, outlined below, to create well-behaved applications that are likely to run properly under future versions of MS-DOS and under multitasking program managers that run on top of MS-DOS, such as Microsoft Windows.

Program structure

Design your programs as .EXE files with separate code, data, and stack segments; shun the use of .COM files. Use the Microsoft conventions for segment names and attributes discussed in Chapter 3. Inspect the environment block at runtime to locate your program's overlays or data files; don't "hard-wire" a directory location into the program.

Check host capabilities

Obtain the MS-DOS version number with Int 21H Function 30H during your program's initialization and be sure that all of the functions your program requires are actually available. If you find that the host MS-DOS version is inadequate, be careful about which functions you call to display an error message and to terminate.

Use the enhanced capabilities of MS-DOS versions 3 and 4 when your program is running under those versions. For example, you can specify a sharing mode when opening a file with Int 21H Function 3DH, you can create temporary or unique files with Int 21H Functions 5AH and 5BH, and you can obtain extended error information (including a recommended recovery strategy) with Int 21H Function 59H. Section II of this book contains version-dependency information for each MS-DOS function.

Input and output

Use the handle file functions exclusively and extend full path support throughout your application (being sure to allow for the maximum possible path length during user input of filenames). Use buffered I/O whenever possible. The device drivers in MS-DOS versions 2.0 and later can handle strings as long as 64 KB, and performance will be improved if you write fewer, larger records as opposed to many short ones.

Avoid the use of FCBs, the Int 25H or Int 26H functions, or the ROM BIOS disk driver. If you must use FCBs, close them when you are done with them and don't move them around while they are open. Avoid reopening FCBs that are already open or reclosing FCBs that have already been closed—these seemingly harmless practices can cause problems when network software is running.

Memory management

During your program's initialization, release any memory that is not needed by the program. (This is especially important for .COM programs.) If your program requires extra memory for buffers or tables, allocate that memory dynamically when it is needed and release it as soon as it is no longer required. Use expanded memory, when it is available, to minimize your program's demands on conventional memory.

As a general rule, don't touch any memory that is not owned by your program. To set or inspect interrupt vectors, use Int 21H Functions 25H and 35H rather than editing the interrupt vector table directly. If you alter the contents of interrupt vectors, save their original values and restore them before the program exits.

Process management

To isolate your program from dependencies on PSP structure and relocation information, use the EXEC function (Int 21H Function 4BH) when loading overlays or other programs. Terminate your program with Int 21H Function 4CH, passing a zero return code if the program executes successfully and a nonzero code if an error is encountered. Your program's parent can then test this return code with Int 21H Function 4DH or, in a batch file, with the IF ERRORLEVEL statement.

Exception handling

Install Ctrl-C (Int 23H) and critical-error (Int 24H) handlers so that your program cannot be terminated unexpectedly by the user's entry of Ctrl-C or Ctrl-Break or by a hardware I/O failure. This is particularly important if your program uses expanded memory or installs its own interrupt handlers.

ROM BIOS and Hardware-Compatible Applications

When you feel the need to introduce ROM BIOS or hardware dependence for performance reasons, keep it isolated to small, well-documented procedures that can be easily modified when the hardware changes. Use macros and equates to hide hardware characteristics and to avoid spreading "magic numbers" throughout your program.

Check host capabilities

If you use ROM BIOS functions in your program, you must check the machine model at runtime to be sure that the functions your program needs are actually available. There is a machine ID byte at F000:FFFEH whose value is interpreted as follows:

F8H	PS/2 Models 70 and 80
F9H	PC Convertible
FAH	PS/2 Model 30
FBH	PC/XT (later models)
FCH	PC/AT, PC/XT-286, PS/2 Models 50 and 60
FDH	PCjr
FEH	PC/XT (early models)
FFH	PC "Classic"

In some cases, submodels can be identified; see Int 15H Function C0H on page 573. Section III of this book contains version-dependency information for each ROM BIOS function.

When writing your own direct video drivers, you must determine the type and capabilities of the video adapter by a combination of Int 10H calls, reading ports, and inspection of the ROM BIOS data area at 0040:0000H and the memory reserved for the EGA or VGA ROM BIOS, among other things. The techniques required are beyond the scope of this book but are well explained in *Programmer's Guide to PC and PS/2 Video Systems* (Microsoft Press, 1987).

Avoid unstable hardware

Some areas of IBM personal computer architecture have remained remarkably stable from the original IBM PC, based on a 4.77 MHz 8088, to today's PS/2 Model 80, based on a 20 MHz 80386. IBM's track record for upward compatibility in its video and serial communications controllers has been excellent; in many cases, the same hardware-dependent code that was written for the original IBM PC runs perfectly well on an IBM PS/2 Model 80. Other areas of relative hardware stability are:

- Sound control via port 61H

- The 8253 timer chip's channels 0 and 2 (ports 40H, 42H, and 43H)

- The game adapter at port 201H

- Control of the interrupt system via the 8259 PIC's mask register at port 21H

However, direct sound generation and manipulation of the 8253 timer or 8259 PIC are quite likely to cause problems if your program is run under a multitasking program manager such as Microsoft Windows or DesqView.

Keyboard mapping, the keyboard controller, and the floppy and fixed disk controllers are areas of relative hardware *instability*. Programs that bypass MS-DOS for keyboard or disk access are much less likely to function properly across the different PC models and are also prone to interfere with each other and with well-behaved applications.

OS/2 Compatibility

MS-DOS is upwardly compatible in several respects with OS/2, Microsoft's multitasking protected-mode virtual memory operating system for 80286 and 80386 computers. The OS/2 graphical user interface (the Presentation Manager) is nearly identical to Microsoft Windows 2.0. OS/2 versions 1.0 and 1.1 use exactly the same disk formats as MS-DOS so that files may easily be moved between MS-DOS and OS/2 systems. Most important, OS/2 includes a module called the "DOS Compatibility Environment" or "3.x Box," which can run one MS-DOS application at a time alongside protected-mode OS/2 applications.

The 3.x Box traps Int 21H function calls and remaps them into OS/2 function calls, emulating an MS-DOS 3.3 environment with the file-sharing module (SHARE.EXE) loaded but returning a major version number of 10 instead of 3 for Int 21H Function 30H. The 3.x Box also supports most ROM BIOS calls, either by emulating their function or by interlocking the device and then calling the original ROM BIOS routine. In addition, the 3.x Box maintains the ROM BIOS data area, provides timer ticks to applications via Int 1CH, and supports certain undocumented MS-DOS services and data structures so that most TSR utilities can function properly. Nevertheless, the 3.x Box's emulation of MS-DOS is not perfect, and you must be aware of certain constraints on MS-DOS applications running under OS/2.

The most significant restriction on an MS-DOS application is that it does not receive any CPU cycles when it is in the background. That is, when a protected-mode application has been "selected," so that the user can interact with it, the MS-DOS application is frozen. If the MS-DOS application has captured any interrupt vectors (such as the serial port or timer tick), these interrupts will not be serviced until the application is again selected and in the foreground. OS/2 must freeze MS-DOS applications when they are in the background because they execute in real mode and are thus not subject to hardware memory protection; nothing else ensures that they will not interfere with a protected-mode process that has control of the screen and keyboard.

Use of FCBs is restricted in the 3.x Box, as it is under MS-DOS 3 or 4 with SHARE.EXE loaded. A file cannot be opened with an FCB if any other process is using it. The number of FCBs that can be simultaneously opened is limited to 16 or to the number specified in a CONFIG.SYS FCBS= directive. Even when the handle file functions are used, these functions may fail unexpectedly due to the activity of other processes (for example, if a protected-mode process has already opened the file with "deny all" sharing mode); most MS-DOS applications are not written with file sharing in mind, and they do not handle such errors gracefully.

Direct writes to a fixed disk using Int 26H or Int 13H are not allowed. This prevents the file system from being corrupted, because protected-mode applications running concurrently with the MS-DOS application may also be writing to the same disk. Imagine the mess if a typical MS-DOS unerase utility were to alter the root directory and FAT at the same time that a protected-mode database program was updating its file and indexes!

MS-DOS applications that attempt to reprogram the 8259 to move the interrupt vector table or that modify interrupt vectors already belonging to an OS/2 device driver are terminated by the operating system. MS-DOS applications *can* change the 8259's interrupt-mask register, disable and reenable interrupts at their discretion, and read or write any I/O port. The obvious corollary is that an MS-DOS program running in the 3.x Box can crash the entire OS/2 system at any time; this is the price for allowing real-mode applications to run at all.

Porting MS-DOS Applications to OS/2

The application program interface (API) provided by OS/2 to protected-mode programs is quite different from the familiar Int 21H interface of MS-DOS and the OS/2 3.x Box. However, the OS/2 API is *functionally* a proper superset of MS-DOS. This makes it easy to convert well-behaved MS-DOS applications to run in OS/2 protected mode, whence they can be enhanced to take advantage of OS/2's virtual memory, multitasking, and interprocess communication capabilities.

To give you a feeling for both the nature of the OS/2 API and the practices that should be avoided in MS-DOS programming if portability to OS/2 is desired, I will outline my own strategy for converting existing MS-DOS assembly-language programs to OS/2. For the purposes of discussion, I have divided the conversion process into five steps and have assigned each an easily remembered buzzword:

1. Segmentation
2. Rationalization
3. Encapsulation
4. Conversion
5. Optimization

The first three stages can (and should) be performed and tested in the MS-DOS environment; only the last two require OS/2 and the protected-mode programming tools. As you read on, you may notice that an MS-DOS program that follows the compatibility guidelines presented earlier in this chapter requires relatively little work to make it run in protected mode. This is the natural benefit of working with the operating system instead of against it.

Segmentation

Most of the 80286's protected-mode capabilities revolve around a change in the way memory is addressed. In real mode, the 80286 essentially emulates an 8088/86 processor, and the value in a segment register corresponds directly to a physical memory address. MS-DOS runs on the 80286 in real mode.

When an 80286 is running in protected mode, as it does under OS/2, an additional level of indirection is added to memory addressing.[1] A segment register holds a *selector*, which is an index to a table of *descriptors*. A descriptor defines the physical address and length of a memory segment, its characteristics (executable, read-only data, or read/write data) and access rights, and whether the segment is currently resident in RAM or has been swapped out to disk. Each time a program loads a segment register or accesses memory, the 80286 hardware checks the associated descriptor and the program's privilege level, generating a *fault* if the selector or memory operation is not valid. The fault acts like a hardware interrupt, allowing the operating system to regain control and take the appropriate action.

This scheme of memory addressing in protected mode has two immediate consequences for application programs. The first is that application programs can no longer perform arithmetic on the contents of segment registers (because selectors are magic numbers and have no direct relationship to physical memory addresses) or use segment registers for storage of temporary values. A program must not load a segment register with anything but a legitimate selector provided by the OS/2 loader or resulting from an OS/2 memory allocation function call. The second consequence is that a program must strictly segregate machine code ("text") from data, placing them in separate segments with distinct selectors (because a selector that is executable is not writable, and vice versa).

Accordingly, the first step in converting a program for OS/2 is to turn it into a .EXE-type program that uses the Microsoft segment, class, and group conventions described in Chapter 3. At minimum, the program must have one code segment and one data segment, and should declare a group—with the special name *DGROUP*—that contains the "near" data segment, stack, and local heap (if any). At the same time, you should remove or rewrite any code that performs direct manipulation of segment values.

---

[1] Although the 80386 has additional modes and addressing capabilities, current versions of OS/2 use the 80386 as though it were an 80286.

After restructuring and segmentation, reassemble and link your program and check to be sure it still works as expected under MS-DOS. Changing or adding segmentation often uncovers hidden addressing assumptions in the code, so it is best to track these problems down before making other substantive changes to the program.

Rationalization

Once you've successfully segmented your program so that it can be linked and executed as a .EXE file under MS-DOS, the next step is to rationalize your code. By rationalization I mean converting your program into a completely well-behaved MS-DOS application.

First, you must ruthlessly eliminate any elements that manipulate the peripheral device adapters directly, alter interrupt priorities, edit the system interrupt-vector table, or depend on CPU speed or characteristics (such as timing loops). In protected mode, control of the interrupt system is completely reserved to the operating system and its device drivers, I/O ports may be read or written by an application only under very specific conditions, and timing loops burn up CPU cycles that can be used by other processes.

As I mentioned earlier in this chapter, display routines constitute the most common area of hardware dependence in an MS-DOS application. Direct manipulation of the video adapter and its regen buffer poses obvious difficulties in a multitasking, protected-memory environment such as OS/2. For porting purposes, you must convert all routines that write text to the display, modify character attributes, or affect cursor shape or position into Int 21H Function 40H calls using ANSI escape sequences or into ROM BIOS Int 10H calls. Similarly, you must convert all hardware-dependent keyboard operations to Int 21H Function 3FH or ROM BIOS Int 16H calls.

Once all hardware dependence has been expunged from your program, your next priority is to make it well-behaved in its use of system memory. Under MS-DOS an application is typically handed all remaining memory in the system to do with as it will; under OS/2 the converse is true: A process is initially allocated only enough memory to hold its code, declared data storage, and stack. You can make the MS-DOS loader behave like the OS/2 loader by linking your application with the /CPARMAXALLOC switch. Alternatively, your program can give up all extra memory during its initialization with Int 21H Function 4AH, as recommended earlier in this chapter.

After your program completes its initialization sequence, it should dynamically obtain and release any additional memory it may require for buffers and tables with MS-DOS Int 21H Functions 48H and 49H. To ensure compatibility with protected mode, limit the size of any single allocated block to 65,536 bytes or less, even though MS-DOS allows larger blocks to be allocated.

Finally, you must turn your attention to file and device handling. Replace any calls to FCB file functions with their handle-based equivalents, because OS/2 does not support FCBs in protected mode at all. Check pathnames for validity within the application; although MS-DOS and the 3.x Box silently truncate a name or extension, OS/2 refuses to open or create a file in protected mode if the name or extension is too long and returns an error instead. Replace any use of the predefined handles for the *standard auxiliary* and *standard list* devices with explicit opens of COM1, PRN, LPT1, and so on, using the resulting handle for read and write operations. OS/2 does not supply processes with standard handles for the serial communications port or printer.

Encapsulation

When you reach this point, with a well-behaved, segmented MS-DOS application in hand, the worst of a port to OS/2 is behind you. You are now ready to prepare your program for true conversion to protected-mode operation by encapsulating, in individual subroutines, every part of the program that is specific to the host operating system. The objective here is to localize the program's "knowledge" of the environment into small procedures that can be subsequently modified without affecting the remainder of the program.

As an example of encapsulation, consider a typical call by an MS-DOS application to write a string to the standard output device (Figure 16-1). In order to facilitate conversion to OS/2, you would replace every instance of such a write to a file or device with a call to a small subroutine that "hides" the mechanics of the actual operating-system function call, as illustrated in Figure 16-2.

Another candidate for encapsulation, which does not necessarily involve an operating-system function call, is the application's code to gain access to command-line parameters, environment-block variables, and the name of the file it was loaded from. Under MS-DOS, this information is divided between the program segment prefix (PSP) and the environment block, as we saw in Chapters 3 and 12; under OS/2, there is no such thing as a PSP, and the program filename and command-line information are appended to the environment block.

```
stdin    equ    0              ; standard input handle
stdout   equ    1              ; standard output handle
stderr   equ    2              ; standard error handle

msg      db     'This is a sample message'
msg_len  equ    $-msg

         .
         .
         .
         mov    dx,seg msg     ; DS:DX = message address
         mov    ds,dx
         mov    dx,offset DGROUP:msg
         mov    cx,msg_len     ; CX = message length
         mov    bx,stdout      ; BX = handle
         mov    ah,40h         ; AH = function 40h write
         int    21h            ; transfer to MS-DOS
         jc     error          ; jump if error
         cmp    ax,msg_len     ; all characters written?
         jne    diskfull       ; no, device is full
         .
         .
         .
```

Figure 16-1. *Typical in-line code for an MS-DOS function call. This particular sequence writes a string to the standard output device. Since the standard output might be redirected to a file without the program's knowledge, it must also check that all of the requested characters were actually written; if the returned length is less than the requested length, this usually indicates that the standard output has been redirected to a disk file and that the disk is full.*

```
stdin    equ    0              ; standard input handle
stdout   equ    1              ; standard output handle
stderr   equ    2              ; standard error handle

msg      db     'This is a sample message'
msg_len  equ    $-msg

         .
         .
         .
```

(continued)

Figure 16-2. *Code from Figure 16-1 after "encapsulation." The portion of the code that is operating-system dependent has been isolated inside a subroutine that is called from other points within the application.*

Figure 16-2. *continued*

```
        mov     dx,seg msg          ; DS:DX = message address
        mov     ds,dx
        mov     dx,offset DGROUP:msg
        mov     cx,msg_len          ; CX = message length
        mov     bx,stdout           ; BX = handle
        call    write               ; perform the write
        jc      error               ; jump if error
        cmp     ax,msg_len          ; all characters written?
        jne     diskfull            ; no, device is full
        .
        .
        .


write   proc    near                ; write to file or device
                                    ; Call with:
                                    ; BX = handle
                                    ; CX = length of data
                                    ; DS:DX = address of data
                                    ; returns:
                                    ; if successful, carry clear
                                    ; and AX = bytes written
                                    ; if error, carry set
                                    ; and AX = error code

        mov     ah,40h              ; function 40h = write
        int     21h                 ; transfer to MS-DOS
        ret                         ; return status in CY and AX

write   endp
        .
        .
        .
```

When you have completed the encapsulation of system services and access to the PSP and environment, subject your program once more to thorough testing under MS-DOS. This is your last chance, while you are still working in a familiar milieu and have access to your favorite debugging tools, to detect any subtle errors you may have introduced during the three conversion steps discussed thus far.

Conversion

Next, you must rewrite each system-dependent procedure you created during the encapsulation stage to conform to the OS/2 protected-mode API. In contrast to MS-DOS functions, which are actuated through software interrupts and pass parameters in registers, OS/2 API functions are requested through a far call to a named entry point. Parameters are passed on the stack, along with the addresses of variables within the calling program's data segment that will receive any results returned by the function. The status of an operation is returned in register AX—zero if the function succeeded, an error code otherwise. All other registers are preserved.

Although it is not my intention here to provide a detailed introduction to OS/2 programming, Figure 16-3 illustrates the final form of our previous example, after conversion for OS/2. Note especially the addition of the *extrn* statement, the *wlen* variable, and the simulation of the MS-DOS function status. This code may not be elegant, but it serves the purpose of limiting the necessary changes to a very small portion of the source file. Some OS/2 functions (such as *DosOpen*) require parameters that have no counterpart under MS-DOS; you can usually select reasonable values for these extra parameters that will make their existence temporarily invisible to the remainder of the application.

```
stdin    equ    0                      ; standard input handle
stdout   equ    1                      ; standard output handle
stderr   equ    2                      ; standard error handle

         extrn  DosWrite:far

msg      db     'This is a sample message'
msg_len equ     $-msg

wlen     dw     ?                       ; receives actual number
                                        ; of bytes written

           .
           .
           .
```

(continued)

Figure 16-3. *Code from Figure 16-2 after "conversion." The MS-DOS function call has been replaced with the equivalent OS/2 function call. Since the knowledge of the operating system has been hidden inside the subroutine by the previous encapsulation step, the surrounding program's requests for write operations should run unchanged. Note that the OS/2 function had to be declared as an external name with the "far" attribute, and that a variable named* wlen *was added to the data segment of the application to receive the actual number of bytes written.*

Figure 16-3. *continued*

```
        mov     dx,seg msg           ; DS:DX = message address
        mov     ds,dx
        mov     dx,offset DGROUP:msg
        mov     cx,msg_len           ; CX = message length
        mov     bx,stdout            ; BX = handle
        call    write                ; perform the write
        jc      error                ; jump if error
        cmp     ax,msg_len           ; all characters written?
        jne     diskfull             ; no, device is full
        .
        .
        .

write   proc    near                 ; write to file or device
                                     ; call with:
                                     ; BX = handle
                                     ; CX = length of data
                                     ; DS:DX = address of data
                                     ; returns:
                                     ; if successful, carry clear
                                     ; and AX = bytes written
                                     ; if error, carry set
                                     ; and AX = error code

        push    bx                   ; handle
        push    ds                   ; address of data
        push    dx
        push    cx                   ; length of data
        push    ds                   ; receives length written
        mov     ax,offset DGROUP:wlen
        push    ax
        call    DosWrite             ; transfer to OS/2
        or      ax,ax                ; did write succeed?
        jnz     write1               ; jump, write failed
        mov     ax,wlen              ; no error, OR cleared CY
        ret                          ; and AX := bytes written

write1: stc                          ; write error, return CY set
        ret                          ; and AX = error number

write   endp
        .
        .
        .
```

Figures 16-4, 16-5, and 16-6 list the OS/2 services that are equivalent to selected MS-DOS and ROM BIOS Int 21H, Int 10H, and Int 16H calls. MS-DOS functions related to FCBs and PSPs are not included in these tables because OS/2 does not support either of these structures. The MS-DOS terminate-and-stay-resident functions are also omitted. Because OS/2 is a true multitasking system, a process doesn't need to terminate in order to stay resident while another process is running.

MS-DOS	Description	OS/2 function
Int 21H Function		
0	Terminate process	DosExit
1	Character input with echo	KbdCharIn
2	Character output	VioWrtTTY
3	Auxiliary input	DosRead
4	Auxiliary output	DosWrite
5	Printer output	DosWrite
6	Direct console I/O	KbdCharIn, VioWrtTTY
7	Unfiltered input without echo	KbdCharIn
8	Character input without echo	KbdCharIn
9	Display string	VioWrtTTY
0AH (10)	Buffered keyboard input	KbdStringIn
0BH (11)	Check input status	KbdPeek
0CH (12)	Reset buffer and input	KbdFlushBuffer, KbdCharIn
0DH (13)	Disk reset	DosBufReset
0EH (14)	Select disk	DosSelectDisk
19H (25)	Get current disk	DosQCurDisk
1BH (27)	Get default drive data	DosQFSInfo
1CH (28)	Get drive data	DosQFSInfo
2AH (42)	Get date	DosGetDateTime
2BH (43)	Set date	DosSetDateTime
2CH (44)	Get time	DosGetDateTime
2DH (45)	Set time	DosSetDateTime
2EH (46)	Set verify flag	DosSetVerify
30H (48)	Get MS-DOS version	DosGetVersion
36H (54)	Get drive allocation information	DosQFSInfo

(continued)

Figure 16-4. *Table of selected MS-DOS function calls and their OS/2 counterparts. Note that OS/2 functions are typically more powerful and flexible than the corresponding MS-DOS functions, and that this is not a complete list of OS/2 services.*

Figure 16-4. *continued*

MS-DOS	Description	OS/2 function
38H (56)	Get or set country information	DosGetCtryInfo
39H (57)	Create directory	DosMkdir
3AH (58)	Delete directory	DosRmdir
3BH (59)	Set current directory	DosChdir
3CH (60)	Create file	DosOpen
3DH (61)	Open file	DosOpen
3EH (62)	Close file	DosClose
3FH (63)	Read file or device	DosRead
40H (64)	Write file or device	DosWrite
41H (65)	Delete file	DosDelete
42H (66)	Set file pointer	DosChgFilePtr
43H (67)	Get or set file attributes	DosQFileMode, DosSetFileMode
44H (68)	I/O control (IOCTL)	DosDevIOCtl
45H (69)	Duplicate handle	DosDupHandle
46H (70)	Redirect handle	DosDupHandle
47H (71)	Get current directory	DosQCurDir
48H (72)	Allocate memory block	DosAllocSeg
49H (73)	Release memory block	DosFreeSeg
4AH (74)	Resize memory block	DosReAllocSeg
4BH (75)	Execute program	DosExecPgm
4CH (76)	Terminate process with return code	DosExit
4DH (77)	Get return code	DosCWait
4EH (78)	Find first file	DosFindFirst
4FH (79)	Find next file	DosFindNext
54H (84)	Get verify flag	DosQVerify
56H (86)	Rename file	DosMove
57H (87)	Get or set file date and time	DosQFileInfo, DosSetFileInfo
59H (89)	Get extended error information	DosErrClass
5BH (91)	Create new file	DosOpen
5CH (92)	Lock or unlock file region	DosFileLocks
65H (101)	Get extended country information	DosGetCtryInfo
66H (102)	Get or set code page	DosGetCp, DosSetCp
67H (103)	Set handle count	DosSetMaxFH
68H (104)	Commit file	DosBufReset
6CH (108)	Extended open file	DosOpen

ROM BIOS	Description	OS/2 function
Int 10H		
Function		
0	Select display mode	VioSetMode
1	Set cursor type	VioSetCurType
2	Set cursor position	VioSetCurPos
3	Get cursor position	VioGetCurPos
6	Initialize or scroll window up	VioScrollUp
7	Initialize or scroll window down	VioScrollDn
8	Read character and attribute	VioReadCellStr
9	Write character and attribute	VioWrtNCell
0AH (10)	Write character	VioWrtNChar
0EH (14)	Write character in teletype mode	VioWrtTTY
0FH (15)	Get display mode	VioGetMode
10H (16)	Set palette, border color, etc.	VioSetState
13H (19)	Write string in teletype mode	VioWrtTTY

Figure 16-5. *Table of ROM BIOS Int 10H video-display driver functions used by MS-DOS applications and their OS/2 equivalents. This is not a complete list of OS/2 video services.*

ROM BIOS	Description	OS/2 function
Int 16H		
Function		
0	Read keyboard character	KbdCharIn
1	Get keyboard status	KbdPeek
2	Get keyboard flags	KbdGetStatus

Figure 16-6. *Table of ROM BIOS Int 16H keyboard driver functions used by MS-DOS applications and their OS/2 equivalents. This is not a complete list of OS/2 keyboard services.*

Optimization

Once your program is running in protected mode, it is time to unravel some of the changes made for purposes of conversion and to introduce various optimizations. Three obvious categories should be considered:

1. Modifying the program's user-interface code for the more powerful OS/2 keyboard and display API functions.

2. Incorporating 80286-specific machine instructions where appropriate.

3. Revamping the application to exploit the OS/2 facilities that are unique to protected mode. (Of course, the application benefits from OS/2's virtual memory capabilities automatically; it can allocate memory until physical memory and disk swapping space are exhausted.)

Modifying subroutines that encapsulate user input and output to take advantage of the additional functionality available under OS/2 is straightforward, and the resulting performance improvements can be quite dramatic. For example, the OS/2 video driver offers a variety of services that are far superior to the screen support in MS-DOS and the ROM BIOS, including high-speed display of strings and attributes at any screen position, "reading back" selected areas of the display into a buffer, and scrolling in all four directions.

The 80286-specific machine instructions can be very helpful in reducing code size and increasing execution speed. The most useful instructions are the shifts and rotates by an immediate count other than one, the three-operand multiply where one of the operands is an immediate (literal) value, and the push immediate value instruction (particularly handy for setting up OS/2 function calls). For example, in Figure 16-3, the sequence

```
mov     ax,offset DGROUP:wlen
push    ax
```

could be replaced by the single instruction

```
push    offset DGROUP:wlen
```

Restructuring an application to take full advantage of OS/2's protected-mode capabilities requires close study of both the application and the OS/2 API, but such study can pay off with sizable benefits in performance, ease of maintenance, and code sharing. Often, for instance, different parts of an application are concerned with I/O devices of vastly different speeds, such as the keyboard, disk, and video display. It both simplifies and enhances the application to separate these elements into subprocesses (called *threads* in OS/2) that execute asynchronously, communicate through shared data structures, and synchronize with each other, when necessary, using semaphores.

As another example, when several applications are closely related and contain many identical or highly similar procedures, OS/2 allows you to centralize those procedures in a *dynamic link library*. Routines in a dynamic link library are bound to a program at its load time (rather than by LINK, as in the case of traditional runtime libraries) and are shared by all the processes that need them. This reduces the size of each application .EXE file and allows more efficient use of memory. Best of all, dynamic link libraries drastically simplify code maintenance; the routines in the libraries can be debugged or improved at any time, and the applications that use them will automatically benefit the next time they are executed.

SECTION II

Notes to the Reader

This section documents the services that the MS-DOS kernel provides to application programs via software interrupts 20H–2FH. Each MS-DOS function is described in the same format:

- A heading containing the function's name, software interrupt and function number, and an icon indicating the MS-DOS version in which the function was first supported. You can assume that the function is available in all subsequent MS-DOS versions unless explicitly noted otherwise.

- A synopsis of the actions performed by the function and the circumstances under which it would be used.

- A summary of the function's arguments.

- The results and/or error indicators returned by the function. A comprehensive list of error codes can be found in the entry for Int 21H Function 59H.

- Notes describing special uses or dependencies of the function.

- A skeleton example of the function's use, written in assembly language.

Version icons used in the synopsis, arguments, results, or Notes sections refer to specific minor or major versions, unless they include a + sign to indicate a version and all subsequent versions.

For purposes of clarity, the examples may include instructions that would not be necessary if the code were inserted into a working program. For example, most of the examples explicitly set the segment registers when passing the address of a filename or buffer to MS-DOS; in real applications, the segment registers are usually initialized once at entry to the program and left alone thereafter.

Int 21H Function Summary by Number

Hex	Dec	Function name	Vers	F/H[1]
00H	0	Terminate Process	1.0+	
01H	1	Character Input with Echo	1.0+	
02H	2	Character Output	1.0+	
03H	3	Auxiliary Input	1.0+	
04H	4	Auxiliary Output	1.0+	
05H	5	Printer Output	1.0+	
06H	6	Direct Console I/O	1.0+	
07H	7	Unfiltered Character Input Without Echo	1.0+	
08H	8	Character Input Without Echo	1.0+	
09H	9	Display String	1.0+	
0AH	10	Buffered Keyboard Input	1.0+	
0BH	11	Check Input Status	1.0+	
0CH	12	Flush Input Buffer and Then Input	1.0+	
0DH	13	Disk Reset	1.0+	
0EH	14	Select Disk	1.0+	
0FH	15	Open File	1.0+	F
10H	16	Close File	1.0+	F
11H	17	Find First File	1.0+	F
12H	18	Find Next File	1.0+	F
13H	19	Delete File	1.0+	F
14H	20	Sequential Read	1.0+	F
15H	21	Sequential Write	1.0+	F
16H	22	Create File	1.0+	F
17H	23	Rename File	1.0+	F
18H	24	Reserved		
19H	25	Get Current Disk	1.0+	
1AH	26	Set DTA Address	1.0+	
1BH	27	Get Default Drive Data	1.0+	
1CH	28	Get Drive Data	2.0+	
1DH	29	Reserved		
1EH	30	Reserved		
1FH	31	Reserved		
20H	32	Reserved		
21H	33	Random Read	1.0+	F
22H	34	Random Write	1.0+	F
23H	35	Get File Size	1.0+	F
24H	36	Set Relative Record Number	1.0+	F
25H	37	Set Interrupt Vector	1.0+	
26H	38	Create New PSP	1.0+	
27H	39	Random Block Read	1.0+	F
28H	40	Random Block Write	1.0+	F
29H	41	Parse Filename	1.0+	

[1] Specifies whether file functions are FCB- or handle-related.

(continued)

Hex	Dec	Function name	Vers	F/H
2AH	42	Get Date	1.0+	
2BH	43	Set Date	1.0+	
2CH	44	Get Time	1.0+	
2DH	45	Set Time	1.0+	
2EH	46	Set Verify Flag	1.0+	
2FH	47	Get DTA Address	2.0+	
30H	48	Get MS-DOS Version Number	2.0+	
31H	49	Terminate and Stay Resident	2.0+	
32H	50	Reserved		
33H	51	Get or Set Break Flag, Get Boot Drive	2.0+	
34H	52	Reserved		
35H	53	Get Interrupt Vector	2.0+	
36H	54	Get Drive Allocation Information	2.0+	
37H	55	Reserved		
38H	56	Get or Set Country Information	2.0+	
39H	57	Create Directory	2.0+	
3AH	58	Delete Directory	2.0+	
3BH	59	Set Current Directory	2.0+	
3CH	60	Create File	2.0+	H
3DH	61	Open File	2.0+	H
3EH	62	Close File	2.0+	H
3FH	63	Read File or Device	2.0+	H
40H	64	Write File or Device	2.0+	H
41H	65	Delete File	2.0+	H
42H	66	Set File Pointer	2.0+	H
43H	67	Get or Set File Attributes	2.0+	
44H	68	IOCTL (I/O Control)	2.0+	
45H	69	Duplicate Handle	2.0+	
46H	70	Redirect Handle	2.0+	
47H	71	Get Current Directory	2.0+	
48H	72	Allocate Memory Block	2.0+	
49H	73	Release Memory Block	2.0+	
4AH	74	Resize Memory Block	2.0+	
4BH	75	Execute Program (EXEC)	2.0+	
4CH	76	Terminate Process with Return Code	2.0+	
4DH	77	Get Return Code	2.0+	
4EH	78	Find First File	2.0+	H
4FH	79	Find Next File	2.0+	H
50H	80	Reserved		
51H	81	Reserved		
52H	82	Reserved		
53H	83	Reserved		

(continued)

Hex	Dec	Function name	Vers	F/H
54H	84	Get Verify Flag	2.0+	
55H	85	Reserved		
56H	86	Rename File	2.0+	
57H	87	Get or Set File Date and Time	2.0+	H
58H	88	Get or Set Allocation Strategy	3.0+	
59H	89	Get Extended Error Information	3.0+	
5AH	90	Create Temporary File	3.0+	H
5BH	91	Create New File	3.0+	H
5CH	92	Lock or Unlock File Region	3.0+	H
5DH	93	Reserved		
5EH	94	Get Machine Name, Get or Set Printer Setup	3.1+	
5FH	95	Device Redirection	3.1+	
60H	96	Reserved		
61H	97	Reserved		
62H	98	Get PSP Address	3.0+	
63H	99	Get DBCS Lead Byte Table	2.25 only	
64H	100	Reserved		
65H	101	Get Extended Country Information	3.3+	
66H	102	Get or Set Code Page	3.3+	
67H	103	Set Handle Count	3.3+	
68H	104	Commit File	3.3+	H
69H	105	Reserved		
6AH	106	Reserved		
6BH	107	Reserved		
6CH	108	Extended Open File	4.0+	H

Int 21H Function Summary by Category

Hex	Dec	Function name	Vers	F/H
Character I/O				
01H	1	Character Input with Echo	1.0+	
02H	2	Character Output	1.0+	
03H	3	Auxiliary Input	1.0+	
04H	4	Auxiliary Output	1.0+	
05H	5	Printer Output	1.0+	
06H	6	Direct Console I/O	1.0+	
07H	7	Unfiltered Character Input Without Echo	1.0+	
08H	8	Character Input Without Echo	1.0+	

(continued)

Hex	Dec	Function name	Vers	F/H
09H	9	Display String	1.0+	
0AH	10	Buffered Keyboard Input	1.0+	
0BH	11	Check Input Status	1.0+	
0CH	12	Flush Input Buffer and Then Input	1.0+	
File Operations				
0FH	15	Open File	1.0+	F
10H	16	Close File	1.0+	F
11H	17	Find First File	1.0+	F
12H	18	Find Next File	1.0+	F
13H	19	Delete File	1.0+	F
16H	22	Create File	1.0+	F
17H	23	Rename File	1.0+	F
23H	35	Get File Size	1.0+	F
29H	41	Parse Filename	1.0+	F
3CH	60	Create File	2.0+	H
3DH	61	Open File	2.0+	H
3EH	62	Close File	2.0+	H
41H	65	Delete File	2.0+	H
43H	67	Get or Set File Attributes	2.0+	
45H	69	Duplicate Handle	2.0+	
46H	70	Redirect Handle	2.0+	
4EH	78	Find First File	2.0+	H
4FH	79	Find Next File	2.0+	H
56H	86	Rename File	2.0+	
57H	87	Get or Set File Date and Time	2.0+	H
5AH	90	Create Temporary File	3.0+	H
5BH	91	Create New File	3.0+	H
67H	103	Set Handle Count	3.3+	
68H	104	Commit File	3.3+	H
6CH	108	Extended Open File	4.0+	H
Record Operations				
14H	20	Sequential Read	1.0+	F
15H	21	Sequential Write	1.0+	F
1AH	26	Set DTA Address	1.0+	
21H	33	Random Read	1.0+	F
22H	34	Random Write	1.0+	F
24H	36	Set Relative Record Number	1.0+	F
27H	39	Random Block Read	1.0+	F
28H	40	Random Block Write	1.0+	F
2FH	47	Get DTA Address	2.0+	
3FH	63	Read File or Device	2.0+	H

(continued)

Hex	Dec	Function name	Vers	F/H
40H	64	Write File or Device	2.0+	H
42H	66	Set File Pointer	2.0+	H
5CH	92	Lock or Unlock File Region	3.0+	H

Directory Operations

39H	57	Create Directory	2.0+	
3AH	58	Delete Directory	2.0+	
3BH	59	Set Current Directory	2.0+	
47H	71	Get Current Directory	2.0+	

Disk Management

0DH	13	Disk Reset	1.0+	
0EH	14	Select Disk	1.0+	
19H	25	Get Current Disk	1.0+	
1BH	27	Get Default Drive Data	1.0+	
1CH	28	Get Drive Data	2.0+	
2EH	46	Set Verify Flag	1.0+	
36H	54	Get Drive Allocation Information	2.0+	
54H	84	Get Verify Flag	2.0+	

Process Management

00H	0	Terminate Process	1.0+	
26H	38	Create New PSP	1.0+	
31H	49	Terminate and Stay Resident	2.0+	
4BH	75	Execute Program (EXEC)	2.0+	
4CH	76	Terminate Process with Return Code	2.0+	
4DH	77	Get Return Code	2.0+	
62H	98	Get PSP Address	3.0+	

Memory Management

48H	72	Allocate Memory Block	2.0+	
49H	73	Release Memory Block	2.0+	
4AH	74	Resize Memory Block	2.0+	
58H	88	Get or Set Allocation Strategy	3.0+	

Network Functions

5EH	94	Get Machine Name, Get or Set Printer Setup	3.1+	
5FH	95	Device Redirection	3.1+	

Time and Date

2AH	42	Get Date	1.0+	
2BH	43	Set Date	1.0+	
2CH	44	Get Time	1.0+	
2DH	45	Set Time	1.0+	

(continued)

Hex	Dec	Function name	Vers	F/H
Miscellaneous System Functions				
25H	37	Set Interrupt Vector	1.0+	
30H	48	Get MS-DOS Version Number	2.0+	
33H	51	Get or Set Break Flag, Get Boot Drive	2.0+	
35H	53	Get Interrupt Vector	2.0+	
38H	56	Get or Set Country Information	2.0+	
44H	68	IOCTL (I/O Control)	2.0+	
59H	89	Get Extended Error Information	3.0+	
63H	99	Get Lead Byte Table	2.25 only	
65H	101	Get Extended Country Information	3.3+	
66H	102	Get or Set Code Page	3.3+	
Reserved Functions				
18H	24	Reserved		
1DH	29	Reserved		
1EH	30	Reserved		
1FH	31	Reserved		
20H	32	Reserved		
32H	50	Reserved		
34H	52	Reserved		
37H	55	Reserved		
50H	80	Reserved		
51H	81	Reserved		
52H	82	Reserved		
53H	83	Reserved		
55H	85	Reserved		
5DH	93	Reserved		
60H	96	Reserved		
61H	97	Reserved		
64H	100	Reserved		
69H	105	Reserved		
6AH	106	Reserved		
6BH	107	Reserved		

Int 20H [1.0]
Terminate process

Terminates the current process. This is one of several methods that a program can use to perform a final exit. MS-DOS then takes the following actions:

- All memory belonging to the process is released.
- File buffers are flushed and any open handles for files or devices owned by the process are closed.
- The termination handler vector (Int 22H) is restored from PSP:000AH.
- The Ctrl-C handler vector (Int 23H) is restored from PSP:000EH.
- [2.0+] The critical-error handler vector (Int 24H) is restored from PSP:0012H.
- Control is transferred to the termination handler.

If the program is returning to COMMAND.COM, control transfers to the resident portion, and the transient portion is reloaded if necessary. If a batch file is in progress, the next line of the file is fetched and interpreted; otherwise, a prompt is issued for the next user command.

Call with:	CS	= segment address of program segment prefix

Returns:	Nothing

Notes:
- Any files that have been written to using FCBs should be closed before performing this exit call; otherwise, data may be lost.
- Other methods of performing a final exit are:
  - Int 21H Function 00H
  - Int 21H Function 31H
  - Int 21H Function 4CH
  - Int 27H
- [2.0+] Int 21H Functions 31H and 4CH are the preferred methods for termination, since they allow a return code to be passed to the parent process.
- [3.0+] If the program is running on a network, it should remove all locks it has placed on file regions before terminating.

Example: Terminate the current program, returning control to the program's parent.

```
        .
        .
        .
        int     20h             ; transfer to MS-DOS
```

Int 21H
Function 00H
Terminate process

Terminates the current process. This is one of several methods that a program can use to perform a final exit. MS-DOS then takes the following actions:

- All memory belonging to the process is released.
- File buffers are flushed and any open handles for files or devices owned by the process are closed.
- The termination handler vector (Int 22H) is restored from PSP:000AH.
- The Ctrl-C handler vector (Int 23H) is restored from PSP:000EH.
- [2.0+] The critical-error handler vector (Int 24H) is restored from PSP:0012H.
- Control is transferred to the termination handler.

If the program is returning to COMMAND.COM, control transfers to the resident portion, and the transient portion is reloaded if necessary. If a batch file is in progress, the next line of the file is fetched and interpreted; otherwise, a prompt is issued for the next user command.

Call with:	AH	= 00H
	CS	= segment address of program segment prefix

Returns:	Nothing

Notes:
- Any files that have been written to using FCBs should be closed before performing this exit call; otherwise, data may be lost.
- Other methods of performing a final exit are:
  - Int 20H
  - Int 21H Function 31H
  - Int 21H Function 4CH
  - Int 27H
- [2.0+] Int 21H Functions 31H and 4CH are the preferred methods for termination, since they allow a return code to be passed to the parent process.
- [3.0+] If the program is running on a network, it should remove all locks it has placed on file regions before terminating.

Example: Terminate the current program, returning control to the program's parent.

```
          .
          .
          .
        mov     ah,0          ; function number
        int     21h           ; transfer to MS-DOS
```

Int 21H
Function 01H
Character input with echo

[1] Inputs a character from the keyboard, then echoes it to the display. If no character is ready, waits until one is available.

[2.0+] Reads a character from the standard input device and echoes it to the standard output device. If no character is ready, waits until one is available. Input can be redirected. (If input has been redirected, there is no way to detect EOF.)

Call with:	AH	= 01H

Returns:	AL	= 8-bit input data

Notes:
- If the standard input is not redirected, and the character read is a Ctrl-C, an Int 23H is executed. If the standard input is redirected, a Ctrl-C is detected at the console, and BREAK is ON, an Int 23H is executed.
- To read extended ASCII codes (such as the special function keys F1 to F10) on the IBM PC and compatibles, you must call this function twice. The first call returns the value 00H to signal the presence of an extended code.
- See also Int 21H Functions 06H, 07H, and 08H, which provide character input with various combinations of echo and/or Ctrl-C sensing.
- [2.0+] You can also read the keyboard by issuing a read (Int 21H Function 3FH) using the predefined handle for the standard input (0000H), if input has not been redirected, or a handle obtained by opening the logical device CON.

Example: Read one character from the keyboard into register AL, echo it to the display, and store it in the variable *char*.

```
char    db      0               ; input character
        .
        .
        .
        mov     ah,1            ; function number
        int     21h             ; transfer to MS-DOS
        mov     char,al         ; save character
        .
        .
        .
```

Int 21H
Function 02H
Character output

[1] Outputs a character to the currently active video display.

[2.0+] Outputs a character to the standard output device. Output can be redirected. (If output is redirected, there is no way to detect disk full.)

Call with:	AH	= 02H
	DL	= 8-bit data for output

Returns:	Nothing

Notes:
- If a Ctrl-C is detected at the keyboard after the requested character is output, an Int 23H is executed.
- If the standard output has not been redirected, a backspace code (08H) causes the cursor to move left one position. If output has been redirected, the backspace code does not receive any special treatment.
- [2.0+] You can also send strings to the display by performing a write (Int 21H Function 40H) using the predefined handle for the standard output (0001H), if output has not been redirected, or a handle obtained by opening the logical device CON.

Example: Send the character "*" to the standard output device.

```
        .
        .
        .
        mov     ah,2        ; function number
        mov     dl,'*'      ; character to output
        int     21h         ; transfer to MS-DOS
        .
        .
        .
```

Int 21H
Function 03H
Auxiliary input

[1] Reads a character from the first serial port.

[2.0+] Reads a character from the standard auxiliary device. The default is the first serial port (COM1).

Call with:	AH	= 03H

Returns: AL   = 8-bit input data

Notes:
- In most MS-DOS systems, the serial device is unbuffered and is not interrupt-driven. If the auxiliary device sends data faster than your program can process it, characters may be lost.
- At startup on the IBM PC, PC-DOS initializes the first serial port to 2400 baud, no parity, 1 stop bit, and 8 data bits. Other implementations of MS-DOS may initialize the serial device differently.
- There is no way for a user program to read the status of the auxiliary device or to detect I/O errors (such as lost characters) through this function call. On the IBM PC, more precise control can be obtained by calling ROM BIOS Int 14H or by driving the communications controller directly.
- If a Ctrl-C is detected at the keyboard, an Int 23H is executed.
- [2.0+] You can also input from the auxiliary device by requesting a read (Int 21H Function 3FH) using the predefined handle for the standard auxiliary device (0003H) or using a handle obtained by opening the logical device AUX.

Example: Read a character from the standard auxiliary input and store it in the variable *char*.

```
char    db      0               ; input character
        .
        .
        .
        mov     ah,3            ; function number
        int     21h             ; transfer to MS-DOS
        mov     char,al         ; save character
        .
        .
        .
```

Int 21H   [1.0]
Function 04H
Auxiliary output

[1] Outputs a character to the first serial port.

[2.0+] Outputs a character to the standard auxiliary device. The default is the first serial port (COM1).

Call with: AH   = 04H
                 DL   = 8-bit data for output

Returns: Nothing

- If the output device is busy, this function waits until the device is ready to accept a character.
- There is no way to poll the status of the auxiliary device using this function. On the IBM PC, more precise control can be obtained by calling ROM BIOS Int 14H or by driving the communications controller directly.
- If a Ctrl-C is detected at the keyboard, an Int 23H is executed.
- [2.0+] You can also send strings to the auxiliary device by performing a write (Int 21H Function 40H) using the predefined handle for the standard auxiliary device (0003H) or using a handle obtained by opening the logical device AUX.

Example: Output a "∗" character to the auxiliary device.

```
          .
          .
          .
     mov    ah,4        ; function number
     mov    dl,'*'      ; character to output
     int    21h         ; transfer to MS-DOS
          .
          .
          .
```

Int 21H   [1.0]
Function 05H
Printer output

[1] Sends a character to the first list device (PRN or LPT1).

[2.0+] Sends a character to the standard list device. The default device is the printer on the first parallel port (LPT1), unless explicitly redirected by the user with the MODE command.

Call with: AH   = 05H
                  DL   = 8-bit data for output

Returns: Nothing

Notes:
- If the printer is busy, this function waits until the printer is ready to accept the character.
- There is no standardized way to poll the status of the printer under MS-DOS.
- If a Ctrl-C is detected at the keyboard, an Int 23H is executed.
- [2.0+] You can also send strings to the printer by performing a write (Int 21H Function 40H) using the predefined handle for the standard printer device (0004H) or using a handle obtained by opening the logical device PRN or LPT1.

Example: Output the character "*" to the list device.

```
        .
        .
        .
        mov    ah,5        ; function number
        mov    dl,'*'      ; character to output
        int    21h         ; transfer to MS-DOS
        .
        .
        .
```

Int 21H   [1.0]
Function 06H
Direct console I/O

Used by programs that need to read and write all possible characters and control codes without any interference from the operating system.

[1] Reads a character from the keyboard or writes a character to the display.

[2.0+] Reads a character from the standard input device or writes a character to the standard output device. I/O may be redirected. (If I/O has been redirected, there is no way to detect EOF or disk full.)

Call with: AH   = 06H
                  DL   = function requested
                        00H–FEH   if output request
                        0FFH   if input request

Returns: If called with DL = 00H–0FEH
                Nothing
                If called with DL = FFH and a character is ready
                Zero flag   = clear
                AL   = 8-bit input data
                If called with DL = FFH and no character is ready
                Zero flag   = set

Notes: ■ No special action is taken upon entry of a Ctrl-C when this service is used.
              ■ To read extended ASCII codes (such as the special function keys F1 to F10) on the IBM PC and compatibles, you must call this function twice. The first call returns the value 00H to signal the presence of an extended code.
              ■ See also Int 21H Functions 01H, 07H, and 08H, which provide character input with various combinations of echo and/or Ctrl-C sensing, and Functions 02H and 09H, which may be used to write characters to the standard output.

- [2.0+] You can also read the keyboard by issuing a read (Int 21H Function 3FH) using the predefined handle for the standard input (0000H), if input has not been redirected, or a handle obtained by opening the logical device CON.

- [2.0+] You can also send characters to the display by issuing a write (Int 21H Function 40H) using the predefined handle for the standard output (0001H), if output has not been redirected, or a handle obtained by opening the logical device CON.

Examples: Send the character "*" to the standard output device.

```
        .
        .
        .
        mov     ah,6            ; function number
        mov     dl,'*'          ; character to output
        int     21h             ; transfer to MS-DOS
        .
        .
        .
```

Read a character from the standard input device and save it in the variable *char*. If no character is ready, wait until one is available.

```
char    db      0               ; input character
        .
        .
        .
wait:   mov     ah,6            ; function number
        mov     dl,0ffh         ; parameter for read
        int     21h             ; transfer to MS-DOS
        jz      wait            ; wait until char ready
        mov     char,al         ; save the character
        .
        .
        .
```

Int 21H [1.0]
Function 07H
Unfiltered character input without echo

[1] Reads a character from the keyboard without echoing it to the display. If no character is ready, waits until one is available.

[2.0+] Reads a character from the standard input device without echoing it to the standard output device. If no character is ready, waits until one is available. Input may be redirected. (If input has been redirected, there is no way to detect EOF.)

Call with:	AH	= 07H

Returns:	AL	= 8-bit input data

Notes:
- No special action is taken upon entry of a Ctrl-C when this function is used. If Ctrl-C checking is required, use Int 21H Function 08H instead.
- To read extended ASCII codes (such as the special function keys F1 to F10) on the IBM PC and compatibles, you must call this function twice. The first call returns the value 00H to signal the presence of an extended code.
- See also Int 21H Functions 01H, 06H, and 08H, which provide character input with various combinations of echo and/or Ctrl-C sensing.
- [2.0+] You can also read the keyboard by issuing a read (Int 21H Function 3FH) using the predefined handle for the standard input (0000H), if input has not been redirected, or a handle obtained by opening the logical device CON.

Example: Read a character from the standard input without echoing it to the display, and store it in the variable *char*.

```
char    db      0               ; input character
        .
        .
        .
        mov     ah,7            ; function number
        int     21h             ; transfer to MS-DOS
        mov     char,al         ; save character
        .
        .
        .
```

Int 21H
Function 08H
Character input without echo

[1.0]

[1] Reads a character from the keyboard without echoing it to the display. If no character is ready, waits until one is available.

[2.0+] Reads a character from the standard input device without echoing it to the standard output device. If no character is ready, waits until one is available. Input may be redirected. (If input has been redirected, there is no way to detect EOF.)

Call with:	AH	= 08H

Returns:	AL	= 8-bit input data

- If the standard input is not redirected, and the character read is a Ctrl-C, an Int 23H is executed. If the standard input is redirected, a Ctrl-C is detected at the console, and BREAK is ON, an Int 23H is executed. To avoid possible interruption by a Ctrl-C, use Int 21H Function 07H instead.

- To read extended ASCII codes (such as the special function keys F1 to F10) on the IBM PC and compatibles, you must call this function twice. The first call returns the value 00H to signal the presence of an extended code.

- See also Int 21H Functions 01H, 06H, and 07H, which provide character input with various combinations of echo and/or Ctrl-C sensing.

- [2.0+] You can also read the keyboard by issuing a read (Int 21H Function 3FH) using the predefined handle for the standard input (0000H), if input has not been redirected, or a handle obtained by opening the logical device CON.

Example: Read a character from the standard input without echoing it to the display, allowing possible detection of Ctrl-C, and store the character in the variable *char*.

```
char    db      0
        .
        .
        .
        mov     ah,8        ; function number
        int     21h         ; transfer to MS-DOS
        mov     char,al     ; save character
        .
        .
        .
```

Int 21H
Function 09H
Display string

[1.0]

---

[1] Sends a string of characters to the display.

[2.0+] Sends a string of characters to the standard output device. Output may be redirected. (If output has been redirected, there is no way to detect disk full.)

Call with:

AH	= 09H
DS:DX	= segment:offset of string

Returns: Nothing

Notes:

- The string must be terminated with the character *$* (24H), which is not transmitted. Any other ASCII codes, including control codes, can be embedded in the string.
- See Int 21H Functions 02H and 06H for single-character output to the video display or standard output device.
- If a Ctrl-C is detected at the keyboard, an Int 23H is executed.
- [2.0+] You can also send strings to the display by performing a write (Int 21H Function 40H) using the predefined handle for the standard output (0001H), if it has not been redirected, or a handle obtained by opening the logical device CON.

Example: Send the string *Hello World*, followed by a carriage return and line feed, to the standard output device.

```
cr      equ     0dh
lf      equ     0ah

msg     db      'Hello World',cr,lf,'$'
        .
        .
        .
        mov     ah,9            ; function number
        mov     dx,seg msg      ; address of string
        mov     ds,dx
        mov     dx,offset msg
        int     21h             ; transfer to MS-DOS
        .
        .
        .
```

Int 21H
Function 0AH (10)
Buffered keyboard input

[1.0]

[1] Reads a line from the keyboard and places it in a user-designated buffer. The characters are echoed to the display.

[2.0+] Reads a string of bytes from the standard input device, up to and including an ASCII carriage return (0DH), and places them in a user-designated buffer. The characters are echoed to the standard output device. Input may be redirected. (If input has been redirected, there is no way to detect EOF.)

Call with: AH   = 0AH
                  DS:DX   = segment:offset of buffer

Returns: Nothing (data placed in buffer)

Notes:

- The buffer used by this function has the following format:

Byte	Contents
0	maximum number of characters to read, set by program
1	number of characters actually read (excluding carriage return), set by MS-DOS
2+	string read from keyboard or standard input, terminated by a carriage return (0DH)

- If the buffer fills to one fewer than the maximum number of characters it can hold, subsequent input is ignored and the bell is sounded until a carriage return is detected.

- This input function is buffered with type-ahead capability, and all of the standard keyboard editing commands are active.

- If the standard input is not redirected, and a Ctrl-C is detected at the console, an Int 23H is executed. If the standard input is redirected, a Ctrl-C is detected at the console, and BREAK is ON, an Int 23H is executed.

- See Int 21H Functions 01H, 06H, 07H, and 08H for single-character input from the keyboard or standard input device.

- [2.0+] You can also read strings from the keyboard by performing a read (Int 21H Function 3FH) using the predefined handle for the standard input (0000H), if it has not been redirected, or a handle obtained by opening the logical device CON.

Example: Read a string that is a maximum of 80 characters long from the standard input device, placing it in the buffer named *buff*.

```
buff    db      81              ; maximum length of input
        db      0               ; actual length of input
        db      81 dup (0)      ; actual input placed here
        .
        .
        .
        mov     ah,0ah          ; function number
        mov     dx,seg buff     ; input buffer address
        mov     ds,dx
        mov     dx,offset buff
        int     21h             ; transfer to MS-DOS
        .
        .
        .
```

[1] Checks whether a character is available from the keyboard.

[2.0+] Checks whether a character is available from the standard input device. Input can be redirected.

Call with:	AH	= 0BH

Returns:	AL	= 00H if no character is available
		FFH if at least one character is available

Notes:
- [1] If a Ctrl-C is detected, an Int 23H is executed.
- [2.0+] If the standard input is not redirected, and a Ctrl-C is detected at the console, an Int 23H is executed. If the standard input is redirected, a Ctrl-C is detected at the console, and BREAK is ON, an Int 23H is executed.
- If a character is waiting, this function will continue to return a true flag until the character is consumed with a call to Int 21H Function 01H, 06H, 07H, 08H, 0AH, or 3FH.
- This function is equivalent to IOCTL Int 21H Function 44H Subfunction 06H.

Example: Test whether a character is available from the standard input.

```
        .
        .
        .
    mov   ah,0bh      ; function number
    int   21h         ; transfer to MS-DOS
    or    al,al       ; character waiting?
    jnz   ready       ; jump if char ready
        .
        .
        .
```

[1] Clears the type-ahead buffer and then invokes one of the keyboard input functions.

[2.0+] Clears the standard input buffer and then invokes one of the character input functions. Input can be redirected.

Call with: AH   = 0CH

AL   = number of input function to be invoked after resetting buffer (must be
01H, 06H, 07H, 08H, or 0AH)

(if AL = 0AH)

DS:DX   = segment:offset of input buffer

Returns: (if called with AL = 01H, 06H, 07H, or 08H)

AL   = 8-bit input data

(if called with AL = 0AH)

Nothing (data placed in buffer)

Notes:
- The function exists to allow a program to defeat MS-DOS's type-ahead feature. It discards any characters that are waiting in MS-DOS's internal type-ahead buffer, forcing the specified input function to wait for a character (usually a keyboard entry) that is truly entered after the program's request.
- The presence or absence of Ctrl-C checking during execution of this function depends on the function number placed in register AL.
- A function number in AL other than 01H, 06H, 07H, 08H, or 0AH simply flushes the input buffer and returns control to the calling program.

Example: Clear the type-ahead buffer, then wait for a character to be entered, echoing it and then returning it in AL. Store the character in the variable *char*.

```
char    db      0
        .
        .
        .
        mov     ah,0ch          ; function number
        mov     al,1            ; subfunction = input char
        int     21h             ; transfer to MS-DOS
        mov     char,al         ; save character
        .
        .
        .
```

Int 21H   [1.0]
Function 0DH (13)
Disk reset

Flushes all file buffers. All data that has been logically written by user programs, but has been temporarily buffered within MS-DOS, is physically written to the disk.

Call with: AH   = 0DH

| Returns: | Nothing |

Notes:

- This function does *not* update the disk directory for any files that are still open. If your program fails to properly close all files before the disk is removed, and files have changed size, the data forced out to the disk by this function may still be inaccessible because the directory entries will not be correct.

- [3.3+] Int 21H Function 68H (Commit File) should be used in preference to this function, since it also updates the disk directory.

Example: Flush all MS-DOS internal disk buffers.

```
        .
        .
        .
    mov   ah,0dh      ; function number
    int   21h         ; transfer to MS-DOS
        .
        .
        .
```

Int 21H
Function 0EH (14)
Select disk

[1.0]

Selects the specified drive to be the current, or default, disk drive and returns the total number of logical drives in the system.

| Call with: | AH | = 0EH |
| | DL | = drive code (0 = A, 1 = B, etc.) |

| Returns: | AL | = number of logical drives in system |

Notes:

- [1] 16 drive designators (0 through 0FH) are available.
- [2] 63 drive designators (0 through 3FH) are available.
- [3.0+] 26 drive designators (0 through 19H) are available.
- To preserve upward compatibility, new applications should limit themselves to the drive letters A–Z (0 = A, 1 = B, etc.).
- *Logical* drives means the total number of block devices: floppy disks, simulated disk drives (RAMdisks), and hard-disk drives. A single physical hard-disk drive is frequently partitioned into two or more logical drives.
- [1] [2] In single-drive IBM PC–compatible systems, the value 2 is returned in AL, because PC-DOS supports two logical drives (A: and B:) on the single physical

floppy-disk drive. The actual number of physical drives in the system can be determined with ROM BIOS Int 11H.

- [3.0+] The value returned in AL is either 5 or the drive code corresponding to the LASTDRIVE entry (if any) in CONFIG.SYS, whichever is greater.

Example: Make drive B the current (default) disk drive. Save the total number of logical drives in the system in the variable *drives*.

```
drives  db      0
        .
        .
        .
        mov     ah,0eh          ; function number
        mov     dl,1            ; drive 1 = B
        int     21h             ; transfer to MS-DOS
        mov     drives,al       ; save total drives
        .
        .
        .
```

Int 21H   [1.0]
Function 0FH (15)
Open file

Opens a file and makes it available for subsequent read/write operations.

Call with:	AH	= 0FH
	DS:DX	= segment:offset of file control block

Returns: If function successful (file found)

AL	= 00H

and FCB filled in by MS-DOS as follows:

drive field (offset 00H)	= *1 for drive A, 2 for drive B, etc.*
current block field (offset 0CH)	= *00H*
record size field (offset 0EH)	= *0080H*
[2.0+] size field (offset 10H)	= *file size from directory*
[2.0+] date field (offset 14H)	= *date stamp from directory*
[2.0+] time field (offset 16H)	= *time stamp from directory*

If function unsuccessful (file not found)

AL	= 0FFH

Notes:
- If your program is going to use a record size other than 128 bytes, it should set the record-size field at FCB offset 0EH *after* the file is successfully opened and *before* any other disk operation.

- If random access is to be performed, the calling program must also set the FCB relative-record field (offset 21H) after successfully opening the file.
- For format of directory time and date, see Int 21H Function 57H.
- [2.0+] Int 21H Function 3DH, which allows full access to the hierarchical directory structure, should be used in preference to this function.
- [3.0+] If the program is running on a network, the file is opened for read/write access in compatibility sharing mode.

Example: Attempt to open the file named QUACK.DAT on the default disk drive.

```
myfcb   db      0                 ; drive = default
        db      'QUACK   '        ; filename, 8 characters
        db      'DAT'             ; extension, 3 characters
        db      25 dup (0)        ; remainder of FCB
          .
          .
          .
        mov     ah,0fh            ; function number
        mov     dx,seg myfcb      ; address of FCB
        mov     ds,dx
        mov     dx,offset myfcb
        int     21h               ; transfer to MS-DOS
        or      al,al             ; check status
        jnz     error             ; jump if open failed
          .
          .
          .
```

Int 21H
Function 10H (16)
Close file

[1.0]

Closes a file, flushes all MS-DOS internal disk buffers associated with the file to disk, and updates the disk directory if the file has been modified or extended.

Call with: AH   = 10H
                   DS:DX   = segment:offset of file control block

Returns: If function successful (directory update successful)
                 AL   = 00H
                 If function unsuccessful (file not found in directory)
                 AL   = FFH

■ [1] [2] MS-DOS versions 1 and 2 do not reliably detect a floppy-disk change, and an error can occur if the user changes disks while a file is still open on that drive. In the worst case, the directory and file allocation table of the newly inserted disk can be damaged or destroyed.

■ [2.0+] Int 21H Function 3EH should be used in preference to this function.

Example: Close the file that was previously opened using the file control block named *myfcb*.

```
myfcb   db      0               ; drive = default
        db      'QUACK   '      ; filename, 8 characters
        db      'DAT'           ; extension, 3 characters
        db      25 dup (0)      ; remainder of FCB
        .
        .
        .
        mov     ah,10h          ; function number
        mov     dx,seg myfcb    ; address of FCB
        mov     ds,dx
        mov     dx,offset myfcb
        int     21h             ; transfer to MS-DOS
        or      al,al           ; check status
        jnz     error           ; jump if close failed
        .
        .
        .
```

Int 21H
Function 11H (17)
Find first file

[1.0]

Searches the current directory on the designated drive for a matching filename.

Call with:
AH = 11H
DS:DX = segment:offset of file control block

Returns:
If function successful (matching filename found)
AL = 00H

and buffer at current disk transfer area (DTA) address filled in as an unopened normal FCB or extended FCB, depending on which type of FCB was input to function

If function unsuccessful (no matching filename found)
AL = FFH

Notes:

- Use Int 21H Function 1AH to set the DTA to point to a buffer of adequate size before calling this function.
- The wildcard character ? is allowed in the filename in all versions of MS-DOS. In versions 3.0 and later, the wildcard character * may also be used in a filename. If ? or * is used, this function returns the first matching filename.
- An extended FCB must be used to search for files that have the system, hidden, read-only, directory, or volume-label attributes.
- If an extended FCB is used, its attribute byte determines the type of search that will be performed. If the attribute byte contains 00H, only ordinary files are found. If the volume-label attribute bit is set, only volume labels will be returned (if any are present). If any other attribute or combination of attributes is set (such as hidden, system, or read-only), those files and all ordinary files will be matched.
- [2.0+] Int 21H Function 4EH, which allows full access to the hierarchical directory structure, should be used in preference to this function.

Example: Search for the first file with the extension *.COM* in the current directory.

```
buff    db      37 dup (0)      ; receives search result

myfcb   db      0               ; drive = default
        db      '????????'      ; wildcard filename
        db      'COM'           ; extension = COM
        db      25 dup (0)      ; remainder of FCB
        .
        .
        .
                                ; set DTA address
        mov     ah,1ah          ; function number
        mov     dx,seg buff     ; buffer address
        mov     ds,dx
        mov     dx,offset buff
        int     21h             ; transfer to MS-DOS

                                ; search for first match
        mov     ah,11h          ; function number
        mov     dx,seg myfcb    ; address of FCB
        mov     ds,dx
        mov     dx,offset myfcb
        int     21h             ; transfer to MS-DOS
        or      al,al           ; check status
        jnz     error           ; jump if no match
        .
        .
        .
```

Int 21H
Function 12H (18)
Find next file

Given that a previous call to Int 21H Function 11H has been successful, returns the next matching filename (if any).

Call with:

AH	= 12H
DS:DX	= segment:offset of file control block

Returns:

If function successful (matching filename found)

AL = 00H

and buffer at current disk transfer area (DTA) address set up as an unopened normal FCB or extended FCB, depending on which type of FCB was originally input to Int 21H Function 11H

If function unsuccessful (no more matching filenames found)

AL = FFH

Notes:

■ This function assumes that the FCB used as input has been properly initialized by a previous call to Int 21H Function 11H (and possible subsequent calls to Int 21H Function 12H) and that the filename or extension being searched for contained at least one wildcard character.

■ As with Int 21H Function 11H, it is important to use Int 21H Function 1AH to set the DTA to a buffer of adequate size before calling this function.

■ [2.0+] Int 21H Functions 4EH and 4FH, which allow full access to the hierarchical directory structure, should be used in preference to this function.

Example:

Assuming a previous successful call to function 11H, search for the next file with the extension *.COM* in the current directory. If the DTA has not been changed since the previous search, another call to Function 1AH is not necessary.

```
buff     db    37 dup (0)      ; receives search result

my_fcb   db    0               ; drive = default
         db    '????????'      ; wildcard filename
         db    'COM'           ; extension = COM
         db    25 dup (0)      ; remainder of FCB
          .
          .
          .
```

```
                                          ; set DTA address
            mov      ah,1ah               ; function number
            mov      dx,seg buff          ; buffer address
            mov      ds,dx
            mov      dx,offset buff
            int      21h                  ; transfer to MS-DOS

                                          ; search for next match
            mov      ah,12h               ; function number
            mov      dx,seg myfcb         ; address of FCB
            mov      ds,dx
            mov      dx,offset myfcb
            int      21h                  ; transfer to MS-DOS
            or       al,al                ; check status
            jnz      error                ; jump if no match
            .
            .
            .
```

Int 21H   [1.0]
Function 13H (19)
Delete file

Deletes all matching files from the current directory on the default or specified disk drive.

| **Call with:** | AH | = 13H |
| | DS:DX | = segment:offset of file control block |

Returns: If function successful (file or files deleted)

AL = 00H

If function unsuccessful (no matching files were found, or at least one matching file was read-only)

AL = FFH

Notes:
- The wildcard character ? is allowed in the filename; if ? is present and there is more than one matching filename, all matching files will be deleted.
- [2.0+] Int 21H Function 41H, which allows full access to the hierarchical directory structure, should be used in preference to this function.
- [3.0+] If the program is running on a network, the user must have Create rights to the directory containing the file to be deleted.

Example: Delete the file MYFILE.DAT from the current disk drive and directory.

```
myfcb    db      0              ; drive = default
         db      'MYFILE  '     ; filename, 8 chars
         db      'DAT'          ; extension, 3 chars
         db      25 dup (0)     ; remainder of FCB
         .
         .
         .

         mov     ah,13h         ; function number
         mov     dx,seg myfcb   ; address of FCB
         mov     ds,dx
         mov     dx,offset myfcb
         int     21h            ; transfer to MS-DOS
         or      al,al          ; check status
         jnz     error          ; jump, delete failed
         .
         .
         .
```

Int 21H   [1.0]
Function 14H (20)
Sequential read

Reads the next sequential block of data from a file, then increments the file pointer appropriately.

| **Call with:** | AH | = 14H |
| | DS:DX | = segment:offset of previously opened file control block |

Returns:	AL	= 00H	if read successful
		01H	if end of file
		02H	if segment wrap
		03H	if partial record read at end of file

Notes:
- The record is read into memory at the current disk transfer area (DTA) address, specified by the most recent call to Int 21H Function 1AH. If the size of the record and the location of the buffer are such that a segment overflow or wraparound would occur, the function fails with a return code of 02H.
- The number of bytes of data to be read is specified by the record-size field (offset 0EH) of the file control block (FCB).
- The file location of the data that will be read is specified by the combination of the current block field (offset 0CH) and current record field (offset 20H) of the file control block (FCB). These fields are also automatically incremented by this function.

- If a partial record is read at the end of file, it is padded to the requested record length with zeros.
- [3.0+] If the program is running on a network, the user must have Read access rights to the directory containing the file to be read.

Example: Read 1024 bytes of data from the file specified by the previously opened file control block *myfcb*.

```
myfcb   db      0                   ; drive = default
        db      'QUACK   '          ; filename, 8 chars
        db      'DAT'               ; extension, 3 chars
        db      25 dup (0)          ; remainder of FCB
        .
        .
        .
        mov     ah,14h              ; function number
        mov     dx,seg myfcb        ; address of FCB
        mov     ds,dx
        mov     dx,offset myfcb
                                    ; set record size
        mov     word ptr myfcb+0eH,1024
        int     21h                 ; transfer to MS-DOS
        or      al,al               ; check status
        jnz     error               ; jump if read failed
        .
        .
        .
```

Int 21H [1.0]
Function 15H (21)
Sequential write

Writes the next sequential block of data into a file, then increments the file pointer appropriately.

Call with:

AH	= 15H	
DS:DX	= segment:offset of previously opened file control block	

Returns:

AL	= 00H	if write successful
	01H	if disk is full
	02H	if segment wrap

Notes:
- The record is written (logically, not necessarily physically) to the disk from memory at the current disk transfer area (DTA) address, specified by the most recent call to Int 21H Function 1AH. If the size of the record and the location of the buffer are such

that a segment overflow or wraparound would occur, the function fails with a return code of 02H.

- The number of bytes of data to be written is specified by the record-size field (offset 0EH) of the file control block (FCB).

- The file location of the data that will be written is specified by the combination of the current block field (offset 0CH) and current record field (offset 20H) of the file control block (FCB). These fields are also automatically incremented by this function.

- [3.0+] If the program is running on a network, the user must have Write access rights to the directory containing the file to be written.

Example: Write 1024 bytes of data to the file specified by the previously opened file control block *myfcb*.

```
myfcb   db      0               ; drive = default
        db      'QUACK   '      ; filename, 8 chars
        db      'DAT'           ; extension, 3 chars
        db      25 dup (0)      ; remainder of FCB
        .
        .
        .

        mov     ah,15h          ; function number
        mov     dx,seg myfcb    ; address of FCB
        mov     ds,dx
        mov     dx,offset myfcb
                                ; set record size
        mov     word ptr myfcb+0eh,1024
        int     21h             ; transfer to MS-DOS
        or      al,al           ; check status
        jnz     error           ; jump if write failed
        .
        .
        .
```

Int 21H   [1.0]
Function 16H (22)
Create file

Creates a new directory entry in the current directory or truncates any existing file with the same name to zero length. Opens the file for subsequent read/write operations.

Call with: AH   = 16H
                 DS:DX   = segment:offset of unopened file control block

Returns: If function successful (file was created or truncated)

AL   = 00H

and FCB filled in by MS-DOS as follows:

drive field (offset 00H)	*= 1 for drive A, 2 for drive B, etc.*
current block field (offset 0CH)	*= 00H*
record size field (offset 0EH)	*= 0080H*
[2.0+] size field (offset 10H)	*= file size from directory*
[2.0+] date field (offset 14H)	*= date stamp from directory*
[2.0+] time field (offset 16H)	*= time stamp from directory*

If function unsuccessful (directory full)

AL   = FFH

Notes:
- Since an existing file with the specified name is truncated to zero length (i.e., all data in that file is irretrievably lost), this function must be used with caution.
- If this function is called with an extended file control block (FCB), the new file may be assigned a special attribute, such as hidden or system, during its creation by setting the appropriate bit in the extended FCB's attribute byte.
- Since this function also opens the file, a subsequent call to Int 21H Function 0FH is not required.
- For format of directory time and date, see Int 21H Function 57H.
- [2.0+] Int 21H Functions 3CH, 5AH, 5BH, and 6CH, which provide full access to the hierarchical directory structure, should be used in preference to this function.
- [3.0+] If the program is running on a network, the user must have Create rights to the directory that will contain the new file.

Example: Create a file in the current directory using the name in the file control block *myfcb*.

```
myfcb   db      0               ; drive = default
        db      'QUACK   '      ; filename, 8 chars
        db      'DAT'           ; extension, 3 chars
        db      25 dup (0)      ; remainder of FCB
        .
        .
        .

        mov     ah,16h          ; function number
        mov     dx,seg myfcb    ; address of FCB
        mov     ds,dx
        mov     dx,offset myfcb
        int     21h             ; transfer to MS-DOS
        or      al,al           ; check status
        jnz     error           ; jump if create failed
        .
        .
        .
```

Alters the name of all matching files in the current directory on the disk in the specified drive.

Call with: AH   = 17H
                  DS:DX   = segment:offset of "special" file control block

Returns: If function successful (one or more files renamed)
                  AL   = 00H

                  If function unsuccessful (no matching files, or new filename matched an existing file)
                  AL   = FFH

Notes: ■ The special file control block has a drive code, filename, and extension in the usual
                    position (bytes 0 through 0BH) and a second filename starting 6 bytes after the first
                    (offset 11H).

                  ■ The ? wildcard character can be used in the first filename. Every file matching the
                    first file specification will be renamed to match the second file specification.

                  ■ If the second file specification contains any ? wildcard characters, the corresponding
                    letters in the first filename are left unchanged.

                  ■ The function terminates if the new name to be assigned to a file matches that of an
                    existing file.

                  ■ [2.0+] An extended FCB can be used with this function to rename a directory.

                  ■ [2.0+] Int 21H Function 56H, which allows full access to the hierarchical directory
                    structure, should be used in preference to this function.

Example: Rename the file OLDNAME.DAT to NEWNAME.DAT.

```
myfcb   db      0               ; drive = default
        db      'OLDNAME '       ; old file name, 8 chars
        db      'DAT'            ; old extension, 3 chars
        db      6 dup (0)        ; reserved area
        db      'NEWNAME '       ; new file name, 8 chars
        db      'DAT'            ; new extension, 3 chars
        db      14 dup (0)       ; reserved area
        .
        .
        .
```

```
        mov     ah,17h              ; function number
        mov     dx,seg myfcb        ; address of FCB
        mov     ds,dx
        mov     dx,offset myfcb
        int     21h                 ; transfer to MS-DOS
        or      al,al               ; check status
        jnz     error               ; jump if rename failed
        .
        .
        .
```

Int 21H
Function 18H (24)
Reserved

Int 21H   [1.0]
Function 19H (25)
Get current disk

Returns the drive code of the current, or default, disk drive.

Call with: AH   = 19H

Returns: AL   = drive code (0 = A, 1 = B, etc.)

Notes:
- To set the default drive, use Int 21H Function 0EH.
- Some other Int 21H functions use drive codes beginning at 1 (that is, 1 = A, 2 = B, etc.) and reserve drive code zero for the default drive.

Example: Get the current disk drive and save the code in the variable *cdrive*.

```
cdrive  db      0                   ; current drive code
        .
        .
        .
        mov     ah,19h              ; function number
        int     21h                 ; transfer to MS-DOS
        mov     cdrive,al           ; save drive code
        .
        .
        .
```

Int 21H
Function 1AH (26)
Set DTA address

[1.0]

Specifies the address of the disk transfer area (DTA) to be used for subsequent FCB-related function calls.

| **Call with:** | AH | = 1AH |
| | DS:DX | = segment:offset of disk transfer area |

| **Returns:** | Nothing |

Notes:
- If this function is never called by the program, the DTA defaults to a 128-byte buffer at offset 0080H in the program segment prefix.
- In general, it is the programmer's responsibility to ensure that the buffer area specified is large enough for any disk operation that will use it. The only exception to this is that MS-DOS will detect and abort disk transfers that would cause a segment wrap.
- Int 21H Function 2FH can be used to determine the current disk transfer address.
- The only handle-type operations that rely on the DTA address are the directory search functions, Int 21H Functions 4EH and 4FH.

Example: Set the current disk transfer area address to the buffer labeled *buff*.

```
buff    db      128 dup (?)
        .
        .
        .
        mov     ah,1ah          ; function number
        mov     dx,seg buff     ; address of disk
        mov     ds,dx           ; transfer area
        mov     dx,offset buff
        int     21h             ; transfer to MS-DOS
        .
        .
        .
```

Int 21H
Function 1BH (27)
Get default drive data

[1.0]

Obtains selected information about the default disk drive and a pointer to the media identification byte from its file allocation table.

Call with:	AH	= 1BH

Returns:	If function successful	
	AL	= sectors per cluster
	DS:BX	= segment:offset of media ID byte
	CX	= size of physical sector (bytes)
	DX	= number of clusters for default drive
	If function unsuccessful (invalid drive or critical error)	
	AL	= FFH

Notes:

- The media ID byte has the following meanings:

0F0H	3.5-inch double-sided, 18 sectors or "other"
0F8H	fixed disk
0F9H	5.25-inch double-sided, 15 sectors or 3.5-inch double-sided, 9 sectors
0FCH	5.25-inch single-sided, 9 sectors
0FDH	5.25-inch double-sided, 9 sectors
0FEH	5.25-inch single-sided, 8 sectors
0FFH	5.25-inch double-sided, 8 sectors

- To obtain information about disks other than the one in the default drive, use Int 21H Function 1CH or 36H.

- [1] The address returned in DS:BX points to a copy of the first sector of the actual FAT, with the media ID byte in the first byte.

- [2.0+] The address returned in DS:BX points only to a copy of the media ID byte from the disk's FAT; the memory above that address cannot be assumed to contain the FAT or any other useful information. If direct access to the FAT is required, use Int 25H to read it into memory.

Example: Determine whether the current disk drive is fixed or removable.

```
        .
        .
        .
        mov     ah,1bh          ; function number
        int     21h             ; transfer to MS-DOS

                                ; check media ID byte
        cmp     byte ptr [bx],0f8h
        je      fixed           ; jump if fixed disk
        jmp     floppy          ; else assume floppy
        .
        .
        .
```

Int 21H
Function 1CH (28)
Get drive data

Obtains allocation information about the specified disk drive and a pointer to the media identification byte from its file allocation table.

Call with: AH = 1CH
DL = drive code (0 = default, 1 = A, etc.)

Returns: If function successful
AL = sectors per cluster
DS:BX = segment:offset of media ID byte
CX = size of physical sector (bytes)
DX = number of clusters for default or specified drive

If function unsuccessful (invalid drive or critical error)
AL = FFH

Notes: ■ The media ID byte has the following meanings:
0F0H   3.5-inch double-sided, 18 sectors
or "other"
0F8H   fixed disk
0F9H   5.25-inch double-sided, 15 sectors
or 3.5-inch double-sided, 9 sectors
0FCH   5.25-inch single-sided, 9 sectors
0FDH   5.25-inch double-sided, 9 sectors
0FEH   5.25-inch single-sided, 8 sectors
0FFH   5.25-inch double-sided, 8 sectors

■ In general, this call is identical to Int 21H Function 1BH, except for the ability to designate a specific disk drive. See also Int 21H Function 36H, which returns similar information.

■ [1] The address returned in DS:BX points to a copy of the first sector of the actual FAT, with the media ID byte in the first byte.

■ [2.0+] The address returned in DS:BX points only to a copy of the media ID byte from the disk's FAT; the memory above that address cannot be assumed to contain the FAT or any other useful information. If direct access to the FAT is required, use Int 25H to read it into memory.

Example: Determine whether disk drive C is fixed or removable.

```
        .
        .
        .
        mov     ah,1ch          ; function number
        mov     dl,3            ; drive code 3 = C
        int     21h             ; transfer to MS-DOS

                                ; check media ID byte
        cmp     byte ptr ds:[bx],0f8h
        je      fixed           ; jump if fixed disk
        jmp     floppy          ; else assume floppy
        .
        .
        .
```

Int 21H
Function 1DH (29)
Reserved

Int 21H
Function 1EH (30)
Reserved

Int 21H
Function 1FH (31)
Reserved

Int 21H
Function 20H (32)
Reserved

Reads a selected record from a file into memory.

Call with:

AH	= 21H	
DS:DX	= segment:offset of previously opened file control block	

Returns:

AL	= 00H	if read successful
	01H	if end of file
	02H	if segment wrap, read canceled
	03H	if partial record read at end of file

Notes:

- The record is read into memory at the current disk transfer area address, specified by the most recent call to Int 21H Function 1AH. It is the programmer's responsibility to ensure that this area is large enough for any record that will be transferred. If the size and location of the buffer are such that a segment overflow or wraparound would occur, the function fails with a return code of 02H.

- The file location of the data to be read is determined by the combination of the relative-record field (offset 21H) and the record-size field (offset 0EH) of the FCB. The default record size is 128 bytes.

- The current block field (offset 0CH) and current record field (offset 20H) are updated to agree with the relative-record field as a side effect of the function.

- The relative-record field of the FCB is not incremented by this function; it is the responsibility of the application to update the FCB appropriately if it wishes to read successive records. Compare with Int 21H Function 27H, which can read multiple records with one function call and automatically increments the relative-record field.

- If a partial record is read at end of file, it is padded to the requested record length with zeros.

- [3.0+] If the program is running on a network, the user must have Read access rights to the directory containing the file to be read.

Example:

Open the file MYFILE.DAT, set the record length to 1024 bytes, then read record number 4 from the file into the buffer named *buff*.

```
myfcb   db      0               ; drive = default
        db      'MYFILE  '      ; filename, 8 chars
        db      'DAT'           ; extension, 3 chars
        db      25 dup (0)      ; remainder of FCB

buff    db      1024 dup (?)    ; receives read data
        .
        .
        .
```

```
                    ; open the file
mov     ah,0fh      ; function number
mov     dx,seg myfcb ; address of FCB
mov     ds,dx
mov     dx,offset myfcb
int     21h         ; transfer to MS-DOS
or      al,al       ; check open status
jnz     error       ; jump if no file

                    ; set DTA address
mov     ah,1ah      ; function number
mov     dx,offset buff ; read buffer address
int     21h         ; transfer to MS-DOS

                    ; set record size
mov     word ptr myfcb+0eh,1024

                    ; set record number
mov     word ptr myfcb+21h,4
mov     word ptr myfcb+23h,0

                    ; read the record
mov     ah,21h      ; function number
mov     dx,offset myfcb ; address of FCB
int     21h         ; transfer to MS-DOS
or      al,al       ; check status
jnz     error       ; jump if read failed
        .
        .
        .
```

Int 21H
Function 22H (34)
Random write

[1.0]

Writes data from memory into a selected record in a file.

Call with:	AH	= 22H	
	DS:DX	= segment:offset of previously opened file control block	

Returns:	AL	= 00H	if write successful
		01H	if disk full
		02H	if segment wrap, write canceled

Notes:

- The record is written (logically, not necessarily physically) to the file from memory at the current disk transfer address, specified by the most recent call to Int 21H Function 1AH. If the size and location of the buffer are such that a segment overflow or wraparound would occur, the function fails with a return code of 02H.

- The file location of the data to be written is determined by the combination of the relative-record field (offset 21H) and the record-size field (offset 0EH) of the FCB. The default record size is 128 bytes.

- The current block field (offset 0CH) and current record field (offset 20H) are updated to agree with the relative-record field as a side effect of the function.

- The relative-record field of the FCB is not incremented by this function; it is the responsibility of the application to update the FCB appropriately if it wishes to write successive records. Compare with Int 21H Function 28H, which can write multiple records with one function call and automatically increments the relative-record field.

- If a record is written beyond the current end of file, the space between the old end of file and the new record is allocated but not initialized.

- [3.0+] If the program is running on a network, the user must have Write access rights to the directory containing the file to be written.

Example:

Open the file MYFILE.DAT, set the record length to 1024 bytes, write record number 4 into the file from the buffer named *buff,* then close the file.

```
myfcb   db      0               ; drive = default
        db      'MYFILE  '      ; filename, 8 chars
        db      'DAT'           ; extension, 3 chars
        db      25 dup (0)      ; remainder of FCB

buff    db      1024 dup (?)    ; buffer for write
        .
        .
        .
                                ; open the file
        mov     ah,0fh          ; function number
        mov     dx,seg myfcb    ; address of FCB
        mov     ds,dx
        mov     dx,offset myfcb
        int     21h             ; transfer to MS-DOS
        or      al,al           ; check status
        jnz     error           ; jump if no file

                                ; set DTA address
        mov     dx,offset buff  ; buffer address
        mov     ah,1ah          ; function number
        int     21h             ; transfer to MS-DOS

                                ; set record size
        mov     word ptr myfcb+0eh,1024
```

```
                            ; set record number
        mov     word ptr myfcb+21h,4
        mov     word ptr myfcb+23h,0

                            ; write the record
        mov     ah,22h      ; function number
        mov     dx,offset myfcb ; address of FCB
        int     21h         ; transfer to MS-DOS
        or      al,al       ; check status
        jnz     error       ; jump if write failed

                            ; close the file
        mov     ah,10h      ; function number
        mov     dx,offset myfcb ; address of FCB
        int     21h         ; transfer to MS-DOS
        or      al,al       ; check status
        jnz     error       ; jump if close failed
        .
        .
        .
```

Int 21H
Function 23H (35)
Get file size

[1.0]

Searches for a matching file in the current directory; if one is found, updates the FCB with the file's size in terms of number of records.

Call with: AH   = 23H
                 DS:DX   = segment:offset of unopened file control block

Returns: If function successful (matching file found)
               AL   = 00H

               and FCB relative-record field (offset 21H) set to the number of records in the file, rounded up if necessary to the next complete record

               If function unsuccessful (no matching file found)
               AL   = FFH

Notes: ■ An appropriate value must be placed in the FCB record-size field (offset 0EH) *before* calling this function. There is no default record size for this function. Compare with the FCB-related open and create functions (Int 21H Functions 0FH and 16H), which initialize the FCB for a default record size of 128 bytes.

         ■ The record-size field can be set to 1 to find the size of the file in bytes.

         ■ Because record numbers are zero based, this function can be used to position the FCB's file pointer to the end of file.

Example: Determine the size in bytes of the file MYFILE.DAT and leave the result in registers DX:AX.

```
myfcb   db      0                   ; drive = default
        db      'MYFILE '           ; filename, 8 chars
        db      'DAT'               ; extension, 3 chars
        db      25 dup (0)          ; remainder of FCB
        .
        .
        .
        mov     ah,23h              ; function number
        mov     dx,seg myfcb        ; address of FCB
        mov     ds,dx
        mov     dx,offset myfcb
                                    ; record size = 1 byte
        mov     word ptr myfcb+0eh,1
        int     21h                 ; transfer to MS-DOS
        or      al,al               ; check status
        jnz     error               ; jump if no file

                                    ; get file size in bytes
        mov     ax,word ptr myfcb+21h
        mov     dx,word ptr myfcb+23h
        .
        .
        .
```

Int 21H   [1.0]
Function 24H (36)
Set relative record number

Sets the relative-record-number field of a file control block (FCB) to correspond to the current file position as recorded in the opened FCB.

Call with: AH   = 24H
                   DS:DX   = segment:offset of previously opened file control block

---

Returns: AL is destroyed (other registers not affected)

                 FCB relative-record field (offset 21H) updated

---

Notes: ■ This function is used when switching from sequential to random I/O within a file. The contents of the relative-record field (offset 21H) are derived from the record size (offset 0EH), current block (offset 0CH), and current record (offset 20H) fields of the file control block.

- All four bytes of the FCB relative-record field (offset 21H) should be initialized to zero before calling this function.

Example: After a series of sequential record transfers have been performed using the file control block *myfcb,* obtain the current relative-record position in the file and leave the record number in DX.

```
myfcb   db      0               ; drive = default
        db      'MYFILE '       ; filename, 8 chars
        db      'DAT'           ; extension, 3 chars
        db      25 dup (0)      ; remainder of FCB
        .
        .
        .
        mov     dx,seg myfcb    ; make FCB addressable
        mov     ds,dx

                                ; initialize relative
                                ; record field to zero
        mov     word ptr myfcb+21h,0
        mov     word ptr myfcb+23h,0

                                ; now set record number
        mov     ah,24h          ; function number
        mov     dx,offset myfcb ; address of FCB
        int     21h             ; transfer to MS-DOS

                                ; load record number in DX
        mov     dx,word ptr myfcb+21h
        .
        .
        .
```

Int 21H [1.0]
Function 25H (37)
Set interrupt vector

Initializes a CPU interrupt vector to point to an interrupt handling routine.

Call with:

AH	= 25H
AL	= interrupt number
DS:DX	= segment:offset of interrupt handling routine

Returns: Nothing

Notes:

- This function should be used in preference to direct editing of the interrupt-vector table by well-behaved applications.

- Before an interrupt vector is modified, its original value should be obtained with Int 21H Function 35H and saved, so that it can be restored using this function before program termination.

Example: Install a new interrupt handler, named *zdiv,* for "divide by zero" CPU exceptions.

```
          .
          .
          .
      mov     ah,25h          ; function number
      mov     al,0            ; interrupt number
      mov     dx,seg zdiv     ; address of handler
      mov     ds,dx
      mov     dx,offset zdiv
      int     21h             ; transfer to MS-DOS
          .
          .
          .
zdiv:                         ; int 00h handler
      iret                    ; (does nothing)
```

Int 21H   [1.0]
Function 26H (38)
Create new PSP

Copies the program segment prefix (PSP) of the currently executing program to a specified segment address in free memory, then updates the new PSP to make it usable by another program.

Call with: AH   = 26H
                   DX   = segment of new program segment prefix

---

Returns: Nothing

Notes:

- After the executing program's PSP is copied into the new segment, the memory size information in the new PSP is updated appropriately and the current contents of the termination (Int 22H), Ctrl-C handler (Int 23H), and critical-error handler (Int 24H) vectors are saved starting at offset 0AH.

- This function does not load another program or in itself cause one to be executed.

- [2.0+] Int 21H Function 4BH (EXEC), which can be used to load and execute programs or overlays in either .COM or .EXE format, should be used in preference to this function.

Example: Create a new program segment prefix 64 KB above the currently executing program. This example assumes that the running program was loaded as a .COM file so that the CS register points to its PSP throughout its execution. If the running program was loaded as a .EXE file, the address of the PSP must be obtained with Int 21H Function 62H (under MS-DOS 3.0 or later) or by saving the original contents of the DS or ES registers at entry.

```
        .
        .
        .
        mov    ah,26h          ; function number
        mov    dx,cs           ; PSP segment of
                               ; this program
        add    dx,1000h        ; add 64 KB as
                               ; paragraph address
        int    21h             ; transfer to MS-DOS
        .
        .
        .
```

Int 21H   [1.0]
Function 27H (39)
Random block read

Reads one or more sequential records from a file into memory, starting at a designated file location.

Call with: AH   = 27H
                 CX   = number of records to read
                 DS:DX = segment:offset of previously opened file control block

Returns: AL   = 00H   if all requested records read
                      01H   if end of file
                      02H   if segment wrap
                      03H   if partial record read at end of file
               CX   = actual number of records read

Notes: ■ The records are read into memory at the current disk transfer area address, specified by the most recent call to Int 21H Function 1AH. It is the programmer's responsibility to ensure that this area is large enough for the group of records that will be transferred. If the size and location of the buffer are such that a segment overflow or wraparound would occur, the function fails with a return code of 02H.

            ■ The file location of the data to be read is determined by the combination of the relative-record field (offset 21H) and the record-size field (offset 0EH) of the FCB. The default record size is 128 bytes.

- After the disk transfer is performed, the current block (offset 0CH), current record (offset 20H), and relative-record (offset 21H) fields of the FCB are updated to point to the next record in the file.
- If a partial record is read at the end of file, the remainder of the record is padded with zeros.
- Compare with Int 21H Function 21H, which transfers only one record per function call and does not update the FCB relative-record field.
- [3.0+] If the program is running on a network, the user must have Read access rights to the directory containing the file to be read.

Example: Read four 1024-byte records starting at record number 8 into the buffer named *buff*, using the file control block *myfcb*.

```
myfcb   db      0                   ; drive = default
        db      'MYFILE '            ; filename, 8 chars
        db      'DAT'                ; extension, 3 chars
        db      25 dup (0)           ; remainder of FCB

buff    db      4096 dup (?)         ; buffer for data
        .
        .
        .
                                     ; set DTA address
        mov     ah,1ah               ; function number
        mov     dx,seg buff          ; address of buffer
        mov     ds,dx
        mov     dx,offset buff
        int     21h                  ; transfer to MS-DOS

                                     ; set relative-record number
        mov     word ptr myfcb+21h,8
        mov     word ptr myfcb+23h,0

                                     ; set record size
        mov     word ptr myfcb+0eh,1024

                                     ; read the records
        mov     ah,27h               ; function number
        mov     cx,4                 ; number of records
        mov     dx,offset myfcb ; address of FCB
        int     21h                  ; transfer to MS-DOS
        or      al,al                ; check status
        jnz     error                ; jump if read error
        .
        .
        .
```

Writes one or more sequential records from memory to a file, starting at a designated file location.

Call with:	AH	= 28H
	CX	= number of records to write
	DS:DX	= segment:offset of previously opened file control block

Returns:	AL	= 00H	if all requested records written
		01H	if disk full
		02H	if segment wrap
	CX	= actual number of records written	

Notes:

- The records are written (logically, not necessarily physically) to disk from memory at the current disk transfer area address, specified by the most recent call to Int 21H Function 1AH. If the size and location of the buffer are such that a segment overflow or wraparound would occur, the function fails with a return code of 02H.

- The file location of the data to be written is determined by the combination of the relative-record field (offset 21H) and the record-size field (offset 0EH) of the FCB. The default record size is 128 bytes.

- After the disk transfer is performed, the current block (offset 0CH), current record (offset 20H), and relative-record (offset 21H) fields of the FCB are updated to point to the next record in the file.

- If this function is called with CX = 0, no data is written to the disk but the file is extended or truncated to the length specified by combination of the record-size (offset 0EH) and the relative-record (offset 21H) fields of the FCB.

- Compare with Int 21H Function 22H, which transfers only one record per function call and does not update the FCB relative-record field.

- [3.0+] If the program is running on a network, the user must have Write access rights to the directory containing the file to be written.

Example: Write four 1024-byte records, starting at record number 8, to disk from the buffer named *buff,* using the file control block *myfcb.*

```
myfcb   db    0            ; drive = default
        db    'MYFILE  '   ; filename, 8 chars
        db    'DAT'        ; extension, 3 chars
        db    25 dup (0)   ; remainder of FCB
```

(continued)

```
buff        db        4096 dup (?)        ; buffer for data
            .
            .
            .
                                          ; set DTA address
            mov       ah,1ah              ; function number
            mov       dx,seg buff         ; address of buffer
            mov       ds,dx
            mov       dx,offset buff
            int       21h                 ; transfer to MS-DOS

                                          ; set relative-record number
            mov       word ptr myfcb+21h,8
            mov       word ptr myfcb+23h,0

                                          ; set record size
            mov       word ptr myfcb+0eh,1024

                                          ; write the records
            mov       ah,28h              ; function number
            mov       cx,4                ; number of records
            mov       dx,offset myfcb     ; address of FCB
            int       21h                 ; transfer to MS-DOS
            or        al,al               ; check status
            jnz       error               ; jump if write error
            .
            .
            .
```

Int 21H
Function 29H (41)
Parse filename

[1.0]

Parses a text string into the various fields of a file control block (FCB).

Call with: AH   = 29H
                AL   = flags to control parsing
                        Bit 3 = 1   *if extension field in FCB will be modified only if an*
                                       extension is specified in the string being parsed.
                                 = 0   *if extension field in FCB will be modified regardless; if no*
                                       extension is present in the parsed string, FCB extension is
                                       set to ASCII blanks.
                        Bit 2 = 1   *if filename field in FCB will be modified only if a filename is*
                                       specified in the string being parsed.
                                 = 0   *if filename field in FCB will be modified regardless; if no*
                                       filename is present in the parsed string, FCB filename is set
                                       to ASCII blanks.

		Bit 1	= 1	*if drive ID byte in FCB will be modified only if a drive was specified in the string being parsed.*

Bit 1 = 1   *if drive ID byte in FCB will be modified only if a drive was specified in the string being parsed.*

      = 0   *if the drive ID byte in FCB will be modified regardless; if no drive specifier is present in the parsed string, FCB drive-code field is set to 0 (default).*

Bit 0 = 1   *if leading separators will be scanned off (ignored).*

      = 0   *if leading separators will not be scanned off.*

DS:SI   = segment:offset of string

ES:DI   = segment:offset of file control block

Returns: AL   = 00H if no wildcard characters encountered

                      01H if parsed string contained wildcard characters

                      FFH if drive specifier invalid

DS:SI   = segment:offset of first character after parsed filename

ES:DI   = segment:offset of formatted unopened file control block

Notes:

- This function regards the following as separator characters:

  [1]   : . ; , = + tab space / " [ ]

  [2.0+]   : . ; , = + tab space

- This function regards all control characters and the following as terminator characters:

  : . ; , = + tab space < > | / " [ ]

- If no valid filename is present in the string to be parsed, upon return ES:DI + 1 points to an ASCII blank.

- If the * wildcard character occurs in a filename or extension, it and all remaining characters in the corresponding field in the FCB are set to ?.

- This function (and file control blocks in general) cannot be used with file specifications that include a path.

Example: Parse the string *fname* into the file control block *myfcb*.

```
fname   db      'D:QUACK.DAT',0 ; filename to be parsed

myfcb   db      37 dup (0)      ; becomes file control block
        .
        .
        .
        mov     ah,29h          ; function number
        mov     al,01h          ; skip leading separators
        mov     si,seg fname    ; address of filename
        mov     ds,si
        mov     si,offset fname
        mov     di,seg myfcb    ; address of FCB
```

(continued)

```
        mov     es,di
        mov     di,offset myfcb
        int     21h             ; transfer to MS-DOS
        cmp     al,0ffh         ; check status
        je      error           ; jump, drive invalid
        .
        .
        .
```

Int 21H
Function 2AH (42)
Get date

[1.0]

Obtains the system day of the month, day of the week, month, and year.

Call with:	AH	= 2AH

Returns:	CX	= year (1980 through 2099)
	DH	= month (1 through 12)
	DL	= day (1 through 31)
	Under MS-DOS versions 1.1 and later	
	AL	= day of the week (0 = Sunday, 1 = Monday, etc.)

Notes:

- This function's register format is the same as that required for Int 21H Function 2BH (Set Date).

- This function can be used together with Int 21H Function 2BH to find the day of the week for an arbitrary date. The current date is first obtained with Function 2AH and saved. The date of interest is then set with Function 2BH, and the day of the week for that date is obtained with a subsequent call to Function 2AH. Finally, the current date is restored with an additional call to Function 2BH, using the values obtained with the original Function 2AH call.

Example: Obtain the current date and save its components in the variables *year, day,* and *month*.

```
year    dw      0
month   db      0
day     db      0
        .
        .
        .
```

```
        mov     ah,2ah          ; function number
        int     21h             ; transfer to MS-DOS
        mov     year,cx         ; save year (word)
        mov     month,dh        ; save month (byte)
        mov     day,dl          ; save day (byte)
        .
        .
        .
```

Int 21H
Function 2BH (43)
Set date

[1.0]

Initializes the system clock driver to a specific date. The system time is not affected.

Call with:	AH	= 2BH
	CX	= year (1980 through 2099)
	DH	= month (1 through 12)
	DL	= day (1 through 31)

| **Returns:** | AL | = 00H | if date set successfully |
| | | FFH | if date not valid (ignored) |

Note: ■ This function's register format is the same as that required for Int 21H Function 2AH (Get Date).

Example: Set the system date according to the contents of the variables *year, day,* and *month.*

```
year    dw      0
month   db      0
day     db      0
        .
        .
        .
        mov     ah,2bh          ; function number
        mov     cx,year         ; get year (word)
        mov     dh,month        ; get month (byte)
        mov     dl,day          ; get day (byte)
        int     21h             ; transfer to MS-DOS
        or      al,al           ; check status
        jnz     error           ; jump if date invalid
        .
        .
        .
```

Int 21H
Function 2CH (44)
Get time

Obtains the time of day from the system real-time clock driver, converted to hours, minutes, seconds, and hundredths of seconds.

Call with: AH   = 2CH

Returns: CH   = hours (0 through 23)
             CL   = minutes (0 through 59)
             DH   = seconds (0 through 59)
             DL   = hundredths of seconds (0 through 99)

Notes:

- This function's register format is the same as that required for Int 21H Function 2DH (Set Time).

- On most IBM PC–compatible systems, the real-time clock does not have a resolution of single hundredths of seconds. On such machines, the values returned by this function in register DL are discontinuous.

Example: Obtain the current time and save its two major components in the variables *hours* and *minutes*.

```
hours    db    0
minutes  db    0
         .
         .
         .
         mov    ah,2ch      ; function number
         int    21h         ; transfer to MS-DOS
         mov    hours,ch    ; save hours (byte)
         mov    minutes,cl  ; save minutes (byte)
         .
         .
         .
```

Int 21H
Function 2DH (45)
Set time

Initializes the system real-time clock to a specified hour, minute, second, and hundredth of second. The system date is not affected.

Call with:	AH	= 2DH
	CH	= hours (0 through 23)
	CL	= minutes (0 through 59)
	DH	= seconds (0 through 59)
	DL	= hundredths of seconds (0 through 99)

| **Returns:** | AL | = 00H | if time set successfully |
| | | FFH | if time not valid (ignored) |

Note:
- This function's register format is the same as that required for Int 21H Function 2CH (Get Time).

Example: Set the system time according to the contents of the variables *hours* and *minutes*. Force the current seconds and hundredths of seconds to zero.

```
hours   db    0
minutes db    0
        .
        .
        .
        mov   ah,2dh        ; function number
        mov   ch,hours      ; get hours (byte)
        mov   cl,minutes    ; get minutes (byte)
        mov   dx,0          ; force seconds and
                            ; hundredths to zero
        int   21h           ; transfer to MS-DOS
        or    al,al         ; check status
        jnz   error         ; jump if time invalid
        .
        .
        .
```

Int 21H
Function 2EH (46)
Set verify flag

[1.0]

Turns off or turns on the operating-system flag for automatic read-after-write verification of data.

Call with:	AH	= 2EH
	AL	= 00H	if turning off verify flag
		01H	if turning on verify flag
	DL	= 00H (MS-DOS versions 1 and 2)

| **Returns:** | Nothing |

- Because read-after-write verification slows disk operations, the default setting of the verify flag is OFF.
- If a particular disk unit's device driver does not support read-after-write verification, this function has no effect.
- The current state of the verify flag can be determined using Int 21H Function 54H.
- The state of the verify flag is also controlled by the MS-DOS commands VERIFY OFF and VERIFY ON.

Example: Save the current state of the system verify flag in the variable *vflag*, then force all subsequent disk writes to be verified.

```
vflag   db      0               ; previous verify flag
        .
        .
        .
                                ; get verify flag
        mov     ah,54h          ; function number
        int     21h             ; transfer to MS-DOS
        mov     vflag,al        ; save current flag state

                                ; set verify flag
        mov     ah,2eh          ; function number
        mov     al,1            ; AL = 1 for verify on
        mov     dl,0            ; DL must be zero
        int     21h             ; transfer to MS-DOS
        .
        .
        .
```

Int 21H
Function 2FH (47)
Get DTA address

[2.0]

Obtains the current address of the disk transfer area (DTA) for FCB file read/write operations.

Call with: AH   = 2FH

Returns: ES:BX   = segment:offset of disk transfer area

Note:

- The disk transfer area address is set with Int 21H Function 1AH. The default DTA is a 128-byte buffer at offset 80H in the program segment prefix.

Example: Obtain the current disk transfer area address and save it in the variable *olddta*.

```
olddta  dd      ?                       ; save disk transfer address
            .
            .
            .
        mov     ah,2fh          ; function number
        int     21h             ; transfer to MS-DOS

                                ; save it as DWORD pointer
        mov     word ptr olddta,bx
        mov     word ptr olddta+2,es
            .
            .
            .
```

Int 21H   [2.0]
Function 30H (48)
Get MS-DOS version number

Returns the version number of the host MS-DOS operating system. This function is used by application programs to determine the capabilities of their environment.

Call with:	AH	= 30H
	AL	= 00H

Returns: If running under MS-DOS version 1

AL   = 00H

If running under MS-DOS versions 2.0 or later

AL   = major version number (MS-DOS 3.10 = 3, etc.)

AH   = minor version number (MS-DOS 3.10 = 0AH, etc.)

BH   = Original Equipment Manufacturer's (OEM's) serial number (OEM-dependent—usually 00H for IBM's PC-DOS, 0FFH or other values for MS-DOS)

BL:CX   = 24-bit user serial number (optional, OEM-dependent)

Notes:
- Because this function was not defined under MS-DOS version 1, it should always be called with AL = 00H. In an MS-DOS version 1 environment, AL will be returned unchanged.
- Care must be taken not to exit in an unacceptable fashion if an MS-DOS version 1 environment is detected. For example, Int 21H Function 4CH (Terminate Process with Return Code), Int 21H Function 40H (Write to File or Device), and the standard error handle are not available in MS-DOS version 1. In such cases a program should display an error message using Int 21H Function 09H and then terminate with Int 20H or Int 21H Function 00H.

Get the MS-DOS version number, terminating the current process with an error message if not running under MS-DOS version 2.0 or later.

```
cr       equ     0dh             ; ASCII carriage return
lf       equ     0ah             ; ASCII line feed

msg      db      cr,lf
         db      'Wrong MS-DOS version'
         db      cr,lf,'$'
         .
         .
         .
         mov     ax,3000h        ; function number
         int     21h             ; transfer to MS-DOS
         cmp     al,2            ; version 2 or later?
         jae     label1          ; yes, jump

                                 ; display error message
         mov     ah,09           ; function number
         mov     dx,offset msg   ; message address
         int     21h             ; transfer to MS-DOS

                                 ; terminate process
         mov     ah,0            ; function number
         int     21h             ; transfer to MS-DOS

label1:  .
         .
         .
```

Int 21H   [2.0]
Function 31H (49)
Terminate and stay resident

Terminates execution of the currently executing program, passing a return code to the parent process, but reserves part or all of the program's memory so that it will not be overlaid by the next transient program to be loaded. MS-DOS then takes the following actions:

- File buffers are flushed and any open handles for files or devices owned by the process are closed.
- The termination handler vector (Int 22H) is restored from PSP:000AH.
- The Ctrl-C handler vector (Int 23H) is restored from PSP:000EH.
- [2.0+] The critical-error handler vector (Int 24H) is restored from PSP:0012H.
- Control is transferred to the termination handler.

If the program is returning to COMMAND.COM, control transfers to the resident portion, and the transient portion is reloaded if necessary. If a batch file is in progress, the next line of the file is fetched and interpreted; otherwise, a prompt is issued for the next user command.

Call with:	AH	= 31H
	AL	= return code
	DX	= amount of memory to reserve (in paragraphs)

| **Returns:** | Nothing |

Notes:

■ This function call is typically used to allow user-written utilities, drivers, or interrupt handlers to be loaded as ordinary .COM or .EXE programs and then remain resident. Subsequent entrance to the code is via a hardware or software interrupt.

■ This function attempts to set the initial memory allocation block to the length in *paragraphs* specified in register DX. If other memory blocks have been requested by the application using Int 21H Function 48H, they will not be released by this function.

■ Other methods of performing a final exit are:
  - Int 20H
  - Int 21H Function 00H
  - Int 21H Function 4CH
  - Int 27H

■ The return code may be retrieved by a parent process with Int 21H Function 4DH (Get Return Code). It can also be tested in a batch file with an IF ERRORLEVEL statement. By convention, a return code of zero indicates successful execution, and a nonzero return code indicates an error.

■ This function should not be called by .EXE programs that are loaded at the high end of the transient program area (that is, linked with the /HIGH switch) because doing so reserves the memory that is normally used by the transient part of COMMAND.COM. If COMMAND.COM cannot be reloaded, the system will fail.

■ [2.0+] This function should be used in preference to Int 27H because it supports return codes, allows larger amounts of memory to be reserved, and does not require CS to contain the segment of the program segment prefix.

■ [3.0+] If the program is running on a network, it should remove all locks it has placed on file regions before terminating.

Example: Exit with a return code of 1 but stay resident, reserving 16 KB of memory starting at the program segment prefix of the process.

```
        .
        .
        .
        mov     ah,31h          ; function number
        mov     al,1            ; return code for parent
        mov     dx,0400h        ; paragraphs to reserve
        int     21h             ; transfer to MS-DOS
        .
        .
        .
```

Int 21H
Function 32H (50)
Reserved

Int 21H   [2.0]
Function 33H (51)
Get or set break flag, get boot drive

Obtains or changes the status of the operating system's break flag, which influences Ctrl-C checking during function calls. Also returns the system boot drive in version 4.0.

Call with: If getting break flag
                   AH   = 33H
                   AL   = 00H

                   If setting break flag
                   AH   = 33H
                   AL   = 01H
                   DL   = 00H   if turning break flag OFF
                             01H   if turning break flag ON

                   [4] If getting boot drive
                   AH   = 33H
                   AL   = 05H

Returns: If called with AL = 00H or 01H
                   DL   = 00H   break flag is OFF
                             01H   break flag is ON

                   [4] If called with AL = 05H
                   DL   = boot drive (1 = A, 2 = B, etc.)

Notes:
- When the system break flag is on, the keyboard is examined for a Ctrl-C entry whenever any operating-system input or output is requested; if Ctrl-C is detected, control is transferred to the Ctrl-C handler (Int 23H). When the break flag is off, MS-DOS only checks for a Ctrl-C entry when executing the traditional character I/O functions (Int 21H Functions 01H through 0CH).
- The break flag is not part of the local environment of the currently executing program; it affects all programs. An application that alters the flag should first save the flag's original status, then restore the flag before terminating.

Example: Save the current state of the system break flag in the variable *brkflag*, then turn the break flag off to disable Ctrl-C checking during most MS-DOS function calls.

```
brkflag db      0                       ; save break flag
        .
        .
        .
                                        ; get current break flag
        mov     ah,33h                  ; function number
        mov     al,0                    ; AL = 0 to get flag
        int     21h                     ; transfer to MS-DOS
        mov     brkflag,dl              ; save current flag

                                        ; now set break flag
        mov     ah,33h                  ; function number
        mov     al,1                    ; AL = 1 to set flag
        mov     dl,0                    ; set break flag OFF
        int     21h                     ; transfer to MS-DOS
        .
        .
        .
```

Int 21H
Function 34H (52)
Reserved

Int 21H   [2.0]
Function 35H (53)
Get interrupt vector

Obtains the address of the current interrupt-handler routine for the specified machine interrupt.

| **Call with:** | AH | = 35H |
| | AL | = interrupt number |

| **Returns:** | ES:BX | = segment:offset of interrupt handler |

Note: ■ Together with Int 21H Function 25H (Set Interrupt Vector), this function is used by well-behaved application programs to modify or inspect the machine interrupt vector table.

Example: Obtain the address of the current interrupt handler for hardware interrupt level 0 (divide by zero) and save it in the variable *oldint0*.

```
oldint0 dd     ?                       ; previous handler address
        .
        .
        .
        mov    ah,35h                   ; function number
        mov    al,0                     ; interrupt level
        int    21h                      ; transfer to MS-DOS

                                        ; save old handler address
        mov    word ptr oldint0,bx
        mov    word ptr oldint0+2,es
        .
        .
        .
```

Int 21H   [2.0]
Function 36H (54)
Get drive allocation information

Obtains selected information about a disk drive, from which the drive's capacity and remaining free space can be calculated.

Call with:	AH	= 36H
	DL	= drive code (0 = default, 1 = A, etc.)

Returns: If function successful

	AX	= sectors per cluster
	BX	= number of available clusters
	CX	= bytes per sector
	DX	= clusters per drive

If function unsuccessful (drive invalid)

	AX	= FFFFH

Notes:
- This function regards "lost" clusters as being in use and does not report them as part of the number of available clusters, even though they are not assigned to a file.
- Similar information is returned by Int 21H Functions 1BH and 1CH.

Example: Calculate the capacity of disk drive C in bytes, leaving the result in the variable *drvsize*. (This code assumes that the product of sectors/cluster • bytes/sector will not overflow 16 bits.)

```
        drvsize dd      ?                   ; drive C size in bytes
                .
                .
                .
                mov     ah,36h              ; function number
                mov     dl,3                ; drive C = 3
                int     21h                 ; transfer to MS-DOS

                mul     cx                  ; sectors/cluster
                                            ; * bytes/sector
                mul     dx                  ; * total clusters
                                            ; result now in DX:AX


                                            ; store low word
                mov     word ptr drvsize,ax
                                            ; store high word
                mov     word ptr drvsize+2,dx
                .
                .
                .
```

Int 21H
Function 37H (55)
Reserved

Int 21H   [2.0]
Function 38H (56)
Get or set country information

---

[2] Obtains internationalization information for the current country.

[3.0+] Obtains internationalization information for the current or specified country or sets the current country code.

Call with: If getting country information (MS-DOS version 2)
AH   = 38H
AL   = 0   to get "current" country information
DS:DX   = segment:offset of buffer for returned information

If getting country information (MS-DOS versions 3.0 and later)
AH   = 38H
AL   = 0   to get "current" country information
          1–FEH   to get information for countries with code < 255
          FFH   to get information for countries with code >= 255

BX	= country code, if AL = FFH
DS:DX	= segment:offset of buffer for returned information

If setting current country code (MS-DOS versions 3.0 and later)

AH	= 38H	
AL	= 1–FEH	country code for countries with code < 255
	FFH	for countries with code >= 255
BX	= country code, if AL = 0FFH	
DX	= FFFFH	

Returns: If function successful

Carry flag   = clear

and, if getting internationalization information

BX	= country code
DS:DX	= segment:offset of buffer holding internationalization information

and buffer filled in as follows:

(for PC-DOS 2.0 and 2.1)

Byte(s)	Contents
00H–01H	date format
	0 = USA m d y
	1 = Europe d m y
	2 = Japan y m d
02H–03H	ASCIIZ currency symbol
04H–05H	ASCIIZ thousands separator
06H–07H	ASCIIZ decimal separator
08H–1FH	reserved

(for MS-DOS versions 2.0 and later, PC-DOS versions 3.0 and later)

Byte(s)	Contents
00H–01H	date format
	0 = USA m d y
	1 = Europe d m y
	2 = Japan y m d
02H–06H	ASCIIZ currency symbol string
07H–08H	ASCIIZ thousands separator character
09H–0AH	ASCIIZ decimal separator character
0BH–0CH	ASCIIZ date separator character
0DH–0EH	ASCIIZ time separator character
0FH	currency format
	bit 0 =0 if currency symbol precedes value
	=1 if currency symbol follows value
	bit 1 =0 if no space between value and currency symbol
	=1 if one space between value and currency symbol
	bit 2 =0 if currency symbol and decimal are separate
	=1 if currency symbol replaces decimal separator
10H	number of digits after decimal in currency
11H	time format
	bit 0 =0 if 12-hour clock
	=1 if 24-hour clock

12H–15H	case-map call address
16H–17H	ASCIIZ data-list separator
18H–21H	reserved

If function unsuccessful

| Carry flag | .= set |
| AX | = error code |

Notes:

- The default country code is determined by the COUNTRY= directive in CONFIG.SYS or by the KEYBxx keyboard driver file if one is loaded. Otherwise, the default country code is OEM-dependent.

- The previous contents of register CX may be destroyed by the Get Country Information subfunction.

- The case-map call address is the segment:offset of a FAR procedure that performs country-specific mapping on character values from 80H through 0FFH. The procedure must be called with the character to be mapped in register AL. If an alternate value exists for that character, it is returned in AL; otherwise, AL is unchanged. In general, lowercase characters are mapped to their uppercase equivalents, and accented or otherwise modified vowels are mapped to their plain vowel equivalents.

- [3.0+] The value in register DX is used by MS-DOS to select between the Set Country and Get Country Information subfunctions.

- [3.3+] Int 21H Function 65H (Get Extended Country Information) returns a superset of the information supplied by this function.

Examples:

Obtain internationalization information for the current country in the buffer *ctrybuf*.

```
ctrybuf db      34 dup (0)
         .
         .
         .
        mov     ah,38h          ; function number
        mov     al,0            ; get current country
        mov     dx,seg ctrybuf  ; address of buffer
        mov     ds,dx           ; for country information
        mov     dx,offset ctrybuf
        int     21h             ; transfer to MS-DOS
        jc      error           ; jump if function failed
         .
         .
         .
```

If the program is running under PC-DOS 3.3 and the current country code is 49 (West Germany), *ctrybuf* is filled in with the following information:

```
        dw      0001h           ; date format
        db      'DM',0,0,0      ; ASCIIZ currency symbol
        db      '.',0           ; ASCIIZ thousands separator
```

(continued)

```
         db      ',',0           ; ASCIIZ decimal separator
         db      '.',0           ; ASCIIZ date separator
         db      '.',0           ; ASCIIZ time separator
         db      02h             ; currency format
         db      02h             ; digits after decimal
         db      01h             ; time format
         dd      026ah:176ch     ; case-map call address
         db      ';',0           ; ASCIIZ data-list separator
         db      10 dup (0)      ; reserved
```

Int 21H
Function 39H (57)
Create directory

[2.0]

Creates a directory using the specified drive and path.

| **Call with:** | AH | = 39H |
| | DS:DX | = segment:offset of ASCIIZ pathname |

Returns:	If function successful	
	Carry flag	= clear
	If function unsuccessful	
	Carry flag	= set
	AX	= error code

Note:
- The function fails if:
  - any element of the pathname does not exist.
  - a directory with the same name at the end of the same path already exists.
  - the parent directory for the new directory is the root directory and is full.
  - [3.0+] the program is running on a network and the user running the program has insufficient access rights.

Example: Create a directory named MYSUB in the root directory on drive C.

```
dname    db      'C:\MYSUB',0
         .
         .
         .
         mov     ah,39h          ; function number
         mov     dx,seg dname    ; address of pathname
         mov     ds,dx
         mov     dx,offset dname
```

```
        int    21h          ; transfer to MS-DOS
        jc     error        ; jump if create failed
        .
        .
        .
```

Int 21H
Function 3AH (58)
Delete directory

Removes a directory using the specified drive and path.

Call with:	AH	= 3AH
	DS:DX	= segment:offset of ASCIIZ pathname

Returns:	If function successful	
	Carry flag	= clear
	If function unsuccessful	
	Carry flag	= set
	AX	= error code

Note:
- The function fails if:
  - any element of the pathname does not exist.
  - the specified directory is also the current directory.
  - the specified directory contains any files.
  - [3.0+] the program is running on a network and the user running the program has insufficient access rights.

Example: Remove the directory named MYSUB in the root directory on drive C.

```
dname   db     'C:\MYSUB',0
        .
        .
        .
        mov    ah,3ah         ; function number
        mov    dx,seg dname   ; address of pathname
        mov    ds,dx
        mov    dx,offset dname
        int    21h            ; transfer to MS-DOS
        jc     error          ; jump if delete failed
        .
        .
        .
```

Int 21H
Function 3BH (59)
Set current directory

Sets the current, or default, directory using the specified drive and path.

Call with:	AH	= 3BH
	DS:DX	= segment:offset of ASCIIZ pathname

Returns: If function successful

Carry flag = clear

If function unsuccessful

Carry flag = set

AX = error code

Notes:
- The function fails if any element of the pathname does not exist.
- Int 21H Function 47H can be used to obtain the name of the current directory before using Int 21H Function 3BH to select another, so that the original directory can be restored later.

Example: Change the current directory for drive C to the directory \MYSUB.

```
dname   db      'C:\MYSUB',0
        .
        .
        .
        mov     ah,3bh          ; function number
        mov     dx,seg dname    ; address of pathname
        mov     ds,dx
        mov     dx,offset dname
        int     21h             ; transfer to MS-DOS
        jc      error           ; jump if bad path
        .
        .
        .
```

Given an ASCIIZ pathname, creates a new file in the designated or default directory on the designated or default disk drive. If the specified file already exists, it is truncated to zero length. In either case, the file is opened and a handle is returned that can be used by the program for subsequent access to the file.

Call with:	AH	= 3CH		
	CX	= file attribute (bits may be combined)		
		Bit(s)	*Significance (if set)*	
		0	read-only	
		1	hidden	
		2	system	
		3	volume label	
		4	reserved (0)	
		5	archive	
		6–15	reserved (0)	
	DS:DX	= segment:offset of ASCIIZ pathname		

Returns:	If function successful	
	Carry flag	= clear
	AX	= handle
	If function failed	
	Carry flag	= set
	AX	= error code

Notes:

- The function fails if:
  - any element of the pathname does not exist.
  - the file is being created in the root directory and the root directory is full.
  - a file with the same name and the read-only attribute already exists in the specified directory.
  - [3.0+] the program is running on a network and the user running the program has insufficient access rights.
- A file is usually given a normal (0) attribute when it is created. The file's attribute can subsequently be modified with Int 21H Function 43H.
- [3.0+] A volume label can be created using an attribute of 0008H, if one does not already exist. When files are created, bit 3 of the attribute parameter should always be clear (0).
- [3.0+] See the entries for Int 21H Functions 5AH and 5BH, which may also be used to create files.
- [4.0+] Int 21H Function 6CH combines the services of Functions 3CH, 3DH, and 5BH.

Example: Create and open, or truncate to zero length and open, the file C:\MYDIR\MYFILE.DAT, and save the handle for subsequent access to the file.

```
fname   db      'C:\MYDIR\MYFILE.DAT',0

fhandle dw      ?
          .
          .
          .
        mov     ah,3ch          ; function number
        xor     cx,cx           ; normal attribute
        mov     dx,seg fname    ; address of pathname
        mov     ds,dx
        mov     dx,offset fname
        int     21h             ; transfer to MS-DOS
        jc      error           ; jump if create failed
        mov     fhandle,ax      ; save file handle
          .
          .
          .
```

Int 21H [2.0]
Function 3DH (61)
Open file

Given an ASCIIZ pathname, opens the specified file in the designated or default directory on the designated or default disk drive. A handle is returned which can be used by the program for subsequent access to the file.

Call with:
AH = 3DH
AL = access mode

Bit(s)	*Significance*
0–2	access mode
	000 = read access
	001 = write access
	010 = read/write access
3	reserved (0)
4–6	sharing mode (MS-DOS versions 3.0 and later)
	000 = compatibility mode
	001 = deny all
	010 = deny write
	011 = deny read
	100 = deny none
7	inheritance flag (MS-DOS versions 3.0 and later)
	0 = child process inherits handle
	1 = child does not inherit handle

DS:DX = segment:offset of ASCIIZ pathname

Returns: If function successful
Carry flag   = clear
AX   = handle

If function unsuccessful
Carry flag   = set
AX   = error code

Notes:
- Any normal, system, or hidden file with a matching name will be opened by this function. If the file is read-only, the success of the operation also depends on the access code in bits 0–2 of register AL. After opening the file, the file read/write pointer is set to offset zero (the first byte of the file).
- The function fails if:
  - any element of the pathname does not exist.
  - the file is opened with an access mode of read/write and the file has the read-only attribute.
  - [3.0+] SHARE.EXE is loaded and the file has already been opened by one or more other processes in a sharing mode that is incompatible with the current program's request.
- The file's date and time stamp can be accessed after a successful open call with Int 21H Function 57H.
- The file's attributes (hidden, system, read-only, or archive) can be obtained with Int 21H Function 43H.
- When a file handle is inherited by a child process or is duplicated with Int 21H Function 45H or 46H, all sharing and access restrictions are also inherited.
- [2] Only bits 0–2 of register AL are significant; the remaining bits should be zero for upward compatibility.
- [3.0+] Bits 4–7 of register AL control access to the file by other programs. (Bits 4–6 have no effect unless SHARE.EXE is loaded.)
- [3.0+] A file-sharing error causes a critical-error exception (Int 24H) with an error code of 02H. Int 21H Function 59H can be used to obtain information about the sharing violation.
- [4.0+] Int 21H Function 6CH combines the services of Functions 3CH, 3DH, and 5BH.

Example: Open the file C:\MYDIR\MYFILE.DAT for both reading and writing, and save the handle for subsequent access to the file.

```
fname    db      'C:\MYDIR\MYFILE.DAT',0

fhandle dw      ?
            .
            .
            .
```

(continued)

```
        mov     ah,3dh          ; function number
        mov     al,2            ; mode = read/write
        mov     dx,seg fname    ; address of pathname
        mov     ds,dx
        mov     dx,offset fname
        int     21h             ; transfer to MS-DOS
        jc      error           ; jump if open failed
        mov     fhandle,ax      ; save file handle
        .
        .
        .
```

Int 21H [2.0]
Function 3EH (62)
Close file

Given a handle that was obtained by a previous successful open or create operation, flushes all internal buffers associated with the file to disk, closes the file, and releases the handle for reuse. If the file was modified, the time and date stamp and file size are updated in the file's directory entry.

Call with:	AH	= 3EH
	BX	= handle

Returns:	If function successful	
	Carry flag	= clear
	If function unsuccessful	
	Carry flag	= set
	AX	= error code

Note:
- If you accidentally call this function with a zero handle, the standard input device is closed, and the keyboard appears to go dead. Make sure you always call the close function with a valid, nonzero handle.

Example: Close the file whose handle is saved in the variable *fhandle*.

```
fhandle dw      0
        .
        .
        .
        mov     ah,3eh          ; function number
        mov     bx,fhandle      ; file handle
        int     21h             ; transfer to MS-DOS
        jc      error           ; jump if close failed
        .
        .
        .
```

Int 21H
Function 3FH (63)
Read file or device

Given a valid file handle from a previous open or create operation, a buffer address, and a length in bytes, transfers data at the current file-pointer position from the file into the buffer and then updates the file pointer position.

Call with:		
	AH	= 3FH
	BX	= handle
	CX	= number of bytes to read
	DS:DX	= segment:offset of buffer

Returns:		
	If function successful	
	Carry flag	= clear
	AX	= bytes transferred
	If function unsuccessful	
	Carry flag	= set
	AX	= error code

Notes:

- If reading from a character device (such as the standard input) in cooked mode, at most one line of input will be read (i.e., up to a carriage return character or the specified length, whichever comes first).
- If the carry flag is returned clear but AX = 0, then the file pointer was already at end of file when the program requested the read.
- If the carry flag is returned clear but AX < CX, then a partial record was read at end of file or there is an error.
- [3.0+] If the program is running on a network, the user must have Read access rights to the directory and file.

Example:

Using the file handle from a previous open or create operation, read 1024 bytes at the current file pointer into the buffer named *buff*.

```
buff     db     1024 dup (?)     ; buffer for read

fhandle dw     ?                 ; contains file handle
         .
         .
         .
```

(continued)

```
        mov     ah,3fh          ; function number
        mov     dx,seg buff     ; buffer address
        mov     ds,dx
        mov     dx,offset buff
        mov     bx,fhandle      ; file handle
        mov     cx,1024         ; length to read
        int     21h             ; transfer to MS-DOS
        jc      error           ; jump, read failed

        cmp     ax,cx           ; check length of read
        jl      done            ; jump, end of file
        .
        .
        .
```

Int 21H   [2.0]
Function 40H (64)
Write file or device

Given a valid file handle from a previous open or create operation, a buffer address, and a length in bytes, transfers data from the buffer into the file and then updates the file pointer position.

Call with: | AH | = 40H
                | BX | = handle
                | CX | = number of bytes to write
                | DS:DX | = segment:offset of buffer

Returns: If function successful
Carry flag = clear
AX   = bytes transferred
If function unsuccessful
Carry flag = set
AX   = error code

Notes:
- If the carry flag is returned clear but AX < CX, then a partial record was written or there is an error. This can be caused by a Ctrl-Z (1AH) embedded in the data if the destination is a character device in cooked mode or by a disk full condition if the destination is a file.
- If the function is called with CX = 0, the file is truncated or extended to the current file pointer position.
- [3.0+] If the program is running on a network, the user must have Write access rights to the directory and file.

Example: Using the handle from a previous open or create operation, write 1024 bytes to disk at the current file pointer from the buffer named *buff*.

```
buff     db     1024 dup (?)      ; buffer for write

fhandle  dw     ?                 ; contains file handle
         .
         .
         .
         mov    ah,40h            ; function number
         mov    dx,seg buff       ; buffer address
         mov    ds,dx
         mov    dx,offset buff
         mov    bx,fhandle        ; file handle
         mov    cx,1024           ; length to write
         int    21h               ; transfer to MS-DOS
         jc     error             ; jump, write failed
         cmp    ax,1024           ; entire record written?
         jne    error             ; no, jump
         .
         .
         .
```

Int 21H
Function 41H (65)
Delete file

[2.0]

Deletes a file from the specified or default disk and directory.

| **Call with:** | AH | = 41H |
| | DS:DX | = segment:offset of ASCIIZ pathname |

Returns: If function successful
Carry flag   = clear

If function unsuccessful
Carry flag   = set
AX   = error code

Notes:
- This function deletes a file by replacing the first character of its filename in the directory with the character *e* (E5H) and marking the file's clusters as "free" in the disk's file allocation table. The actual data stored in those clusters is not overwritten.
- Only one file at a time may be deleted with this function. Unlike the FCB-related Delete File function (Int 21H Function 13H), the * and ? wildcard characters are not allowed in the file specification.

- The function fails if:
  - any element of the pathname does not exist.
  - the designated file exists but has the read-only attribute. (Int 21H Function 43H can be used to examine and modify a file's attribute before attempting to delete it.)
  - [3.0+] the program is running on a network, and the user running the program has insufficient access rights.

Example: Delete the file named MYFILE.DAT from the directory \MYDIR on drive C.

```
fname   db      'C:\MYDIR\MYFILE.DAT',0
        .
        .
        .
        mov     ah,41h          ; function number
        mov     dx,seg fname    ; filename address
        mov     ds,dx
        mov     dx,offset fname
        int     21h             ; transfer to MS-DOS
        jc      error           ; jump if delete failed
        .
        .
        .
```

Int 21H   [2.0]
Function 42H (66)
Set file pointer

Sets the file location pointer relative to the start of file, end of file, or current file position.

Call with:	AH	= 42H
	AL	= method code
		00H absolute offset from start of file
		01H signed offset from current file pointer
		02H signed offset from end of file
	BX	= handle
	CX	= most significant half of offset
	DX	= least significant half of offset

Returns:	If function successful	
	Carry flag	= clear
	DX	= most significant half of resulting file pointer
	AX	= least significant half of resulting file pointer
	If function unsuccessful	
	Carry flag	= set
	AX	= error code

- This function uses a method code and a double-precision (32-bit) value to set the file pointer. The next record read or written in the file will begin at the new file pointer location. No matter what method is used in the call to this function, the file pointer returned in DX:AX is always the resulting absolute byte offset from the start of file.

- Method 02H may be used to find the size of the file by calling Int 21H Function 42H with an offset of 0 and examining the pointer location that is returned.

- Using methods 01H or 02H, it is possible to set the file pointer to a location that is before the start of file. If this is done, no error is returned by this function, but an error will be encountered upon a subsequent attempt to read or write the file.

Examples: Using the file handle from a previous open or create operation, set the current file pointer position to 1024 bytes after the start of file.

```
fhandle dw      ?
        .
        .
        .
        mov     ah,42h          ; function number
        mov     al,0            ; method = absolute
        mov     bx,fhandle      ; file handle
        mov     cx,0            ; upper half of offset
        mov     dx,1024         ; lower half of offset
        int     21h             ; transfer to MS-DOS
        jc      error           ; jump, function failed
        .
        .
        .
```

The following subroutine accepts a record number, record size, and handle and sets the file pointer appropriately.

```
; call this routine with BX = handle
;                         AX = record number
;                         CX = record size
; returns all registers unchanged
;
setptr  proc    near
        push    ax              ; save record number
        push    cx              ; save record size
        push    dx              ; save whatever's in DX
        mul     cx              ; size * record number
        mov     cx,ax           ; upper part to CX
        xchg    cx,dx           ; lower part to DX
        mov     ax,4200h        ; function number & method
        int     21h             ; transfer to MS-DOS
        pop     dx              ; restore previous DX
        pop     cx              ; restore record size
        pop     ax              ; restore record number
        ret                     ; back to caller
setptr  endp
```

Obtains or alters the attributes of a file (read-only, hidden, system, or archive) or directory.

Call with:	AH	= 43H	
	AL	= 00H	to get attributes
		01H	to set attributes
	CX	= file attribute, if AL = 01H (bits can be combined)	

	Bit(s)	**Significance (if set)**
	0	read-only
	1	hidden
	2	system
	3–4	reserved (0)
	5	archive
	6–15	reserved (0)

	DS:DX	= segment:offset of ASCIIZ pathname

Returns: If function successful

	Carry flag	= clear
	CX	= file attribute

	Bit(s)	**Significance (if set)**
	0	read-only
	1	hidden
	2	system
	3	volume label
	4	directory
	5	archive
	6–15	reserved (0)

If function unsuccessful

	Carry flag	= set
	AX	= error code

Notes:

- Bits 3 and 4 of register CX must always be clear (0) when this function is called; in other words, you cannot change an existing file into a directory or volume label. However, you can assign the "hidden" attribute to an existing directory with this function.
- [3.0+] If the program is running on a network, the user must have Create access rights to the directory containing the file whose attribute is to be modified.

Example: Change the attribute of the file D:\MYDIR\MYFILE.DAT to read-only, so that it cannot be accidentally modified or deleted by other application programs.

```
rdonly  equ     01h             ; file attributes
hidden  equ     02h
system  equ     04h
volume  equ     08h
subdir  equ     10h
archive equ     20h

fname   db      'D:\MYDIR\MYFILE.DAT',0
         .
         .
         .
        mov     ah,43h          ; function number
        mov     al,01h          ; subfunction = modify
        mov     cx,rdonly       ; read-only attribute
        mov     dx,seg fname    ; filename address
        mov     ds,dx
        mov     dx,offset fname
        int     21h             ; transfer to MS-DOS
        jc      error           ; jump if modify failed
         .
         .
         .
```

Int 21H   [2.0]
Function 44H (68)
IOCTL (I/O control)

Provides a direct path of communication between an application program and a device driver. Allows a program to obtain hardware-dependent information and to request operations that are not supported by other MS-DOS function calls.

The IOCTL subfunctions and the MS-DOS versions in which they first became available are:

Subfunction	*Name*	*MS-DOS version*
00H	Get Device Information	2.0
01H	Set Device Information	2.0
02H	Receive Control Data from Character Device Driver	2.0
03H	Send Control Data to Character Device Driver	2.0
04H	Receive Control Data from Block Device Driver	2.0
05H	Send Control Data to Block Device Driver	2.0
06H	Check Input Status	2.0

(continued)

Subfunction	Name	MS-DOS version
07H	Check Output Status	2.0
08H	Check If Block Device Is Removable	3.0
09H	Check If Block Device Is Remote	3.1
0AH (10)	Check If Handle Is Remote	3.1
0BH (11)	Change Sharing Retry Count	3.1
0CH (12)	Generic I/O Control for Character Devices	
	CL = 45H: Set Iteration Count	3.2
	CL = 4AH: Select Code Page	3.3
	CL = 4CH: Start Code Page Preparation	3.3
	CL = 4DH: End Code Page Preparation	3.3
	CL = 5FH: Set Display Information	4.0
	CL = 65H: Get Iteration Count	3.2
	CL = 6AH: Query Selected Code Page	3.3
	CL = 6BH: Query Prepare List	3.3
	CL = 7FH: Get Display Information	4.0
0DH (13)	Generic I/O Control for Block Devices	
	CL = 40H: Set Device Parameters	3.2
	CL = 41H: Write Track	3.2
	CL = 42H: Format and Verify Track	3.2
	CL = 47H: Set Access Flag	4.0
	CL = 60H: Get Device Parameters	3.2
	CL = 61H: Read Track	3.2
	CL = 62H: Verify Track	3.2
	CL = 67H: Get Access Flag	4.0
0EH (14)	Get Logical Drive Map	3.2
0FH (15)	Set Logical Drive Map	3.2

Only IOCTL Subfunctions 00H, 06H, and 07H may be used for handles associated with files. Subfunctions 00H–08H are not supported on network devices.

Int 21H [2.0]
Function 44H (68) Subfunction 00H
IOCTL: get device information

Returns a device information word for the file or device associated with the specified handle.

Call with:	AH	= 44H
	AL	= 00H
	BX	= handle

Returns: If function successful
                Carry flag = clear
                DX   = device information word

        For a file:

Bit(s)	Significance
0–5	drive number (0 = A, 1 = B, etc.)
6	0 if file has been written
	1 if file has not been written
7	0, indicating a file
8–15	reserved

        For a device:

Bit(s)	Significance
0	1 if standard input
1	1 if standard output
2	1 if NUL device
3	1 if clock device
4	reserved
5	0 if handle in ASCII mode
	1 if handle in binary mode
6	0 if end of file on input
7	1, indicating a device
8–13	reserved
14	0 if IOCTL subfunctions 02H and 03H not supported
	1 if IOCTL subfunctions 02H and 03H supported
15	reserved

        If function unsuccessful
        Carry flag = set
        AX   = error code

Notes:
- Bits 8–15 of DX correspond to the upper 8 bits of the device-driver attribute word.
- Bit 5 of the device information word for a handle associated with a character device signifies whether MS-DOS considers that handle to be in binary ("raw") mode or ASCII ("cooked") mode. In ASCII mode, MS-DOS filters the character stream and may take special action when the characters Ctrl-C, Ctrl-S, Ctrl-P, Ctrl-Z, and carriage return are detected. In binary mode, all characters are treated as data, and the exact number of characters requested is always read or written.

Example: See Int 21H Function 44H Subfunction 01H.

Sets certain flags for a handle associated with a character device. This subfunction may not be used for a handle that is associated with a file.

Call with:

AH	= 44H	
AL	= 01H	
BX	= handle	
DX	= device information word	

Bit(s)	Significance
0	1 if standard input
1	1 if standard output
2	1 if NUL device
3	1 if clock device
4	reserved (0)
5	0 to select ASCII mode
	1 to select binary mode
6	reserved (0)
7	1, indicating a device
8–15	reserved (0)

Returns:

If function successful
Carry flag = clear

If function unsuccessful
Carry flag = set
AX = error code

Notes:

- If register DH does not contain 00H, control returns to the program with the carry flag set and error code 0001H (invalid function) in register AX.
- Bit 5 of the information word for a handle associated with a character device signifies whether MS-DOS considers that handle to be in binary ("raw") or ASCII ("cooked") mode. See Notes for Int 21H Function 44H Subfunction 00H.

Example:

Place the standard output handle into binary ("raw") mode. This speeds up output by disabling checking for Ctrl-C, Ctrl-S, and Ctrl-P between each character.

```
                              .
                              .
                              .
                                        ; get device information
        mov     ax,4400h                ; function & subfunction
        mov     bx,1                    ; standard output handle
        int     21h                     ; transfer to MS-DOS

        mov     dh,0                    ; force DH = 0
        or      dl,20h                  ; set binary mode bit

                                        ; set device information
        mov     ax,4401h                ; function & subfunction
        int     21h                     ; transfer to MS-DOS
                              .
                              .
                              .
```

Int 21H   [2.0]
Function 44H (68) Subfunction 02H
IOCTL: read control data from character device driver

Reads control data from a character-device driver. The length and contents of the data are specific to each device driver and do not follow any standard format. This function does not necessarily result in any input from the physical device.

Call with:	AH	= 44H
	AL	= 02H
	BX	= handle
	CX	= number of bytes to read
	DS:DX	= segment:offset of buffer

Returns:	If function successful
	Carry flag	= clear
	AX	= bytes read
	and buffer contains control data from driver
	If function unsuccessful
	Carry flag	= set
	AX	= error code

Notes: ■ If supported by the driver, this subfunction can be used to obtain hardware-dependent status and availability information that is not supported by other MS-DOS function calls.

- Character-device drivers are not required to support IOCTL Subfunction 02H. A program can test bit 14 of the device information word returned by IOCTL Subfunction 00H to determine whether the driver supports this subfunction. If Subfunction 02H is requested and the driver does not have the ability to process control data, control returns to the program with the carry flag set and error code 0001H (invalid function) in register AX.

| **Example:** | Read a control string from the standard list driver into the buffer *buff*. |

```
stdprn  equ    4                ; standard list handle
buflen  equ    64               ; length of buffer

ctllen  dw     ?                ; length of control string
buff    db     buflen dup (0)   ; receives control string
        .
        .
        .
        mov    ax,4402h         ; function & subfunction
        mov    bx,stdprn        ; standard list handle
        mov    cx,buflen        ; buffer length
        mov    dx,seg buff      ; buffer address
        mov    ds,dx
        mov    dx,offset buff
        int    21h              ; transfer to MS-DOS
        jc     error            ; jump if read failed
        mov    ctllen,ax        ; save control string length
        .
        .
        .
```

Int 21H [2.0]
Function 44H (68) Subfunction 03H
IOCTL: write control data to character-device driver

Transfers control data from an application to a character-device driver. The length and contents of the data are specific to each device driver and do not follow any standard format. This function does not necessarily result in any output to the physical device.

Call with:

	AH	= 44H
	AL	= 03H
	BX	= handle
	CX	= number of bytes to write
	DS:DX	= segment:offset of data

Returns: If function successful
Carry flag   = clear
AX   = bytes transferred

If function unsuccessful
Carry flag   = set
AX   = error code

Notes: ■ If supported by the driver, this subfunction can be used to request hardware-dependent operations (such as setting baud rate for a serial port) that are not supported by other MS-DOS function calls.

■ Character-device drivers are not required to support IOCTL Subfunction 03H. A program can test bit 14 of the device information word returned by IOCTL Subfunction 00H to determine whether the driver supports this subfunction. If Subfunction 03H is requested and the driver does not have the ability to process control data, control returns to the program with the carry flag set and error code 0001H (invalid function) in register AX.

Example: Write a control string from the buffer *buff* to the standard list device driver. The length of the string is assumed to be in the variable *ctllen*.

```
stdprn  equ   4               ; standard list handle
buflen  equ   64              ; length of buffer

ctllen  dw    ?               ; length of control data
buff    db    buflen dup (?)  ; contains control data
        .
        .
        .
        mov   ax,4403h        ; function & subfunction
        mov   bx,stdprn       ; standard list handle
        mov   dx,seg buff     ; buffer address
        mov   ds,dx
        mov   dx,offset buff
        mov   cx,ctllen       ; length of control data
        int   21h             ; transfer to MS-DOS
        jc    error           ; jump if write failed
        .
        .
        .
```

Transfers control data from a block-device driver directly into an application program's buffer. The length and contents of the data are specific to each device driver and do not follow any standard format. This function does not necessarily result in any input from the physical device.

Call with:		
	AH	= 44H
	AL	= 04H
	BL	= drive code (0 = default, 1 = A, 2 = B, etc.)
	CX	= number of bytes to read
	DS:DX	= segment:offset of buffer

Returns:

If function successful

Carry flag	= clear
AX	= bytes transferred

and buffer contains control data from device driver

If function unsuccessful

Carry flag	= set
AX	= error code

Notes:

- When supported by the driver, this subfunction can be used to obtain hardware-dependent status and availability information that is not provided by other MS-DOS function calls.

- Block-device drivers are not required to support IOCTL Subfunction 04H. If this subfunction is requested and the driver does not have the ability to process control data, control returns to the program with the carry flag set and error code 0001H (invalid function) in register AX.

Example:

Read a control string from the block-device driver for drive C into the buffer *buff*.

```
buflen  equ    64              ; length of buffer

ctllen  dw     ?               ; length of control string
buff    db     buflen dup (0)  ; receives control string
          .
          .
          .
        mov    ax,4404h        ; function & subfunction
        mov    bl,3            ; drive C = 3
        mov    cx,buflen       ; buffer length
        mov    dx,seg buff     ; buffer address
```

```
        mov     ds,dx
        mov     dx,offset buff
        int     21h             ; transfer to MS-DOS
        jc      error           ; jump if read failed
        mov     ctllen,ax       ; save control string length
        .
        .
        .
```

Int 21H
Function 44H (68) Subfunction 05H
IOCTL: write control data to block-device driver

Transfers control data from an application program directly to a block-device driver. The length and contents of the control data are specific to each device driver and do not follow any standard format. This function does not necessarily result in any output to the physical device.

Call with: AH = 44H
AL = 05H
BL = drive code (0 = default, 1 = A, 2 = B, etc.)
CX = number of bytes to write
DS:DX = segment:offset of data

Returns: If function successful
Carry flag = clear
AX = bytes transferred

If function unsuccessful
Carry flag = set
AX = error code

Notes:
- When supported by the driver, this subfunction can be used to request hardware-dependent operations (such as tape rewind or disk eject) that are not provided by other MS-DOS function calls.
- Block-device drivers are not required to support IOCTL Subfunction 05H. If this subfunction is requested and the driver does not have the ability to process control data, control returns to the program with the carry flag set and error code 0001H (invalid function) in register AX.

Example: Write a control string from the buffer *buff* to the block-device driver for drive C. The length of the string is assumed to be in the variable *ctllen*.

```
buflen  equ     64              ; length of buffer

ctllen  dw      ?               ; length of control data
```

(continued)

```
buff    db      buflen dup (?)   ; contains control data
        .
        .
        .
        mov     ax,4405h         ; function & subfunction
        mov     bl,3             ; drive C = 3
        mov     dx,seg buff      ; buffer address
        mov     ds,dx
        mov     dx,offset buff
        mov     cx,ctllen        ; length of control data
        int     21h              ; transfer to MS-DOS
        jc      error            ; jump if write failed
        .
        .
        .
```

Int 21H
Function 44H (68) Subfunction 06H
IOCTL: check input status

[2.0]

Returns a code indicating whether the device or file associated with a handle is ready for input.

Call with:	AH	= 44H
	AL	= 06H
	BX	= handle

Returns:	If function successful		
	Carry flag	= clear	
	and, for a device:		
	AL	= 00H	if device not ready
		FFH	if device ready
	or, for a file:		
	AL	= 00H	if file pointer at EOF
		FFH	if file pointer not at EOF
	If function unsuccessful		
	Carry flag	= set	
	AX	= error code	

| **Note:** | ■ This function can be used to check the status of character devices, such as the serial port, that do not have their own "traditional" MS-DOS status calls. |

Example: Check whether a character is ready from the standard auxiliary device (usually COM1).

```
stdaux  equ    3                 ; standard auxiliary handle
        .
        .
        .
        mov    ax,4406h          ; function & subfunction
        mov    bx,stdaux         ; standard auxiliary handle
        int    21h               ; transfer to MS-DOS
        jc     error             ; jump if function failed
        or     al,al             ; test status flag
        jnz    ready             ; jump if character ready
        .
        .
        .
```

Int 21H   [2.0]
Function 44H (68) Subfunction 07H
IOCTL: check output status

Returns a code indicating whether the device associated with a handle is ready for output.

Call with: AH   = 44H
                   AL   = 07H
                   BX   = handle

Returns: If function successful
                 Carry flag   = clear
                 and, for a device:
                 AL   = 00H   if device not ready
                            FFH   if device ready
                 or, for a file:
                 AL   = FFH
                 If function unsuccessful
                 Carry flag   = set
                 AX   = error code

Note: ■ When used with a handle for a file, this function always returns a ready status, even
              if the disk is full or no disk is in the drive.

Example: Check whether the standard auxiliary device (usually COM1) can accept a character for output.

```
stdaux  equ    3                      ; standard auxiliary handle
          .
          .
          .
        mov    ax,4407h               ; function & subfunction
        mov    bx,stdaux              ; standard auxiliary handle
        int    21h                    ; transfer to MS-DOS
        jc     error                  ; jump if function failed
        or     al,al                  ; test status flag
        jnz    ready                  ; jump if not busy
          .
          .
          .
```

Int 21H [3.0]
Function 44H (68) Subfunction 08H
IOCTL: check if block device is removable

Checks whether the specified block device contains a removable storage medium, such as a floppy disk.

Call with:

AH	= 44H	
AL	= 08H	
BL	= drive number (0 = default, 1 = A, 2 = B, etc.)	

Returns:

If function successful

Carry flag	= clear	
AL	= 00H	if medium is removable
	01H	if medium is not removable

If function unsuccessful

Carry flag	= set	
AX	= error code	

Notes:

- If a file is not found as expected on a particular drive, a program can use this subfunction to determine whether the user should be prompted to insert another disk.
- This subfunction may not be used for a network drive.
- Block drivers are not required to support Subfunction 08H. If this subfunction is requested and the block device cannot supply the information, control returns to the program with the carry flag set and error code 0001H (invalid function) in register AX.

Example: Check whether drive C is removable.

```
        .
        .
        .
    mov     ax,4408h    ; function & subfunction
    mov     bl,3        ; drive 3 = C
    int     21h         ; transfer to MS-DOS
    jc      error       ; jump if function failed
    and     al,1        ; test type of medium
    jnz     fixed       ; jump if not removable
        .
        .
        .
```

Int 21H   [3.1]
Function 44H (68) Subfunction 09H
IOCTL: check if block device is remote

Checks whether the specified block device is local (attached to the computer running the program) or remote (redirected to a network server).

Call with:	AH	= 44H
	AL	= 09H
	BL	= drive number (0 = default, 1 = A, 2 = B, etc.)

Returns: If function successful
Carry flag   = clear
DX   = device attribute word
        bit 12   = *0 if drive is local*
                         1 if drive is remote

If function unsuccessful
Carry flag   = set
AX   = error code

Note: ■ Use of this subfunction should be avoided. Application programs should not distinguish between files on local and remote devices.

Example: Check whether drive D is mounted on the machine running the program or is a network drive.

```
          .
          .
          .
      mov    ax,4409h      ; function & subfunction
      mov    bl,4          ; drive 4 = D
      int    21h           ; transfer to MS-DOS
      jc     error         ; jump if function failed
      and    dx,1000h      ; test local/remote bit
      jnz    remote        ; jump if network drive
          .
          .
          .
```

Int 21H   [3.1]
Function 44H (68) Subfunction 0AH (10)
IOCTL: check if handle is remote

Checks whether the specified handle refers to a file or device that is local (located on the PC that is running the program) or remote (located on a network server).

Call with:	AH	= 44H
	AL	= 0AH
	BX	= handle

Returns: If function successful
Carry flag   = clear
DX   = attribute word for file or device
                   bit 15   = 0 if local
                   1 if remote

If function unsuccessful
Carry flag   = set
AX   = error code

Notes: ■ Application programs should not ordinarily attempt to distinguish between files on local and remote devices.

■ If the network has not been started, control returns to the calling program with the carry flag set and error code 0001H (invalid function) in register AX.

Example: Check if the handle saved in the variable *fhandle* is associated with a file or device on the machine running the program or on a network server.

```
fhandle dw      ?                   ; device handle
        .
        .
        .
        mov     ax,440ah            ; function & subfunction
        mov     bx,fhandle          ; file/device handle
        int     21h                 ; transfer to MS-DOS
        jc      error               ; jump if function failed
        and     dx,8000h            ; test local/remote bit
        jnz     remote              ; jump if network handle
        .
        .
        .
```

Int 21H   [3.1]
Function 44H (68) Subfunction 0BH (11)
IOCTL: change sharing retry count

Sets the number of times MS-DOS retries a disk operation after a failure caused by a file-sharing violation before it returns an error to the requesting process. This subfunction is not available unless the file-sharing module (SHARE.EXE) is loaded.

Call with:
AH	= 44H
AL	= 0BH
CX	= delays per retry (default = 1)
DX	= number of retries (default = 3)

Returns:
If function successful
Carry flag = clear
If function unsuccessful
Carry flag = set
AX = error code

Notes:
- The length of a delay is a machine-dependent value determined by the CPU type and clock speed. Each delay consists of the following instruction sequence:

```
        xor     cx,cx
        loop    $
```

which executes 65,536 times before falling out of the loop.
- The sharing retry count affects the behavior of the system as a whole and is not a local parameter for the process. If a program changes the sharing retry count, it should restore the default values before terminating.

Example: Change the number of automatic retries for a file-sharing violation to five.

```
        .
        .
        .
mov     ax,440bh        ; function & subfunction
mov     cx,1            ; delays per retry
mov     dx,5            ; number of retries
int     21h            ; transfer to MS-DOS
jc      error          ; jump if function failed
        .
        .
        .
```

Int 21H   [3.2]
Function 44H (68) Subfunction 0CH (12)
IOCTL: generic I/O control for character devices

Provides a general-purpose mechanism for communication between application programs and character-device drivers.

Call with: AH   = 44H

                 AL   = 0CH

                 BX   = handle

                 CH   = category (major) code:
                             00H = unknown
                             01H = COM1, COM2, COM3, or COM4 (3.3)
                             03H = CON (keyboard and display) (3.3)
                             05H = LPT1, LPT2, or LPT3 (3.2)

                 CL   = function (minor) code:
                             45H = Set Iteration Count (3.2)
                             4AH = Select Code Page (3.3)
                             4CH = Start Code Page Preparation (3.3)
                             4DH = End Code Page Preparation (3.3)
                             5FH = Set Display Information (4.0)
                             65H = Get Iteration Count (3.2)
                             6AH = Query Selected Code Page (3.3)
                             6BH = Query Prepare List (3.3)
                             7FH = Get Display Information (4.0)

                 DS:DX   = segment:offset of parameter block

Returns: If function successful

                 Carry flag   = clear

                 and, if called with CL = 65H, 6AH, 6BH, or 7FH

                 DS:DX   = segment:offset of parameter block

If function unsuccessful
Carry flag   = set
AX   = error code

Notes:

- If the minor code is 45H (Set Iteration Count) or 65H (Get Iteration Count), the parameter block is simply a 2-byte buffer containing or receiving the iteration count for the printer. This call is valid only for printer drivers that support *Output Until Busy,* and determines the number of times the device driver will wait for the device to signal *ready* before returning from the output call.

- The parameter block for minor code 4DH (End Code Page Preparation) has the following format:

```
dw      2                   ; length of following data
dw      0                   ; (reserved)
```

- For MS-DOS version 3.3, the parameter block for minor codes 4AH (Select Code Page) and 6AH (Query Code Page) has the following format:

```
dw      2                   ; length of following data
dw      ?                   ; code page ID
```

For MS-DOS version 4.0, minor codes 4AH and 6AH also set or get the double-byte character set (DBCS) lead byte table, and the following format is used:

```
dw      (n+2)*2+1           ; length of following data
dw      ?                   ; code page ID
db      start,end           ; DBCS lead byte range 1
.
.
.
db      start,end           ; DBCS lead byte range n
db      0,0
```

- The parameter block for minor code 4CH (Start Code Page Preparation) has the following format:

```
dw      0                   ; font type
                            ; bit 0   = 0 downloaded
                            ;         = 1 cartridge
                            ; bits 1-15 = reserved (0)
dw      (n+1)*2             ; length of remainder of
                            ;   parameter block
dw      n                   ; number of code pages in
                            ;   the following list
dw      ?                   ; code page 1
dw      ?                   ; code page 2
.
.
.
dw      ?                   ; code page n
```

- The parameter block for minor code 6BH (Query Prepare List) has the following format, assuming n hardware code pages and m prepared code pages ($n <= 12$, $m <= 12$):

```
dw       (n+m+2)*2            ; length of following data
dw       n                    ; number of hardware code pages
dw       ?                    ; hardware code page 1
dw       ?                    ; hardware code page 2
  .
  .
  .
dw       ?                    ; hardware code page n
dw       m                    ; number of prepared code pages
dw       ?                    ; prepared code page 1
dw       ?                    ; prepared code page 2
  .
  .
  .
dw       ?                    ; prepared code page m
```

■ After a minor code 4CH (Start Code Page Preparation) call, the data defining the code page font is written to the driver using one or more calls to the IOCTL Write Control Data subfunction (Interrupt 21H, Function 44H, Subfunction 03H). The format of the data is device- and driver-specific. After the font data has been written to the driver, a minor code 4DH (End Code Page Preparation) call must be issued. If no data is written to the driver between the minor code 4CH and 4DH calls, the driver interprets the newly prepared code pages as hardware code pages.

■ A special variation of the minor code 4CH (Start Code Page Preparation) call, called "Refresh," is required to actually load the peripheral device with the prepared code pages. The refresh operation is obtained by requesting minor code 4CH with each code page position in the parameter block set to −1, followed by an immediate call for minor code 4DH (End Code Page Preparation).

■ [4.0+] For minor codes 5FH (Set Display Information) and 7FH (Get Display Information), the parameter block is formatted as follows:

```
db       0                    ; level (0 in MS-DOS 4.0)
db       0                    ; reserved (must be 0)
dw       14                   ; length of following data
dw       ?                    ; control flags
                              ; bit 0     = 0 intensity
                              ;            = 1 blink
                              ; bits 1-15 = reserved (0)
db       ?                    ; mode type (1 = text, 2 = APA)
db       0                    ; reserved (must be 0)
dw       ?                    ; colors
                              ; 0 = monochrome compatible
                              ; 1 = 2 colors
                              ; 2 = 4 colors
                              ; 4 = 16 colors
                              ; 8 = 256 colors
dw       ?                    ; pixel columns
dw       ?                    ; pixel rows
dw       ?                    ; character columns
dw       ?                    ; character rows
```

Example: Get the current code page for the standard list device.

```
stdprn  equ   4                ; standard list handle

pars    dw    2                ; length of data
        dw    ?                ; receives code page
         .
         .
         .
        mov   ax,440ch         ; function & subfunction
        mov   bx,stdprn        ; standard list handle
        mov   ch,5             ; LPTx category
        mov   cl,6ah           ; query code page
        mov   dx,seg pars      ; parameter block address
        mov   ds,dx
        mov   dx,offset pars
        int   21h             ; transfer to MS-DOS
        jc    error           ; jump if function failed
         .
         .
         .
```

Int 21H   [3.2]
Function 44H Subfunction 0DH (13)
IOCTL: generic I/O control for block devices

Provides a general-purpose mechanism for communication between application programs and block-device drivers. Allows a program to inspect or change device parameters for a logical drive and to read, write, format, and verify disk tracks in a hardware-independent manner.

Call with: AH   = 44H
              AL   = 0DH
              BL   = drive code (0 = default, 1 = A, 2 = B, etc.)
              CH   = category (major) code:
                           08H = disk drive
              CL   = function (minor) code:
                           40H = Set Device Parameters
                           41H = Write Track
                           42H = Format and Verify Track
                           47H = Set Access Flag (4.0)
                           60H = Get Device Parameters
                           61H = Read Track
                           62H = Verify Track
                           67H = Get Access Flag (4.0)
              DS:DX   = segment:offset of parameter block

Returns: If function successful
Carry flag   = clear
and, if called with CL = 60H or 61H
DS:DX   = segment:offset of parameter block
If function unsuccessful
Carry flag   = set
AX   = error code

Notes: ■ The minor code 40H (Set Device Parameters) function must be used before an attempt to write, read, format, or verify a track on a logical drive. In general, the
following sequence applies to any of these operations:

   – Get the current parameters (minor code 60H). Examine and save them.
   – Set the new parameters (minor code 40H).
   – Perform the task.
   – Retrieve the original parameters and restore them with minor code 40H.

   ■ For minor codes 40H (Set Device Parameters) and 60H (Get Device Parameters), the
parameter block is formatted as follows:

Special-functions field: offset 00H, length = 1 byte

Bit(s)	Value	Meaning
0	0	device BPB field contains a new default BPB
	1	use current BPB
1	0	use all fields in parameter block
	1	use track layout field only
2	0	sectors in track may be different sizes (*should always be avoided*)
	1	sectors in track are all same size; sector numbers range from 1 to the total number of sectors in the track (*should always be used*)
3–7	0	reserved

Device type field: offset 01H, length 1 byte

Value	Meaning
0	320/360 KB, 5.25-inch disk
1	1.2 MB, 5.25-inch disk
2	720 KB, 3.5-inch disk
3	single-density, 8-inch disk
4	double-density, 8-inch disk
5	fixed disk
6	tape drive
7	other type of block device

Device attributes field: offset 02H, length 1 word

Bit(s)	Value	Meaning
0	0	removable storage medium
	1	nonremovable storage medium
1	0	door lock not supported
	1	door lock supported
2–15	0	reserved

Number of cylinders field: offset 04H, length 1 word
Maximum number of cylinders supported on the block device

Media type field: offset 06H, length 1 byte

Value	Meaning
0	1.2 MB, 5.25-inch disk
1	320/360 KB, 5.25-inch disk

Device BPB field: offset 07H, length 31 bytes
For format of the device BPB, see separate Note below.
If bit 0 = 0 in special-functions field, this field contains the new default BPB for the device.
If bit 0 = 1 in special-functions field, the BPB in this field is returned by the device driver in response to subsequent Build BPB requests.

Track layout field: offset 26H, variable-length table

Length	Meaning
Word	number of sectors in track
Word	number of first sector in track
Word	size of first sector in track
.	
.	
.	
Word	number of last sector in track
Word	size of last sector in track

- The device BPB field is a 31-byte data structure that describes the current disk and its control areas. The field is formatted as follows:

Byte(s)	Meaning
00H–01H	bytes per sector
02H	sectors per cluster (allocation unit)
03–04H	reserved sectors, beginning at sector 0
05H	number of file allocation tables (FATs)
06H–07H	maximum number of root-directory entries
08H–09H	number of sectors
0AH	media descriptor
0BH–0CH	sectors per FAT
0DH–0EH	sectors per track
0FH–10H	number of heads
11H–14H	number of hidden sectors
15H–18H	large number of sectors (if bytes 08H–09H=0)
19H–1EH	reserved

- When minor code 40H (Set Device Parameters) is used, the number of cylinders should not be altered, or some or all of the volume may become inaccessible.

- For minor codes 41H (Write Track) and 61H (Read Track), the parameter block is formatted as follows:

Byte(s)	Meaning
00H	special-functions field (must be 0)
01H–02H	head
03H–04H	cylinder
05H–06H	starting sector
07H–08H	sectors to transfer
09H–0CH	transfer buffer address

- For minor codes 42H (Format and Verify Track) and 62H (Verify Track), the parameter block is formatted as follows:

Byte(s)	Meaning
00H	special-functions field

	Bit(s)	Significance
	0	0 = Format/Verify track
		1 = Format status call (MS-DOS 4.0 only)
	1–7	reserved (0)

Byte(s)	Meaning
01H–02H	head
03H–04H	cylinder

In MS-DOS 4.0, this function may be called with bit 0 of the special-functions field set after a minor code 40H call (Set Device Parameters) to determine whether the driver supports the specified number of tracks and sectors per track. A status is returned in the special-functions field which is interpreted as follows:

Value	Meaning
0	specified number of tracks and sectors per track supported
1	this function not supported by the ROM BIOS
2	specified number of tracks and sectors per track not supported
3	no disk in drive

- For minor codes 47H (Set Access Flag) and 67H (Get Access Flag), the parameter block is formatted as follows:

Byte	Meaning
00H	special-functions field (must be 0)
01H	disk access flag

When the disk access flag is zero, access to the medium is blocked by the driver. The flag is set to zero when the driver detects an unformatted medium or a medium with an invalid boot record. When the access flag is nonzero, read/write operations to the medium are allowed by the driver. A formatting program must clear the disk access flag with minor code 47H before it requests minor code 42H (Format and Verify Track).

Example: Get the device parameter block for disk drive C.

```
dbpb    db      128 dup (0)     ; device parameter block
        .
        .
        .
        mov     ax,440dh        ; function & subfunction
        mov     bl,3            ; drive C = 3
        mov     ch,8            ; disk category
        mov     cl,60h          ; get device parameters
        mov     dx,seg dbpb     ; buffer address
        mov     ds,dx
        mov     dx,offset dbpb
        int     21h             ; transfer to MS-DOS
        jc      error           ; jump if function failed
        .
        .
        .
```

Int 21H
Function 44H (68) Subfunction 0EH (14)
IOCTL: get logical drive map

Returns the logical drive code that was most recently used to access the specified block device.

Call with:	AH	= 44H
	AL	= 0EH
	BL	= drive code (0 = default, 1 = A, 2 = B, etc.)

Returns:	If function successful	
	Carry flag	= clear
	AL	= mapping code
	00H	*if only one logical drive code assigned to the block device*
	01H–1AH	*logical drive code (1 = A, 2 = B, etc.) mapped to the block device*
	If function unsuccessful	
	Carry flag	= set
	AX	= error code

Note:	■ If a drive has not been assigned a logical mapping with Function 44H Subfunction 0FH, the logical and physical drive codes are the same.

Example: Check whether drive A has more than one logical drive code.

```
        .
        .
        .
        mov     ax,440eh      ; function & subfunction
        mov     bl,1          ; drive 1 = A
        int     21h           ; transfer to MS-DOS
        jc      error         ; jump if function failed
        or      al,al         ; test drive code
        jz      label1        ; jump, no drive aliases
        .
        .
        .
```

Function 44H (68) Subfunction 0FH (15)
IOCTL: set logical drive map

Sets the next logical drive code that will be used to reference a block device.

Call with:	AH	= 44H
	AL	= 0FH
	BL	= drive code (0 = default, 1 = A, 2 = B, etc.)

Returns:	If function successful	
	Carry flag	= clear
	AL	= mapping code
	00H	*if only one logical drive code assigned to the block device*
	01H–1AH	*logical drive code (1 = A, 2 = B, etc.) mapped to the block device*
	If function unsuccessful	
	Carry flag	= set
	AX	= error code

Note:
- When a physical block device is aliased to more than one logical drive code, this function can be used to inform the driver which drive code will next be used to access the device.

Example: Notify the floppy-disk driver that the next access will be for logical drive B.

```
        .
        .
        .
        mov     ax,440fh        ; function & subfunction
        mov     bl,2            ; drive 2 = B
        int     21h             ; transfer to MS-DOS
        jc      error           ; jump if function failed
        .
        .
        .
```

Int 21H
Function 45H (69)
Duplicate handle

Given a handle for a currently open device or file, returns a new handle that refers to the same device or file at the same position.

Call with:	AH	= 45H
	BX	= handle to be duplicated

Returns: If function successful
Carry flag = clear
AX = new handle

If function unsuccessful
Carry flag = set
AX = error code

Notes:
- A seek, read, or write operation that moves the file pointer for one of the two handles also moves the file pointer associated with the other.
- This function can be used to efficiently update the directory for a file that has changed in length, without incurring the overhead of closing and then reopening the file. The handle for the file is simply duplicated with this function and the duplicate is closed, leaving the original handle open for further read/write operations.
- [3.3] See also Int 21H Function 68H (Commit File).

Example: Duplicate the handle stored in the variable *fhandle,* then close the duplicate. This ensures that all buffered data is physically written to disk and that the directory entry for the corresponding file is updated, but leaves the original handle open for subsequent file operations.

```
fhandle dw      0               ; file handle
         .
         .
         .
                                ; get duplicate handle
         mov    ah,45h          ; function number
         mov    bx,fhandle      ; original file handle
         int    21h             ; transfer to MS-DOS
         jc     error           ; jump if dup failed
                                ; now close dup'd handle
         mov    bx,ax           ; put handle into BX
         mov    ah,3eh          ; function number
         int    21h             ; transfer to MS-DOS
```

(continued)

```
                    jc      error           ; jump if close failed
                    .
                    .
                    .
```

Int 21H
Function 46H (70)
Redirect handle

[2.0]

Given two handles, makes the second handle refer to the same device or file at the same location as the first handle. The second handle is then said to be redirected.

Call with:	AH	= 46H
	BX	= handle for file or device
	CX	= handle to be redirected

Returns: If function successful
Carry flag = clear
If function unsuccessful
Carry flag = set
AX = error code

Notes:
- If the handle passed in CX already refers to an open file, that file is closed first.
- A seek, read, or write operation that moves the file pointer for one of the two handles also moves the file pointer associated with the other.
- This function is commonly used to redirect the standard input and output handles to another file or device before a child process is executed with Int 21H Function 4BH.

Example: Redirect the standard output to the list device, so that all output directed to the console will appear on the printer instead. Later, restore the original meaning of the standard output handle.

```
stdin    equ     0
stdout   equ     1
stderr   equ     2
stdaux   equ     3
stdprn   equ     4

dhandle dw       0               ; duplicate handle
         .
         .
         .
```

```
                                   ; get dup of stdout
          mov     ah,45h           ; function number
          mov     bx,stdout        ; standard output handle
          int     21h              ; transfer to MS-DOS
          jc      error            ; jump if dup failed
          mov     dhandle,ax       ; save dup'd handle
                                   ;
                                   ; redirect standard output
                                   ; to standard list device
          mov     ah,46h           ; function number
          mov     bx,stdprn        ; standard list handle
          mov     cx,stdout        ; standard output handle
          int     21h              ; transfer to MS-DOS
          jc      error            ; jump if redirect failed
          .
          .
          .
                                   ; restore standard output
                                   ; to original meaning
          mov     ah,46h           ; function number
          mov     bx,dhandle       ; saved duplicate handle
          mov     cx,stdout        ; standard output handle
          int     21h              ; transfer to MS-DOS
          jc      error            ; jump if redirect failed
                                   ; close duplicate handle
                                   ; because no longer needed
          mov     ah,3eh           ; function number
          mov     bx,dhandle       ; saved duplicate handle
          int     21h              ; transfer to MS-DOS
          jc      error            ; jump if close failed
          .
          .
          .
```

Int 21H
Function 47H (71)
Get current directory

[2.0]

Obtains an ASCIIZ string that describes the path from the root to the current directory, and the name of that directory.

Call with:

AH	= 47H	
DL	= drive code (0 = default, 1 = A, etc.)	
DS:SI	= segment:offset of 64-byte buffer	

Returns: If function successful
Carry flag   = clear

and buffer is filled in with full pathname from root of current directory.

If function unsuccessful
Carry flag   = set
AX   = error code

Notes:
- The returned path name does not include the drive identifier or a leading backslash (\). It is terminated with a null (00H) byte. Consequently, if the current directory is the root directory, the first byte in the buffer will contain 00H.
- The function fails if the drive code is invalid.
- The current directory may be set with Int 21H Function 3BH.

Example: Get the name of the current directory for drive C into the buffer named *dbuff*.

```
dbuff   db      64 dup (0)      ; receives path string
        .
        .
        .
        mov     ah,47h          ; function number
        mov     dl,03           ; drive C = 3
        mov     si,seg dbuff    ; buffer address
        mov     ds,si
        mov     si,offset dbuff
        int     21h             ; transfer to MS-DOS
        jc      error           ; jump if error
        .
        .
        .
```

Int 21H   [2.0]
Function 48H (72)
Allocate memory block

Allocates a block of memory and returns a pointer to the beginning of the allocated area.

Call with: AH   = 48H
BX   = number of paragraphs of memory needed

Returns: If function successful
Carry flag   = clear
AX   = base segment address of allocated block

If function unsuccessful
Carry flag   = set
AX   = error code
BX   = size of largest available block (paragraphs)

Notes:
- If the function succeeds, the base address of the newly allocated block is AX:0000.
- The default allocation strategy used by MS-DOS is "first fit"; that is, the memory block at the lowest address that is large enough to satisfy the request is allocated. The allocation strategy can be altered with Int 21H Function 58H.
- When a .COM program is loaded, it ordinarily already "owns" all of the memory in the transient program area, leaving none for dynamic allocation. The amount of memory initially allocated to a .EXE program at load time depends on the MINALLOC and MAXALLOC fields in the .EXE file header. See Int 21H Function 4AH.

Example: Request a 64 KB block of memory for use as a buffer.

```
bufseg  dw      ?               ; segment base of new block
        .
        .
        .
        mov     ah,48h          ; function number
        mov     bx,1000h        ; block size (paragraphs)
        int     21h             ; transfer to MS-DOS
        jc      error           ; jump if allocation failed
        mov     bufseg,ax       ; save segment of new block
        .
        .
        .
```

Int 21H   [2.0]
Function 49H (73)
Release memory block

Releases a memory block and makes it available for use by other programs.

Call with: AH   = 49H
                 ES   = segment of block to be released

Returns: If function successful
               Carry flag   = clear
               If function unsuccessful
               Carry flag   = set
               AX   = error code

Notes:
- This function assumes that the memory block being released was previously obtained by a successful call to Int 21H Function 48H.
- The function will fail or can cause unpredictable system errors if:
  - the program releases a memory block that does not belong to it.
  - the segment address passed in register ES is not a valid base address for an existing memory block.

Example: Release the memory block that was previously allocated in the example for Int 21H Function 48H (page 438).

```
bufseg  dw      ?                       ; segment base of block
        .
        .
        .
        mov     ah,49h                  ; function number
        mov     es,bufseg               ; base segment of block
        int     21h                     ; transfer to MS-DOS
        jc      error                   ; jump if release failed
        .
        .
```

Int 21H [2.0]
Function 4AH (74)
Resize memory block

Dynamically shrinks or extends a memory block, according to the needs of an application program.

Call with:
AH	= 4AH
BX	= desired new block size in paragraphs
ES	= segment of block to be modified

Returns:

If function successful
Carry flag	= clear

If function unsuccessful
Carry flag	= set
AX	= error code
BX	= maximum block size available (paragraphs)

Notes:
- This function modifies the size of a memory block that was previously allocated with a call to Int 21H Function 48H.
- If the program is requesting an increase in the size of an allocated block, and this function fails, the maximum possible size for the specified block is returned in register BX. The program can use this value to determine whether it should terminate, or continue in a degraded fashion with less memory.

- A program that uses EXEC (Int 21H Function 4BH) to load and execute a child program must call this function first to make memory available for the child, passing the address of its PSP in register ES and the amount of memory needed for its own code, data, and stacks in register BX.

Example: Resize the memory block that was allocated in the example for Int 21H Function 48H (page 438), shrinking it to 32 KB.

```
bufseg  dw      ?                       ; segment base of block
        .
        .
        .
        mov     ah,4ah                  ; function number
        mov     bx,0800h                ; new size (paragraphs)
        mov     es,bufseg               ; segment base of block
        int     21h                     ; transfer to MS-DOS
        jc      error                   ; jump, resize failed
        .
        .
        .
```

Int 21H
Function 4BH (75)
Execute program (EXEC)

[2.0]

Allows an application program to run another program, regaining control when it is finished. Can also be used to load overlays, although this use is uncommon.

Call with: AH   = 4BH
                  AL   = subfunction
                          00H = Load and Execute Program
                          03H = Load Overlay
                  ES:BX = segment:offset of parameter block
                  DS:DX = segment:offset of ASCIIZ program pathname

---

Returns: If function successful
               Carry flag   = clear
               [2]   all registers except for CS:IP may be destroyed
               [3.0+]   registers are preserved in the usual fashion
               If function unsuccessful
               Carry flag   = set
               AX   = error code

Notes:

- The parameter block format for Subfunction 00H (Load and Execute Program) is as follows:

Bytes	*Contents*
00H–01H	segment pointer to environment block
02H–03H	offset of command line tail
04H–05H	segment of command line tail
06H–07H	offset of first FCB to be copied into new PSP + 5CH
08H–09H	segment of first FCB
0AH–0BH	offset of second FCB to be copied into new PSP + 6CH
0CH–0DH	segment of second FCB

- The parameter block format for Subfunction 03H (Load Overlay) is as follows:

Bytes	*Contents*
00H–01H	segment address where overlay is to be loaded
02H–03H	relocation factor to apply to loaded image

- The environment block must be paragraph-aligned. It consists of a sequence of ASCIIZ strings in the form:

```
db      'COMSPEC=A:\COMMAND.COM',0
```

  The entire set of strings is terminated by an extra null (00H) byte.

- The command tail format consists of a count byte, followed by an ASCII string, terminated by a carriage return (which is not included in the count). The first character in the string should be an ASCII space (20H) for compatibility with the command tail passed to programs by COMMAND.COM. For example:

```
db      6,' *.DAT',0dh
```

- Before a program uses Int 21H Function 4BH to run another program, it must release all memory it is not actually using with a call to Int 21H Function 4AH, passing the segment address of its own PSP and the number of paragraphs to retain.

- Ordinarily, all active handles of the parent program are inherited by the child program, although the parent can prevent this in MS-DOS 3.0 and later by setting the inheritance bit when the file or device is opened. Any redirection of the standard input and/or output in the parent process also affects the child process.

- The environment block can be used to pass information to the child process. If the environment block pointer in the parameter block is zero, the child program inherits an exact copy of the parent's environment. In any case, the segment address of the child's environment is found at offset 002CH in the child's PSP.

- After return from the EXEC function call, the termination type and return code of the child program may be obtained with Int 21H Function 4DH.

Example: See Chapter 12.

Terminates the current process, passing a return code to the parent process. This is one of several methods that a program can use to perform a final exit. MS-DOS then takes the following actions:

- All memory belonging to the process is released.
- File buffers are flushed and any open handles for files or devices owned by the process are closed.
- The termination handler vector (Int 22H) is restored from PSP:000AH.
- The Ctrl-C handler vector (Int 23H) is restored from PSP:000EH.
- [2.0+] The critical-error handler vector (Int 24H) is restored from PSP:0012H.
- Control is transferred to the termination handler.

If the program is returning to COMMAND.COM, control transfers to the resident portion and the transient portion is reloaded if necessary. If a batch file is in progress, the next line of the file is fetched and interpreted; otherwise, a prompt is issued for the next user command.

| **Call with:** | AH | = 4CH |
| | AL | = return code |

| **Returns:** | Nothing |

Notes:
- [2.0+] This is the preferred method of termination for application programs because it allows a return code to be passed to the parent program and does not rely on the contents of any segment register. Other methods of performing a final exit are:
  - Int 20H
  - Int 21H Function 00H
  - Int 21H Function 31H
  - Int 27H
- Any files that have been opened using FCBs and modified by the program should be closed before program termination; otherwise, data may be lost.
- The return code can be retrieved by the parent process with Int 21H Function 4DH (Get Return Code). It can also be tested in a batch file with an IF ERRORLEVEL statement. By convention, a return code of zero indicates successful execution, and a non-zero return code indicates an error.
- [3.0+] If the program is running on a network, it should remove all locks it has placed on file regions before terminating.

Terminate the current process, passing a return code of 1 to the parent process.

```
        .
        .
        .
mov     ah,4ch          ; function number
mov     al,01h          ; return code
int     21h             ; transfer to MS-DOS
```

Int 21H
Function 4DH (77)
Get return code

[2.0]

Used by a parent process, after the successful execution of an EXEC call (Int 21H Function 4BH), to obtain the return code and termination type of a child process.

Call with:	AH	= 4DH

Returns:	AH	= exit type
		00H if normal termination by Int 20H, Int 21H Function 00H, or Int 21H Function 4CH
		01H if termination by user's entry of CtrlDC
		02H if termination by critical-error handler
		03H if termination by Int 21H Function 31H or Int 27H
	AL	= return code passed by child process (0 if child terminated by Int 20H, Int 21H Function 00H, or Int 27H)

Notes:

■ This function will yield the return code of a child process only once. A subsequent call without an intervening EXEC (Int 21H Function 4BH) will not necessarily return any valid information.

■ This function does not set the carry flag to indicate an error. If no previous child process has been executed, the values returned in AL and AH are undefined.

Example:

Get the return code and termination kind of child process that was previously executed with Int 21H Function 4BH (EXEC).

```
retcode dw      ?               ; return code, termination type
        .
        .
        .
mov     ah,4dh          ; function number
int     21h             ; transfer to MS-DOS
mov     retcode,ax      ; save child process info
        .
        .
        .
```

Int 21H
Function 4EH (78)
Find first file

Given a file specification in the form of an ASCIIZ string, searches the default or specified directory on the default or specified drive for the first matching file.

Call with: AH = 4EH

CX = search attribute (bits may be combined)

Bit(s)	Significance (if set)
0	read-only
1	hidden
2	system
3	volume label
4	directory
5	archive
6–15	reserved (0)

DS:DX = segment:offset of ASCIIZ pathname

Returns: If function successful (matching file found)

Carry flag = clear

and search results returned in current disk transfer area as follows:

Byte(s)	Description
00H–14H	reserved (0)
15H	attribute of matched file or directory
16H–17H	file time
	bits 00H–04H = 2-second increments (0–29)
	bits 05H–0AH = minutes (0–59)
	bits 0BH–0FH = hours (0–23)
18H–19H	file date
	bits 00H–04H = day (1–31)
	bits 05H–08H = month (1–12)
	bits 09H–0FH = year (relative to 1980)
1AH–1DH	file size
1EH–2AH	ASCIIZ filename and extension

If function unsuccessful (no matching files)

Carry flag = set

AX = error code

Notes:
- This function assumes that the DTA has been previously set by the program with Int 21H Function 1AH to point to a buffer of adequate size.
- The * and ? wildcard characters are allowed in the filename. If wildcard characters are present, this function returns only the first matching filename.

- If the attribute is 0, only ordinary files are found. If the volume label attribute bit is set, only volume labels will be returned (if any are present). Any other attribute or combination of attributes (hidden, system, and directory) results in those files *and* all normal files being matched.

Example: Find the first .COM file in the directory \MYDIR on drive C.

```
fname    db       'C:\MYDIR\*.COM',0

dbuff    db       43 dup (0)     ; receives search results
         .
         .
         .
                                 ; set DTA address
         mov      ah,1ah         ; function number
         mov      dx,seg dbuff   ; result buffer address
         mov      ds,dx
         mov      dx,offset dbuff
         int      21h            ; transfer to MS-DOS

                                 ; search for first match
         mov      ah,4eh         ; function number
         mov      cx,0           ; normal attribute
         mov      dx,seg fname   ; address of filename
         mov      ds,dx
         mov      dx,offset fname
         int      21h            ; transfer to MS-DOS
         jc       error          ; jump if no match
         .
         .
         .
```

Int 21H
Function 4FH (79)
Find next file

[2.0]

Assuming a previous successful call to Int 21H Function 4EH, finds the next file in the default or specified directory on the default or specified drive that matches the original file specification.

Call with: AH   = 4FH

Assumes DTA points to working buffer used by previous successful Int 21H Function 4EH or 4FH.

Returns: If function successful (matching file found)

Carry flag   = clear

and search results returned in current disk transfer area as described for Int 21H Function 4EH

If function unsuccessful (no more matching files)

Carry flag = set
AX   = error code

Notes:
- Use of this call assumes that the original file specification passed to Int 21H Function 4EH contained one or more ∗ or ? wildcard characters.
- When this function is called, the current disk transfer area (DTA) must contain information from a previous successful call to Int 21H Function 4EH or 4FH.

Example: Continuing the search operation in the example for Int 21H Function 4EH, find the next .COM file (if any) in the directory \MYDIR on drive C.

```
fname   db      'C:\MYDIR\*.COM',0

dbuff   db      43 dup (0)      ; receives search results
        .
        .
        .
                                ; search for next match
        mov     ah,4fh          ; function number
        int     21h             ; transfer to MS-DOS
        jc      error           ; jump if no more files
        .
        .
        .
```

Int 21H
Function 50H (80)
Reserved

Int 21H
Function 51H (81)
Reserved

Int 21H
Function 52H (82)
Reserved

Int 21H
Function 53H (83)
Reserved

Int 21H
Function 54H (84)
Get verify flag

[2.0]

Obtains the current value of the system verify (read-after-write) flag.

Call with: AH   = 54H

Returns: AL   = current verify flag value
00H if verify off
01H if verify on

Notes:
- Because read-after-write verification slows disk operations, the default state of the system verify flag is OFF.
- The state of the system verify flag can be changed through a call to Int 21H Function 2EH or by the MS-DOS commands VERIFY ON and VERIFY OFF.

Example: Obtain the state of the system verify flag.

```
        .
        .

        mov     ah,54h          ; function number
        int     21h             ; transfer to MS-DOS
        cmp     al,01h          ; check verify state
        je      label1          ; jump if verify on
                                ; else assume verify off
        .
        .
        .
```

Int 21H
Function 55H (85)
Reserved

Renames a file and/or moves its directory entry to a different directory on the same disk. In MS-DOS version 3.0 and later, this function can also be used to rename directories.

Call with:

AH	= 56H	
DS:DX	= segment:offset of current ASCIIZ pathname	
ES:DI	= segment:offset of new ASCIIZ pathname	

Returns:

If function successful

Carry flag = clear

If function unsuccessful

Carry flag = set

AX = error code

Notes:

- The function fails if:
  - any element of the pathname does not exist.
  - a file with the new pathname already exists.
  - the current pathname specification contains a different disk drive than does the new pathname.
  - the file is being moved to the root directory, and the root directory is full.
  - [3.0+] the program is running on a network and the user has insufficient access rights to either the existing file or the new directory.
- The * and ? wildcard characters are not allowed in either the current or new pathname specifications.

Example:

Change the name of the file MYFILE.DAT in the directory \MYDIR on drive C to MYTEXT.DAT. At the same time, move the file to the directory \SYSTEM on the same drive.

```
oldname  db      'C:\MYDIR\MYFILE.DAT',0

newname  db      'C:\SYSTEM\MYTEXT.DAT',0
         .
         .
         .
         mov     ah,56h          ; function number
         mov     dx,seg oldname  ; old filename address
         mov     ds,dx
         mov     dx,offset oldname
         mov     di,seg newname  ; new filename address
         mov     es,di
         mov     di,offset newname
```

(continued)

```
        int     21h            ; transfer to MS-DOS
        jc      error          ; jump if rename failed
        .
        .
        .
```

Int 21H
Function 57H (87)
Get or set file date and time

Obtains or modifies the date and time stamp in a file's directory entry.

Call with: If getting date and time
    AH   = 57H
    AL   = 00H
    BX   = handle

If setting date and time
    AH   = 57H
    AL   = 01H
    BX   = handle
    CX   = time
          bits 00H–04H = 2-second increments (0–29)
          bits 05H–0AH = minutes (0–59)
          bits 0BH–0FH = hours (0–23)
    DX   = date
          bits 00H–04H = day (1–31)
          bits 05H–08H = month (1–12)
          bits 09H–0FH = year (relative to 1980)

Returns: If function successful
    Carry flag   = clear

and, if called with AL = 00H
    CX   = time
    DX   = date

If function unsuccessful
    Carry flag   = set
    AX   = error code

Notes:
- The file must have been previously opened or created via a successful call to Int 21H Function 3CH, 3DH, 5AH, 5BH, or 6CH.
- If the 16-bit date for a file is set to zero, that file's date and time are not displayed on directory listings.
- A date and time set with this function will prevail, even if the file is modified afterwards before the handle is closed.

Example: Get the date that the file MYFILE.DAT was created or last modified, and then decompose the packed date into its constituent parts in the variables *month, day,* and *year*.

```
fname   db      'MYFILE.DAT',0

month   dw      0
day     dw      0
year    dw      0
        .
        .
        .
                                ; first open the file
        mov     ah,3dh          ; function number
        mov     al,0            ; read-only mode
        mov     dx,seg fname    ; filename address
        mov     ds,dx
        mov     dx,offset fname
        int     21h             ; transfer to MS-DOS
        jc      error           ; jump if open failed

                                ; get file date/time
        mov     bx,ax           ; copy handle to BX
        mov     ah,57h          ; function number
        mov     al,0            ; 0 = get subfunction
        int     21h             ; transfer to MS-DOS
        jc      error           ; jump if function failed

        mov     day,dx          ; decompose date
        and     day,01fh        ; isolate day
        mov     cl,5
        shr     dx,cl
        mov     month,dx        ; isolate month
        and     month,0fh
        mov     cl,4
        shr     dx,cl           ; isolate year
        and     dx,03fh         ; relative to 1980
        add     dx,1980         ; correct to real year
        mov     year,dx         ; save year

                                ; now close file,
                                ; handle still in BX
        mov     ah,3eh          ; function number
        int     21h             ; transfer to MS-DOS
        jc      error           ; jump if close failed
        .
        .
        .
```

Int 21H
Function 58H (88)
Get or set allocation strategy

Obtains or changes the code indicating the current MS-DOS strategy for allocating memory blocks.

Call with: If getting strategy code
         AH   = 58H
         AL   = 00H

         If setting strategy code
         AH   = 58H
         AL   = 01H
         BX   = desired strategy code
               00H   = *first fit*
               01H   = *best fit*
               02H   = *last fit*

Returns: If function successful
         Carry flag   = clear

         and, if called with AL = 00H
         AX   = current strategy code

         If function unsuccessful
         Carry flag   = set
         AX   = error code

Notes:
- The memory allocation strategies are:
  - First fit: MS-DOS searches the available memory blocks from low addresses to high addresses, assigning the first one large enough to satisfy the block allocation request.
  - Best fit: MS-DOS searches all available memory blocks and assigns the smallest available block that will satisfy the request, regardless of its position.
  - Last fit: MS-DOS searches the available memory blocks from high addresses to low addresses, assigning the highest one large enough to satisfy the block allocation request.
- The default MS-DOS memory allocation strategy is First Fit (code 0).

Example: Save the code indicating the current memory allocation strategy in the variable *strat*, then change the system's memory allocation strategy to "best fit."

```
strat   dw      0                    ; previous strategy code
        .
        .
        .
```

```
                                   ; get current strategy
        mov     ah,58h             ; function number
        mov     al,0               ; 0 = get strategy
        int     21h                ; transfer to MS-DOS
        jc      error              ; jump if function failed
        mov     strat,ax           ; save strategy code

                                   ; now set new strategy
        mov     ah,58h             ; function number
        mov     al,1               ; 1 = set strategy
        mov     bx,1               ; 1 = best fit
        int     21h                ; transfer to MS-DOS
        jc      error              ; jump if function failed
        .
        .
        .
```

Int 21H
Function 59H (89)
Get extended error information

[3.0]

Obtains detailed error information after a previous unsuccessful Int 21H function call, including the recommended remedial action.

| **Call with:** | AH | = 59H |
| | BX | = 00H |

Returns:	AX	= extended error code
		01H	*function number invalid*
		02H	*file not found*
		03H	*path not found*
		04H	*too many open files*
		05H	*access denied*
		06H	*handle invalid*
		07H	*memory control blocks destroyed*
		08H	*insufficient memory*
		09H	*memory block address invalid*
		0AH (10)	*environment Invalid*
		0BH (11)	*format invalid*
		0CH (12)	*access code invalid*
		0DH (13)	*data invalid*
		0EH (14)	*unknown unit*
		0FH (15)	*disk drive invalid*
		10H (16)	*attempted to remove current directory*
		11H (17)	*not same device*

12H (18)	*no more files*
13H (19)	*disk write-protected*
14H (20)	*unknown unit*
15H (21)	*drive not ready*
16H (22)	*unknown command*
17H (23)	*data error (CRC)*
18H (24)	*bad request structure length*
19H (25)	*seek error*
1AH (26)	*unknown media type*
1BH (27)	*sector not found*
1CH (28)	*printer out of paper*
1DH (29)	*write fault*
1EH (30)	*read fault*
1FH (31)	*general failure*
20H (32)	*sharing violation*
21H (33)	*lock violation*
22H (34)	*disk change invalid*
23H (35)	*FCB unavailable*
24H (36)	*sharing buffer exceeded*
25H–31H	*reserved*
32H (50)	*unsupported network request*
33H (51)	*remote machine not listening*
34H (52)	*duplicate name on network*
35H (53)	*network name not found*
36H (54)	*network busy*
37H (55)	*device no longer exists on network*
38H (56)	*netBIOS command limit exceeded*
39H (57)	*error in network adapter hardware*
3AH (58)	*incorrect response from network*
3BH (59)	*unexpected network error*
3CH (60)	*remote adapter incompatible*
3DH (61)	*print queue full*
3EH (62)	*not enough space for print file*
3FH (63)	*print file canceled*
40H (64)	*network name deleted*
41H (65)	*network access denied*
42H (66)	*incorrect network device type*
43H (67)	*network name not found*
44H (68)	*network name limit exceeded*
45H (69)	*netBIOS session limit exceeded*
46H (70)	*file sharing temporarily paused*
47H (71)	*network request not accepted*
48H (72)	*print or disk redirection paused*
49H–4FH	*reserved*
50H (80)	*file already exists*
51H (81)	*reserved*
52H (82)	*cannot make directory*
53H (83)	*fail on Int 24H (critical error)*

	54H (84)	*too many redirections*
	55H (85)	*duplicate redirection*
	56H (86)	*invalid password*
	57H (87)	*invalid parameter*
	58H (88)	*network device fault*
	59H (89)	*function not supported by network*
	5AH (90)	*required system component not installed*
BH	= error class	
	01H	*if out of resource (such as storage or handles)*
	02H	*if not error, but temporary situation (such as locked region in file) that can be expected to end*
	03H	*if authorization problem*
	04H	*if internal error in system software*
	05H	*if hardware failure*
	06H	*if system software failure not the fault of the active process (such as missing configuration files)*
	07H	*if application program error*
	08H	*if file or item not found*
	09H	*if file or item of invalid type or format*
	0AH (10)	*if file or item locked*
	0BH (11)	*if wrong disk in drive, bad spot on disk, or storage medium problem*
	0CH (12)	*if item already exists*
	0DH (13)	*unknown error*
BL	= recommended action	
	01H	*retry reasonable number of times, then prompt user to select abort or ignore*
	02H	*retry reasonable number of times with delay between retries, then prompt user to select abort or ignore*
	03H	*get corrected information from user (typically caused by incorrect filename or drive specification)*
	04H	*abort application with cleanup (i.e., terminate the program in as orderly a manner as possible: releasing locks, closing files, etc.)*
	05H	*perform immediate exit without cleanup*
	06H	*ignore error*
	07H	*retry after user intervention to remove cause of error*
CH	= error locus	
	01H	*unknown*
	02H	*block device (disk or disk emulator)*
	03H	*network*
	04H	*serial device*
	05H	*memory*

and, for MS-DOS 3.0 and later,

ES:DI	= ASCIIZ volume label of disk to insert, if AX = 0022H (invalid disk change)

- This function may be called after any other Int 21H function call that returned an error status, in order to obtain more detailed information about the error type and the recommended action. If the previous Int 21H function call had no error, 0000H is returned in register AX. This function may also be called during the execution of a critical-error (Int 24H) handler.

- The contents of registers CL, DX, SI, DI, BP, DS, and ES are destroyed by this function.

- Note that extended error codes 13H–1FH (19–31) and 34 (22H) correspond exactly to the error codes 0–0CH (0–12) and 0FH (15) returned by Int 24H.

- You should not code your programs to recognize only specific error numbers if you wish to ensure upward compatibility, because new error codes are added in each version of MS-DOS.

Example: Attempt to open the file named NOSUCH.DAT using a file control block; if the open request fails, get the extended error code.

```
myfcb   db      0                   ; drive = default
        db      'NOSUCH  '          ; filename, 8 chars
        db      'DAT'               ; extension, 3 chars
        db      25 dup (0)          ; remainder of FCB
        .
        .
        .

label1:                             ; open the file
        mov     ah,0fh              ; function number
        mov     dx,seg myfcb        ; address of FCB
        mov     ds,dx
        mov     dx,offset myfcb
        int     21h                 ; transfer to MS-DOS
        or      al,al               ; check open status
        jz      success             ; jump if opened OK

                                    ; open failed, get
                                    ; extended error info
        mov     ah,59h              ; function number
        xor     bx,bx               ; BX must = 0
        int     21h                 ; transfer to MS-DOS
        or      ax,ax               ; double check for error
        jz      success             ; jump if no error

        cmp     bl,2                ; should we retry?
        jle     label1              ; yes, jump
        jmp     error               ; no, give up
        .
        .
        .
```

Int 21H
Function 5AH (90)
Create temporary file

Creates a file with a unique name, in the current or specified directory on the default or specified disk drive, and returns a handle that can be used by the program for subsequent access to the file. The name generated for the file is also returned in a buffer specified by the program.

Call with:

AH	= 5AH
CX	= attribute (bits may be combined)

Bit(s)	Significance (if set)
0	read-only
1	hidden
2	system
3–4	reserved (0)
5	archive
6–15	reserved (0)

DS:DX	= segment:offset of ASCIIZ path

Returns:

If function successful

Carry flag	= clear
AX	= handle
DS:DX	= segment:offset of complete ASCIIZ pathname

If function unsuccessful

Carry flag	= set
AX	= error code

Notes:

- The ASCIIZ path supplied to this function should be followed by at least 13 additional bytes of buffer space. MS-DOS adds a backslash (\) to the supplied path, if necessary, then appends a null-terminated filename that is a function of the current time.

- Files created with this function are not automatically deleted when the calling program terminates.

- The function fails if
  - any element of the pathname does not exist.
  - the file is being created in the root directory, and the root directory is full.

- See also Int 21H Functions 3CH, 5BH, and 6CH, which provide additional facilities for creating files.

- [3.0+] If the program is running on a network, the file is created and opened for read/write access in compatibility sharing mode.

Create a temporary file with a unique name and normal attribute in directory \TEMP of drive C. Note that you must allow room for MS-DOS to append the generated filename to the supplied path. The complete file specification should be used to delete the temporary file before your program terminates.

```
fname    db      'C:\TEMP\'       ; pathname for temp file
         db      13 dup (0)       ; receives filename

fhandle dw      ?                 ; file handle
         .
         .
         .
         mov     ah,5ah           ; function number
         mov     cx,0             ; normal attribute
         mov     dx,seg fname     ; address of pathname
         mov     ds,dx
         mov     dx,offset fname
         int     21h              ; transfer to MS-DOS
         jc      error            ; jump if create failed
         mov     fhandle,ax       ; save file handle
         .
         .
         .
```

Int 21H
Function 5BH (91)
Create new file

[3.0]

Given an ASCIIZ pathname, creates a file in the designated or default directory on the designated or default drive, and returns a handle that can be used by the program for subsequent access to the file. If a file with the same name already exists, the function fails.

Call with:

AH	= 5BH	
CX	= attribute (bits may be combined)	

Bit(s)	Significance (if set)
0	read-only
1	hidden
2	system
3	volume label
4	reserved (0)
5	archive
6–15	reserved (0)

DS:DX	= segment:offset of ASCIIZ pathname

Returns: If function successful
Carry flag   = clear
AX   = handle

If function unsuccessful
Carry flag   = set
AX   = error code

Notes:
- The function fails if:
  - any element of the specified path does not exist.
  - a file with the identical pathname (i.e., the same filename and extension in the same location in the directory structure) already exists.
  - the file is being created in the root directory, and the root directory is full.
  - [3.0+] the program is running on a network, and the user has insufficient access rights to the directory that will contain the file.
- The file is usually given a normal attribute (0) when it is created, and is opened for both read and write operations. The attribute can subsequently be modified with Int 21H Function 43H.
- See also Int 21H Functions 3CH, 5AH, and 6CH, which provide alternative ways of creating files.
- This function may be used to implement semaphores in a network or multitasking environment. If the function succeeds, the program has acquired the semaphore. To release the semaphore, the program simply deletes the file.

Example: Create and open a file named MYFILE.DAT in the directory \MYDIR on drive C; MS-DOS returns an error if a file with the same name already exists in that location.

```
fname    db      'C:\MYDIR\MYFILE.DAT',0

fhandle dw       ?                ; file handle
         .
         .
         .
         mov     ah,5bh           ; function number
         xor     cx,cx            ; normal attribute
         mov     dx,seg fname     ; filename address
         mov     ds,dx
         mov     dx,offset fname
         int     21h              ; transfer to MS-DOS
         jc      error            ; jump if create failed
         mov     fhandle,ax       ; save file handle
         .
         .
         .
```

Int 21H
Function 5CH (92)
Lock or unlock file region

Locks or unlocks the specified region of a file. This function is not available unless the file-sharing module (SHARE.EXE) is loaded.

Call with:	AH	= 5CH	
	AL	= 00H	if locking region
		01H	if unlocking region
	BX	= handle	
	CX	= high part of region offset	
	DX	= low part of region offset	
	SI	= high part of region length	
	DI	= low part of region length	

Returns: If function successful
Carry flag   = clear

If function unsuccessful
Carry flag   = set
AX   = error code

Notes:
- This function is useful for file and record synchronization in a multitasking environment or network. Access to the file as a whole is controlled by the attribute and file-sharing parameters passed in open or create calls and by the file's attributes, which are stored in its directory entry.

- The beginning location in the file to be locked or unlocked is supplied as a positive double precision integer, which is a byte offset into the file. The length of the region to be locked or unlocked is similarly supplied as a positive double precision integer.

- For every call to lock a region of a file, there must be a subsequent unlock call with exactly the same file offset and length.

- Locking beyond the current end of file is not an error.

- Duplicate handles created with Int 21H Function 45H, or handles redirected to the file with Int 21H Function 46H, are allowed access to locked regions within the same process.

- Programs that are loaded with the EXEC call (Int 21H Function 4BH) inherit the handles of their parent but not any active locks.

- If a process terminates without releasing active locks on a file, the result is undefined. Therefore, programs using this function should install their own Int 23H and Int 24H handlers so that they cannot be terminated unexpectedly.

Example: Assume that a file was previously opened and that its handle was saved in the variable *fhandle*. Lock a 4096 byte region of the file, starting at 32,768 bytes from the beginning of the file, so that it cannot be accessed by other programs.

```
fhandle dw      ?                   ; file handle
        .
        .
        .
        mov     ah,5ch              ; function number
        mov     al,0                ; subfunction 0 = lock
        mov     bx,fhandle          ; file handle
        mov     cx,0                ; upper part of offset
        mov     dx,32768            ; lower part of offset
        mov     si,0                ; upper part of length
        mov     di,4096             ; lower part of length
        int     21h                 ; transfer to MS-DOS
        jc      error               ; jump if lock failed
        .
        .
        .
```

Int 21H
Function 5DH (93)
Reserved

Int 21H   [3.1]
Function 5EH (94) Subfunction 00H
Get machine name

Returns the address of an ASCIIZ (null-terminated) string identifying the local computer. This function call is only available when Microsoft Networks is running.

Call with:	AH	= 5EH
	AL	= 00H
	DS:DX	= segment:offset of buffer to receive string

Returns:	If function successful	
	Carry flag	= clear
	CH	= 00H	if name not defined
		<> 00H	if name defined
	CL	= netBIOS name number (if CH <> 0)
	DX:DX	= segment:offset of identifier (if CH <> 0)

If function unsuccessful
Carry flag   = set
AX   = error code

Notes:
- The computer identifier is a 15-byte string, padded with spaces and terminated with a null (00H) byte.
- The effect of this call is unpredictable if the file-sharing support module is not loaded.

Example: Get the machine name of the local computer into the buffer named *mname*.

```
mname   db      16 dup (?)
        .
        .
        .
        mov     ax,5e00h        ; function & subfunction
        mov     dx,seg mname    ; address of buffer
        mov     ds,dx
        mov     dx,offset mname
        int     21h             ; transfer to MS-DOS
        jc      error           ; jump if function failed

        or      ch,ch           ; make sure name exists
        jz      error           ; jump if no name defined
        .
        .
        .
```

Int 21H   [3.1]
Function 5EH (94) Subfunction 02H
Set printer setup string

Specifies a string to be sent in front of all files directed to a particular network printer, allowing users at different network nodes to specify individualized operating modes on the same printer. This function call is only available when Microsoft Networks is running.

Call with: AH   = 5EH
              AL   = 02H
              BX   = redirection list index
              CX   = length of setup string
              DS:SI   = segment:offset of setup string

Returns: If function successful
              Carry flag   = clear

If function unsuccessful

Carry flag   = set

AX   = error code

Notes:
- The redirection list index passed in register BX is obtained with Function 5FH Subfunction 02H (Get Redirection List Entry).
- See also Function 5EH Subfunction 03H, which may be used to obtain the existing setup string for a particular network printer.

Example: Initialize the setup string for the printer designated by redirection list index 2 so that the device is put into boldface mode before printing a file requested by this network node.

```
setup   db      01bh,045h       ; selects boldface mode
        .
        .
        .
        mov     ax,5e02h        ; function & subfunction
        mov     bx,2            ; redirection list index 2
        mov     cx,2            ; length of setup string
        mov     si,seg setup    ; address of setup string
        mov     ds,si
        mov     si,offset setup
        int     21h             ; transfer to MS-DOS
        jc      error           ; jump if function failed
        .
        .
        .
```

Int 21H [3.1]
Function 5EH (94) Subfunction 03H
Get printer setup string

Obtains the printer setup string for a particular network printer. This function call is only available when Microsoft Networks is running.

Call with:

AH   = 5EH

AL   = 03H

BX   = redirection list index

ES:DI   = segment:offset of buffer to receive setup string

Returns:

If function successful

Carry flag   = clear

CX   = length of printer setup string

ES:DI   = address of buffer holding setup string

If function unsuccessful
Carry flag   = set
AX   = error code

Notes:
- The redirection list index passed in register BX is obtained with Function 5FH Subfunction 02H (Get Redirection List Entry).
- See also Int 21H Function 5EH Subfunction 02H, which is used to specify a setup string for a network printer.

Example: Get the setup string for this network node associated with the printer designated by redirection list index 2.

```
setup   db      64 dup (?)       ; receives setup string
        .
        .
        .
        mov     ax,5e03h         ; function & subfunction
        mov     bx,2             ; redirection list index 2
        mov     di,seg setup     ; address of buffer
        mov     es,di
        mov     di,offset setup
        int     21h              ; transfer to MS-DOS
        jc      error            ; jump if function failed
        .
        .
        .
```

Int 21H   [3.1]
Function 5FH (95) Subfunction 02H
Get redirection list entry

Allows inspection of the system redirection list, which associates local logical names with network files, directories, or printers. This function call is only available when Microsoft Networks is running and the file-sharing module (SHARE.EXE) has been loaded.

Call with: AH   = 5FH
                 AL   = 02H
                 BX   = redirection list index
                 DS:SI   = segment:offset of 16-byte buffer to receive local device name
                 ES:DI   = segment:offset of 128-byte buffer to receive network name

Returns: If function successful
                Carry flag   = clear
                BH   = device status flag
                       bit 0   = 0 if device valid
                                    = 1 if not valid

BL = device type

     03H   *if printer*

     04H   *if drive*

CX = stored parameter value

DX = destroyed

BP = destroyed

DS:SI = segment:offset of ASCIIZ local device name

ES:DI = segment:offset of ASCIIZ network name

If function unsuccessful

Carry flag = set

AX = error code

Note:

■ The parameter returned in CX is a value that was previously passed to MS-DOS in register CX with Int 21H Function 5FH Subfunction 03H (Redirect Device). It represents data that is private to the applications which store and retrieve it and has no meaning to MS-DOS.

Example: Get the local and network names for the device specified by the first redirection list entry.

```
local   db      16 dup (?)      ; receives local device name

network db      128 dup (?)     ; receives network name
        .
        .
        .
        mov     ax,5f02h        ; function & subfunction
        mov     bx,0            ; redirection list entry 0
        mov     si,seg local    ; local name buffer addr
        mov     ds,si
        mov     si,offset local
        mov     di,seg network  ; network name buffer addr
        mov     es,di
        mov     di,offset network
        int     21h             ; transfer to MS-DOS
        jc      error           ; jump if call failed

        or      bh,bh           ; check device status
        jnz     error           ; jump if device not valid
        .
        .
        .
```

Int 21H
Function 5FH (95) Subfunction 03H
Redirect device

Establishes redirection across the network by associating a local device name with a network name. This function call is only available when Microsoft Networks is running and the file-sharing module (SHARE.EXE) has been loaded.

Call with:

AH	= 5FH	
AL	= 03H	
BL	= device type	
	03H	*if printer*
	04H	*if drive*
CX	= parameter to save for caller	
DS:SI	= segment:offset of ASCIIZ local device name	
ES:DI	= segment:offset of ASCIIZ network name, followed by ASCIIZ password	

Returns:

If function successful

Carry flag = clear

If function unsuccessful

Carry flag = set

AX = error code

Notes:

- The local name can be a drive designator (a letter followed by a colon, such as "D:"), a printer name, or a null string. Printer names must be one of the following: PRN, LPT1, LPT2, or LPT3. If a null string followed by a password is used, MS-DOS attempts to grant access to the network directory with the specified password.

- The parameter passed in CX can be retrieved by later calls to Int 21H Function 5FH Subfunction 02H. It represents data that is private to the applications which store and retrieve it and has no meaning to MS-DOS.

Example:

Redirect the local drive E to the directory \FORTH on the server named LMI, using the password FRED.

```
locname db      'E:',0          ; local drive

netname db      '\\LMI\FORTH',0
        db      'FRED',0
        .
        .
        .
```

```
        mov     ax,5f03h        ; function & subfunction
        mov     bl,4            ; code 4 = disk drive
        mov     si,seg locname  ; address of local name
        mov     ds,si
        mov     si,offset locname
        mov     di,seg netname  ; address of network name
        mov     es,di
        mov     di,offset netname
        int     21h             ; transfer to MS-DOS
        jc      error           ; jump if redirect failed
        .
        .
        .
```

Int 21H
Function 5FH (95) Subfunction 04H
Cancel device redirection

Cancels a previous redirection request by removing the association of a local device name with a network name. This function call is only available when Microsoft Networks is running and the file-sharing module (SHARE.EXE) has been loaded.

Call with:	AH	= 5FH
	AL	= 04H
	DS:SI	= segment:offset of ASCIIZ local device name

Returns:	If function successful	
	Carry flag	= clear
	If function unsuccessful	
	Carry flag	= set
	AX	= error code

Note:
- The supplied name can be a drive designator (a letter followed by a colon, such as "D:"), a printer name, or a string starting with two backslashes (\\). Printer names must be one of the following: PRN, LPT1, LPT2, or LPT3. If the string with two backslashes is used, the connection between the local machine and the network directory is terminated.

Example: Cancel the redirection of local drive E to the network server.

```
locname db      'E:',0
        .
        .
        .
```

(continued)

```
        mov    ax,5f04h      ; function & subfunction
        mov    si,seg locname  ; address of local name
        mov    ds,si
        mov    si,offset locname
        int    21h           ; transfer to MS-DOS
        jc     error         ; jump if cancel failed
        .
        .
        .
```

Int 21H
Function 60H (96)
Reserved

Int 21H
Function 61H (97)
Reserved

Int 21H   [3.0]
Function 62H (98)
Get PSP address

Obtains the segment (paragraph) address of the program segment prefix (PSP) for the currently executing program.

Call with:	AH	= 62H

Returns:	BX	= segment address of program segment prefix

Notes:
- Before a program receives control from MS-DOS, its program segment prefix is set up to contain certain vital information, such as:
  - the segment address of the program's environment block
  - the command line originally entered by the user
  - the original contents of the terminate, Ctrl-C, and critical-error handler vectors
  - the top address of available RAM
- The segment address of the PSP is normally passed to the program in registers DS and ES when it initially receives control from MS-DOS. This function allows a program to conveniently recover the PSP address at any point during its execution, without having to save it at program entry.

Example: Get the segment base of the program segment prefix, then copy the command tail from the PSP into the local buffer named *buff*.

```
ctail   equ    080H            ; PSP offset, command tail

buff    db     80 dup (?)      ; copy of command tail
        .
        .
        .
                               ; get PSP address
        mov    ah,62H          ; function number
        int    21h             ; transfer to MS-DOS

                               ; copy command tail
        mov    ds,bx           ; PSP segment to DS
        mov    si,offset ctail ; offset of command tail
        mov    di,seg buff     ; local buffer address
        mov    es,di
        mov    di,offset buff
        mov    cl,[si]         ; length of command tail
        inc    cl              ; include count byte
        xor    ch,ch
        cld
        rep movsb              ; copy to local buffer
        .
        .
        .
```

Int 21H   [2.25 only]
Function 63H (99)
Get DBCS lead byte table

Obtains the address of the system table of legal lead byte ranges for double-byte character sets (DBCS), or sets or obtains the interim console flag. Int 21H Function 63H is available only in MS-DOS version 2.25; it is not supported in MS-DOS versions 3.0 and later.

Call with: AH   = 63H
                AL   = subfunction
                        00H   *if getting address of DBCS lead byte table*
                        01H   *if setting or clearing interim console flag*
                        02H   *if obtaining value of interim console flag*

                If AL = 01H
                DL   = 00H   if clearing interim console flag
                          01H   if setting interim console flag

Returns: If function successful

Carry flag   = clear

and, if called with AL = 00H

DS:SI   = segment:offset of DBCS lead byte table

or, if called with AL = 02H

DL   = value of interim console flag

If function unsuccessful

Carry flag   = set

AX   = error code

Notes:

- The DBCS lead byte table consists of a variable number of two byte entries, terminated by two null (00H) bytes. Each pair defines the beginning and ending value for a range of lead bytes. The value of a legal lead byte is always in the range 80–0FFH.
- Entries in the lead byte table must be in ascending order. If no legal lead bytes are defined in a given system, the table consists only of the two null bytes.
- If the interim console flag is set, Int 21H Functions 07H (Unfiltered Character Input), 08H (Character Input without Echo), and 0BH (Keyboard Status) will support interim characters.
- Unlike most other MS-DOS services, this function call does not necessarily preserve any registers except SS:SP.
- [4.0] The address of the DBCS lead byte table can also be obtained with Int 21H Function 65H.

Int 21H
Function 64H (100)
Reserved

Int 21H   [3.3]
Function 65H (101)
Get extended country information

Obtains information about the specified country and/or code page.

Call with: AH   = 65H

AL   = subfunction

           01H = Get General Internationalization Information

           02H = Get Pointer to Uppercase Table

           04H = Get Pointer to Filename Uppercase Table

           06H = Get Pointer to Collating Table

           07H = Get Pointer to Double-Byte Character Set (DBCS) Vector

           (MS-DOS versions 4.0 and later)

BX	= code page of interest (−1 = active CON device)
CX	= length of buffer to receive information (must be >= 5)
DX	= country ID (−1 = default)
ES:DI	= address of buffer to receive information

Returns:

If function successful

Carry flag   = clear

and requested data placed in calling program's buffer

If function unsuccessful

Carry flag   = set

AX   = error code

Notes:

- The information returned by this function is a superset of the information returned by Int 21H Function 38H.
- This function may fail if either the country code or the code page number is invalid, or if the code page does not match the country code.
- The function fails if the specified buffer length is less than five bytes. If the buffer to receive the information is at least five bytes long but is too short for the requested information, the data is truncated and no error is returned.
- The format of the data returned by Subfunction 01H is:

Byte(s)	*Contents*
00H	information ID code (1)
01H–02H	length of following buffer
03H–04H	country ID
05H–06H	code page number
07H–08H	date format
	0 = USA *m d y*
	1 = Europe *d m y*
	2 = Japan *y m d*
09H–0DH	ASCIIZ currency symbol
0EH–0FH	ASCIIZ thousands separator
10H–11H	ASCIIZ decimal separator
12H–13H	ASCIIZ date separator
14H–15H	ASCIIZ time separator
16H	currency format flags
	bit 0 =0 if currency symbol precedes value
	=1 if currency symbol follows value
	bit 1 =0 if no space between value and currency symbol
	=1 if one space between value and currency symbol
	bit 2 =0 if currency symbol and decimal are separate
	=1 if currency symbol replaces decimal separator
17H	number of digits after decimal in currency
18H	time format
	bit 0 =0 if 12-hour clock
	=1 if 24-hour clock
19H–1CH	case-map routine call address
1DH–1EH	ASCIIZ data list separator
1FH–28H	reserved

- The format of the data returned by Subfunctions 02H, 04H, 06H, and 07H is:

  Byte(s)   ***Contents***
  00H   information ID code (2, 4, or 6)
  01H–05H   double-word pointer to table

- The uppercase and filename uppercase tables are a maximum of 130 bytes long. The first two bytes contain the size of the table; the following bytes contain the uppercase equivalents, if any, for character codes 80H–FFH. The main use of these tables is to map accented or otherwise modified vowels to their plain vowel equivalents. Text translated with the help of this table can be sent to devices that do not support the IBM graphics character set, or used to create filenames that do not require a special keyboard configuration for entry.

- The collating table is a maximum of 258 bytes long. The first two bytes contain the table length, and the subsequent bytes contain the values to be used for the corresponding character codes (0–FFH) during a sort operation. This table maps uppercase and lowercase ASCII characters to the same collating codes so that sorts will be case-insensitive, and it maps accented vowels to their plain vowel equivalents.

- [4.0+] Subfunction 07H returns a pointer to a variable length table of that defines ranges for double-byte character set (DBCS) lead bytes. The table is terminated by a pair of zero bytes, unless it must be truncated to fit in the buffer, and has the following format:

```
dw      length
db      start1,end1
db      start2,end2
.
.
.
db      0,0
```

  For example:

```
dw      4
db      81h,9fh
db      0e0h,0fch
db      0,0
```

- In some cases a truncated translation table may be presented to the program by MS-DOS. Applications should always check the length at the beginning of the table, to make sure it contains a translation code for the particular character of interest.

Examples: Obtain the extended country information associated with the default country and code page 437.

```
buffer  db      41 dup (0)       ; receives country info
        .
        .
        .
        mov     ax,6501h         ; function & subfunction
        mov     bx,437           ; code page
```

```
        mov     cx,41               ; buffer length
        mov     dx,-1               ; default country
        mov     di,seg buffer       ; buffer address
        mov     es,di
        mov     di,offset buffer
        int     21h                 ; transfer to MS-DOS
        jc      error               ; jump if function failed
        .
        .
        .
```

In this case, MS-DOS filled the following extended country information into the buffer:

```
buffer  db      1                   ; info ID code
        dw      38                  ; length of following buffer
        dw      1                   ; country ID (USA)
        dw      437                 ; code page number
        dw      0                   ; date format
        db      '$',0,0,0,0         ; currency symbol
        db      ',',0               ; thousands separator
        db      '.',0               ; decimal separator
        db      '-',0               ; date separator
        db      ':',0               ; time separator
        db      0                   ; currency format flags
        db      2                   ; digits in currency
        db      0                   ; time format
        dd      026ah:176ch         ; case map entry point
        db      ',',0               ; data list separator
        db      10 dup (0)          ; reserved
```

Obtain the pointer to the uppercase table associated with the default country and code page 437.

```
buffer  db      5 dup (0)           ; receives pointer info
        .
        .
        .
        mov     ax,6502h            ; function number
        mov     bx,437              ; code page
        mov     cx,5                ; length of buffer
        mov     dx,-1               ; default country
        mov     di,seg buffer       ; buffer address
        mov     es,di
        mov     di,offset buffer
        int     21h                 ; transfer to MS-DOS
        jc      error               ; jump if function failed
        .
        .
        .
```

In this case, MS-DOS filled the following values into the buffer:

```
buffer  db     2                ; info ID code
        dw     0204h            ; offset of uppercase table
        dw     1140h            ; segment of uppercase table
```

and the table at 1140:0204H contains the following data:

```
             0  1  2  3  4  5  6  7  8  9  A  B  C  D  E  F  0123456789ABCDEF
1140:0200                80 00 80 9A 45 41 8E 41 8F 80 45 45     ....EA.A..EE
1140:0210    45 49 49 49 8E 8F 90 92 92 4F 99 4F 55 55 59 99    EIII.....O.OUUY.
1140:0220    9A 9B 9C 9D 9E 9F 41 49 4F 55 A5 A5 A6 A7 A8 A9    ......AIOU......
1140:0230    AA AB AC AD AE AF B0 B1 B2 B3 B4 B5 B6 B7 B8 B9    ................
1140:0240    BA BB BC BD BE BF C0 C1 C2 C3 C4 C5 C6 C7 C8 C9    ................
1140:0250    CA CB CC CD CE CF D0 D1 D2 D3 D4 D5 D6 D7 D8 D9    ................
1140:0260    DA DB DC DD DE DF E0 E1 E2 E3 E4 E5 E6 E7 E8 E9    ................
1140:0270    EA EB EC ED EE EF F0 F1 F2 F3 F4 F5 F6 F7 F8 F9    ................
1140:0280    FA FB FC FD FE FF                                  ......
```

Int 21H
Function 66H (102)
Get or set code page

[3.3]

Obtains or selects the current code page.

Call with:	AH	= 66H
	AL	= subfunction
		01H = Get Code Page
		02H = Select Code Page
	BX ˙	= code page to select, if AL = 02H

Returns:	If function successful	
	Carry flag	= clear
	and, if called with AL = 01H	
	BX	= active code page
	DX	= default code page
	If function unsuccessful	
	Carry flag	= set
	AX	= error code

Note:

- When the Select Code Page subfunction is used, MS-DOS gets the new code page from the COUNTRY.SYS file. The device must be previously prepared for code page switching with the appropriate DEVICE= directive in the CONFIG.SYS file and NLSFUNC and MODE CP PREPARE commands (placed in the AUTOEXEC.BAT file, usually).

Example: Force the active code page to be the same as the system's default code page, that is, restore the code page that was active when the system was first booted.

```
                                      ; get current and
                                      ; default code page
                  mov    ax,6601h     ; function number
                  int    21h          ; transfer to MS-DOS
                  jc     error        ; jump if function failed

                                      ; set code page
                  mov    bx,dx        ; active = default
                  mov    ax,6602h     ; function number
                  int    21h          ; transfer to MS-DOS
                  jc     error        ; jump if function failed
```

Int 21H   [3.3]
Function 67H (103)
Set handle count

Sets the maximum number of files and devices that may be opened simultaneously using handles by the current process.

| **Call with:** | AH | = 67H |
| | BX | = number of desired handles |

Returns: If function successful
Carry flag   = clear

If function unsuccessful
Carry flag   = set
AX   = error code

Notes:
- This function call controls the size of the table that relates handle numbers for the current process to MS-DOS's internal, global table for all of the open files and devices in the system. The default table is located in the reserved area of the process's PSP and is large enough for 20 handles.
- The function fails if the requested number of handles is greater than 20 and there is not sufficient free memory in the system to allocate a new block to hold the enlarged table.

- If the number of handles requested is larger than the available entries in the system's global table for file and device handles (controlled by the FILES entry in CONFIG.SYS), no error is returned. However, a subsequent attempt to open a file or device, or create a new file, will fail if all the entries in the system's global file table are in use, even if the requesting process has not used up all its own handles.

Example: Set the maximum handle count for the current process to thirty, so that the process can have as many as 30 files or devices opened simultaneously. (Five of the handles are already assigned to the standard devices when the process starts up.) Note that a FILES=30 (or greater value) entry in the CONFIG.SYS file would also be required for the process to successfully open 30 files or devices.

```
        .
        .
        .
mov     ah,67h      ; function number
mov     bx,30       ; maximum number of handles
int     21h         ; transfer to MS-DOS
jc      error       ; jump if function failed
        .
        .
        .
```

Int 21H
Function 68H (104)
Commit file

[3.3]

Forces all data in MS-DOS's internal buffers associated with a specified handle to be physically written to the device. If the handle refers to a file, and the file has been modified, the time and date stamp and file size in the file's directory entry are updated.

Call with:
AH = 68H
BX = handle

Returns:
If function successful
Carry flag = clear
If function unsuccessful
Carry flag = set
AX = error code

Notes:
- The effect of this function is equivalent to closing and reopening a file, or to duplicating a handle for the file with Int 21H Function 45H and then closing the duplicate. However, this function has the advantage that it will not fail due to lack of handles, and the application does not risk losing control of the file in multitasking or network environments.

- If this function is requested for a handle associated with a character device, a success flag is returned, but there is no other effect.

Example: Assume that the file MYFILE.DAT has been previously opened and that the handle for that file is stored in the variable *fhandle.* Call the Commit File function to ensure that any data in MS-DOS's internal buffers associated with the handle is written out to disk and that the directory and file allocation table are up to date.

```
fname    db      'MYFILE.DAT',0  ; ASCIIZ filename
fhandle  dw      ?               ; file handle
         .
         .
         .
         mov     ah,68h          ; function number
         mov     bx,fhandle      ; file handle
         int     21h             ; transfer to MS-DOS
         jc      error           ; jump if commit failed
         .
         .
         .
```

Int 21H
Function 69H (105)
Reserved

Int 21H
Function 6AH (106)
Reserved

Int 21H
Function 6BH (107)
Reserved

Int 21H
Function 6CH (108)
Extended open file

Given an ASCIIZ pathname, opens, creates or replaces a file in the designated or default directory on the designated or default disk drive. Returns a handle that can be used by the program for subsequent access to the file.

Call with:

AH	= 6CH	
AL	= 00H	
BX	= open mode	

Bit(s)	Significance
0–2	access type
	000 = read-only
	001 = write-only
	010 = read/write
3	reserved (0)
4–6	sharing mode
	000 = compatibility
	001 = deny read/write (deny all)
	010 = deny write
	011 = deny read
	100 = deny none
7	inheritance
	0 = child process inherits handle
	1 = child does not inherit handle
8–12	reserved (0)
13	critical error handling
	0 = execute Int 24H
	1 = return error to process
14	write-through
	0 = writes may be buffered and deferred
	1 = physical write at request time
15	reserved (0)

CX = file attribute (bits may be combined; ignored if open)

Bit(s)	Significance (if set)
0	read-only
1	hidden
2	system
3	volume label
4	reserved (0)
5	archive
6–15	reserved (0)

	DX	= open flag	
		Bits	**Significance**
		0–3	action if file exists
			0000 = fail
			0001 = open file
			0010 = replace file
		4–7	action if file doesn't exist
			0000 = fail
			0001 = create file
		8–15	reserved (0)
	DS:SI	= segment:offset of ASCIIZ pathname	

Returns: If function successful

Carry flag = clear

AX = handle

CX = action taken

1 = file existed and was opened

2 = file did not exist and was created

3 = file existed and was replaced

If function failed

Carry flag = set

AX = error code

Notes:
- The function fails if:
  - any element of the pathname does not exist.
  - the file is being created in the root directory and the root directory is full.
  - the file is being created and a file with the same name and the read-only attribute already exists in the specified directory.
  - the program is running on a network and the user running the program has insufficient access rights.
- A file is usually given a normal (0) attribute when it is created. The file's attribute can subsequently be modified with Int 21H Function 43H.
- This function combines the capabilities of Int 21H Functions 3CH, 3DH, and 5BH. It was added to MS-DOS for compatibility with the DosOpen function of OS/2.

Example: Create the file MYFILE.DAT, if it does not already exist, in directory \MYDIR on drive C, and save the handle for subsequent access to the file.

```
fname    db      'C:\MYDIR\MYFILE.DAT',0

fhandle dw       ?
         .
         .
         .
```

(continued)

```
        mov     ax,6c00h          ; function number
        mov     bx,4042h          ; read/write, deny none,
                                  ; write-through mode
        xor     cx,cx             ; normal attribute
        mov     dx,0010h          ; create if doesn't exist,
                                  ; fail if exists
        mov     si,seg fname      ; address of pathname
        mov     ds,si
        mov     si,offset fname
        int     21h               ; transfer to MS-DOS
        jc      error             ; jump if open failed
        mov     fhandle,ax        ; save file handle
        .
        .
        .
```

Int 22H   [1.0]
Terminate handler address

The machine interrupt vector for Int 22H (memory locations 0000:0088H through 0000:008BH) contains the address of the routine that receives control when the currently executing program terminates via Int 20H, Int 27H, or Int 21H Functions 00H, 31H, or 4CH. The address in this vector is also copied into offsets 0AH through 0DH of the program segment prefix (PSP) when a program is loaded but before it begins executing, and is restored from the PSP (in case it was modified by the application) as part of MS-DOS's termination handling.

This interrupt should never be issued directly.

Int 23H   [1.0]
Ctrl-C handler address

The machine interrupt vector for Int 23H (memory locations 0000:008CH though 0000:008FH) contains the address of the routine which receives control when a Ctrl-C is detected during any character I/O function and, if the Break flag is ON, during most other MS-DOS function calls. The address in this vector is also copied into locations 0EH through 11H of the program segment prefix (PSP) when a program is loaded but before it begins executing, and is restored from the PSP (in case it was modified by the application) as part of MS-DOS's termination handling.

This interrupt should never be issued directly.

Notes: ■ The initialization code for an application can use Int 21H Function 25H to reset the Interrupt 23H vector to point to its own routine for Ctrl-C handling. In this way, the program can avoid being terminated unexpectedly as the result of the user's entry of a Ctrl-C or Ctrl-Break.

- When a Ctrl-C is detected and the program's Int 23H handler receives control, all registers are set to their values at the point of the original function call. The handler can then do any of the following:
  - Set a local flag for later inspection by the application, or take any other appropriate action, and perform an IRET. All registers must be preserved. The MS-DOS function in progress will be restarted from scratch and will proceed to completion, control finally returning to the application in the normal manner.
  - Take appropriate action and then perform a RET FAR to give control back to MS-DOS. The state of the carry flag is used by MS-DOS to determine what action to take. If the carry flag is set, the application will be terminated; if the carry flag is clear, the application will continue in the normal manner.
  - Retain control by transferring to an error-handling routine within the application and then resume execution or take other appropriate action, never performing a RET FAR or IRET to end the interrupt-handling sequence. This option will cause no harm to the system.
- Any MS-DOS function call may be used within the body of an Int 23H handler.

Example: See Chapter 5.

Int 24H   [1.0]
Critical-error handler address

The machine interrupt vector for Int 24H (memory locations 0000:0090H through 0000:0093H) contains the address of the routine that receives control when a critical error (usually a hardware error) is detected. This address is also copied into locations 12H through 15H of the program segment prefix (PSP) when a program is loaded but before it begins executing, and is restored from the PSP (in case it was modified by the application) as part of MS-DOS's termination handling.

This interrupt should never be issued directly.

Notes:
- On entry to the critical-error interrupt handler, bit 7 of register AH is clear (0) if the error was a disk I/O error; otherwise, it is set (1). BP:SI contains the address of a device-driver header from which additional information can be obtained. Interrupts are disabled. The registers will be set up for a retry operation, and an error code will be in the lower half of the DI register, with the upper half undefined.
  The lower byte of DI contains:

00H	write-protect error
01H	unknown unit
02H	drive not ready
03H	unknown command
04H	data error (CRC)
05H	bad request structure length
06H	seek error
07H	unknown media type
08H	sector not found

09H	printer out of paper
0AH	write fault
0BH	read fault
0CH	general failure
0DH	reserved
0EH	reserved
0FH	invalid disk change (MS-DOS version 3 only)

Note that these are the same error codes returned by the device driver in the request header. Also, upon entry, the stack is set up as shown in Figure 8-8, page 149.

- When a disk I/O error occurs, MS-DOS automatically retries the operation before issuing a critical-error Int 24H. The number of retries varies in different versions of MS-DOS, but is typically in the range three to five.

- Int 24H handlers must preserve the SS, SP, DS, ES, BX, CX, and DX registers. Only Int 21H Functions 01H–0CH and 59H can be used by an Int 24H handler; other function calls will destroy the MS-DOS stack and its ability to retry or ignore an error.

- When the Int 24H handler issues an IRET, it should return an action code in AL that will be interpreted by DOS as follows:

0	ignore the error
1	retry the operation
2	terminate the program
3	[3.0+] fail the function call in progress

- If the Int 24H handler returns control directly to the application program rather than to MS-DOS, it must restore the program's registers, removing all but the last three words from the stack, and issue an IRET. Control returns to the instruction immediately following the function call that caused the error. This option leaves MS-DOS in an unstable state until a call to an Int 21H function higher than Function 0CH is made.

Example: See Chapter 8.

Int 25H   [1.0]
Absolute disk read

Provides a direct linkage to the MS-DOS BIOS module to read data from a logical disk sector into memory.

Call with: For access to partitions <= 32 MB

AL	= drive number (0 = A, 1 = B, etc)
CX	= number of sectors to read
DX	= starting sector number
DS:BX	= segment:offset of buffer

For access to partitions > 32 MB (MS-DOS 4.0 and later)

AL	= drive number (0 = A, 1 = B, etc)
CX	= −1
DS:BX	= segment:offset of parameter block (see Notes)

Returns:	If function successful
	Carry flag = clear
	If function unsuccessful
	Carry flag = set
	AX = error code (see Notes)

Notes:

- All registers except the segment registers may be destroyed.
- When this function returns, the CPU flags originally pushed on the stack by the INT 25H instruction are *still* on the stack. The stack must be cleared by a POPF or ADD SP,2 to prevent uncontrolled stack growth and to make accessible any other values that were pushed on the stack before the call to INT 25H.
- Logical sector numbers are obtained by numbering each disk sector sequentially from cylinder 0, head 0, sector 1, and continuing until the last sector on the disk is counted. The head number is incremented before the track number. Logically adjacent sectors may not be physically adjacent, due to interleaving that occurs at the device-adapter level for some disk types.
- The error code is interpreted as follows: The lower byte (AL) is the same error code that is returned in the lower byte of DI when an Int 24H is issued. The upper byte (AH) contains:

01H	if bad command
02H	if bad address mark
04H	if requested sector not found
08H	if direct memory access (DMA) failure
10H	if data error (bad CRC)
20H	if controller failed
40H	if seek operation failed
80H	if attachment failed to respond

- [4.0+] When accessing partitions larger than 32 MB under MS-DOS version 4, this function uses a parameter block with the following format:

Bytes	*Description*
00H–03H	32-bit sector number
04H–05H	number of sectors to read
06H–07H	offset of buffer
08H–09H	segment of buffer

Example: Read logical sector 1 of drive A into the memory area named *buff*. (On most MS-DOS floppy disks, this sector contains the beginning of the file allocation table.)

```
buff    db      512 dup (?)     ; receives data from disk
        .
        .
        .
```

(continued)

```
mov     al,0            ; drive A
mov     cx,1            ; number of sectors
mov     dx,1            ; beginning sector number
mov     bx,seg buff     ; buffer address
mov     ds,bx
mov     bx,offset buff
int     25h             ; request disk read
jc      error           ; jump if read failed
add     sp,2            ; clear stack
        .
        .
        .
```

Int 26H
Absolute disk write

[1.0]

Provides a direct linkage to the MS-DOS BIOS module to write data from memory to a logical disk sector.

Call with:

For access to partitions <= 32 MB

AL = drive number (0 = A, 1 = B, etc)
CX = number of sectors to write
DX = starting sector number
DS:BX = segment:offset of buffer

For access to partitions > 32 MB (MS-DOS 4.0 and later)

AL = drive number (0 = A, 1 = B, etc)
CX = −1
DS:BX = segment:offset of parameter block (see Notes)

Returns:

If function successful
Carry flag = clear

If function unsuccessful
Carry flag = set
AX = error code (see Notes)

Notes:

- All registers except the segment registers may be destroyed.
- When this function returns, the CPU flags originally pushed onto the stack by the INT 26H instruction are *still* on the stack. The stack must be cleared by a POPF or ADD SP,2 to prevent uncontrolled stack growth and to make accessible any other values that were pushed on the stack before the call to INT 26H.
- Logical sector numbers are obtained by numbering each disk sector sequentially from cylinder 0, head 0, sector 1, and continuing until the last sector on the disk is counted. The head number is incremented before the track number. Logically adjacent sectors may not be physically adjacent, due to interleaving that occurs at the device-adapter level for some disk types.

- The error code is interpreted as follows: The lower byte (AL) is the same error code that is returned in the lower byte of DI when an Int 24H is issued. The upper byte (AH) contains:

01H	if bad command
02H	if bad address mark
03H	if write-protect fault
04H	if requested sector not found
08H	if direct memory access (DMA) failure
10H	if data error (bad CRC)
20H	if controller failed
40H	if seek operation failed
80H	if attachment failed to respond

- [4.0+] When accessing partitions larger than 32 MB under MS-DOS version 4, this function uses a parameter block with the following format:

Bytes	Description
00H–03H	32-bit sector number
04H–05H	number of sectors to read
06H–07H	offset of buffer
08H–09H	segment of buffer

Example: Write the contents of the memory area named *buff* into logical sector 3 of drive C.

Warning: Verbatim use of the following code could damage the file system on your fixed disk. There is, unfortunately, no way to provide a really safe example of this function.

```
buff    db      512 dup (?)     ; contains data for write
        .
        .
        .
        mov     al,2            ; drive C
        mov     cx,1            ; number of sectors
        mov     dx,3            ; beginning sector number
        mov     bx,seg buff     ; buffer address
        mov     ds,bx
        mov     bx,offset buff
        int     26h             ; request disk write
        jc      error           ; jump if write failed
        add     sp,2            ; clear stack
        .
        .
        .
```

Int 27H [1.0]
Terminate and stay resident

Terminates execution of the currently executing program, but reserves part or all of its memory so that it will not be overlaid by the next transient program to be loaded. MS-DOS then takes the following actions:

- File buffers are flushed and any open handles for files or devices owned by the process are closed.
- The termination handler vector (Int 22H) is restored from PSP:000AH.
- The Ctrl-C handler vector (Int 23H) is restored from PSP:000EH.
- [2.0+] The critical-error handler vector (Int 24H) is restored from PSP:0012H.
- Control is transferred to the termination handler.

If the program is returning to COMMAND.COM, control transfers to the resident portion and the transient portion is reloaded if necessary. If a batch file is in progress, the next line of the file is fetched and interpreted; otherwise a prompt is issued for the next user command.

| **Call with:** | DX | = offset of the last byte plus one (relative to the program segment prefix) of program to be protected |
| | CS | = segment of program segment prefix |

| **Returns:** | Nothing |

Notes:
- This function call is typically used to allow user-written utilities, drivers, or interrupt handlers to be loaded as ordinary .COM or .EXE programs, then remain resident. Subsequent entrance to the code is via a hardware or software interrupt.
- This function attempts to set the initial memory allocation block to the length in bytes specified in register DX. If other memory blocks have been requested by the application via Int 21H Function 48H, they will not be released by this function.
- Other methods of performing a final exit are:
  - Int 20H
  - Int 21H Function 00H
  - Int 21H Function 31H
  - Int 21H Function 4CH
- This function should not be called by .EXE programs that are loaded at the high end of the transient program area (i.e., linked with the /HIGH switch), because doing so reserves the memory normally used by the transient part of COMMAND.COM. If COMMAND.COM cannot be reloaded, the system will fail.
- This function does not work correctly when DX contains values in the range 0FFF1H–0FFFFH. In this case, MS-DOS discards the high bit of the value in DX, resulting in the reservation of 32 KB less memory than was requested by the program.
- [2.0+] Int 21H Function 31H should be used in preference to this function, because it supports return codes, allows larger amounts of memory to be reserved, and does not require CS to contain the segment of the program segment prefix.

- [3.0+] If the program is running on a network, it should remove all locks it has placed on file regions before terminating.

Example: Terminate and stay resident, reserving enough memory to contain the entire program.

```
          .
          .
          .
          mov    dx,offset pend  ; DX = bytes to reserve
          int    27h             ; terminate, stay resident
          .
          .
          .
pend      equ    $               ; offset, end of program

          end
```

Int 28H
Reserved

Int 29H
Reserved

Int 2AH
Reserved

Int 2BH
Reserved

Int 2CH
Reserved

Int 2DH
Reserved

Int 2EH
Reserved

Int 2FH   [3.0]
Multiplex interrupt

Provides a general-purpose avenue of communication with another process or with MS-DOS extensions, such as the print spooler, ASSIGN, SHARE, and APPEND. The multiplex number in register AH specifies the process or extension being communicated with. The range 00H–BFH is reserved for MS-DOS; applications may use the range C0H–FFH.

Int 2FH   [3.0]
Function 01H
Print spooler

Submits a file to the print spooler, removes a file from the print spooler's queue of pending files, or obtains the status of the printer. The print spooler, which is contained in the file PRINT.COM, was first added to MS-DOS in version 2.0, but the application program interface to the spooler was not documented until MS-DOS version 3.

Call with:	AH	= 01H
	AL	= subfunction
		00H = Get Installed State
		01H = Submit File to be Printed
		02H = Remove File from Print Queue
		03H = Cancel All Files in Queue
		04H = Hold Print Jobs for Status Read
		05H = Release Hold
	DS:DX	= segment:offset of packet (Subfunction 01H)
		segment:offset of ASCIIZ pathname (Subfunction 02H)

Returns:　　If function successful
Carry flag　= clear
and, if called with AL = 00H
AL　　　　= print spooler state
   00H　　*if not installed, ok to install*
   01H　　*if not installed, not ok to install*
   FFH　　*if installed*
or, if called with AL = 04H
DX　　　　= error count
DS:SI　　 = segment:offset of print queue file list
If function unsuccessful
Carry flag　= set
AX　　　　= error code

Notes:　　■ The packet passed to Subfunction 01H consists of five bytes. The first byte contains the *level,* which should be 00H for current versions of MS-DOS. The following four bytes contain the segment:offset of an ASCIIZ pathname, which may not include wildcard characters. If the specified file exists, it is added to the print queue.

　　■ The * and ? wildcard characters may be included in a pathname passed to Subfunction 02H, making it possible to delete multiple files from the print queue with one call.

　　■ The address returned by Subfunction 04H points to a list of 64-byte entries, each containing an ASCIIZ pathname. The first pathname in the list is the file currently being printed. The last entry in the list is a null string (a single 00H byte).

Int 2FH　　　　　　　　　　　　　　　　　　　　　　[3.2]
Function 02H
ASSIGN

Returns a code indicating whether the resident portion of the ASSIGN utility has been loaded.

Call with:　　AH　　= 02H
AL　　= subfunction
  00H = Get Installed State

Returns:　　If function successful
Carry flag　= clear
AL　　　　= ASSIGN installed status
   00H　　*if not installed, ok to install*
   01H　　*if not installed, not ok to install*
   FFH　　*if installed*
If function unsuccessful
Carry flag　= set
AX　　　　= error code

Int 2FH
Function 10H (16)
SHARE

[3.2]

Returns a code indicating whether the SHARE.EXE file-sharing module has been loaded.

Call with:	AH	= 10H
	AL	= subfunction
		00H = Get Installed State

Returns:	If function successful	
	Carry flag	= clear
	AL	= SHARE installed status
		00H *if not installed, ok to install*
		01H *if not installed, not ok to install*
		FFH *if installed*
	If function unsuccessful	
	Carry flag	= set
	AX	= error code

Int 2FH
Function B7H (183)
APPEND

[3.3]

Allows an application to test whether APPEND has been installed. If APPEND is resident, returns the APPEND version, state, and the path used to search for data files.

Call with:	AH	= B7H
	AL	= subfunction
		00H = Get Installed State
		02H = Get Append Version (4.0)
		04H = Get Append Path Pointer (4.0)
		06H = Get Append Function State (4.0)
		07H = Set Append Function State (4.0)
		11H = Set Return Found Name State (4.0, see Note)
	BX	= APPEND state (if AL = 07H)

			Bit(s)	*Significance (if set)*
			0	APPEND enabled
			1–12	Reserved (0)
			13	/PATH switch active
			14	/E switch active
			15	/X switch active

Returns:　　If function successful

Carry flag　= clear

and, if called with AL = 00H

AL　　　　= APPEND installed status

　　　　00H　　*if not installed, ok to install*

　　　　01H　　*if not installed, not ok to install*

　　　　FFH　　*if installed*

or, if called with AL = 02H (MS-DOS 4.0)

AX　　　　= FFFFH if MS-DOS 4.0 APPEND

or, if called with AL = 04H (MS-DOS 4.0)

ES:DI　　　= segment:offset of active APPEND path

or, if called with AL = 06H (MS-DOS 4.0)

BX　　　　= APPEND state (see above)

If function unsuccessful

Carry flag　= set

AX　　　　= error code

Note:　　■　If the Return Found Name State is set with Subfunction 11H, the fully qualified file-name is returned to the next application to call Int 21H Function 3DH, 43H, or 6CH. The name is placed at the same address as the ASCIIZ parameter string for the Int 21H function, so the application must be sure to provide a buffer of adequate size. The Return Found Name State is reset after APPEND processes one Int 21H function call.

SECTION III

IBM ROM BIOS
and Mouse
Functions
Reference

Notes to the Reader

In the headers for ROM BIOS video driver (Int 10H) function calls, the following icons are used:

[MDA]   Monochrome Display Adapter
[CGA]   Color/Graphics Adapter
[PCjr]   PCjr system board video controller
[EGA]   Enhanced Graphics Adapter
[MCGA]   Multi-Color Graphics Array (PS/2 Models 25 & 30)
[VGA]   Video Graphics Array (PS/2 Models 50 and above)

In the remainder of this section, the following icons are used:

[PC]   Original IBM PC, PC/XT, and PCjr, unless otherwise noted.
[AT]   PC/AT and PC/XT-286, unless otherwise noted.
[PS/2]   All PS/2 models (including Models 25 and 30), unless other-
                 wise noted.

ROM BIOS functions that are unique to the PC Convertible have been omitted.

Some functions are supported only in very late revisions of a particular machine's ROM BIOS (such as Int 1AH Functions 00H and 01H on the PC/XT). In general, such functions are not given an icon for that machine since a program could not safely assume that they were available based on the machine ID byte(s).

Summary of ROM BIOS and Mouse Function Calls

Int	Function	Subfunction	Name
10H			Video Driver
10H	00H		Set Video Mode
10H	01H		Set Cursor Type
10H	02H		Set Cursor Position
10H	03H		Get Cursor Position
10H	04H		Get Light Pen Position
10H	05H		Set Display Page
10H	06H		Initialize or Scroll Window Up
10H	07H		Initialize or Scroll Window Down
10H	08H		Read Character and Attribute at Cursor
10H	09H		Write Character and Attribute at Cursor
10H	0AH (10)		Write Character at Cursor
10H	0BH (11)		Set Palette, Background, or Border

(continued)

Int	Function	Subfunction	Name
10H	0CH (12)		Write Graphics Pixel
10H	0DH (13)		Read Graphics Pixel
10H	0EH (14)		Write Character in Teletype Mode
10H	0FH (15)		Get Video Mode
10H	10H (16)	00H	Set Palette Register
10H	10H (16)	01H	Set Border Color
10H	10H (16)	02H	Set Palette and Border
10H	10H (16)	03H	Toggle Blink/Intensity Bit
10H	10H (16)	07H	Get Palette Register
10H	10H (16)	08H	Get Border Color
10H	10H (16)	09H	Get Palette and Border
10H	10H (16)	10H (16)	Set Color Register
10H	10H (16)	12H (18)	Set Block of Color Registers
10H	10H (16)	13H (19)	Set Color Page State
10H	10H (16)	15H (21)	Get Color Register
10H	10H (16)	17H (23)	Get Block of Color Registers
10H	10H (16)	1AH (26)	Get Color Page State
10H	10H (16)	1BH (27)	Set Gray-Scale Values
10H	11H (17)	00H	Load User Font
10H	11H (17)	01H	Load ROM 8-by-14 Font
10H	11H (17)	02H	Load ROM 8-by-8 Font
10H	11H (17)	03H	Set Block Specifier
10H	11H (17)	04H	Load ROM 8-by-16 Font
10H	11H (17)	10H (16)	Load User Font, Reprogram Controller
10H	11H (17)	11H (17)	Load ROM 8-by-14 Font, Reprogram Controller
10H	11H (17)	12H (18)	Load ROM 8-by-8 Font, Reprogram Controller
10H	11H (17)	14H (20)	Load ROM 8-by-16 Font, Reprogram Controller
10H	11H (17)	20H (32)	Set Int 1FH Pointer
10H	11H (17)	21H (33)	Set Int 43H for User's Font
10H	11H (17)	22H (34)	Set Int 43H for ROM 8-by-14 Font
10H	11H (17)	23H (35)	Set Int 43H for ROM 8-by-8 Font
10H	11H (17)	24H (36)	Set Int 43H for Rom 8-by-16 Font
10H	11H (17)	30H (48)	Get Font Information
10H	12H (18)	10H (16)	Get Configuration Information
10H	12H (18)	20H (32)	Select Alternate PrintScreen
10H	12H (18)	30H (48)	Set Scan Lines
10H	12H (18)	31H (49)	Enable/Disable Palette Loading
10H	12H (18)	32H (50)	Enable/Disable Video
10H	12H (18)	33H (51)	Enable/Disable Gray-Scale Summing
10H	12H (18)	34H (52)	Enable/Disable Cursor Emulation

(continued)

Int	Function	Subfunction	Name
10H	12H (18)	35H (53)	Switch Active Display
10H	12H (18)	36H (54)	Enable/Disable Screen Refresh
10H	13H (19)		Write String in Teletype Mode
10H	1AH (26)		Get or Set Display Combination Code
10H	1BH (27)		Get Functionality/State Information
10H	1CH (28)		Save or Restore Video State
11H			Get Equipment Configuration
12H			Get Conventional Memory Size
13H			Disk Driver
13H	00H		Reset Disk System
13H	01H		Get Disk System Status
13H	02H		Read Sector
13H	03H		Write Sector
13H	04H		Verify Sector
13H	05H		Format Track
13H	06H		Format Bad Track
13H	07H		Format Drive
13H	08H		Get Drive Parameters
13H	09H		Initialize Fixed Disk Characteristics
13H	0AH (10)		Read Sector Long
13H	0BH (11)		Write Sector Long
13H	0CH (12)		Seek
13H	0DH (13)		Reset Fixed Disk System
13H	0EH (14)		Read Sector Buffer
13H	0FH (15)		Write Sector Buffer
13H	10H (16)		Get Drive Status
13H	11H (17)		Recalibrate Drive
13H	12H (18)		Controller RAM Diagnostic
13H	13H (19)		Controller Drive Diagnostic
13H	14H (20)		Controller Internal Diagnostic
13H	15H (21)		Get Disk Type
13H	16H (22)		Get Disk Change Status
13H	17H (23)		Set Disk Type
13H	18H (24)		Set Media Type for Format
13H	19H (25)		Park Heads
13H	1AH (26)		Format ESDI Drive
14H			Serial Communications Port Driver
14H	00H		Initialize Communications Port
14H	01H		Write Character to Communications Port

(continued)

Int	Function	Subfunction	Name
14H	02H		Read Character from Communications Port
14H	03H		Get Communications Port Status
14H	04H		Extended Initialize Communications Port
14H	05H		Extended Communications Port Control
15H			I/O Subsystem Extensions
15H	00H		Turn On Cassette Motor
15H	01H		Turn Off Cassette Motor
15H	02H		Read Cassette
15H	03H		Write Cassette
15H	0FH (15)		Format ESDI Drive Periodic Interrupt
15H	21H (33)	00H	Read POST Error Log
15H	21H (33)	01H	Write POST Error Log
15H	4FH (79)		Keyboard Intercept
15H	80H (128)		Device Open
15H	81H (129)		Device Close
15H	82H (130)		Process Termination
15H	83H (131)		Event Wait
15H	84H (132)		Read Joystick
15H	85H (133)		SysReq Key
15H	86H (134)		Delay
15H	87H (135)		Move Extended Memory Block
15H	88H (136)		Get Extended Memory Size
15H	89H (137)		Enter Protected Mode
15H	90H (144)		Device Wait
15H	91H (145)		Device Post
15H	C0H (192)		Get System Environment
15H	C1H (193)		Get Address of Extended BIOS Data Area
15H	C2H (194)	00H	Enable/Disable Pointing Device
15H	C2H (194)	01H	Reset Pointing Device
15H	C2H (194)	02H	Set Sample Rate
15H	C2H (194)	03H	Set Resolution
15H	C2H (194)	04H	Get Pointing Device Type
15H	C2H (194)	05H	Initialize Pointing Device Interface
15H	C2H (194)	06H	Set Scaling or Get Status
15H	C2H (194)	07H	Set Pointing Device Handler Address
15H	C3H (195)		Set Watchdog Time-Out
15H	C4H (196)		Programmable Option Select

(continued)

Int	Function	Subfunction	Name
16H			Keyboard Driver
16H	00H		Read Character from Keyboard
16H	01H		Get Keyboard Status
16H	02H		Get Keyboard Flags
16H	03H		Set Repeat Rate
16H	04H		Set Keyclick
16H	05H		Push Character and Scan Code
16H	10H (16)		Read Character from Enhanced Keyboard
16H	11H (17)		Get Enhanced Keyboard Status
16H	12H (18)		Get Enhanced Keyboard Flags
17H			Parallel Port Printer Driver
17H	00H		Write Character to Printer
17H	01H		Initialize Printer Port
17H	02H		Get Printer Status
18H			ROM BASIC
19H			Reboot System
1AH			Real-time (CMOS) Clock Driver
1AH	00H		Get Tick Count
1AH	01H		Set Tick Count
1AH	02H		Get Time
1AH	03H		Set Time
1AH	04H		Get Date
1AH	05H		Set Date
1AH	06H		Set Alarm
1AH	07H		Reset Alarm
1AH	0AH (10)		Get Day Count
1AH	0BH (11)		Set Day Count
1AH	80H (128)		Set Sound Source
33H			Microsoft Mouse Driver
33H	00H		Reset Mouse and Get Status
33H	01H		Show Mouse Pointer
33H	02H		Hide Mouse Pointer
33H	03H		Get Mouse Position and Button Status
33H	04H		Set Mouse Pointer Position
33H	05H		Get Button Press Information
33H	06H		Get Button Release Information
33H	07H		Set Horizontal Limits for Pointer
33H	08H		Set Vertical Limits for Pointer
33H	09H		Set Graphics Pointer Shape

(continued)

Int	Function	Subfunction	Name
33H	0AH (10)		Set Text Pointer Type
33H	0BH (11)		Read Mouse Motion Counters
33H	0CH (12)		Set User-defined Mouse Event Handler
33H	0DH (13)		Turn On Light Pen Emulation
33H	0EH (14)		Turn Off Light Pen Emulation
33H	0FH (15)		Set Mickeys to Pixels Ratio
33H	10H (16)		Set Mouse Pointer Exclusion Area
33H	13H (19)		Set Double Speed Threshold
33H	14H (20)		Swap User-defined Mouse Event Handlers
33H	15H (21)		Get Mouse Save State Buffer Size
33H	16H (22)		Save Mouse Driver State
33H	17H (23)		Restore Mouse Driver State
33H	18H (24)		Set Alternate Mouse Event Handler
33H	19H (25)		Get Address of Alternate Mouse Event Handler
33H	1AH (26)		Set Mouse Sensitivity
33H	1BH (27)		Get Mouse Sensitivity
33H	1CH (28)		Set Mouse Interrupt Rate
33H	1DH (29)		Select Pointer Page
33H	1EH (30)		Get Pointer Page
33H	1FH (31)		Disable Mouse Driver
33H	20H (32)		Enable Mouse Driver
33H	21H (33)		Reset Mouse Driver
33H	22H (34)		Set Language for Mouse Driver Messages
33H	23H (35)		Get Language Number
33H	24H (36)		Get Mouse Information

Int 10H
Function 00H
Set video mode

Selects the current video display mode. Also selects the active video controller, if more than one video controller is present.

Call with:	AH	= 00H
	AL	= video mode (see Notes)

Returns: Nothing

Notes:
- The video modes applicable to the various IBM machine models and video adapters are as follows:

Mode	Resolution	Colors	Text/ graphics	MDA	CGA	PCjr	EGA	MCGA	VGA
00H	40-by-25 color burst off	16	text		•	•	•	•	•
01H	40-by-25	16	text		•	•	•	•	•
02H	80-by-25 color burst off	16	text		•	•	•	•	•
03H	80-by-25	16	text		•	•	•	•	•
04H	320-by-200	4	graphics		•	•	•	•	•
05H	320-by-200 color burst off	4	graphics		•	•	•	•	•
06H	640-by-200	2	graphics		•	•	•	•	•
07H	80-by-25	2^1	text	•			•		•
08H	160-by-200	16	graphics			•			
09H	320-by-200	16	graphics			•			
0AH	640-by-200	4	graphics			•			
0BH	reserved								
0CH	reserved								
0DH	320-by-200	16	graphics				•		•
0EH	640-by-200	16	graphics				•		•
0FH	640-by-350	2^2	graphics				•		•
10H	640-by-350	4	graphics				•^{3}		
10H	640-by-350	16	graphics				•^{4}		•
11H	640-by-480	2	graphics					•	•
12H	640-by-480	16	graphics						•
13H	320-by-200	256	graphics					•	•

1 Monochrome monitor only.
2 Monochrome monitor only.
3 EGA with 64 KB of RAM.
4 EGA with 128 KB or more of RAM.

- The presence or absence of color burst is only significant when a composite monitor is being used. For RGB monitors, there is no functional difference between modes 00H and 01H or modes 02H and 03H. On the CGA, two palettes are available in mode 04H and one in mode 05H.

- On the PC/AT, PCjr, and PS/2, if bit 7 of AL is set, the display buffer is not cleared when a new mode is selected. On the PC or PC/XT, this capability is available only when an EGA or VGA (which have their own ROM BIOS) is installed.

Int 10H Function 01H Set cursor type
[MDA] [CGA] [PCjr] [EGA] [MCGA] [VGA]

Selects the starting and ending lines for the blinking hardware cursor in text display modes.

Call with:
AH = 01H
CH bits 0–4 = starting line for cursor
CL bits 0–4 = ending line for cursor

Returns: Nothing

Notes:
- In text display modes, the video hardware causes the cursor to blink, and the blink cannot be disabled. In graphics modes, the hardware cursor is not available.
- The default values set by the ROM BIOS are:

Display	Start	End
monochrome mode 07H	11	12
text modes 00H–03H	6	7

- On the EGA, MCGA, and VGA in text modes 00H–03H, the ROM BIOS accepts cursor start and end values as though the character cell were 8 by 8 and remaps the values as appropriate for the true character cell dimensions. This mapping is called cursor emulation.
- You can turn off the cursor in several ways. On the MDA, CGA, and VGA, setting register CH = 20H causes the cursor to disappear. Techniques that involve setting illegal starting and ending lines for the current display mode are unreliable. An alternative is to position the cursor to a nondisplayable address, such as $(x,y)=(0,25)$.

Int 10H Function 02H Set cursor position
[MDA] [CGA] [PCjr] [EGA] [MCGA] [VGA]

Positions the cursor on the display, using text coordinates.

Call with:
AH = 02H
BH = page
DH = row (y coordinate)
DL = column (x coordinate)

Returns:	Nothing

Notes:

- A separate cursor is maintained for each display page, and each can be set independently with this function regardless of the currently active page. The number of available display pages depends on the video adapter and current display mode. See Int 10H Function 05H.
- Text coordinates $(x,y)=(0,0)$ are the upper left corner of the screen.
- The maximum value for each text coordinate depends on the video adapter and current display mode, as follows:

Mode	Maximum x	Maximum y
00H	39	24
01H	39	24
02H	79	24
03H	79	24
04H	39	24
05H	39	24
06H	79	24
07H	79	24
08H	19	24
09H	39	24
0AH	79	24
0BH	reserved	
0CH	reserved	
0DH	39	24
0EH	79	24
0FH	79	24
10H	79	24
11H	79	29
12H	79	29
13H	39	24

Int 10H
Function 03H
Get cursor position

[MDA] [CGA] [PCjr] [EGA] [MCGA] [VGA]

Obtains the current position of the cursor on the display, in text coordinates.

Call with:	AH	= 03H
	BH	= page

Returns:	CH	= starting line for cursor
	CL	= ending line for cursor
	DH	= row (y coordinate)
	DL	= column (x coordinate)

■ A separate cursor is maintained for each display page, and each can be inspected independently with this function regardless of the currently active page. The number of available display pages depends on the video adapter and current display mode. See Int 10H Function 05H.

Int 10H
Function 04H
Get light pen position

[CGA] [PCjr] [EGA]

Obtains the current status and position of the light pen.

Call with:	AH	= 04H	

Returns:	AH	= 00H	if light pen not down/not triggered
		01H	if light pen down/triggered
	BX	= pixel column (graphics *x* coordinate)	
	CH	= pixel row (graphics *y* coordinate, modes 04H–06H)	
	CX	= pixel row (graphics *y* coordinate, modes 0DH–13H)	
	DH	= character row (text *y* coordinate)	
	DL	= character column (text *x* coordinate)	

Notes:

■ The range of text and graphics coordinates returned by this function depends on the current display mode.

■ On the CGA, the graphics coordinates returned by this function are not continuous. The *y* coordinate is always a multiple of two; the *x* coordinate is either a multiple of four (for 320-by-200 graphics modes) or a multiple of eight (for 640-by-200 graphics modes).

■ Careful selection of background and foreground colors is necessary to obtain maximum sensitivity from the light pen across the full screen width.

Int 10H
Function 05H
Set display page

[CGA] [PCjr] [EGA] [MCGA] [VGA]

Selects the active display page for the video display.

Call with: For CGA, EGA, MCGA, VGA

AH   = 05H
AL   = page

        0–7   *for modes 00H and 01H (CGA, EGA, MCGA, VGA)*
        0–3   *for modes 02H and 03H (CGA)*
        0–7   *for modes 02H and 03H (EGA, MCGA, VGA)*
        0–7   *for mode 07H (EGA, VGA)*
        0–7   *for mode 0DH (EGA, VGA)*
        0–3   *for mode 0EH (EGA, VGA)*
        0–1   *for mode 0FH (EGA, VGA)*
        0–1   *for mode 10H (EGA, VGA)*

For PCjr only

AH   = 05H
AL   = subfunction

        80H = read CRT/CPU page registers
        81H = set CPU page register
        82H = set CRT page register
        83H = set both CPU and CRT page registers

BH   = CRT page (Subfunctions 82H and 83H)
BL   = CPU page (Subfunctions 81H and 83H)

Returns: If CGA, EGA, MCGA, or VGA adapter
Nothing

If PCjr and if function called with AL= 80H–83H
BH   = CRT page register
BL   = CPU page register

Notes:

- Video mode and adapter combinations not listed above support one display page (for example, a Monochrome Adapter in mode 7).

- Switching between pages does not affect their contents. In addition, text can be written to any video page with Int 10H Functions 02H, 09H, and 0AH, regardless of the page currently being displayed.

- On the PCjr, the CPU page determines the part of the physical memory region 00000H–1FFFFH that will be hardware mapped onto 16 KB of memory beginning at segment B800H. The CRT page determines the starting address of the physical memory used by the video controller to refresh the display. Smooth animation effects can be achieved by manipulation of these registers. Programs that write directly to the B800H segment can reach only the first 16 KB of the video refresh buffer. Programs requiring direct access to the entire 32 KB buffer in modes 09H and 0AH can obtain the current CRT page from the ROM BIOS variable PAGDAT at 0040:008AH.

Int 10H   [MDA] [CGA] [PCjr] [EGA] [MCGA] [VGA]
Function 06H
Initialize or scroll window up

Initializes a specified window of the display to ASCII blank characters with a given attribute or scrolls up the contents of a window by a specified number of lines.

Call with: AH   = 06H
              AL   = number of lines to scroll (if zero, entire window is blanked)
              BH   = attribute to be used for blanked area
              CH   = y coordinate, upper left corner of window
              CL   = x coordinate, upper left corner of window
              DH   = y coordinate, lower right corner of window
              DL   = x coordinate, lower right corner of window

Returns: Nothing

Notes:
- In video modes that support multiple pages, this function affects only the page currently being displayed.
- If AL contains a value other than 00H, the area within the specified window is scrolled up by the requested number of lines. Text that is scrolled beyond the top of the window is lost. The new lines that appear at the bottom of the window are filled with ASCII blanks carrying the attribute specified by register BH.
- To scroll down the contents of a window, see Int 10H Function 07H.

Int 10H   [MDA] [CGA] [PCjr] [EGA] [MCGA] [VGA]
Function 07H
Initialize or scroll window down

Initializes a specified window of the display to ASCII blank characters with a given attribute, or scrolls down the contents of a window by a specified number of lines.

Call with: AH   = 07H
              AL   = number of lines to scroll (if zero, entire window is blanked)
              BH   = attribute to be used for blanked area
              CH   = y coordinate, upper left corner of window
              CL   = x coordinate, upper left corner of window
              DH   = y coordinate, lower right corner of window
              DL   = x coordinate, lower right corner of window

Returns: Nothing

- In video modes that support multiple pages, this function affects only the page currently being displayed.
- If AL contains a value other than 00H, the area within the specified window is scrolled down by the requested number of lines. Text that is scrolled beyond the bottom of the window is lost. The new lines that appear at the top of the window are filled with ASCII blanks carrying the attribute specified by register BH.
- To scroll up the contents of a window, see Int 10H Function 06H.

Int 10H   [MDA] [CGA] [PCjr] [EGA] [MCGA] [VGA]
Function 08H
Read character and attribute at cursor

Obtains the ASCII character and its attribute at the current cursor position for the specified display page.

Call with:	AH	= 08H
	BH	= page

Returns:	AH	= attribute
	AL	= character

Note:

- In video modes that support multiple pages, characters and their attributes may be read from any page, regardless of the page currently being displayed.

Int 10H   [MDA] [CGA] [PCjr] [EGA] [MCGA] [VGA]
Function 09H
Write character and attribute at cursor

Writes an ASCII character and its attribute to the display at the current cursor position.

Call with:	AH	= 09H
	AL	= character
	BH	= page
	BL	= attribute (text modes) or color (graphics modes)
	CX	= count of characters to write (replication factor)

Returns:	Nothing

Notes:

- In graphics modes, the replication factor in CX produces a valid result only for the current row. If more characters are written than there are remaining columns in the current row, the result is unpredictable.
- All values of AL result in some sort of display; control characters, including bell, backspace, carriage return, and line feed, are not recognized as special characters and do not affect the cursor position.
- After a character is written, the cursor must be moved explicitly with Int 10H Function 02H to the next position.
- To write a character without changing the attribute at the current cursor position, use Int 10H Function 0AH.
- If this function is used to write characters in graphics mode and bit 7 of BL is set (1), the character will be exclusive-OR'd (XOR) with the current display contents. This feature can be used to write characters and then "erase" them.
- For the CGA and PCjr in graphics modes 04H–06H, the bit patterns for character codes 80H–FFH are obtained from a table whose address is stored in the vector for Int 1FH. On the PCjr, the address of the table for character codes 00H–7FH is stored in the vector for Int 44H. Alternative character sets may be installed by loading them into memory and updating this vector.
- For the EGA, MCGA, and VGA in graphics modes, the address of the character definition table is stored in the vector for Int 43H. See Int 10H Function 11H.

Int 10H [MDA] [CGA] [PCjr] [EGA] [MCGA] [VGA]
Function 0AH (10)
Write character at cursor

Writes an ASCII character to the display at the current cursor position. The character receives the attribute of the previous character displayed at the same position.

Call with:

AH	= 0AH
AL	= character
BH	= page
BL	= color (graphics modes, PCjr only)
CX	= count of characters to write (replication factor)

Returns: Nothing

Notes:

- In graphics modes, the replication factor in CX produces a valid result only for the current row. If more characters are written than there are remaining columns in the current row, the result is unpredictable.
- All values of AL result in some sort of display; control characters, including bell, backspace, carriage return, and line feed, are not recognized as special characters and do not affect the cursor position.

- After a character is written, the cursor must be moved explicitly with Int 10H Function 02H to the next position.
- To write a character and attribute at the current cursor position, use Int 10H Function 09H.
- If this function is used to write characters in graphics mode and bit 7 of BL is set (1), the character will be exclusive-OR'd (XOR) with the current display contents. This feature can be used to write characters and then "erase" them.
- For the CGA and PCjr in graphics modes 04H–06H, the bit patterns for character codes 80H–FFH are obtained from a table whose address is stored in the vector for Int 1FH. On the PCjr, the address of the table for character codes 00H–7FH is stored in the vector for Int 44H. Alternative character sets may be installed by loading them into memory and updating this vector.
- For the EGA, MCGA, and VGA in graphics modes, the address of the character definition table is stored in the vector for Int 43H. See Int 10H Function 11H.

Int 10H [CGA] [PCjr] [EGA] [MCGA] [VGA]
Function 0BH (11)
Set palette, background, or border

Selects a palette, background, or border color.

Call with: To set the background color and border color for graphics modes or the border color for text modes

AH   = 0BH
BH   = 00H
BL   = color

To select the palette (320-by-200 4-color graphics modes)

AH   = 0BH
BH   = 01H
BL   = palette (see Notes)

Returns: Nothing

Notes:
- In text modes, this function selects only the border color. The background color of each individual character is controlled by the upper 4 bits of that character's attribute byte.
- On the CGA and EGA, this function is valid for palette selection only in 320-by-200 4-color graphics modes.

- In 320-by-200 4-color graphics modes, if register BH = 01H, the following palettes may be selected:

Palette	Pixel value	Color
0	0	same as background
	1	green
	2	red
	3	brown or yellow
1	0	same as background
	1	cyan
	2	magenta
	3	white

- On the CGA in 640-by-200 2-color graphics mode, the background color selected with this function actually controls the display color for nonzero pixels; zero pixels are always displayed as black.

- On the PCjr in 640-by-200 2-color graphics mode, if BH = 00H and bit 0 of register BL is cleared, pixel value 1 is displayed as white; if bit 0 is set, pixel value 1 is displayed as black.

- See also Int 10H Function 10H, which is used for palette programming on the PCjr, EGA, MCGA, and VGA.

Int 10H   [CGA] [PCjr] [EGA] [MCGA] [VGA]
Function 0CH (12)
Write graphics pixel

Draws a point on the display at the specified graphics coordinates.

Call with: AH   = 0CH
                AL   = pixel value
                BH   = page
                CX   = column (graphics x coordinate)
                DX   = row (graphics y coordinate)

Returns: Nothing

Notes:
- The range of valid pixel values and (x,y) coordinates depends on the current video mode.
- If bit 7 of AL is set, the new pixel value will be exclusive-OR'd (XOR) with the current contents of the pixel.
- Register BH is ignored for display modes that support only one page.

Int 10H   [CGA] [PCjr] [EGA] [MCGA] [VGA]
Function 0DH (13)
Read graphics pixel

Obtains the current value of the pixel on the display at the specified graphics coordinates.

Call with:	AH	= 0DH
	BH	= page
	CX	= column (graphics x coordinate)
	DX	= row (graphics y coordinate)

Returns:	AL	= pixel value

Notes:
- The range of valid (x,y) coordinates and possible pixel values depends on the current video mode.
- Register BH is ignored for display modes that support only one page.

Int 10H   [MDA] [CGA] [PCjr] [EGA] [MCGA] [VGA]
Function 0EH (14)
Write character in teletype mode

Writes an ASCII character to the display at the current cursor position, using the specified color (if in graphics modes), and then increments the cursor position appropriately.

Call with:	AH	= 0EH
	AL	= character
	BH	= page
	BL	= foreground color (graphics modes)

Returns:	Nothing

Notes:
- The special ASCII codes for bell (07H), backspace (08H), carriage return (0DH), and line feed (0AH) are recognized, and the appropriate action is taken. All other characters are written to the display (even if they are control characters), and the cursor is moved to the next position.
- In video modes that support multiple pages, characters can be written to any page, regardless of the page currently being displayed.
- Line wrapping and scrolling are provided. If the cursor is at the end of a line, it is moved to the beginning of the next line. If the cursor reaches the end of the last line on the screen, the screen is scrolled up by one line and the cursor is placed at the

beginning of a new blank line. The attribute for the entire new line is taken from the last character that was written on the preceding line.

- The default MS-DOS console driver (CON) uses this function to write text to the screen. You cannot use this function to specify the attribute of a character. One method of writing a character to the screen with a specific attribute is to first write an ASCII blank (20H) with the desired attribute at the current cursor location using Int 10H Function 09H and then write the actual character with Int 10H Function 0EH. This technique, although somewhat clumsy, does not require the program to explicitly handle line wrapping and scrolling.

- See also Int 10H Function 13H.

Int 10H [MDA] [CGA] [PCjr] [EGA] [MCGA] [VGA]
Function 0FH (15)
Get video mode

Obtains the current display mode of the active video controller.

Call with:	AH	= 0FH

Returns:	AH	= number of character columns on screen
	AL	= display mode (see Int 10H Function 00H)
	BH	= active display page

Note:
- This function can be called to obtain the screen width before clearing the screen with Int 10H Functions 06H or 07H.

Int 10H [PCjr] [EGA] [MCGA] [VGA]
Function 10H (16) Subfunction 00H
Set palette register

Sets the correspondence of a palette register to a displayable color.

Call with:	On the PCjr, EGA, or VGA	
	AH	= 10H
	AL	= 00H
	BH	= color value
	BL	= palette register (00–0FH)
	On the MCGA	
	AH	= 10H
	AL	= 00H
	BX	= 0712H

Returns:	Nothing

Note:	■ On the MCGA, this function can only be called with BX = 0712H and selects a color register set with eight consistent colors.

Int 10H
Function 10H (16) Subfunction 01H
Set border color

[PCjr] [EGA] [VGA]

Controls the color of the screen border (overscan).

Call with:	AH	= 10H
	AL	= 01H
	BH	= color value

Returns:	Nothing

Int 10H
Function 10H (16) Subfunction 02H
Set palette and border

[PCjr] [EGA] [VGA]

Sets all palette registers and the border color (overscan) in one operation.

Call with:	AH	= 10H
	AL	= 02H
	ES:DX	= segment:offset of color list

Returns:	Nothing

Notes:	■ The color list is 17 bytes long. The first 16 bytes are the color values to be loaded into palette registers 0–15, and the last byte is stored in the border color register.
	■ In 16-color graphics modes, the following default palette is set up:

Pixel value	Color
01H	blue
02H	green
03H	cyan
04H	red
05H	magenta
06H	brown

Pixel value	Color
07H	white
08H	gray
09H	light blue
0AH	light green
0BH	light cyan
0CH	light red
0DH	light magenta
0EH	yellow
0FH	intense white

Int 10H [PCjr] [EGA] [MCGA] [VGA]
Function 10H (16) Subfunction 03H
Toggle blink/intensity bit

Determines whether the most significant bit of a character attribute will select blinking or intensified display.

Call with:

AH	= 10H
AL	= 03H
BL	= blink/intensity toggle
	0 = enable intensity
	1 = enable blinking

Returns: Nothing

Int 10H [VGA]
Function 10H (16) Subfunction 07H
Get palette register

Returns the color associated with the specified palette register.

Call with:

AH	= 10H
AL	= 07H
BL	= palette register

Returns:

BH	= color

Int 10H

[VGA]

Function 10H (16) Subfunction 08H
Get border color

Returns the current border color (overscan).

| **Call with:** | AH | = 10H |
| | AL | = 08H |

| **Returns:** | BH | = color |

Int 10H

[VGA]

Function 10H (16) Subfunction 09H
Get palette and border

Gets the contents of all palette registers and the border color (overscan) in one operation.

Call with:	AH	= 10H
	AL	= 09H
	ES:DX	= segment:offset of 17-byte buffer

| **Returns:** | ES:DX | = segment:offset of buffer |
| | *and* buffer contains palette values in bytes 00H–0FH and border color in byte 10H. | |

Int 10H

[MCGA] [VGA]

Function 10H (16) Subfunction 10H (16)
Set color register

Programs an individual color register with a red-green-blue (RGB) combination.

Call with:	AH	= 10H
	AL	= 10H
	BX	= color register
	CH	= green value
	CL	= blue value
	DH	= red value

| **Returns:** | Nothing |

| **Note:** | ■ If gray-scale summing is enabled, the weighted gray-scale value is calculated as described under Int 10H Function 10H Subfunction 1BH and is stored into all three components of the color register. See also Int 10H Function 12H Subfunction 33H. |

Int 10H [MCGA] [VGA]
Function 10H (16) Subfunction 12H (18)
Set block of color registers

Programs a group of consecutive color registers in one operation.

Call with:	AH	= 10H
	AL	= 12H
	BX	= first color register
	CX	= number of color registers
	ES:DX	= segment:offset of color table

| **Returns:** | Nothing |

| **Notes:** | ■ The table consists of a series of 3-byte entries, one entry per color register to be programmed. The bytes of an individual entry specify the red, green, and blue values (in that order) for the associated color register. |
| | ■ If gray-scale summing is enabled, the weighted gray-scale value for each register is calculated as described under Int 10H Function 10H Subfunction 1BH and is stored into all three components of the color register. See also Int 10H Function 12H Subfunction 33H. |

Int 10H [VGA]
Function 10H (16) Subfunction 13H (19)
Set color page state

Selects the paging mode for the color registers, or selects an individual page of color registers.

Call with:	To select the paging mode		
	AH	= 10H	
	AL	= 13H	
	BH	= paging mode	
		00H	*for 4 pages of 64 registers*
		01H	*for 16 pages of 16 registers*
	BL	= 00H	

To select a color register page

AH	= 10H
AL	= 13H
BH	= page
BL	= 01H

Returns: Nothing

Note: ■ This function is not valid in mode 13H (320-by-200 256-color graphics).

Int 10H   [MCGA] [VGA]
Function 10H (16) Subfunction 15H (21)
Get color register

Returns the contents of a color register as its red, green, and blue components.

Call with:

AH	= 10H
AL	= 15H
BX	= color register

Returns:

CH	= green value
CL	= blue value
DH	= red value

Int 10H   [MCGA] [VGA]
Function 10H (16) Subfunction 17H (23)
Get block of color registers

Allows the red, green, and blue components associated with each of a set of color registers to be read in one operation.

Call with:

AH	= 10H
AL	= 17H
BX	= first color register
CX	= number of color registers
ES:DX	= segment:offset of buffer to receive color list

Returns:

ES:DX	= segment:offset of buffer

and buffer contains color list

- The color list returned in the caller's buffer consists of a series of 3-byte entries corresponding to the color registers. Each 3-byte entry contains the register's red, green, and blue components in that order.

Int 10H [VGA]
Function 10H (16) Subfunction 1AH (26)
Get color page state

Returns the color register paging mode and current color page.

Call with:	AH	= 10H
	AL	= 1AH

Returns:	BH	= color page	
	BL	= paging mode	
		00H	*if 4 pages of 64 registers*
		01H	*if 16 pages of 16 registers*

Note:

- See Int 10H Function 10H Subfunction 13H, which allows selection of the paging mode or current color page.

Int 10H [MCGA] [VGA]
Function 10H (16) Subfunction 1BH (27)
Set gray-scale values

Transforms the red, green, and blue values of one or more color registers into the gray-scale equivalents.

Call with:	AH	= 10H
	AL	= 1BH
	BX	= first color register
	CX	= number of color registers

Returns: Nothing

Note:

- For each color register, the weighted sum of its red, green, and blue values is calculated (30% red + 59% green + 11% blue) and written back into all three components of the color register. The original red, green, and blue values are lost.

Int 10H [EGA] [MCGA] [VGA]
Function 11H (17) Subfunctions 00H and 10H (16)
Load user font

Loads the user's font (character definition) table into the specified block of character generator RAM.

Call with:	AH	= 11H
	AL	= 00H or 10H (see Notes)
	BH	= points (bytes per character)
	BL	= block
	CX	= number of characters defined by table
	DX	= first character code in table
	ES:BP	= segment:offset of font table

Returns:	Nothing

Notes:
- This function provides font selection in text (alphanumeric) display modes. For font selection in graphics (all-points-addressable) modes, see Int 10H Function 11H Subfunctions 20H–24H.

- If AL = 10H, page 0 must be active. The points (bytes per character), rows, and length of the refresh buffer are recalculated. The controller is reprogrammed with the maximum scan line ($points - 1$), cursor start ($points - 2$), cursor end ($points - 1$), vertical display end (($rows * points) - 1$), and underline location ($points - 1$, mode 7 only).

  If Subfunction 10H is called at any time other than immediately after a mode set, the results are unpredictable.

- On the MCGA, a Subfunction 00H call should be followed by a Subfunction 03H call so that the ROM BIOS will load the font into the character generator's internal font pages.

- Subfunction 10H is reserved on the MCGA. If it is called, Subfunction 00H is executed.

Int 10H [EGA] [VGA]
Function 11H (17) Subfunctions 01H and 11H (17)
Load ROM 8-by-14 font

Loads the ROM BIOS default 8-by-14 font table into the specified block of character generator RAM.

Call with:	AH	= 11H
	AL	= 01H or 11H (see Notes)
	BL	= block

Returns: Nothing

Notes:
- This function provides font selection in text (alphanumeric) display modes. For font selection in graphics (all-points-addressable) modes, see Int 10H Function 11H Subfunctions 20H–24H.
- If AL = 11H, page 0 must be active. The points (bytes per character), rows, and length of the refresh buffer are recalculated. The controller is reprogrammed with the maximum scan line (*points – 1*), cursor start (*points – 2*), cursor end (*points – 1*), vertical display end ((*rows* * *points*) – *1*), and underline location (*points – 1*, mode 7 only).

  If Subfunction 11H is called at any time other than immediately after a mode set, the results are unpredictable.
- Subfunctions 01H and 11H are reserved on the MCGA. If either is called, Subfunction 04H is executed.

Int 10H   [EGA] [MCGA] [VGA]
Function 11H (17) Subfunctions 02H and 12H (18)
Load ROM 8-by-8 font

Loads the ROM BIOS default 8-by-8 font table into the specified block of character generator RAM.

Call with: AH   = 11H
                 AL   = 02H or 12H (see Notes)
                 BL   = block

Returns: Nothing

Notes:
- This function provides font selection in text (alphanumeric) display modes. For font selection in graphics (all-points-addressable) modes, see Int 10H Function 11H Subfunctions 20H–24H.
- If AL = 12H, page 0 must be active. The points (bytes per character), rows, and length of the refresh buffer are recalculated. The controller is reprogrammed with the maximum scan line (*points – 1*), cursor start (*points – 2*), cursor end (*points – 1*), vertical display end ((*rows* * *points*) – *1*), and underline location (*points – 1*, mode 7 only).

  If Subfunction 12H is called at any time other than immediately after a mode set, the results are unpredictable.
- On the MCGA, a Subfunction 02H call should be followed by a Subfunction 03H call, so that the ROM BIOS will load the font into the character generator's internal font pages.
- Subfunction 12H is reserved on the MCGA. If it is called, Subfunction 02H is executed.

Int 10H

Function 11H (17) Subfunction 03H
Set block specifier

Determines the character blocks selected by bit 3 of character attribute bytes in alphanumeric (text) display modes.

Call with:	AH	= 11H
	AL	= 03H
	BL	= character generator block select code (see Notes)

Returns:	Nothing

Notes:
- On the EGA and MCGA, the bits of BL are used as follows:

Bits	**Significance**
0–1	character block selected by attribute bytes with bit 3 = 0
2–3	character block selected by attribute bytes with bit 3 = 1
4–7	not used (should be 0)

- On the VGA, the bits of BL are used as follows:

Bits	**Significance**
0,1,4	character block selected by attribute bytes with bit 3 = 0
2,3,5	character block selected by attribute bytes with bit 3 = 1
6–7	not used (should be 0)

- When using a 256-character set, both fields of BL should select the same character block. In such cases, character attribute bit 3 controls the foreground intensity. When using 512-character sets, the fields of BL designate the blocks holding each half of the character set, and bit 3 of the character attribute selects the upper or lower half of the character set.
- When using a 512-character set, a call to Int 10H Function 10H Subfunction 00H with BX = 0712H is recommended to set the color planes to eight consistent colors.

Int 10H
[MCGA] [VGA]

Function 11H (17) Subfunctions 04H and 14H (20)
Load ROM 8-by-16 font

Loads the ROM BIOS default 8-by-16 font table into the specified block of character generator RAM.

Call with:	AH	= 11H
	AL	= 04H or 14H (see Notes)
	BL	= block

Returns: Nothing

Notes:
- This function provides font selection in text (alphanumeric) display modes. For font selection in graphics (all-points-addressable) modes, see Int 10H Function 11H Subfunctions 20H–24H.
- If AL = 14H, page 0 must be active. The points (bytes per character), rows, and length of the refresh buffer are recalculated. The controller is reprogrammed with the maximum scan line (*points* – *1*), cursor start (*points* – *2*), cursor end (*points* – *1*), vertical display end (*rows* * *points* – *1* for 350- and 400-line modes, or *rows* * *points* * 2 – 1 for 200-line modes), and underline location (*points* – *1*, mode 7 only).

  If Subfunction 14H is called at any time other than immediately after a mode set, the results are unpredictable.
- On the MCGA, a Subfunction 04H call should be followed by a Subfunction 03H call so that the ROM BIOS will load the font into the character generator's internal font pages.
- Subfunction 14H is reserved on the MCGA. If it is called, Subfunction 04H is executed.

Int 10H   [EGA] [MCGA] [VGA]
Function 11H (17) Subfunction 20H (32)
Set Int 1FH font pointer

Sets the Int 1FH pointer to the user's font table. This table is used for character codes 80H–FFH in graphics modes 04H–06H.

Call with: AH   = 11H
               AL   = 20H
               ES:BP   = segment:offset of font table

Returns: Nothing

Note:
- This function provides font selection in graphics (all-points-addressable) display modes. For font selection in text (alphanumeric) modes, see Int 10H Function 11H Subfunctions 00H–14H.
- If this subfunction is called at any time other than immediately after a mode set, the results are unpredictable.

Int 10H [EGA] [MCGA] [VGA]
Function 11H (17) Subfunction 21H (33)
Set Int 43H for user's font

Sets the vector for Int 43H to point to the user's font table and updates the video ROM BIOS data area. The video controller is not reprogrammed.

Call with:

AH	= 11H	
AL	= 21H	
BL	= character rows specifier	
	00H	*if user specified (see register DL)*
	01H	*= 14 (0EH) rows*
	02H	*= 25 (19H) rows*
	03H	*= 43 (2BH) rows*
CX	= points (bytes per character)	
DL	= character rows per screen (if BL = 00H)	
ES:BP	= segment:offset of user font table	

Returns: Nothing

Notes:
- This function provides font selection in graphics (all-points-addressable) display modes. For font selection in text (alphanumeric) modes, see Int 10H Function 11H Subfunctions 00H–14H.
- If this subfunction is called at any time other than immediately after a mode set, the results are unpredictable.

Int 10H [EGA] [MCGA] [VGA]
Function 11H (17) Subfunction 22H (34)
Set Int 43H for ROM 8-by-14 font

Sets the vector for Int 43H to point to the ROM BIOS default 8-by-14 font and updates the video ROM BIOS data area. The video controller is not reprogrammed.

Call with:

AH	= 11H	
AL	= 22H	
BL	= character rows specifier	
	00H	*if user specified (see register DL)*
	01H	*= 14 (0EH) rows*
	02H	*= 25 (19H) rows*
	03H	*= 43 (2BH) rows*
DL	= character rows per screen (if BL = 00H)	

Returns: Nothing

Notes:
- This function provides font selection in graphics (all-points-addressable) display modes. For font selection in text (alphanumeric) modes, see Int 10H Function 11H Subfunctions 00H–14H.
- If this subfunction is called at any time other than immediately after a mode set, the results are unpredictable.
- When this subfunction is called on the MCGA, Subfunction 24H is substituted.

Int 10H   [EGA] [MCGA] [VGA]
Function 11H (17) Subfunction 23H (35)
Set Int 43H for ROM 8-by-8 font

Sets the vector for Int 43H to point to the ROM BIOS default 8-by-8 font and updates the video ROM BIOS data area. The video controller is not reprogrammed.

Call with: AH   = 11H
                 AL   = 23H
                 BL   = character rows specifier
                         00H   *if user specified (see register DL)*
                         01H   *= 14 (0EH) rows*
                         02H   *= 25 (19H) rows*
                         03H   *= 43 (2BH) rows*
                 DL   = character rows per screen (if BL = 00H)

Returns: Nothing

Notes:
- This function provides font selection in graphics (all-points-addressable) display modes. For font selection in text (alphanumeric) modes, see Int 10H Function 11H Subfunctions 00H–14H.
- If this subfunction is called at any time other than immediately after a mode set, the results are unpredictable.

Int 10H   [MCGA] [VGA]
Function 11H (17) Subfunction 24H (36)
Set Int 43H for ROM 8-by-16 font

Sets the vector for Int 43H to point to the ROM BIOS default 8-by-16 font and updates the video ROM BIOS data area. The video controller is not reprogrammed.

Call with:	AH	= 11H
	AL	= 24H
	BL	= row specifier
		00H	*if user specified (see register DL)*
		01H	= *14 (0EH) rows*
		02H	= *25 (19H) rows*
		03H	= *43 (2BH) rows*
	DL	= character rows per screen (if BL = 00H)

| **Returns:** | Nothing |

| **Note:** | ■ This function provides font selection in graphics (all-points-addressable) display modes. For font selection in text (alphanumeric) modes, see Int 10H Function 11H Subfunctions 00H–14H. |
| | ■ If this subfunction is called at any time other than immediately after a mode set, the results are unpredictable. |

Int 10H [EGA] [MCGA] [VGA]
Function 11H (17) Subfunction 30H (48)
Get font information

Returns a pointer to the character definition table for a font and the points (bytes per character) and rows for that font.

Call with:	AH	= 11H
	AL	= 30H
	BH	= font code
		00H	= *current Int 1FH contents*
		01H	= *current Int 43H contents*
		02H	= *ROM 8-by-14 font (EGA, VGA only)*
		03H	= *ROM 8-by-8 font (characters 00H–7FH)*
		04H	= *ROM 8-by-8 font (characters 80H–FFH)*
		05H	= *ROM alternate 9-by-14 font (EGA, VGA only)*
		06H	= *ROM 8-by-16 font (MCGA, VGA only)*
		07H	= *ROM alternate 9-by-16 font (VGA only)*

Returns:	CX	= points (bytes per character)
	DL	= rows (character rows on screen − 1)
	ES:BP	= segment:offset of font table

Int 10H
Function 12H (18) Subfunction 10H (16)
Get configuration information

Obtains configuration information for the active video subsystem.

| Call with: | AH | = 12H |
| | BL | = 10H |

Returns:	BH	= display type
		0 *if color display*
		1 *if monochrome display*
	BL	= memory installed on EGA board
		00H *if 64 KB*
		01H *if 128 KB*
		02H *if 192 KB*
		03H *if 256 KB*
	CH	= feature bits (see Notes)
	CL	= switch setting (see Notes)

Notes:

■ The feature bits are set from Input Status register 0 in response to an output on the specified Feature Control register bits:

Feature bit(s)	*Feature control output bit*	*Input status bit*
0	0	5
1	0	6
2	1	5
3	1	6
4–7	not used	

■ The bits in the switch settings byte indicate the state of the EGA's configuration DIP switch (1 = off, 0 = on).

Bit(s)	*Significance*
0	configuration switch 1
1	configuration switch 2
2	configuration switch 3
3	configuration switch 4
4–7	not used

Int 10H [EGA] [VGA]
Function 12H (18) Subfunction 20H (32)
Select alternate printscreen

Selects an alternate print-screen routine for the EGA and VGA that works properly if the screen length is not 25 lines. The ROM BIOS default print-screen routine always prints 25 lines.

| Call with: | AH | = 12H |
| | BL | = 20H |

Returns: Nothing

Int 10H [VGA]
Function 12H (18) Subfunction 30H (48)
Set scan lines

Selects the number of scan lines for alphanumeric modes. The selected value takes effect the next time Int 10H Function 00H is called to select the display mode.

Call with:	AH	= 12H	
	AL	= scan line code	
		00H	*= 200 scan lines*
		01H	*= 350 scan lines*
		02H	*= 400 scan lines*
	BL	= 30H	

Returns:	If the VGA is active	
	AL	= 12H
	If the VGA is not active	
	AL	= 00H

Int 10H [MCGA] [VGA]
Function 12H (18) Subfunction 31H (49)
Enable/disable default palette loading

Enables or disables loading of a default palette when a video display mode is selected.

Call with: AH = 12H
AL = 00H to enable default palette loading
01H to disable default palette loading
BL = 31H

Returns: If function supported
AL = 12H

Int 10H [MCGA] [VGA]
Function 12H (18) Subfunction 32H (50)
Enable/disable video

Enables or disables CPU access to the video adapter's I/O ports and video refresh buffer.

Call with: AH = 12H
AL = 00H to enable access
01H to disable access
BL = 32H

Returns: If function supported
AL = 12H

Int 10H [MCGA] [VGA]
Function 12H (18) Subfunction 33H (51)
Enable/disable gray-scale summing

Enables or disables gray-scale summing for the currently active display.

Call with: AH = 12H
AL = 00H to enable gray-scale summing
01H to disable gray-scale summing
BL = 33H

Returns: If function supported
AL = 12H

Note: ■ When enabled, gray-scale summing occurs during display mode selection, palette programming, and color register loading.

Int 10H [VGA]
Function 12H (18) Subfunction 34H (52)
Enable/disable cursor emulation

Enables or disables cursor emulation for the currently active display. When cursor emulation is enabled, the ROM BIOS automatically remaps Int 10H Function 01H cursor starting and ending lines for the current character cell dimensions.

Call with:	AH	= 12H
	AL	= 00H to enable cursor emulation
		01H to disable cursor emulation
	BL	= 34H

Returns:	If function supported	
	AL	= 12H

Int 10H [MCGA] [VGA]
Function 12H (18) Subfunction 35H (53)
Switch active display

Allows selection of one of two video adapters in the system when memory usage or port addresses conflict between the two adapters.

Call with:	AH	= 12H	
	AL	= switching function	
		00H	*to disable initial video adapter*
		01H	*to enable system board video adapter*
		02H	*to disable active video adapter*
		03H	*to enable inactive video adapter*
	BL	= 35H	
	ES:DX	= segment:offset of 128-byte buffer (if AL = 00H, 02H, or 03H)	

Returns:	If function supported	
	AL	= 12H

and, if called with AL = 00H or 02H
Video adapter state information saved in caller's buffer

or, if called with AL = 03H
Video adapter state restored from information in caller's buffer

- This subfunction cannot be used unless both video adapters have a disable capability (Int 10H Function 12H Subfunction 32H).

- If there is no conflict between the system board video and the adapter board video in memory or port usage, both video controllers can be active simultaneously and this subfunction is not required.

Int 10H [VGA]
Function 12H (18) Subfunction 36H (54)
Enable/disable screen refresh

Enables or disables the video refresh for the currently active display.

Call with:

AH	= 12H	
AL	= 00H to enable refresh	
	01H to disable refresh	
BL	= 36H	

Returns: If function supported

AL	= 12H

Int 10H [MDA] [CGA] [PCjr] [EGA] [MCGA] [VGA]
Function 13H (19)
Write string in teletype mode

Transfers a string to the video buffer for the currently active display, starting at the specified position.

Call with:

AH	= 13H	
AL	= write mode	
	0	*attribute in BL;*
		string contains character codes only; and cursor position is not updated after write
	1	*attribute in BL;*
		string contains character codes only; and cursor position is updated after write
	2	*string contains alternating character codes and attribute bytes; and cursor position is not updated after write*
	3	*string contains alternating character codes and attribute bytes; and cursor position is updated after write*

BH	= page	
BL	= attribute, if AL = 00H or 01H	
CX	= length of character string	
DH	= y coordinate (row)	
DL	= x coordinate (column)	
ES:BP	= segment:offset of string	

Returns: Nothing

Notes:
- This function is not available on the original IBM PC or PC/XT unless an EGA video adapter (which contains its own ROM BIOS) is installed.
- This function may be thought of as an extension to Int 10H Function 0EH. The control characters bell (07H), backspace (08H), line feed (0AH), and carriage return (0DH) are recognized and handled appropriately.

Int 10H   [PS/2]
Function 1AH (26)
Get or set display combination code

Returns a code describing the installed display adapter(s) or updates the ROM BIOS's variable describing the installed adapter(s).

Call with:
AH	= 1AH
AL	= subfunction
	00H = get display combination code
	01H = set display combination code
BH	= inactive display code (if AL = 01H)
BL	= active display code (if AL = 01H)

Returns: If function supported

AL	= 1AH

and, if called with AL = 00H

BH	= inactive display code
BL	= active display code

Note:
- The display codes are interpreted as follows:

Code(s)	Video subsystem type
00H	no display
01H	MDA with 5151 monitor
02H	CGA with 5153 or 5154 monitor
03H	reserved
04H	EGA with 5153 or 5154 monitor

Code(s)	Video subsystem type
05H	EGA with 5151 monitor
06H	PGA with 5175 monitor
07H	VGA with analog monochrome monitor
08H	VGA with analog color monitor
09H	reserved
0AH	MCGA with digital color monitor
0BH	MCGA with analog monochrome monitor
0CH	MCGA with analog color monitor
0DH–FEH	reserved
FFH	unknown

Int 10H
Function 1BH (27)
Get functionality/state information

[PS/2]

Obtains information about the current display mode as well as a pointer to a table describing the characteristics and capabilities of the video adapter and monitor.

Call with:

AH	= 1BH
BX	= implementation type (always 00H)
ES:DI	= segment:offset of 64-byte buffer

Returns:

If function supported

AL	= 1BH

and information placed in caller's buffer (see Notes)

Notes:

- The caller's buffer is filled in with information that depends on the current video display mode:

Byte(s)	Contents
00H–03H	pointer to functionality information (see next Note)
04H	current video mode
05H–06H	number of character columns
07H–08H	length of video refresh buffer (bytes)
09H–0AH	starting address in buffer of upper left corner of display
0BH–1AH	cursor position for video pages 0–7 as eight 2-byte entries; first byte of each pair is y coordinate, second byte is x coordinate
1BH	cursor starting line
1CH	cursor ending line
1DH	active display page
1EH–1FH	adapter base port address (3BXH monochrome, 3DXH color)
20H	current setting of register 3B8H or 3D8H

Byte(s)	Contents
21H	current setting of register 3B9H or 3D9H
22H	number of character rows
23H–24H	character height in scan lines
25H	active display code (see Int 10H Function 1AH)
26H	inactive display code (see Int 10H Function 1AH)
27H–28H	number of displayable colors (0 for monochrome)
29H	number of display pages
2AH	number of scan lines

00H	*= 200 scan lines*
01H	*= 350 scan lines*
02H	*= 400 scan lines*
03H	*= 480 scan lines*
04H–FFH	*= reserved*

Byte(s)	Contents
2BH	primary character block (see Int 10H Function 11H Subfunction 03H)
2CH	secondary character block
2DH	miscellaneous state information

Bit(s)	Significance
0	= 1 if all modes on all displays active (always 0 on MCGA)
1	= 1 if gray-scale summing active
2	= 1 if monochrome display attached
3	= 1 if mode set default palette loading disabled
4	= 1 if cursor emulation active (always 0 on MCGA)
5	= state of I/B toggle (0 = intensity, 1 = blink)
6–7	= reserved

Byte(s)	Contents
2EH–30H	reserved
31H	video memory available

00H	*= 64 KB*
01H	*= 128 KB*
02H	*= 192 KB*
03H	*= 256 KB*

Byte(s)	Contents
32H	save pointer state information

Bit(s)	Significance
0	= 1 if 512-character set active
1	= 1 if dynamic save area active
2	= 1 if alpha font override active
3	= 1 if graphics font override active
4	= 1 if palette override active
5	= 1 if display combination code (DCC) extension active
6–7	= reserved

Byte(s)	Contents
33H–3FH	reserved

- Bytes 0–3 of the caller's buffer contain a DWORD pointer (offset in lower word, segment in upper word) to the following information about the display adapter and monitor:

Byte(s)	Contents
00H	video modes supported

Bit	Significance
0	= 1 if mode 00H supported
1	= 1 if mode 01H supported
2	= 1 if mode 02H supported
3	= 1 if mode 03H supported
4	= 1 if mode 04H supported
5	= 1 if mode 05H supported
6	= 1 if mode 06H supported
7	= 1 if mode 07H supported

Byte(s)	Contents
01H	video modes supported

Bit	Significance
0	= 1 if mode 08H supported
1	= 1 if mode 09H supported
2	= 1 if mode 0AH supported
3	= 1 if mode 0BH supported
4	= 1 if mode 0CH supported
5	= 1 if mode 0DH supported
6	= 1 if mode 0EH supported
7	= 1 if mode 0FH supported

Byte(s)	Contents
02H	video modes supported

Bit(s)	Significance
0	= 1 if mode 10H supported
1	= 1 if mode 11H supported
2	= 1 if mode 12H supported
3	= 1 if mode 13H supported
4–7	= reserved

Byte(s)	Contents
03H–06H	reserved
07H	scan lines available in text modes

Bit(s)	Significance
0	= 1 if 200 scan lines
1	= 1 if 350 scan lines
2	= 1 if 400 scan lines
3–7	= reserved

Byte(s)	Contents
08H	character blocks available in text modes (see Int 10H Function 11H)
09H	maximum number of active character blocks in text modes
0AH	miscellaneous BIOS capabilities

Bit	Significance
0	= 1 if all modes active on all displays (always 0 for MCGA)
1	= 1 if gray-scale summing available
2	= 1 if character font loading available
3	= 1 if mode set default palette loading available
4	= 1 if cursor emulation available
5	= 1 if EGA (64-color) palette available
6	= 1 if color register loading available
7	= 1 if color register paging mode select available

Byte(s)	Contents		
0BH	miscellaneous BIOS capabilities		
	Bit(s)	**Significance**	
	0	= 1 if light pen available	
	1	= 1 if save/restore video state available (always 0 on MCGA)	
	2	= 1 if background intensity/blinking control available	
	3	= 1 if get/set display combination code available	
	4–7	= reserved	
0CH–0DH	reserved		
0EH	save area capabilities		
	Bit(s)	**Significance**	
	0	= 1 if supports 512-character sets	
	1	= 1 if dynamic save area available	
	2	= 1 if alpha font override available	
	3	= 1 if graphics font override available	
	4	= 1 if palette override available	
	5	= 1 if display combination code extension available	
	6–7	= reserved	
0FH	reserved		

Int 10H [PS/2]
Function 1CH (28)
Save or restore video state

Saves or restores the digital-to-analog converter (DAC) state and color registers, ROM BIOS video driver data area, or video hardware state.

Call with:

	AH	= 1CH	
	AL	= subfunction	
		00H	*to get state buffer size*
		01H	*to save state*
		02H	*to restore state*
	CX	= requested states	
		Bit(s)	**Significance (if set)**
		0	save/restore video hardware state
		1	save/restore video BIOS data area
		2	save/restore video DAC state and color registers
		3–15	reserved
	ES:BX	= segment:offset of buffer	

Returns: If function supported

	AL	= 1CH

and, if called with AL = 00H

BX   = buffer block count (64 bytes per block)

or, if called with AL = 01H

State information placed in caller's buffer

or, if called with AL = 02H

Requested state restored according to contents of caller's buffer

---

Notes:
- Subfunction 00H is used to determine the size of buffer that will be necessary to contain the specified state information. The caller must supply the buffer.
- The current video state is altered during a save state operation (AL = 01H). If the requesting program needs to continue in the same video state, it can follow the save state request with an immediate call to restore the video state.
- This function is supported on the VGA only.

Int 11H   [PC] [AT] [PS/2]
Get equipment configuration

Obtains the equipment list code word from the ROM BIOS.

Call with: Nothing

Returns: AX   = equipment list code word

Bit(s)	Significance
0	= 1 if floppy disk drive(s) installed
1	= 1 if math coprocessor installed
2	= 1 if pointing device installed (PS/2)
2–3	system board ram size (PC, see Note)
	00 = 16 KB
	01 = 32 KB
	10 = 48 KB
	11 = 64 KB
4–5	initial video mode
	00 reserved
	01 40-by-25 color text
	10 80-by-25 color text
	11 80-by-25 monochrome
6–7	number of floppy disk drives (if bit 0 = 1)
	00 = 1
	01 = 2
	10 = 3
	11 = 4
8	reserved
9–11	number of RS-232 ports installed
12	= 1 if game adapter installed

Bit(s)	Significance
13	= 1 if internal modem installed (PC and XT only)
	= 1 if serial printer attached (PCjr)
14–15	number of printers installed

Note:

- Bits 2–3 of the returned value are used only in the ROM BIOS for the original IBM PC with the 64 KB system board and on the PCjr.

Int 12H
Get conventional memory size

[PC] [AT] [PS/2]

Returns the amount of conventional memory available for use by MS-DOS and application programs.

Call with: Nothing

Returns: AX = memory size (in KB)

Notes:

- On some early PC models, the amount of memory returned by this function is controlled by the settings of the dip switches on the system board and may not reflect all the memory that is physically present.

- On the PC/AT, the value returned is the amount of *functional* memory found during the power-on self-test, regardless of the memory size configuration information stored in CMOS RAM.

- The value returned does not reflect any extended memory (above the 1 MB boundary) that may be installed on 80286 or 80386 machines such as the PC/AT or PS/2 (Models 50 and above).

Int 13H
Function 00H
Reset disk system

[PC] [AT] [PS/2]

Resets the disk controller, recalibrates its attached drives (the read/write arm is moved to cylinder 0), and prepares for disk I/O.

Call with:
AH	= 00H	
DL	= drive	
	00H–7FH	*floppy disk*
	80H–FFH	*fixed disk*

Returns: If function successful
Carry flag = clear
AH   = 00H

If function unsuccessful
Carry flag = set
AH   = status (see Int 13H Function 01H)

Notes:
- This function should be called after a failed floppy disk Read, Write, Verify, or Format request before retrying the operation.
- If called with DL >= 80H (i.e., selecting a fixed disk drive), the floppy disk controller and then the fixed disk controller are reset. See also Int 13H Function 0DH, which allows the fixed disk controller to be reset without affecting the floppy disk controller.

Int 13H
Function 01H
Get disk system status

[PC] [AT] [PS/2]

Returns the status of the most recent disk operation.

Call with: AH   = 01H
DL   = drive
        00H–7FH   *floppy disk*
        80H–FFH   *fixed disk*

Returns: AH   = 00H
AL   = status of previous disk operation
        00H   *no error*
        01H   *invalid command*
        02H   *address mark not found*
        03H   *disk write-protected (F)*
        04H   *sector not found*
        05H   *reset failed (H)*
        06H   *floppy disk removed (F)*
        07H   *bad parameter table (H)*
        08H   *DMA overrun (F)*
        09H   *DMA crossed 64 KB boundary*
        0AH   *bad sector flag (H)*
        0BH   *bad track flag (H)*
        0CH   *media type not found (F)*
        0DH   *invalid number of sectors on format (H)*
        0EH   *control data address mark detected (H)*
        0FH   *DMA arbitration level out of range (H)*

10H	uncorrectable CRC[1] or ECC[2] data error
11H	ECC corrected data error (H)
20H	controller failed
40H	seek failed
80H	disk timed-out (failed to respond)
AAH	drive not ready (H)
BBH	undefined error (H)
CCH	write fault (H)
E0H	status register error (H)
FFH	sense operation failed (H)

H = fixed disk only, F = floppy disk only

[1] Cyclic Redundancy Check code
[2] Error Checking and Correcting code

Note: ■ On fixed disks, error code 11H (ECC data error) indicates that a recoverable error was detected during a preceding Read Sector (Int 13H Function 02H) function.

Int 13H
Function 02H
Read sector

[PC] [AT] [PS/2]

Reads one or more sectors from disk into memory.

Call with:

AH	= 02H
AL	= number of sectors
CH	= cylinder
CL	= sector
DH	= head
DL	= drive
	00H–7FH *floppy disk*
	80H–FFH *fixed disk*
ES:BX	= segment:offset of buffer

Returns:

If function successful

Carry flag	= clear
AH	= 00H
AL	= number of sectors transferred

If function unsuccessful

Carry flag	= set
AH	= status (see Int 13H Function 01H)

■ On fixed disks, the upper 2 bits of the 10-bit cylinder number are placed in the upper 2 bits of register CL.

■ On fixed disks, error code 11H indicates that a read error occurred that was corrected by the ECC algorithm; in this event, register AL contains the burst length. The data returned is probably good, although there is a small chance that the data was not corrected properly. If a multi-sector transfer was requested, the operation was terminated after the sector containing the read error.

■ On floppy disk drives, an error may result from the drive motor being off at the time of the request. The ROM BIOS does not automatically wait for the drive to come up to speed before attempting the read operation. The requesting program should reset the floppy disk system (Int 13H Function 00H) and retry the operation three times before assuming that the error results from some other cause.

Int 13H
Function 03H
Write sector

[PC] [AT] [PS/2]

Writes one or more sectors from memory to disk.

Call with:

AH	= 03H	
AL	= number of sectors	
CH	= cylinder	
CL	= sector	
DH	= head	
DL	= drive	
	00H–7FH	*floppy disk*
	80H–FFH	*fixed disk*
ES:BX	= segment:offset of buffer	

Returns:

If function successful

Carry flag	= clear
AH	= 00H
AL	= number of sectors transferred

If function unsuccessful

Carry flag	= set
AH	= status (see Int 13H Function 01H)

Notes:

■ On fixed disks, the upper 2 bits of the 10-bit cylinder number are placed in the upper 2 bits of register CL.

■ On floppy disk drives, an error may result from the drive motor being off at the time of the request. The ROM BIOS does not automatically wait for the drive to come up to speed before attempting the write operation. The requesting program should reset the floppy disk system (Int 13H Function 00H) and retry the operation three times before assuming that the error results from some other cause.

Int 13H
Function 04H
Verify sector

[PC] [AT] [PS/2]

Verifies the address fields of one or more sectors. No data is transferred to or from memory by this operation.

Call with:

AH	= 04H
AL	= number of sectors
CH	= cylinder
CL	= sector
DH	= head
DL	= drive
	00H–7FH floppy disk
	80H–FFH fixed disk
ES:BX	= segment:offset of buffer (see Notes)

Returns:

If function successful

Carry flag	= clear
AH	= 00H
AL	= number of sectors verified

If function unsuccessful

Carry flag	= set
AH	= status (see Int 13H Function 01H)

Notes:

- On PCs, PC/XTs, and PC/ATs with ROM BIOS dated earlier than 11/15/85, ES:BX should point to a valid buffer.
- On fixed disks, the upper 2 bits of the 10-bit cylinder number are placed in the upper 2 bits of register CL.
- This function can be used to test whether a readable media is in a floppy disk drive. An error may result from the drive motor being off at the time of the request, because the ROM BIOS does not automatically wait for the drive to come up to speed before attempting the verify operation. The requesting program should reset the floppy disk system (Int 13H Function 00H) and retry the operation three times before assuming that a readable floppy disk is not present.

Int 13H
Function 05H
Format track

Initializes disk sector and track address fields on the specified track.

Call with: AH   = 05H
                AL   = interleave (PC/XT fixed disks)
                CH   = cylinder
                DH   = head
                DL   = drive

                       00H–7FH   floppy disk
                       80H–FFH   fixed disk

                ES:BX   = segment:offset of address field list (except PC/XT fixed disk, see Note)

Returns: If function successful
             Carry flag   = clear
             AH   = 00H

             If function unsuccessful
             Carry flag   = set
             AH   = status (see Int 13H Function 01H)

Notes:

- On floppy disks, the address field list consists of a series of 4-byte entries, one entry per sector, in the following format:

Byte	*Contents*
0	cylinder
1	head
2	sector
3	sector-size code

          00H   *if 128 bytes per sector*
          01H   *if 256 bytes per sector*
          02H   *if 512 bytes per sector (standard)*
          03H   *if 1024 bytes per sector*

- On floppy disks, the number of sectors per track is taken from the BIOS floppy disk parameter table whose address is stored in the vector for Int 1EH.

- When this function is used for floppy disks on the PC/AT or PS/2, it should be preceded by a call to Int 13H Function 17H to select the type of medium to be formatted.

- On fixed disks, the upper 2 bits of the 10-bit cylinder number are placed in the upper 2 bits of register CL.

- On PC/XT-286, PC/AT, and PS/2 fixed disks, ES:BX points to a 512-byte buffer containing byte pairs for each physical disk sector, as follows:

Byte	Contents
0	00H for good sector
	80H for bad sector
1	sector number

For example, to format a track with 17 sectors and an interleave of two, ES:BX would point to the following 34-byte array at the beginning of a 512-byte buffer:

```
db    00h,01h,00h,0ah,00h,02h,00h,0bh,00h,03h,00h,0ch
db    00h,04h,00h,0dh,00h,05h,00h,0eh,00h,06h,00h,0fh
db    00h,07h,00h,10h,00h,08h,00h,11h,00h,09h
```

Int 13H
Function 06H
Format bad track

Initializes a track, writing disk address fields and data sectors and setting bad sector flags.

Call with:

AH	= 06H	
AL	= interleave	
CH	= cylinder	
DH	= head	
DL	= drive	
	80H–FFH	*fixed disk*

Returns:

If function successful
Carry flag = clear
AH = 00H

If function unsuccessful
Carry flag = set
AH = status (see Int 13H Function 01H)

Notes:

- This function is defined for PC/XT fixed disk drives only.
- For additional information, see Notes for Int 13H Function 05H.

Int 13H
Function 07H
Format drive

Formats the entire drive, writing disk address fields and data sectors, starting at the specified cylinder.

Call with: AH   = 07H
                   AL   = interleave
                   CH   = cylinder
                   DL   = drive
                          80H–FFH   fixed disk

Returns: If function successful
                   Carry flag   = clear
                   AH   = 00H
                   If function unsuccessful
                   Carry flag   = set
                   AH   = status (see Int 13H Function 01H)

Notes: ▪ This function is defined for PC/XT fixed disk drives only.
               ▪ For additional information, see Notes for Int 13H Function 05H.

Int 13H
Function 08H
Get drive parameters

Returns various parameters for the specified drive.

Call with: AH   = 08H
                   DL   = drive
                          00H–7FH   floppy disk
                          80H–FFH   fixed disk

Returns: If function successful
                   Carry flag   = clear
                   BL   = drive type (PC/AT and PS/2 floppy disks)
                          01H   if 360 KB, 40 track, 5.25"
                          02H   if 1.2 MB, 80 track, 5.25"
                          03H   if 720 KB, 80 track, 3.5"
                          04H   if 1.44 MB, 80 track, 3.5"

CH	= low 8 bits of maximum cylinder number
CL	= bits 6–7 high-order 2 bits of maximum cylinder number
	bits 0–5 maximum sector number
DH	= maximum head number
DL	= number of drives
ES:DI	= segment:offset of disk drive parameter table

If function unsuccessful

Carry flag	= set
AH	= status (see Int 13H Function 01H)

Notes:
- On the PC and PC/XT, this function is supported on fixed disks only.
- The value returned in register DL reflects the true number of physical drives attached to the adapter for the requested drive.

Int 13H
Function 09H
Initialize fixed disk characteristics

[PC] [AT] [PS/2]

Initializes the fixed disk controller for subsequent I/O operations, using the values found in the ROM BIOS disk parameter block(s).

Call with:

AH	= 09H
DL	= drive
	80H–FFH fixed disk

and, on the PC/XT
Vector for Int 41H must point to disk parameter block

or, on the PC/AT and PS/2
Vector for Int 41H must point to disk parameter block for drive 0
Vector for Int 46H must point to disk parameter block for drive 1

Returns:

If function successful

Carry flag	= clear
AH	= 00H

If function unsuccessful

Carry flag	= set
AH	= status (see Int 13H Function 01H)

Notes:

- This function is supported on fixed disks only.
- For PC and PC/XT fixed disks, the parameter block format is as follows:

Byte(s)	Contents
00H–01H	maximum number of cylinders
02H	maximum number of heads
03H–04H	starting reduced write current cylinder
05H–06H	starting write precompensation cylinder
07H	maximum ECC burst length
08H	drive options

Bit(s)	Significance (if set)
0–2	drive option
3–5	reserved (0)
6	disable ECC retries
7	disable disk-access retries

Byte(s)	Contents
09H	standard time-out value
0AH	time-out value for format drive
0BH	time-out value for check drive
0CH–0FH	reserved

- For PC/AT and PS/2 fixed disks, the parameter block format is as follows:

Byte(s)	Contents
00H–01H	maximum number of cylinders
02H	maximum number of heads
03H–04H	reserved
05H–06H	starting write precompensation cylinder
07H	maximum ECC burst length
08H	drive options

Bit(s)	Significance (if set)
0–2	not used
3	more than 8 heads
4	not used
5	manufacturer's defect map present at maximum cylinder + 1
6–7	nonzero (10, 01, or 11) if retries disabled

Byte(s)	Contents
09H–0BH	reserved
0CH–0DH	landing zone cylinder
0EH	sectors per track
0FH	reserved

Int 13H
Function 0AH (10)
Read sector long

[PC] [AT] [PS/2]

Reads a sector or sectors from disk into memory, along with a 4-byte ECC code for each sector.

Call with:

AH	= 0AH	
AL	= number of sectors	
CH	= cylinder	
CL	= sector (see Notes)	
DH	= head	
DL	= drive	
	80H–FFH fixed disk	
ES:BX	= segment:offset of buffer	

Returns:

If function successful

Carry flag	= clear
AH	= 00H
AL	= number of sectors transferred

If function unsuccessful

Carry flag	= set
AH	= status (see Int 13H Function 01H)

Notes:

- This function is supported on fixed disks only.
- The upper 2 bits of the 10-bit cylinder number are placed in the upper 2 bits of register CL.
- Unlike the normal Read Sector function (Int 13H Function 02H), ECC errors are not automatically corrected. Multisector transfers are terminated after any sector with a read error.

Int 13H
Function 0BH (11)
Write sector long

[PC] [AT] [PS/2]

Writes a sector or sectors from memory to disk. Each sector's worth of data must be followed by its 4-byte ECC code.

Call with:

AH	= 0BH	
AL	= number of sectors	
CH	= cylinder	
CL	= sector (see Notes)	
DH	= head	
DL	= drive	
	80H–FFH fixed disk	
ES:BX	= segment:offset of buffer	

Returns: If function successful
Carry flag   = clear
AH   = 00H
AL   = number of sectors transferred

If function unsuccessful
Carry flag   = set
AH   = status (see Int 13H Function 01H)

Notes:
- This function is supported on fixed disks only.
- The upper 2 bits of the 10-bit cylinder number are placed in the upper 2 bits of register CL.

Int 13H
Function 0CH (12)
Seek

Positions the disk read/write heads to the specified cylinder, but does not transfer any data.

Call with: AH   = 0CH
CH   = lower 8 bits of cylinder
CL   = upper 2 bits of cylinder in bits 6–7
DH   = head
DL   = drive
        80H–FFH fixed disk

Returns: If function successful
Carry flag   = clear
AH   = 00H

If function unsuccessful
Carry flag   = set
AH   = status (see Int 13H Function 01H)

Notes:
- This function is supported on fixed disks only.
- The upper 2 bits of the 10-bit cylinder number are placed in the upper 2 bits of register CL.
- The Read Sector, Read Sector Long, Write Sector, and Write Sector Long functions include an implied seek operation and need not be preceded by an explicit call to this function.

Int 13H
Function 0DH (13)
Reset fixed disk system

[PC] [AT] [PS/2]

Resets the fixed disk controller, recalibrates attached drives (moves the read/write arm to cylinder 0), and prepares for subsequent disk I/O.

Call with:	AH	= 0DH
	DL	= drive
		80H–FFH fixed disk

Returns:	If function successful	
	Carry flag	= clear
	AH	= 00H
	If function unsuccessful	
	Carry flag	= set
	AH	= status (see Int 13H Function 01H)

| Note: | ■ This function is supported on fixed disks only. It differs from Int 13H Function 00H in that the floppy disk controller is not reset. |

Int 13H
Function 0EH (14)
Read sector buffer

[PC]

Transfers the contents of the fixed disk adapter's internal sector buffer to system memory. No data is read from the physical disk drive.

| Call with: | AH | = 0EH |
| | ES:BX | = segment:offset of buffer |

Returns:	If function successful	
	Carry flag	= clear
	If function unsuccessful	
	Carry flag	= set
	AH	= status (see Int 13H Function 01H)

| Note: | ■ This function is supported by the PC/XT's fixed disk adapter only. It is not defined for fixed disk adapters on the PC/AT or PS/2. |

Int 13H
Function 0FH (15)
Write sector buffer

Transfers data from system memory to the fixed disk adapter's internal sector buffer. No data is written to the physical disk drive.

Call with:	AH	= 0FH
	ES:BX	= segment:offset of buffer

Returns:	If function successful
	Carry flag = clear
	If function unsuccessful
	Carry flag = set
	AH = status (see Int 13H Function 01H)

Notes:
- This function is supported by the PC/XT's fixed disk adapter only. It is not defined for fixed disk adapters on the PC/AT or PS/2.
- This function should be called to initialize the contents of the sector buffer before formatting the drive with Int 13H Function 05H.

Int 13H
Function 10H (16)
Get drive status

Tests whether the specified fixed disk drive is operational and returns the drive's status.

Call with:	AH	= 10H
	DL	= drive
		80H–FFH fixed disk

Returns:	If function successful
	Carry flag = clear
	AH = 00H
	If function unsuccessful
	Carry flag = set
	AH = status (see Int 13H Function 01H)

Note:
- This function is supported on fixed disks only.

Int 13H
Function 11H (17)
Recalibrate drive

Causes the fixed disk adapter to recalibrate itself for the specified drive, positioning the read/write arm to cylinder 0, and returns the drive's status.

Call with:	AH	= 11H
	DL	= drive
		80H–FFH fixed disk

Returns:	If function successful	
	Carry flag	= clear
	AH	= 00H
	If function unsuccessful	
	Carry flag	= set
	AH	= status (see Int 13H Function 01H)

Note:	■ This function is supported on fixed disks only.

Int 13H
Function 12H (18)
Controller RAM diagnostic

Causes the fixed disk adapter to carry out a built-in diagnostic test on its internal sector buffer, indicating whether the test was passed by the returned status.

Call with:	AH	= 12H

Returns:	If function successful	
	Carry flag	= clear
	If function unsuccessful	
	Carry flag	= set
	AH	= status (see Int 13H Function 01H)

Note:	■ This function is supported on PC/XT fixed disks only.

Int 13H
Function 13H (19)
Controller drive diagnostic

Causes the fixed disk adapter to run internal diagnostic tests of the attached drive, indicating whether the test was passed by the returned status.

Call with:	AH	= 13H

Returns:	If function successful	
	Carry flag	= clear
	If function unsuccessful	
	Carry flag	= set
	AH	= status (see Int 13H Function 01H)

Note:	■ This function is supported on PC/XT fixed disks only.

Int 13H
Function 14H (20)
Controller internal diagnostic

Causes the fixed disk adapter to carry out a built-in diagnostic self-test, indicating whether the test was passed by the returned status.

Call with:	AH	= 14H

Returns:	If function successful	
	Carry flag	= clear
	AH	= 00H
	If function unsuccessful	
	Carry flag	= set
	AH	= status (see Int 13H Function 01H)

Note:	■ This function is supported on fixed disks only.

Int 13H
Function 15H (21)
Get disk type

Returns a code indicating the type of floppy or fixed disk referenced by the specified drive code.

Call with: AH   = 15H

                 DL   = drive

                               00H–7FH floppy disk

                               80H–FFH fixed disk

Returns: If function successful

             Carry flag   = clear

             AH   = drive type code

                              00H   *if no drive present*

                              01H   *if floppy disk drive without change-line support*

                              02H   *if floppy disk drive with change-line support*

                              03H   *if fixed disk*

             and, if fixed disk (AH = 03H)

             CX:DX   = number of 512-byte sectors

             If function unsuccessful

             Carry flag   = set

             AH   = status (see Int 13H Function 01H)

Note: ■   This function is not supported on the PC or PC/XT.

Int 13H
Function 16H (22)
Get disk change status

Returns the status of the change line, indicating whether the disk in the drive may have been replaced since the last disk access.

Call with: AH   = 16H

                 DL   = drive

                               00H–7FH floppy disk

Returns: If change line inactive (disk has not been changed)
Carry flag   = clear
AH   = 00H

If change line active (disk may have been changed)
Carry flag   = set
AH   = 06H

Notes: ■ If this function returns with the carry flag set, the disk has not necessarily been changed; the change line can be activated by simply unlocking and locking the disk drive door without removing the floppy disk.

■ This function is not supported for floppy disks on the PC or PC/XT.

Int 13H   [AT] [PS/2]
Function 17H (23)
Set disk type

Selects a floppy disk type for the specified drive.

Call with: AH   = 17H
AL   = floppy disk type code
        00H   not used
        01H   320/360 KB floppy disk in 360 KB drive
        02H   320/360 KB floppy disk in 1.2 MB drive
        03H   1.2 MB floppy disk in 1.2 MB drive
        04H   720 KB floppy disk in 720 KB drive
SL   = drive
        00H–7FH floppy disk

Returns: If function successful
Carry flag   = clear
AH   = 00H

If function unsuccessful
Carry flag   = set
AH   = status (see Int 13H Function 01H)

Notes: ■ This function is not supported for floppy disks on the PC or PC/XT.

■ If the change line is active for the specified drive, it is reset. The ROM BIOS then sets the data rate for the specified drive and media type.

Int 13H
Function 18H (24)
Set media type for format

Selects media characteristics for the specified drive.

Call with:	AH	= 18H
	CH	= number of cylinders
	CL	= sectors per track
	DL	= drive
		00H–7FH floppy disk

Returns:	If function successful	
	Carry flag	= clear
	AH	= 00H
	ES:DI	= segment:offset of disk parameter table for media type
	If function unsuccessful	
	Carry flag	= set
	AH	= status (see Int 13H Function 01H)

Notes:
- A floppy disk must be present in the drive.
- This function should be called prior to formatting a disk with Int 13H Function 05H so that the ROM BIOS can set the correct data rate for the media.
- If the change line is active for the specified drive, it is reset.

Int 13H
Function 19H (25)
Park heads

Moves the read/write arm to a track that is not used for data storage, so that data will not be damaged when the drive is turned off.

Call with:	AH	= 19H
	DL	= drive
		80H–FFH fixed disk

Returns:	If function successful	
	Carry flag	= clear
	AH	= 00H

If function unsuccessful
Carry flag   = set
AH   = status (see Int 13H Function 01H)

Note: ■ This function is defined for PS/2 fixed disks only.

Int 13H
Function 1AH (26)
Format ESDI drive

Initializes disk sector and track address fields on a drive attached to the ESDI Fixed Disk Drive Adapter/A.

Call with: AH   = 1AH
                 AL   = relative block address (RBA) defect table count
                            0   *if no RBA table*
                            >0   *if RBA table used*
                 CL   = format modifier bits

Bit(s)	*Significance (if set)*
0	ignore primary defect map
1	ignore secondary defect map
2	update secondary defect map (see Notes)
3	perform extended surface analysis
4	generate periodic interrupt (see Notes)
5–7	reserved (must be 0)

                 DL   = drive
                            80H–FFH fixed disk
                 ES:BX   = segment:offset of RBA table

Returns: If function successful
                Carry flag   = clear
                AH   = 00H
                If function unsuccessful
                Carry flag   = set
                AH   = status (see Int 13H Function 01H)

Notes: ■ This operation is sometimes called a "low level format" and prepares the disk for physical read/write operations at the sector level. The drive must be subsequently partitioned with the FDISK command and then given a "high level format" with the FORMAT command to install a file system.

- If bit 4 of register CL is set, Int 15H is called with AH = 0FH and AL = phase code after each cylinder is formatted or analyzed. The phase code is defined as:

  0 = reserved
  1 = surface analysis
  2 = formatting

  See also Int 15H Function 0FH.

- If bit 2 of register CL is set, the drive's secondary defect map is updated to reflect errors found during surface analysis. If both bit 2 and bit 1 are set, the secondary defect map is replaced.

- For an extended surface analysis, the disk should first be formatted by calling this function with bit 3 cleared, then analyzed by calling this function with bit 3 set.

Int 14H   [PC] [AT] [PS/2]
Function 00H
Initialize communications port

Initializes a serial communications port to a desired baud rate, parity, word length, and number of stop bits.

Call with:	AH	= 00H
	AL	= initialization parameter (see Notes)
	DX	= communications port number (0 = COM1, 1 = COM2, etc.)

Returns: AH = port status

Bit	Significance (if set)
0	receive data ready
1	overrun error detected
2	parity error detected
3	framing error detected
4	break detected
5	transmit holding register empty
6	transmit shift register empty
7	timed-out

AL = modem status

Bit	Significance (if set)
0	change in clear-to-send status
1	change in data-set-ready status
2	trailing edge ring indicator
3	change in receive line signal detect
4	clear-to-send
5	data-set-ready
6	ring indicator
7	receive line signal detect

Notes:

- The initialization parameter byte is defined as follows:

7 6 5 *Baud rate*	4 3 *Parity*	2 *Stop bits*	1 0 *Word length*
000 = 110	X0 = none	0 = 1 bit	10 = 7 bits
001 = 150	01 = odd	1 = 2 bits	11 = 8 bits
010 = 300	11 = even		
011 = 600			
100 = 1200			
101 = 2400			
110 = 4800			
111 = 9600			

- To initialize the serial port for data rates greater than 9600 baud on PS/2 machines, see Int 14H Functions 04H and 05H.

Int 14H [PC] [AT] [PS/2]
Function 01H
Write character to communications port

Writes a character to the specified serial communications port, returning the current status of the port.

Call with: AH   = 01H
AL   = character
DX   = communications port number (0 = COM1, 1 = COM2, etc.)

Returns: If function successful
AH bit 7   = 0
AH bits 0–6 = port status

Bit	Significance (if set)
0	receive data ready
1	overrun error detected
2	parity error detected
3	framing error detected
4	break detected
5	transmit holding register empty
6	transmit shift register empty

AL   = character (unchanged)

If function unsuccessful (timed-out)
AH bit 7   = 1
AL   = character (unchanged)

Int 14H
Function 02H
Read character from communications port

Reads a character from the specified serial communications port, also returning the port's status.

| **Call with:** | AH | = 02H |
| | DX | = communications port number (0 = COM1, 1 = COM2, etc.) |

Returns: If function successful
AH bit 7 = 0
AH bits 0–6 = status

	Bit	*Significance (if set)*
	1	overrun error detected
	2	parity error detected
	3	framing error detected
	4	break detected

AL = character

If function unsuccessful (timed-out)
AH bit 7 = 1

Int 14H
Function 03H
Get communications port status

Returns the status of the specified serial communications port.

| **Call with:** | AH | = 03H |
| | DX | = communications port number (0 = COM1, 1 = COM2, etc.) |

| **Returns:** | AH | = port status (see Int 14H Function 00H) |
| | AL | = modem status (see Int 14H Function 00H) |

Int 14H
Function 04H
Extended initialize communications port

Initializes a serial communications port to a desired baud rate, parity, word length, and number of stop bits. Provides a superset of Int 14H Function 00H capabilities for PS/2 machines.

AH	= 04H	
AL	= break flag	
	00H	*no break*
	01H	*break*
BH	= parity	
	00H	*none*
	01H	*odd*
	02H	*even*
	03H	*stick parity odd*
	04H	*stick parity even*
BL	= stop bits	
	00H	*1 stop bit*
	01H	*2 stop bits if word length = 6–8 bits*
	01H	*1.5 stop bits if word length = 5 bits*
CH	= word length	
	00H	*5 bits*
	01H	*6 bits*
	02H	*7 bits*
	03H	*8 bits*
CL	= baud rate	
	00H	*110 baud*
	01H	*150 baud*
	02H	*300 baud*
	03H	*600 baud*
	04H	*1200 baud*
	05H	*2400 baud*
	06H	*4800 baud*
	07H	*9600 baud*
	08H	*19,200 baud*
DX	= communications port number (0 = COM1, 1 = COM2, etc.)	

Returns:

AH	= port status (see Int 14H Function 00H)
AL	= modem status (see Int 14H Function 00H)

Int 14H [PS/2]
Function 05H
Extended communications port control

Reads or sets the modem control register (MCR) for the specified serial communications port.

Call with:

AH	= 05H	
AL	= subfunction	
	00H	*to read modem control register*
	01H	*to write modem control register*

BL	= modem control register contents (if AL = 01H)

Bit(s)	Significance
0	data-terminal ready
1	request-to-send
2	Out1
3	Out2
4	loop (for testing)
5–7	reserved

DX	= communications port number (0 = COM1, 1 = COM2, etc.)

Returns: If called with AL = 00H

BL   = modem control register contents (see above)

If called with AL = 01H

AH   = port status (see Int 14H Function 00H)

AL   = modem status (see Int 14H Function 00H)

Int 15H   [PC]
Function 00H
Turn on cassette motor

Turns on the motor of the cassette tape drive.

Call with: AH   = 00H

Returns: If function successful

Carry flag = clear

If function unsuccessful

Carry flag = set

AH   = status

            86H   *if cassette not present*

Note: ■ This function is available only on the PC and the PCjr. It is not supported on the PC/XT and all subsequent models.

Int 15H   [PC]
Function 01H
Turn off cassette motor

Turns off the motor of the cassette tape drive.

Call with:	AH	= 01H

Returns:	If function successful	
	Carry flag	= clear
	If function unsuccessful	
	Carry flag	= set
	AH	= status
		86H *if cassette not present*

Note:	■ This function is available only on the PC and the PCjr. It is not supported on the PC/XT and all subsequent models.

Int 15H   [PC]
Function 02H
Read cassette

Reads one or more 256-byte blocks of data from the cassette tape drive to memory.

Call with:	AH	= 02H
	CX	= number of bytes to read
	ES:BX	= segment:offset of buffer

Returns:	If function successful	
	Carry flag	= clear
	DX	= number of bytes actually read
	ES:BX	= segment:offset + 1 of last byte read
	If function unsuccessful	
	Carry flag	= set
	AH	= status
		01H *if CRC error*
		02H *if bit signals scrambled*
		04H *if no data found*
		80H *if invalid command*
		86H *if cassette not present*

Note:	■ This function is available only on the PC and on the PCjr. It is not supported on the PC/XT and all subsequent models.

Int 15H [PC]
Function 03H
Write cassette

Writes one or more 256-byte blocks of data from memory to the cassette tape drive.

Call with:	AH	= 03H
	CX	= number of bytes to write
	ES:BX	= segment:offset of buffer

Returns:	If function successful	
	Carry flag	= clear
	CX	= 00H
	ES:BX	= segment:offset + 1 of last byte written
	If function unsuccessful	
	Carry flag	= set
	AH	= status
		80H *if invalid command*
		86H *if cassette not present*

Note: ■ This function is available only on the PC and on the PCjr. It is not supported on the PC/XT and all subsequent models.

Int 15H [PS/2]
Function 0FH (15)
Format ESDI drive periodic interrupt

Invoked by the ROM BIOS on the ESDI Fixed Disk Drive Adapter/A during a format or surface analysis operation after each cylinder is completed.

Call with:	AH	= 0FH
	AL	= phase code
		0 = reserved
		1 = surface analysis
		2 = formatting

Returns:	If formatting or analysis should continue
	Carry flag = clear
	If formatting or analysis should be terminated
	Carry flag = set

- This function call can be captured by a program so that it will be notified as each cylinder is formatted or analyzed. The program can count interrupts for each phase to determine the current cylinder number.

- The default ROM BIOS handler for this function returns with the carry flag set.

Int 15H [PS/2]
Function 21H (33) Subfunction 00H
Read POST error log

Returns error information that was accumulated during the most recent power-on self-test (POST).

| **Call with:** | AH | = 21H |
| | AL | = 00H |

Returns:	If function successful	
	Carry flag	= clear
	AH	= 00H
	BX	= number of POST error codes stored
	ES:DI	= segment:offset of POST error log
	If function unsuccessful	
	Carry flag	= set
	AH	= status
		80H	*= invalid command*
		86H	*= function not supported*

Notes:

- The error log consists of single-word entries. The first byte of an entry is the device error code, and the second is the device identifier.

- This function is not available on the PS/2 Models 25 and 30.

Int 15H [PS/2]
Function 21H (33) Subfunction 01H
Write POST error log

Adds an entry to the power-on self-test (POST) error log.

Call with:	AH	= 21H
	AL	= 01H
	BH	= device identifier
	BL	= device error code

Returns: If function successful
Carry flag   = clear
AH   = 00H

If function unsuccessful
Carry flag   = set
AH   = status
  01H   = *error list full*
  80H   = *invalid command*
  86H   = *function not supported*

Note: ■   This function is not available on the PS/2 Models 25 and 30.

Int 15H   [PS/2]
Function 4FH (79)
Keyboard intercept

Invoked for each keystroke by the ROM BIOS's Int 09H keyboard interrupt handler.

Call with: AH   = 4FH
AL   = scan code

Returns: If scan code consumed
Carry flag   = clear

If scan code not consumed
Carry flag   = set
AL   = unchanged or new scan code

Notes: ■   An operating system or a resident utility can capture this function to filter the raw keyboard data stream. The new handler can substitute a new scan code, return the same scan code, or return the carry flag clear causing the keystroke to be discarded. The default ROM BIOS routine simply returns the scan code unchanged.

■   A program can call Int 15H Function C0H to determine whether the host machine's ROM BIOS supports this keyboard intercept.

Int 15H   [AT] [PS/2]
Function 80H (128)
Device open

Acquires ownership of a logical device for a process.

Call with:	AH	= 80H
	BX	= device ID
	CX	= process ID

Returns:	If function successful	
	Carry flag	= clear
	AH	= 00H
	If function unsuccessful	
	Carry flag	= set
	AH	= status

Note:	■ This function call, along with Int 15H Functions 81H and 82H, defines a simple protocol that can be used to arbitrate usage of devices by multiple processes. A multitasking program manager would be expected to capture Int 15H and provide the appropriate service. The default BIOS routine for this function simply returns with the carry flag clear and AH = 00H.

Int 15H
Function 81H (129)
Device close

[AT] [PS/2]

Releases ownership of a logical device for a process.

Call with:	AH	= 81H
	BX	= device ID
	CX	= process ID

Returns:	If function successful	
	Carry flag	= clear
	AH	= 00H
	If function unsuccessful	
	Carry flag	= set
	AH	= status

Note:	■ A multitasking program manager would be expected to capture Int 15H and provide the appropriate service. The default BIOS routine for this function simply returns with the carry flag clear and AH = 00H. See also Int 15H Functions 80H and 82H.

Int 15H
Function 82H (130)
Process termination

Releases ownership of all logical devices for a process that is about to terminate.

Call with: AH   = 82H
            BX   = process ID

Returns: If function successful
            Carry flag   = clear
            AH   = 00H
            If function unsuccessful
            Carry flag   = set
            AH   = status

Note: ■ A multitasking program manager would be expected to capture Int 15H and provide the appropriate service. The default BIOS routine for this function simply returns with the carry flag clear and AH = 00H. See also Int 15H Functions 80H and 81H.

Int 15H
Function 83H (131)
Event wait

Requests setting of a semaphore after a specified interval or cancels a previous request.

Call with: If requesting event wait
            AH   = 83H
            AL   = 00H
            CX:DX   = microseconds
            ES:BX   = segment:offset of semaphore byte
            If canceling event wait
            AH   = 83H
            AL   = 01H

Returns: If called with AL = 00H, and function successful
            Carry flag   = clear
            If called with AL = 00H, and function unsuccessful (Event Wait already active)
            Carry flag   = set
            If called with AL = 01H
            Nothing

- The function call returns immediately. If the function is successful, bit 7 of the semaphore byte is set when the specified interval has elapsed. The calling program is responsible for clearing the semaphore before requesting this function.

- The actual duration of an event wait is always an integral multiple of 976 microseconds. The CMOS date/clock chip interrupts are used to implement this function.

- Use of this function allows programmed, hardware-independent delays at a finer resolution than can be obtained through use of the MS-DOS Get Time function (Int 21H Function 2CH, which returns time in hundredths of a second).

- See also Int 15H Function 86H, which suspends the calling program for the specified interval in milliseconds.

- This function is not supported on the PS/2 Models 25 and 30.

Int 15H   [AT] [PS/2]
Function 84H (132)
Read joystick

Returns the joystick switch settings and potentiometer values.

Call with: AH   = 84H
                 DX   = subfunction
                      00H   *to read switch settings*
                      01H   *to read resistive inputs*

Returns: If function successful
                 Carry flag   = clear
                 and, if called with DX = 00H
                 AL   = switch settings (bits 4–7)
                 or, if called with DX = 01H
                 AX   = A(x) value
                 BX   = A(y) value
                 CX   = B(x) value
                 DX   = B(y) value
                 If function unsuccessful
                 Carry flag   = set

Notes:

- An error condition is returned if DX does not contain a valid subfunction number.

- If no game adapter is installed, AL is returned as 00H for Subfunction 00H (i.e., all switches open); AX, BX, CX, and DX are returned containing 00H for Subfunction 01H.

- Using a 250 KOhm joystick, the potentiometer values usually lie within the range 0–416 (0000–01A0H).

Int 15H
Function 85H (133)
SysReq key

Invoked by the ROM BIOS keyboard driver when the SysReq key is detected.

Call with:	AH	= 85H
	AL	= key status
		00H *if key make (depression)*
		01H *if key break (release)*

Returns:	If function successful	
	Carry flag	= clear
	AH	= 00H
	If function unsuccessful	
	Carry flag	= set
	AH	= status

Note: ■ The ROM BIOS handler for this function call is a dummy routine that always returns a success status unless called with an invalid subfunction number in AL. A multitasking program manager would be expected to capture Int 15H so that it can be notified when the user strikes the SysReq key.

Int 15H
Function 86H (134)
Delay

[AT] [PS/2]

Suspends the calling program for a specified interval in microseconds.

Call with:	AH	= 86H
	CX:DX	= microseconds to wait

Returns:	If function successful (wait was performed)	
	Carry flag	= clear
	If function unsuccessful (wait was not performed)	
	Carry flag	= set

Notes: ■ The actual duration of the wait is always an integral multiple of 976 microseconds.

■ Use of this function allows programmed, hardware-independent delays at a finer resolution than can be obtained through use of the MS-DOS Get Time function (Int 21H Function 2CH, which returns time in hundredths of a second).

- See also Int 15H Function 83H, which triggers a semaphore after a specified interval but does not suspend the calling program.

Int 15H
Function 87H (135)
Move extended memory block

Transfers data between conventional memory and extended memory.

Call with:	AH	= 87H
	CX	= number of words to move
	ES:SI	= segment:offset of Global Descriptor Table (see Notes)

Returns:

If function successful

Carry flag	= clear
AH	= 00H

If function unsuccessful

Carry flag	= set	
AH	= status	
	01H	*if RAM parity error*
	02H	*if exception interrupt error*
	03H	*if gate address line 20 failed*

Notes:

- Conventional memory lies at addresses below the 640 KB boundary, and is used for the execution of MS-DOS and its application programs. Extended memory lies at addresses above 1 MB, and can only be accessed by an 80286 or 80386 CPU running in protected mode. As much as 15 MB of extended memory can be installed in an IBM PC/AT or compatible.

- The Global Descriptor Table (GDT) used by this function must be set up as follows:

Byte(s)	*Contents*
00H–0FH	reserved (should be 0)
10H–11H	segment length in bytes (2∗CX − 1 or greater)
12H–14H	24-bit source address
15H	access rights byte (always 93H)
16H–17H	reserved (should be 0)
18H–19H	segment length in bytes (2∗CX − 1 or greater)
1AH–1CH	24-bit destination address
1DH	access rights byte (always 93H)
1EH–2FH	reserved (should be 0)

The table is composed of six 8-byte descriptors to be used by the CPU in protected mode. The four descriptors in offsets 00H–0FH and 20H–2FH are filled in by the ROM BIOS before the CPU mode switch.

- The addresses used in the descriptor table are linear (physical) 24-bit addresses in the range 000000H–FFFFFFH—not segments and offsets—with the least significant byte at the lowest address and the most significant byte at the highest address.
- The block move is performed with interrupts disabled; thus, use of this function may interfere with the operation of communications programs, network drivers, or other software that relies on prompt servicing of hardware interrupts.
- Programs and drivers that access extended memory with this function cannot be executed in the Compatibility Environment of OS/2.
- This function is not supported on the PS/2 Models 25 and 30.

Int 15H   [AT] [PS/2]
Function 88H (136)
Get extended memory size

Returns the amount of extended memory installed in the system.

Call with:	AH	= 88H

Returns:	AX	= amount of extended memory (in KB)

Notes:
- Extended memory is memory at addresses above 1 MB, which can only be accessed by an 80286 or 80386 CPU running in protected mode. Because MS-DOS is a real-mode operating system, extended memory can be used for storage of volatile data but cannot be used for execution of programs.
- Programs and drivers that use this function cannot be executed in the Compatibility Environment of OS/2.
- This function is not supported on the PS/2 Models 25 and 30.

Int 15H   [AT] [PS/2]
Function 89H (137)
Enter protected mode

Switches the CPU from real mode into protected mode.

Call with:	AH	= 89H
	BH	= interrupt number for IRQ0, written to ICW2 of 8259 PIC #1 (must be evenly divisible by 8, determines IRQ0–IRQ7)
	BL	= interrupt number for IRQ8, written to ICW2 of 8259 PIC #2 (must be evenly divisible by 8, determines IRQ8–IRQ15)
	ES:SI	= segment:offset of Global Descriptor Table (GDT)

Returns: If function successful (CPU is in protected mode)

Carry flag	= clear
AH	= 00H
CS	= user-defined selector
DS	= user-defined selector
ES	= user-defined selector
SS	= user-defined selector

If function unsuccessful (CPU is in real mode)

Carry flag	= set
AH	= FFH

Notes: ■ The Global Descriptor Table must contain eight descriptors set up as follows:

Offset	*Descriptor usage*
00H	dummy descriptor (initialized to 0)
08H	Global Descriptor Table (GDT)
10H	Interrupt Descriptor Table (IDT)
18H	user's data segment (DS)
20H	user's extra segment (ES)
28H	user's stack segment (SS)
30H	user's code segment (CS)
38H	BIOS code segment

The user must initialize the first seven descriptors; the eighth is filled in by the ROM BIOS to provide addressability for its own execution. The calling program may modify and use the eighth descriptor for any purpose after return from this function call.

■ This function is not supported on the PS/2 Models 25 and 30.

Int 15H [AT] [PS/2]
Function 90H (144)
Device wait

Invoked by the ROM BIOS fixed disk, floppy disk, printer, network, and keyboard drivers prior to performing a programmed wait for I/O completion.

Call with:

AH	= 90H
AL	= device type
	00H–7FH serially reusable devices
	80H–BFH reentrant devices
	C0H–FFH wait-only calls, no corresponding Post function
ES:BX	= segment:offset of request block for device types 80H–FFH

Returns: If no wait (driver must perform its own time-out)
Carry flag   = clear
AH   = 00H

If wait was performed
Carry flag   = set

Notes:
- Predefined device types are:
00H	disk (may time-out)
01H	floppy disk (may time-out)
02H	keyboard (no time-out)
03H	pointing device (PS/2, may time-out)
80H	network (no time-out)
FCH	fixed disk reset (PS/2, may time-out)
FDH	floppy disk drive motor start (may time-out)
FEH	printer (may time-out)
- For network adapters, ES:BX points to a network control block (NCB).
- A multitasking program manager would be expected to capture Int 15H Function 90H so that it can dispatch other tasks while I/O is in progress. The default BIOS routine for this function simply returns with the carry flag clear and AH = 00H.

Int 15H   [AT] [PS/2]
Function 91H (145)
Device post

Invoked by the ROM BIOS fixed disk, floppy disk, network, and keyboard drivers to signal that I/O is complete and/or the device is ready.

Call with: AH   = 91H
AL   = device type
            00H–7FH   serially reusable devices
            80H–BFH   reentrant devices
ES:BX   = segment:offset of request block for device types 80H–BFH

Returns: AH   = 00H

Notes:
- Predefined device types that may use Device Post are:
00H	disk (may time-out)
01H	floppy disk (may time-out)
02H	keyboard (no time-out)
03H	pointing device (PS/2, may time-out)
80H	network (no time-out)

- The ROM BIOS printer routine does not invoke this function because printer output is not interrupt driven.
- A multitasking program manager would be expected to capture Int 15H Function 91H so that it can be notified when I/O is completed and awaken the requesting task. The default BIOS routine for this function simply returns with the carry flag clear and AH = 00H.

Int 15H
Function C0H (192)
Get system environment

[AT] [PS/2]

Returns a pointer to a table containing various information about the system configuration.

Call with: AH = C0H

Returns: ES:BX = segment:offset of configuration table (see Notes)

Notes:
- The format of the system configuration table is as follows:

Byte(s)	Contents
00H–01H	length of table in bytes
02H	system model (see following Note)
03H	system submodel (see following Note)
04H	BIOS revision level
05H	configuration flags

Bit	Significance (if set)
0	reserved
1	Micro Channel implemented
2	extended BIOS data area allocated
3	Wait for External Event is available
4	keyboard intercept (Int 15H Function 4FH) available
5	real-time clock available
6	slave 8259 present (cascaded IRQ2)
7	DMA channel 3 used

| 06H–09H | reserved |

- The system model and type bytes are assigned as follows:

Machine	Model byte	Submodel byte
PC	FFH	
PC/XT	FEH	
PC/XT	FBH	00H or 01H
PCjr	FDH	
PC/AT	FCH	00H or 01H
PC/XT-286	FCH	02H
PC Convertible	F9H	

Machine	Model byte	Submodel byte
PS/2 Model 30	FAH	00H
PS/2 Model 50	FCH	04H
PS/2 Model 60	FCH	05H
PS/2 Model 70	F8H	04H *or* 09H
PS/2 Model 80	F8H	00H *or* 01H

Int 15H [PS/2]
Function C1H (193)
Get address of extended BIOS data area

Returns the segment address of the base of the extended BIOS data area.

Call with: AH　　　= C1H

Returns: If function successful
Carry flag　= clear
ES　　　　= segment of extended BIOS data area
If function unsuccessful
Carry flag　= set

Notes:
- The extended BIOS data area is allocated at the high end of conventional memory during the POST (Power-On-Self-Test) sequence. The word at 0040:0013H (memory size) is updated to reflect the reduced amount of memory available for MS-DOS and application programs. The first byte in the extended BIOS data area is initialized to its length in KB.
- A program can determine whether the extended BIOS data area exists with Int 15H Function C0H.

Int 15H [PS/2]
Function C2H (194) Subfunction 00H
Enable/disable pointing device

Enables or disables the system's mouse or other pointing device.

Call with: AH　　　= C2H
AL　　　= 00H
BH　　　= enable/disable flag
　　　　　00H　　= *disable*
　　　　　01H　　= *enable*

If function successful
Carry flag   = clear
AH   = 00H

If function unsuccessful
Carry flag   = set
AH   = status
　　　　　　　01H   *if invalid function call*
　　　　　　　02H   *if invalid input*
　　　　　　　03H   *if interface error*
　　　　　　　04H   *if resend*
　　　　　　　05H   *if no far call installed*

Int 15H   [PS/2]
Function C2H (194) Subfunction 01H
Reset pointing device

Resets the system's mouse or other pointing device, setting the sample rate, resolution, and other characteristics to their default values.

Call with:　　AH　　= C2H
　　　　　　　　　AL　　= 01H

Returns:　　If function successful
　　　　　　　　Carry flag   = clear
　　　　　　　　AH   = 00H
　　　　　　　　BH   = device ID

　　　　　　　　If function unsuccessful
　　　　　　　　Carry flag   = set
　　　　　　　　AH   = status (see Int 15H Function C2H Subfunction 00H)

Notes:　　■　After a reset operation, the state of the pointing device is as follows:
　　　　　　　　– disabled;
　　　　　　　　– sample rate at 100 reports per second;
　　　　　　　　– resolution at 4 counts per millimeter;
　　　　　　　　– and scaling at 1 to 1.
　　　　　　　　The data package size is unchanged by this function.

　　　　　　■　The application can use the other Int 15H Function C2H subfunctions to initialize the pointing device to other sample rates, resolution, and scaling, and then enable the device with Int 15H Function C2H Subfunction 00H.

　　　　　　■　See also Int 15H Function C2H Subfunction 05H, which incidentally resets the pointing device in a similar manner.

Sets the sampling rate of the system's mouse or other pointing device.

Call with: AH = C2H
AL = 02H
BH = sample rate value

00H	*= 10 reports per second*
01H	*= 20 reports per second*
02H	*= 40 reports per second*
03H	*= 60 reports per second*
04H	*= 80 reports per second*
05H	*= 100 reports per second*
06H	*= 200 reports per second*

Returns: If function successful
Carry flag = clear
AH = 00H

If function unsuccessful
Carry flag = set
AH = status (see Int 15H Function C2H Subfunction 00H)

Note: ■ The default sample rate is 100 reports per second after a reset operation (Int 15H Function C2H Subfunction 01H).

Sets the resolution of the system's mouse or other pointing device.

Call with: AH = C2H
AL = 03H
BH = resolution value

00H	*= 1 count per millimeter*
01H	*= 2 counts per millimeter*
02H	*= 4 counts per millimeter*
03H	*= 8 counts per millimeter*

Returns: If function successful
Carry flag   = clear
AH   = 00H

If function unsuccessful
Carry flag   = set
AH   = status (see Int 15H Function C2H Subfunction 00H)

Note: ▪ The default resolution is 4 counts per millimeter after a reset operation (Int 15H Function C2H Subfunction 01H).

Int 15H   [PS/2]
Function C2H (194) Subfunction 04H
Get pointing device type

Returns the identification code for the system's mouse or other pointing device.

Call with: AH   = C2H
AL   = 04H

Returns: If function successful
Carry flag   = clear
AH   = 00H
BH   = device ID

If function unsuccessful
Carry flag   = set
AH   = status (see Int 15H Function C2H Subfunction 00H)

Int 15H   [PS/2]
Function C2H (194) Subfunction 05H
Initialize pointing device interface

Sets the data package size for the system's mouse or other pointing device, and initializes the resolution, sampling rate, and scaling to their default values.

Call with: AH   = C2H
AL   = 05H
BH   = data package size in bytes (1–8)

Returns: If function successful
Carry flag   = clear
AH   = 00H

If function unsuccessful
Carry flag   = set
AH   = status (see Int 15H Function C2H Subfunction 00H)

Note: ■ After this operation, the state of the pointing device is as follows:
  – disabled;
  – sample rate at 100 reports per second;
  – resolution at 4 counts per millimeter;
  – and scaling at 1 to 1.

Int 15H   [PS/2]
Function C2H (194) Subfunction 06H
Set scaling or get status

Returns the current status of the system's mouse or other pointing device or sets the device's scaling factor.

Call with: AH   = C2H
AL   = 06H
BH   = extended command
      00H   *= return device status*
      01H   *= set scaling at 1:1*
      02H   *= set scaling at 2:1*

Returns: If function successful
Carry flag   = clear
AH   = 00H

and, if called with BH = 00H
BL   = status byte

Bit	*Significance*
0	= 1 if right button pressed
1	= reserved
2	= 1 if left button pressed
3	= reserved
4	= 0 if 1:1 scaling
	1 if 2:1 scaling
5	= 0 if device disabled
	1 if device enabled
6	= 0 if stream mode
	1 if remote mode
7	= reserved

CL   = resolution
            00H   = *1 count per millimeter*
            01H   = *2 counts per millimeter*
            02H   = *4 counts per millimeter*
            03H   = *8 counts per millimeter*
DL   = sample rate
            0AH   = *10 reports per second*
            14H   = *20 reports per second*
            28H   = *40 reports per second*
            3CH   = *60 reports per second*
            50H   = *80 reports per second*
            64H   = *100 reports per second*
            C8H   = *200 reports per second*

If function unsuccessful
Carry flag = set
AH   = status (see Int 15H Function C2H Subfunction 00H)

Int 15H   [PS/2]
Function C2H (194) Subfunction 07H
Set pointing device handler address

Notifies the ROM BIOS pointing device driver of the address for a routine to be called each time pointing device data is available.

Call with: AH   = C2H
                   AL   = 07H
                   ES:BX   = segment:offset of user routine

Returns: If function successful
                   Carry flag = clear
                   If function unsuccessful
                   Carry flag = set
                   AH   = status (see Int 15H Function C2H Subfunction 00H)

Notes: ■ The user's handler for pointing device data is entered via a far call with four parameters on the stack:
               SS:SP+0AH   status
               SS:SP+08H   *x* coordinate
               SS:SP+06H   *y* coordinate
               SS:SP+04H   *z* coordinate (always 0)

               The handler must exit via a far return without removing the parameters from the stack.

- The status parameter passed to the user's handler is interpreted as follows:

Bit(s)	Significance (if set)
0	left button pressed
1	right button pressed
2–3	reserved
4	sign of x data is negative
5	sign of y data is negative
6	x data has overflowed
7	y data has overflowed
8–15	reserved

Int 15H
Function C3H (195)
Set watchdog time-out

[PS/2]

Enables or disables a watchdog timer.

Call with:	AH	= C3H
	AL	= subfunction
		00H to disable watchdog time-out
		01H to enable watchdog time-out
	BX	= watchdog timer counter (if AL = 01H)

Returns:	If function successful
	Carry flag = clear
	If function unsuccessful
	Carry flag = set

Notes:
- The watchdog timer generates an NMI interrupt.
- This function is not available on the PS/2 Models 25 and 30.

Int 15H
Function C4H (196)
Programmable option select

[PS/2]

Returns the base Programmable Option Select register address, enables a slot for setup, or enables an adapter.

Call with:	AH	= C4H
	AL	= subfunction
		00H *to return base POS adapter register address*
		01H *to enable slot*
		02H *to enable adapter*
	BL	= slot number (if AL = 01H)

Returns: If function successful

Carry flag   = clear

and, if called with AL = 00H

DX   = base POS adapter register address

If function unsuccessful

Carry flag   = set

Notes:
- This function is available only on machines using the Micro Channel Architecture (MCA) bus.
- After a slot is enabled with Subfunction 01H, specific information can be obtained for the adapter in that slot by performing port input operations:

Port	*Function*
100H	MCA ID (low byte)
101H	MCA ID (high byte)
102H	Option Select Byte 1
	bit 0 = 1 if enabled, = 0 if disabled
103H	Option Select Byte 2
104H	Option Select Byte 3
105H	Option Select Byte 4
	bits 6–7 = channel check indicators
106H	Subaddress Extension (low byte)
107H	Subaddress Extension (high byte)

Int 16H
Function 00H
Read character from keyboard

[PC] [AT] [PS/2]

Reads a character from the keyboard, also returning the keyboard scan code.

| **Call with:** | AH | = 00H |

| **Returns:** | AH | = keyboard scan code |
| | AL | = ASCII character |

Int 16H
Function 01H
Get keyboard status

Determines whether a character is ready for input, returning a flag and also the character itself, if one is waiting.

Call with: AH   = 01H

Returns: If key waiting to be input
Zero flag   = clear
AH   = keyboard scan code
AL   = character

If no key waiting
Zero flag   = set

Note:
■ The character returned by this function when the zero flag is clear is not removed from the type-ahead buffer. The same character and scan code will be returned by the next call to Int 16H Function 00H.

Int 16H
Function 02H
Get keyboard flags

Returns the ROM BIOS flags byte that describes the state of the various keyboard toggles and shift keys.

Call with: AH   = 02H

Returns: AL   = flags

Bit	Significance (if set)
0	right Shift key is down
1	left Shift key is down
2	Ctrl key is down
3	Alt key is down
4	Scroll Lock on
5	Num Lock on
6	Caps Lock on
7	Insert on

Note:
■ The keyboard flags byte is stored in the ROM BIOS data area at 0000:0417H.

Int 16H
Function 03H
Set repeat rate

Sets the ROM BIOS key repeat ("typematic") rate and delay.

Call with: On the PC/AT and PS/2

AH	= 03H
AL	= 05H
BH	= repeat delay (see Notes)
BL	= repeat rate (see Notes)

On the PCjr

AH	= 03H
AL	= subfunction

00H	to restore default rate and delay
01H	to increase initial delay
02H	to decrease repeat rate by one-half
03H	to increase delay and decrease repeat rate by one-half
04H	to turn off keyboard repeat

Returns: Nothing

Notes:

- Subfunctions 00H–04H are available on the PCjr but are not supported by the PC or PC/XT ROM BIOS. Subfunction 05H is available on PC/ATs with ROM BIOS's dated 11/15/85 and later, and on the PS/2.

- On the PC/AT and PS/2, the value in BH controls the amount of delay before the first repeat key is generated. The delay is always a multiple of 250 milliseconds:

Value	Delay (msec.)
00H	250
01H	500
02H	750
03H	1000

- On the PC/AT and PS/2, the value for the repeat rate in characters per second can be chosen from the following table:

Value	Repeat rate (characters per second)
00H	30.0
01H	26.7
02H	24.0
03H	21.8
04H	20.0
05H	18.5
06H	17.1
07H	16.0
08H	15.0

Value	Repeat rate (characters per second)
09H	13.3
0AH	12.0
0BH	10.9
0CH	10.0
0DH	9.2
0EH	8.6
0FH	8.0
10H	7.5
11H	6.7
12H	6.0
13H	5.5
14H	5.0
15H	4.6
16H	4.3
17H	4.0
18H	3.7
19H	3.3
1AH	3.0
1BH	2.7
1CH	2.5
1DH	2.3
1EH	2.1
1FH	2.0

Int 16H [PC]
Function 04H
Set keyclick

Turns the keyboard click on or off.

Call with:	AH	= 04H	
	AL	= subfunction	
		00H	*to turn off keyboard click*
		01H	*to turn on keyboard click*

Returns:	Nothing

Note:	■ This function is supported by the PCjr BIOS only.

Function 05H
Push character and scan code

Places a character and scan code in the keyboard type-ahead buffer.

Call with:	AH	= 05H
	CH	= scan code
	CL	= character

Returns:	If function successful	
	Carry flag	= clear
	AL	= 00H
	If function unsuccessful (type-ahead buffer is full)	
	Carry flag	= set
	AL	= 01H

Note: ■ This function can be used by keyboard enhancers and other utilities to interpolate keys into the data stream seen by application programs.

Function 10H (16)
Read character from enhanced keyboard

Reads a character and scan code from the keyboard type-ahead buffer.

| **Call with:** | AH | = 10H |

| **Returns:** | AH | = keyboard scan code |
| | AL | = ASCII character |

Note: ■ Use this function for the enhanced keyboard instead of Int 16H Function 00H. It allows applications to obtain the scan codes for the additional F11, F12, and cursor control keys.

Int 16H
Function 11H (17)
Get enhanced keyboard status

Determines whether a character is ready for input, returning a flag and also the character itself, if one is waiting.

Call with:	AH	= 11H

Returns:	If key waiting to be input	
	Zero flag	= clear
	AH	= keyboard scan code
	AL	= character
	If no key waiting	
	Zero flag	= set

Notes:

- Use this function for the enhanced keyboard instead of Int 16H Function 00H. It allows applications to test for the additional F11, F12, and cursor control keys.

- The character returned by this function when the zero flag is clear is not removed from the type-ahead buffer. The same character and scan code will be returned by the next call to Int 16H Function 10H.

Int 16H
Function 12H (18)
Get enhanced keyboard flags

Obtains the status of various enhanced keyboard special keys and keyboard driver states.

Call with:	AH	= 12H

Returns:	AX	= flags	
		Bit	**Significance (if set)**
		0	right Shift key is down
		1	left Shift key is down
		2	either Ctrl key is down
		3	either Alt key is down
		4	Scroll Lock toggle is on
		5	Num Lock toggle is on
		6	Caps Lock toggle is on
		7	Insert toggle is on
		8	left Ctrl key is down

Bit	Significance (if set)
9	left Alt key is down
10	right Ctrl key is down
11	right Alt key is down
12	Scroll key is down
13	Num Lock key is down
14	Caps Lock key is down
15	SysReq key is down

Note:
- Use this function for the enhanced keyboard instead of Int 16H Function 02H.

Int 17H   [PC] [AT] [PS/2]
Function 00H
Write character to printer

Sends a character to the specified parallel printer interface port and returns the current status of the port.

Call with: AH   = 00H
AL   = character
DX   = printer number (0 = LPT1, 1 = LPT2, 2 = LPT3)

Returns: AH   = status

Bit	Significance (if set)
0	printer timed-out
1	unused
2	unused
3	I/O error
4	printer selected
5	out of paper
6	printer acknowledge
7	printer not busy

Int 17H   [PC] [AT] [PS/2]
Function 01H
Initialize printer port

Initializes the specified parallel printer interface port and returns its status.

Call with: AH   = 01H
DX   = printer number (0 = LPT1, 1 = LPT2, 2 = LPT3)

Returns: AH   = status (see Int 17H Function 00H)

Int 17H
Function 02H
Get printer status

Returns the current status of the specified parallel printer interface port.

Call with:	AH	= 02H
	DX	= printer number (0 = LPT1, 1 = LPT2, 2 = LPT3)

Returns: AH   = status (see Int 17H Function 00H)

Int 18H
ROM BASIC

Transfers control to ROM BASIC.

Call with: Nothing

Returns: Nothing

Note: ■ This function is invoked when the system is turned on or restarted if attempts to read a boot sector from the fixed disk or floppy disk drives are unsuccessful.

Int 19H
Reboot system

Reboots the operating system from the floppy disk or fixed disk drive.

Call with: Nothing

Returns: Nothing

Notes: ■ The bootstrap routine reads Sector 1, Track 0 into memory at location 0000:7C00H and transfers control to the same address. If attempts to read a boot sector from the floppy disk or fixed disk are unsuccessful, control is transferred to ROM BASIC by execution of an Int 18H.

- If location 0000:0472H does not contain the value 1234H, a memory test will be performed before reading the boot sector.

Int 1AH
Function 00H
Get tick count

Returns the contents of the clock tick counter.

Call with:	AH	= 00H

Returns:	AL	= rolled-over flag
		00H if midnight not passed since last read
		<>00H if midnight was passed since last read
	CX:DX	= tick count (high 16 bits in CX)

Notes:
- This function is supported by the PC/XT and PCjr ROM BIOS, but is not present in the ROM BIOS for the original PC.
- The returned value is the cumulative number of clock ticks since midnight. There are 18.2 clock ticks per second. When the counter reaches 1,573,040, it is cleared to zero, and the rolled-over flag is set.
- The rolled-over flag is cleared by this function call, so the flag will only be returned nonzero once per day.
- Int 1AH Function 01H can be used to set the clock tick counter to an arbitrary 32-bit value.

Int 1AH
Function 01H
Set tick count

Stores a 32-bit value in the clock tick counter.

Call with:	AH	= 01H
	CX:DX	= tick count (high 16 bits in CX)

Returns:	Nothing

Notes:

- This function is supported by the PC/XT and PCjr ROM BIOS, but is not present in the ROM BIOS for the original PC.
- Int 1AH Function 00H is used to read the value of the clock tick counter.
- The rolled-over flag is cleared by this function call.

Int 1AH
Function 02H
Get time

[AT] [PS/2]

Reads the current time from the CMOS time/date chip.

Call with:	AH	= 02H

Returns:	CH	= hours in binary coded decimal (BCD)
	CL	= minutes in BCD
	DH	= seconds in BCD
	DL	= daylight-saving-time code
		00H *if standard time*
		01H *if daylight saving time*

and, if clock running
Carry flag   = clear

or, if clock stopped
Carry flag   = set

Int 1AH
Function 03H
Set time

[AT] [PS/2]

Sets the time in the CMOS time/date chip.

Call with:	AH	= 03H
	CH	= hours in binary coded decimal (BCD)
	CL	= minutes in BCD
	DH	= seconds in BCD
	DL	= daylight-saving-time code
		00H *if standard time*
		01H *if daylight saving time*

Returns:	Nothing

Int 1AH
Function 04H
Get date

Reads the current date from the CMOS time/date chip.

Call with:	AH	= 04H

Returns:	CH	= century (19 or 20) in binary coded decimal (BCD)
	CL	= year in BCD
	DH	= month in BCD
	DL	= day in BCD

and, if clock running

Carry flag = clear

or, if clock stopped

Carry flag = set

Int 1AH
Function 05H
Set date

Sets the date in the CMOS time/date chip.

Call with:	AH	= 05H
	CH	= century (19 or 20) in binary coded decimal (BCD)
	CL	= year in BCD
	DH	= month in BCD
	DL	= day in BCD

Returns:	Nothing

Int 1AH
Function 06H
Set alarm

Sets an alarm in the CMOS date/time chip.

Call with:	AH	= 06H
	CH	= hours in binary coded decimal (BCD)
	CL	= minutes in BCD
	DH	= seconds in BCD

Returns:	If function successful
	Carry flag = clear
	If function unsuccessful (alarm already set, or clock stopped)
	Carry flag = set

Notes:	■ A side effect of this function is that the clock chip's interrupt level (IRQ8) is enabled.
	■ Only one alarm may be active at any given time. The alarm occurs every 24 hours at the specified time until it is reset with Int 1AH Function 07H.
	■ The program using this function must place the address of its interrupt handler for the alarm in the vector for Int 4AH.

Int 1AH
Function 07H
Reset alarm

[AT] [PS/2]

Cancels any pending alarm request on the CMOS date/time chip.

Call with:	AH	= 07H

Returns:	Nothing

Note:	■ This function does not disable the clock chip's interrupt level (IRQ8).

Int 1AH
Function 0AH (10)
Get day count

[PS/2]

Returns the contents of the system's day counter.

Call with:	AH	= 0AH

Returns:	If function successful
	Carry flag = clear
	CX = count of days since January 1, 1980
	If function unsuccessful
	Carry flag = set

Int 1AH
Function 0BH (11)
Set day count

Stores an arbitrary value in the system's day counter.

Call with:	AH	= 0BH
	CX	= count of days since January 1, 1980

Returns:	If function successful	
	Carry flag	= clear
	If function unsuccessful	
	Carry flag	= set

Int 1AH
Function 80H (128)
Set sound source

Sets up the source for tones that will appear on the PCjr's "Audio Out" or RF modulator.

Call with:	AH	= 80H	
	AL	= sound source	
		00H	*if 8253 programmable timer, channel 2*
		01H	*if cassette input*
		02H	*if "Audio In" line on I/O channel*
		03H	*if sound generator chip*

Returns:	Nothing

Note:	■ This function is supported on the PCjr only.

Int 33H
Microsoft Mouse driver

The Microsoft Mouse driver makes its functions available to application programs via Int 33H. These functions have become a de facto standard for pointer device drivers of all varieties. Unlike the other function calls described in this section, the Microsoft Mouse driver is not part of the ROM BIOS but is loaded by a DEVICE= directive in the CONFIG.SYS file. All mouse-function information applies to the Microsoft Mouse driver version 6. Earlier versions of the driver may not support all of these functions.

Int 33H
Function 00H
Reset mouse and get status

Initializes the mouse driver and returns the driver status. If the mouse pointer was previously visible, it is removed from the screen, and any previously installed user handlers for mouse events are disabled.

Call with:	AX	= 0000H

Returns:	If mouse support is available	
	AX	= FFFFH
	BX	= number of mouse buttons
	If mouse support is not available	
	AX	= 0000H

Note:
- After a call to this function, the mouse driver is initialized to the following state:
  - Mouse pointer at screen center (see Int 33H Functions 03H and 04H)
  - Display page for mouse pointer set to zero (see Int 33H Functions 1DH and 1EH)
  - Mouse pointer hidden (see Int 33H Functions 01H, 02H, and 10H)
  - Mouse pointer set to default arrow shape in graphics modes, or reverse block in text modes (see Int 33H Functions 09H and 0AH)
  - User mouse event handler disabled (see Int 33H Functions 0CH and 14H)
  - Light pen emulation enabled (see Int 33H Functions 0DH and 0EH)
  - Horizontal mickeys to pixels ratio at 8 to 8, vertical ratio at 16 to 8 (see Int 33H Function 0FH)
  - Double speed threshold set to 64 mickeys/second (see Int 33H Function 19H)
  - Minimum and maximum horizontal and vertical pointer position limits set to include the entire screen in the current display mode (see Int 33H Functions 07H and 08H)

Int 33H
Function 01H
Show mouse pointer

Displays the mouse pointer, and cancels any mouse pointer exclusion area previously defined with Int 33H Function 10H.

Call with:	AX	= 0001H

Returns:	Nothing

Note: ■ A counter is maintained which is decremented by calls to Int 33H Function 02H (Hide Mouse Pointer) and incremented (if nonzero) by this function. When the counter is zero or becomes zero, the mouse pointer is displayed. When the mouse driver is reset with Int 33H Function 00H, the counter is forced to –1.

Int 33H
Function 02H
Hide mouse pointer

Removes the mouse pointer from the display. The driver continues to track the mouse position.

Call with:	AX	= 0002H

Returns:	Nothing

Note: ■ A counter is maintained which is decremented by calls to this function and incremented (if nonzero) by Int 33H Function 01H (Show Mouse Pointer). When the counter is zero, the mouse pointer is displayed. When the mouse driver is reset with Int 33H Function 00H, the counter is forced to –1.

Int 33H
Function 03H
Get mouse position and button status

Returns the current mouse button status and pointer position.

Call with:	AX	= 0003H

Returns: BX = mouse button status

Bit(s)	*Significance (if set)*
0	left button is down
1	right button is down
2	center button is down
3–15	reserved (0)

CX = horizontal (*X*) coordinate
DX = vertical (*Y*) coordinate

Note: ■ Coordinates are returned in pixels regardless of the current display mode. Position (*x,y*) = (0,0) is the upper left corner of the screen.

Int 33H
Function 04H
Set mouse pointer position

Sets the position of the mouse pointer. The pointer is displayed at the new position unless it has been hidden with Int 33H Function 02H, or the new position lies within an exclusion area defined with Int 33H Function 10H.

Call with:	AX	= 0004H
	CX	= horizontal (X) coordinate
	DX	= vertical (Y) coordinate

| **Returns:** | Nothing |

Notes:
- Coordinates are specified in pixels regardless of the current display mode. Position $(x,y) = (0,0)$ is the upper left corner of the screen.
- The position is adjusted if necessary to lie within the horizontal and vertical limits specified with a previous call to Int 33H Functions 07H and 08H.

Int 33H
Function 05H
Get button press information

Returns the current status of all mouse buttons, and the number of presses and position of the last press for a specified mouse button since the last call to this function for that button. The press counter for the button is reset to zero.

Call with:	AX	= 0005H	
	BX	= button identifier	
		0	= *left button*
		1	= *right button*
		2	= *center button*

Returns:	AX	= button status	
		Bit(s)	***Significance (if set)***
		0	left button is down
		1	right button is down
		2	center button is down
		3–15	reserved (0)
	BX	= button press counter	
	CX	= horizontal (X) coordinate of last button press	
	DX	= vertical (Y) coordinate of last button press	

Int 33H
Function 06H
Get button release information

Returns the current status of all mouse buttons, and the number of releases and position of the last release for a specified mouse button since the last call to this function for that button. The release counter for the button is reset to zero.

Call with:	AX	= 0006H
	BX	= button identifier
	0	*= left button*
	1	*= right button*
	2	*= center button*

Returns:	AX	= button status

Bit(s)	*Significance (if set)*
0	left button is down
1	right button is down
2	center button is down
3–15	reserved (0)

	BX	= button release counter
	CX	= horizontal (*X*) coordinate of last button release
	DX	= vertical (*Y*) coordinate of last button release

Int 33H
Function 07H
Set horizontal limits for pointer

Limits the mouse pointer display area by assigning minimum and maximum horizontal (*X*) coordinates for the mouse pointer.

Call with:	AX	= 0007H
	CX	= minimum horizontal (*X*) coordinate
	DX	= maximum horizontal (*X*) coordinate

Returns:	Nothing

Notes:	■ If the minimum value is greater than the maximum value, the two values are swapped.
	■ The mouse pointer will be moved if necessary so that it lies within the specified horizontal coordinates.

- See also Int 33H Function 10H, which defines an exclusion area for the mouse pointer.

Int 33H
Function 08H
Set vertical limits for pointer

Limits the mouse pointer display area by assigning minimum and maximum vertical (Y) coordinates for the mouse pointer.

Call with:	AX	= 0008H
	CX	= minimum vertical (Y) coordinate
	DX	= maximum vertical (Y) coordinate

| **Returns:** | Nothing |

Notes:	■ If the minimum value is greater than the maximum value, the two values are swapped.
	■ The mouse pointer will be moved if necessary so that it lies within the specified vertical coordinates.
	■ See also Int 33H Function 10H, which defines an exclusion area for the mouse pointer.

Int 33H
Function 09H
Set graphics pointer shape

Defines the shape, color, and hot spot of the mouse pointer in graphics modes.

Call with:	AX	= 0009H
	BX	= hot spot offset from left
	CX	= hot spot offset from top
	ES:DX	= segment:offset of pointer image buffer

| **Returns:** | Nothing |

| **Notes:** | ■ The pointer image buffer is 64 bytes long. The first 32 bytes contain a bit mask which is ANDed with the screen image, and the second 32 bytes contain a bit mask which is XORed with the screen image. |
| | ■ The hot spot is relative to the upper left corner of the pointer image, and each pixel offset must be in the range −16 through 16. In display modes 4 and 5, the horizontal offset must be an even number. |

Int 33H
Function 0AH (10)
Set text pointer type

Defines the shape and attributes of the mouse pointer in text modes.

Call with:	AX	= 000AH
	BX	= pointer type
		$\quad$ 0 $\qquad$ = *software cursor*
		$\quad$ 1 $\qquad$ = *hardware cursor*
	CX	= AND mask value (if BX = 0) *or*
		$\quad$ starting line for cursor (if BX = 1)
	DX	= XOR mask value (if BX = 0) *or*
		$\quad$ ending line for cursor (if BX = 1)

Returns: Nothing

Notes:
- If the software text cursor is selected (BX = 0), the masks in CX and DX are mapped as follows:

Bit(s)	*Significance*
0–7	character code
8–10	foreground color
11	intensity
12–14	background color
15	blink

  For example, the following values would yield a software mouse cursor that inverts the foreground and background colors:

AX	= 000AH
BX	= 0000H
CX	= 77FFH
DX	= 7700H

- When the hardware text cursor is selected (BX = 1), the values in CX and DX are the starting and ending scan lines for the blinking cursor generated by the video adapter. The maximum scan line which may be used depends on the type of adapter and the current display mode.

Int 33H
Function 0BH (11)
Read mouse motion counters

Returns the net mouse displacement since the last call to this function. The returned value is in mickeys; a positive number indicates travel to the right or downwards, a negative number indicates travel to the left or upwards. One mickey represents approximately $\frac{1}{200}$ of an inch of mouse movement.

Returns:	CX	= horizontal (*X*) mickey count
	DX	= vertical (*Y*) mickey count

Int 33H
Function 0CH (12)
Set user-defined mouse event handler

Sets the address and event mask for an application program's mouse event handler. The handler is called by the mouse driver whenever the specified mouse events occur.

Call with:	AX	= 000CH
	CX	= event mask

Bit(s)	Significance (if set)
0	mouse movement
1	left button pressed
2	left button released
3	right button pressed
4	right button released
5	center button pressed
6	center button released
7–15	reserved (0)

	ES:DX	= segment:offset of handler

Returns:	Nothing

Notes:

- The user-defined event handler is entered from the mouse driver by a far call with registers set up as follows:

AX	mouse event flags (see event mask)
BX	button state

Bit(s)	Significance (if set)
0	left button is down
1	right button is down
2	center button is down
3–15	reserved (0)

CX	horizontal (*X*) pointer coordinate
DX	vertical (*Y*) pointer coordinate
SI	last raw vertical mickey count
DI	last raw horizontal mickey count
DS	mouse driver data segment

- If an event does not generate a call to the user-defined handler because its bit is not set in the event mask, it is still reported in the event flags during calls to the handler for events which *are* enabled.

- Calls to the handler are disabled with Int 33H Function 00H or by calling this function with an event mask of zero.
- See also Int 33H Functions 14H and 18H.

Int 33H
Function 0DH (13)
Turn on light pen emulation

Enables light pen emulation by the mouse driver for IBM BASIC. A "pen down" condition is created by pressing the left and right mouse buttons simultaneously.

Call with: AX   = 000DH

Returns: Nothing

Int 33H
Function 0EH (14)
Turn off light pen emulation

Disables light pen emulation by the mouse driver for IBM BASIC.

Call with: AX   = 000EH

Returns: Nothing

Int 33H
Function 0FH (15)
Set mickeys to pixels ratio

Sets the number of mickeys per 8 pixels for horizontal and vertical mouse motion. One mickey represents approximately $1/200$ of an inch of mouse travel.

Call with: AX   = 000FH
                   CX   = horizontal mickeys (1–32,767, default = 8)
                   DX   = vertical mickeys (1–32,767, default = 16)

Returns: Nothing

Int 33H
Function 10H (16)
Set mouse pointer exclusion area

Defines an exclusion area for the mouse pointer. When the mouse pointer lies within the specified area, it is not displayed.

Call with:	AX	= 0010H
	CX	= upper left X coordinate
	DX	= upper left Y coordinate
	SI	= lower right X coordinate
	DI	= lower right Y coordinate

Returns:	Nothing

Note:	■ The exclusion area is replaced by another call to this function or cancelled by Int 33H Functions 00H or 01H.

Int 33H
Function 13H (19)
Set double speed threshold

Sets the threshold speed for doubling pointer motion on the screen. The default threshold speed is 64 mickeys/second.

Call with:	AX	= 0013H
	DX	= threshold speed in mickeys/second

Returns:	Nothing

Note:	■ Doubling of pointer motion can be effectively disabled by setting the threshold to a very large value (such as 10,000).

Int 33H
Function 14H (20)
Swap user-defined mouse event handlers

Sets the address and event mask for an application program's mouse event handler and returns the address and event mask for the previous handler. The newly installed handler is called by the mouse driver whenever the specified mouse events occur.

Call with:	AX	= 0014H		
	CX	= event mask		
		Bit(s)	*Significance (if set)*	
		0	mouse movement	
		1	left button pressed	
		2	left button released	
		3	right button pressed	
		4	right button released	
		5	center button pressed	
		6	center button released	
		7–15	reserved (0)	
	ES:DX	= segment:offset of event handler		

Returns:	CX	= previous event mask
	ES:DX	= segment:offset of previous handler

Notes:	■ The Notes for Int 33H Function 0CH describe the information passed to the user-defined event handler. See also Int 33H Function 18H.
	■ Calls to the event handler are disabled with Int 33H Function 00H or by setting an event mask of zero.

Int 33H
Function 15H (21)
Get mouse save state buffer size

Gets the size of the buffer required to store the current state of the mouse driver.

Call with:	AX	= 0015H

Returns:	BX	= buffer size (bytes)

Note:	■ See also Int 33H Functions 16H and 17H.

Int 33H
Function 16H (22)
Save mouse driver state

Saves the mouse driver state in a user buffer. The minimum size for the buffer must be determined by a previous call to Int 33H Function 15H.

| **Call with:** | AX | = 0016H |
| | ES:DX | = segment:offset of buffer |

| **Returns:** | Nothing |

| **Note:** | ■ Call this function before executing a child program with Int 21H Function 4BH (EXEC), in case the child also uses the mouse. After the EXEC call, restore the previous mouse driver state with Int 33H Function 17H. |

Int 33H
Function 17H (23)
Restore mouse driver state

Restores the mouse driver state from a user buffer.

| **Call with:** | AX | = 0017H |
| | ES:DX | = segment:offset of buffer |

| **Returns:** | Nothing |

| **Note:** | ■ The mouse driver state must have been previously saved into the same buffer with Int 33H Function 16H. The format of the data in the buffer is undocumented and subject to change. |

Int 33H
Function 18H (24)
Set alternate mouse event handler

Sets the address and event mask for a an application program mouse event handler. As many as three handlers with distinct event masks can be registered with this function. When an event occurs that matches one of the masks, the corresponding handler is called by the mouse driver.

Call with:

AX = 0018H
CX = event mask

Bit(s)	Significance (if set)
0	mouse movement
1	left button pressed
2	left button released
3	right button pressed
4	right button released
5	Shift key pressed during button press or release
6	Ctrl key pressed during button press or release
7	Alt key pressed during button press or release
8–15	reserved (0)

ES:DX = segment:offset of handler

Returns:

If function successful
AX = 0018H

If function unsuccessful
AX = FFFFH

Notes:

- When this function is called, at least one of the bits 5, 6, and 7 must be set in register CX.
- The user-defined event handler is entered from the mouse driver by a far call with registers set up as follows:

AX   mouse event flags (see event mask)
BX   button state

Bit(s)	Significance (if set)
0	left button is down
1	right button is down
2	center button is down
3–15	reserved (0)

CX   horizontal (X) pointer coordinate
DX   vertical (Y) pointer coordinate
SI   last raw vertical mickey count
DI   last raw horizontal mickey count
DS   mouse driver data segment

- If an event does not generate a call to the user-defined handler because its bit is not set in the event mask, it can still be reported in the event flags during calls to the handler for events that *are* enabled.
- Calls to the handler are disabled with Int 33H Function 00H.
- See also Int 33H Functions 0CH and 14H.

Int 33H
Function 19H (25)
Get address of alternate mouse event handler

Returns the address for the mouse event handler matching the specified event mask.

Call with:	AX	= 0019H
	CX	= event mask (see Int 33H Function 18H)

Returns:	If function successful	
	CX	= event mask
	ES:DX	= segment:offset of alternate event handler

If function unsuccessful (no handler installed or event mask does not match any installed handler)

	CX	= 0000H

Note:
- Int 33H Function 18H allows as many as three event handlers with distinct event masks to be installed. This function can be called to search for a handler that matches a specific event, so that it can be replaced or disabled.

Int 33H
Function 1AH (26)
Set mouse sensitivity

Sets the number of mickeys per 8 pixels for horizontal and vertical mouse motion and the threshold speed for doubling pointer motion on the screen. One mickey represents approximately $1/200$ of an inch of mouse travel.

Call with:	AX	= 001AH
	BX	= horizontal mickeys (1–32,767, default = 8)
	CX	= vertical mickeys (1–32,767, default = 16)
	DX	= double speed threshold in mickeys/second (default = 64)

Returns:	Nothing

Note:
- See also Int 33H Functions 0FH and 13H, which allow the mickeys to pixels ratio and threshold speed to be set separately, and Int 33H Function 1BH, which returns the current sensitivity values.

Int 33H
Function 1BH (27)
Get mouse sensitivity

Returns the current mickeys to pixels ratios for vertical and horizontal screen movement and the threshold speed for doubling of pointer motion.

Call with:	AX	= 001BH

Returns:	BX	= horizontal mickeys (1–32,767, default = 8)
	CX	= vertical mickeys (1–32,767, default = 16)
	DX	= double speed threshold in mickeys/second (default = 64)

Note:	■ See also Int 33H Functions 0FH, 13H, and 1AH.

Int 33H
Function 1CH (28)
Set mouse interrupt rate

Sets the rate at which the mouse driver polls the status of the mouse. Faster rates provide better resolution in graphics mode but may degrade the performance of application programs.

Call with:	AX	= 001CH	
	BX	= interrupt rate flags	
		Bit(s)	*Significance*
		0	no interrupts allowed
		1	30 interrupts/second
		2	50 interrupts/second
		3	100 interrupts/second
		4	200 interrupts/second
		5–15	reserved (0)

Returns:	Nothing

Notes:	■ This function is applicable for the InPort Mouse only.
	■ If more than one bit is set in register BX, the lowest order bit prevails.

Int 33H
Function 1DH (29)
Select pointer page

Selects the display page for the mouse pointer.

Call with: AX   = 001DH
                  BX   = page

Returns: Nothing

Note: ■ The valid page numbers depend on the current display mode. See Int 10H
             Function 05H.

Int 33H
Function 1EH (30)
Get pointer page

Returns the current display page for the mouse pointer.

Call with: AX   = 001EH

Returns: BX   = page

Int 33H
Function 1FH (31)
Disable mouse driver

Disables the mouse driver and returns the address of the previous Int 33H handler.

Call with: AX   = 001FH

Returns: If function successful
              AX   = 001FH
              ES:BX   = segment:offset of previous Int 33H handler
              If function unsuccessful
              AX   = FFFFH

Notes:

- When this function is called, the mouse driver releases any interrupt vectors it has captured *other* than Int 33H (which may include Int 10H, Int 71H, and/or Int 74H). The application program can *complete* the process of logically removing the mouse driver by restoring the original contents of the Int 33H vector with Int 21H Function 25H, using the address returned by this function in ES:BX.

- See also Int 33H Function 20H.

Int 33H
Function 20H (32)
Enable mouse driver

Enables the mouse driver and the servicing of mouse interrupts.

Call with:	AX	= 0020H

Returns:	Nothing

Note:

- See also Int 33H Function 1FH.

Int 33H
Function 21H (33)
Reset mouse driver

Resets the mouse driver and returns driver status. If the mouse pointer was previously visible, it is removed from the screen, and any previously installed user handlers for mouse events are disabled.

Call with:	AX	= 0021H

Returns:	If mouse support is available	
	AX	= FFFFH
	BX	= number of mouse buttons
	If mouse support is not available	
	AX	= 0021H

Note:

- This function differs from Int 33H Function 00H in that there is no initialization of the mouse hardware.

Int 33H
Function 22H (34)
Set language for mouse driver messages

Selects the language that will be used by the mouse driver for prompts and error messages.

Call with:	AX	= 0022H
	BX	= language number

	0	= *English*
	1	= *French*
	2	= *Dutch*
	3	= *German*
	4	= *Swedish*
	5	= *Finnish*
	6	= *Spanish*
	7	= *Portuguese*
	8	= *Italian*

Returns:	Nothing

Note:
- This function is only available in international versions of the Microsoft Mouse driver.

Int 33H
Function 23H (35)
Get language number

Returns the number of the language that is used by the mouse driver for prompts and error messages.

Call with:	AX	= 0023H

Returns:	BX	= language number (see Int 33H Function 22H)

Note:
- This function is only available in international versions of the Microsoft Mouse driver.

Int 33H
Function 24H (36)
Get mouse information

Returns the mouse driver version number, mouse type, and the IRQ number of the interrupt used by the mouse adapter.

Call with:	AX	= 0024H

Returns:	BH	= major version number (6 for version 6.10, etc.)
	BL	= minor version number (0AH for version 6.10, etc.)
	CH	= mouse type
		1 = *bus mouse*
		2 = *serial mouse*
		3 = *InPort mouse*
		4 = *PS/2 mouse*
		5 = *HP mouse*
	CL	= IRQ number
		0 = *PS/2*
		2, 3, 4, 5, or 7 = *IRQ number*

SECTION IV

Lotus/Intel/
Microsoft EMS
Functions
Reference

Notes to the Reader

The Lotus/Intel/Microsoft Expanded Memory Specification (EMS) defines a hardware/software subsystem, compatible with 80x86-based microcomputers running MS-DOS, that allows applications to access as much as 32 MB of bank-switched random-access memory. The software component, called the Expanded Memory Manager (EMM), is installed during system initialization by a DEVICE= directive in the CONFIG.SYS file in the root directory on the boot disk.

After ensuring that the EMM is present (see Chapter 11), an application program communicates directly with the EMM using software interrupt 67H. A particular EMM function is selected by the value in register AH and a success or error status is returned in register AH (error codes are listed on pages 207–209). Other parameters and results are passed or returned in registers or buffers.

An icon in each function heading indicates the EMS version in which that function was first supported. You can assume that the function is available in all subsequent EMS versions unless explicitly noted otherwise.

Version icons used in the synopsis, parameters, results, or Notes section refer to specific minor or major EMS versions, unless they include a + sign to indicate a version and all subsequent versions.

The material in this section has been verified against the Expanded Memory Specification version 4.0, dated October 1987, Intel part number 300275-005. This document can be obtained from Intel Corporation, 5200 N.E. Elam Young Parkway, Hillsboro, OR 97124.

Summary of EMM Functions

Function	Subfunction	Description
40H (64)		Get Status
41H (65)		Get Page Frame Address
42H (66)		Get Number of Pages
43H (67)		Allocate Handle and Pages
44H (68)		Map Expanded Memory Page
45H (69)		Release Handle and Expanded Memory
46H (70)		Get Version
47H (71)		Save Page Map
48H (72)		Restore Page Map
49H (73)		Reserved
4AH (74)		Reserved
4BH (75)		Get Handle Count

(continued)

Function	Subfunction	Description
4CH (76)		Get Handle Pages
4DH (77)		Get Pages for All Handles
4EH (78)	00H	Save Page Map
4EH (78)	01H	Restore Page Map
4EH (78)	02H	Save and Restore Page Map
4EH (78)	03H	Get Size of Page Map Information
4FH (79)	00H	Save Partial Page Map
4FH (79)	01H	Restore Partial Page Map
4FH (79)	02H	Get Size of Partial Page Map Information
50H (80)	00H	Map Multiple Pages by Number
50H (80)	01H	Map Multiple Pages by Address
51H (81)		Reallocate Pages for Handle
52H (82)	00H	Get Handle Attribute
52H (82)	01H	Set Handle Attribute
52H (82)	02H	Get Attribute Capability
53H (83)	00H	Get Handle Name
53H (83)	01H	Set Handle Name
54H (84)	00H	Get All Handle Names
54H (84)	01H	Search for Handle Name
54H (84)	02H	Get Total Handles
55H (85)	00H	Map Pages by Number and Jump
55H (85)	01H	Map Pages by Address and Jump
56H (86)	00H	Map Pages by Number and Call
56H (86)	01H	Map Pages by Address and Call
56H (86)	02H	Get Space for Map Page and Call
57H (87)	00H	Move Memory Region
57H (87)	01H	Exchange Memory Regions
58H (88)	00H	Get Addresses of Mappable Pages
58H (88)	01H	Get Number of Mappable Pages
59H (89)	00H	Get Hardware Configuration
59H (89)	01H	Get Number of Raw Pages
5AH (90)	00H	Allocate Handle and Standard Pages
5AH (90)	01H	Allocate Handle and Raw Pages
5BH (91)	00H	Get Alternate Map Registers
5BH (91)	01H	Set Alternate Map Registers
5BH (91)	02H	Get Size of Alternate Map Register Save Area
5BH (91)	03H	Allocate Alternate Map Register Set
5BH (91)	04H	Deallocate Alternate Map Register Set
5BH (91)	05H	Allocate DMA Register Set
5BH (91)	06H	Enable DMA on Alternate Map Register Set
5BH (91)	07H	Disable DMA on Alternate Map Register Set
5BH (91)	08H	Deallocate DMA Register Set
5CH (92)		Prepare Expanded Memory Manager for Warm Boot
5DH (93)	00H	Enable EMM Operating-System Functions
5DH (93)	01H	Disable EMM Operating-System Functions
5DH (93)	02H	Release Access Key

Int 67H
Function 40H (64)
Get status

Returns a status code indicating whether the expanded memory software and hardware are present and functional.

Call with:	AH	= 40H

Returns:	If function successful	
	AH	= 00H
	If function unsuccessful	
	AH	= error code

Note:	■ This call should be used only after an application has established that the Expanded Memory Manager is in fact present, using one of the techniques described in Chapter 11.

Int 67H
Function 41H (65)
Get page frame address

Returns the segment address of the page frame used by the Expanded Memory Manager.

Call with:	AH	= 41H

Returns:	If function successful	
	AH	= 00H
	BX	= segment base of page frame
	If function unsuccessful	
	AH	= error code

Notes:	■ The page frame is divided into four 16 KB pages, which are used to map logical expanded memory pages into the physical memory space of the CPU.
	■ The application need not have already acquired an EMM handle to use this function.
	■ [EMS 4.0] Mapping of expanded memory pages is not necessarily limited to the 64 KB page frame. See also Int 67H Function 58H Subfunction 00H.

Int 67H
Function 42H (66)
Get number of pages

Obtains the total number of logical expanded memory pages present in the system and the number of pages that are not already allocated.

Call with: AH   = 42H

Returns: If function successful
                AH   = 00H
                BX   = unallocated pages
                DX   = total pages
                If function unsuccessful
                AH   = error code

Notes: ▪ The application need not have already acquired an EMM handle to use this function.
            ▪ [EMS 4.0] See also Int 67H Function 59H Subfunction 01H.

Int 67H
Function 43H (67)
Allocate handle and pages

Obtains an EMM handle and allocates logical pages of expanded memory to be controlled by that handle.

Call with: AH   = 43H
                BX   = number of pages to allocate (must be nonzero)

Returns: If function successful
                AH   = 00H
                DX   = EMM handle
                If function unsuccessful
                AH   = error code

- This is the equivalent of a file open function for the expanded memory manager. The handle that is returned is analogous to a file handle and owns a certain number of expanded memory pages. The handle must be used with every subsequent request to map memory and must be released by a close operation before the application terminates.

- This function may fail because there are no handles left to allocate or because there is an insufficient number of expanded memory pages to satisfy the request. In the latter case, Int 67H Function 42H can be used to determine the actual number of pages available.

- [EMS 4.0] Int 67H Function 51H can be called to change the number of pages allocated to an EMM handle.

- [EMS 4.0] The pages allocated by this function are always 16 KB for compatibility with earlier versions of EMS. See also Int 67H Function 5AH Subfunctions 00H and 01H.

- [EMS 4.0] Handle 0000H is always available for use by the operating system, and a prior call to this function is not required. The operating system must call Int 67H Function 51H to assign the desired number of pages to its reserved handle.

Int 67H   [EMS 3.0]
Function 44H (68)
Map expanded memory page

Maps one of the logical pages of expanded memory assigned to a handle onto a physical memory page that can be accessed by the CPU.

Call with: AH   = 44H
                  AL   = physical page
                  BX   = logical page
                  DX   = EMM handle

Returns: If function successful
                AH   = 00H

                If function unsuccessful
                AH   = error code

Notes:
- The logical page number is in the range {0 ... $n-1$}, where n is the number of pages allocated or reallocated to the handle by a previous call to Int 67H Function 43H, 51H, or 5AH. Logical pages allocated by Int 67H Function 43H or Function 5AH Subfunction 00H are always 16 KB long; logical pages allocated by Int 67H Function 5AH Subfunction 01H are referred to as raw pages and are not necessarily 16 KB.

- [EMS 3] The physical page is in the range 0–3 and lies within the EMM page frame, whose base address is obtained from Int 67H Function 41H.

- [EMS 4.0] A list of the available physical pages and their addresses may be obtained from Int 67H Function 58H Subfunction 00H.
- [EMS 4.0] If this function is called with BX = −1, the specified physical page is unmapped (made inaccessible for reading or writing).

Int 67H [EMS 3.0]
Function 45H (69)
Release handle and expanded memory

Deallocates the expanded memory pages assigned to a handle and then releases the handle.

Call with: AH   = 45H
DX   = EMM handle

Returns: If function successful
AH   = 00H
If function unsuccessful
AH   = error code

Notes:
- If this function is not called before a program terminates, the EMS pages it owned remain unavailable until the system is restarted. Programs that use EMS should install their own Ctrl-C handlers and critical-error handlers (Ints 23H and 24H) so that they cannot be terminated unexpectedly.
- [EMS 4.0] When a handle is released, its name is set to all ASCII nulls.

Int 67H [EMS 3.0]
Function 46H (70)
Get version

Returns the EMS version supported by the expanded memory manager.

Call with: AH   = 46H

Returns: If function successful
AH   = 00H
AL   = version number
If function unsuccessful
AH   = error code

- The version number is returned in binary code decimal (BCD) format, with the integer portion in the upper 4 bits of AL and the fractional portion in the lower 4 bits. For example, under an EMM that supports EMS version 3.2, AL is returned as the value 32H.
- Applications should always check the EMM version number to ensure that all of the EMM functions they require are available.

Int 67H   [EMS 3.0]
Function 47H (71)
Save page map

Saves the contents of the page-mapping registers on the expanded memory hardware, associating those contents with a particular EMM handle.

Call with:	AH	= 47H
	DX	= EMM handle

Returns:	If function successful	
	AH	= 00H
	If function unsuccessful	
	AH	= error code

Notes:
- This function is used by interrupt handlers or device drivers that must access expanded memory. The EMM handle supplied to this function is the handle that was assigned to the handler or driver during its own initialization sequence, *not* to the program that was interrupted.
- The mapping context is restored by a subsequent call to Int 67H Function 48H.
- [EMS 4.0] This function saves only the mapping state for the 64 KB page frame defined in EMS 3. Programs that are written to take advantage of the additional capabilities of EMS 4.0 should use Int 67H Function 4EH or 4FH in preference to this function.

Int 67H   [EMS 3.0]
Function 48H (72)
Restore page map

Restores the contents of the page-mapping registers on the expanded memory hardware to the values associated with the specified handle by a previous call to Int 67H Function 47H.

| **Call with:** | AH | = 48H |
| | DX | = EMM handle |

Returns:	If function successful	
	AH	= 00H
	If function unsuccessful	
	AH	= error code

Notes:
- This function is used by interrupt handlers or device drivers that must access expanded memory. The EMM handle supplied to this function is the handle that was assigned to the handler or driver during its own initialization sequence, *not* to the program that was interrupted.
- [EMS 4.0] This function restores only the mapping state for the 64 KB page frame defined in EMS 3. Programs that are written to take advantage of the additional capabilities of EMS 4.0 should use Int 67H Function 4EH or 4FH in preference to this function.

Int 67H [EMS 3.0]
Function 49H (73)
Reserved

This function was defined in EMS version 3.0 but is not documented for later EMS versions, so it should be avoided in application programs.

Int 67H [EMS 3.0]
Function 4AH (74)
Reserved

This function was defined in EMS version 3.0 but is not documented for later EMS versions, so it should be avoided in application programs.

Int 67H [EMS 3.0]
Function 4BH (75)
Get handle count

Returns the number of active expanded memory handles.

Call with:	AH	= 4BH

Returns:	If function successful	
	AH	= 00H
	BX	= number of active EMM handles
	If function unsuccessful	
	AH	= error code

Notes:
- If the returned number of EMM handles is zero, the expanded memory manager is idle, and none of the expanded memory is in use.
- The value returned by this function is not necessarily the same as the number of programs using expanded memory because one program may own multiple EMM handles.
- The number of active EMM handles never exceeds 255.

Int 67H [EMS 3.0]
Function 4CH (76)
Get handle pages

Returns the number of expanded memory pages allocated to a specific EMM handle.

Call with:	AH	= 4CH
	DX	= EMM handle

Returns:	If function successful	
	AH	= 00H
	BX	= number of EMM pages
	If function unsuccessful	
	AH	= error code

Notes:
- [EMS 3] The total number of pages allocated to a handle never exceeds 512. A handle never has zero pages allocated to it.
- [EMS 4.0] The total number of pages allocated to a handle never exceeds 2048. A handle may have zero pages of expanded memory.

Int 67H [EMS 3.0]
Function 4DH (77)
Get pages for all handles

Returns an array that contains all the active handles and the number of expanded memory pages associated with each handle.

Call with:	AH	= 4DH
	ES:DI	= segment:offset of buffer (see Notes)

Returns:	If function successful	
	AH	= 00H
	BX	= number of active EMM handles
	and buffer filled in as described in Notes	
	If function unsuccessful	
	AH	= error code

Notes:
- The buffer is filled in with a series of DWORD (32-bit) entries, one per active EMM handle. The first word of an entry contains the handle, and the second word contains the number of pages allocated to that handle.
- The maximum number of active handles is 256 (including the operating system handle 0), so a buffer size of 1024 bytes is adequate in all cases.

Int 67H [EMS 3.2]
Function 4EH (78) Subfunction 00H
Save page map

Saves the current page-mapping state of the expanded memory hardware in the specified buffer.

Call with:	AH	= 4EH
	AL	= 00H
	ES:DI	= segment:offset of buffer (see Notes)

Returns:	If function successful	
	AH	= 00H
	and buffer filled in with mapping information (see Notes)	
	If function unsuccessful	
	AH	= error code

Notes:

- The buffer receives the information necessary to restore the state of the mapping registers using Int 67H Function 4EH Subfunction 01H. The format of the information may vary.

- The size of the buffer required by this function can be determined with Int 67H Function 4EH Subfunction 03H.

- Unlike Int 67H Function 47H, this function does not require a handle.

Int 67H [EMS 3.2]
Function 4EH (78) Subfunction 01H
Restore page map

Restores the page-mapping state of the expanded memory hardware using the information in the specified buffer.

Call with:

AH	= 4EH	
AL	= 01H	
DS:SI	= segment:offset of buffer (see Notes)	

Returns:

If function successful
AH   = 00H

If function unsuccessful
AH   = error code

Notes:

- The buffer contains information necessary to restore the state of the mapping registers from a previous call to Int 67H Function 4EH Subfunction 00H or 02H. The format of the information may vary.

- Unlike Int 67H Function 48H, this function does not require a handle.

Int 67H [EMS 3.2]
Function 4EH (78) Subfunction 02H
Save and restore page map

Saves the current page-mapping state of the expanded memory hardware in a buffer and then sets the mapping state using the information in another buffer.

Call with:

AH	= 4EH	
AL	= 02H	
DS:SI	= segment:offset of buffer containing mapping information (see Notes)	
ES:DI	= segment:offset of buffer to receive mapping information (see Notes)	

Returns: If function successful

AH   = 00H

and buffer pointed to by ES:DI filled in with mapping information (see Notes)

If function unsuccessful

AH   = error code

Notes:
- The buffer addressed by DS:SI contains information necessary to restore the state of the mapping registers from a previous call to Int 67H Function 4EH Subfunction 00H or 02H. The format of the information may vary.
- The sizes of the buffers required by this function can be determined with Int 67H Function 4EH Subfunction 03H.
- Unlike Int 67H Functions 47H and 48H, this function does not require a handle.

Int 67H [EMS 3.2]
Function 4EH (78) Subfunction 03H
Get size of page map information

Returns the size of the buffer that is required to receive page-mapping information using Int 67H Function 4EH Subfunctions 00H and 02H.

Call with: AH   = 4EH

AL   = 03H

Returns: If function successful

AH   = 00H

AL   = size of buffer (bytes)

If function unsuccessful

AH   = error code

Int 67H [EMS 4.0]
Function 4FH (79) Subfunction 00H
Save partial page map

Saves the state of a subset of the expanded memory page-mapping registers in the specified buffer.

Call with: AH   = 4FH

AL   = 00H

DS:SI = segment:offset of map list (see Notes)

ES:DI = segment:offset of buffer to receive mapping state (see Notes)

Returns: If function successful

AH   = 00H

and buffer filled in with mapping information (see Notes)

If function unsuccessful

AH   = error code

Notes:
- The map list contains the number of mappable segments in the first word, followed by the segment addresses of the mappable memory regions (one segment per word).
- To determine the size of the buffer required for the mapping state, use Int 67H Function 4FH Subfunction 02H.

Int 67H   [EMS 4.0]
Function 4FH (79) Subfunction 01H
Restore partial page map

Restores the state of a subset of the expanded memory page-mapping registers.

Call with: AH   = 4FH

AL   = 01H

DS:SI   = segment:offset of buffer (see Note)

Returns: If function successful

AH   = 00H

If function unsuccessful

AH   = error code

Note:
- The buffer contains mapping information and must have been prepared by a previous call to Int 67H Function 4FH Subfunction 00H.

Int 67H   [EMS 4.0]
Function 4FH (79) Subfunction 02H
Get size of partial page map information

Returns the size of the buffer which will be required to receive partial page-mapping information using Int 67H Function 4FH Subfunction 00H.

Call with: AH   = 4FH

AL   = 02H

BX   = number of pages

Returns: If function successful
AH   = 00H
AL   = size of array (bytes)

If function unsuccessful
AH   = error code

Int 67H   [EMS 4.0]
Function 50H (80) Subfunction 00H
Map multiple pages by number

Maps one or more of the logical expanded memory pages assigned to a handle onto physical memory pages that can be accessed by the CPU. Physical pages are referenced by their numbers.

Call with: AH   = 50H
AL   = 00H
CX   = number of pages to map
DX   = EMM handle
DS:SI   = segment:offset of buffer (see Note)

Returns: If function successful
AH   = 00H

If function unsuccessful
AH   = error code

Note: ■ The buffer contains a series of DWORD (32-bit) entries that control the pages to be mapped. The first word of each entry contains the logical expanded memory page number, and the second word contains the physical page number to which it should be mapped. If the logical page is −1, the physical page is unmapped (made inaccessible for reading or writing).

Int 67H   [EMS 4.0]
Function 50H (80) Subfunction 01H
Map multiple pages by address

Maps one or more of the logical expanded memory pages assigned to a handle onto physical memory pages that can be accessed by the CPU. Physical pages are referenced by their segment addresses.

Call with:	AH	= 50H
	AL	= 01H
	CX	= number of pages to map
	DX	= EMM handle
	DS:SI	= segment:offset of buffer (see Notes)

Returns:	If function successful	
	AH	= 00H
	If function unsuccessful	
	AH	= error code

Notes:
- The buffer contains a series of DWORD (32-bit) entries that control the pages to be mapped. The first word of each entry contains the logical page number, and the second word contains the physical page segment address to which it should be mapped. If the logical page is –1, the physical page is unmapped (made inaccessible for reading or writing).
- The mappable segment addresses may be obtained by calling Int 67H Function 58H Subfunction 00H.

Int 67H   [EMS 4.0]
Function 51H (81)
Reallocate pages for handle

Modifies the number of expanded memory pages allocated to an EMM handle.

Call with:	AH	= 51H
	BX	= new number of pages
	DX	= EMM handle

Returns:	If function successful	
	AH	= 00H
	BX	= logical pages owned by EMM handle
	If function unsuccessful	
	AH	= error code

Note:
- If the requested number of pages is zero, the handle is still active, and pages can be reallocated to the handle at a later time; also, the handle must still be released with Int 67H Function 45H before the application terminates.

Int 67H
Function 52H (82) Subfunction 00H
Get handle attribute

Returns the attribute (volatile or nonvolatile) associated with the specified handle. A nonvolatile memory handle and the contents of the expanded memory pages that are allocated to it are maintained across a warm boot operation (system restart using Ctrl-Alt-Del).

Call with: AH   = 52H
                  AL   = 00H
                  DX   = EMM handle

Returns: If function successful
                  AH   = 00H
                  AL   = attribute
                           0   = *volatile*
                           1   = *nonvolatile*

                  If function unsuccessful
                  AH   = error code

Int 67H
Function 52H (82) Subfunction 01H
Set handle attribute

Sets the attribute (volatile or nonvolatile) associated with the specified handle. A nonvolatile memory handle and the contents of the expanded memory pages that are allocated to it are maintained across a warm boot operation (system restart using Ctrl-Alt-Del).

Call with: AH   = 52H
                  AL   = 01H
                  BL   = attribute
                           0   = *volatile*
                           1   = *nonvolatile*
                  DX   = EMM handle

Returns: If function successful
                  AH   = 00H
                  If function unsuccessful
                  AH   = error code

Note: ■ If the expanded memory hardware cannot support nonvolatile pages, this function returns an error.

Int 67H
Function 52H (82) Subfunction 02H
Get attribute capability

Returns a code indicating whether the Expanded Memory Manager and hardware can support the non-volatile attribute for EMM handles.

Call with:	AH	= 52H
	AL	= 02H

Returns:	If function successful	
	AH	= 00H
	AL	= attribute capability
	0	= *only volatile handles supported*
	1	= *volatile and nonvolatile handles supported*
	If function unsuccessful	
	AH	= error code

Int 67H
Function 53H (83) Subfunction 00H
Get handle name

Returns the 8-character name assigned to a handle.

Call with:	AH	= 53H
	AL	= 00H
	DX	= EMM handle
	ES:DI	= segment:offset of 8-byte buffer

Returns:	If function successful	
	AH	= 00H
	and name for handle in specified buffer	
	If function unsuccessful	
	AH	= error code

Note:	■ A handle's name is initialized to 8 zero bytes when it is allocated or deallocated. Another name may be assigned to an active handle with Int 67H Function 53H Subfunction 01H. The bytes in a handle name need not be ASCII characters.

Int 67H
Function 53H (83) Subfunction 01H
Set handle name

Assigns a name to an EMM handle.

Call with:

AH	= 53H	
AL	= 01H	
DX	= EMM handle	
DS:SI	= segment:offset of 8-byte name	

Returns:

If function successful

AH   = 00H

If function unsuccessful

AH   = error code

Notes:

- The bytes in a handle name need not be ASCII characters, but the sequence of 8 zero bytes is reserved for no name (the default after a handle is allocated or deallocated). A handle name should be padded with zero bytes, if necessary, to a length of 8 bytes.
- A handle may be renamed at any time.
- All handle names are initialized to 8 zero bytes when the system is turned on. The name of a nonvolatile handle is preserved across a warm boot. (See Int 67H Function 52H Subfunctions 00H and 02H.)

Int 67H
Function 54H (84) Subfunction 00H
Get all handle names

Returns the names for all active handles.

Call with:

AH	= 54H	
AL	= 00H	
ES:DI	= segment:offset of buffer (see Notes)	

Returns:

If function successful

AH   = 00H

AL   = number of active handles

and buffer filled in with handle-name information (see Notes)

If function unsuccessful

AH   = error code

Notes:

- The function fills the buffer with a series of 10-byte entries. The first 2 bytes of each entry contain an EMM handle, and the next 8 bytes contain the name associated with the handle. Handles that have never been assigned a name have 8 bytes of 0 as a name.

- Because there is a maximum of 255 active handles, the buffer need not be longer than 2550 bytes.

Int 67H   [EMS 4.0]
Function 54H (84) Subfunction 01H
Search for handle name

Returns the EMM handle associated with the specified name.

Call with:
AH	= 54H	
AL	= 01H	
DS:SI	= segment:offset of 8-byte handle name	

Returns:

If function successful

AH	= 00H
DX	= EMM handle

If function unsuccessful

AH	= error code

Int 67H   [EMS 4.0]
Function 54H (84) Subfunction 02H
Get total handles

Returns the total number of handles that are supported by the Expanded Memory Manager, including the operating-system handle (0).

Call with:
AH	= 54H
AL	= 02H

Returns:

If function successful

AH	= 00H
BX	= number of handles

If function unsuccessful

AH	= error code

Int 67H [EMS 4.0]
Function 55H (85) Subfunctions 00H and 01H
Map pages and jump

Alters the expanded memory mapping context and transfers control to the specified address.

Call with:	AH	= 55H	
	AL	= subfunction	
		0	= *map using physical page numbers*
		1	= *map using physical page segments*
	DX	= EMM handle	
	DS:SI	= segment:offset of buffer (see Notes)	

Returns:	If function successful	
	AH	= 00H
	If function unsuccessful	
	AH	= error code

Notes:
- The buffer contains map-and-jump entries in the following format:

Offset	*Length*	*Description*
00H	4	far pointer to jump target
04H	1	number of pages to map before jump
05H	4	far pointer to map list (see below)

  The map list in turn consists of DWORD (32-bit) entries, one per page. The first word of each entry contains the logical page number, and the second word contains the physical page number or segment (depending on the value in register AL) to which it should be mapped.

- A request to map zero pages and jump is not considered an error; the effect is a simple far jump.

Int 67H [EMS 4.0]
Function 56H (86) Subfunctions 00H and 01H
Map pages and call

Alters the expanded memory mapping context and performs a far call to the specified address. When the destination routine executes a far return, the EMM again alters the page-mapping context as instructed and then returns control to the original caller.

Call with: AH   = 56H
                  AL   = subfunction
                         0   = *map using physical page numbers*
                         1   = *map using physical page segments*
                  DX   = EMM handle
                  DS:SI = segment:offset of buffer (see Notes)

Returns: If function successful
                AH   = 00H

                If function unsuccessful
                AH   = error code

Notes: ■ The format of the buffer containing map and call information is:

Offset	Length	Description
00H	4	far pointer to call target
04H	1	number of pages to map before call
05H	4	far pointer to list of pages to map before call (see below)
09H	1	number of pages to map before return
0AH	4	far pointer to list of pages to map before return (see below)
0EH	8	reserved (0)

Both map lists have the same format and consist of a series of double-word entries, one per page. The first word of each entry contains the logical page number, and the second word contains the physical page number or segment (depending on the value in register AL) to which it should be mapped.

■ A request to map zero pages and call is not an error; the effect is a simple far call.

■ This function uses extra stack space to save information about the mapping context; the amount of stack space required can be determined by calling Int 67H Function 56H Subfunction 02H.

Int 67H   [EMS 4.0]
Function 56H (86) Subfunction 02H
Get stack space for map page and call

Returns the number of bytes of stack space required by Int 67H Function 56H Subfunction 00H or 01H.

Call with: AH   = 56H
                  AL   = 02H

Returns: If function successful
                AH   = 00H
                BX   = stack space required (bytes)

                If function unsuccessful
                AH   = error code

Int 67H [EMS 4.0]
Function 57H (87) Subfunction 00H
Move memory region

Copies a memory region from any location in conventional or expanded memory to any other location without disturbing the current expanded memory mapping context.

Call with:	AH	= 57H
	AL	= 00H
	DS:SI	= segment:offset of buffer (see Notes)

Returns:	If function successful	
	AH	= 00H
	If function unsuccessful	
	AH	= error code

Notes:
- The format of the buffer controlling the move operation is:

Offset	Length	Description
00H	4	region length in bytes
04H	1	source memory type (0 = conventional, 1 = expanded)
05H	2	source memory handle
07H	2	source memory offset
09H	2	source memory segment or physical page number
0BH	1	destination memory type (0 = conventional, 1 = expanded)
0CH	2	destination memory handle
0EH	2	destination memory offset
10H	2	destination memory segment or physical page number

- A length of zero bytes is not an error. The maximum length of a move is 1 MB. If the length exceeds a single expanded memory page, consecutive expanded memory pages (as many as are required) supply or receive the data.

- If the source and destination addresses overlap, the move will be performed in such a way that the destination receives an intact copy of the original data, and a nonzero status is returned.

Int 67H [EMS 4.0]
Function 57H (87) Subfunction 01H
Exchange memory regions

Exchanges any two memory regions in conventional or expanded memory without disturbing the current expanded memory mapping context.

Call with:	AH	= 57H
	AL	= 01H
	DS:SI	= segment:offset of buffer (see Notes)

Returns:	If function successful	
	AH	= 00H
	If function unsuccessful	
	AH	= error code

Notes:	■ The format of the buffer controlling the exchange operation is the same as for Int 67H Function 57H Subfunction 00H.
	■ An exchange of zero bytes is not an error. The maximum length of an exchange is 1 MB. If the length exceeds a single expanded memory page, consecutive expanded memory pages (as many as are required) supply or receive the data.
	■ If the source and destination addresses overlap, the exchange is not performed and an error is returned.

Int 67H [EMS 4.0]
Function 58H (88) Subfunction 00H
Get addresses of mappable pages

Returns the segment base address and physical page number for each mappable page in the system.

Call with:	AH	= 58H
	AL	= 00H
	ES:DI	= segment:offset of buffer (see Notes)

Returns:	If function successful	
	AH	= 00H
	CX	= number of entries in mappable physical page array
	and page number/address information in buffer (see Notes)	
	If function unsuccessful	
	AH	= error code

Notes:	■ Upon return from the function, the buffer contains a series of double-word entries, one per mappable page. The first word of an entry contains the page's segment base address, and the second contains its physical page number. The entries are sorted in order of ascending segment addresses.
	■ The size of the buffer required can be calculated with the information returned by Int 67H Function 58H Subfunction 01H.

Int 67H [EMS 4.0]
Function 58H (88) Subfunction 01H
Get number of mappable pages

Returns the number of mappable physical pages.

Call with:	AH	= 58H
	AL	= 01H

Returns:	If function successful	
	AH	= 00H
	CX	= number of mappable physical pages
	If function unsuccessful	
	AH	= error code

Note:	■ The information returned by this function can be used to calculate the size of the buffer that will be needed by Int 67H Function 58H Subfunction 00H.

Int 67H [EMS 4.0]
Function 59H (89) Subfunction 00H
Get hardware configuration

Returns information about the configuration of the expanded memory hardware.

Call with:	AH	= 59H
	AL	= 00H
	ES:DI	= segment:offset of buffer (see Notes)

Returns:	If function successful	
	AH	= 00H
	and hardware configuration information in buffer.	
	If function unsuccessful	
	AH	= error code

Notes: ■ Upon return from the function, the buffer has been filled in with hardware configuration information in the following format:

Offset	*Length*	*Description*
00H	2	size of raw expanded memory pages (in paragraphs)
02H	2	number of alternate register sets
04H	2	size of mapping-context save area (in bytes)

Offset	Length	Description
06H	2	number of register sets that can be assigned to DMA channels
08H	2	DMA operation type (0 = DMA may be used with alternate register sets; 1 = only one DMA register set available)

- The size returned for the mapping-context save area is the same as the size returned by Int 67H Function 4EH Subfunction 03H.

- This function is intended for use by operating systems only and can be disabled by the operating system at any time.

Int 67H   [EMS 4.0]
Function 59H (89) Subfunction 01H
Get number of raw pages

Obtains the total number of raw expanded memory pages present in the system and the number of raw pages that are not already allocated. Raw memory pages may have a size other than 16 KB.

Call with: AH   = 59H
                  AL   = 01H

Returns: If function successful
                AH   = 00H
                BX   = unallocated raw pages
                DX   = total raw pages
                If function unsuccessful
                AH   = error code

Note: ■ If the Expanded Memory Manager supports only pages of standard size, the values returned by this function are the same as those returned by Int 67H Function 42H.

Int 67H   [EMS 4.0]
Function 5AH (90) Subfunction 00H
Allocate handle and standard pages

Allocates an EMM handle and associates standard (16 KB) expanded memory pages with that handle.

Call with: AH   = 5AH
                  AL   = 00H
                  BX   = number of standard pages to allocate

Returns: If function successful

AH   = 00H

DX   = EMM handle

If function unsuccessful

AH   = error code

Note: ■ Unlike Int 67H Function 43H, allocating zero pages with this function is not an error.

Int 67H [EMS 4.0]
Function 5AH (90) Subfunction 01H
Allocate handle and raw pages

Allocates a raw EMM handle and associates raw expanded memory pages with that handle.

Call with: AH   = 5AH

AL   = 01H

BX   = number of raw pages to allocate

Returns: If function successful

AH   = 00H

DX   = handle for raw EMM pages

If function unsuccessful

AH   = error code

Notes: ■ Raw memory pages may have a size other than 16 KB.

■ Allocation of zero pages is not an error.

Int 67H [EMS 4.0]
Function 5BH (91) Subfunction 00H
Get alternate map registers

Returns the number of the active alternate register set or, if no alternate set is active, saves the state of the mapping registers into a buffer and returns its address.

Call with: AH   = 5BH

AL   = 00H

Returns: If function successful and alternate map register set active

AH	= 00H
BL	= current active alternate map register set

If function successful and alternate map register set not active

AH	= 00H
BL	= 00H
ES:DI	= segment:offset of alternate map register save area (if BL = 0)

If function unsuccessful

AH	= error code

Notes:
- The address of the save area must have been specified in a previous call to Int 67H Function 5BH Subfunction 01H, and the save area must have been initialized by a previous call to Int 67H Function 4EH Subfunction 00H. If there was no previous call to Int 67H Function 5BH Subfunction 01H, the address returned is zero, and the registers are not saved.
- This function is intended for use by operating systems only and can be disabled by the operating system at any time.

Int 67H   [EMS 4.0]
Function 5BH (91) Subfunction 01H
Set alternate map registers

Selects an alternate map register set or (if alternate sets are not supported) restores the mapping context from the specified buffer.

Call with:

AH	= 5BH
AL	= 01H
BL	= alternate register set number or 00H
ES:DI	= segment:offset of map register context restore area (if BL = 0)

Returns: If function successful

AH	= 00H

If function unsuccessful

AH	= error code

Notes:
- The buffer address specified in this call is returned by subsequent calls to Int 67H Function 5BH Subfunction 00H with BL = 00H.
- The save area must have been initialized by a previous call to Int 67H Function 4EH Subfunction 00H.
- This function is intended for use by operating systems only and can be disabled by the operating system at any time.

Int 67H [EMS 4.0]
Function 5BH (91) Subfunction 02H
Get size of alternate map register save area

Returns the amount of storage needed by Int 67H Function 5BH Subfunctions 00H and 01H.

Call with:	AH	= 5BH
	AL	= 02H

Returns:	If function successful	
	AH	= 00H
	DX	= size of buffer (bytes)
	If function unsuccessful	
	AH	= error code

Note:	■ This function is intended for use by operating systems only and can be disabled by the operating system at any time.

Int 67H [EMS 4.0]
Function 5BH (91) Subfunction 03H
Allocate alternate map register set

Allocates an alternate map register set for use with Int 67H Function 5BH Subfunctions 00H and 01H. The contents of the currently active map registers are copied into the newly allocated alternate map registers in order to provide an initial context when they are selected.

Call with:	AH	= 5BH
	AL	= 03H

Returns:	If function successful	
	AH	= 00H
	BL	= alternate map register set number or zero, if no alternate sets are available
	If function unsuccessful	
	AH	= error code

Note:	■ This function is intended for use by operating systems only and can be disabled by the operating system at any time.

Int 67H
Function 5BH (91) Subfunction 04H
Deallocate alternate map register set

Releases an alternate map register set that was previously allocated with Int 67H Function 5BH Subfunction 03H.

Call with:	AH	= 5BH
	AL	= 04H
	BL	= alternate register set number

Returns:	If function successful	
	AH	= 00H
	If function unsuccessful	
	AH	= error code

Notes:	■ The current alternate map register set cannot be deallocated.
	■ This function is intended for use by operating systems only and can be disabled by the operating system at any time.

Int 67H
Function 5BH (91) Subfunction 05H
Allocate DMA register set

Allocates a DMA register set.

Call with:	AH	= 5BH
	AL	= 05H

Returns:	If function successful	
	AH	= 00H
	BL	= DMA register set number (0 = none available)
	If function unsuccessful	
	AH	= error code

Note:	■ This function is intended for use by operating systems only and can be disabled by the operating system at any time.

Int 67H
Function 5BH (91) Subfunction 06H
Enable DMA on alternate map register set

Associates a DMA channel with an alternate map register set.

Call with:	AH	= 5BH
	AL	= 06H
	BL	= alternate map register set
	DL	= DMA channel number

Returns:	If function successful	
	AH	= 00H
	If function unsuccessful	
	AH	= error code

Notes:
- If a DMA channel is not assigned to a specific register set, DMA for that channel will be mapped through the current register set.
- If zero is specified as the alternate map register set, no special action is taken on DMA accesses for the specified DMA channel.
- This function is intended for use by operating systems only and can be disabled by the operating system at any time.

Int 67H
Function 5BH (91) Subfunction 07H
Disable DMA on alternate map register set

Disables DMA accesses for all DMA channels associated with a specific alternate map register set.

Call with:	AH	= 5BH
	AL	= 07H
	BL	= alternate register set number

Returns:	If function successful	
	AH	= 00H
	If function unsuccessful	
	AH	= error code

Int 67H   [EMS 4.0]
Function 5BH (91) Subfunction 08H
Deallocate DMA register set

Deallocates a DMA register set that was previously allocated with Int 67H Function 5BH Subfunction 05H.

Call with: AH   = 5BH
               AL   = 08H
               BL   = DMA register set number

Returns: If function successful
               AH   = 00H
               If function unsuccessful
               AH   = error code

Note: ■ This function is intended for use by operating systems only and can be disabled by the operating system at any time.

Int 67H   [EMS 4.0]
Function 5CH (92)
Prepare Expanded Memory Manager for warm boot

Prepares the expanded memory hardware for an impending warm boot. This function affects the current mapping context, the alternate register set in use, and any other expanded memory hardware dependencies that would ordinarily be initialized at system boot time.

Call with: AH   = 5CH

Returns: If function successful
               AH   = 00H
               If function unsuccessful
               AH   = error code

Note:

- If an application maps expanded memory at addresses below 640 KB, the application must trap all possible conditions that might lead to a warm boot, so that this function can be called first.

Int 67H [EMS 4.0]
Function 5DH (93) Subfunction 00H
Enable EMM operating-system functions

Enables the operating-system–specific EMM functions (Int 67H Functions 59H, 5BH, and 5DH) for calls by any program or device driver. (This is the default condition.)

Call with:	AH	= 5DH
	AL	= 00H
	BX:CX	= access key (if not first call to function)

Returns:	If function successful	
	AH	= 00H
	BX:CX	= access key (if first call to function)
	If function unsuccessful	
	AH	= error code

Notes:

- An access key is returned in registers BX and CX on the first call to Int 67H Function 5DH Subfunction 00H or 01H. The access key is required for all subsequent calls to either function.
- This function is intended for use by operating systems only.

Int 67H [EMS 4.0]
Function 5DH (93) Subfunction 01H
Disable EMM operating-system functions

Disables the operating-system–specific EMM functions (Int 67H Functions 59H, 5BH, and 5DH) for calls by application programs and device drivers, reserving the use of these functions for the operating system.

Call with:	AH	= 5DH
	AL	= 01H
	BX:CX	= access key (if not first call to function)

Returns: If function successful

AH   = 00H

BX:CX   = access key (if first call to function)

If function unsuccessful

AH   = error code

Notes:
- An access key is returned in registers BX and CX on the first call to Int 67H Function 5DH Subfunction 00H or 01H. The access key is required for all subsequent calls to either function.
- This function is intended for use by operating systems only.

Int 67H   [EMS 4.0]
Function 5DH (93) Subfunction 02H
Release access key

Releases the access key obtained by a previous call to Int 67H Function 5DH Subfunction 00H or 01H.

Call with: AH   = 5DH

AL   = 02H

BX:CX   = access key

Returns: If function successful

AH   = 00H

If function unsuccessful

AH   = error code

Notes:
- With respect to the operating-system–specific expanded memory functions, the EMM is returned to the state it had when the system was initialized. A new access key is returned by the next call to Int 67H Function 5DH Subfunction 00H or 01H.
- This function is intended for use by operating systems only and can be disabled by the operating system at any time.

Index

References to tables and illustrations are in italics.

Special Characters

! 298–99
. 187
.. 187–88
; 60
< 298–99
> 298–99
>> 298–99
@ 60
86-DOS operating system 4

A

Absolute disk read 482–84
Absolute disk write 484–85
adapters, video display 86–87
alarm
   reset 592
   set 591–92
align type 38
Allocate alternate map register set (EMS)
   641
Allocate DMA register set (EMS) 642
Allocate handle and pages (EMS) 617–18
Allocate handle and raw pages (EMS) 639
Allocate handle and standard pages
   (EMS) 638–39
Allocate memory block 438–39
ANSI.SYS device driver, screen control 91
   escape sequences used with *92–93*
APPEND 490–91
application program interface (API) 320
application programs. *See* MS-DOS
      application programs, porting to
      OS/2; MS-DOS application
      programs, structure of; MS-DOS
      application programs, writing
      compatible
arena entries 196
arena headers 196, 201
   diagram example *202*
ASCII escape code *92–93*
ASCII mode 69
   character-device drivers in 261–62
ASCII text files 56
ASCIIZ strings 24, 139, 168

.ASM files 45. *See also* assembly-language
     programs
assembly-language programs 37–42
   to access file allocation table *191*
   BREAK.ASM 75–78
   CLEAN.ASM *304–9*
   DRIVER.ASM *283–91*
   DUMP.ASM 152–61
   HELLO.COM example 27–30, 33–36
   program modules 37
   program procedures 41–42
   program segments 38–41
   PROTO.ASM *301–2*
   SHELL.ASM program 229–38
   TALK.ASM 113–26
   ZERODIV.ASM 254, *255–58*
ASSIGN 489
ASSUME statement 29, 33
attribute byte
   color text display *98*
   monochrome text display *97*
attribute word, device *264*
Auxiliary device (AUX) 12, 106, 298. *See*
     also serial port
Auxiliary input 344–45
Auxiliary output 345–46

B

background, set 508–9
BACKUP command 15
.BAT (batch) files 15
Batch files 15
binary mode 69
   character-device drivers in 261–62
   output 93–94
BIOS module 12–13, 17
   get address of extended, 574
BIOS parameter block (BPB) 181, 189
   build 272
   structure *269*
bit planes 101
blink/intensity bit, toggle 513
block-device drivers 260, 262
   check for remoteness 423–24
   check removability of 422–23
   generic I/O control of 429–32

D

data segment 38
data segment (DS) register 31, 35
Date and time device (CLOCK$) 12
day count
  get 592–93
  set 593
Deallocate alternate map register set
  (EMS) 642
Deallocate DMA register set (EMS) 644
.DEF files 45
Delay 568–69
DEL(ETE) command 14
Delete directory 399
Delete file 361–62, 407–8
dependency statements 61
descriptors, memory segment 321
device
  cancel redirection 467–68
  close 565
  get device information 412–13
  open 564–65
  post 572–73
  read file or 405–6
  redirect 466–67
  set device information 414–15
  wait 571
  write file or 406–7
Device Close (command code function
  0EH) 277–78
Device close (MS-DOS function) 565
DEVICE commands 12
device drivers, installable 12–13, 259–96
  CLOCK driver 282
  command-code routines 267–81
  debugging 295–96
  chain before/after driver installation
    294
  chain listing *295*
  device attribute word *264*
  error codes *267*
  MS-DOS type 260–63
  processing of typical input/output
    requests 281–82
  structure of MS-DOS 263–67
    device header 263–64
    interrupt routine 266–67
    strategy routine 265
  writing and installing 282–95
    assembly 283–92
    installation 293–95
    linking 293

device drivers, resident 12–13
Device Open (command-code function
  0DH) 277
Device open (MS-DOS function) 564–65
Device post 572–73
Device wait 571–72
Digital Research 4
DIR command 14, 167, 174
Direct console I/O 347–48
directory 166, 167–73
  create 398–99
  delete 399
  format of a single entry in a disk
    184, 185
  functions controlling 167–68
  get current 437–38
  hierarchical (tree) structure 166, *167*
  moving files 173
  root 184–86
  searching 168–73
  set current 400
directory operations, Int 21H functions
  summary 339
Disable DMA on alternate map register
  set (EMS) 643–44
Disable EMM operating system functions
  (EMS) 645–46
Disable mouse driver 608–9
disk(s) 177–94. *See also* drive, logical;
  ESDI Fixed Disk Drive Adapter
  absolute read 482–84
  absolute write 484–85
  boot sector 179–82
  controller drive diagnostic 551
  controller internal diagnostic 551
  controller RAM diagnostic 550
  file allocation table 182–84
    interpreting the 188–92
  files area 186–88
  fixed-disk partitions 192–94
  format 543
  format bad track 542
  format track 541–42
  get change status 552–53
  get current 367
  get default drive data 368–69
  get drive allocation information
    394–95
  get drive data 370
  get drive parameters 543–44
  get drive status 549
  get type 552
  initialize fixed disk characteristics
    544–45

E

W

watchdog time-out, set 580
window
    initialize or scroll down 505–6
    initialize or scroll up 505
Windows 7, 318
Write (function 08H) 275
Write cassette 562
Write character and attribute at cursor
    506–7
Write character at cursor 507–8
Write character in teletype mode 510–11
Write character to communications port
    557
Write character to printer 587

Write control data to block-device driver
    419–20
Write control data to character-device
    driver 416–17
Write File or Device 406–7
Write graphics pixel 509
Write POST error log 563–64
Write screen in teletype mode 529–30
Write sector 539
Write sector buffer 549
Write sector long 546–47
Write with Verify (function 09H) 276

Z

ZERODIV.ASM program 254, *255–58*
Zilog Z-80 microprocessor 4

Ray Duncan received a B.A. in chemistry at the University of California, Riverside, and an M.D. at the University of California, Los Angeles; he specialized in pediatrics and neonatology at the Cedars-Sinai Medical Center in Los Angeles. Duncan has been involved with microcomputers since the Altair days and has written many articles for personal computer magazines, including *Dr. Dobb's Journal, Programmer's Journal,* and *BYTE;* he is currently a contributing editor to *PC Magazine.* In addition, Duncan is the founder of Laboratory Microsystems Incorporated, a software house specializing in FORTH interpreters and compilers. Duncan was the general editor of THE MS-DOS ENCYCLOPEDIA.

The manuscript for this book was prepared and submitted to Microsoft Press in electronic form. Text files were processed and formatted using Microsoft Word.

Cover design adapted by Becky Geisler-Johnson from original design by Ted Mader and Associates.

Interior text design by Darcie S. Furlan

Principal typography by Lisa G. Iversen and Jean Trenary

Text composition by Microsoft Press in Garamond with display in Garamond Bold, using the Magna composition system and the Linotronic 300 laser imagesetter.